THE ROUTLEDGE COMPANION TO GLOBAL VALUE CHAINS

This Companion provides a review of global value chains (GVCs) and the megatrends that are shaping them and will continue to reshape them in deep-set trajectories of change over the next few decades. Megatrends herald both challenges and opportunities. With the growing interest among business leaders and researchers in GVCs, this is a reference work which fills a gap in current literature by focusing on the new features of GVCs, including the shift of global purchasing power towards developing economies, the significance of emerging technologies and data analytics, the increasing tensions between globalisation and de-globalisation, and the role of micro-multinationals, start-up entrepreneurs, the public sector and middle markets in a fast-changing global economy.

The early chapters are essentially *intradisciplinary* in character, with the first seeking to explore some historical aspects of GVCs. Subsequent chapters cover the theory and practice of operations and supply chain management, emerging supply chain technologies, and the impact of inter-firm collaboration across sectors and economies. The final chapters take a more *interdisciplinary* approach and examine topics at the interface of GVCs with the economy, society, culture and politics.

This comprehensive handbook provides a timely analysis of leading-edge global megatrends and practices in one volume.

Renu Agarwal is Associate Professor, Operations and Supply Chain Management, and the Director of Strategic Supply Chain Management Programs at the University of Technology Sydney. Agarwal has extensive industry experience and now provides leadership in the disciplinary fields of service innovation, service value networks, supply chain management, dynamic capability building, management practices, innovation and productivity. Agarwal has undertaken research for many organisations, in particular federal and state governments, and industry groups and associations. Agarwal has published in several edited books and top-tier refereed management journal articles.

Christopher Bajada is Associate Professor of Economics at the University of Technology Sydney. Bajada's research is primarily in applied macroeconomics, with a special interest in management practices, supply chains, tax compliance, circular economy and productivity. Bajada has published widely, including in top-tier journals, research books and academic textbooks.

Bajada has undertaken research for many organisations, including federal and state governments, and industry groups and associations.

Roy Green is Emeritus Professor and Special Innovation Adviser at the University of Technology Sydney. Green also chairs the Port of Newcastle and Advanced Robotics for Manufacturing Hub and is a board member of the Innovative Manufacturing Cooperative Research Centre.

Katrina Skellern is a post-doctoral research fellow with the Centre for Business & Social Innovation at the University of Technology Sydney (UTS) Business School. She has over 20 years of experience in project management, policy development, program evaluation, business model innovation, and community and stakeholder engagement in Australia and internationally. Skellern is currently working on a business model transformation project with the Innovative Manufacturing Cooperative Research Centre.

"The rise of Global Value Chains in the 1990s and 2000s has transformed international trade. Today, about 70% of global trade flows through GVCs. This has a large impact on trade policy and the tools available to policymakers for shaping international trade. This handbook is a great resource for researchers and policymakers to navigate their way through the complexities of GVCs and design better and more accurate solutions to the challenges of today."

Xiaozhun Yi, Deputy Director-General, World Trade Organization, Geneva, Switzerland

"The Covid-19 pandemic showed us the importance – and fragility – of global value chains and the need to rethink our established paradigms. This handbook assembles the who's who of researchers, analysts, strategic thinkers and doers in the field of supply chain management in a global context. What interests me most is the role intangible assets such as management practices, collaboration and dynamic capabilities in global value chains. We've always known intangible assets are an essential ingredient of a successful supply chain – as it turns out, their importance is amplified during these challenging times. This handbook provides a solid overview of the state of the art in this field and has plenty of inspiration for future GVCs design and management which will inspire future research and practice alike."

Tim Reed, President, Business Council of Australia, Australia

"Over the past decade, my position at OECD has allowed me to witness how global value chains analysis has profoundly changed policymaking at national and international level. This authoritative book provides an excellent account of where the concept comes from, why it matters, how it is changing and the implications for different policy domains. Perhaps most importantly, the book also offers relevant insights on future trends from the best experts in the field."

Andrew Wyckoff, Director, OECD Directorate for Science, Technology and Innovation, Paris, France

"Today, global value chains are evolving because of trade wars, technology, demands for more inclusiveness and sustainability, and now COVID. Given the importance of global value chains in trade, and the importance of trade for development, it is key to understand the new dynamics driving them. This book provides an incredible analysis of the new trends, their drivers, and the way forward. It is extremely timely as changes are happening now and it is critical to provide sound advice to policymakers in the developing world based on thorough analysis and evidence. Having been at the World Bank Group for over 20 years providing trade policy advice to countries around the world, this book is a necessary input into the current debate on the role of trade in development and how best to go about recalibrating globalisation, to take new factors into account."

Mona Haddad, Practice Manager, East Asia and Pacific, Trade & Competitiveness, World Bank Group, Washington DC, USA

"In today's turbulent and uncertain world, the challenges facing organisations dependent upon global demand and supply networks have never been greater. This timely and scholarly book brings new insights into how global value chains need to be re-shaped to adapt to the changed conditions that they must confront."

Professor Martin Christopher, Emeritus Professor of Marketing & Logistics, Cranfield School of Management, Cranfield University, UK

"Bringing together the wide and diverse field of global value chains into a single, comprehensive and insightful text is a daunting challenge. Yet, this is exactly what *The Routledge Companion to Global Value Chains* handbook does. With Covid-19, this is a hugely important area and this handbook contains chapters from some of the leading academics and practitioners in the field covering a range of topics such as the historical evolution of global value chains, its theory and practice, future megatrends in GVCs amongst many. Based on my 20 years of teaching and research experience in the area of supply chain management, this handbook is great and compelling to read, which I wholeheartedly recommend."

Professor A. Gunasekaran, Dean and Professor, School of Business and Public Administration, California State University, USA

"When emphasizing today the need for a digital transformation of organizations and industries, we sometimes overlook that we predominantly live in a material, physical world that is built on a complex global network of supply chains moving physical goods around the world (and, soon, into and from space as well). This handbook provides a solid introduction into the principles, models, and success factors of this field – also illustrating how digital technologies are creating smart supply chains utilizing information and communication technologies in novel ways."

Professor Frank Piller, Professor of Management and Co-Director, Institute for Technology & Innovation Management; Scientific Director, Institute for Management Cybernetics (IfU e.V.), RWTH Aachen, Germany

"As we emerge into the new world – either post Covid or living with Covid – the fabric of our economic interactions are forever changed. The success of strong global value chains in a world grappling with technological change, increasing protectionist sentiment and the need to upscale industry are now more important than ever in driving our economic success, building competitiveness and developing our skills base. In these times of challenge and opportunity, this collection is more needed than ever for policymakers, business leaders and decision makers."

Innes Willox, Chief Executive, Australian Industry Group, Australia

"Global Value Chains make up over two-thirds of global trade. Yet despite centuries of evolution and rapidly developing digital systems, Global Value Chains are inherently unstable – continuously evolving to market and technology drivers and megatrends. Will global megatrends such as offshoring be reversed by new technology such as blockchain and Industry 4.0? As demonstrated in 2020 – unplanned events can throw even the best plans into disarray. This book provides a survival guide."

Professor Graham Wren OBE FREng, FIMechE, FIET, FCIM, FIoD, FRSA, EurIng, CEng, CDir, CMar, Special Advisor to the Principal and Major Projects Director, University of Strathclyde, UK

"This volume is comprehensive and deeply steeped in both theory and practice. Readers will quickly come to appreciate that value chains are the heart of wealth creation and that their effective design, management and improvement are core to economic, environmental and societal progress. We learn from the studies and contributions of this book that globalisation has many ongoing challenges and opportunities that manifest in both risks and returns, such as new technologies. The contributions on megatrends in global value chains are particularly insightful, as both practitioners and researchers will be able to use these to project forward from today's challenges into the future. Congratulations to the authors and editors on integrating this body of knowledge."

Professor Danny Samson, Department of Management and Marketing, University of Melbourne, Australia

"The opportunity for investment and participation in local and global supply chains – particularly for SMEs – will continue to increase, with a shift to competing on value rather than cost, and through unique and service-based business models. This handbook comes at an important time – supply chain disruptions and uncertainty creates an opportunity for those who can competitively and collaboratively embrace Industry 4.0 technologies to design, manufacture and build service platforms for local and global markets."

David Chuter, CEO and Managing Director, Innovative Manufacturing Cooperative Research Centre, Australia

"Given the incredible turbulence in trade, understanding global value chains is so topical and even more important than ever as we emerge into the new world – either post Covid-19 or living with Covid-19. The fabric of our global economic interactions are forever changed. This handbook provides an excellent account of various theoretical concepts, why they matter, their enablers which help identify implications for different policy domains. This handbook as a knowledge resource is even more pertinent especially when the new factors of intangible resources such as management practices and dynamic capability are deemed essential in modern days. No matter what, this book provides an ideal map for academics, researchers, practitioners and policymakers on how best they should go about transforming and recalibrating globalization."

Professor Nicholas Bloom, William D. Eberle Professor of Economics, Stanford University, USA

Routledge Companions in Business, Management and Marketing

Routledge Companions are prestige volumes which provide an overview of a research field or topic. Surveying the business disciplines, the books in this series incorporate both established and emerging research themes. Compiled and edited by an array of highly regarded scholars, these volumes also benefit from global teams of contributors reflecting disciplinary diversity.

Individually, *Routledge Companions in Business, Management and Marketing* provide impactful one-stop-shop publications. Collectively, they represent a comprehensive learning and research resource for researchers, postgraduate students and practitioners.

The Routledge Handbook of Critical Finance Studies
Edited by Christian Borch and Robert Wosnitzer

The Routledge Handbook of Financial Geography
Edited by Janelle Knox-Hayes and Dariusz Wójcik

The Routledge Companion to Asian Family Business
Governance, Succession, and Challenges in the Age of Digital Disruption
Edited by Ho-Don Yan and Fu-Lai Tony Yu

The Routledge Companion to Marketing Research
Edited by Len Tiu Wright, Luiz Moutinho, Merlin Stone and Richard P. Bagozzi

The Routledge Companion to Talent Management
Edited by Ibraiz Tarique

The Routledge Companion to Corporate Social Responsibility
Edited by Thomas Maak, Nicola M. Pless, Sukhbir Sandhu and Marc Olitzky

The Routledge Companion to Global Value Chains
Reinterpreting and Reimagining Megatrends in the World Economy
Edited by Renu Agarwal, Christopher Bajada, Roy Green and Katrina Skellern

For more information about this series, please visit: www.routledge.com/Routledge-Compani ons-in-Business-Management-and-Marketing/book-series/RCBUS

THE ROUTLEDGE COMPANION TO GLOBAL VALUE CHAINS

Reinterpreting and Reimagining Megatrends in the World Economy

Edited by Renu Agarwal, Christopher Bajada, Roy Green and Katrina Skellern

Routledge
Taylor & Francis Group

LONDON AND NEW YORK

First published 2022
by Routledge
2 Park Square, Milton Park, Abingdon, Oxon OX14 4RN

and by Routledge
605 Third Avenue, New York, NY 10158

Routledge is an imprint of the Taylor & Francis Group, an informa business

British Library Cataloguing-in-Publication Data
A catalogue record for this book is available from the British Library

Library of Congress Cataloging-in-Publication Data
Names: Agarwal, Renu (Professor of Operations and Supply Chain Management), editor.
Title: The Routledge companion to global value chains: reinterpreting and reimagining megatrends in the world economy/edited by Renu Agarwal, Christopher Bajada, Roy Green and Katrina Skellern.
Description: Abingdon, Oxon; New York, NY: Routledge, 2022. |
Series: Routledge companions in business, management & marketing |
Includes bibliographical references and index. |
Identifiers: LCCN 2021009443 | ISBN 9780415787918 (hardback) |
ISBN 9781032059891 (paperback) | ISBN 9781315225661 (ebook)
Subjects: LCSH: International trade. | Business logistics.
Classification: LCC HF1379 .R68 2022 | DDC 382–dc23
LC record available at https://lccn.loc.gov/2021009443

ISBN: 978-0-415-78791-8 (hbk)
ISBN: 978-1-032-05989-1 (pbk)
ISBN: 978-1-315-22566-1 (ebk)

DOI: 10.4324/9781315225661

Typeset in Bembo
by Deanta Global Publishing Services, Chennai, India

Printed in the United Kingdom
by Henry Ling Limited

CONTENTS

Contents

FIGURES

CASE STUDY

TABLES

CONTRIBUTORS

Renu Agarwal is Associate Professor, Operations and Supply Chain Management in the Management Discipline Group, University of Technology Sydney (UTS) Business School. She is currently the director of Strategic Supply Chain Management Programs and in this role she provides leadership within the UTS Business School in the disciplinary fields of service innovation, service value networks, supply chain management, dynamic capability building, management practices, management education, innovation and productivity. Agarwal is also the director of management practices projects and has been instrumental in managing several federal and state government research project grants, including the 2009 landmark study "Management Matters in Australia – Just how productive are we?" which has had an impact on government policy and contributed to the broader international WMS study. Agarwal has published in many top-tier international journals; edited *The Handbook Service Innovation* published by Springer-Verlag UK; and edited *Global Value Chains, Flexibility and Sustainability* published by Springer. Agarwal is also amidst editing a book titled *Innovation* to be published by Routledge UK (Taylor & Francis Group) in 2022.

Felix Arndt is the John F. Wood Chair in Entrepreneurship in the Department of Management; a Research Fellow at the Center for Business and Sports of the Stockholm School of Economics, Sweden; and a Visiting Professor at the University of Agder, Norway. Arndt's research intersects strategy, entrepreneurship and innovation. He looks at how firms use organisational renewal and technological innovation to stay ahead of the competition (dynamic capabilities, ecosystems, business models). A second field of interest is best captured by the question of how entrepreneurs overcome extreme challenges (e.g. of socio-economic or medical nature). His research has frequently used the emerging market context (e.g. China). Some of his research uses corporate social responsibility questions and the context of contested industries (tobacco, nuclear power, etc.). His work has been published in the *Academy of Management Review, Journal of Business Ethics, Journal of Business Venturing Insights, Industrial and Corporate Change, Entrepreneurship and Regional Development, Technological Forecasting and Social Change,* and *Technovation,* among others. Teaching has been a passion and privilege. Arndt has taught in top MBA and EMBA programs around the world. He was involved in the foundation of several entrepreneurship centres, and entrepreneurship and executive programmes teaching a range of topics from innovation, entrepreneurship, strategy, leadership to international business. Arndt is an active entrepreneur and investor. As an engineer by training, he is fascinated by new technologies and their application. He has held patents, has experience as an entrepreneur (including scaling and exits), on the director level in consulting and as a lobbyist. Arndt is a recognised executive and start-up coach, provides consulting services to the private sector and policy advice to the government. He is currently a board member of Innovation Guelph. Prior to coming to Guelph, Arndt was affiliated with universities in the UK (Leicester Castle Business School), USA (Wharton School) and China (University of Nottingham) in various faculty and director positions. He has appeared in print, radio and TV media outlets.

Menaka Arudchelvan has a keen interest in applied economics, trade, regional integration, SME and inclusive growth. She has worked as a data analyst, consultant and economist for several organisations, including Teikoku Databank, Asian Development Bank Institute, New Zealand Ministry of Foreign Affairs, and Trade and Statistics New Zealand. Arudchelvan graduated from Victoria University of Wellington in New Zealand.

Koen De Backer is Head of Division in the Directorate for Science, Technology and Innovation (STI) of the Organisation for Economic Co-operation and Development (OECD) with special oversight of the steel and shipbuilding sectors. De Backer joined the OECD in 2006 and has worked on different topics in the Directorate for Science, Technology and Industry and the Statistics Directorate: economic globalisation, multinational enterprises, offshoring/outsourcing, R&D internationalisation, industrial policy, open innovation, entrepreneurship, structural business statistics and micro-data. He was one of the persons leading the OECD work on global value chains. Prior to joining the OECD, De Backer held post-doctoral positions at the Universitat Pompeu Fabre in Barcelona (Spain) and at the Department of Applied Economics of the KU Leuven, acted as adviser to the Minister of Economic Affairs in Belgium, and was professor at the Vlerick Leuven Gent Management School. De Backer holds a PhD degree from KU Leuven (Belgium) and a Master of Business Administration degree from KU Leuven/UCI (USA).

Christopher Bajada is Associate Professor of Economics at the University of Technology Sydney. Bajada has previously been the Associate Dean (Education) and Chair of the University's Teaching and Learning Committee. Bajada has held several external appointments, including council member of the Economic Society of Australia (NSW Branch), member of the Australian Taxation Office's Cash Economy Task Force and on the expert committee for developing Economics Learning Standards for Australian Higher Education. Bajada's research is primarily in applied macroeconomics, with a special interest in management practices, tax compliance, circular economy, productivity and curriculum design. Bajada has published several research books, academic textbooks and refereed journal articles in highly reputable economics journals. Bajada has undertaken research for several organisations, including the Department of Industry, Innovation and Science; Australian Bureau of Statistics; Export Council of Australia; Deloitte Access Economics; NSW Office of Environment and Heritage; National Association of Testing Authorities; NSW Innovation and Productivity Council; and the NSW Department of Industry.

Manjot Singh Bhatia is Assistant Professor at Jindal Global Business School, O. P. Jindal Global University, India. He has completed a Doctorate in Operations Management from the Indian Institute of Management, Lucknow, India (AACSB accredited). His research has been published/ accepted in reputed journals such as the *International Journal of Production Research, Production Planning and Control; IEEE Transactions on Engineering Management;* and *Annals of Operations*

Research. His current research areas include closed loop supply chain, Industry 4.0, blockchain and sustainability.

Martin Bliemel is the Director of Research at TD School, a new pan-university transdisciplinary school at the University of Technology Sydney (UTS). Bliemel's research interests include entrepreneurial networks, accelerators, education, research commercialisation and entrepreneurial ecosystems. In particular, his work on accelerators played a key role in the design of the $23 million Incubator Support Programme by the Department of Industry. Bliemel's research has been published in several prestigious journals, including *Nature Nanotechnology*, *Technovation*, *Entrepreneurship Theory and Practice*, *Entrepreneurship and Regional Development*, *Education + Training*, *International Journal of Entrepreneurial Behavior and Research*, and the *Entrepreneurship Research Journal*, where one of his articles on entrepreneurship education is *ERJ*'s most downloaded article. Bliemel is a recipient of the nationally competitive Office of Learning and Teaching Citation for "For preparing students studying management to become entrepreneurs by creating authentic and respectful learning experiences that immerse students in collaborative interactions with external stakeholders." He is a member of the advisory committee for the Australian Centre for Entrepreneurship Research Exchange (ACERE), and a repeat member of committees of the NSW Innovation & Productivity Council.

Paul Childerhouse is Director of Quality and Supply Chain Management at Massey University and one of New Zealand's leading supply chain academics. His research into supply chain integration and supply chain auditing is internationally renowned. The latter focuses on the assessment of organisational supply chain competence and has led to the development of a string of collaborative relationships with industry. Over time he has become interested in the behavioural aspects of supply chain management. For example, he is currently working with scholars from around the world investigating the effects of different national cultures on supply chain management. Together with his current crop of doctoral students he is researching the power and dependency of logistical service providers and the effects of social networks on supply chain relationships.

Md. Maruf Hossan Chowdhury is a senior lecturer of Operations and Supply Chain Management in the University of Technology Sydney (UTS). He has extensive teaching and research experience in operations, supply chain management and decision modelling. He has published his research papers in the top-tier journals of operations and supply chain management. Chowdhury has multiple methodological skills and has worked extensively in different national and international projects. As an expert of supply chain management Chowdhury has taught at several universities in Australia, including the University of Technology Sydney, University of Western Australia (UWA) and Curtin University. Chowdhury has professional experience in different industrial settings such as textile and apparel, and petroleum refinery.

Mesbahuddin Chowdhury, PhD, is Senior Lecturer in Operations and Supply Chain Management in the Department of Management, Marketing and Entrepreneurship at the University of Canterbury, New Zealand. He received his PhD in supply chain management from Monash University, Australia; MBA (major – management of technology) from Asian Institute of Technology, Thailand; and a master's in industrial management from Katholieke Universiteit Leuven, Belgium. He also served as a research fellow in the Department of Accounting at Monash University for two years. Chowdhury teaches strategic management, operations management, purchasing and supply chain management, and business research methods. He earned his Postgraduate Certificate on Tertiary Teaching from the University of Canterbury in 2016. His current research interests are on social capital, supply chain resilience, organisational resilience, certification, and health and safety management practice. His works have appeared in leading operations and supply chain management journals such as the *International Journal of Production Economics, International Journal of Production Research, Supply Chain Management: An International Journal, International Journal of Disaster Risk Reduction*, and *Australasian Journal of Environmental Management*. He has also published in top-tier tourism journals such as the *Journal of Travel Research, Annals of Tourism Research* and *Current Issues in Tourisms*.

Rameshwar Dubey is Reader in Operations Management at Liverpool Business School. Dubey is also a senior editor of the *International Journal of Physical Distribution and Logistics Management* and associate editor of the *Journal of Humanitarian Logistics and Supply Chain Management, International Journal of Information Management, Benchmarking: An International Journal, Global Journal of Flexible Systems Management* and *Management of Environmental Quality*. Before joining the Liverpool Business School, Dubey was a full-time associate professor in Supply Chain Management at Montpellier Business School, Montpellier, France, in which he is still associated as an affiliate professor. He also has taught at some of the leading international schools, including the Indian Institute of Management, Jammu, India; the Faculty of Engineering, UNESP, Bauru, São Paulo, Brazil; Southern University of Science and Technology of China; Stockholm School of Business, Stockholm, Sweden; Audencia Business School, Nantes, France; SIBM, Pune, India; SIOM, Nashik, India; SCMHRD, Pune; MDI, Murshidabad; MDI, Gurgaon; and School of Management Studies, MNNIT Allahabad. Dubey's research interests include supply chain management, operations management and business analytics with a strong focus on humanitarian operations management, sustainable supply chain management, supply chain design issues and application of emerging technologies in disaster relief operations. Dubey has published some of the most cited papers in the *International Journal of Operations and Production Management; International Journal of Production Economics; International Journal of Production Research; British Journal of Management, Production, Planning & Control; IEEE Transactions on Engineering Management; Journal of Business Research; Journal of Cleaner Production; Annals of Operations Research; Technological Forecasting and Social Change*; and *Management Decision*. For his academic work, Dubey has received several awards: outstanding reviewer award, *International Journal of Production Economics, Journal of Business Research*, and *Journal of Cleaner Production*; best reviewer award, *Journal of Humanitarian Logistics and Supply Chain Management* (2014, 2016), and *Management Decision* (2018); and received a title on 8 November 2019 at Bauru, São Paulo, Brazil, for life-time commitment to advancing scientific knowledge on supply chain management, operations management, information systems and technology for promoting innovation, enhancing indus-trial competitiveness and improving quality of life, both in Brazil and worldwide. Dubey is an active member of several professional societies, active reviewer of over 75 leading international scientific journals, and reviewer of PhD theses and other professional bodies engaged in the dissemination of grants.

Jakob Engel is an economist in the World Bank's Macroeconomics, Trade and Investment Global Practice. His research focus is on issues related to the economics and politics of regional integration, the emergence and impact of global value chains and production networks, trade and industrial policy, and financial regulation. He is the author of multiple publications in journals and edited volumes, including the recently published *The Distributional Impacts of Trade: Empirical Innovations, Analytical Tools, and Policy Responses* (with Deeksha Kokas, Maryla Maliszewska and Gladys Lopez-Acevedo, World Bank 2021). He previously worked for the UK Department for International Development, the Overseas Development Institute, and the Smith School for Enterprise and Environment at the University of Oxford.

Cyril Foropon is Full Professor of Operations and Supply Chain Management, and Director of Doctorate in Business Administration (DBA) Programs at Montpellier Business School (MBS). He holds a PhD in management from HEC Paris. His research interests are in the fields of quality management and humanitarian supply chain management. He is particularly interested in the implementation of Lean management within both service and manufacturing organisations, quality management practices within ISO 9000 candidate organisations, process management within humanitarian non-governmental organisations, the impact of emerging technologies in the field of operations and supply chain management, and the use of metaphors in operations management theory building. His articles are published in *IJPE, IJPR, IJOPM, AOR, JCP, MD, IJIM, JEIM, IJLM* and *TFSC*, amongst other leading academic journals. He serves as an associate editor of the *Global Journal of Flexible Systems Management*.

Derek Friday is Lecturer of Operations and Supply Schain Management at the University of Newcastle Australia. His PhD research focused on developing a new collaborative risk management framework to improve the resilience of supply chains against disruptions. Friday has over ten years of experience in supply chain management as an academic and practitioner. Friday is passionate about engaging with industry and is a chartered member of the Chartered Institute of Logistics and Transport Australia. He has worked as a consultant and project manager for inland transportation and related services projects with the United Nations missions in Africa. Friday has co-authored several refereed journal articles.

John Gattorna has spent the last four decades working inside numerous multi-national companies, seeking to shape theory from observed practice, and has succeeded. It is through this indepth applied research that he and his co-workers formulated the Dynamic Alignment™ business model, which has been progressively refined through use over time. Those companies that have applied John's concepts have exhibited large improvements in operational and financial performance, and corresponding increases in customer satisfaction.

Janet Godsell joined WMG in October 2013 from her prior position of Senior Lecturer at Cranfield University School of Management. Her career has been split between both industry and academia. She joined the faculty of Cranfield in 2001, following the completion of her Executive MBA there. She also completed her PhD at Cranfield, researching the development of a customer responsive supply chain. Prior to her return to academia, Godsell developed a successful career within industry, beginning at ICI/Zeneca Pharmaceuticals. Following this, she worked up to senior management level at Dyson, in both supply chain and operations management functions. At Dyson, she undertook a number of operational and process improvement roles within research and development, customer logistics, purchasing and manufacturing. Godsell is a chartered engineer and member of the IMechE. She is on the board and scientific committee of the European Operations Management Association (EurOMA), the cabinet of the UK roundtable of the Council of Supply Chain Management Professionals (CSCMP), and the manufacturing steering committee of the IMechE. She is on the editorial board of three journals, including the *International Journal of Operations and Production Management*, and she is an advocate for improving the uptake of STEM subjects by schoolchildren.

Anwara Happy is a PhD candidate of operations and supply chain management at the School of Business in the University of Technology Sydney (UTS), Sydney, Australia. She has completed her master's of philosophy in 2020 from Western Sydney University, Sydney, Australia. She received her master's of business in operations and supply chain management (procurement stream) degree in 2014 from UTS. Happy has professional experience both in government and private sectors in Australia and Bangladesh with specialisation in supply chain–related fields.

As part of the job, she trained fellow employees on various aspects of operational issues. Her ten years of experience as a procurement professional in Technicolor Australia (from 2001 to 2011) provided her with an opportunity to understand profound practical knowledge relating to supply chain management. Along with the industrial experience, Happy has academic experience; she has presented a paper at the international conference of ANZIBA 2020. She has successfully contributed two book chapters. Her current research interests are in emerging technologies such as blockchain, cloud computing in the context of operations and supply chain management, including the adoption of Lean, Agile and Six Sigma philosophies in supply chain management.

Norma Harrison is Professor of Management, Macquarie Business School, and Past Dean at the Macquarie Graduate School of Management (MGSM). She has served as professor of operations management at the China Europe International Business School, and as the foundation head of the Graduate School of Business at the University of Technology, Sydney. Harrison's teaching, research and consulting interests are in the areas of innovation and technology management, sustainable supply chains, the globalisation of operations and performance improvement. She continues to publish in academic journals and to serve on journal editorial review boards. She chaired and conducted the Production and Operations Management Society (POMS) 2017 International Conference in Sydney (http://pomssydney2017.com) and she is the co-chair of the 2020 International Conference of Operations and Supply Chain Management (ICOSCM) (https://www.icoscm-anzam2020.com). Since May 2020, Harrison has conducted a series of public webinars titled "Response and Resilience in Supply Chains Amid COVID-19" involving panellists from industry, government and academia.

Mile Katic is a multi-disciplinary management scholar with expertise that spans the likes of technology and innovation management, operations management as well as strategic management. He has been involved in facilitating teaching and learning across multiple faculties, disciplines and education levels at both the University of Technology Sydney and other institutions abroad. With professional experience in the Australian manufacturing industry, Mile is particularly interested in boundary-spanning research that helps transfer leading edge management theory into practical know-how. To this end, he has collaborated with various government agencies as well as other universities to deliver practice-centred research concerning Australian management capabilities, the nexus between strategic management and technology convergence and, more recently, the managerial implications of industrial energy efficiency and strategic decision making under uncertainty.

Arshinder Kaur is currently working as Professor in the Department of Management Studies, IIT Madras, Chennai. She worked at Curtin University, Australia, for one year in the Curtin Business School in 2014 as a senior lecturer. She has more than 35 publications in reputed international journals like *Omega, Journal of Cleaner Production* and *International Journal of Production Economics*. Her doctoral work on the topic supply chain coordination has been accepted as a Highly Commended Award Winner of the 2008 Emerald/EFMD Outstanding Doctoral Research Award. Her areas of research interests are supply chain coordination and contracts, and sustainable food supply chains. She has coordinated many industry programmes.

Jodie-Anne Keane is Senior Research Fellow with the International Economic Development Group at the ODI, London, having rejoined in 2020 where she was previously a Research Fellow 2007–2015. She is a trade economist who has worked with multiple governments across the developing world to secure their trade and development aspiration over the last 15 years. This includes supporting the smooth transition strategies of Least Developed Countries graduating from the category over the coming years. Between 2015 and 2020, Keane was an economic adviser within the Trade, Oceans and Natural Resources Directorate of the Commonwealth Secretariat, with responsibility for global advocacy on emerging trade issues and the supporting global trade architecture. She began her career in Vietnam and Cambodia, including working on non-market economy issues for the World Bank in 2006. She has a PhD in Development Economics from SOAS, University of London. She has taught seminars on comparative growth and more recently on the political economy of trade, Department of International Relations, London School of Economics. She has published journal articles, book chapters and edited a volume on Global Value Chains for the Commonwealth Secretariat.

Ramesh Krishnan is currently doing a joint PhD at the Department of Management Studies of the Indian Institute of Technology Madras, India, and Business School of the University of Technology Sydney, Australia. His research interest includes operations research, supply chain network design, sustainability and circular economy. He has publications in the *International Journal of Production Research, Journal of Cleaner Production, Cleaner Technologies and Environmental Policy*, and *Total Quality Management and Business Excellence*. He has also reviewed articles for the *International Journal of Production Research, Computers and Industrial Engineering*, and *International Journal of Lean Six Sigma*. He obtained his master's degree in industrial engineering from the National Institute of Technology, Tiruchirappalli, India, and bachelor's degree in mechanical engineering from Anna University, Tiruchirappalli, India.

Raymond Markey joined Macquarie University at the end of 2011 as Professor of Employment Relations in the Department of Marketing and Management and Director of the new Centre for Workforce Futures. He had previously spent almost seven years as a professor of employment relations at the Auckland University of Technology Business School (2005–11), and was foundation director of the New Zealand Work and Labour Market Institute (2006–2011) as well as associate dean of research (2006–2009). Prior to that he was convenor of the Industrial Relations Programme at the University of Wollongong from 1979 to 2005, where he also established and led the Centre for Work and Labour Market Studies.

Donato Masi is Senior Lecturer in Operations Management at Aston Business School in Birmingham. He holds a PhD in management engineering and an MSc in mechanical engineering from Politecnico di Milano, Italy. He is a specialist in sustainable operations and supply chain management, and he published several scientific papers in top-ranked international journals for this area. He actively collaborates with industry through private and publicly funded research projects. He is currently focusing on how digitalisation and the emerging Industry 4.0 approach can enhance the sustainability of operations and supply chains.

Mark Matthews is a public policy and innovation strategy specialist who has worked in both academia and consulting. He has a doctorate in science and technology policy studies from the Science Policy Research Unit (SPRU), University of Sussex. Matthews has held senior positions in universities in the UK and Australia, and has also worked on innovation strategy for a number of consulting firms. In addition to innovation strategy and economic development, he has a research interest in the management (and mismanagement) of uncertainty and risk in the public sector. His work on global value chains (GVCs) has a strong focus on empirical analyses of the structure and performance of GVCs using the new global data sets now becoming available. Matthews is currently Director in the Ipsos MORI Social Research Institute based in London, UK.

Steven A. Melnyk (PhD, Western, 1981) is Professor of Supply Chain Management at Michigan State University. He has co-authored 21 books, over 100 refereed journal articles and numerous practitioner articles. His research focus includes supply chain risk and resilience, strategic supply chain management, supply chain cyber security, and certified management standards. Melnyk sits on the editorial review board for numerous journals, including the *Journal of Business Logistics*, the *International Journal of Production Research*, and the *International Journal of Operations and Production Management*. From 2014 to 2016, Melnyk was a member of the APICS Board of Directors. From 2017 to 2019, Melnyk had a joint appointment from the University of Newcastle (Australia) where he was the Newcastle Global Innovation Chair in Supply Chain Management. In 2017, the Academy of Management, the Operations and Supply Chain Division, recognised Melnyk as a Distinguished Scholar in the field. Melnyk is recognised for this ability to bridge the gap between theory and practice. In 2018, Melnyk received the Withrow Teacher-Scholar Award from the Eli Broad School of Business, Michigan State University, in recognition of his work as both a researcher and a teacher. His recent work has included a study for the Department of the Navy addressing the question of how good a customer was the Navy and a study for the National Defense Industry Association regarding supply chain cybersecurity.

Sébastien Miroudot is senior trade policy analyst in the Trade in Services Division of the OECD Trade and Agriculture Directorate. He has spent 15 years working on trade and investment issues, including the creation of trade statistics in value-added terms (TiVA), the construction of a services trade restrictiveness index (STRI) and the analysis of the policy implications of global value chains. Before joining the OECD, he was researcher at Sciences Po in Groupe d'Economie Mondiale and taught international economics. In 2016-2017, he was visiting professor at the Graduate School of International Studies (GSIS) of Seoul National University. His research interests focus on trade in services, the role of multinational enterprises in trade and the analysis of global value chains. He holds a PhD in international economics from Sciences Po, Paris.

Anushree Mistry recently completed her PhD in engineering with a focus on complex systems and energy systems with a view to providing policy recommendations. Mistry is also an active member of the School of Information, Systems and Modelling in the Faculty of Engineering and IT and the Management Discipline Group in the UTS Business School at the University of Technology Sydney as a casual academic involved in subject development, coordination and facilitating learning at both undergraduate and postgraduate levels in a variety of subjects revolving around energy systems and management. Mistry is open to collaboration and co-authorship in research projects involving complex systems and policy decision-making.

Sarwat Nafei is a cybersecurity expert with 20 years of experience in the information technology field. He held many executive positions at the fortune 500 corporations and the Big 4 firms (i.e. Deloitte, EY, PwC, and KPMG). Recently he was the vice president for National Cybersecurity CGI-Canada (one of the largest multinational IT corporations). He also served on the cybersecurity committee of the International Telecom Union, a United Nations organisation. He has a degree in Electrical Engineering, MBA, and is currently a PhD researcher at Leicester Castle Business School. He holds multiple industry certifications, including certified information system security professional (CISSP), certified information system auditor (CISA), and PSEC System Engineer, and was the head of an International Association of Privacy Professionals (IAPP) chapter. He has a passion for education and taught at well-ranked universities, including York University and American University. In his capacity as a program director and professor he was developing courses, exams and teaching cybersecurity, IT management, IT audit for undergrads as well as for graduate programs and EMBAs.

Rema Padman is Trustees Professor of Management Science and Healthcare Informatics in the Heinz College of Information Systems and Public Policy at Carnegie Mellon University in Pittsburgh, Pennsylvania. She is also Thrust Leader of Healthcare Informatics Research at iLab, research area director for Operations and Informatics at the Center for Health Analytics at the Heinz College, and adjunct professor in the Department of Biomedical Informatics at the University of Pittsburgh School of Medicine. Her research investigates healthcare informatics, analytics and operations, data-driven decision support, and process modelling and risk analysis in the context of clinical (using electronic health records) and consumer-facing IT interventions in healthcare, such as e-health, m-health, chronic and infectious disease management, and workflow analysis. She has developed, applied, and evaluated models and methods drawn from operations research, machine learning, and behavioural science for designing and investigating these IT interventions in the emergency, inpatient, ambulatory, and consumer self-health management settings. She has published extensively in major academic journals and served on their editorial boards; been a keynote speaker at multiple conferences; and advised healthcare informatics projects for provider, payer, pharmaceutical, consulting and non-profit organisations. She has also served on proposal review panels of the US and international funding agencies, and received funding from federal agencies and foundations. *Becker's Hospital Review* recognised her as one of the top 110 women in MedTech in 2017 and she was nominated for the 2018 HIMSS Most Influential Women in Health IT Award.

Sanjoy Kumar Paul is currently working as Senior Lecturer in Operations and Supply Chain Management at UTS Business School of the University of Technology Sydney. He has published more than 60 articles in top-tier journals and conferences, including the *European Journal of Operational Research*, *International Journal of Production Economics*, *Computers and Operations Research*, *International Journal of Production Research*, *Annals of Operations Research*, *Journal of Management in Engineering*, *Journal of Cleaner Production*, *Computers and Industrial Engineering*, *Journal of Retailing and Consumer Services*, and *Journal of Intelligent Manufacturing*. He is also an active reviewer of many reputed journals. Paul has received several awards in his career, including the ASOR Rising Star Award to recognise early career researchers in operations research, the Excellence in Early Career Research Award from the UTS Business School, the Stephen Fester prize for most outstanding thesis and the high impact publications award from UNSW. His research interest includes supply chain risk management, modelling, applied operations research and intelligent decision-making.

Phi Yen Phan is a third year PhD student and a research assistant in the business school at the University of Technology Sydney. Her doctoral research investigates supply chain innovation in the context of Vietnamese agricultural supply chain, based on mixed methods of qualitative and quantitative research. She is also a lecturer at the University of Economics and Law, Vietnam National University HCMC. She holds a master's degree in logistics and supply chain management from Sheffield Hallam University, England, and a bachelor's degree in management information systems from Vietnam National University HCMC. Yen's research interests span a wide range of disciplines: operations management, logistics, supply chain management, innovation, e-commerce and management information systems. She was a core member of the e-commerce project at Vietnam National University and co-authored a book *Electronic Commerce* published by Vietnam National University in 2015.

Kazi Waziur Rahman is a final year postgraduate student at the University of Technology Sydney (UTS). He is pursuing a master's of strategic supply chain and will be eligible for CIPS

(Chartered Institute of Procurement and Supply) membership. He received his bachelor's of business (major – management) degree in 2009 from Southern Cross University, Australia. He has several years professional experience in Australian retail and the Bangladeshi apparel supply chain segment. He has successfully co-authored two book chapters and is currently serving as a research assistant at UTS. His current research interests are on supply chain resilience, disruptive innovation and design, modularity in system design, understanding ripple effect dynamics and time criticality, due diligence in global food supply chain, and operational sustainability.

Göran Roos is a Visiting Professor in Business Performance and Intangible Asset Management, Centre for Business Performance, Cranfield School of Management, Cranfield University and a Visiting Professor at Australian Industrial Transformation Institute, Flinders University. He is a CSIRO fellow and a fellow of the Australian Academy of Technological Sciences and Engineering (ATSE) and of the Royal Swedish Academy of Engineering Sciences (IVA). He has published extensively on strategy, industry policy and intellectual capital and is advising companies and governments globally on these topics.

Moira Scerri, PhD, is Lecturer in Operations and Supply Chain Management at the University of Technology Sydney. She is also a director of the Centre of Business and Social Innovation (CBSI). She teaches in the areas of operations and quality management, problem solving, creativity and solution setting, and supply chain technology management. Her research interests include digital transforming with a focus on new and emerging technologies such as blockchain, 3D printing, artificial intelligence, machine learning, cloud-based computing and the sharing economy. She is also the recipient of a number of internal and external competitive research grants. Her work has appeared in leading journals such as *Service Theory and Practice*, *Technology Forecasting* and *Social Change*.

Wenwen Sheng is Associate Professor at the Economic Institute, National Development and Reform Commission of China. She worked at the Division of Market Development, International Trade Centre (ITC) from 2019 to 2020 as the Junior Professional Officer. Previously, she worked at the State Administration of Foreign Exchange and Research Bureau of the People's Bank of China during 2014–2016. She holds a PhD in economics (2014) from Renmin University of China. Her research interests include financial development, monetary policy and international finance.

Katrina Skellern is Post-Doctoral Research Fellow with the Centre for Business & Social Innovation at the University of Technology Sydney (UTS) Business School. She has over 20 years of experience in project management, policy development, program evaluation, business model innovation, and community and stakeholder engagement in Australia and internationally. Skellern is currently working on a business model transformation project with the Innovative Manufacturing Cooperative Research Centre.

Jimena Sotelo is Project Lead of Digital Trade at the Centre for the Fourth Industrial Revolution of the World Economic Forum, based in San Francisco. Her work focuses on the intersection of new technologies and trade. She has ten years of experience working on trade in international organisations and the private sector. She worked for the International Trade Centre and the think tank ICTSD in Geneva, as well as for the Organization of American States in Washington DC. Her experience in the private sector was at Banco Comafi SA and DuPont, in Buenos Aires. She has a bachelor's degree in international trade and a postgraduate course in international business from the Universidad Argentina de la Empresa (UADE), where she was awarded top honours. She also holds a master's in international law and economics from the World Trade Institute (WTI) at the University of Bern, where she graduated summa cum laude.

Daria Taglioni is Lead Economist in the World Bank Chief Economist Office. She has been with the World Bank Group since 2011, covering issues of international trade and countries' trade competitiveness. Her career started with the Organisation for Economic Co-operation and Development in Paris and she also worked at the European Central Bank for several years. She has published extensively in peer-reviewed journals, and her work has been cited in the *New York Times* and *Forbes*. She has authored various books on international trade, including *Making Global Value Chains Work for Development* (with Deborah Winkler), *Inclusive Global Value Chains* (with Ana Paula Cusolito and Raed Safadi), *Vietnam at a Crossroads: Engaging in the Next Generation of Global Value Chains* (with Claire Hollweg and Tanya Smith), and *Valuing Services in Trade* (with Sebastian Saez, Erik van der Marel, Claire Hollweg and Veronika Zavaka). She was also the Task Team Leader for the World Development Report 2020, *Trading for Development in the Age of Global Value Chains*. She is Italian and holds a PhD in international economics from the Graduate Institute, Geneva.

V. G. Venkatesh is a faculty member with EM Normandie Business School, France. He has years of industrial and teaching experience in the supply chain domain from Honduras, Sri Lanka, New Zealand, Colombia, USA, France and Bangladesh. He has been actively publishing his academic research in reputable journals in the areas of supplier networks, social sustainability, transportation infrastructure and strategic procurement.

Ganeshan Wignaraja is a Non-Resident Senior Fellow at the Institute of South Asian Studies at the National Univeristy of Singapore and a Senior Research Associate at the Overseas Development Institute in London. Previously, Wignaraja was the Executive Director of the Lakshman Kadirgamar Institute of International Relations and Strategic Studies in Sri Lanka, Director of Research at the ADB Institute in Tokyo and a Visiting Scholar at the IMF in Washington DC. He has published widely on international economics and regional economic integration in Asia including *Production Neworks and Enterprises in East Asia and Asia's Free Trade Agreements: How is Business Responding?* Wignaraja has a DPhil in economics from Oxford University.

Deborah Winkler is Senior Consultant in the World Bank Group's Macroeconomics, Trade and Investment Global Practice. Winkler has worked on issues of global value chains; export competitiveness; foreign direct investment; trade in services; offshoring; and their determinants, welfare and distributional effects. She is the author of *Making Global Value Chains Work for Development* (with Daria Taglioni, World Bank, 2016), *Outsourcing Economics* (with William Milberg, Cambridge University Press, 2013) and *Services Offshoring and Its Impact on the Labor Market* (Springer, 2009). Winkler is the editor of *Making Foreign Direct Investment Work for Sub-Saharan Africa* (with Thomas Farole, World Bank, 2014). She has published over 30 articles in peer-reviewed journals and edited volumes. Winkler was a core team member of the *World Development Report 2020*. She is a former research associate of the New School for Social Research and received her PhD in economics from the University of Hohenheim in Germany.

Brian Wixted is an Adjunct Professor at the Johnson-Shoyama Graduate School of Public Policy at the University of Saskatchewan and a member of The Centre for the Study of Science and Innovation Policy (CSIP). Brian has worked for the Australian Government on science and innovation policy issues and for a research centre at what is now known as Western Sydney University. His research work has focused particularly on global cluster and value chains in science, technology and innovation. His interests cover a broad range of topics related to the changing global economy as emerging technologies restructure the economic and technological landscapes. He is the author of *Innovation System Frontiers: Cluster Networks and Global Value* (Springer 2009).

Abraham Zhang is Senior Lecturer in Supply Chain Management at Auckland University of Technology (AUT), where he received the Emerging Scholar Award from the Faculty of Business, Economics and Law in 2018. He is an honorary Senior Research Fellow of Lumen Research Institute, Excelsia College (Australia) and Indiana Wesleyan University (USA). He obtained his PhD from the University of Hong Kong in 2011. He received the Dean's Award for Outstanding Emerging Scholar in 2015 from the University of Waikato Management School. Before he moved into academia, he was a production supervisor in Singapore and a Lean management consultant serving the Asia-Pacific region. He has been actively publishing his research and consulting works in reputable academic journals, including *Omega, International Journal of Production Economics, International Journal of Operations and Production Research, Supply Chain Management: An International Journal, International Journal of Production Research* and *Journal of Cleaner Production*. His current research focuses on supply chain sustainability, especially on circular supply chain management and blockchain-based sustainable supply chain management.

Wei Zhang is Economic Affairs Officer in the Accessions Division of the World Trade Organization (WTO). She serves as co-secretary of a number of accession working parties, and covers technical assistance and publications. Prior to that, she served as a trade negotiator at the Permanent Mission of China to the WTO and Ministry of Commerce, China. Zhang holds a summa cum laude master's in international law and economics from the World Trade Institute, University of Bern. Her research focuses on digital trade, global value chain and WTO accessions.

Quan Zhao is Trade Policy Adviser in the Office of the Chief Economist, International Trade Centre (ITC). He leads the trade in services team at ITC and is responsible for policy research and project management in the areas of trade in services, e-commerce, digital economy and cross-border investment. He also advises the senior management on trade and investment issues in the context of the G20. Prior to joining the ITC, Zhao was a trade negotiator and diplomat at the Permanent Mission of China to the World Trade Organization (WTO) and the Ministry of Commerce of China. He served as the chair of the WTO's Committee on Trade in Financial Services, and lead services negotiator in a number of China's free trade agreement (FTA) negotiations.

Ray Y. Zhong is Assistant Professor in the Department of Industrial and Manufacturing Systems Engineering, University of Hong Kong. He was a Lecturer in the Department of Mechanical Engineering, University of Auckland, New Zealand, from June 2016 to January 2019. Zhong gained his MPhil and PhD in signal and information processing and industrial and manufacturing systems engineering from the Guangdong University of Technology (China) and the University of Hong Kong (Hong Kong), respectively. His research interests include internet of things (IoT)-enabled manufacturing, big data in manufacturing and supply chain management, and data-driven APS. He has published over 160 research publications (~80 Science Citation Index journals and ~80 conference papers). The total citations from Google Scholar is over 4700 with the H-index: 32, i10-index: 70 (as of 14 August 2020). He has five of the most cited papers from Web of Science. In addition, he has participated in a set of projects sponsored by the NSFC, National R&D Department, HK ITF and HKU. He is a member of CIRP RA (2017–2020), ASME (USA), HKIE (Hong Kong), IET (UK), IEEE (USA) and LSCM Hong Kong. Zhong was awarded the Young Author Prize in the 15th IFAC/IEEE/IFIP/IFORS Symposium on Information Control Problems in Manufacturing, Young Scientist Award (2017) from New Zealand Chinese Scientist Association (Only Awardee), and several best conference papers in reputable IEEE conferences.

PREFACE

The rise of global value chains

GVCs have become the world economy's backbone and central nervous system.

O. Cattaneo, G. Gereffi, and C. Staritz, 2010,
Global Value Chains in a Postcrisis World: A
Development Perspective, *Washington, DC: The*
World Bank, p. 7

This Companion provides a review of global value chains (GVCs) and the megatrends shaping them. We have seen over the last century the various ways in which the world manages the production and delivery of goods and services, sometimes summarised as "made-here-sold-there goods crossing borders" (Daria and Winkler, 2016). Globalisation has now evolved alongside automation and digitalisation such that finished products are now the result of manufacturing and assembly across multiple countries around the globe. In particular, GVCs have expanded each country's reach into international trade by enabling them to "make things, not just sell things" (Daria and Winkler, 2016). While multinational enterprises account for one-third of world production and half of world trade (OECD, 2018), GVCs now make up more than two-thirds of world trade. They have become an all-pervasive mechanism that facilitates the exchange of raw materials and intermediate parts for the production of goods and services, services for businesses, and capital goods (OECD, 2020).

Significantly, the scale and pervasiveness of the 2008–2009 global financial crisis (GFC) reflected the increased complexity of globalisation, and the COVID-19 pandemic has even more viscerally exposed the vulnerability of GVCs and the loss of "sovereign capability." Overlayering the impact of the pandemic is the re-emergence of geopolitical conflict and the struggle for technological pre-eminence, particularly between the US and China. As a result, while globalisation is unlikely to go into full-scale retreat, organisations are actively seeking new ways to diversify and shorten their supply chains, so as to become less dependent on any single country's production and assembly. For example, in an attempt to mitigate risk, organisations are changing the locations from which they source their resource requirements (Wu, 2020), while also instigating new collaborative relationships not previously entered into or possibly even considered (see Chapter 4). Consequently, the future growth and sustainability of GVCs will need to accommodate some element of "deglobalisation" as businesses reshore identified strategic activities and avoid excessive dependence on externally developed and controlled technologies ("The changes Covid-19," 2020).

Characteristics of GVCs

It is sometimes said that the global economy can be viewed either through the lens of growth and structural change in individual countries, developed and developing, or through GVCs, the complex network structure of flows of goods, services, capital and technology across national borders (World Bank, 2019a). This Companion covers both aspects as they are complementary to one another and demonstrate the underlying technological and broader economic forces at work in shaping the patterns of interconnectedness at both the regional and global levels. Over the last two decades, the world has been transformed and energised by GVCs, which have reduced trade barriers, lowered the costs of logistics and distribution, precipitated a massive structural change, and created many new jobs in developing countries. Combined with technological advances, GVCs are transforming the way international trade operates and have become a major driver of global economic growth, which must also be re-engineered for environmental sustainability (World Bank, 2019a).

A major contribution of GVCs has been to source inputs more efficiently and effectively, as well as access knowledge and capital through innovative collaborations and internationalisation that have facilitated expansion into new markets (OECD, 2013; also see Chapter 4). The evidence suggests that GVCs have had a pivotal role in reducing poverty and have been instrumental in offering opportunities to developing countries to grow and catch up with more affluent nations (World Bank, 2019b). Yet the growth of GVCs has slowed since the GFC. From 2000 to 2007, complex GVCs expanded at a faster rate than world production. During the GFC there was naturally some retrenchment of GVCs followed by recovery during 2010–2011, but subsequently GVC growth was sluggish. It was only recently, since 2017, that complex GVCs again began to grow faster than world production, and until COVID-19 their rise was considered unstoppable due to the fragmentation and dispersion of business activities across the globe. Now we see as a result of technological change and an increasing emphasis in business models on core competences, an increasing tension between on-shoring through the move of production and sourcing closer to the end user (Clarke-Sather and Cobb, 2019) and outsourcing enabling more cost-competitive externalisation of business activities (Kano et al., 2019).

GVCs are both global and regional, and their characteristics have varied over time. Between 2000 and 2017, intra-regional GVC trade increased in "Factory Asia" reflecting, in part, upgrading by China and other Asian economies. In contrast, intra-regional GVC trade in "Factory Europe" and "Factory North America" decreased slightly relative to inter-regional GVC trade reflecting stronger linkages with Factory Asia. Among leading economies, China has emerged as an important hub in traditional trade and "simple GVC networks," but the US and Germany remain the most important hubs in "complex GVC networks."

Global collaboration, integration and alignment

According to the Organisation for Economic Co-operation and Development (OECD), there is evidence of a decline in fragmentation of production across the world, and even when the growth of GVCs declined during 2011, firms were not only reducing their use of foreign inputs but became part of shorter GVCs (Miroudot and Nordström, 2019). Essentially there are two GVC megatrends in progress here. The first megatrend involves a shift in the share of global purchasing power towards developing economies with major changes in the characteristics of

GVCs. Regional trade has risen as a share, especially in Asia, resulting in more production being consumed in domestic markets in these developing countries instead of being exported to countries outside the region. This is shifting the trade paradigm from being one based on comparative advantage to one based on differential labour costs and labour arbitrage. Whilst this megatrend is still in transition, these low-income developing countries will continue to depend on access to global demand using traditional, labour-intensive processes in manufacturing.

The second megatrend involves digitalisation of GVCs (Schniederjans, Curado, and Khalajhedayati, 2020) through emergence of blockchain (Chalmers, Matthews, and Hyslop, 2019), Industry 4.0 technologies (Bibby and Dehe, 2018; Fatorachian and Kazemi, 2018) and data analytics (Sivarajah et al., 2017; Yasmin et al., 2020). This will over time transform entire economies and the way in which manufacturing and trade take place. Future GVCs will ultimately be built on digital foundations, and these new technologies and skills will become core across GVCs. In Asia, GVCs have already displaced the labour-intensive technologies, especially in the textile and clothing sector. The future of GVCs not only relies on the traditional growth model but also increasingly on the ability of the "industries of the future" to adopt Supply Chain 4.0 principles. By this is meant the reorganisation of supply chains – design and planning, production, distribution, consumption, and reverse logistics functions – using big data, 3D printing, advanced (autonomous) robotics, smart sensors, augmented reality, artificial intelligence, cloud computing and the internet of things (IoT). With the adoption of these emerging technologies, complex GVC activities will be reshaped and reimagined (World Bank, 2019a).

Small and medium enterprises

Whilst the rise of GVCs is a phenomenon of our time as a result of the fragmentation and dispersion of business activities throughout most of the world, the benefits have so far primarily been accrued by large multinationals, which are best placed to take advantage of the new opportunities. However, with the shift from vertically integrated mass production to smaller, more specialised interdependent units of the production process, small and medium-sized enterprises (SMEs) have also become more globalised. Even during the broader productivity slowdown in the advanced economies over recent years, SMEs have become the "frontier firms" experiencing significantly greater productivity growth than the "laggards," which still comprise the vast majority of SMEs. The problem is that many SMEs have not taken the step to becoming "micromultinationals," as there is limited awareness of the benefits they gain from participation in international trade (Gonzalez et al., 2019).

SMEs face a range of challenges, including limited access to resources and finances for new investments, lower skills related to management, limited access information and technology, and lower levels of productivity, thus making it harder for them to grow and scale globally (Gonzalez et al., 2019). GVCs can help SMEs access better and cheaper inputs to increase their global presence and competitiveness, and offer new opportunities through "smart specialisation" in intermediate products rather than attempting to master all the tasks required to produce final goods. New research finds that when a manufacturing SME has a fully functional, interactive website, not surprisingly its participation in GVCs and trade generally significantly increases. In particular, such SMEs are more likely to use foreign inputs for production and export a larger share of their output. Further, digital connectivity is found to be more important for smaller firms than for large ones whether or not the firm participates in trade. As such, with the rise of the digital economy, being able to exploit the potential of digital platforms will allow SMEs to improve their international trade performance and build a competitive advantage in global ecosystems (OECD, 2008).

To maximise the potential gains for SMEs, a holistic approach is crucial, particularly one that combines high-quality management, investment in information and communications technology (ICT) infrastructure and human capital, access to finance and logistics, and trade-based reforms. Additionally, more resilient GVC networks can be achieved by strategies at the firm level that place an emphasis on risk awareness, risk mitigation and greater transparency, integration, and alignment across the network. It has been noted that this can be achieved through programs supporting greater agility and adaptability, as SMEs operate under extremely volatile, uncertain, complex and ambiguous (VUCA) environments (Schoemaker, 2018). Improving the availability of historical data also helps to better understand and integrate SMEs in GVC networks.

Impact of COVID-19: A future megatrend

Change can be so profound and dislocating that it is challenging to distinguish disaster from opportunity.

> *"The changes covid-19 is forcing on to business,"*
> 2020, The Economist, *https://www.economist.com*
> */briefing/2020/04/11/the-changes-covid-19-is-forci*
> *ng-on-to-business*

For some time GVCs have been hailed as "the world economy's backbone and central nervous system" (Cattaneo, Gereffi and Staritz, 2010, p. 7) and they are recognised as the vital governance structures of business value creation. However, according to a new McKinsey report, "supply chain disruptions lasting a month or longer now happen every 3.7 years on average" (Lund et al., 2020). In addition, the operation of GVCs has been challenged by the COVID-19 pandemic, reigniting an old debate about the supply chain risks associated with international production systems. The pandemic has exposed the vulnerabilities of interconnected and interdependent trade relationships that involve multiple actors spanning multiple countries with supply chain activities and resources running both upstream and downstream (Gereffi, Humphrey and Sturgeon, 2005).

The COVID-19 outbreak shook the world and not only restricted the value chain flow of medical supplies needed for patient treatment, protection and control (World Health Organization, 2020), but also brought the movement of people and goods across national boundaries almost to a complete halt. In some countries, particularly the US, the pandemic has been characterised as more a policy failure than a market failure necessitating more resilient supply chains and diversified sourcing patterns (Gereffi, 2020). Whilst in other similar health-related crises, such as SARS, Ebola and swine flu, serious supply chain disruptions were experienced, the devastating long-term economic impact of COVID-19 is on a different, more far-reaching scale. At the same time that it offers new opportunities for inclusive, low emissions growth paths, along with active fiscal and monetary policies, this crisis must be placed into a unique category of global socioeconomic disruptions (Gupta, 2020), where "companies need an understanding of their exposure, vulnerabilities, and potential losses to inform reliance strategies" (Lund et al., 2020).

While businesses, governments and researchers are grappling with the fallout from the pandemic, those engaged in GVCs and the revival and reinvention of manufacturing capability are already identifying the new opportunities created by this disruption (Green, 2020). Certainly, the pandemic has triggered alarm bells about the pitfalls of reliance in any GVC on a single country or market, but it has also accelerated the trend to the shorter, more manageable GVCs associated with digitalisation, artificial intelligence and the rise of Industry 4.0. It has also refocused attention on the role of GVCs in addressing the major issues of climate change and worker protections. This will signify not a reversal of globalisation but the transition to new forms of global connectivity with production and sourcing closer to the end user and a discontinuous shift in the choices and expectations of consumers, suppliers and organisations (Harari, 2020). While it is not possible to predict exactly how globalisation will evolve from here, we can be sure that COVID-19 will have a major impact in accelerating current observable trends and preparing the way for new ones.

References

Bibby, L., & Dehe, B. (2018). Defining and assessing Industry 4.0 maturity levels—case of the defence sector. *Production Planning & Control, 29*(12), 1030–1043.

Cattaneo, O., Gereffi, G., & Staritz, C. (2010). *Global Value Chains in a Postcrisis World: A Development Perspective.* Washington, DC: The World Bank.

Chalmers, D., Matthews, R., & Hyslop, A. (2019). Blockchain as an external enabler of new venture ideas: Digital entrepreneurs and the disintermediation of the global music industry. *Journal of Business Research.*

Clarke-Sather, A., & Cobb, K. (2019). Onshoring fashion: Worker sustainability impacts of global and local apparel production. *Journal of Cleaner Production, 208*, 1206–1218.

Fatorachian, H., & Kazemi, H. (2018). A critical investigation of Industry 4.0 in manufacturing: Theoretical operationalisation framework. *Production Planning & Control, 29*(8), 633–644.

Gereffi, G. (2020). What does the COVID-19 pandemic teach us about global value chains? The case of medical supplies. *Journal of International Business Policy, 3*, 287–301.

Gereffi, G., Humphrey, J., & Sturgeon, T. (2005). The governance of global value chains. *Review of International Political Economy, 12*(1), 78–104.

Green, R. (2020). "Making it in Australia," in E. Dawson & J. McCalman (eds.), *What Happens Next? Reconstructing Australia after COVID-19.* Melbourne University Publishing.

Gupta, A. (Producer). (2020). "After Covid: The new normal webinar." Retrieved 7 August 2020 from https ://www.youtube.com/watch?v=uqBqSIl3ItU&app=desktop.

Harari, Y. N. (2020). The world after Coronavirus. Retrieved 7 August 2020 from https://www.ft.com/c ontent/19d90308-6858-11ea-a3c9-1fe6fedcca75.

Kano, L., Tsang, E.W., & Yeung, H.W.-C. (2020). Global value chains: A review of the multi-disciplinary literature. *Journal of International Business Studies, 51*, 577–622.

López González, J., Munro, L., Gourdon, J, Mazzini, G., & Andrenelli, A. (2019). Participation and benefits of SMEs in GVCs in Southeast Asia, OECD Trade Policy Papers, No. 231, OECD Publishing, Paris. http://dx.doi.org/10.1787/3f5f2618-en.

Lund, S., Manyika, J., Woetzel, J. Barriball, E., Krishnan, M., Alicke, K., Birshan, M., George, K., Smit, S., Swan, D., & Hutzler, K. (2020). "Risk, resilience, and rebalancing in global value chains." McKinsey Global Institute. https://www.mckinsey.com/business-functions/operations/our-insights/risk-resilie nce-and-rebalancing-in-global-value-chains?cid=other-eml-alt-mip-mck&hlkid=613f28d440d54d8 fbd394c7d3eb20aca&hctky=2749456&hdpid=6f558006-aeb4-489b-9c38-d1d9421f2077

Miroudot, S., & H. Nordström (2019), "Made in the world revisited," RSCAS Applied Network Science Working Paper No. 2019/84, European University Institute.

OECD. (2008). *Enhancing the Role of SMEs in Global Value Chains.* Paris: OECD Publishing. https://doi.org /10.1787/9789264051034-en.

OECD. (2013). *Interconnected Economies: Benefiting from Global Value Chains.* Paris: OECD Publishing. https://doi.org/10.1787/9789264189560-en.

OECD. (2018). *Multinational Enterprises in the Global Economy: Heavily Debated but Hardly Measured.* Paris: OECD Publishing. https://www.oecd.org/industry/ind/MNEs-in-the-global-economy-policy-note .pdf.

OECD. (2020a). "COVID-19 and global value chains: Policy options to build more resilient production networks." Retrieved 28 July 2020 from http://www.oecd.org/coronavirus/policy-responses/covid-19-and-global-value-chains-policy-options-to-build-more-resilient production-networks-04934ef4/.

OECD. (2020b). "Trade policy implications of global value chains." https://issuu.com/oecd.publishing/d ocs/trade_policy_implications_of_global.

Schniederjans, D.G., Curado, C., & Khalajhedayati, M. (2020). Supply chain digitisation trends: An integration of knowledge management. *International Journal of Production Economics*, *220*, 107439.

Schoemaker, P. J. H., Heaton, S., & Teece, D. (2018). Innovation, dynamic capabilities, and leadership. *California Management Review*, *61*(1), 15–42.

Sivarajah, U., Kamal, M.M., Irani, Z., & Weerakkody, V. (2017). Critical analysis of big data challenges and analytical methods. *Journal of Business Research*, *70*, 263–286.

Taglioni, Daria, & Deborah Winkler. 2016. *Making Global Value Chains Work for Development*. Trade and Development series. Washington, DC: World Bank.

"The changes Covid-19 is forcing on to business." (2020). *The Economist*. Retrieved 24 July 2020 from https://www.economist.com/briefing/2020/04/11/the-changes-covid-19-is-forcing-on-to-business.

World Bank. (2019a). "The global value chain development report 2019: Technological innovation, supply chain trade, and workers in a globalized world." Retrieved 31 July 2020 from https://www.worldbank.org/en/topic/trade/publication/global-value-chain-development-report-2019.

World Bank. (2019b). *World Development Report 2020: Trading for Development in the Age of Global Value Chains*. Washington, DC: The World Bank.

World Health Organization (WHO). (2020). Novel coronavirus (2019-ncov) situation report – 18 [Press release]. Retrieved 2 August 2020 from https://www.who.int/docs/default-source/coronaviruse/situation-reports/20200207-sitrep-18-ncov.pdf?sfvrsn=fa644293_2

Wu, D. (2020). "Supply lines: Not made in china is global tech's next big trend." *Bloomberg*. Retrieved 2 August 2020 from https://www.bloomberg.com/news/articles/2020-03-31/supply-chains-latest-not-made-in-china-is-tech-s-next-move.

Yasmin, M., Tatoglu, E., Kilic, H.S., Zaim, S., & Delen, D. (2020). Big data analytics capabilities and firm performance: An integrated MCDM approach. *Journal of Business Research*, *114*, 1–15.

HANDBOOK STRUCTURE

The *Routledge Companion to Global Value Chains: Reinterpreting and Reimagining Megatrends in the World Economy* is organised into five parts that draw together key insights into the megatrends driving global value chains:

Part I: History of global value chains
Part II: Global value chains: Theory and practice
Part III: Role of emerging technologies and data analytics in global value chains
Part IV: Megatrends in global value chains
Part V: Implications

These five parts cover a range of topics, both emergent and traditional. The aim of this GVC companion handbook, as with others in the Routledge series, is to provide a state-of-the-art and an up-to-date, enduring and authoritative account of the GVC field.

ABBREVIATIONS

Following is a list of terms used as abbreviations in *The Routledge Companion to Global Value Chains*, along with their extended form. The abbreviations are listed in alphabetical order and by no means are exhaustive.

Abbreviation	Expanded form
3D	three dimensional
3PL	third-party logistics
G20	Group of Twenty
AD	Anno Domini
ADB	Asian Development Bank
ACP	African, Caribbean and Pacific
ADBI	Asian Development Bank Institute
AfCFTA	African Continental Free Trade Area
AFTA	ASEAN Free Trade Area
AHP	analytic hierarchy process
ASCM	agri-food supply chain management
ASEAN	Association of Southeast Asian Nations
Ai	Australian Industry
B2B	business-to-business
B2C	business-to-consumer
BCMA	barcoded medication administration
BERD	business expenditure on R&D
BC	Before Christ
BIT	bilateral investment treaty
BTD	Bilateral Trade Database
CEPT	Common Effective Preferential Tariff
CFA	confirmatory factor analysis
CEO	chief executive officer
CMB	common method bias
CoV	coefficient of variation
COVID-19	2019 novel coronavirus or 2019-nCoV

CR	consistency ratio
CRM	customer relationship management
DC	dynamic capabilities
DDMRP	Demand Driven Materials Requirements Planning
EEF	(now Make UK)
E2E	end to end
ERP	enterprise resource planning
EU	European Union
FDI	foreign direct investment
FOIK	first of a kind
FTA	free trade agreement
FVA	foreign value added
FVC	food value chain
GATT	General Agreement on Trade and Tariffs
GDP	gross domestic product
GM	General Motors
GPN	Global Production Network
GSP	Generalised System of Preferences
GFVC	global food value chain
GVA	global value architecture
GVC	**global value chain**
IAS	Innovation Activity Separability
ICIO	inter-country input–output
ICT	information and communications technology
ICTSD	International Centre for Trade and Sustainable Development
IoT	internet of things
IP	intellectual property
IPR	intellectual property rights
ITA	Information Technology Agreement
KPIs	key performance indicators
LDC	least developed country
LBE	learning by exporting
LCD	liquid crystal display
M&A	mergers and acquisitions
MAR	medical administration record
MNC	multinational corporation
MNE	multinational enterprise
MRIO	multi-regional input–output
MRP	materials requirement planning
NAIT	National Animal Identification and Tracing
NGO	non-government organisation
NIC	newly industrialised country
NSW	New South Wales
OEA	original equipment assembling
OECD	Organisation for Economic Co-operation and Development
OBM	original brand manufacturing
OEM	original equipment manufacturing
ODM	original design manufacturing

OSCM	operations and supply chain management
PPID	positive patient identification
PwC	PricewaterhouseCoopers
R&D	research and development
RBV	resource-based view
RCEP	Regional Comprehensive Economic Partnership
RFID	radio frequency identification
RI	Random Index
RTA	regional trade agreement
S&OP	sales and operations planning
SC	supply chain
SKU	stock-keeping unit
SME	small and medium enterprise
SOE	state-owned enterprise
SPE	sourcing pathways per economy
TiVA	OECD–WTO Trade in Value Added
TFA	Trade Facilitation Agreement
TOC	theory of constraints
TQM	total quality management
UK	United Kingdom
UNCTAD	United Nations Conference on Trade and Development
UNCTAD-EORA	UNCTAD-Eora Global Value Chain database
US	United States
VA	value added
VMI	vendor management inventory
VUCA	volatile, uncertain, complex and ambiguous
WEF	World Economic Forum
WIOD	World Input-Output Database
WRI	Working Relations Index
WTO	World Trade Organization

PART I

History of global value chains

Before being able to understand the changing nature of global value chains, it is paramount to first understand how global value chains have evolved over time. In Chapter 1, Donato Masi and Janet Godsell outline how global supply chains throughout history have undergone substantial change adapting to the many different innovations that ultimately have shaped this trajectory. They provide an overview of the history of supply chains, from ancient times to more recent times, and discuss some trends that will determine the nature of supply chains of the future.

DOI: 10.4324/9781315225661-1

1

PAST, PRESENT AND FUTURE PERSPECTIVES OF SUPPLY CHAINS

Donato Masi and Janet Godsell

1.1 Ancient times

In ancient times, the vast majority of supply chains were local, limited to a city or a small region. The exchange of materials relied on a set of basic transportation technologies, such as horses or boats; the cost of moving materials was therefore relatively high. However, the exchange of information was quite efficient, since customers could directly communicate with the producer and specify what they wanted. This was the case of pre-industrial artisan manufacturing, which included village weavers, potters, blacksmiths and cobblers. Similarly, in the agrarian supply chain, a farmer would cut the wheat, send it to a mill for grinding into flour, then send it to a baker to make into bread and finally it would be sold at a market stall.

Because of the high transportation costs, long-distance supply chains only traded high-value items such as spices, weapons and luxury goods. For these high-value items, however, there are some noticeable examples of global supply chains that mirror modern ones, at least in terms of geographical extension.

A noticeable example is the olive oil supply chain of the Roman Empire. This supply chain originated in North Africa, where people were effectively cultivating olive trees. These cultivations dramatically influenced the characteristics of the local landscapes, and traces of the roads, ditches and waterworks used to support the cultivation of olives are still visible today. Oil warehouses stored oil in shipping containers called amphorae. Large ships of the grain fleet would then carry wheat and olive oil from Africa to the port of Rome. The technology of the time facilitated the trade, with some examples of solutions like cargo loading cranes that are surprisingly similar to the ones currently employed.

Other noticeable examples of global supply chains in ancient times are the Silk Road through Central Asia and the spice route over the Indian Ocean. The Silk Road was an ancient network of trade routes, formally established during the Han Dynasty of China, which linked the regions of the ancient world in commerce between 130 BC and 1453 AD (Ancient History Encyclopedia, 2018). The goods transported from West to East include wool, carpets, textiles, gold, silver and camels. The goods transported from East to West included silk, tea, dyes and precious stones. These ancient supply chains had the power of influencing the imagination of artists: the Italian explorer Marco Polo travelled on the silk routes and described them in depth in his book *Il Milione*.

 DOI: 10.4324/9781315225661-2

1.2 The Industrial Revolution

The Industrial Revolution that started in the late 18th century radically changed the scale and the nature of global supply chains. Several technological shifts created radical changes in the way of producing and transporting goods.

In 1781 the inventor James Watt built the rotary action steam engine. This engine represented a breakthrough and provided an alternative power source for several industries, such as textile, coal and iron. The textile industry exemplifies well the changes that transformed the supply chains of the time. Textiles were initially slow to adopt the steam engine because of its costs and risks. However, in 1830 steam was the main source of power in the industry and it enabled the creation of new factories as well as large increases of productivity. A global supply network progressively emerged, and it involved shipping cotton from the United States to mills in England. The finished cloth was then shipped out to the rest of the world. Similarly, the coal, iron and steel industries used the new engines for deeper mines and greater coal production; these changes lowered the prices of fuel and steam, thus increasing the demand for coal.

Other innovations in the field of logistics also contributed to modifying the scale and the nature of global supply chains. Railways enabled faster, easier and cheaper transport of goods over longer distances. Rudimentary hand trucks and other tools made it easier to handle goods. Communications improved thanks to steamships and railways able to carry letters.

The industrial structure and the supply chains of the early 20th century were the results of all these innovations in manufacturing and logistics, with communication tools that were still relatively rudimental. The difficult communication between the various echelons of supply chains produced vertically integrated industrial structures, where Fordist production lines would mass manufacture goods, later centralised at major transportation hubs.

The advent of mass production also created strong social tensions. From 1800 to 1850, the population of England and Wales doubled, from 9 million to 18 million. At the same time, the proportion of people living in cities rose from 10 per cent to 50 per cent. The flow of rural people into cities overwhelmed the physical facilities. Poorly built houses were hosting crowded masses of people, and suburbs lacking adequate facilities could not keep pace with the growth in population. In 1845 Engels published "The Condition of the Working Class in England," a study that denounced the poor living conditions of the industrial working class in Victorian England, suffering from long hours, monotonous labour, widespread employment of children and low wages. Serious environmental changes also started to emerge. Coal was the universal fuel to power factories and heat homes, and burnt coal covered English cities, turning many buildings black over time and contributing to air pollution, both inside poorly ventilated factories and outside.

Supply chains became very important during World War II, as military organisations needed efficient supply chains. Supply chains manufactured military hardware and supplies, and the demands of war pushed a consolidation of industrial engineering and operations research into supply chain engineering.

1.3 Supply chains from postwar to current: From offshoring to reshoring to right-shoring

1.3.1 Offshoring

After World War II the decline in barriers to the free flow of goods and services and important technological changes determined the beginning of the globalisation phenomenon. Globalisation implied a shift toward a more interdependent and integrated global economic system, the merging of historically separate national markets into one huge global marketplace, and the possibility of sourcing good and services from locations around the globe. The internationalisation of business activities implied the creation of institutions to govern the global marketplace, such as the International Monetary Fund and the World Bank, both created in 1944, and the General Agreement on Tariffs and Trade (GATT), created in 1948. Industries worldwide thus entered a new era of intense global competition. Manufacturers in particular had to achieve world-class status to compete effectively in global markets, and they had to interlink and incorporate marketing strategy and manufacturing strategy with the corporate strategy (Skinner, 1969, as cited in Deshmukh, 2001). In this context, manufacturers also started to recognise the strategic importance of factory location decisions, also called 'shoring decision' (Kinkel and Maloca, 2009). Offshoring, namely the relocation of parts of production processes to locations abroad irrespective of the ownership mode (Kinkel and Maloca 2009), progressively became one of the most popular location strategies. The outsourced processes were initially operational or supporting processes such as manufacturing or accounting; however, after some time companies started to also offshore technical and administrative services.

Historically, most outsourcing has been directed at the developed nations of the world, as firms based in advanced countries invested in others' markets. During the 1980s and 1990s, the United States was often the favourite target for foreign direct investment (FDI) inflows. Investors include firms based in Great Britain, Japan, Germany, Holland and France. The developed nations of Europe have also been recipients of significant FDI inflows, principally from the United States and other European nations. These developed nations still account for the largest share of FDI inflows (te Velde, 2006; UNCTAD, 2019).

The outsourcing location had a different direction for manufacturing companies with non-advanced manufacturing technologies that perceived labour cost as a large proportion of the overall manufacturing cost. Several of these companies started to relocate their manufacturing plants to Far Eastern locations, where the labour cost was a fraction of the cost in the original locations in developed countries. FDI into developing nations and the transition economies of Eastern Europe and the old Soviet Union progressively increased. The majority of FDI inflows into developing nations had been targeted at the emerging economies of Southeast Asia. Recently, the world economy saw the growing importance of China as a recipient of FDI; the country attracted about $60 billion of FDI in 2004 which steadily rose to a record of $139 billion in 2018 (UNCTAD, 2019).

A key reason for offshoring was the possibility of exploiting national differences in the cost and quality of factors of production such as labour, energy, land and capital. The cost of labour has always been among the most important drivers for offshoring among manufacturing firms. A survey of 1663 German companies by Kinkel and Maloca (2009) revealed that the cost of wages was the most popular driver for offshoring in emerging markets in the years 1999 to 2006. Access to new markets and the vicinity to foreign markets were two other key reasons for offshoring. The United States has been an attractive target for FDI because of its large and wealthy domestic markets, dynamic and stable economy, favourable political environment, and the openness of the country to FDI. The reasons for the strong flow of investments into emerging markets and into China are similar, considering that China represents the world's largest market with its population of more than 1.3 billion people. The presence of related and supporting industries was another important reason for offshoring, since manufacturing companies are often dependent on alliances and partnerships with other companies in order to create additional value for customers and become more competitive. Suppliers were especially mindful to enhancing innovation through more efficient and higher-quality inputs, timely feedback and short lines of communication. Other offshoring drivers included access to a skilled labour force, access to new technologies, capacity constraints in the home country, increasing speed to market and vicinity to foreign customers.

1.3.2 The global economic crisis and the emergence of reshoring

Since 2005 some changes in the business environment started to call into question the paradigm of offshored manufacturing. Firstly, the global economic crisis implied a significant increase in the price of major commodities, raw materials and oil. Therefore, the transportation costs for long-distance deliveries increased significantly. Secondly, a survey conducted by Manning (2014) revealed that companies were starting to feel the difficulty of dealing with communication barriers and cultural differences generated by their offshoring strategy. Thirdly, the macroeconomic situation of some offshoring destinations changed, and increases in labour wages reduced the cost related advantages of offshoring. Fourthly, the business environment saw an increased attention for customer satisfaction, with supply chains forced to be more flexible and responsive, in opposition to the cost advantages given by offshoring strategies (Fratocchi et al., 2011).

As a result, offshoring lost many of its initial strategic advantages. An increasingly high number of firms started to question the real benefits of their 'offshoring' strategies (Holweg, Reichhart and Hong, 2011) and they started to move their offshored production back to their original countries (Kinkel and Maloca, 2009).

This was the beginning of the phenomenon called 'reshoring.' Fratocchi et al. (2014) defined it as "the back relocation of earlier off-shored production activities, and one of the strategic options available to manufacturing firms in terms of international relocation of manufacturing activities irrespective of the ownership mode (in-sourced and out-sourced)" (p. 56). Simply put, right-shoring is "the placement of a business' components and processes in localities and countries that provide the best combination of cost and efficiency" (Investopedia, 2019). In this context, companies make location decisions trying to achieve the best combination of a set of production factors, rather than moving factories overseas to profit from economies of scale or reduction in the cost of the workforce.

Since reshoring started, many manufacturing companies in the United States and in Europe have announced the return to the home countries of all or part of their offshored production (Fratocchi et al., 2014). These manufacturing companies include industrial giants such as Caterpillar, Bosch and Philips.

Some data can help estimate the extent of the reshoring phenomenon. Data from 2007 and 2009 has shown that there were 249 companies involved in reshoring activities in the United States and in Europe (Ancarani et al., 2015). Similarly, the "European Manufacturing Survey" revealed that offshoring activities of German manufacturing firms declined by 17 per cent from the mid-1900s to 2012 (Kinkel, 2014; Kinkel and Maloca, 2009). A report from EEF (2014) confirmed that some companies are bringing production closer to the UK, either to Western Europe (9 per cent) or Eastern Europe (12 per cent). Similar studies confirm that the phenomenon has started. Fratocchi et al. (2015) analysed secondary data revealing that there are 377 companies engaged in reshoring globally, including 177 in North America and 194 in Western Europe. However, it is necessary to highlight that despite the emergence of reshoring, offshoring is still the choice of the majority of firms.

Reshoring decisions can have direct and important implications on the competitive position of a firm. A well-formulated reshoring decision implies an analysis of the reasons for reshoring, the content of the reshored activities, the reshoring location and the reshoring mode.

The reasons for reshoring include a blend of internal competitive priorities, external incentives and risk mitigation. A recent study of Godsell et al. (2019) demonstrated that companies that have reshored focused on the competitive priorities of time and flexibility, while also considering other factors such as access to qualified personnel, skills, technology, innovation and the reduction of risk. The proximity to a main market triggered 38 per cent of direct and 37 per cent of indirect reshoring decisions.

Reshoring decisions can affect the full production volume or a percentage of it, and the reshored activities can range from the production of a finished product to the production of a component. The finished products or the components that are reshored can belong to new or consolidated product lines. Similarly, the selection of the reshoring location implies the consideration of several factors such as the proximity to research and development (R&D) facilities, the country of registration or a main market. Regarding the reshoring mode, the company can offshore production capacity back to the home country (direct reshoring) or increase capacity at home instead of abroad (indirect reshoring).

Reshoring decisions have an impact on the performance of the company and of the supply chain. The study of Godsell et al. (2019) focused on the impact of reshoring at the firm level and supply chain level, and analysed the implications of direct and indirect reshoring. Regarding the firm level, the study highlighted that 57 per cent of companies that directly reshored saw an increase in production output, and 75 per cent of companies that indirectly reshored saw an increase in production output. The study also suggests that reshoring provides benefits in terms of flexibility and delivery times, based on the analysis of data collected from companies operating in the automotive industry. Regarding the supply chain level, the study highlighted that the impact on the supply base was not as extensive as expected, with 66 per cent of the 144 companies that reshored reporting no impact on their supply base as a result.

At a macroeconomic level, some preliminary evidence suggests that reshoring has several advantages for the home countries, especially in terms of employment. PWC (2014) estimated that in the UK reshoring could create up to 200,000 jobs and boost GDP by 0.8 per cent in the next decade.

Researchers also started to look beyond the difference between reshoring and offshoring to consider the 'right-shoring' decision, namely the location of the supply chain assets around the globe (Ellram et al., 2013; Gray et al., 2013; Tate, 2014). The factors considered for the right-shoring decision partially overlap with the factors considered for reshoring, and include input/product, cost, labour, logistics, supply chain interruptions risk, strategic access, country risk and government trade policies (Ellram et al., 2013).

Change seems to be the only constant today for supply chains. Christopher and Holweg (2011) observed that supply chains had entered into the 'era of turbulence,' characterised by an unstable business environment and a range of crises or shocks. Classic supply chain managerial models are unfit for this turbulence. The offshoring location strategy, based on the economies of scale, is one of these dated supply chain practices. New supply chain archetypes are emerging, such as the idea of moving from 'dynamic flexibility' to 'structural flexibility.' There is a difference between structural flexibility and dynamic flexibility. Dynamic flexibility reflects the agility of a supply chain and its ability to respond rapidly to variations in volume and mix. This is the traditional measure that characterised the flexibility of the supply chain in the dichotomy between the lean and the agile supply chain. Structural flexibility on the other hand is the ability of the supply chain to adapt to fundamental change. An example of fundamental change is the modification of the 'centre of gravity' of a supply chain, that is the ideal location for a distribution centre that minimises the transportation cost. A dynamically flexible supply chain is able to modify its structure after a change of the centre of gravity.

The achievement of structural flexibility requires five key steps.

The first step consists of considering the supply chain assets needed in the network, namely the number and the nature of the production and distribution plants.

The second step consists in understanding where to position the supply chain assets. In making this decision, managers typically use the mentioned criteria for right-shoring.

The third step consists in deciding what is the best ownership model for the assets. There are two polar choices regarding the ownership model. On the one side, there is the vertically integrated supply chain, or the 'make' model in the make/buy dichotomy. In this model the OEM also owns the assets to produce components or the supporting functions for their production processes. This model emphasises functional integration, protection from market pressure and information integration. On the other side, there is the market-based supply chain, or the 'buy' model in the make/buy dichotomy. In this model the OEM buys in the market the components or the supporting functions for their production processes. This model emphasises functional specialism and market efficiency. Figure 1.1 highlights the difference between the vertically integrated and the market-based supply chain.

The fourth step consists in deciding who will manage the network. The complexity of modern supply chains as well as the need of aligning and optimising the processes requires an actor able to coordinate the whole network beyond the boundaries of the specific firm. An example of actors that can have this type of role for modern supply chains is the fourth-party logistics providers (4PLs) that manage resources, technology, infrastructure and even external logistics providers to design, build and provide supply chain solutions.

The fifth and last step consists of ensuring that the network remains dynamic and refreshed. This step highlights the fact that designing a supply chain is a continuous improvement process, rather than a one-off and isolated activity. In keeping the network dynamic and refreshed, managers have to observe and track the changes and the dynamics of the market, and adapt the choices of the preceding four steps accordingly.

1.4 Future trends

The landscape of supply chain management continues to evolve, and there are two key trends that are profoundly influencing the nature of supply chains and that will play an even greater role in the future. These trends are the Fourth Industrial Revolution and the pressure for a better performance from a triple bottom line perspective.

1.4.1 Supply chains 4.0

The Fourth Industrial Revolution, known as Industry 4.0 (I4.0), refers to recent technological advances where the internet and supporting technologies serve as a backbone to integrate physical objects, human actors, intelligent machines, production lines and processes across supply chains.

Godsell et al. (2020) highlighted that the Fourth Industrial Revolution is changing the nature of supply chains by intervening on six different dimensions: products and services, manufacturing and operations, strategy and organisation, supply chain, business model, and legal considerations.

Products and services are typically made in large batch sizes with limited late differentiation. The I4.0 technologies are enabling late differentiation for most make-to-order products, up to the case in which a production batch has a size of one unit. The digital features of products are

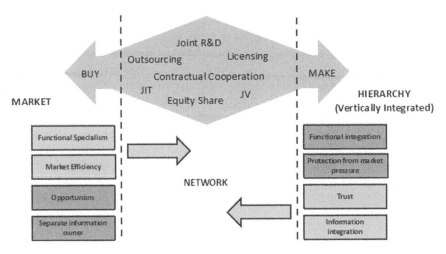

Figure 1.1 Difference between the vertically integrated and the market-based supply chain. (Adapted from Hinterhuber and Hirsch, 1998.)

also changing towards a situation in which products exhibit high digital features and value from intellectual property licensing. Data-driven services are gaining an increasingly important role, and while they currently account for a minor share of revenue (<2.5 per cent), they will play an important role in revenue (>10 per cent) in the near future.

The nature of manufacturing and operations is evolving from situations in automation that control a few machines to a situation in which automation can completely control machines and systems, with the adoption of autonomously guided workpieces and self-optimising processes. While currently only a few processes use digital modelling, the I4.0 technologies create production plants that adopt complete digital modelling for all the relevant processes. IT security solutions are now in their infancy and in the near future they will guarantee the safe exchange of data for all the mentioned applications and they will continuously evolve with the complexity of the systems and of the data exchanged.

Industry 4.0 is also changing the way of defining the strategy and organisation of companies. Connected and automated machines will increase productivity and dynamically adapt to the priorities and the objectives of the firm. In this context, Industry 4.0 will evolve from a functional specialism to a strategy fully implemented across the business and departments, and it will enable a more efficient cross-company collaboration for mutual improvements. Higher levels of Industry 4.0 maturity will require widespread support of the leadership team as well as leading edge digital and analytics skills across the business. This represents an evolution from the current situation in which only some technology-focused areas of the companies have employees with evolved digital skills.

The implementation of I4.0 can make a revolutionary change to the traditional way of managing supply chains, by providing real-time information about upcoming demand, inventories, site location, capacity and operations. This enhanced visibility will guarantee higher levels of supply chain integration, a more agile response from upstream suppliers to downstream logistics providers and ultimately a better response to customers' needs. From a situation in which the response to market changes is relatively slow, the digital supply chain will be able to give an immediate response to changes in the market environment as well as a response that is tailored to individual customer requirements.

The new technologies are facilitating the creation of new business models, and an example is the shift from 'ownership-based' to 'service-based' business models, in which periodic payments ensure dedicated access to services. Service-based business models will require real-time tracking of the products as well as real-time and automated scheduling of maintenance activities. These new business models will benefit from the more integrated supply chains, especially in terms of customer integration, and IT-supported business will continue proliferating, with IT systems supporting and integrating all company processes.

It is finally necessary to consider that for companies to successfully harness the full potential of Industry 4.0, new regulations will be needed. Innovations in the legal profession will follow the challenges opened by the new configuration of business models and supply chains, and they will include new contracting models, legal risk, data access procedures and intellectual property enforcement. These dimensions pose the areas of greatest legal risk but also the greatest opportunity when handled in the most effective way.

1.4.2 Sustainable supply chains

Several societal and environmental challenges are increasing the relevance of the concept of sustainability for companies and supply chains. Among the environmental challenges it is necessary to mention CO_2 emissions and the related climate changes consequences, the production of solid waste, and the depletion of natural resources. Societal challenges created by the way in which modern supply chains operate include modern slavery, decent wages, and occupational health and safety in the production plants and building sites of hazardous industries.

Although a tension between the needs of companies and the protection of the environment and humans was born with the First Industrial Revolution, the scale of this tension has dramatically grown in terms of importance, in parallel with the growth of the impact of business activities on the natural environment.

The news of the last few months have seen the younger generations protesting the consequences of climate change, and the top management of the largest corporations is fully aware of the urgency of adopting sustainable business practices. An example is David Taylor, Procter & Gamble Company's chairman, president and chief executive officer, who recently stated that

> consumers expect the brands they trust to deliver superior performance and to also help solve some of the most complex challenges facing our world. Our global reach, our understanding of the five billion consumers we serve, and our innovation capabilities give us a unique ability to make a positive difference.
>
> *(P&G webpage)*

It is easily possible to find similar statements among the CEOs of other companies operating in different industries.

The environmental challenges are promoting the transition to a circular economy (CE) that proposes new patterns of production, consumption and use based on circular flows of resources (Ghisellini et al. 2016). Traditional supply chains are being progressively replaced by closed-loop supply chains that maximise value creation over the entire life cycle of a product and the dynamic recovery of value from different types and volumes of returns over time (Guide and Van Wassenhove 2009). The introduction of closed-loop supply chains is increasing the importance of activities that were marginal just a few years ago, such as the collection of used products from customers, reverse logistics, inspections and sorting, recovery operations, and finally remarketing.

Supply chain managers of the future will have to manage these new activities, and the nature of the business models and of the traditional linear supply chain activities will change to better accommodate the design and the implementation of the reverse flows. New actors such as NGOs and interest groups are playing a more active role within supply chains, by facilitating awareness at the different levels and by promoting and facilitating the adoption of practices that guarantee the protection of the environment.

The social challenges within supply chains are prompting changes in terms of better supply chain visibility and supply chain integration. Supply chain managers realised that the tool traditionally adopted to ensure the social sustainability of supply chains, such as certification schemes, can only work in a limited number of cases, and they are difficult to implement beyond the first tiers of the supply chains. Suppliers in developing countries often do not have the resources or the capabilities to afford these certification schemes. In light of this situation, supply chain managers are realising that a close integration with suppliers and a diffusion of a sustainability culture can trigger an authentic change and spread its positive effect along the upstream side of supply chains.

It is increasingly clear that these transitions towards more sustainable business practices also have positive implications from a business perspective. The mechanisms creating synergies between environmental sustainability and business objectives are often straightforward, since cutting the consumption of energy and resources and optimising efficiency implies direct cost savings. Similarly, the mechanisms creating synergies between social sustainability and business objectives include a better perception of the brand and all the positive implications of a more integrated supply chain, which have been widely documented in the scientific literature. It is important to highlight that this transition regards not only the Western developed economies but also the companies operating in developing economies that are currently putting sustainability at the heart of their agendas. The future therefore looks bright, and supply chains are more and more contributing to making the world a better place.

References

Ancarani, A., Di Mauro, C., Fratocchi, L., Orzes, G. and Sartor, M., 2015. Prior to reshoring: A duration analysis of foreign manufacturing ventures. *International Journal of Production Economics, 169*, pp.141–155.

Ancient History Encyclopedia, 2018, May 1. Silk road. Available online: https://www.ancient.eu/Silk _Road/

Christopher, M. and Holweg, M., 2011. "Supply Chain 2.0": Managing supply chains in the era of turbulence. *International Journal of Physical Distribution & Logistics Management, 41*(1), pp.63–82.

Deshmukh, D., 2001. Manufacturing strategy: Literature review and some issues [J]. *International Journal of Operations & Production Management, 21*(7), pp.884–932.

EEF, 2014. Backing Britain: A manufacturing base for the future. London. Available online: https://www .themanufacturer.com/wp-content/uploads/2014/03/Backing-Britain-a-manufacturing-base-for-the -future-FINAL.pdf

Ellram, L.M., Tate, W.L. and Petersen, K.J., 2013. Offshoring and reshoring: An update on the manufacturing location decision. *Journal of Supply Chain Management, 49*(2), pp.14–22.

Fratocchi, L., Nassimbeni, G., Zanoni, A., Ancarani, A., Valente, M., Sartor, M., Barbieri, P., Di Mauro, C. and Vignoli, M., 2011, July. Manufacturing back-shoring: A research agenda for an emerging issue in international business. In 37th European International Business Academy Annual Conference.

Fratocchi, L., Di Mauro, C., Barbieri, P., Nassimbeni, G. and Zanoni, A., 2014. When manufacturing moves back: Concepts and questions. *Journal of Purchasing and Supply Management, 20*(1), pp.54–59.

Fratocchi, L., Ancarani, A., Barbieri, P., Di Mauro, C., Nassimbeni, G., Sartor, M., Vignoli, M. and Zanoni, A., 2015. Manufacturing back-reshoring as a nonlinear internationalization process. In *The Future of Global Organizing*, edited by Rob Van Tulder, Alain Verbeke, and Rian Drogendijk (Progress in International

Business Research, Vol. 10), Emerald Group Publishing Limited, United Kingdom, pp. 365–403. https://doi.org/10.1108/S1745-886220150000010011

Ghisellini, P., Cialani, C. and Ulgiati, S., 2016. A review on circular economy: The expected transition to a balanced interplay of environmental and economic systems. *Journal of Cleaner Production*, *114*, pp.11–32.

Godsell, J., Ignatius, J., Karatzas, A. King, J., Li, D. and Moore, J., 2019. Realities of Reshoring: A UK Perspective. WMG. Available online: https://warwick.ac.uk/fac/sci/wmg/research/scip/reports/wmg_realities_of_reshoring_report.pdf

Godsell, J., Agca, O., Gibson, J., Ignatius, J. Davies, C.W., Xu, O., 2020. An Industry 4 readiness assessment tool. WMG. Available online: https://warwick.ac.uk/fac/sci/wmg/research/scip/reports/final_version_of_i4_report_for_use_on_websites.pdf

Gray, J.V., Skowronski, K., Esenduran, G. and Johnny Rungtusanatham, M., 2013. The reshoring phenomenon: What supply chain academics ought to know and should do. *Journal of Supply Chain Management*, *49*(2), pp.27–33.

Guide Jr, V.D.R. and Van Wassenhove, L.N., 2009. OR FORUM—The evolution of closed-loop supply chain research. *Operations Research*, *57*(1), pp.10–18.

Hinterhuber, H.H. and Hirsch, A., 1998. Starting up a strategic network. *Thunderbird International Business Review*, *40*(3), pp.185–207.

Holweg, M., Reichhart, A. and Hong, E., 2011. On risk and cost in global sourcing. *International Journal of Production Economics*, 131(1), pp.333–341.

Investopedia, 2019, September 2. Right-shoring. https://www.investopedia.com/terms/r/right-shoring.asp

Kinkel, S. and Maloca, S., 2009. Drivers and antecedents of manufacturing offshoring and backshoring—A German perspective. *Journal of purchasing and Supply Management*, *15*(3), pp.154–165.

Kinkel, S., 2014. Future and impact of backshoring—Some conclusions from 15 years of research on German practices. *Journal of Purchasing and Supply Management*, *20*(1), pp.63–65.

Manning, S., 2014. Mitigate, tolerate or relocate? Offshoring challenges, strategic imperatives and resource constraints. *Journal of World Business*, *49*(4), pp.522–535.

PwC, 2014, UK Economic Outlook.

P&G webpage, 2019, April 16. P&G announces new environmental sustainability goals focused on enabling and inspiring positive impact in the world. https://news.pg.com/news-releases/news-details/2018/PG-Announces-New-Environmental-Sustainability-Goals-Focused-on-Enabling-and-Inspiring-Positive-Impact-in-the-World/default.aspx

Skinner, W., 1969. Manufacturing-missing link in corporate strategy. *Harvard Business Review*, pp.136–145.

Tate, W.L., 2014. Offshoring and reshoring: US insights and research challenges. *Journal of Purchasing and Supply Management*, *20*(1), pp.66–68.

te Velde, D.W. and United Nations Conference on Trade and Development, 2006. *Foreign Direct Investment and Development: An Historical Perspective*. Overseas Development Institute (ODI). Available online: https://www.odi.org/sites/odi.org.uk/files/odi-assets/publications-opinion-files/850.pdf

UNCTAD (United Nations Conference on Trade and Development), 2019. World investment report 2019. Available online: https://unctad.org/en/PublicationsLibrary/wir2019_en.pdf

PART II

Global value chains

Theory and practice

Part II commences with Chapter 2 written by John Gattorna. The days of one-size-fits-all are dead and buried. We now know that customers and consumers in all market–product combinations exhibit several different buying behaviours, and suppliers in each case have to find ways to align with these and move between these buying behaviours. The collaborative buying behaviour (in particular has been largely ignored to date, yet it promises significant rewards to suppliers who recognise the opportunity and pay special attention to their genuinely collaborative customers. It is a subset of the transactional segment, served by the Lean supply chain type. Gattorna discusses what a genuine collaborative supply chain looks like in design terms, and how it can be implemented successfully in practice by shaping the appropriate underlying subculture. Examples and a short case study are used to support this explanation.

In Chapter 3, Felix Arndt, Mile Katic, Anushree Mistry and Sarwat Nafei go on to discuss dynamic capability building in global value chains. Organisational dynamic capabilities (ODCs) and global value chains (GVCs) are currently hot issues in strategy and management, but not yet cross-fertilised. Drawing on earlier work by Pitelis and Teece that has defined ecosystem co-creation as the mother of all DCs, Arndt et al. argue that a key constituent part of successful GVC creation and management involves the purposeful development and leverage of good for purpose ODCs (ODCs4GVCs). They go on to look at how the traditional functions of ODCs, namely sensing, seizing and reconfiguring/maintaining, are applied in the case of ODCs4GVCs, how they are modified for the purpose in question, and how they can be developed and leveraged to create a sustainable competitive advantage (SCA).

In Chapter 4, Katrina Skellern and Raymond Markey bring the theme of sustainability to the forefront of the global value chain. The transition literature has given little attention to the role that interfirm customer–supplier relationships might play in sustainable projects. This chapter draws on the contributions from technological innovation systems and sustainable collaboration literature to examine whether and how collaborations between the customer–supplier in a traditional manufacturing context can influence a shift towards a sustainable transition. An analysis of four cases of collaborations between the supplier (manufacturer) and the customer (original equipment manufacturer or OEM) highlight that a collaborative alliance can indeed influence a shift of the traditional manufacturing mindset. By blending regional and extraregional proximity, this transition is achieved by employing seven key resource formation processes: a direction

DOI: 10.4324/9781315225661-3

and vision for sustainability, knowledge creation and diffusion, market-niche formation, resource investment, creation of legitimacy, demand articulation, and policy coordination.

In Chapter 5, Rameshwar Dubey, Cyril Foropon and V. G. Venkatesh discuss the climate-resilient supply chain that is becoming increasingly important for its impact on sustainability. Growing complexity and increased supply chain disruptions have raised questions for supply chain managers with limited answers from current literature. To answer these questions and explain resilience in supply chain networks, Dubey et al. conceptualized a theoretical framework firmly grounded in resource-based view (RBV) and relationship theories. A survey instrument was developed with data collected from 250 Indian manufacturing organizations for testing 11 research hypotheses. The authors tested their theoretical model using confirmatory factor analysis (CFA), their research hypotheses using hierarchical regression analyses, and the interaction effect using hierarchical moderation regression analysis. Supply chain visibility and cooperation have a significant impact on supply chain resilience. The results offer a more nuanced understanding of the implications of supply chain resilience, visibility, cooperation, trust, commitment, behavioural uncertainty, and addressing the crucial question of why resources and capabilities have limited benefits under external influences.

A case study by Abraham Zhang and Paul Childerhouse stresses the importance of effective supply chain management in the horticultural industry, using the success of Zespri as an example.

2

THE USE OF REQUISITE COLLABORATION TO BETTER ALIGN AND DRIVE VALUE IN CONTEMPORARY VALUE CHAINS

John Gattorna

Introduction

The world has changed, and customers, especially at the consumer/end user level in the distribution channel, are having their day in the sun. With the coming of the eCommerce revolution, consumers are the new disruptors, and this influence is spreading into the business-to-business (B2B) world of industry and commerce. Businesses are becoming increasingly demanding in terms of ever-shorter lead times.

Rapidly rising technology is the enabler, which consumers and customers are making use of, but it is the consumer that is at the heart of the *continuous disruption* being felt by supply chains everywhere. Consumers (and intermediate customers) are king, and we would do well to get on board with the move to 'outside-in' thinking, where we listen to and interpret their expectations, and use the insights gained to reverse engineer the design of our enterprise supply chains. The world of 'one-size-fits-all' is dead, and more companies are recognising the need to re-engineer their supply chains to cater to a range of consumer and customer expectations, with embedded flexibility. But how to go about this fundamental transformation is the big question everyone is asking.

For purposes of this chapter, we define 'value chain' as a supply chain well done. In other words, if we define the supply chain as fully end-to-end (E2E), from customer/consumer on the demand side back through the business to the supply base, we are in effect defining the value chain.

The Dynamic Alignment™ business model

What we now know about customers is that they all have in-built biases about the way they prefer to buy products and services, and that despite this, they can and do change their buying behaviours for short periods when the situation demands. So, we have to study the target market for our products/services and better understand the structure in terms of the customer segments present. And also, we have to allow for shifts *between* these segments as the situation arises. In other words, we need a supply chain capability that is able to satisfy a range of buying behaviours, without the huge cost imposed by creating a myriad of exceptions. In other words, we need embedded flexibility without the associated cost.

 DOI: 10.4324/9781315225661-4

Introducing the overarching framework of Dynamic Alignment™

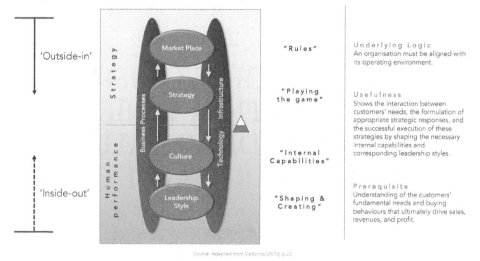

Source: Adapted from Gattorna (2015) p.25

Figure 2.1 Dynamic Alignment™ business model.

In 1989, the author and a small group of co-researchers set out to answer the following question: *If one-size-fits-all is a flawed concept, how many different supply chain configurations does the enterprise typically have to design in order to align with and service its target market?* The conceptual model we developed for this purpose was presented at the 10th Annual International Conference of the Strategic Management Society in Stockholm in 1990,[1] and is depicted in Figure 2.1. Essentially, the four-level model involves aligning the business [composed of its internal culture (L3) and leadership style (L4)], with the external market [including customers (L1), linked by strategy (L2)].

In our experience, in the best performing companies, leadership (L4) is in close touch with and understands the target market (L1); this is fundamental. In such cases, the alignment of levels 2 and 3 becomes more feasible, and so the overall alignment leading to higher performance prevails.

Our own field research across hundreds of product/market/geography combinations found that there were up to 16 archetypes of buying behaviour possible in a given marketplace for a particular product/service category, but only the five most dominant behaviours were needed in any market situation to provide an estimated 80 per cent coverage of the target market. This insight led us to the conclusion that enterprises need at least five matching supply chain configurations to best align with their target market.

For each identified behavioural segment, there is a corresponding value proposition and associated operational strategy. This in turn is underpinned by the appropriate internal cultural capabilities. And finally, these cultural capabilities are shaped and supported by a particular leadership style in each case. The result is five uniquely different supply chains running in parallel through the business, as depicted in Figure 2.2.

From our extensive empirical work[2] with clients in multiple industries across multiple geographies, we found that the most common combination of customer segments were the five behavioural segments described in detail in Figure 2.3. In each case, the attributes of each behavioural segment are described. Finally, the corresponding supply chain type for each segment is indicated at the bottom of the diagram.

Five supply chain configurations provide approximately an 80% coverage of the market

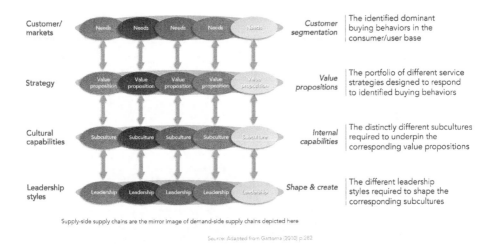

Figure 2.2 Multiple supply chain alignment: demand side.

This insight in itself was a massive breakthrough, because it provided a definitive answer to the question that we had originally posed and, in the same breath, provided a *direct link* between the target customers and the enterprise itself. No more guessing and approximation required.

In this chapter we will focus our attention on the first of these behavioural segments only, because this is what gave rise to the Collaborative Supply Chain™. We have trademarked this segment because we were the first to recognise it.

Collaboration and the Collaborative Supply Chain™

We found a customer segment that had always existed but had largely been ignored to date: the *Collaborative* segment with its associated collaborative buying behaviour. This group of customers is mostly predictable, likes regular delivery, buys only mature or augmented products, and seeks a trusting relationship with the supplier over time. Indeed, they tend to focus on a single supplier as the primary source of supply, and are very willing to share data about their current operations and future intentions. And they are very forgiving, which is a danger because it lulls suppliers into a false sense of security. This group of customers will put up with a lot of poor performance, but when they have had enough of being ignored, they leave and never come back. And no amount of effort will entice them back.

In the B2B world, these customers willingly get involved in joint developments, are very forgiving and tend to be less price sensitive. What they don't like are surprises and unreliable behaviour by suppliers.

In any given market for particular product/service categories, the Collaborative customer segment is usually small in number, although they can represent a disproportionately high share by volume and revenue. And they certainly return good margins to suppliers that are reliable and accommodating.

Our advice to clients is to identify which of their customers are Collaborative, as a matter of priority, and then lock them in with the appropriate strategies. But collaboration is not a strat-

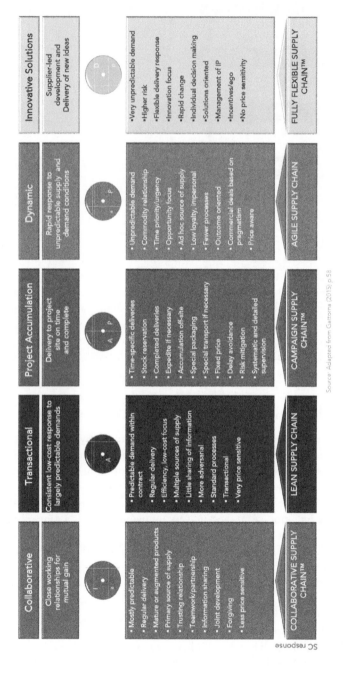

Figure 2.3 The five most common behavioural segments and corresponding supply chains.

egy that you should pursue with your entire customer base, because if you do you will surely waste a lot of resources overservicing many customers who just do not appreciate the effort and cost involved. Hence the term *requisite* collaboration, i.e., you should only collaborate with those customers who genuinely have collaborative values, who will appreciate your efforts on their behalf, and reward you for that via their ongoing loyalty in the form of repeat business.

Indeed, for most companies, if you can find 10 per cent of your customers (by number) who are 'collaborative,' you are doing well, and these could easily represent up to 40 per cent of the total volume of your business, which is well worth focusing on.

The 'value proposition' for Collaborative customers

The *value proposition* to the Collaborative customer segment is to 'win together,' i.e., *we will provide you with a consistent-quality product, delivered on time, at a stable price. We will use our capacity, and your information, to provide you with assured supply. We aim to be an integral part of your business and to engage with you on joint developments for mutual advantage.*

The important thing to note here is that all functions of the firm must contribute to this value proposition, as the supply chain flows horizontally across the business from the supply side to the demand side. This embodies the philosophy that all functions in the firm must buy into, otherwise the supply chain will be broken and customer satisfaction impaired as a direct result.

Protective strategy for the Collaborative Supply Chain™

To reinforce the point about embracing a genuine supply chain philosophy in the firm, every function must contribute to the operational strategies in ways outlined below.

Sales and Marketing: should emphasise mature, branded products; build brand loyalty; distribute via direct and/or trusted outlets; set moderate prices; and only engage in low promotional activity.

Procurement: should carefully select suppliers on the basis of relationships and share information with them; it is vital that procurement strategies are aligned to the front end of the business.

Production: set a stable production schedule, collaborate to reduce costs and seek to maximise capacity utilisation.

Logistics: offer reliable/scheduled delivery and shared forecasts.

Systems/IT: place emphasis on customer account management and apply the customer relationship management (CRM) system at all times.

Finance and Administration: offer more relaxed credit terms and undertake customer account profitability analyses.

Practical implications of Collaborative Supply Chain™ configurations: Network considerations

In terms of the company network, the flow of product through the Collaborative Supply Chain™ has particular characteristics as follows:

- Supply side: best to seek long-term supplier contracts, with stable volumes and stable supply paths.
- Production: seek a base load, with known committed capacity and agreed production schedules.

- Distribution centre network: minimise stock levels by removing products with variable demand, and optimise stock-holding locations between supplier and customer, in some cases shared.
- Transport: seek firm third-party logistics (3PL) provider contracts, with assured volumes and routine deliveries to minimise rates. If possible, eliminate echelons in the network and go directly to customers from production, thus reducing distribution costs.

Practical implications of Collaborative Supply Chain™ configurations: Planning considerations

In terms of planning, the Collaborative Supply Chain™ can be managed in the following ways:

- Demand planning/forecasting: this can be done efficiently at the SKU level using collaborative planning and forecasting techniques.
- Production planning: it is possible to have firm plans and meet fixed commitments; this is a sweet spot for sales and operations planning (S&OP).
- Inventory: minimal inventory holding is possible, because of low variability and high visibility.
- Deployment: where volumes justify, more direct plant-to-customer movements.
- Demand/order capture: VMI (vendor-managed inventory) procedures are possible, and full visibility of true demand can be achieved.

The collaboration sweet spot

Once you establish who exactly are your collaborative customers, it is possible to focus efforts on solidifying relationships with them for mutual benefit. McDonald's does this particularly well, working with its two main worldwide distributors: HAVI Logistics and Martin Brouwer. Both these suppliers enjoy long-term contracts, but in return they must submit to 'open book' costing and carrying extra headroom capacity to ensure McDonald's is never short of products at the all-important store level.

The McDonald's guiding philosophy is that employees, owner-operators and suppliers have to be in equal balance; that all three stakeholders must be subservient to the 'system' as a whole; and the primacy of the customer interface trumps everything else, i.e., it is all about the restaurant and its patrons.

On this basis, McDonald's enters only a few global relationships with suppliers, insists on mutual reward/shared risk, and expects all innovation to be shared. Long-term contracts are on a 'handshake' basis.

More generally, genuine two-way collaboration in the supply chain means that it is possible to separate *baseload* demand from the more *volatile* demand that surely accompanies it. This leads to more efficient logistics operations in the baseload component, and avoids the complications that inevitably arise from mixing baseload and volatile components. The advantages of following this practice are outlined next:

a. Lower demand variability from standing orders and reduced coefficient of variation (CoV).
b. Lower logistics costs due to increased use of full loads and higher vehicle utilisation.
c. More stable plans in manufacturing, and therefore higher plant utilisation.

d. Increased cash from lower raw materials and finished-goods stocks.
e. Increased revenue from higher stock availability and higher customer and distributor satisfaction.

We have demonstrated all these advantages are real and realisable through our work with Unilever in Asia.

Benefits of partnering with suppliers

Perhaps the industry that has best documented the benefits of partnering is the automotive industry. Figure 2.4 depicts the Supplier Working Relations Index (WRI) between automotive original equipment manufacturers (OEMs) and their component suppliers. Clearly, Toyota has shown the way in the last five years, and benefited greatly as a result, recording a 2-point improvement in 2020/21 to 347 on the index, the highest of all six manufacturers surveyed. This upward trend has a positive impact on Toyota's margin per vehicle; the reverse is true for those manufacturers with a downward trend on the WRI.

A special type of subculture

Consistent with our Dynamic Alignment™ model referred to earlier, it is not possible to properly service collaborative customers unless you have in place in the organisation a *group* subculture as described next.

The best way of establishing such a subculture is to put together a cluster (or team) of people, drawn from all the major disciplines in the firm, and selected on the basis of their technical skills and their individual mindsets. By this we mean, the cluster should have a clear *bias* for 'relationships,' even though there will be other counter-pressures coming from personnel in the group who represent cost, speed, and innovation values.

This cluster should be co-located and given joint key performance indicators (KPIs) to work towards, the two main ones being *customer retention* and *increased share of wallet*.

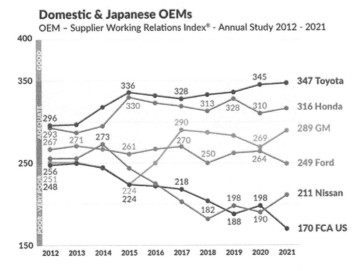

Figure 2.4 Benefits of partnering with suppliers. (Source: Plante Moran 2021 North American Automotive OEM – Tier 1 Supplier Working Relations Index® Study.)

This internal team should work together on the basis of consensus decision-making, and where possible include their collaborative customers in the decision-making process too. Time is not a factor that concerns collaborative customers, but change minimisation and a requirement for stability are factors.

The team would be held together through a participative incentive scheme in which all members are included and benefit equally. This is not the place for lone wolves!

Training and development in this cluster would focus on team-building ahead of everything else. Over time, a natural leader will usually arise among the cluster members, with a coaching style that seeks to get the best out of other team members, and to develop them individually and as a team.

Finally, when recruiting team members to cover gaps or rotations back to the functions (after perhaps one to two years), the emphasis should be on finding suitable replacement team players.

All in all, what you should be trying to do here is mirror as much as possible in your Collaborative Supply Chain™ team, the same relationship bias that is evident among your Collaborative customer segment. This is alignment working in practice and leads directly to growth in revenues and margins.

A final word

In the last two decades, there has been a preoccupation with Lean and Agile supply chain operations. While these two supply chain configurations account for a big part of the demand side, the impact of collaborative customers has been largely overlooked, and in effect lost in all the noise created by demanding customers and complex operating environments.

It is also true that collaboration has been overused as a possible solution to all the ills in supply chain performance. This is not valid either, because only a relatively small percentage of customers in any given product–market situation will exhibit genuine collaborative values; you have to be very precise in your selection.

In this regard, more sophisticated companies have identified and singled out the Collaborative customer segment in their target market and developed more finely tuned operations to better align with them, and in the process benefited greatly from this precision. Put simply, you can't afford to ignore this segment, because if you do, they will simply leave, and no amount of effort, retrospectively, will entice them back.

These are customers who quite rightly should be the first priority to identify and serve appropriately in your business, because they are a source of stable ongoing revenue and stable margins. Ignore them at your peril.

Notes

1 N H Chorn, K L Myres, and J L Gattorna, 'Bridging Strategy Formulation and Implementation,' unpublished paper presented at the 10th Annual International Conference of the Strategic Management Society, Stockholm, 1990.
2 Mostly involving consulting assignments, and therefore not published because of confidentiality reasons. In effect, our clients provided us with the laboratories to study buyer behaviour.

Further reading

Gattorna, John, and Ellis, Deborah, *Transforming Supply Chains: Realign Your Business to Better Serve Customers in a Disruptive World*, FT Publishing, Harlow, 2020.

3

DYNAMIC CAPABILITIES OF GLOBAL VALUE CHAINS

From selection to deployment

Felix Arndt, Mile Katic, Anushree Mistry and Sarwat Nafei[1]

3.1 Introduction

Global Value Chains have become the world economy's backbone and central nervous system.

(Cattaneo, Gereffi & Staritz 2010)

Global value chains (GVCs) have shaped our picture of the world economy in times of globalisation. Both start-ups that are international from their inception – often called "born globals" – and large multi-national enterprises have equally triggered literature streams built on the larger dynamic capability framework. This framework has been powerful in accommodating environmental characteristics such as velocity, complexity, ambiguity and unpredictability typically present in GVCs (Davis, Eisenhardt & Bingham, 2009). Teece, Peteraf and Leih (2016) argue that today's GVCs even host deep uncertainty, the "unknown unknowns". A new era of "semi-globalisation" (Ghemawat, 2003) that involves political players deeply involved in economic activity outside of a Western understanding of the rule of law add to the deep uncertainty through, often non-transparent, institutional complexities and voids (Arndt & Ashkanasy, 2015).

A focus on GVCs is imperative not only in light of deep uncertainty but also due to potentially altered supply chain costs as one of the consequences of the Covid-19 pandemic. The pandemic may trigger changes in national security policies that render current value chain arrangements unsustainable (e.g. when it comes to national food security). In addition, the political conflict between China and the USA may alter supply chain costs if Pacific shipping routes will not be secured anymore through the USA. Political conflict and a tension between interconnectedness and independence (particularly in times of crisis) of economies increase the challenges for GVCs and dynamically capable firms.

Dynamically capable firms stimulate meaningful change to address volatile, uncertain, complex and ambiguous (VUCA) environments. In this chapter, we focus on the selection of capabilities and the deployment of capabilities. Capability selection is core to dynamically capable firms in VUCA environments (Eisenhardt & Martin, 2000). In a global context, selection and deployment may not be independent, as being dynamically capable may require fundamentally

        DOI: 10.4324/9781315225661-5

different capability portfolios in different institutional contexts. As such, the question of what capabilities a firm needs in global environments cannot always be answered without knowing how problems can be addressed.

GVCs are on the verge of a transformation through shifting political landscapes and unprecedented government interventions to reduce the spread of a global pandemic (Covid-19) that has affected economies in vastly different ways; has triggered large variation in responses of nations and also firms; and will necessarily lead to a reprioritisation of national agendas very possibly with long-lasting implications for markets, economies and firms.

We start with a brief literature overview of the current debate on dynamic capabilities for GVCs. Then, we elaborate in more depth how capability selection and deployment benefits firms that possess dynamic capabilities to address the challenges of VUCA environments inherent to GVCs. Finally, we discuss the implications of these two crucial stops within the context of GVCs and for dynamic capabilities more generally.

3.2 Dynamic capabilities in global value chains: An overview

Dynamic capabilities are the creation of difficult-to-imitate combinations of resources, including the effective coordination of interorganisational relationships, local differentiation, global integration and innovation as part of the global value chains that can enable a firm to coordinate key activities and respond rapidly in a flexible manner. Dynamic capabilities require the capacity to extract economic benefits from current resources and to develop new capabilities. In the global economy of today, the competitive advantage of a firm appears to rest on the ability of the firm to go beyond the static role of its resources. Firms that are able to develop and deploy intangible assets, relationships and human capital in the global market may gain competitive advantage over their rivals. Dynamic capabilities in GVCs therefore consist of developing a systemic global coherence while recognising the unique feature of each country's environment to facilitate customisation of individual country strategies.

Entrepreneurial management – as a central part of dynamic capabilities – is viewed as one of the resources of the firm (Arndt & Pierce, 2018). Penrose (1959: 86) viewed entrepreneurship as one of the resources of the firm, stating, "we include 'entrepreneurs' among the resources of the firm and the range of ideas of entrepreneurs among the services rendered". Expanding the firm's operations into new geographic markets presents an important opportunity for growth and value creation (Lu & Beamish, 2001). Entrepreneurial management and the ability to reconfigure capabilities have a positive and significant effect on a firm's performance both domestically as well as globally. Cantwell recognises that in a global firm the active role of management offers endogenous ownership advantages and allows the firm to develop strategies that allow it to extend its capabilities and overall innovation potential using global networks (Cantwell, 1989).

One example of such a firm is Apple. Well known for the ingenuity of its designs, it owns none of its own manufacturing. It has tight supply relations with many companies globally – some pure contractors such as Foxconn (headquartered in Taiwan with factories in China) and at least one competitor, Samsung (headquartered in Korea). Apple helps provide financing to some of its global suppliers and may obtain exclusive purchase arrangements from them for short periods. Contractual agreements appear to suffice for Apple to achieve the necessary coordination, while retaining the flexibility needed to respond to market forces.

Global firms with strong dynamic capabilities exhibit technological and market agility. Dynamic capabilities also help characterise how a firm obtains strengths, extends these strengths by developing new business models, synchronises business processes and models with the business environment, and/or shapes the business environment in its favour (Teece, Pisano & Shuen,

1997). An essential characteristic of firms is that they can generate and embody knowledge that cannot be easily bought and sold (Arndt, Fourne & MacInerney-May, 2018). Signature processes and signature business models illustrate the path-dependent nature of the firm. Such signature processes embody a company's history, experience, culture and creativity (Gratton & Ghoshal, 2005). Because of their deep roots, they are not so easily replicated by others who do not share this history, and may have different values, too. For example, Coca-Cola's vast number of bottling facilities worldwide is not an organisationally embedded critical resource. Its formulas (syrups and concentrates), however, are a critical capability that gives the firm a sustained competitive edge in the global beverage market. This inevitably requires that firms constantly create new technologies, differentiated and superior processes, and better business models to stay ahead of the competition, stay in tune with the market and even shape the market if necessary. The firm must be able to simultaneously cope with changes in the external environment and with changes caused by processes internal to the firm (Greiner, 1998). As stated by Apple CEO Tim Cook in February 2013: "Apple has the ability to innovate in resources, processes and business models and create magic ... This isn't something you can just write a cheque for. This is something you build over decades" (Agence France-Presse, 2013). A global firm competing in diverse contexts has the opportunity and hence the advantage to develop distinct signature processes and models in different geographies than a pure domestic enterprise.

The focus of dynamic capabilities in GVCs is on how firms can create, extend, integrate, modify and deploy their resources and assets globally while simultaneously managing competitive threats and effectuating necessary transformations. As noted by Geoffrey Jones (2005: 289), "the recognition that global firms are profoundly heterogeneous is one of the most important lessons". Dynamic capabilities will help organisations stay relevant to marketplace needs and technological opportunities. Dynamic capabilities (involving sensing, seizing and, ultimately, transforming) can in most cases be sequenced over time and across different geographic markets. For example, Yum! Brands (the owner of fast-food brands KFC, Taco Bell and Pizza Hut) has simultaneously engaged in rapid expansion in China, and in retrenchment and transformation in one of its established markets, the United Kingdom. The company's mission to build the world's most loved, trusted and fastest-growing restaurant brands led to the development of its three iconic global brands, increasing its franchise ownership and creating a leaner, more efficient cost structure (Yum Brands, 2016).

The need to balance the dynamic tension between multiple forces (geographic, product, market, technological) has resulted in firms extending their presence all over the globe for a multitude of purposes and in a multitude of forms. Possessing, deploying and upgrading capabilities is a primary driver of global success and an important predictor of competitive position. With a well-developed global coordination and integration system, global firms can be efficient agents for internalising and transferring resources. For example, GM's "simultaneous engineering" used in its Shanghai joint venture, a strategy in which designers, engineers and marketers from various specialties team up to reduce production costs and improve innovation, significantly contributed to the rapid growth of Volvo's market share in China. Similarly, Hitachi's new management system, which divides its global operations into ten independent divisions while cutting the number of board members, has noticeably sped up the decision-making process and made its overseas managers more motivated.

Value chains are more dynamic in nature than casual markets. This is because of the constant change in the behaviour of the customers or a significant change of non-governmental institutions (Hall, 2000). Dynamic capabilities are defined as "the firm's ability to integrate, build and reconfigure internal and external competencies to address rapidly changing environments" (Teece et al., 1997). Dynamic capabilities are especially relevant to global firms due to their business environment being open to international commerce and exposed to the opportunities and threats associated with rapid technological change. Therefore, dynamic capabilities require a strong base of established capabilities or resources as well as the ability to efficiently deploy these resources and to continuously create bundles of new resources and knowledge in order to respond more efficiently in a field of its activity. Dynamic capabilities require a longer-term focus and involve subordinating short-term cost cutting, optimisation and other best practices to longer-term innovation-enhancing strategies (Teece et al., 2016).

The general dynamic capabilities framework focuses on the foundation of enterprise-level competitive advantage in terms of rapid technological change. The framework indicates the extent to which an enterprise develops and employs superior dynamic capabilities will determine the nature and amount of intangible assets it will generate and the level of economic profits it can earn.

3.3 Capability selection in global value chains

Today's GVCs are characterised by an increasing dynamism stemming from uncertainties in relation to both technological and market changes, but also those associated with global trade policy and the rise of what some label bifurcated governance and a culture of protectionism (Petricevic & Teece, 2019). Despite these seemingly disruptive phenomena for organisations participating in GVCs, there remains a lucrative opportunity for competitive advantage that transcends the direct effects on organisations to those of their communities and, ultimately, their constituent economies. Indeed, investments in competencies (or capabilities, for that matter) in order to syphon some of these benefits related to participation in GVCs require careful consideration of competency gaps and elements relating to strategic priorities as well as direction. Here, we outline some of these competencies that constitute an overarching schema for capability selection in GVCs.

3.3.1 Identification

The identification of competency gaps relates, for the most part, to the *sensing* functional block of the DC framework typified as an "inherently entrepreneurial set of capabilities that involves exploring technological opportunities, probing markets and listening to customers, along with scanning the other elements of the business ecosystem" (Teece, 2017: 20). Whilst this presents itself as a key managerial capability in the context of supply chains in general (Tatham et al., 2017), their contribution towards supply chain success remains largely ignored (Aslam et al., 2018).

From the perspective of a typical buyer–supplier relationship, a supply chain manager's role may be more concerned with forecasting activities associated with demand and supply planning, and ensuring a smooth and uninterrupted flow of physical goods and information. In this instance, key information required in order to plan for and sense operational disruptions include those in relation to inventory levels, tracking data and perceived demand (amongst a host of others). Technology adoption in, for instance, integrated customer relationship management (CRM) software, has also been well observed in improving market sensing capabilities and, by virtue, supply chain disruption mitigation. Indeed, these perhaps ordinary capabilities can certainly help an organisation in achieving efficiency gains through the exploitation of existing capabilities and resources. Alone, however, they offer little support in times of discontinuous change, as is often the case for GVCs.

A recent example is highlighted by Hendry et al. (2019) in their exploratory study of UK food supply chains affected by the UK's decision to exit the European Union. Here, the authors exemplify the key role of sensing opportunities and threats stemming from the impending constitutional changes in building what they label as supply chain resilience. In this instance, building fruitful relationships with members of the GVC that operate in the same tier (as well as vertically) has seen increased opportunities to collectively build effective disruption mitigation strategies. In the same vein, literature concerning supply chain learning in dynamic environments (Yang, Jia & Xu, 2019) as well as those associated with market-focussed learning (Weerawardena et al., 2007) would consistently advocate the necessity towards building trusting and collaborative relationships with GVC partners in order to facilitate a firm's sensing capabilities. The question then becomes, how and with whom?

In a general sense, alliance capabilities are said to consist of three overarching dimensions in alliance management, integration and learning capabilities (Kohtamäki et al., 2018). The antecedents of which often include the likes of market turbulence, sufficient resources, an open corporate culture and a host of others (Kohtamäki et al., 2018). From a sensing perspective, then, this becomes a firm-level construct that necessitates a sound foundation and willingness to participate in interfirm collaboration in the first place, though the same extends to external parties that should experience a sense of mutual dependence and complementarity in the collaborative relationship (Schreiner et al., 2009). From a more generalised capabilities-based perspective, sensing activities in collaborative ventures has also been found to require internal capabilities in innovation, information infrastructure and integrated knowledge among participating organisations (Wang et al., 2015). However, the impact of these capabilities on the financial and market performance of organisations, as in the previous discussion, depends on the volatility of the markets in which the firm operates – the more turbulent, the stronger the link (Wang et al., 2015). As such, from a selection perspective, the capabilities of participating firms are of significant concern.

3.3.2 Choice

The dynamic capabilities view of the firm is one that is fundamentally centred on the theory of strategic choice (Stacey & Mowles, 2016) where the central question concerns identifying and selecting the right organisational capabilities to deploy at the right time (Pisano, 2017). Indeed, for the organisation that is participating in GVCs, a particular capability such as supply chain integration and alignment may well yield to greater performance by way of competitive advantage, though such capabilities can also hinder an organisation's capabilities to do the same – given the characteristics of the market within which the firm operates.

In the context of GVCs, the strategic task of choice could concern decisions relating to firm investments in capabilities associated with the exploitation of existing competencies as well as those more concerned with the exploration of new opportunities of growth (Lee & Rha, 2016). In this instance, organisations with an imperative to leverage GVCs towards sustained growth could, for example, extend their existing capabilities through collaborative endeavours with fellow GVC members or augment their capabilities entirely through strategic acquisitions abroad (c.f. Meyer, 2015). As part of the foundational logic guiding investment decisions in international business (Narula & Dunning, 2000), the choice to augment or extend capabilities through GVC activities also carries significant implications.

In addition to strategic considerations concerning the state of an organisation's existing resource pool, integration and alignment processes as well as strategic trajectory (Teece, 2017), today's organisations operating in GVCs must also contend with changes to the institutional environment and the increased risk of key capabilities leaking into the hands of offshore competitors. Multinational enterprises (MNEs) seem to hold a distinct advantage in this regard through greater control over

GVC operations where they are observed to consistently outperform local counterparts (Bloom et al., 2012). Measures including a conscious attempt to distribute competencies across global sites have seen MNEs decrease the likelihood of competitor intervention, though such measures require substantial effort in building and/or buying key resource integration capabilities at the host site (Teece, 2014). On the other hand, organisations without a global presence that utilise GVCs in sourcing or distribution activities are more susceptible to losing their competitive edge through imitation, often at the expense of costly IP activities. Here, capability investment should consider, in addition to geographical location, the state (and nature) of trade relationships with GVC partners whereby trust becomes a precursor for evolutionary fitness by way of supply chain alignment.

It is also important to keep in mind an organisation would typically participate in collaborate ventures if the pursuit of knowledge exchange is not hindered by the market system through, for instance, licencing (Hennart, 1982, as cited in Luo, 2000). Thus, an organisation participating in GVCs should also consider the degree (Luo, 2000) and type (Chen, Park & Newburry, 2009) of control in the collaborative relationship necessary to protect its strategic interests whilst allowing for the seamless flow of knowledge and other resources that are required to benefit from GVC operations. Along the same vein, the firm-level capabilities that facilitate better resource allocation choices are, themselves, resource intensive. Greater controlling interest coincides with greater responsibility in allocation and flow of resources between GVC members – get the balance wrong and participating organisations may find themselves in an expensive pursuit of collaboration with little return on investment. That said, partner selection based on equity agreements through formal control mechanisms seems to be detrimental to collaborative efforts, unless there is not any prior collaborative experience amongst the participating firms (Zollo, Reuer & Singh, 2002). From this perspective, it is also imperative to uncover the required nature of GVC relationships during sensing activities. A mismatch can indeed lead to detrimental consequences.

3.4 Capability deployment in global value chains

The deployment of capabilities is the next step when addressing competency gaps. In GVCs the deployment of capabilities is especially important since firms need to ambidextrously orchestrate capabilities of local and global reach as well as adaptations of global capabilities to local needs. These GVC-related issues are discussed in the following sections.

3.4.1 Producer-driven vs. buyer-driven value chains

Understanding the intricacies of dynamic capabilities in VUCA environments requires a clear picture of what value chains look like. A value chain includes the following activities: design, production, marketing, distribution and support to the final consumer. These activities can be performed within the same firm or divided among different firms. The fact that they are increasingly spread over several countries explains why the value chain is regarded as "global". An important difference emphasised in the literature is between "producer-driven" and "buyer-driven" chains.

Producer-driven GVCs are found in high-tech sectors such as the semiconductor or the pharmaceuticals industry. Because these industries rely on technology and research and development (R&D), lead firms are placed upstream and control the design of products as well as most of the assembly, which is fragmented in different countries.

In buyer-driven chains, retailers and branded marketers control the production, which can be totally outsourced, the focus being on marketing and sales (Backer & Miroudot, 2014). For services, they are not just the "glue" in value chains; they are also essential inputs in key stages of the production process, starting with design and engineering at the beginning of the value chain and finishing with marketing, distribution, sales and after-sales services at the end.

While services inputs can be outsourced and provided by independent companies, they are also produced in-house; it is often the case for R&D or IT activities.

Firms tend to produce in-house services that correspond to core strategic functions for which they are interested in investing in the human skills and training that will contribute to the productivity of the firm and guarantee that it remains more competitive than other firms. On the contrary, activities that are too costly to maintain in-house, are more efficiently carried out by external providers and are not part of the core functions of the firm are outsourced (Miroudot & Cadestin, 2017).

Since GVCs spread across all industries, electronics, mostly a "producer-driven" GVC, is probably the industry where GVCs are the most pervasive. An important reason for the high value chain character of the electronics industry is the high modularity of its products. Standardisation, codification and computerisation allow for a large interoperability of parts and components, which in turn allow for the fragmentation of the production process across different stages. Product design, logistics and different parts of the production process are often executed by different firms in the value chain.

The electronics GVC consists of a very large number of firms across different countries, from large MNEs to small and medium enterprises (SMEs). Sturgeon and Kawakami (2010) distinguish between lead firms and contract manufacturers in discussing the most important actors within the electronics GVC. Lead firms are the firms that carry brands and sell branded products to final customers; these firms have typically a lot of market power over suppliers more upstream in the electronics GVC because of technological leaderships and large investments in brand development.

In some segments of the electronics industry, such as PCs and mobile phones, these lead firms have grown to platform leaders, as their technology is incorporated in the products of other companies like the giants Intel and Apple. On the other hand, contract manufacturers assemble products for lead firms and have limited market power, notwithstanding they are typically large and often have operations in different countries (comparable to the first-tier suppliers in the automotive industry). The actual activities undertaken by contract manufacturers differ across companies; original equipment manufacturers (OEMs) provide only production services while original design manufacturers (ODMs) undertake production as well as design activities. Contract manufacturers work with smaller suppliers, although the supplying pyramid in electronics is less developed than in the automotive industry (Backer & Miroudot, 2014).

3.4.2 *Market contingencies*

Capability deployment in GVCs depends on the type of market. These markets are dynamic, and increasingly the old wisdom of value chain logic between developed and emerging markets underlies more complex dynamics. Most lead firms in the electronics industry are located in developed economies, especially Europe, Japan and the United States; Korea has recently joined this group (Sturgeon & Kawakami, 2010). Emerging countries are more often represented in the category of contract manufacturers; some companies like Acer and Huawei have successfully moved up the value chain from OEM over ODM to true original brand manufacturer (OBM), while others have failed (Backer & Miroudot, 2014).

Generally, firms in traditional emerging markets have been found to adopt a short-term focus and avoid more risky strategies requiring considerable investment (cf. Awate et al., 2012). The main focus of firms from this type of emerging market is on knowledge from external sources and on objective knowledge rather than on internal sources of knowledge resulting in only small increases in absorptive capacity (Sinkovics, Sinkovics & Hoque, 2018). Absorptive capacity can be defined as "the ability of a firm to recognise the value of new, external information, assimilate it, and apply it to commercial ends" (Cohen and Levinthal, 1990: 218).

The relationship between developing country suppliers and their multinational buyers within a GVC is often characterised by an extensive power and knowledge asymmetry that affects the strategies and routines which these firms adopt to develop capabilities (cf. Bradley et al., 2006; Hoque et al., 2016). While GVC studies consider the role of supplier capabilities within the context of governance, there is less emphasis on the way in which capabilities are developed (Mahutga, 2012).

3.4.3 Transferability

To ensure survival and growth in the global market, MNEs must be able to successfully transfer critical capabilities within their international networks to give their operations in a foreign country a competitive advantage and to fulfil a strategy derived from local operations. Transferability is one such capability to which a parent firm is equipped or controls the distinctive capabilities that can be transferred to the foreign subunit. The foreign subunits could rely on local resources or develop capabilities as needed in a local setting, but this is an inefficient strategy as the indigenous firms are already more effective at developing such capabilities; hence the movement from parent to foreign subunits is the most practical transfer of critical capabilities (Tallman, 1992). For instance, McDonald's tremendous success overseas has been built on the firm's ability to rapidly transfer the capacity to operate its entire complex business system to foreign entrepreneurs (Mujtaba & Patel, 2007). Similar is the case for KFC, which shares more profits in some of its overseas joint ventures than the percentage of its ownership allows because of its ability to transfer developed organisational skills that are in demand at the local partner markets (Bell & Shelman, 2011).

Leveraging critical capabilities within or between markets is complex. MNEs need to decide what should be transferred from the home base to subunits in foreign markets based on what will give the firm a competitive edge. Technological capabilities are generally more transferable than organisational skills. For instance, in the efforts to globalise its R&D activities worth $2.6 billion in 1998, Sony did not face difficulties in transferring core technologies to the overseas R&D units, but management was raised with the question of which R&D management approach to use. After several years of implementation, Sony finally realised the top-down management approach used at home did not work and changed to the bottom-up approach (Arimura, 1999). Thus, Sony's ability to identify, develop and leverage a specialised management approach is one of its core dynamic capabilities (Pitelis & Teece, 2010).

Further, international experience and reputation are more easily transferable across borders compared to experience and reputation in the home country. The knowledge of how to establish and manage a successful distribution network is a critical capability that can be transferred to the foreign market. For instance, Nestlé's application of promotion and distribution experience accumulated in China to other emerging markets in Vietnam and Russia has proven successful in these regions (Nestlé, 2018).

3.4.4 Value chain flexibility

MNEs increasingly recognise that each of its globally distributed subunits can be a source of new innovation, and they must organise themselves appropriately to capture these benefits. One way to untether these effects is to preserve maximum flexibility. This can be achieved by outsourcing business processes or business units. For instance, Apple has achieved flexibility by outsourcing its manufacturing of iPhone to China. Such an arrangement allows Apple flexibility with respect to manufacturing. Further, Steve Jobs's decision to change the face of the iPhone from plastic to glass just before the launch required an additional 8000 workers to work 12-hour shifts fitting glass screens into bevelled frames; within 96 hours the plant produced over 10,000 iPhones a day (Teece et al., 2016). On the other hand, organisations such as Google and Honda have demonstrated flexibility through partnerships and outsourcing to strategically gain access to new markets. Honda partnered with GE to manufacture engines for its light jet, while Google has developed car-specific capabilities such as Android Auto and virtual maps to help autonomous vehicles navigate without a need to necessarily engineer a whole vehicle. The dynamic capabilities perspective on these MNEs is about rapid innovation, adaptation and flexibility across multiple jurisdictions (Pitelis & Teece, 2010).

Another set of approaches involves building agility into the organisation itself. The organisational structure also has strong implications for agility. Entry into a new market requires the organisation to upgrade from its existing general-purpose capabilities. It requires breaking conventional modes of thinking. For instance, if Google were to enter into the car market directly it would need to develop a host of car-specific engineering and design capabilities derived from mechanical engineering. This for Google is far more challenging than deepening its existing capabilities in data science, artificial intelligence and machine learning. Thus, organisations such as Google have greater incentive to deepen their general-purpose capabilities that are also firm-specific because these presumably offer greater returns. It is the ability of the organisation to enhance its entrepreneurial skills and develop a practical approach enabled by the dynamic capabilities of the organisation and restrained by the cost of attaining a given level of organisational agility.

3.5 Discussion

Participating in GVCs and promoting technology upgrading is a universal topic, as all countries have policies in place to address this issue (Kergroach, 2019). Participation in GVCs contributes to national economies. Moving up in these chains contributes to the development and upgrading of the economy itself.

Although the rapid spread of GVCs has provided organisations the opportunities to reap the benefits of innovation offshoring, developing countries are not as fully integrated into MNE networks as they are in global trade (Cadestin et al., 2018). In addition, developing economies may face difficulties in meeting international capability requirements and standards, and according to the mode of governance prevailing in the value chain, they may be locked-in to "hierarchical" or "captive" relationships that prevent any further functional upgrading (Gereffi et al., 2005). Therefore, further upgrading through GVCs requires building stronger capabilities autonomously and reshaping supply firms' relationships with chain partners, especially lead firms and MNEs. In this respect, it has become crucial for emerging economies to create indigenous innovation systems that are able to absorb new knowledge drawn from GVC participation (Ernst, 2008; Fu et al., 2011; Pietrobelli & Raboletti, 2011).

These developments will be accelerated through the implications of the current pandemic shakeout. For example, when securing food, technological innovation and automatisation are likely to increase. If that happens, GVCs, for example, in the agrifood sector, are likely to reduce the competitiveness of non-tech and non-premium food solutions. In the case of economies that highly rely on exports from traditional agriculture, these developments imply a complete loss of competitiveness on the world market, making GVCs increasingly difficult to access and potentially more competitive due to a surge of national solutions.

A gradually increasing number of GVC studies conclude that the development of supplier capabilities may be a function of their firm-level strategic behaviour and their relational setting with their buyers (e.g. Fujita, 2011; Kawakami, 2011). However, further research is needed to achieve a deeper understanding of how suppliers in different relational settings strategise and set up appropriate routines for building capabilities within GVCs, and how those capabilities feed into the process of step-by-step upgrading (Sinkovics et al., 2018).

The current environment offers ample opportunity to understand selection and deployment logics in GVCs. The pandemic lockdowns have caused interruptions in supply chains and require adaptation to new regulations and policies emerging from this event. As a consequence, GVCs will undergo a reorganisation. We invite scholars to take this opportunity to follow these adaptation processes closely.

Note

1 All authors contributed equally.

References

Agence France-Presse. (2013, February). Apple CEO says company still has "Magic." *Industry Week*. Retrieved from https://www.industryweek.com/leadership/article/21960995/apple-ceo-says-com pany-still-has-magic

Arndt, F., Fourné, S.P., & MacInerney-May, K. (2018). The merits of playing it by the book: Routine versus deliberate learning and the development of dynamic capabilities. *Industrial and Corporate Change*, *27*(4), 723–743.

Arndt, F., & Pierce, L. (2018). The behavioral and evolutionary roots of dynamic capabilities. *Industrial and Corporate Change*, *27*(2), 413–424.

Arndt, F.F., & Ashkanasy, N. (2015). Integrating ambiculturalism and fusion theory: A world with open doors. *Academy of Management Review*, *40*(1), 144–147.

Aslam, H., Blome, C., Roscoe, S., & Azhar, T. (2018). Dynamic supply chain capabilities: How market sensing, supply chain agility and adaptability affect supply chain ambidexterity. *International Journal of Operations and Production Management*, *38*(12), 226–2285.

Backer, K., & Miroudot, S. (2014). *Mapping Global Value Chains*. European Central Bank (ECB), Frankfurt a. M. Retrieved from https://www.openaire.eu/search/publication?articleId=dedup_wf_001::b4dfde5 1b6cfadeda3418432795f67a4

Bloom, N., Genakos, C., Sadun, R., & Van Reenen, J. (2012). Management practices across firms and countries. *The Academy of Management Perspectives*, *26*(1), 12–33.

Cadestin, C., De Backer, K., Desnoyers-James, I., Miroudot, S., Ye, M., & Rigo, D. (2018). *Multinational Enterprises and Global Value Chains: New Insights on the Trade-investment Nexus, OECD Directorate for Science*. Technology and Industry Working Papers 2018/5. OECD Publishing, Paris

Cantwell, J. (1989). Technological innovation and multinational corporations. In *The Eclectic Paradigm*. Basil Blackwell, Cambridge, MA.

Cattaneo, O., Gereffi, G., & Staritz, C. (Eds.). (2010). *Global Value Chains in a Postcrisis World: A Development Perspective*. The World Bank.

Chen, D., Park, S.H., & Newburry, W. (2009). Parent contribution and organizational control in international joint ventures. Strategic Management Journal, *30*(11), 1133–1156.

Corrado, C.A., Hulten, C.R., & Sichel, D.E. (2005). Measuring capital and technology: An expanded framework. In C. Corrado, J. Haltiwanger, & D. Sichel (Eds.), *Measuring Capital in the New Economy*. The University of Chicago Press, Chicago, IL, pp. 11–45.

Davis, J. P., Eisenhardt, K. M., & Bingham, C. B. (2009). Optimal structure, market dynamism, and the strategy of simple rules. *Administrative Science Quarterly*, *54*(3), 413–452.

De Backer, K., & S. Miroudot (2013, December 19). "*Mapping Global Value Chains*", OECD Trade Policy Papers, No. 159, OECD Publishing, Paris, http://dx.doi.org/10.1787/5k3v1trgnbr4-en

Dyer, J.H., & Singh, H. (1998). The relational view: Cooperative strategy and sources of interorganizational competitive advantage. *Academy of Management Review, 23*(4), 660–679.

Eisenhardt, K. M., & Martin, J. A. (2000). Dynamic capabilities: What are they? *Strategic Management Journal, 21*(10-11), 1105–1121.

Ernst, D. (2008). Asia's upgrading through innovation 31 strategies and global innovation networks: An extension of Sanjaya Lall's research agenda. *Transnational Corporation, 17*(3), 31–58.

Fu, X., Pietrobelli, C., & Soete, L. (2011). The role of foreign technology and indigenous innovation in the emerging economies: Technological change and catching-up. *World Development, 39*(7), 1204–1212.

Fujita, Mai (2011). Value chain dynamics and local suppliers' capability building: An analysis of the Vietnamese motorcycle industry. In Kawakami, Momoko, & Sturgeon, Timothy J. (Eds.), *The Dynamics of Local Learning in Global Value Chains: Experiences from East Asia.* Palgrave Macmillan, Hampshire, UK, pp. 68–99.

Galvin, P., & Arndt, F. (2014). Strategic management: Building depth as well as breadth. *Journal of Management & Organization, 20*(2), 139–147.

Gereffi, Gary, Humphrey, John, & Sturgeon, Timothy (2005). The governance of global value chains. Review of International Political Economy, *12*(1), 78–104.

Ghemawat, P. (2003). Semiglobalization and international business strategy. *Journal of international business studies, 34*(2), 138–152.

Gratton, L., & Ghoshal, S. (2005). Beyond best practice. *MIT Sloan Management Review, 46*(3), 49–57+92.

Greiner, L. (1998). Evolution and revolution as organizations grow. *Harvard Business Review,* (May-June). Retrieved from https://hbr.org/1998/05/evolution-and-revolution-as-organizations-grow

Hendry, L.C., Stevenson, M., MacBryde, J., Ball, P., Sayed, M., & Liu, L. (2019). Local food supply chain resilience to constitutional change: The Brexit effect. *International Journal of Operations & Production Management.*

Hennart, J. (1982). *A Theory of Multinational Enterprise,* University of Michigan.

Jones, G. (2005). *Multinationals and Global Capitalism: From the Nineteenth to the Twenty First Century.* Oxford University Press.

Kawakami, Momoko, & Sturgeon, Timothy J. (Eds.) (2011). *The Dynamics of Local Learning in Global Value Chains: Experiences from East Asia.* Palgrave Macmillan, Hampshire, UK.

Kergroach, S. (2019). National innovation policies for technology upgrading through GVCs: A cross-country comparison. *Technological Forecasting and Social Change, 145*, 258–272.

Kohtamäki, M., Rabetino, R., & Möller, K. (2018). Alliance capabilities: A systematic review and future research directions. Industrial Marketing Management, *68*, 188–201.

Lee, S.M., & Rha, J.S. (2016). Ambidextrous supply chain as a dynamic capability: Building a resilient supply chain. *Management Decision.*

Lu, J.W., & Beamish, P.W. (2001). The Internationalization and Performance of SMEs. *Strategic Management Journal, 22*(6/7), 565–586.

Luo, Y. (2000). Dynamic capabilities in international expansion. *Journal of World Business, 35*(4), 355–378.

Meyer, K.E. (2015). What is "strategic asset seeking FDI"? *The Multinational Business Review.*

Miroudot, S., & Cadestin, C. (2017). *Services in Global Value Chains: From Inputs to Value-Creating Activities.* OECD Publishing, Paris. doi:10.1787/465f0d8b-en Retrieved from http://dmu.summon.serialssolut ions.com.proxy.library.dmu.ac.uk/2.0.0/link/0/eLvHCXMwpV1NT8MwDI0YuyAhPgSIMZhy4l bWpWnXcEFj2qASbKjrKsGlShpPIKAbsIm_j9O1IEDiwjmXyM95sePnmBCHndjWD05QwDWm EphtpAyEtrmSvpZMc4x2BZMG- uw3Ym92y6PC3GhaY0p4C5ZMqduPU3Nq3mzZSpsLfNycTZ 7scwcKVNvLYZqVEiVYV6PR7V63rsL4qI1D92zyT13YmtfWZAhD08h1b94OL9c-pvksdzHU lPyKbh-Lr_z__514792vEU2ihiUdpZOs01WINshQckaNMjochIAjeXTAmj3Xj5kb6e0Hw6vaTC4 GUcjGg1p3Lka96xu2OtEweCCGjVKHEQYXe6SqN-LupdWMWfBAl-4FrjMmyjMxXzVFsrzwA EzSghslykOIBxgtq-YTrXQAheERgSl0v4EJNrYc_bIujRy_Gyet-3pfUIIEinXZjKSk3Lfk1KnUnjcBk C-EAJq5NgYPnlfVgRmcobBbmISEkQoKRHCk1sj9dKUSVFFSb7MePDnap2sMXMJ54qxQ7I6 f13AEakgeo3CKxqkEo6GH_hVyko

Narula, R., & Dunning, J.H. (2000). Industrial development, globalization and multinational enterprises: New realities for developing countries. *Oxford development studies, 28*(2), 141–167.

Penrose, E.T. (1959). *The Theory of the Growth of the Firm.* John Wiley, New York.

Petricevic, O., & Teece, D. J. (2019). The structural reshaping of globalization: Implications for strategic sectors, profiting from innovation, and the multinational enterprise. *Journal of International Business Studies, 50*(9), 1487–1512.

Pietrobelli, C., & Raboletti, R. (2011). Global value chains meet innovation systems: Are there learning opportunities for developing countries? *World Development, 39*(7), 1261–1269.

Pisano, G.P. (2017). Toward a prescriptive theory of dynamic capabilities: Connecting strategic choice, learning, and competition. *Industrial and Corporate Change, 26*(5), 747–762.

Pitelis, C. N., & Teece, D. J. (2010). Cross-border market co-creation, dynamic capabilities and the entrepreneurial theory of the multinational enterprise. *Industrial and corporate change, 19*(4), 1247–1270.

Schoemaker, P.J., Heaton, S., & Teece, D. (2018). Innovation, dynamic capabilities, and leadership. *California Management Review, 61*(1), 15–42.

Schreiner, M., Kale, P., & Corsten, D. (2009). What really is alliance management capability and how does it impact alliance outcomes and success? *Strategic Management Journal, 30*(13), 1395–1419.

Sinkovics, R. R., Sinkovics, N., & Hoque, S. F. (2018). Supplier strategies and routines for capability development: Implications for upgrading. *Journal of International Management, 24*(4), 348–368. doi:10.1016/j.intman.2018.04.005

Stacey, R., & Mowles, C. (2016). *Strategic Management and Organisational Dynamics: The Challenge of Complexity to Ways of Thinking about Organisations.* Pearson Education.

Tatham, P., Wu, Y., Kovács, G., & Butcher, T. (2017). Supply chain management skills to sense and seize opportunities. *The International Journal of Logistics Management.*

Teece, D., Pisano, G., & Shuen, A. (1997). Dynamic capabilities and strategic management. *Strategic Management Journal, 18*(7), 509–533.

Teece, D.J. (2014). A dynamic capabilities-based entrepreneurial theory of the multinational enterprise. *Journal of international business studies, 45*(1), 8–37.

Teece, D.J. (2017). A capability theory of the firm: an economics and (strategic) management perspective. *New Zealand Economic Papers, 53*(1), 1–43.

Teece, D., Peteraf, M., & Leih, S. (2016). Dynamic capabilities and organizational agility: Risk, uncertainty, and strategy in the innovation economy. *California Management Review, 58*(4), 13–35.

Wang, G., Dou, W., Zhu, W., & Zhou, N. (2015). The effects of firm capabilities on external collaboration and performance: The moderating role of market turbulence. *Journal of Business Research, 68*(9), 1928–1936.

Weerawardena, J., Mort, G.S., Liesch, P.W. & Knight, G. (2007). Conceptualizing accelerated internationalization in the born global firm: A dynamic capabilities perspective. *Journal of World Business, 42*(3), 294–306.

Yang, Y., Jia, F., & Xu, Z. (2019). Towards an integrated conceptual model of supply chain learning: an extended resource-based view. *Supply Chain Management: An International Journal.*

Yum Brands. (2016). Yum! Brands details transformation plans to drive growth of KFC, Pizza Hut and Taco Bell after China separation at annual investor conference today. Retrieved July 6, 2020, from https://www.yum.com/wps/portal/yumbrands/Yumbrands/news/press-releases/yum%21+brands+details+transformation+plans+to+drive+growth+of+kfc%2C+pizza+hut+and+taco+bell+after+china+separation+at+annual+investor+conference+today

Zollo, M., Reuer, J.J., & Singh, H. (2002). Interorganizational routines and performance in strategic alliances. *Organization science, 13*(6), 701–713.

4

INTERFIRM CUSTOMER–SUPPLIER COLLABORATION FOR A SUSTAINABLE TRANSITION

Katrina Skellern and Raymond Markey

Introduction

This chapter aims to build knowledge on interfirm customer–supplier approaches to sustainability. Focusing on the traditional manufacturing value chain in an Australian setting, this chapter develops an innovative conceptual model, drawing on the concepts of technological innovations systems, sustainable collaboration studies and global value chains. We explore theoretical and practical dimensions for sustainable change by applying our innovative theoretical model to four case studies.

The research findings here demonstrate that maintaining entrenched socio-technical regime behaviours often anchor manufacturers into 'business as usual' thinking. This makes it less likely that they will engage with the notion of sustainability. However, external collaboration (beyond the firm boundary) with 'new' customers and suppliers in emerging markets such as clean technology and sustainability can articulate new demands, provide fresh opportunities for niche manufacturing solutions, and influence possibilities for sustainable transitions and supplier value-add.

The importance of understanding this transition dynamic is underlined by the global concentration of production and supplier relationships, which are facilitated by multi-national interfirm partnerships. According to Kiron et al. (2015), almost one-third of the global economy passes through 1000 large companies and associated suppliers. In 2012, the world's largest 1000 firms generated US$34 trillion, approximately 40 per cent of the world's $85 trillion wealth. In the process, these companies 'influenced billions of people around the world, from employees to suppliers, customers and regulators' (UNEP Finance Initiative 2014, p. 34). If this corporate influence was to be strategically oriented towards attaining global sustainability goals, the conventional production–consumption regime would exhibit significantly less environmental impact than it does today. Norton et al. (2015) have noted that for large business enterprises, the supply chain is one of the most opportune areas to develop sustainable practices, both through reducing carbon emissions and building adaptive capacity.

The business case for sustainability has steadily grown in importance over the past two decades (Hart and Milstein 2003; Loorbach and Rotmans 2006; Jovane and Westkämper 2009; Qian 2014). More specifically, the concept of sustainable manufacturing has been positioned as not only offering resource savings through production efficiencies, ecologically sensitive design and

 DOI: 10.4324/9781315225661-6

cleaner production, but also by creating fresh opportunities along the value chain (Qian 2014; Halldórsson and Kovács 2010). Jovane and Westkamper (2009) propose that linking production values with consumption behaviour increases public awareness of environmental pressures and demand for technological and social solutions. This would establish manufacturing as a key enabler of change. While many businesses recognise that profitability depends upon establishing a balance across the economic, social and ecological context in which they operate (Kiron et al. 2015), the 'incumbent manufacturer' (mainly heavy engineering, machining and metals, chemical, and steel fabrication sectors) often struggles to adopt such a perspective (Van Winden et al. 2010). Manufacturing firms that are juggling multiple pressures associated with technological innovation and global competition are at the same time impacted by climate change, limits to finite resources and increasingly discerning customers, in terms of product selection or choice. As a shift towards a lower carbon economy becomes more globally accepted and a preferred corporate modus operandi, traditional manufacturing firms are realising that they cannot achieve such a transformation alone. Sheffi (2005) argues that the number and types of threats from various sources, which are now greater than ever, can undermine a supply chain. Thus, the notion of resilience in manufacturing supply chains has gained significant importance in recent years (Bakshi and Kleindorfer 2009; Liu et al. 2015).

The next section of this chapter explores the research literature in sustainable transition in firms and develops from it the innovative conceptual model applied to the cases studies. The methodology for the cases studies is then outlined, and main findings are presented. A broader discussion of the findings then ensues, followed by conclusions regarding theoretical and practical implications for firms.

Literature review and conceptual model

Sustainability as a concept has evolved from a simple expression of good intentions and searching for internal operational efficiencies to a strategy that addresses critical business issues involving a complex network of strategic relationships and activities across the value chain (Hart and Milstein 2003). A missing perspective within transition research is the role of the consumer in forming relationships for sustainable change. Currently, transition studies focus on understanding the production or supply traits for change; but increasingly apparent within these contributions are new types of consumer–producer combinations that enable decentralised technology strategies, knowledge diffusion and transformative reorientation to take place. Through one such value-based relationship – interfirm customer and supplier – the supplier can, and arguably must, tackle some of the difficult sustainability issues related to production and consumption. Rather than the conventional customer (household end-consumer) market, the manufacturer has a customer base predominantly centred on the original equipment manufacturer. Presently, a four-tiered supply chain system makes up this manufacturing model. Whilst the original equipment manufacturer customer assembles the final product (e.g. wind turbine, solar panel) for the end-consumer marketplace, tier one manufacturing suppliers produce components, such as brackets for solar panels or gear boxes for wind turbines, directly for the original equipment manufacturer. Tier two manufacturing suppliers provide products and services to the customer at the next level in the chain, supplying fittings and operational equipment, with tier three and the smaller tier four niche producers delivering specialised components such a technical design elements of the build. In the Australian context, Goennemann (2015) argues that these latter two tiers comprise the majority of the manufacturing supply chain, but by contrast currently contribute just 1 per cent towards an available 41 per cent share of the global manufacturing trade base. By employing collaborative initiatives, global supplier value and innovative sustainable solutions, Goennemann (2015) claims that Australian manufacturing's niche production market share could grow exponentially.

There is an absence of practical and readily accessible information for manufacturing firms on how to develop interfirm customer–supplier partnerships and sustainable supply chains, engage external stakeholders, and manage these ongoing relationships to stimulate beneficial innovation and sustainability activity (Wilcox 2014). Published examples illustrate the actions of business conglomerates such as Lotus, which combined high-speed and lightweight techno-logical expertise to build a sports car. Engineers from Lotus partnered with a global aluminium company to acquire knowledge on emerging materials for future automotive vehicle produc-tion. The alliance yielded a highly innovative product and renewed capability within Lotus (Assembly Automotion 1996). Similarly, the corporate multi-national firms of Mercedes and Swatch joined forces to develop the Smart Car, while Philips Electronics and Nike partnered to combine digital technology and sporting prowess to design and create niche products and services, such as portable radios to be worn whilst exercising, to increase sales in the personal training market (Von Stamm 2004). These cases demonstrate that the selection of global supply chain partners in the creation of sustainable and innovative products can be a critical decision factor in forging successful interfirm customer–supplier alliances.

Previous work (Skellern, Markey and Thornwaite 2017) identifies challenges and opportu-nities experienced by incumbent manufacturing firms when undertaking collaboration initia-tives. The research findings indicate that longstanding customer collaboration styles 'lock-in' the manufacturer to an existing regime, preventing the firm from searching for sustainable and inno-vative value-add. Instead, firms respond to the development of a sustainability agenda through incremental process innovation, such as adopting carbon management systems and corporate social responsibility activities (Hockerts and Wüstenhagen 2010). Further research findings illus-trate that extra-regional collaboration attributes contribute to system innovation, subsequently motivating traditional manufacturing firms to explore sustainable business alternatives.

Skellern, Markey and Thornwaite (2017) also suggest that a manufacturing firm's capacity to build innovative and sustainable alliances varies. In Australia, an Ai Group (2016) study of businesses found firms tend to be good problem-solvers by exploiting existing knowledge and relationships. However, firms are less willing to collaborate when exploring niche and innova-tive opportunities, resulting in fewer visionary outputs generated internally. An estimated 45 per cent of collaborative relationships were found to be between businesses that already had an established supply chain network. Clearly, many companies turn inwardly to people they already know and trust to help solve problems. The same study illustrated that firms are much more likely to align with each other to develop new products, processes or business models (59 per cent of medium-sized business respondents) than with public sector researchers (23 per cent). This indicates the importance of united interfirm models as a mechanism for change. Subsequently, this evidence suggests such value-based networks need to extend beyond local and regional boundaries and the importance of building greater interconnectedness within the wider manufacturing innovation sector (Australian Government 2011; Roos 2014; Ai Group 2016; Altey et al. 2018).

Enriching manufacturing links both domestically and internationally to maximise the flow and exchange of knowledge, resources and ideas can create value-based opportunities for sus-tainable learning, creativity and ultimately niche innovation. Kiron et al. (2015) has called for the business community to join forces to address sustainability challenges, help reshape the social context in which they operate and explore vital new market sectors. The network of interde-pendencies among firms, governments and society has created a world of mutual reliance, in which collaboration is a necessary route to stimulate transformative change.

An enriched transitions analysis

Skellern, Markey and Thornwaite (2017) analysed a socio-technical systems approach towards sustainable transition research in stimulating systemic change towards environmental and socially sustainable alternatives (Geels 2011). Of particular relevance to analyses of socio-technical systems is the concept of 'path-dependence', which is a core feature of evolutionary economic geography studies. The notion of path-dependence emerged from research conducted by Cooke (2013), who explored industrial district transformations in the 1980s and 1990s. This work is now significant in understanding the complex challenges firms face when initiating a sustainable transition. For instance, when firms rely on following a particular path, they tend to optimise existing capital investment scenarios, technology strategies and operating systems that maintain the existing socio-technical regime and ignore future opportunities for new path creation (Boschma et al. 2016). Skellern, Markey and Thornwaite (2017) draw on this theoretical assessment, to demonstrate the sustainable transition attributes of traditional manufacturing sectors in Australian city regions. This study provides a detailed insight into the transition attributes of 24 manufacturers, systematically analysing the firm context for a reorientation towards achieving a sustainable economy. In recent times, interest has grown in where and how new industries emerge, existing industries adapt (Tödtling and Trippl 2005), supply chains innovate, and how to steer or coordinate a reconfiguration of the traditional manufacturing sector (Cooke 2013; Gibbs and O'Neill 2014). In spite of this interest, to date the interfirm customer–supplier alliance has been a missing ingredient in comprehending the manufacturing transition dynamic, particularly with regards to the significance of regional and extra-regional interfirm collaborations.

Collaborations for sustainability

Research on collaborations, aimed at improving sustainability outcomes of firms and suppliers, has historically focused on relations between firms, non-government organisations and government organisations (Niesten et al. 2016). Few studies have addressed customer–supplier collaborations with interfirm, supplier or competitor alliances, and none have focused on the manufacturing sector (Wassmer, Paquin and Sharma 2014). Several recent contributions have utilised institutional and strategic management theoretical frameworks to explain why firms prefer to collaborate; they consider how institutions influence collaboration and when a choice for alliance building can enhance performance (Niesten et al. 2016; Tether 2002). For example, Kishna et al. (2016) argue that the development of sustainable technologies should be accompanied by organisations legitimising technology with the end-user. To achieve this, Fischer and Pascucci (2016) describe new organisational forms of interfirm collaborations that are required for a shift to a more sustainable society. Using empirical evidence from a study in the Dutch textile industry, Fischer and Pascucci (2016) illustrate how global supply chain engagement, contract implementation and investment in human and financial resources (resource investment) are key organisational strategies that facilitate a sustainable transition. Evidence from Aschemann-Witzel et al. (2016) and Zhu, Feng and Choi (2016) show that sustainable collaboration involves understanding business-to-business relationships and articulating the demand features between the business and consumer. Zeng et al. (2016) suggest that institutional pressures embedded in standards and policies such as environmental laws and regulations are pivotal for developing sustainable global value-chain initiatives, but these same pressures can also stymie progress towards achieving transformative sustainability performance (Ramanathan et al. 2016).

These contributions reinforce the important role that collaboration, governance and institutional forms play in facilitating transformative change in different contexts. However, innovation system attributes, including knowledge creation, market-niche development, visionary and strategic concepts (Jacobsson and Bergek 2011), and endogenous and exogenous mechanisms for collaboration are less visible. Tödtling and Trippl (2005) argue that whilst emerging and transitioning industries are influenced by existing dense local knowledge and actor networks, they can also be mobilised by external regional, national and global triggers. Similarly, Asheim and Gertler (2005) claim that if a firm is exposed to a very few 'outside' contacts, relations become too durable; this may be good for developing trust but a disadvantage for stimulating learning and innovation, resulting in maintaining lock-in and path-dependence. Likewise, Tether (2002) describes the concept of innovation as an interactive and distributed process that involves strategic technological alliances and a range of blended internal and external networks (Freeman 1991). Consequently, firms that collaborate with customers and global value chains in pursuing innovative and sustainable outcomes increase their knowledge of customer needs and improve user confidence in the product–service offerings; this subsequently reduces potential risks associated with bringing an innovation to market. Jensen et al. (2007) describe this mode of firm collaboration as 'Doing, Using and Interacting'. For interfirm customer–supplier partnerships in the 'Doing, Using and Interacting' camp, a transition involves the 'know-who' and 'know-how' needed at any given point in time. These attributes are obtained through informal and formal exchanges internal to the firm, but also with suppliers, customers and competitors that share the same practical problems and experiences (Tether 2002). Thus, constant and repeated interaction within such network environments generates the tacit knowledge which responds to user demands and drives innovation within the firm (Jensen et al. 2007). Contrary to what is frequently stressed in the literature regarding clusters and industrial districts (Cooke and Morgan 1998; Boschma et al. 2016), innovative and collaborative practices do not seem to be restricted to incremental product innovation. In fact, the likelihood of radical product innovation is estimated to be 71 per cent higher for firms that cooperate with new customers and suppliers in a mix of informal and formal interaction (Fitjar and Rodriguez Pose 2013).

Niesten et al. (2016) call for further research on how resources and transactions in sustainable global supply chains differ from those activities in traditional supply chains, which may enable a more thorough understanding of why some forms of collaboration are more effective for a sustainable transition. For example, Husted and De Sousa-Filho (2016, p. 9) suggest that 'sustainability problems by their nature are complex and different from the products and services with which firms typically deal. Such complexity needs to be matched by more complex forms of collaboration that draw upon resources and capabilities that may live outside the boundaries of the firm'. This chapter makes a critical contribution by demonstrating that conventional and traditional forms of collaboration are unsatisfactory for stimulating a systematic transition and require adjustment to advance sustainable manufacturing and associated supply chain initiatives. Understanding firm socio-technical dynamics is essential in order to identify the opportunities and challenges associated with regional and extra-regional customer–supplier alliances, whether identified by the firms themselves or as initiatives to stimulate change by policymakers. Therefore, an innovation systems analysis is employed here to complement the sustainable collaboration literature.

Technological innovation systems

Innovation systems theory was developed as a policy concept in the mid-1980s for application across different system boundaries, including national innovation systems (Freeman 1991), sectoral innovation systems (Malerba 2002), technological innovation systems (Carlsson and Stankiewicz 1991) and regional innovation systems (Cooke, Gomez and Etxebarria 1997). Each construct advocates that the innovation and diffusion process is both a collective and an individual act. In the study of sustainable transitions, such a notion assists in identifying and addressing system strengths and weaknesses for change, not only for developing new products, emerging technologies and markets, but also for building parallel support mechanisms and global supply chain capacity (Jacobsson and Bergek 2011).

Whilst each system concept is important, for this analysis a technological innovation system lens assists in defining the characteristics and dynamic disparities of traditional manufacturers attempting to forge alliances with new customers and value chains. More specifically, technological innovation systems examine the wider innovation system, including the nature of endogenous and exogenous learning processes and relevant bottlenecks that inhibit production and transition processes. For industry renewal to occur, Bergek et al. (2008) introduce six key resource dimensions as being necessary conditions to support innovation of the system. These are knowledge development and diffusion, entrepreneurial experimentation, resource mobilisation, legitimation, influences on the direction of search (or incentives/pressures for organisations to enter the technological field), and new market formation. Drawing upon Jacobsson and Bergek (2011), Truffer and Coenen (2012), Weber and Rohracher (2012), and Binz, Truffer and Coenen (2015), these key elements have been adapted to reveal seven fundamental resource attributes:

- *Knowledge creation and diffusion* is central to the transition process and a decisive mechanism through which firms create and sustain competitiveness (Binz, Truffer and Coenen 2015). As Jacobsson and Bergek (2011) suggest, whole new global value chains often need to be created, requiring that knowledge development and diffusion occurs among a range of firms connected vertically.
- *Market-niche development* is considered a key output of entrepreneurial experimentation, since demand for radically new technologies and products often does not pre-exist but must be created by the actors themselves. For example, the early German solar photovoltaic industry did not begin as a functional global market, but rather technology experts, environmental activists and policymakers aligned to construct a new market segment and lobbied policymakers to regulate the integration of solar into the grid (Binz, Truffer and Coenen 2015).
- *Resource investment and mobilisation* of financial and human assets are essential to facilitate adaptation within new manufacturing arenas, but can be challenging for actors to obtain.
- *Creating legitimacy* requires an alignment of the new industry and its products with relevant institutional contexts to obtain social acceptance of change and reduce potential scepticism.
- *Directionality*, leadership or the vision created to steer a transition involves implementing institutional elements of change, such as incentive structures, cognitive frames and expectations.
- *Demand articulation* steers the formation of new markets (Jacobsson and Bergek 2011). Articulating customer demand is required to understand and be responsive to user practices and preferences that shape innovation and transformative change reflected in the socio-technical arrangements of products (Weber and Rohracher 2012).

A missing key resource attribute of technological innovation systems is the identification of policy coordination initiatives (standard settings, codes, laws and regulations) that may be internally introduced by the firm or externally facilitated by government. In the context of transformative change Weber and Rohracher (2012), in work on system failures of transformative change, illustrate that a parallel analysis of private and public sector policy coordination initiatives needs to be included to understand the transition process. Such an approach ensures coherence between activities of national, regional, sectoral and technological institutions with those of the corporate sector for driving sustainability-related transformation, but this is currently a shortcoming in innovation systems thinking. Hence, a seventh key resource dimension, namely *policy coordination*, is added to complement the conceptual lens.

The main task for an organisation instigating a sustainable transition is to break down the value system into these seven key resource components so as to identify potential challenges and opportunities that could hinder or stimulate reorientation of the system. Therefore, a sustainable transition of the traditional manufacturing firm will depend on how the seven technological innovation system functions emerge, as a consequence of systematic interactions and alignment within the interfirm customer–suppler relationship. Binz, Truffer and Coenen (2015) argue that if any technological innovation system features are deficient, the industry in transition will face a significant development barrier. In saying that, critics of technological innovation system theory claim that the conceptual approach focuses more on elements of weakness than on understanding constructive system changes and interfirm dynamics.

To address this perceived limitation, this chapter refines a technological innovation system analysis using insights from the sustainable collaboration literature to present the conceptual framework. Figure 4.1 illustrates the theoretical framing of this approach and the importance of the seven key features of knowledge, market niche, legitimacy, resource investment, directionality, demand articulation and policy contribution for stimulating regional and extra-regional

Figure 4.1 Theoretical framework: customer–supplier attributes for a sustainable transition.

collaborations. This framework is applied in investigating four interfirm customer–supplier relationships for steering future sustainable transitions. All seven key attributes of the framework need to be present to ensure a sustainable transition.

Methodology

The chapter identifies multi-national corporation original equipment manufacturer entities as customers with an Australian-based headquarters or subsidiary, together with specific manufacturer supplier organisations. These are employed as experiential consumer–production case studies.

Identifying interfirm customer–supplier dynamics for a sustainable transition requires an analysis of actors as well as the social construction of relationships and situations. We investigated the status of collaborations with suppliers for nine original equipment manufacturer customers which were developing a broad range of new products and services focusing on clean technology and sustainability market sectors. These customers had established or were developing supplier alliances to generate niche opportunities within sustainable global value chains. Each customer was extra-regionally located in proximity to its manufacturing supply chain and internally connected within a multi-national group structure.

Nine semi-structured interviews were conducted with the relevant manager of each customer. Interviews were designed to explore the seven key attributes outlined in Figure 4.1 to identify factors that customers determined were important for delivering sustainability-related projects and creating a successful supply chain alliance. All interviews were transcribed verbatim and analysed using qualitative discourse analysis (Foucault 1972).

Table 4.1 illustrates the status of collaborations with suppliers for nine original equipment manufacturer customers. Four customers were actively collaborating with manufacturing suppliers to deliver sustainable value-added outputs, and strategically reconfiguring existing alliances or creating new ones. Another four customers, were seeking to develop new sustainability-oriented supply chain collaborations, but had not yet initiated such transition efforts. One customer case study (C6) was not pursuing new interfirm customer–supplier relationships, citing that existing global partnerships for supply and manufacture were already meeting corporate expectations.

Table 4.2 indicates the case study indicators aligned with the seven key resource attributes and necessary conditions to support sustainable transition. The following analysis details the attributes of the four functioning interfirm customer–supplier collaborations for a sustainable transition, as summarised in Table 4.2.

Table 4.1 Interfirm customer–supplier collaborations

Customer	Functioning 'real-time' collaborations with suppliers	New collaborations being sought	No new collaborations sought
CI	✓		
C2	✓		
C3		✓	
C4	✓		
C5		✓	
C6			✓
C7		✓	
C8		✓	
C9	✓		

Table 4.2 Interfirm customer–supplier resource alignment across four case study customers

Key resource	Formation process	Definition – activities that…	Case study indicators	Literature source
Knowledge	Knowledge creation	Create new knowledge and related competencies	Number of R&D projects, collaborative platforms/open innovation, number of actors involved, learning by doing, key stakeholder/intermediary linkages, tacit knowledge exchange, spatial dynamics	Knowledge development and diffusion (Bergek et al. 2008)
Market–niche	Market formation and innovation	Create protected spaces for new technology, processes and markets	Number of niche markets, new business models, EPDs, incubators, process and production innovation (incremental/radical), spatial dynamics	Entrepreneurial experimentation (Bergek et al. 2008)
Resource investment	Investment mobilisation	Mobilise financial inputs e.g. loans, venture capital	Corporate investment in local initiatives, funding partnerships	Resource mobilisation…. (Bergek et al. 2008)
Legitimacy	Technology legitimation	Embed a new technology in existing institutional structures or adapt the institutional environment to the needs of the technology	Institutional entrepreneurship, corporate investment, lobbying of industry, spin-offs, business case for sustainability, off-shoring, niche value-add	Legitimisation (Bergek et al. 2008)
Directionality	Vision and goal formation	Create a shared vision for the transformation process	Philosophy for local, shared vision platforms, mindset, attitude	Influence on the direction of search (Bergek et al. 2008)
Demand articulation	User need formation	Understand the needs of users for uptake of innovations	Addressing challenges and problems – value-add, Lean, learning by doing, keeping it local, spatial dynamics	Market formation (Bergek et al. 2008; Weber and Rohracher 2012)
Policy coordination	Policy creation	Stimulate change, investment, systematic transformation attributes and barriers	Lack of agility, policy direction, business case, investment, level playing field, private/public policy More of internal policy for sustainability	Policy coordination (Weber and Rohracher 2012)

Source: Adapted from C. Binz, B. Truffer and L. Coenen, 2015, Path creation as a process of resource alignment and anchoring: Industry formation for on-site water recycling in Beijing, *Economic Geography*, vol. 92, pp. 1–29.
Notes: R&D, research and Development; EPD, environmental product declaration.

Case study C1

As part of an iconic building and construction project awarded to C1 by the New South Wales (NSW) government, strategic *directionality* was aimed at reducing the development's carbon footprint by 20 per cent compared to similar ventures. To achieve this vision, C1 initiated a contractor selection process to identify and engage appropriate suppliers in a formal partnership alliance. Once formed, these interfirm customer–supplier relationships were nurtured within an open innovation business model and built on sustainability-related principles that facilitated innovative *knowledge* creation and capability exchange. As a result of such a 'learning by doing' strategy, alliance suppliers were able to adapt existing products or services or design alternatives to meet the sustainability vision of the customer, and subsequently form a new *market-niche*. For example, one supplier introduced a stewardship service to encourage the return of retired or unwanted goods for recycling, thus creating a value-added component to its existing production line. Following C1's implementing Environmental Product Declarations[1] (internal *policy coordination* program to encourage sustainable supply chain practices), a second supplier conducted a systematic assessment of material content within its plasterboard product. Subsequently, this analysis initiated a series of innovative changes, including significantly reducing the volume of raw materials used to create the product. These improvements resulted in creating a lighter, more efficient item and decreased installation time and cost. Consequently, a highly innovative sustainable solution achieved a level of product *legitimacy* and met the *demand articulation* requirements of the end-user by expediting delivery to market. A third supplier applied Environmental Product Declaration policy principles to its carpet manufacturing operation, and, as a result, was able to identify and remove a toxic substance from the product by replacing it with recycled ingredients. In addition, C1 established an in-house 'incubator', a protected space in the factory, away from core business, for experimentation and to work with other stakeholders on innovation and transforming ideas into commercial reality. The incubator explored alternative timber construction techniques and niche experimentation with relevant supplier partners to streamline the building process.

Table 4.3 illustrates that C1 mobilised appropriate *resource investment* attributes to finance projects such as community renewable energy schemes. The funding model enabled program contributors to invest in 1 KW amounts of solar generation with the NSW government paying a dividend for power generated. Such a feature of *demand articulation* motivated suppliers to be more closely aligned with end-consumer needs; this resulted in innovative product design that attained user 'function', as opposed to focusing on physical value only. A similar approach was deployed by C1 in a commercial context. In seeking to develop alternative capital investment models for new building ventures, C1 partnered with its supply chain to articulate the views of the client. As a result, Cl was able to design and implement a 'user pays function' to supply water rather than owning the physical asset, freeing up resources to be invested in future initiatives. However, longer-term corporate *policy coordination* initiatives that stimulated future sustainable building design beyond the awarded NSW project were limited, inhibited by the existing sociotechnical regime. Whilst on one hand reducing the project's carbon footprint was a pivotal criterion for C1 in winning a significant government contract, scaling up the project to achieve internal sustainability-oriented change created challenges for C1 and its conventionally oriented procurement channels. On the other hand, a practical and strategic vision for pursuing sustainability goals enabled C1 to demonstrate the ongoing operational benefits of sustainable product choices and associated supplier innovations.

The introduction of the sustainable supplier alliance is an integrated feature of C1's value chain, incentivising suppliers to generate in-house sustainability-oriented policies and standards for this project. As a result, suppliers shifted from a 'cost'-oriented mindset to developing a 'busi-

Table 4.3 Summary of key interfirm customer–supplier functions and attributes for a sustainable transition

		Knowledge	Market niche	Legitimacy	Resource investment	Directionality	Demand articulation	Policy coordination
C1	Extra-regional Regional	Open innovation platform for collaboration and external knowledge exchange Learning by doing to adapt products and services	EPDs implemented, incubator Process, product and business model innovation	State government awarded sustainable build Supplier alliance developed	Internal investment within the global group Community- and corporate-funded projects	Carbon reductions for regional build, business case for sustainability	Deliver the function instead of the technology	Preference for sustainable design but limited general policy for scaling up Challenges scaling up corporate sustainability principles
C2	Extra-regional Regional	External knowledge shared across the global group and diffused, open innovation framework Learning by doing to problem-solve and value-add	Technological innovation stimulates market shift Downstream influence for recycled content, business model innovation	Sustainability reputation and credentials, unique selling point, certification process Suppliers leverage off credibility, present at conference and schools to educate stakeholders	Internal investment within the global group, tax incentives	Sustainability is key to production and part of core vision Business case for sustainability built within supply chain	Front-end design process Supply chain integration	National economic stimulus triggered innovation, sustainability criteria in development approvals Process innovation, increase landfill and regulatory fees

(Continued)

Table 4.3 (Continued)

C4	Extra-regional Regional	External engineering construction knowledge procured within group Intermediary know-how selected suppliers	Niche process innovation for installation Modular design and manufacture, product stewardship	Formal supplier process critical to development strategy Related expertise led to supplier alliance	Internal global investment, partnership funding	Policy to build domestic capability base Forms to impart knowledge/direction, value add via sustainability	Process innovation to meet customer demand	'Local content' requested around the world, unequal for Australia Cost of doing business, regulations, globalisation
C9	Extra-regional Regional	Open innovation model; global and local experts Innovation Council and local interactive learning and knowledge spillover	Downstream niche innovation Business model innovation	Company managers and system intermediaries present to stakeholders about product and process	Internal investment, global research partnerships	Sustainability = smart product design for the customer = business case Business case for sustainability	Work along value chain to understand customer	Unequal playing field, cost of doing business, regulations, globalisation

Source: Adapted from C. Binz, B. Truffer and L. Coenen, 2015, Path creation as a process of resource alignment and anchoring: Industry formation for on-site water recycling in Beijing, *Economic Geography*, vol. 92, pp. 1–29.

ness case for sustainability'. This shift was motivated by interfirm customer–supplier relationship outcomes and subsequent participation in industry workshops, facilitated by intermediaries such as the Green Building Council of Australia.[2] However, in contrast to *policy coordination* driven from the bottom-up, our research findings additionally indicate that government top-down instigated policy initiatives tended to place limited value on reducing carbon levels in the building process. This weakened sustainability commitment and suggested that C1's NSW project was a one-off rather than a systematic signal of change from the top.

Case study C2

Column seven in Table 4.3 illustrates that *directionality* and creating a sustainable vision were critical resource formation elements for steering a sustainable transition across all four case study scenarios. These attributes were philosophical features and core elements guiding C2's operational strategy and its corporate sustainable *policy coordination* efforts to increase efficiencies, reduce costs and gain a competitive market edge. For example, to reduce waste in the manufacturing process and compete across globalised production channels, C2 invested in state-of-the-art carpet tile manufacturing technology which was designed to operate within a highly automated, innovative and sustainable manner.

In collaboration with internal multi-national corporation group resources, C2 diffused global *knowledge* across its supply chain. Such partnership arrangements enabled C2 to introduce a new product into an Australian market context. External and internal corporate experts specialising in Lean manufacturing[3] and biomimicry[4] techniques, operated within an open innovation framework to engage suppliers, imparting *knowledge*, solving problems and generating value-added innovation as part of the company's transformative journey. However, not all suppliers benefited from such an approach. One supplier's reluctance to explore recycling solutions, for example, prompted C2 to terminate the partnership and collaborate with an alternate supplier in order to achieve its sustainability goals. This particular interfirm customer–supplier challenge triggered C2 to consider mentoring other suppliers in how to adopt sustainable practices beyond its own supply chain pool.

> Do we start acquiring other companies and make them more sustainable?… go beyond our own boundaries and influence and reduce impact elsewhere.
>
> *(C2)*

Such sustainable *directionality* attributes stimulated internal *resource investment* within the multinational corporation group structure, building upon the founder's corporate sustainability principles, which are shared by employees and suppliers alike. This also speaks to the need for building resilience amongst supply chain partners to be able to remain competitive in a changing industry (Bakshi and Kleindorfer 2009; Liu et al. 2015).

In addition, external *policy coordination* activities, such as those facilitated by the Building Education Revolution[5] program, stimulated new interfirm customer–supplier innovations to measure and reduce building inefficiencies. Consequently, C2 introduced a recycled product, replacing a fossil-fuel-based option with a superior, eco-friendly building material alternative and established a *market-niche*. At the same time, C2 implemented a technology road map that delivered the first 're-entry' facility[6] to an Australian market. This technology enabled a niche product to be scaled up by recycling large volumes of carpet on-site rather than off-shoring the process. Existing suppliers were encouraged to increase the content of recycled materials within their product. In this way, C2's influence was leveraged for reduced manufacturing environmental pressures and impact. However, whilst the Building Education Revolution government *policy coordination* program stimulated a niche in the market, research indicates that C2 is continuing its efforts to advocate for further state and local government intervention to accelerate the business case for sustainability, particularly in relation to re-use and recycling of waste products. For instance, to increase the amount of recycled content in building construction products, C2 called for such criteria to be stipulated in local government development applications and for landfill fees to be increased. However, such policies are yet to eventuate.

Corporate *policy coordination* initiatives involved the implementation of a standardised certification process to ensure environmental and sustainable obligations were met internally, creating product and firm *legitimacy* and end-user reassurance:

> Certification is our business … we have a program to remove all substances and emissions … so we are down to 0.1% of some compounds as our process has removed them … the architects that we deal with are aware of that.
>
> *(C2)*

Building corporate *legitimacy* was also accomplished by participating and presenting at relevant conferences and universities. These presentations complemented factory tours conducted by C2 to showcase its sustainability and advanced manufacturing credentials, key points of difference, and value creation attributes for the organisation. Such strategic collaboration initiatives to ascertain user *demand articulation* attributes were key to customising product and reducing waste, at the same time benefiting key suppliers with access to new *knowledge*.

Case study C4

For C4, creating engineering procurement and construction *knowledge* were key resource features generating large solar projects in remote locations and in turn, building and strengthening their supplier capability base. When managing projects around the world, C4 organised global supplier engagement forums to clearly articulate a project's *directionality* and vision, and in the process identify and recruit appropriate suppliers. For example, in executing an Australian renewables contract, C4, assisted by supporting intermediary organisations, selected suppliers with the capability to streamline product design, manufacture and installation in order to meet the logistic and timeframe challenges of building in remote locations. C4 sought appropriate and capable suppliers who could contribute to solving these complexities through value-adding, experimentation, innovation and agile practices:

> I had to do a roadshow … if you mention solar they think 'you put something on your roof and you get hot water', no. So I actually had to go down and do a full presentation to them and show them what we were about.
>
> *(C4)*

Hence, undertaking supplier selection was a critical and *directional* exercise in securing the sustainable positioning of C4. New interfirm customer–supplier alliances were established with traditional engineering and technical manufacturing suppliers, which had not previously been involved in sustainability or clean-technology-related projects, but had the demand attributes and formation processes for adaptation and innovation. Such collaborative exchange facilitated *legitimacy* and dissemination of sustainable product knowledge, while complementing a typical non-traditional area for the manufacturing supplier and establishment of a new *market-niche* for

C4, applicable to global like-minded projects. For instance, C4 developed a niche solar photovoltaic module to replace diesel power generation in remote mining locations. By applying the supplier's engineering and technical expertise, the solar components were produced and installed using modular design techniques, enabling C4 to create a unique barcode for each individual asset. Consequently, the product was able to be monitored and identified in any location, allowing C4 to collect, re-use or recycle modules at the end of their life, generating a *legitimate* and unique corporate product stewardship framework for the solar industry as well as meeting its own corporate sustainability goals.

Financial *resource investment* for solar projects in Australia was primarily mobilised by corporate ventures and external funding, while project developers aligned with suppliers, energy utilities and relevant levels of government to manage the project. Two large-scale projects in remote Australia were developed by C4 in this manner. By employing innovative and agile manufacturing suppliers to develop unique modular components, C4 was able to manage rigorous construction timeframes, stagger financial payments and enable space for innovation to occur throughout the project and not just at the design phase. These initiatives met the client's *demand articulation* goals which would have proven problematic if the product was pre-manufactured and shipped from overseas. It would have been subsequently exposed to risks of time delays, logistical complexity and rigidities that constrain innovation. As a global company, external *policy coordination* programs that prioritise a percentage of local content in manufacturing negotiations provide certainty for projecting the costs, labour and skills required for each job. However, in Australia, these policy conditions are rarely a requirement in contractual tenders. The research suggests that such unequal global trading circumstances disadvantage Australian industry from acquiring and scaling up clean-technology manufacturing capability to compete on a global stage unless customers, as in the case of C4, strategically seek these collaborative relationships with suppliers on the ground.

Case study C9

The development of an open innovation platform was a key manufacturing supplier collaboration strategy for C9, and illustrated in column three of Table 4.3. Such a mechanism was designed to create and facilitate *knowledge* exchange in partnership with relevant suppliers to develop the best possible technological solutions. Embedding innovative principles within corporate *directionality* and vision enabled C9's multi-national corporation research and development heads to collaborate with smaller suppliers through internal network channels. In turn, regional knowledge spillover triggered a renewed trajectory across the local supplier base. The research suggested that such interactive learning alliances generated a *legitimate* innovative manufacturing system that attracted external experts to work with the customer and supplier; this further extended and built upon existing regional knowledge foundations. As a result, C9 established sustainable *market-niches* in downstream businesses. For example, a manager from C9 described 'a solar thermal roofing system that combines solar heating and cooling with photovoltaic electricity production, ventilation and fresh looking aesthetics' as one new market opportunity. To strengthen product *legitimacy*, C9 consulted customers beyond the immediate tiers two and three to gauge an understanding of *demand articulation* influences within the market. Based on these consultation initiatives, C9 engaged with appropriate suppliers and stakeholders, *legitimising* the product and process to build alliances to meet future customer demand. Additionally, C9 complemented internal *resource investment* activities, of research and product innovation, by collaborating in a number of external university research partnerships; these included those funded by the Australian Research Council to explore future technology applications.

Column nine in Table 4.3 illustrates external government *policy coordination* initiatives to support Australian manufacturing or sustainability programs were lacking and posed a significant challenge for C9 in pursuing its transition in Australia. As a subsidiary site within a multinational corporation competing in a global marketplace, such policy foresight is a requirement for developing future sustainable markets:

> I think it is noble to say that Australia needs to stand on its own two feet and for us to try and survive, this would be the right stance if it was a level playing field. I know businesses that we compete with in China who get free land, interest-free loans, subsidies and enormous help ... the government is good in changing policy regulation to create less red tape for us ... but until we get our heads around the cost of doing business in Australia ... it is going to be very difficult.
>
> *(C9)*

Discussion

This chapter has combined the key features of technological innovation systems with insights from the global collaboration literature to identify the interfirm customer–supplier attributes of a sustainable transition in four manufacturing case studies. Previous research has identified a lack of understanding of how sustainable supply chains emerge or differ from traditional models (Niesten et al. 2016). The conceptual frame adopted here enables a systematic analysis of the key features that influence and determine how the manufacturing supplier can innovate and adapt a process or product to meet the customer's sustainability vision. This process stimulated a sustainable internal reconfiguration beyond the firm's traditional production roots.

Table 4.3 summarises the sustainable transition attributes in the four observed case studies. Five major findings derived from these results, confirming the importance of the seven combined key resource alignment features for a sustainable transition.

First, Table 4.3 illustrates the relevance of extra-regional and regional proximity attributes for stimulating a transition. In all four case studies, extra-regional customer collaboration introduced new resource formation attributes creating key building blocks for change. These were then aligned to endogenous regional path creation across the supply chain (Binz, Truffer and Coenen 2015). Many traditional manufacturers are part of small and self-contained city regions, and excessive cognitive or organised proximity amongst local suppliers can be detrimental to a transition, leading to lock-in and limiting innovation. Furthermore, the research indicates that manufacturers who engage in extra-regional, novel customer collaboration tend to increase the uptake of innovative opportunities, compared to firms that rely on internal resources or existing customer interactions for innovation. Hence, the heterogeneity and extra-regionality among interfirm customer–suppliers adds *legitimacy* and *directionality* to innovative relations, setting them apart from others. Table 4.3 also illustrates that most resource formation processes were retained and aligned in a regional yet internationally well-connected innovation system formed around a global technology (e.g. modular design of solar systems, re-entry recycling facility), as a result of internal multi-national corporation relationship subsidiary structures. Binz, Truffer and Coenen (2015) argue that possessing a range of mobilising attributes to stimulate a transition contradicts Crevoisier and Jeannerat (2009), who suggest that *knowledge* is the only anchoring resource formation process. Whilst knowledge creation is important, Tether (2002) claims that 'group firms' are able to internally draw upon other resource qualities such as *legitimacy*, market access, *investment*, power, *demand articulation*, security, and the branding and prestige of a global reputation in seeking partners for innovation. Leveraging these processes enables a supplier to access a variety of resources beyond knowledge, which is a significant research finding in all four case studies.

Second, Table 4.3 articulates each customer's sustainable vision and *directionality* attributes. Our findings support Kiron et al.'s (2015) claim that firms which prioritise a sustainability agenda are more than twice as likely to pursue collaborations that are strategic and transformational. Promoting sustainability strategies enables each customer to identify and engage with like-minded suppliers and partners to achieve its goals, and presents a compelling case for organisational change and business model innovation. The presence of robust sustainability principles and integrity embedded in each case study customer's operations consequently influenced a supply chain reconfiguration. Subsequently, if a vision for sustainability was activated, all other key resource formation processes were mobilised. When both sustainability-oriented collaboration and business model change occur, the combination is strongly correlated with sustainability-based profits and new market creation.

Third, echoing contributions within the 'Doing, Using and Interacting' literature, Table 4.3 illustrates each interfirm customer–supplier relationship was formed within a model of open innovation, demonstrating that 'learning by doing' attributes are an essential ingredient for a transition. In a survey of 1604 Norwegian firms, Fitjar and Rodríguez-Pose (2013) found that innovation tended to develop in open collaborative environments, by drawing innovative capacity from a mix of internal and external interaction. The imported sustainability *knowledge* and know-how obtained and exchanged from within the customer multi-national corporation group structure presented new learning opportunities for the supplier and transformed the incumbent firm in a localised 'learning by doing' process. Jensen et al. (2007) suggest that 'Doing, Using and Interacting'–type collaborations involve more transmission of tacit knowledge and practical know-how, which is less easily transferred across geographical distance. Such a claim may explain the success of the open innovation model analysed in this article. However, in contrast, when mapping extra-regional supplier relationships across the four research case studies, collaboration was associated with a high degree of sustainable product innovation regardless of spatial proximity. Each customer employed a mix of regional and extra-regional suppliers and, therefore, was indifferent about the need to be geographically proximate, citing a preference to appoint a supplier that met the needs of the customer. This indicates that customers favoured cognitive proximity over geographic proximity. Thus, system building dynamics on the customer side (with differing, yet related market 'clean technology' segments), together with pre-existing competence in designing and manufacturing-related technologies (fabrication, machining, engineering and technical expertise) were crucial factors to the interfirm partnership and success of the supplier transition, integrated within a 'learning by doing' and open innovation framework.

Fourth, Teece (2010) argues that for innovation to occur, a wide variety of assets and competencies need to be accessed, which are unlikely to be provided by one company. To produce a personal computer, for example, a company needs access to multiple levels of expertise in developing semi-conductor and display technologies, disk drive, networking and keyboard technology, and many other areas usually enabled by aligning with relevant third parties. This chapter demonstrates the value of involving suppliers in the product development journey, including understanding aspects such as time to market, competitive positioning, quality control, costing estimates and process efficiencies, rather than each stakeholder working independently to introduce a new product.

Tether (2002) insists that innovation is becoming increasingly distributed, as fewer firms are able to go it alone in technology development. This results in a transition to more sustainable production, due to alignment with external industry partners. Mobilising a range of stakeholders, imported knowledge and resources from other places enabled new *market-niches* to be formed across each case study observed (Table 4.3), subsequently encouraging technological development, new business model formations and other associated changes. Where creativity and entrepreneurial enterprise were limited across the case studies, a collaborative environment for experimentation opened a 'protected space' for innovative activity and trialling of niche initiatives for both the customer and supplier (Loorbach 2010). Such a strategy assisted both customer and supplier firms to *articulate the demand* of future end-users, leverage resources, share risk, build new capability, compete globally and create *legitimate* sustainable *market-niches*.

Fifth, Table 4.3 demonstrates that public and private *policy coordination* and government intervention are seen as both key ingredients and detriments to a sustainable transition (Binz, Truffer and Coenen 2015). On one hand, in-house corporate policy instruments (e.g. contracts, standards and disclosures) as well as external regulations that support sustainable projects stimulate the market and foster *market-niche* development. Structural mechanisms such as certification were used, not only to *legitimise* sustainability initiatives but also to ensure transparent and accountable practices were incorporated; these were crucial to building a business case for sustainability and mobilising necessary *resource investment*. On the other hand, inconsistent and confusing public policy statements inhibited transformative change for the customer and supplier which, in turn, limited scaling up of niche innovations, *resource investment* strategies and capability building opportunities. This research suggests that although Australian government policy initiatives lack clarity for guiding future sustainability and manufacturing industry change, the market is able to find a way to internally reconfigure by employing innovative, collaborative solutions. So, internal corporate sustainability *policy coordination* was critical for driving a sustainable transition.

Drawing more general conclusions from this research, selecting and appointing suppliers for involvement in sustainable product development was a significant decision factor in forging interfirm customer–supplier alliances, but has not received much attention in the literature. Wagner (2010) points out that the degree to which a supplier's sustainable business ethos complements the customer's business culture is an important collaboration characteristic. Whilst internal knowledge creation, technology development and manufacturing expertise are important, other factors considered critical in the selection process included a supplier's competence and innovation mindset combined with the qualities of trustworthiness, reliability, openness, mutual support, and goal congruence. Such an implicit contribution counters the suggestion in the literature that interaction simply happens because 'something is in the air' or as a result of 'being there' or sharing the same geographical location (Gertler 1995).

Whilst the transition literature emphasises the role of path-dependency as a factor that can inhibit the transition process for incumbent manufacturing firms, this research illustrates that forming interfirm customer–supplier alliances contribute to the types of system shifts required to overcome such a mindset. In turn, the partnership generates benefits for both actors, particularly in the shape of encouraging risk taking, entering new markets, engaging in cognitive learning settings and opening space for innovation (Tether 2002).

Sheffi (2005) also argues that the number and types of threats, which are now greater than ever, within the macro environment can undermine a supply chain's potential. The notion of resilience building in supply chains can be viewed as a source of competitive advantage (Sheffi 2005; Jüttner and Maklan 2011; Brandon-Jones et al. 2014; Altay et al. 2018). Our findings demonstrate how customer–supplier relationships can build this resilient capacity for the purpose of competitive advantage.

The key emerging features presented in this article could be strategically considered by manufacturing firms and the wider industry sector to influence the change process, address challenges of optimisation and support enabling mechanisms for sustainability across global supply chains. Understanding the socio-technical regime dynamics, regional path and place-dependent characteristics, and organisational routines that inhibit change, whether at the firm or sector or city region level, is crucial to activating a sustainable transition of the manufacturing system. The chapter findings particularly illustrate the significance of three key characteristics for stimulating a sustainable transition. These are developing a core vision for sustainability, building the transition capability of managers and the workforce, and improving interfirm and external collaboration:

Developing a core vision. By investing in transition management techniques, the strategic vision of the traditional manufacturing firm can be reimagined. A sustainable transition vision embraced at the top and throughout the organisation provides the enabling conditions to deliver internal policies for change. Such leadership motivates product and process innovation, based not only on efficiencies and cost but also productivity gains, when entering new niche markets.

Building transition capability. The research findings suggest that over three-quarters of respondent firms are either optimising operational status quo or managing resources to increase efficiency and cut costs. In order to trigger a future sustainable and innovative transition of the manufacturing sector and meet the shifting needs of its future end-users, higher level skillsets, capability, and education across firm management and workforce levels need to be improved.

Improving interfirm and external collaboration. This research illustrates the range of opportunities manufacturing firms have to collaborate with a mixture of businesses, research organisations, competitors and customers. However, limited time, resources, expertise, know-how and capacity restrict many small to medium firms from taking opportunities to build new alliances. Empirical findings from case studies show the advantages of instigating diverse and multiple collaborations. But a collaborative mindset and subsequent internal behaviour need to be encouraged to activate such external connections beyond the boundaries of the city region and internal firm resources.

Conclusion

This chapter has demonstrated limitations within both the technological innovation systems and sustainable collaboration literature. The technological innovation system concept on innovating systems does little to assist in understanding the role of firm collaboration activity, particularly interfirm or customer–supplier alliances and the role of public or private policy initiatives to stimulate sustainable change. As a result, the typology's prime motivation has been on analysing firm technological approaches, which overlook interaction with other system environments (Jacobson and Bergek 2011) and do not fully tackle the problem of transformative change in the existing socio-technical regime. Whilst the sustainable collaboration literature places emphasis on individual elements of the system, or incremental approaches for transformation, it too lacks a holistic overview of systematic innovation for a sustainable transition (Niesten et al. 2016). Interposing a technological innovation systems framework more systematically with a sustainable collaboration lens responds to filling these gaps and provides an explanation for this phenomena in a way which has yet to be theoretically and practically articulated.

Our research demonstrates that both knowledge and market-niche creation are important attributes to stimulate an interfirm customer–supplier sustainable transition. But it also shows that each of the seven features of the combined technological innovation system and sustainable collaboration framework are needed to develop a successful collaborative environment and a systematic sustainable pathway.

Each of the factors Binz, Truffer and Coenen (2015) identified helps to explain the variables of path creation, beyond firm-based organisational routines and traditional production mindsets. These attributes include the disentangling of actor networks and institutional contexts of knowledge creation, market-niche formation, legitimation, mobilisation of financial and resource investment, vision and direction setting, articulation of demand, and the transformative nature of policy coordination initiatives.

The conceptual framework developed here contributes towards a more nuanced response regarding whether sustainability-based interfirm customer–supplier alliances stimulate a transition of the traditional manufacturer. It also demonstrates that new and adapting industries depend on the co-evolution of both proximate and socio-technical embedded innovation processes as well as extra-regional alliances within the global innovation system to stimulate change. In terms of wider implications for sustainable transitions, this work contributes to the understudied topic of the role of incumbent firms and regime-level actors in transition processes (Geels, Tyfield and Urry 2014). Whilst much of the literature focuses on the role of institutional factors that inhibit sustainable transitions of incumbent manufacturing firms, this article demonstrates the equally important role that interfirm and collaborative relations have on influencing systematic change. Such findings signal the value of paying attention to the role of collaboration in order to understand the development of future manufacturing sector transitions. Further research could apply the conceptual framework described in this article to a wider range of manufacturing firm contexts or other traditional industries. Ongoing research could also examine confounding case studies that display less collaborative environments, in pursuit of systematic transitions, in the manufacturing sector. In addition, the transformative failure perspective on innovation systems in this chapter considers the impact of denying a true understanding of the demand articulation and policy coordination attributes of the end-user market; it only goes so far in identifying the end-user consumer–producer relationship. A perspective missing from transitions research is not only that of the original equipment manufacturer customer in a consumer–producer type combination, but also in extending that of the end-user consumer–producer analysis.

Notes

1 International accreditation standard enabling a life-cycle and environmental impact assessment of the product to be completed. An Environmental Product Declaration is created and verified in accordance with the international standard ISO 14025 developed by the International Organisation of Standards.

2 The Green Building Council of Australia was established in 2002 to introduce and drive the adoption of sustainable practices in the Australian property industry. Membership of the organisation represents 600-plus individual companies with a collective annual turnover of more than $40 billion.

3 Systematic method for the elimination of waste within a manufacturing system (Krafcik 1988).

4 From the term 'bios', meaning life, and 'mimesis', meaning to imitate – a discipline that studies nature's best ideas and then imitates these designs and processes to solve human problems; studying a leaf to invent a better solar cell is an example (Benyus 1997).

5 An Australian government program designed to provide new and refurbished infrastructure to eligible Australian schools. The program was part of the Rudd Labor government's economic stimulus package in response to the 2007–2010 global financial crisis.

6 Technology that separates old carpet tiles into face cloth and backing, and sends the face materials to other companies for recycling. The proprietary technology can turn the old backing into new backing and convert the separated backing into pellets.

References

Ai Group 2016, *Joining Forces: Innovation Success Through Partnerships*, viewed 28 November 2016, http://cdn.aigroup.com.au/Reports/2016/JoiningForces_Innovation_success_through_partnerships_Sept_2016.pdf

Altay, N., Gunasekaran, A., Dubey, R. and Childe, S. J. 2018, Agility and resilience as antecedents of supply chain performance under moderating effects of organizational culture within the humanitarian setting: a dynamic capability view, *Production Planning & Control*, vol. 29, no. 14, pp. 1158–1174.

Aschemann-Witzel, J. 2016, Waste not, want not, emit less, *Science*, vol. 352, no. 6284, pp. 408–409.

Asheim, B. and Gertler, M.S. 2005, The geography of innovation: Regional innovation systems. In Manfred M. Fischer and Peter Nijkamp (eds.), *The Oxford Handbook Of Innovation*, Oxford University Press, Oxford.

Australian Government 2011, *Trends in Manufacturing to 2020*, A foresighting paper, Future Manufacturing Industry Innovation Council, Canberra, viewed 8 September 2015, <http://webcache.googleusercontent.com/search?q=cache:QuL12zZXcVAJ:db.foresight.kr/sub03/research/filedown/id/215/field/file_saved_name/rfile/73165ade29bf75e460accbf7cf4d07cb+&cd=3&hl=en&ct=clnk&gl=au>.

Bakshi, N., and Kleindorfer, P. 2009, Co-opetition and investment for supply-chain resilience, *Production and Operations Management*, vol. 18, no. 6, pp. 583–603.

Benyus, J.M. 1997, *Biomimicry*, William Morrow, New York.

Bergek, A., Jacobsson, S., Carlsson, B., Lindmark, S. and Rickne, A. 2008, Analyzing the functional dynamics of technological innovation systems: A scheme of analysis, *Research Policy*, vol. 37, no. 3, pp. 407–429.

Binz, C., Truffer, B. and Coenen, L. 2015, Path creation as a process of resource alignment and anchoring: Industry formation for on-site water recycling in Beijing, *Economic Geography*, vol. 92, pp. 1–29.

Boschma, R., Coenen, L., Frenken, K. and Truffer, B. 2016, Towards a theory of regional diversification: combining insights from evolutionary economic geography and transition studies, *Regional Studies*, vol. 51, no. 1, pp. 31–45.

Brandon-Jones, E., Squire, B., Autry, C.W. and Petersen, K.J. 2014, A contingent resource-based perspective of supply chain resilience and robustness, *Journal of Supply Chain Management*, vol. 50, no. 3, pp. 55–73. https://doi.org/10.1111/jscm.12050

Carlsson, B. and Stankiewicz, R. 1991, On the nature, function and composition of technological systems, *Journal of Evolutionary Economics*, vol. 1, no. 2, pp. 93–118.

Cooke 2013, Transition regions: Green innovation and economic development. In J.J.M. Ferreira, M. Raposo, R. Rutten and A. Varga (eds.), *Cooperation, Clusters, and Knowledge Transfer*, Springer, Berlin Heidelberg, pp. 105–25, DOI: 10.1007/978-3-642-33194-7_6, http://dx.doi.org/10.1007/978-3-642-33194-7_6.

Cooke, Gomez and Etxebarria 1997, Regional innovation systems: Institutional and organisational dimensions, *Research Policy*, vol. 26, no. 4–5, pp. 475–491.

Cooke and Morgan, K. 1998, *The Associational Economy: Firms, Regions and Innovation*, Oxford University Press, Oxford.

Crevoisier, O. and Jeannerat, H. 2009, Territorial knowledge dynamics: From the proximity paradigm to multi-location milieus, *European Planning Studies*, vol. 17, no. 8, pp. 1223–1241.

Fischer, A. and Pascucci, S. 2016, Institutional incentives in circular economy transition: The case of material use in the Dutch textile industry, *Journal of Cleaner Production*, vol. 155, no. 2, pp. 17–32.

Fitjar, R.D. and Rodríguez-Pose, A. 2013, Firm collaboration and modes of innovation in Norway, *Research Policy*, vol. 42, no. 1, pp. 128–138.

Foucault, M. 1972, *The Archaeology of Knowledge*, trans, A.M.S. Smith, Pantheon, New York, vol. 24.

Freeman, C. 1991, Innovation, changes of techno-economic paradigm and biological analogies in economics, *Revue économique*, pp. 211–231.

Geels 2011, The multi-level perspective on sustainability transitions: Responses to seven criticisms, *Environmental Innovation and Societal Transitions*, vol. 1, no. 1, pp. 24–40.

Geels, Tyfield, D. and Urry, J. 2014, Regime resistance against low-carbon transitions: Introducing politics and power into the multi-level perspective, *Theory, Culture & Society*, vol. 31, no. 5, pp. 21–40.

Gertler, M.S. 1995, "Being There": Proximity, organization, and culture in the development and adoption of advanced manufacturing technologies, *Economic Geography*, vol. 71, pp. 1–26.

Gibbs and O'Neill 2014, The green economy, sustainability transitions and transition regions: a case study of Boston, *Geografiska Annaler: Series B, Human Geography*, vol. 96, no. 3, pp. 201–16.

Goennemann, J. 2015, Collaboration for innovation, *Australian Manufacturing Week*, Sydney, NSW.

Halldórsson, Á. and Kovács, G. 2010, The sustainable agenda and energy efficiency: Logistics solutions and supply chains in times of climate change, *International Journal of Physical Distribution & Logistics Management*, vol. 40, no. 1/2, pp. 5–13.

Hart, S.L. and Milstein, M.B. 2003, Creating sustainable value, *The Academy of Management Executive*, vol. 17, no. 2, pp. 56–67.

Hockerts, K. and Wüstenhagen, R. 2010, Greening Goliaths versus emerging Davids—Theorizing about the role of incumbents and new entrants in sustainable entrepreneurship, *Journal of Business Venturing*, vol. 25, no. 5, pp. 481–492.

Husted, B.W. and de Sousa-Filho, J.M. 2016, The impact of sustainability governance, country stakeholder orientation, and country risk on environmental, social, and governance performance, *Journal of Cleaner Production*, vol. 155, pp. 93–102.

Jacobsson, S. and Bergek, A. 2011, Innovation system analyses and sustainability transitions: Contributions and suggestions for research, *Environmental Innovation and Societal Transitions*, vol. 1, no. 1, pp. 41–57.

Jensen, M.B., Johnson, B., Lorenz, E. and Lundvall, B.Å. 2007, Forms of knowledge and modes of innovation, *Research Policy*, vol. 36, no. 5, pp. 680–693.

Jovane and Westkämper 2009, Towards Competitive Sustainable Manufacturing. In *The ManuFuture Road: Towards Competitive and Sustainable High-Adding-Value Manufacturing*, Springer-Verlag, Berlin Heidelberg, p. 22.

Juettner, U. and Maklan, S. 2011, Supply chain resilience in the global financial crisis: an empirical study, *Supply Chain Management*, vol. 16, pp. 246–259.

Kiron, D., Kruschwitz, N., Haanaes, K., Reeves, M., Fuisz-Kehrbach, S.-K. and Kell, G. 2015, Joining forces: Collaboration and leadership for sustainability, *MIT Sloan Management Review*, vol. 56, no. 3, pp. 1–32.

Kishna, M., Niesten, E., Negro, S. and Hekkert, M.P. 2016, The role of alliances in creating legitimacy of sustainable technologies: A study on the field of bio-plastics, *Journal of Cleaner Production*, vol. 155, pp. 7–16.

Kochan, A. 1996, Lotus: Aluminium extrusions and adhesives, *Assembly Automation*, vol. 16, no. 4, pp. 19–21.

Krafcik, J.F. 1988, Triumph of the lean production system, *MIT Sloan Management Review*, vol. 30, no. 1, p. 41.

Liu, W., Xie, D., Liu, Y. and Liu, X.Y. 2015, Service capability procurement decision in logistics service supply chain: A research under demand updating and quality guarantee, *International Journal of Production Research*, vol. 53, pp. 488–510.

Loorbach, D. and Rotmans, J. 2006, Managing transitions for sustainable development. In Olsthoorn, X., and Wieczorek, A. (eds) *Understanding Industrial Transformation. Environment & Policy*, vol. 44, pp. 187–206, Springer, Dordrecht.

Loorbach, D. 2010, Transition management for sustainable development: a prescriptive, complexity-based governance framework, *Governance*, vol. 23, no. 1, pp. 161–183.

Malerba, F. 2002, Sectoral systems of innovation and production, *Research Policy*, vol. 31, no. 2, pp. 247–264.

Niesten, E., Jolink, A., de Sousa Jabbour, A.B.L., Chappin, M. and Lozano, R. 2016, Sustainable collaboration: The impact of governance and institutions on sustainable performance, *Journal of Cleaner Production*, vol. 155, pp. 1–6.

Norton, T., Ryan, M., & Wang, F. 2015, *Business Action for Climate-Resilient Supply Chains: A Practical Framework for identifying priorities to Evaluating Impact*. BSR Working Paper. BSR, San Francisco

Qian, Y. 2014, New industrial revolution and environmental protection, *Frontiers of Engineering Management*, vol. 1, pp. 71–76.

Ramanathan, R., He, Q., Black, A., Ghobadian, A. and Gallear, D. 2016, Environmental regulations, innovation and firm performance: a revisit of the Porter hypothesis, *Journal of Cleaner Production*, vol. 155 (2017), pp. 79–92.

Roos, G. 2014, Manufacturing in a high cost environment: Basis for future success on the national level. In *Global Perspectives on Achieving Success in High and Low Cost Operating Environments*, IGI Global, Hershey, PA, USA, pp. 1–51, DOI 10.4018/978-1-4666-5828-8.ch001, http://services.igi-global.com/resolvedoi/resolve.aspx?doi=10.4018/978-1-4666-5828-8.ch001.

Sheffi, Y. 2005, Building a resilient supply chain, *Harvard Business Review*, vol. 1, no. 8, pp. 1–4.

Skellern, K., Markey, R. and Thornthwaite, L. 2017, Identifying attributes of sustainable transitions for traditional regional manufacturing industry sectors—A conceptual framework, *Journal of Cleaner Production*, vol. 140, pp. 1782–1793.

Teece, D.J. 2010, Business models, business strategy and innovation, *Long Range Planning*, vol. 43, no. 2, pp. 172–194.

Tether, B.S. 2002, Who co-operates for innovation, and why: an empirical analysis, *Research Policy*, vol. 31, no. 6, pp. 947–967.

Tödtling, F. and Trippl, M. 2005, One size fits all?: Towards a differentiated regional innovation policy approach, *Research Policy*, vol. 34, no. 8, pp. 1203–1219.

Truffer, B. and Coenen, L. 2012, Environmental innovation and sustainability transitions in regional studies, *Regional Studies*, vol. 46, no. 1, pp. 1–21.

United Nations Environment Program 2014, Green Economy, viewed 2 September 2014, http://www .unep.org/greeneconomy/AboutGEI/WhatisGEI/tabid/29784/Default.aspx

Van Winden, W., Van den Berg, L., Carvalho, L. and Van Tuijl, E. 2010, *Manufacturing in the New Urban Economy*, Routledge, London.

Von Stamm, B. 2004, Collaboration with other firms and customers: innovation's secret weapon, *Strategy & Leadership*, vol. 32, no. 3, pp. 16–20.

Wagner, S.M. 2010, Supplier traits for better customer firm innovation performance, *Industrial Marketing Management*, vol. 39, no. 7, pp. 1139–1149.

Wassmer, U., Paquin, R. and Sharma, S. 2014, The engagement of firms in environmental collaborations: existing contributions and future directions, *Business & Society*, vol. 53, no. 6, pp. 754–786. doi:10.1177/0007650312439865.

Weber, K.M. and Rohracher, H. 2012, Legitimizing research, technology and innovation policies for transformative change: Combining insights from innovation systems and multi-level perspective in a comprehensive 'failures' framework, *Research Policy*, vol. 41, no. 6, pp. 1037–1047.

Wilcox 2014, *Advanced Australian Manufacturing*, paper presented to Advanced Manufacturing Summit 2014, Sydney, 11 November 2014, http://www.aigroup.com.au/portal/binary/com.epicentric.contentman agement.servlet.ContentDeliveryServlet/LIVE_CONTENT/Publications/Speeches/2014/Advanc ing_Australian_Manufacturing.pdf

Zeng, H., Chen, X., Xiao, X. and Zhou, Z. 2016, Institutional pressures, sustainable supply chain management, and circular economy capability: Empirical evidence from Chinese eco-industrial park firms, *Journal of Cleaner Production*, vol. 155, pp. 54–65.

Zhu, Q., Feng, Y. and Choi, S.-B. 2016, The role of customer relational governance in environmental and economic performance improvement through green supply chain management, *Journal of Cleaner Production*, vol. 155, pp. 46–53.

5

CLIMATE-RESILIENT SUPPLY CHAINS

A mixed-methods approach

Rameshwar Dubey, Cyril Foropon and V. G. Venkatesh

5.1 Introduction

In recent years, climate change has attracted significant attention from practitioners and academia (Kolk and Pinkse 2004; Park et al. 2015). Most of the scholars have noted in their study that "climate change threatens irreversible and dangerous impacts," which may have a significant influence on global supply chains (Norton et al. 2015). It has been argued that irresponsible human activities have caused severe damage to the planet (IPCC 2014; Jacobs et al. 2014), and to address the pressing global threat, there is a unanimous call for an immediate reduction in carbon emission levels (Park et al. 2015; Norton et al. 2015). Norton et al. (2015) have noted that for large business enterprises, the supply chain is one of the most opportune areas to develop climate resilience, both through reducing carbon emissions and building adaptive capacity. In a carbon disclosure report (CDP 2011), it was noted that over 50% of the carbon emissions in any corporation is due to its supply chain, and in some industries, the level of carbon emission is estimated to be even higher. For example, in food, beverage, and agriculture companies, up to 90% of their total emissions can be found in the supply chain. Cuevas (2011) has noted that climate change vulnerability has a major influence on the risk.

Norton et al. (2015) have noted that most of the companies that have participated in their research have acquiesced that climate change is a major influential factor in their supply chains. In response, organizations have outlined major changes in quality and availability of specific raw materials (Hart 1997), a degradation in biodiversity, and an impact on the human work-force in their global supply chains (Halldórsson and Kovács 2010). In recent years, supply chain risk management has been the subject of much debate (Wagner and Bode 2008; Bakshi and Kleindorfer 2009; Altay and Ramirez 2010; Wu et al. 2013; Brandon-Jones et al. 2014; Mogre et al. 2016). However, the literature focusing on sustainability and resilience is still in the nascent stage (Derissen et al. 2011; Fiksel 2006). As a result, many organizations are working within to build resilience to climate change and make themselves more adaptable (Ivanov, 2018). We define climate resilient supply chains as the capacity of businesses and their supply chains to minimize their contribution to climate change, and to cope with and adapt to climate-related hazardous events, trends, or disturbances, including disrupted supply chains, reduced availability

DOI: 10.4324/9781315225661-7

of natural resources, infrastructure impacts, disrupted transport and logistical routes, and other unpredictable impacts (Norton et al. 2015).

Despite the growing literature focusing on climate-resilient supply chains or sustainability embedded in the disaster relief chain (Papadopoulos et al. 2017; Fahimnia and Jabbarzadeh 2016; Ivanov, 2018), there are few studies that utilize a theory-focused approach to understanding the role of key factors in building a climate-resilient supply chain.

Drawing on resource-based view (RBV) (Barney 1991) and relationship theory (Kwon and Suh 2004) literature, we developed a theoretical model to help our understanding of how and when an organization can create a climate-resilient supply chain. The RBV argues that an organization can achieve a competitive advantage through a combination of strategic resources that create distinct, organizational capabilities. The commitment–trust theory argues that commitment and trust among members in the supply chain network can build coordination. A CDP report (2011) notes how PepsiCo built trust and commitment among its suppliers to reduce carbon emissions in their supply chains.

Wieland and Wallenburg (2013) observed that communicative and cooperative relationships have a positive effect on supply chain resilience. Following Brandon-Jones et al. (2014), we have considered supply chain visibility as an important antecedent of supply chain resilience. The visibility helps organizations to proactively track products and identify potential disruptions. Brandon-Jones et al. (2014) noted that in the absence of visibility, organizations are more prone to risks.

By empirically validating a theoretically derived climate-resilient supply chain model, this study offers three major contributions to the literature focusing on the climate-resilient supply chain. First, as a novel contribution, we study to what extent relationship factors, such as trust and commitment, mediate between resources of the firm and supply chain visibility. Second, by recognizing the role of supply chain visibility as one of the antecedents of a climate-resilient supply chain, we make a noteworthy contribution to existing literature. Our findings of the study enrich the theory on climate-resilient supply chains by confirming that resources of the organization and relationship management among the partners in the supply chain network help create supply chain visibility. This, in turn, positively influences building a climate-resilient supply chain. Finally, our study extends the research of Brandon-Jones et al. (2014) by using arguments derived from Oliver (1997). The RBV has not looked beyond the properties of resources and resource markets to explain enduring firm heterogeneity. The RBV has failed to address the social context within which an organization, or organizations, operates toward a common goal. How relationships among the partners in the supply chain help mitigate the risk resulting from climate change may offer better insights into the existing debate surrounding climate-resilient supply chains. The relevance of studying climate-resilient supply chains using an integrated approach becomes clearer as we describe the difficulties in building coordination among the players in the supply chain.

The rest of the chapter is structured as follows. The next section deals with a review of RBV and relationship theory from a theoretical perspective. We then present literature on supply chain visibility and resilience before embarking on hypothesis development. Next, we describe our research design, which consisted of questionnaire development, pretesting of the questionnaire, sampling design, data collection approach, and non-response bias testing of the cross-sectional data collected using the questionnaire. This section is followed by data analyses and research findings. We then discuss our research findings in the context of theoretical contributions, managerial implications, limitations, and further research directions. Finally, concluding remarks from this study are offered.

5.2 Underpinning theory

5.2.1 Resource-based view (RBV)

The RBV of an organization helps to understand how organizational resources – tangible and intangible – can be utilized to gain competitive advantage (Barney 1991; Barney et al. 2011; Hoopes et al. 2003; Brandon-Jones et al. 2014). Scholars have noted that supply chain management has the potential to generate a competitive advantage (Barney 2012; Priem and Swink 2012) as long as the resources or capabilities have properties that put them into four categories: valuable, rare, inimitable, and non-substitutable (Barney 1991). The selection of the resources is guided by an economic rationality and motives of efficiency, effectiveness, and profitability (Conner 1991). Recently, the literature has been extensively differentiating between resources and capabilities. Barney (1991) has categorized resources as physical capital, human capital, and organizational capital. Grant (1991) further extends this to include financial capital, technological capital, and reputational capital. Simon et al. (2008) add that the bundling of strategic resources is necessary to build the organization through exploiting opportunities or mitigating threats. Organizational capabilities are referred to as a higher-order construct, which relies on the bundling of resources (Wu 2010; Brandon-Jones et al. 2014). The resources and capabilities of the firm are regarded as the predictors of the organization's success (Ravichandran and Lertwongsatien 2005). Brandon-Jones et al. (2014) have further argued that resources and capabilities have a positive impact on supply chain resilience and supply chain robustness. Following these arguments, we also form the RBV as one of the basis of our theoretical model to predict the climate-resilient supply chain.

5.2.2 Relationship theory

Morgan and Hunt (1994) argue that cooperative aspects of economic behavior are often neglected. This statement still holds true in present contexts noted by behavioral operations management scholars (Bendoly et al. 2006; Gans and Croson 2008; Gino and Pisano 2008; Tokar 2010). In one of Tatham and Kovács's studies (2010), they noted the importance of building swift trust to improve coordination among humanitarian actors coming from diverse cultures, speaking different languages, and coming from different nations that may be meeting for the first time for a common goal. Morgan and Hunt (1994) contended that trust and commitment are important antecedents for building coordination. Kwon and Suh (2004) further argued that the degree of information sharing among supply chain partners reduces behavioral uncertainty among partners, which further enhances trust among supply chain partners. The trust further leads to commitment to each other, which is critical for building coordination among supply chain partners. Moreover, the interplay between technology and trust can further enhance collaboration (Welt and Becerra-Fernandez 2001). Wieland and Wallenburg (2013) discuss relationship theory, arguing that communicative and cooperative relationships have a positive effect on supply chain resilience. Sheffi (2005) asserts that relationships with partners provide the organization the flexibility to negotiate any degree of uncertainties and exploit the uncertainties to achieve a competitive advantage. Relationship theory argues that reduction in behavioral uncertainty can help to enhance trust and commitment in relationships. Thus we have formed relationship theory as one of the basis, along with RBV, to develop our theoretical model.

5.2.3 Supply chain visibility

There was a significant rise in supply chain visibility literature following the Barratt and Oke (2007) seminal study. Williams et al. (2013) suggested that supply chain visibility can be used to improve supply chain responsiveness. Supply chain visibility, from the RBV perspective, can be visualized as one of the desired capabilities of a supply chain (see Barratt and Oke 2007; Jüttner and Maklan 2011), which may reduce the negative impacts of supply chain disruption (Christopher and Lee 2004). Brandon-Jones et al. (2014) argued on the basis of Cao and Zhang's (2011) contributions that supply chain visibility is largely undefined. There is a lack of consistent understanding among operations and supply chain management (OSCM) scholars (Brandon-Jones et al. 2014). In fact, at times scholars have failed to distinguish between supply chain visibility and information sharing (Francis, 2008; Cao and Zhang 2011). Barratt and Oke (2007) noted that the relationship between information sharing is mediated by visibility, which in turn further enhances operational performance. Further, supply chain visibility helps improve resilience and robustness in a supply chain (Brandon-Jones et al. 2014). On the basis of the research findings of Brandon-Jones et al. (2014), we assume that supply chain visibility may reduce negative impacts of rapid change in climate due to carbon emissions in a supply chain. Therefore, we assume supply chain visibility to be a mediating construct between information sharing, data connectivity, and reduction in behavioral uncertainty, which further enhances trust and commitment among supply chain partners to improve coordination to achieve a climate-resilient supply chain.

5.2.4 Supply chain resilience

Sheffi (2005) argues that the number and types of threats, which are now greater than ever, from various sources can undermine a supply chain's potential. Thus the notion of resilience in supply chains has gained significant importance in recent years (Bakshi and Kleindorfer 2009; Liu et al. 2016). Resilience in supply chains can be viewed as a source of competitive advantage (Sheffi 2005; Jüttner and Maklan 2011; Brandon-Jones et al. 2014; Altay et al. 2018). Supply chain resilience has attracted a significant amount of attention from researchers (Ponomarov and Holcomb 2009; Pettit et al. 2010; Jüttner and Maklan 2011; Ivanov et al. 2014; Gunasekaran et al. 2015; Munoz and Dunbar 2015; Kamalahmadi and Mellat-Parast 2016; Kamalahmadi and Mellat-Parast 2016a; Purvis et al. 2016; Papadopoulos et al. 2017; Ivanov and Dolgui, 2019; Dubey et al. 2021) guided by the common objective of how to build a resilient supply chain. We use the Norton et al. (2015) definition as the basis of our study.

5.3 Theoretical framework and hypothesis development

The foundation of our theoretical framework comprises two elements: RBV and relationship theory (see Figure 5.1). During the last two decades, RBV (Barney 1991) has emerged as a powerful explanation to account for the competitive advantage of a firm. However, following some antagonist RBV criticisms, we also integrated the relationship theory construct to improve the explanation of RBV. Relationship theory, in recent years, has attracted significant attention from operations and supply chain management researchers to explain complexities in supply chains. Following Kwon and Suh's (2004) arguments, we have introduced three constructs, namely, reduction in behavioral uncertainty, trust, and commitment. Morgan and Hunt (1994) argued in one of their seminal works that the commitment–trust theory can be a useful theory to explain coordination among partners. We have grounded our framework in these two theories to predict climate resilience.

5.3.1 Supply chain connectivity and information sharing

According to RBV arguments we can assume that the bundling of supply chain connectivity and information sharing can improve supply chain visibility (Brandon-Jones et al. 2014). Supply chain connectivity can be regarded as a tangible resource following Barratt and Oke's (2007)

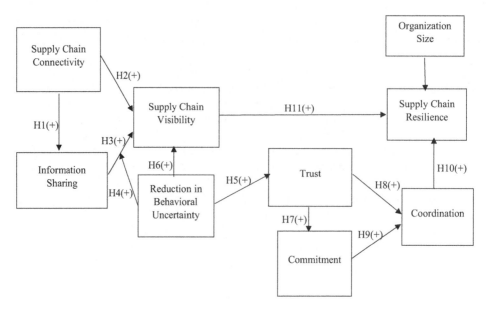

Figure 5.1 Theoretical framework. (Adapted from Dubey et al. 2019a.)

arguments. Connectivity is an example of a technological resource that facilitates the effective sharing of information (Fawcett et al. 2009). On the other hand, information sharing may be categorized as organizational capital, a resource that focuses on the flow of information (Premkumar and King 1994). Following the argument of Brandon-Jones et al. (2014), we can hypothesize:

H1: Supply chain connectivity has a positive impact on information sharing.

5.3.2 The impacts of supply chain connectivity and information sharing on supply chain visibility

Fahimnia and Jabbarzadeh (2016) argued that the bundling of resources and capabilities may lead to a competitive advantage. Größler and Grübner (2006) further suggested that resources may be either tangible or intangible. Zhu and Kraemer (2002) argued that connectivity might be referred to as organizational IT infrastructure, which is regarded as one of the most important business resources. Singh and Garg (2015) noted that information sharing within the supply chain significantly reduces inventory levels and the bullwhip effect. Wu (2006) argued that connectivity is an important resource that is exploited to build capabilities in the supply chain. Following Fawcett et al.'s (2011) arguments, we can argue that supply chain connectivity may enhance supply chain visibility. However, the utility of the supply chain connectivity is dependent on the quality of the information sharing. Brandon-Jones et al. (2014) found that supply chain connectivity and information sharing both have positive impacts on supply chain visibility, which may be regarded as an extension to Barratt and Oke's (2007) findings. Therefore, based on these arguments of scholars, we also hypothesize:

H2: Supply chain connectivity has a positive impact on supply chain visibility.

H3: Information sharing has a positive impact on supply chain visibility.

5.3.3 Reduction in behavioral uncertainty, information sharing, and supply chain visibility

Park and Ungson (2001) have noted that the degree of behavioral uncertainty among partners is a major source of tension in strategic alliances. Krishnan et al. (2006) argued that behavioral uncertainty leads to situations in which it becomes difficult for an organization to anticipate and predict the actions of their partners. Chen et al. (2011) have further argued that behavioral uncertainty has negative consequences on organizational performance, and it negatively impacts the information-sharing mechanism. Conversely, we can argue that reduction in behavioral uncertainty can improve the impact of information sharing on supply chain visibility. Chen et al. (2011) found a moderating effect in the reduction of behavioral uncertainty on the impact of information sharing on supply chain visibility. They also found a positive influence on trust with information sharing. However, literature focusing on the reduction of behavioral uncertainty and its impact on supply chain visibility is still underdeveloped. We extended the work of Chen et al. (2011) by arguing that if a reduction in behavioral uncertainty has a moderating effect on the impact of information sharing on supply chain visibility, then we assume that reduction in behavioral uncertainty may have a positive impact on supply chain visibility. We have hypothesized our arguments on the basis of supporting literature and the transitive property logic. Therefore, we have drawn three research hypotheses:

H4: Reduction in behavioral uncertainty has a moderating effect on information sharing.

H5: Reduction in behavioral uncertainty has a positive impact on trust.

H6: Reduction in behavioral uncertainty has a positive impact on supply chain visibility.

5.3.4 Trust, commitment, and coordination

Several studies have found a positive relationship between trust and commitment (Morgan and Hunt 1994; Kwon and Suh 2004; Trust and Kovacs, 2010; Chen et al. 2011). Morgan and Hunt (1994) asserted that trust is an important antecedent for building commitment among partners, which was further extended to supply chain partnering by Kwon and Suh (2004). Morgan and Hunt (1994) also found positive impacts of trust and commitment on coordination among the partners. On the basis of supporting literature, we can hypothesize:

H7: Trust has a positive impact on commitment.

H8: Trust has a positive impact on coordination.

H9: Commitment has a positive impact on coordination.

5.3.5 Coordination and supply chain resilience

Wieland and Wallenburg (2013) argued that coordination among the partners in a supply chain has a positive impact on supply chain agility and robustness, which together constitute supply chain resilience. Therefore, on the basis of this work, we hypothesize:

H10: Coordination has a positive impact on supply chain resilience.

5.3.6 Supply chain visibility and supply chain resilience

The relationship between supply chain visibility and supply chain resilience is still an underdeveloped area. However, the findings of Brandon-Jones et al. (2014) support a positive relationship between supply chain visibility and supply chain resilience. Christopher and Lee (2004) argue that supply chain visibility capability may reduce the probability and impacts of a supply chain disruption, which may lead to enhanced resilience (Jüttner and Maklan 2011). Kleindorfer and Saad (2005) have noted that supply chain visibility may be one of the desired requirements to mitigate supply chain risk. Tang (2006) has further argued that supply chain visibility would enable supply chain partners to generate a common demand forecast that, if combined with the proportional restoration rule, could further help to manage deviation in the observed inventory levels. We therefore hypothesize:

H11: Supply chain visibility has a positive impact on supply chain resilience.

5.3.7 Statistical controls

We included organization size as a statistical control that appeared to have a confounding effect on other variables used in the study. Here we have included two measures following Ryu et al. (2015): number of employees and sales revenue of the organization. Organizational size is an important control variable, because it has enough slack resources to withstand any degree of supply chain disruption arising from climate change. Appendix A provides the definitions of constructs examined in this study.

5.4 Methods

5.4.1 Measures

To test our hypothesized framework (see Figure 5.1), we have derived testable research hypotheses (H1–H11). Since the framework consists of latent constructs, we used a survey-based approach. A survey was developed by identifying appropriate measures following a comprehensive literature review. The scales were adopted from existing literature and we further modified the scales to make it suitable for our context. We selected manufacturing organizations as our target organizations for research because prior research (see Bozarth et al. 2009; Brandon-Jones et al. 2014) argues that manufacturing organizations provide a detailed understanding of how supply chain design affects performance. Before we finalized our questionnaire, we pretested it with three academicians who have published extensively and have strong research credentials in a similar area and with five senior managers. A few changes were made based on the input of these experts to ensure high reliability and validity. All of the exogenous constructs in Figure 5.1 were operationalized (see Table 5.1) as reflective constructs. The dependent construct, supply chain resilience, is a formative construct.

5.4.2 Data collection

The target sample was composed of managers included in the Indian Institute of Materials Management database. We selected 780 potential respondents by their job function (supply chain manager, materials management manager, logistics management manager, or purchasing manager) (see Table 5.2) and industry codes reflecting manufacturing organizations (16 "manu-

Table 5.1 Operationalization of constructs

Construct	Measures	Reference
Supply chain connectivity	SC1: Current information systems meet the supply chain communications requirements. SC2: Information applications are highly integrated within firm and supply chain. SC3: Adequate information linkages exist with supply chain partners.	Brandon-Jones et al. 2014; Fawcett et al. 2011
Information sharing	IS1: Our firm exchanges relevant information with partners. IS2: Our firm exchanges timely information with partners. IS3: Our firm exchanges accurate information with partners. IS4: Our firm exchanges complete information with partners. IS5: Our firm exchanges confidential information with partners.	Brandon-Jones et al. 2014; Cao and Zhang 2011
Supply chain visibility	SCV1: Inventory levels are visible throughout the supply chain. SCV2: Demand levels are visible throughout the supply chain.	Braunscheidel and Suresh 2009
Reduction in behavioral uncertainty	BU1: We can accurately predict the performance of our partners for our next business cycle. BU2: We know that our partners will adapt quickly, should we change our specifications at short notice. BU3: We can predict changes in the pricing of our partner's products/services for the next year. BU4: We can predict the introduction of our partner's new product/services.	Chen et al. 2011; Kwon and Suh 2004
Trust	T1: Even when our partners give us rather unlikely explanation, we are confident that they are telling the truth. T2: Our partners have often provided us with information that has later proved to be accurate. T3: Our partners usually keep the promises that they make to the firm. T4: Whenever our partners give us advice on our business operation we know that they are sharing their best judgement. T5: Our organizations can count on our partners to be sincere. T6: Though circumstances change, we believe that our partners will be ready and willing to offer assistance and support. T7: When making important decisions, our partners are concerned about our welfare. T8: When we share our problems with our partners, we know that they will respond with understanding. T9: In future, we can count on our partners to consider how their decisions and action will affect us. T10: When it comes to things that are important to us, we can depend on our partner's support.	Chen et al. 2011

(Continued)

Table 5.1 (Continued)

Construct	Measures	Reference
Commitment	C1: Even if we could, we would not drop our partners because we like being associated with them. C2: We want to remain a member of our partner's network because we genuinely enjoy our relationship with them. C3: Our positive feelings towards our partners are a major reason we continue working with them. C4: We expect our relationships with our partners to continue for a long time. C5: The renewal of our relationships with our partners is virtually automatic.	Chen et al. 2011
Coordination	CO1: No matter who is at fault, problems are joint responsibilities. CO2: One party will not take unfair advantage of a strong bargaining position. CO3: We are willing to make cooperative changes. CO4: We do not mind owing each other favors.	Wieland and Wallenburg 2013
Supply chain resilience	SCR1: Material flow would be quickly restored. SCR2: It would not take a long time to recover normal operating performance. SCR3: The supply chain would easily recover to its original state. SCR4: Disruptions would be dealt with quickly.	Brandon-Jones et al. 2014
Organization size	OS1: Number of employees. OS2: Revenue.	Ryu et al. 2015

facturer of wood and products of wood and cork, except furniture"; 17 "manufacturer of paper and paper products"; 19 "manufacturer of coke and refined petroleum products"; 20 "manufacturer of chemicals and chemical products"; 22 "manufacturer of rubber and plastic products"; and 25 "manufacturer of fabricated metal products, except machinery and equipment"). After selecting potential respondents, we e-mailed the questionnaires. Each questionnaire included a cover letter in which the purpose of the study was explained to the target respondents, following Dillman's total-test design method (see Dillman 2011), offering comprehensive guidelines for an electronic mode survey. After five weeks we had received 120 usable responses. We sent further reminders via e-mail and followed up by phone. After four weeks we had received an additional 130 usable responses. We received a total of 250 usable responses, which represents 32.05% (250/780 = 32.05%). Compared with prior studies adopting a survey based study (see Braunscheidel and Suresh 2009; Eckstein et al. 2015), our sample size is sufficient for a hypotheses test.

Before we proceeded with data analyses, it was recommended to undertake a non-response bias test on data gathered using the survey-based instrument. Following Armstrong and Overton's 1977 non-response bias test, we compared the responses of the early and late waves of our returned survey, based on the assumption that the opinions of the late respondents are representative of the opinions of the non-respondents (see Armstrong and Overton 1977). The t-tests yielded no statistically significant differences (p = 0.76) between early-wave (120 responses) and late-wave (130 responses) responses. This suggested that non-response bias was

Table 5.2 Sample profile (N = 250)

Industry code (NIC)	Count	Percent
16 (Wood and products of wood)	12	4.8
17 (Manufacture of paper and paper products)	18	7.2
19 (Manufacture of coke and refined petroleum products)	22	8.8
20 (Manufacture of chemicals and chemical products)	53	21.2
22 (Manufacture of rubber and rubber products)	78	31.2
25 (Manufacture of fabricated metal products, except machinery and equipment)	67	26.8
Number of employees		
Less than 100	35	14
101–500	63	25.2
501–1000	72	28.8
1000 or more	80	32
Annual sales ($)		
150 million and above	67	26.8
More than 100 million and less than 150 million	130	52
Less than 100 million	53	21.2
Position of the respondents		
Directors	30	12
Vice presidents	75	30
General managers	145	58

Source: Dubey et al. 2019a.

not a problem. The final sample consisted of 30 directors (12%), 75 vice presidents (30%) and 145 general managers (58%). The respondents primarily worked for medium to large firms, with 32% of the respondents working for large firms with more than 1000 employees and a gross income of more than US$150 million. The respondents were evenly distributed among the six NIC codes selected.

5.5 Data analyses and results

It has been suggested by prior research to examine assumptions of constant variance, the existence of outliers, and normality before checking the reliability and validity of the constructs (see Dubey and Gunasekaran 2015; Eckstein et al. 2015; Chen and Paulraj 2004). Therefore, we used plots of residuals by predicted values and statistics of skewness and kurtosis. To detect multivariate outliers, we used Mahalanobis distances of predicted variables (Dubey and Gunasekaran 2015; Eckstein et al. 2015). The maximum absolute values of skewness and kurtosis of the measures in the remaining data set were found to be 1.66 and 2.07, respectively (see Appendix B). These values were well within the limits recommended by past research (univariates skewness <2, kurtosis <7) (Curran, West, and Finch 1996). We did not find any plots, nor did the statistics indicate any significant deviances from the assumptions.

5.5.1 Measurement validation

We used a three-stage process (see Chen and Paulraj 2004) to develop measures that satisfied all the requirements for reliability, validity, and unidimensionality. To evaluate reliability, we used the

Table 5.3 Convergent validity

Construct	Indicator	λi	Variance	Error	SCR	AVE
Supply chain connectivity	SC1	0.60	0.36	0.64	0.83	0.63
(α = 0.96)	SC2	0.89	0.79	0.21		
	SC3	0.85	0.72	0.28		
Information sharing	IS1	0.67	0.45	0.55	0.85	0.53
(α = 0.95)	IS2	0.67	0.45	0.55		
	IS3	0.83	0.68	0.32		
	IS4	0.84	0.70	0.30		
	IS5	0.59	0.35	0.65		
Supply chain visibility	SCV1	0.87	0.75	0.25	0.86	0.75
(α = 0.95)	SCV2	0.87	0.75	0.25		
Behavioral uncertainty	BU1	0.64	0.41	0.59	0.89	0.67
(α = 0.95)	BU2	0.91	0.82	0.18		
	BU3	0.83	0.69	0.31		
	BU4	0.86	0.74	0.26		
Trust (α = 0.95)	T1	0.73	0.53	0.47	0.92	0.53
	T2	0.70	0.48	0.52		
	T3	0.59	0.34	0.66		
	T4	0.81	0.66	0.34		
	T5	0.87	0.75	0.25		
	T6	0.79	0.63	0.37		
	T7	0.71	0.51	0.49		
	T8	0.80	0.64	0.36		
	T9	0.55	0.30	0.70		
	T10	0.64	0.41	0.59		
Commitment (α = 0.95)	C1	0.59	0.35	0.65	0.89	0.67
	C2	0.90	0.80	0.20		
	C3	0.89	0.80	0.20		
	C4	0.84	0.71	0.29		
Coordination (α = 0.95)	CO1	0.89	0.80	0.20	0.86	0.61
	CO2	0.80	0.64	0.36		
	CO3	0.64	0.41	0.59		
	CO4	0.76	0.58	0.42		
Supply chain resilience	SCR1	0.80	0.63	0.37	0.86	0.62
(α = 0.95)	SCR2	0.79	0.62	0.38		
	SCR3	0.85	0.73	0.27		
	SCR4	0.70	0.48	0.52		

average correlation among items in a scale (Nunnally 1978). We can see from Table 5.3 that the Cronbach's α (alpha) for each variable are well above the cutoff 0.7 (Hair et al. 2006).

Next, we assessed two types of validity: convergent and discriminant (Fawcett et al. 2014). As shown in Table 5.3, item load on the intended constructs had standardized loadings greater than 0.5, the structural composite reliability (SCR) was greater than 0.7, and the average variance extracted (AVE) was greater than 0.5. Therefore, we can argue that there is sufficient evidence for convergent validity. Fawcett et al. (2014) noted that for discriminant validity, all the items should have higher loadings on their assigned constructs than any other constructs.

Table 5.4 Intercorrelation matrix

	SC	IS	SCV	BU	T	C	CO	SCR
SC	**0.79**							
IS	0.34	**0.73**						
SCV	0.55	0.26	**0.87**					
BU	0.59	0.29	0.50	**0.82**				
T	0.59	0.32	0.48	0.42	**0.73**			
C	0.43	0.16	0.27	0.24	0.38	**0.82**		
CO	0.30	0.08	0.31	0.26	0.29	0.29	**0.78**	
SCR	0.42	0.30	0.29	0.23	0.32	0.32	0.29	**0.79**

Furthermore, the mean shared variance should be below 0.50. Alternatively, the square root of the AVE for each construct should be greater than any correlation estimate (see Table 5.4). Therefore, we can argue that there is sufficient evidence for discriminant validity.

Finally, we assessed the unidimensionality of our theoretical framework constructs via adherence to two conditions (Gerbing and Anderson 1988). First, an item must be significantly associated with the empirical indicators of the construct, and second, it must be associated with one and only one construct (Chen and Paulraj 2004). To check for unidimensionality, we tested the overall fit of our model. Based on the literature (see Bentler 1990; Hu and Bentler 1999; Brandon-Jones et al. 2014; Chen and Paulraj 2004), multiple fit criteria were utilized to assess model fit (see Appendix C). On the basis of Appendix C, we can conclude that constructs exhibit unidimensionality.

5.5.2 Common method bias

Since we have gathered data using a questionnaire designed for a single respondent, there is the potential for common method bias (CMB) (Ketokivi and Schroeder, 2004; Dubey et al. 2019a, b). Podsakoff et al. (2003) argued that in the case of self-reported data, there is a high possibility of common method biases resulting from multiple sources, such as consistency motif, implicit theories, social desirability, leniency biases, and acquiescence biases. We attempted to enforce procedural remedy by asking respondents not to estimate SCR on the basis of their own experience, but rather to obtain this information from minutes of organizational meetings or from documentation (Podsakoff and Organ 1986). Furthermore, we performed statistical analyses to assess the severity of common method bias. We conducted a conservative version of Harman's one-factor test – following the suggestions of Podsakoff and Organ (1986) – on seven variables in our theoretical model. The results showed that the seven factors were present and the most covariance explained by any one factor was 14.61% (see Appendix D), indicating that common method bias was not likely to contaminate our results. Next, following the suggestions of Malhotra et al. (2006) we further conducted a confirmatory factor analysis (CFA) loading all the items on a single factor, and examined the fit indices. The main logic behind this test is that the single factor is the equivalent of a "methods factor" that signifies the presence of bias due to the method of data collection. The fit for the single factor model is very poor ($\chi^2/df = 15{,}012.64$; RMSEA = 0.432; NNFI = 0.093; CFI = 0.234) and the chi-square change ($\Delta\chi^2 = 13{,}209.324$; $\Delta df = 26$; $p < 0.000$) from the hypothesized model is highly significant. Finally, we tested for CMB using the marker variable test (Lindell and Whitney, 2001). In this case we used an unrelated variable to partial out the correlations using the equations suggested by Lindell and Whitney (2001, p. 116). We observed minimal differences between adjusted and unadjusted correlations. Moreover, the significance of the correlations did not change. Hence, we can argue based on multiple analyses that CMB is not a major issue in our study. However, we also acknowledge that CMB cannot be eliminated. Hence, in such cases we must develop our instrument to be suitable for multiple informants (see Ketokivi and Schroeder, 2004).

5.5.3 Hypothesis testing

We tested our research hypotheses following the arguments of Brandon-Jones et al. (2014), Ryu et al. (2015), and Eckstein et al. (2015). Eckstein et al. (2015) argued that hierarchical regression analysis is considered to be the most appropriate and more conservative technique than covariance-based modeling approaches, due to the complexity of the model, the available data points, and the great robustness of the technique. Hypotheses H1–H3 were tested using hierarchical regression analysis as shown in Table 5.5. The results suggest that H1 ($\beta = 0.57$; p = 0.00), H2 ($\beta = 0.14$; p = 0.044) and H3 ($\beta = 0.42$; p = 0.00) are supported, which is consistent with Brandon-Jones et al.'s (2014) findings, and the results of H1 and H3 are consistent with Barratt and Oke's (2007) findings. The control variable "organization size" did not have any significant effect on the model (see Table 5.5). We interpreted that the size of the organization has little to do with the impact of supply chain connectivity on information sharing and supply chain visibility.

Next we address H4, which was tested using hierarchical moderated regression analysis (see Table 5.5). We found that reduction in behavioral uncertainty has a positive significant interaction effect. We interpreted that the reduction in behavioral uncertainty may enhance the positive effect of information sharing on supply chain visibility. Addressing H5 and H6, we found support (see Table 5.6). H5 ($\beta = 0.60$; p = 0.00) is supported. We interpreted that reduction in behavioral uncertainty helps to enhance trust among the partners in the supply chain. H6 ($\beta = 0.56$; p = 0.00) is also supported. Therefore, we can argue that a reduction in behavioral uncertainty improves supply chain visibility. These findings extend the findings of Barratt and Oke (2007) and Brandon-Jones et al. (2014).

Addressing H7 ($\beta = 0.774$; p = 0.00) and H8 ($\beta = 0.17$; p = 0.004), we find they are supported. Consequently, we can argue that trust among supply chain partners enhances commitment and coordination among them. These findings are consistent with the findings of Morgan and Hunt (1994) and Chen et al. (2011). H9 ($\beta = 0.71$; p = 0.00) is also supported. We interpreted this result to show that an increase in commitment level among supply chain partners helps to build coordination among supply chain partners.

Table 5.5 Multiple regression results for supply chain visibility and information sharing (for H1–H4)

Variable	DV = Information sharing		DV = Supply chain visibility	
Controls	Beta	t-value	Beta	t-value
Organization size	**0.22**	0.993	0.20	0.79
Main effects				
Supply chain connectivity (SC)	0.57	12.42	0.14	2.028
Information sharing (IS)			0.42	5.58
Interaction effects				
IS*BU			0.11	11.77
R²	0.383		0.244	
Adj R²	0.381		0.238	
Model F	154.2		39.942	
ΔR²			0.12	
ΔF			29.84	

Table 5.6 Hierarchical regression results (for H5–H11)

Variable	DV = Trust		DV = Supply chain visibility		DV= Commitment		DV= Coordination		DV = Supply chain resilience	
	Beta	t-value	Beta	t-value	Beta	t-value	Beta	t-value	Beta	t-value
Controls										
Organization Size	0.20	1.44								
Main effects										
BU	0.60	21.23	0.56	11.53						
Trust					0.774	18.67	0.17	2.78		
C							0.71	11.67		
CO									0.67	11.3
SCV									0.371	7.43
R^2	0.646		0.351		0.587		0.655		0.461	
Adj R^2	0.643		0.346		0.583		0.651		0.454	
Model F	225.3		66.87		175.37		155.59		70.01	

Next we addressed H10 and H11. H10 ($\beta = 0.67$; $p = 0.00$) is supported, so we can interpret that coordination has a significant impact on resilience. This result is found to be consistent with Wieland and Wallenburg (2013). H11 ($\beta = 0.37$; $p = 0.00$) is also supported. With this we can interpret that SCV has a significant impact on supply chain resilience. This result is consistent with prior studies like Christopher and Lee (2004) and Brandon-Jones et al. (2014). Based on these results, we can argue that coordination and supply chain visibility are both significant antecedents of supply chain resilience.

5.5.4 Post-hoc analyses

Ivanov (2014) argued that supply chain resilience and supply chain sustainability have several commonalities between them. However, despite the number of intersections between them, literature focusing on integration of resilience and sustainability has largely remained elusive. Most of the literature offers anecdotal evidence (see Redman 2014; Fahimnia and Jabbarzadeh 2016), and empirical study on how resilience affects sustainability is scant (Ivanov 2014). Informed by the Ivanov (2014) study we performed supplemental analyses to examine the direct effects of resilience on environmental sustainability. We validated our results with the supply chain managers of Renault Trucks, France. Renault Trucks is a leading French commercial truck and military vehicles manufacturer. The automotive company needs to constantly adapt to volatile, uncertain, complex, and ambiguous (VUCA) environments. Renault Trucks has built greater visibility to demand and supply via bundling of information technology and effective sharing of information. It has invested in big data and predictive analytics capability and distributed ledger technology to enhance visibility in the supply chain. However, these insights are less valuable if the supply chain managers are unable to build trust among the partners. For instance, in order to improve cooperative behavior, effort has to be taken to reduce the opportunistic behavior among the partners. We interviewed senior managers at Renault Trucks engaged in logistics and purchasing who have a deep understanding of global supply chain strategy, resilience, the role of emerging technologies, and sustainability (environmental and economic). Our interview generated some interesting insights. Since they have to manage a greater number of suppliers, the visibility capabilities allow organizations to understand the strengths and weakness in the system and thereby create higher supply chain resilience. Moreover, higher supply chain resilience may lead to better environmental and economic performance. However, with proper coordination the emissions level can be significantly reduced. Hence, with proper alignment, the resilience has positive effects on the reduction of wastage of raw materials and further helps to focus on improving environmental sustainability. This may take some time and requires significant efforts in improving visibility, trust among the partners, and better coordination. We also found via interview that agility and resilience are complementary to each other.

In this study, we used total interpretive structural modeling (TISM) to examine the complex relationship among the key drivers obtained through in-depth interviews with the managers. In TISM, the group expert judgment methodology was used to capture the relationships among the drivers. Opinions from managers having core experience in the supply chain domain were incorporated in the study using a structural self-interaction matrix (SSIM). The experts approached had more than 15 years of industry experience in the supply chain domain. Warfield (1974) and Malone (1975) were the first operation research experts to introduce the ISM technique. The major steps involved in TISM can be listed in sequence as (Sushil, 2012; Dubey and Ali, 2014; Dubey et al. 2017; Shibin et al. 2018) literature collection on the topic; review of collected literature to identify the variables; explaining the VAXO matrix allocation rules to the experts; formulation of the structural self-interaction matrix (SSIM) with the help of experts in the domain (see Table 5.7); conversion of the structural self-interaction matrix to a binary matrix and then to a final reachability matrix by considering the transitivity property (see Table 5.8); deriving the total driving power and dependence based on the binary matrixes to find out the level of variables (see Table 5.9); and making the directed graph (DIGRAPH) based on the levels of variables identified (see Table 5.10). The ISM model can be finalized by preparing a structural model from the DIGRAPH, which will be self-explanatory on the relationship among the variables. Reviewing the structural model may be required to validate the conceptual stability and make necessary changes to the model. There are two possible responses, such as yes or no, for any question regarding the relationship between two variables. And thus there will be nC_2 possible number of paired comparisons, which will tally into 45 for 10 drivers in our case. The ISM model can be taken to the next level of TISM by incorporating the interpretive logic between the drivers based on the expert explanation (see Figure 5.2). These interpretive logics are the contextual relationships among the variables, which are derived through brainstorming.

Table 5.7 Structural self-interaction matrix of drivers (SSIM)

	E10	E9	E8	E7	E6	E5	E4	E3	E2	E1
E1	V	V	O	O	V	V	V	O	X	X
E2	V	V	V	O	O	X	O	X	X	
E3	O	V	V	V	V	X	O	X		
E4	O	V	A	X	X	O	X			
E5	V	X	X	A	A	X				
E6	A	V	A	X	X					
E7	A	O	A	X						
E8	X	A	X							
E9	V	X								
E10	X									

Note: E1, supply chain connectivity; E2, supply chain visibility; E3, information sharing; E4, agility; E5, environmental performance; E6, resilience; E7, coordination; E8, commitment; E9, economic performance; E10, trust.

Table 5.8 Final reachability matrix drivers

	E10	E9	E8	E7	E6	E5	E4	E3	E2	E1	Driving power
E1	1	1	0	1*	1	1	1	0	1	1	8
E2	1	1	1	1*	1*	1	1*	1	1	1	10
E3	0	1	1	1	1	1	1*	1	1	0	8
E4	0	1	0	1	1	0	1	0	0	0	4
E5	1	1	1	0	0	1	0	1	1	0	6
E6	0	1	0	1	1	1	1	0	0	0	5
E7	0	0	0	1	1	1	1	0	0	0	4
E8	1	1*	1	1	1	1	1	0	0	0	7
E9	1	1	1	0	0	1	0	0	0	0	4
E10	1	1*	1	1	1	1*	0	0	0	0	6
Dependence	6	9	6	8	8	9	7	3	4	2	

* Transitivity property checked.
Note: E1, supply chain connectivity; E2, supply chain visibility; E3, information sharing; E4, agility; E5, environmental performance; E6, resilience; E7, coordination; E8, commitment; E9, economic performance; E10, trust.

Table 5.9 Binary matrix of drivers

	E10	E9	E8	E7	E6	E5	E4	E3	E2	E1	Driving power
E1	1	1	0	1	1	1	1	0	1	—	8
E2	1	1	1	1	1	1	1	1	—	1	10
E3	0	1	1	1	1	1	1	—	1	0	8
E4	0	1	0	1	1	0	—	0	0	0	4
E5	1	1	1	0	0	—	0	1	1	0	6
E6	0	1	0	1	—	1	1	0	0	0	5
E7	0	0	0	—	1	1	1	0	0	0	4
E8	1	1	—	1	1	1	1	0	0	0	7
E9	1	—	1	0	0	1	0	0	0	0	4
E10	—	1	1	1	1	1	0	0	0	0	6
Dependence	6	9	6	8	8	9	7	3	4	2	

Note: E1, supply chain connectivity; E2, supply chain visibility; E3, information sharing; E4, agility; E5, environmental performance; E6, resilience; E7, coordination; E8, commitment; E9, economic performance; E10, trust.

5.6 Discussion

5.6.1 Theoretical implications

The RBV argues that the bundling of resources and capabilities are utilized to create a competitive advantage (Barney 1991). Following the Barney (1991) logic, we considered supply chain connectivity and information sharing as complementary resources that may be bundled together to create supply chain visibility as a capability (Simon et al. 2008; Brandon-Jones et al. 2014). Following the arguments of Brandon-Jones et al. (2014), we hypothesized that both supply chain connectivity

Table 5.10 Level matrix of drivers

Variable	Level
E5, E9	Level 1
E4, E6, E7	Level 2
E8, E10	Level 3
E1, E2, E3	Level 4

Note: E1, supply chain connectivity; E2, supply chain visibility; E3, information sharing; E4, agility; E5, environmental performance; E6, resilience; E7, coordination; E8, commitment; E9, economic performance; E10, trust.

and information sharing are useful for creating supply chain visibility. Consequently, supply chain visibility may be exploited to expose sources of the supply chain risk and exploit the opportunities (Simon et al. 2008; Brandon-Jones et al. 2014). However, Oliver (1997) noted that RBV has its own limitations, and thus the resources of the firm may not provide a better explanation of supply chain resilience, which are exposed to various external factors, including social and political issues.

The Brandon-Jones et al. (2014) framework can further be extended using the integration framework. Wieland and Wallenburg (2013) argue that coordination among supply chain partners enhances resilience. We argue, on the basis of Morgan and Hunt (1994) and Kwon and Suh (2004), that reduction in behavioral uncertainty further enhances trust among partners, which further improves the commitment level and coordination among the partners. With this chapter we have attempted to answer some of the unanswered questions in prior studies, which have failed to reflect upon behavioral complexity among supply chain partners. This in turn impacted the degree of coordination, which is argued as one of the important antecedents of supply chain resilience (Wieland and Wallenburg 2013). Thus, by integrating relationship theory with RBV, we have attempted to address the concerns in operations management (see Bendoly et al. 2006; Gans and Croson 2008; Gino and Pisano 2008).

We believe that our framework is unique in terms of its theoretical implications to the existing literature in three ways. First, we demonstrate that behavioral dimensions have a significant impact on resilience, along with other important resources of the firm. Second, we have shown empirically that reduction in behavioral uncertainty has a positive interaction effect on information sharing and its impact on supply chain visibility. These results further extend the work of Barratt and Oke (2007) and Brandon-Jones et al. (2014), where they have not considered the role of the reduction of behavioral uncertainty on the positive effect of information sharing on supply chain visibility. Finally, we have shown in our framework that supply chain visibility and coordination are immediate antecedents of supply chain resilience, which explains nearly 46.1% of the total variance (R^2) in supply chain resilience. If we compare our model R^2 with the existing models, then our explanatory power of the model is comparatively high. We can argue that coordination among supply chain partners and supply chain visibility may help to build a climate-resilient supply chain.

5.6.2 Managerial implications

This study stems from current business challenges. Therefore, by empirically testing a theoretical framework grounded in existing literature, we offer a number of useful implications for supply chain managers. First, investing in the right kind of technology and quality information shar-

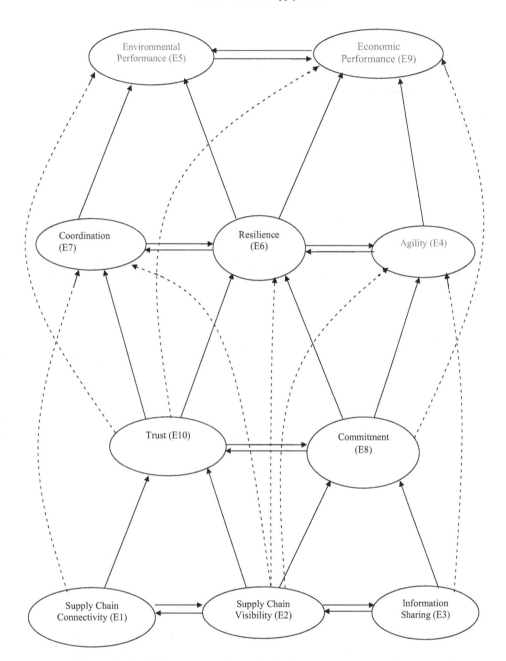

Figure 5.2 TISM model of drivers. Note: E1, supply chain connectivity; E2, supply chain visibility; E3, information sharing; E4, agility; E5, environmental performance; E6, resilience; E7, coordination; E8, commitment; E9, economic performance; E10, trust.

ing may help to improve supply chain visibility. Second, by reducing behavioral uncertainty, the organization might achieve better results of information sharing on supply chain visibility. Third, the reduction in behavioral uncertainty can help to generate trust among supply chain partners, which may help to build commitment and a desired level of coordination, which in turn may help significantly in building a climate-resilient supply chain.

We recognize that the idea of advising organizations on the basis of data gathered from selected manufacturing organizations may sound ill-advised, as service organizations have their own challenges. This study has also been conducted in the context of Indian manufacturing organizations, and thus we cannot claim to generalize our research findings. However, it should be noted that our study is based on organizations that have already invested in technology and information sharing to create visibility across the supply chain. Presumably, it is in the best interest for such companies to invest in the right kind of technologies and training programs for their employees to improve their behavioral skills.

5.6.3 Implications for policymakers

First, the findings of the study may encourage senior leaders from the manufacturing sector to invest in building supply chain visibility capability. Further, the study promotes the recommendation for a fundamental foundation of "resilience sustainability" studies in the manufacturing sector that enfolds a multilevel thought for formulating practices that can foster and hone climate-resilient supply chains. It is well understood that the precondition for successful organizational sustainability is well-designed organizational policies and the collective effort of all the industry stakeholders. The finding of the study endeavors to spark dialogue among various manufacturing organizations, and for research & development personnel and corporate leaders to maintain a healthy, innovative, thought-provoking, and zero-tolerance work environment for their employees. Hence, this empirical study necessarily reinforces industry enthusiasts to augment the trust and commitment among the employees via technology as the foremost priority to attain resilience and agility, which in turn influence the environmental and economic performance.

Second, the government can create industry-friendly policies that can benefit manufacturing companies operating under extreme conditions with scarce resources. The policies include foreign investment and tax benefits for companies taking steps to prioritize and produce innovative products.

Third, the industry associations can unite and lay a solid foundation to understand the role of emerging technologies to achieve climate resilience.

5.6.4 Limitations and future research directions

Like other studies, we also acknowledge that this study has some limitations that may further advance our current effort to a next level. We enumerate our limitations and unanswered questions in this section. First, the current study adopts a theory-focused approach, meaning that we have used RBV and relationship theory to explain resilience in supply chains. However, we have only considered supply chain connectivity and information sharing as tangible and intangible resources. However, other resources like human skills (i.e., managerial skills and technical skills) and learning culture might have a significant effect on supply chain visibility as a desired capability of the organization. However, besides supply chain visibility, other organizational capabilities like supply chain agility, supply chain adaptability, and supply chain alignment could be explored. We admit that due to our survey-based approach (Choi and Krause 2006,) we could not further measure complexity associated with behavioral uncertainty. However, qualitative research methods may answer some of these unanswered questions.

Second, in this study we have only considered resilience. However, other components may be explored, like redundancy, robustness, and rapidity (which are considered to be important characteristics of supply chain resilience). A simulation-based modeling approach can further help to quantify these aspects.

Third, our model considers the climate-resilient supply chain. In this model we have limited our discussion to the impact of carbon emissions on the supply chains of organizations.

However, in the future, other dimensions could be explored, such as ethical sourcing, child labor, gender workforce ratio, gender equity, and health standards of the workers in the context of supply chain resilience.

5.7 Conclusion

Drawing broadly on RBV and relationship theory, we argued that resources, capabilities, behavioral uncertainty, trust, commitment, and coordination are the predictors of supply chain resilience. Our theoretical framework reconciled the independent contributions of two well-established streams in the literature: bundling of resources and capabilities; and the impact of behavioral uncertainty, trust, and commitment on coordination. We attempted to explain the interaction effect of the reduction of behavioral uncertainty on paths connecting information sharing and supply chain visibility, and the effect of trust and commitment on coordination among supply chain partners. Analyses based on 250 Indian manufacturing organizations support the hypothesized relationships in the framework. This research makes significant contributions to the supply chain resilience field by focusing on much neglected behavioral dimensions, and extending and enriching existing studies, and confirms that coordination and supply chain visibility have a significant influence on resilience. Finally, we enumerated some limitations and further research directions to take the current study to the next level.

Appendix A: Definitions of the main constructs

Construct	Definition
Supply chain connectivity (Srinivasan and Swink 2018)	Supply chain connectivity may be defined as tangible resources of the firm that include terminals, computers, devices, and other analytic tools that may help to process data to extract meaningful information.
Information sharing (Pemkumar and King 1994)	Information sharing can be defined as an organizational capital, an intangible resource that focuses on the flow of information.
Supply chain visibility (Zhou and Benton Jr. 2007)	Supply chain visibility is defined by the availability (currency) and quality (accuracy, usefulness) of information.
Behavioral uncertainty (Kwon and Suh 2004)	Behavioral uncertainty is defined as the inability to predict a supply chain partner's behavior or changes in the external environment.
Trust (adapted from Kwon and Suh 2004)	Here trust is defined as the organization's belief that another organization will perform actions that will result in positive outcomes for the organization as well as not take any unexpected actions for the organization that result in negative outcomes.
Commitment (Morgan and Hunt 1994)	Commitment is defined as an exchange partner believing that an ongoing relationship with another is so important as to warrant maximum efforts at maintaining it.
Coordination (Xu and Beamon 2006)	Coordination within the supply chain network is defined as a strategic response to the problems that often arise from interorganizational dependencies within the supply chain.
Supply chain resilience (Brandon-Jones et al. 2014)	Supply chain resilience is defined as the ability of a supply chain to return to normal operating performance, within an acceptable time, after being disturbed.

Appendix B: Descriptive statistics

	N	Minimum	Maximum	Mean	Std. deviation	Skewness		Kurtosis	
	Statistic	Statistic	Statistic	Statistic	Statistic	Statistic	Std. error	Statistic	Std. error
SC1	250	1.00	5.00	2.7200	1.18288	.000	.154	-1.198	.307
SC2	250	1.00	5.00	3.6440	1.04000	-.843	.154	.420	.307
SC3	250	1.00	5.00	3.6040	1.12617	-1.044	.154	.269	.307
IS1	250	1.00	5.00	3.1840	1.26354	-.411	.154	-.971	.307
IS2	250	1.00	5.00	3.5960	1.08327	-.861	.154	.224	.307
IS3	250	1.00	5.00	3.9200	1.03046	-1.038	.154	.722	.307
IS4	250	1.00	5.00	3.6520	1.05420	-.697	.154	.007	.307
IS5	250	1.00	5.00	3.5160	1.11297	-.507	.154	-.609	.307
SCV1	250	1.00	5.00	3.8960	.96795	-.888	.154	.141	.307
SCV2	250	1.00	5.00	3.7680	.97878	-.556	.154	-.532	.307
BU1	250	2.00	5.00	3.7800	.87100	-.513	.154	-.292	.307
BU2	250	1.00	5.00	4.1160	1.14358	-1.659	.154	2.070	.307
BU3	250	1.00	5.00	3.9880	1.19397	-1.218	.154	.717	.307
BU4	250	1.00	5.00	3.9960	1.15990	-1.424	.154	1.305	.307
T1	250	1.00	5.00	4.0400	.99315	-1.048	.154	.550	.307
T2	250	1.00	5.00	3.8080	.98336	-.730	.154	.310	.307
T3	250	1.00	5.00	3.7320	1.08484	-.782	.154	-.211	.307
T4	250	1.00	5.00	3.9680	1.08614	-1.453	.154	1.839	.307
T5	250	2.00	5.00	3.7760	.85835	-.742	.154	.058	.307
T6	250	1.00	5.00	3.8840	.88639	-.852	.154	.530	.307
T7	250	1.00	5.00	3.7880	.85907	-.956	.154	1.450	.307
T8	250	2.00	5.00	3.9960	.91616	-.813	.154	-.009	.307
T9	250	1.00	5.00	3.7640	.87140	-.697	.154	.614	.307
T10	250	2.00	5.00	3.8200	.76284	-.340	.154	-.100	.307

	N	Minimum	Maximum	Mean	Std. Deviation	Skewness Statistic	Skewness Std. Error	Kurtosis Statistic	Kurtosis Std. Error
C1	250	1.00	5.00	3.8800	.75090	-.717	.154	1.930	.307
C2	250	1.00	5.00	3.5680	.95972	-.800	.154	.323	.307
C3	250	1.00	5.00	3.8400	.89980	-.846	.154	.249	.307
C4	250	1.00	5.00	3.6720	.93805	-.449	.154	-.521	.307
C5	250	1.00	5.00	3.2320	1.10592	-.237	.154	-.483	.307
CO1	250	1.00	5.00	3.8640	.98048	-1.322	.154	1.887	.307
CO2	250	1.00	5.00	3.6520	.95842	-.688	.154	.478	.307
CO3	250	1.00	5.00	3.8120	.80701	-.754	.154	1.529	.307
CO4	250	2.00	5.00	4.0080	.89169	-.906	.154	.315	.307
SCR1	250	2.00	5.00	3.8960	.88107	-.612	.154	-.194	.307
SCR2	250	1.00	5.00	3.8160	.86321	-.428	.154	-.028	.307
SCR3	250	1.00	5.00	3.8840	1.07479	-1.234	.154	1.354	.307
SCR4	250	1.00	5.00	3.8880	.90262	-.735	.154	.378	.307
Valid N (listwise)	250								

Appendix C: Unidimensionality test (fit indices and their acceptable limits)

Absolute fit index	Acceptable threshold levels	Our observed values	Description
Relative (κ^2/df)	2:1 (Tabachnick and Fidell 2007) 3:1 (Kline 2005)	1.56	This value adjusts for sample size.
CFI (comparative fit index)	Values should be greater than 0.98.	0.98	
GFI (goodness of fit)	Values should be greater than 0.95.	0.97	The GFI values lie between 0 to 1, with higher values reflecting better model fit.
AGFI (adjusted goodness of fit)		0.95	
RMSEA (root mean square error of approximation)	Values less than 0.07 (Steiger and Mayer 2008).	0.05	Represents that sample has known distribution. Favors parsimony.
NFI (normed fit index)	Values greater than 0.95	0.96	Assesses fit relative to baseline model, which assumes no covariance between the observed variables.

Appendix D: Common method bias

	SC	IS	SCV	BU	T	C	CO	SCR
SC1	0.60							
SC2	0.89							
SC3	0.85							
IS1		0.67						
IS2		0.67						
IS3		0.83						
IS4		0.84						
IS5		0.59						
SCV1			0.87					
SCV2			0.87					
BU1				0.64				
BU2				0.91				
BU3				0.83				
BU4				0.86				
T1					0.73			
T2					0.70			
T3					0.59			
T4					0.81			
T5					0.87			

(Continued)

	SC	IS	SCV	BU	T	C	CO	SCR
T6					0.79			
T7					0.71			
T8					0.80			
T9					0.55			
T10					0.64			
C1						0.59		
C2						0.90		
C3						0.89		
C4						0.84		
C5								
CO1							0.89	
CO2							0.80	
CO3							0.64	
CO4							0.76	
SCR1								0.80
SCR2								0.79
SCR3								0.85
SCR4								0.70
Variance	1.88	2.64	1.50	2.67	5.26	2.67	2.43	2.46
%	5.21	7.34	4.17	7.41	14.61	7.41	6.75	6.84

References

Altay, N., Gunasekaran, A., Dubey, R., & Childe, S. J. (2018). Agility and resilience as antecedents of supply chain performance under moderating effects of organizational culture within the humanitarian setting: A dynamic capability view. *Production Planning & Control*, *29*(14), 1158–1174.

Altay, N., & Ramirez, A. (2010). Impact of disasters on firms in different sectors: Implications for supply chains. *Journal of Supply Chain Management*, *46*(4), 59–80.

Armstrong, J. S., & Overton, T. S. (1977). Estimating nonresponse bias in mail surveys. *Journal of Marketing Research*, *14*(3), 396–402.

Bakshi, N., & Kleindorfer, P. (2009). Co-opetition and investment for supply-chain resilience. *Production and Operations Management*, *18*(6), 583–603.

Barney, J. (1991). Firm resources and sustained competitive advantage. *Journal of Management*, *17*(1), 99–120.

Barney, J. B. (2012). Purchasing, supply chain management and sustained competitive advantage: The relevance of resource-based theory. *Journal of Supply Chain Management*, *48*(2), 3–6.

Barney, J.B., Ketchen, D.J., & Wright, M. (2011). The future of resource-based theory – Revitalization or decline? *Journal of Management*, *37*(5), 1299–1315.

Barratt, M., & Oke, A. (2007). Antecedents of supply chain visibility in retail supply chains: A resource-based theory perspective. *Journal of Operations Management*, *25*(6), 1217–1233.

Bendoly, E., Donohue, K., & Schultz, K. L. (2006). Behavior in operations management: Assessing recent findings and revisiting old assumptions. *Journal of Operations Management*, *24*(6), 737–752.

Bentler, P. M. (1990). Comparative fit indexes in structural models. *Psychological Bulletin*, *107*(2), 238–246.

Bozarth, C. C., Warsing, D. P., Flynn, B. B., & Flynn, E. J. (2009). The impact of supply chain complexity on manufacturing plant performance. *Journal of Operations Management*, *27*(1), 78–93.

Brandon-Jones, E., Squire, B., Autry, C.W., & Petersen, K.J. (2014). A contingent resource-based perspective of supply chain resilience and robustness. *Journal of Supply Chain Management*, *50*(3), 55–73.

Braunscheidel, M. J., & Suresh, N. C. (2009). The organizational antecedents of a firm's supply chain agility for risk mitigation and response. *Journal of Operations Management*, *27*(2), 119–140.

Cao, M., & Zhang, Q. (2011). Supply chain collaboration: Impact on collaborative advantage and firm performance. *Journal of Operations Management, 29*(3), 163–180.

CDP (2011). Supply Chain Report 2011. https://www.cdp.net/CDPResults/CDP-2011-Supply-Chain -Report.pdf (Date of access: 15th August, 2016).

Chen, I. J., & Paulraj, A. (2004). Towards a theory of supply chain management: The constructs and measurements. *Journal of Operations Management, 22*(2), 119–150.

Chen, J. V., Yen, D. C., Rajkumar, T. M., & Tomochko, N. A. (2011). The antecedent factors on trust and commitment in supply chain relationships. *Computer Standards & Interfaces, 33*(3), 262–270.

Choi, T. Y., & Krause, D. R. (2006). The supply base and its complexity: Implications for transaction costs, risks, responsiveness, and innovation. *Journal of Operations Management, 24*(5), 637–652.

Christopher, M., & Lee, H. (2004). Mitigating supply chain risk through improved confidence. *International Journal of Physical Distribution & Logistics Management, 34*(5), 388–396.

Conner, K. R. (1991). A historical comparison of resource-based theory and five schools of thought within industrial organization economics: Do we have a new theory of the firm? *Journal of Management, 17*(1), 121–154.

Cuevas, S. C. (2011). Climate change, vulnerability, and risk linkages. *International Journal of Climate Change Strategies and Management, 3*(1), 29–60.

Curran, P. J., West, S. G., & Finch, J. F. (1996). The robustness of test statistics to nonnormality and specification error in confirmatory factor analysis. *Psychological Methods, 1*(1), 16–29.

Derissen, S., Quaas, M. F., & Baumgärtner, S. (2011). The relationship between resilience and sustainability of ecological-economic systems. *Ecological Economics, 70*(6), 1121–1128.

Dillman, D. A. (2011). *Mail and Internet surveys: The tailored design method--2007 Update with new Internet, visual, and mixed-mode guide.* John Wiley & Sons: NJ, USA.

Dubey, R., & Ali, S. S. (2014). Identification of flexible manufacturing system dimensions and their interrelationship using total interpretive structural modelling and fuzzy MICMAC analysis. *Global Journal of Flexible Systems Management, 15*(2), 131–143.

Dubey, R., & Gunasekaran, A. (2015). Exploring soft TQM dimensions and their impact on firm performance: Some exploratory empirical results. *International Journal of Production Research, 53*(2), 371–382.

Dubey, R., Gunasekaran, A., Childe, S. J., Fosso Wamba, S., Roubaud, D., & Foropon, C. (2021). Empirical investigation of data analytics capability and organizational flexibility as complements to supply chain resilience. *International Journal of Production Research, 59*(1), 110–128.

Dubey, R., Gunasekaran, A., Childe, S. J., Papadopoulos, T., Blome, C., & Luo, Z. (2019a). Antecedents of resilient supply chains: An empirical study. *IEEE Transactions on Engineering Management, 66*(1), 8–19.

Dubey, R., Gunasekaran, A., Childe, S. J., Roubaud, D., Wamba, S. F., Giannakis, M., & Foropon, C. (2019b). Big data analytics and organizational culture as complements to swift trust and collaborative performance in the humanitarian supply chain. *International Journal of Production Economics, 210,* 120-136.

Dubey, R., Gunasekaran, A., Papadopoulos, T., Childe, S. J., Shibin, K. T., & Wamba, S. F. (2017). Sustainable supply chain management: Framework and further research directions. *Journal of cleaner production, 142,* 1119–1130.

Eckstein, D., Goellner, M., Blome, C., & Henke, M. (2015). The performance impact of supply chain agility and supply chain adaptability: The moderating effect of product complexity. *International Journal of Production Research, 53*(10), 3028–3046.

Fahimnia, B., & Jabbarzadeh, A. (2016). Marrying supply chain sustainability and resilience: A match made in heaven. *Transportation Research Part E: Logistics and Transportation Review, 91,* 306–324.

Fawcett, S. E., Waller, M. A., Miller, J. W., Schwieterman, M. A., Hazen, B. T., & Overstreet, R. E. (2014). A trail guide to publishing success: Tips on writing influential conceptual, qualitative, and survey research. *Journal of Business Logistics, 35*(1), 1–16.

Fawcett, S. E., Wallin, C., Allred, C., Fawcett, A. M., & Magnan, G. M. (2011). Information technology as an enabler of supply chain collaboration: A dynamic-capabilities perspective. *Journal of Supply Chain Management, 47*(1), 38–59.

Fawcett, S. E., Wallin, C., Allred, C., & Magnan, G. (2009). Supply chain information-sharing: benchmarking a proven path. *Benchmarking: An International Journal, 16*(2), 222–246.

Fiksel, J. (2006). Sustainability and resilience: Toward a systems approach. *Sustainability: Science, Practice, & Policy, 2*(2), 14–21.

Francis, V. (2008). Supply chain visibility: lost in translation? *Supply Chain Management: An International Journal, 13*(3), 180–184.

Gans, N., & Croson, R. (2008). Introduction to the special issue on behavioral operations. *Manufacturing & Service Operations Management*, *10*(4), 563–565.

Gerbing, D. W., & Anderson, J. C. (1988). An updated paradigm for scale development incorporating unidimensionality and its assessment. *Journal of Marketing Research*, *25*(2), 186–192.

Gino, F., & Pisano, G. (2008). Toward a theory of behavioral operations. *Manufacturing & Service Operations Management*, *10*(4), 676–691.

Grant, R. M. (1991). The resource-based theory of competitive advantage: Implications for strategy formulation. *California Management Review*, *33*(3), 114–135.

Größler, A., & Grübner, A. (2006). An empirical model of the relationships between manufacturing capabilities. *International Journal of Operations & Production Management*, *26*(5), 458–485.

Gunasekaran, A., Subramanian, N., & Rahman, S. (2015). Supply chain resilience: Role of complexities and strategies. *International Journal of Production Research*, *53*(22), 6809–6819.

Hair, J. F., Black, W. C., Babin, B. J., Anderson, R. E., & Tatham, R. L. (2006). Multivariate data analysis (Vol. 6), Pearson, New Jersey, USA.

Halldórsson, Á., & Kovács, G. (2010). The sustainable agenda and energy efficiency: Logistics solutions and supply chains in times of climate change. *International Journal of Physical Distribution & Logistics Management*, *40*(1/2), 5–13.

Hart, S. L. (1997). Beyond greening: Strategies for a sustainable world. *Harvard Business Review*, *75*(1), 66–76.

Hoopes, D. G., Madsen, T. L., & Walker, G. (2003). Guest editors' introduction to the special issue: Why is there a resource-based view? Toward a theory of competitive heterogeneity. *Strategic Management Journal*, *24*(10), 889–902.

Hu, L. T., & Bentler, P. M. (1999). Cutoff criteria for fit indexes in covariance structure analysis: Conventional criteria versus new alternatives. *Structural Equation Modeling: A Multidisciplinary Journal*, *6*(1), 1–55.

IPCC (2014). *Press Release: Concluding Instalment of the Fifth Assessment Report: Climate change threatens irreversible and dangerous impacts, but options exist to limit its effects.* IPCC, Copenhagen. http://www.ipcc.ch/pdf/ar5/prpc_syr/11022014_syr_copenhagen.pdf. (Date of access: 5th June, 2016).

Ivanov, D. (2018). Revealing interfaces of supply chain resilience and sustainability: A simulation study. *International Journal of Production Research*, *56*(10), 3507–3523.

Ivanov, D., & Dolgui, A. (2019). Low-Certainty-Need (LCN) supply chains: A new perspective in managing disruption risks and resilience. *International Journal of Production Research*, 57(15-16),5119-5136.

Ivanov, D., Sokolov, B., & Dolgui, A. (2014). The Ripple effect in supply chains: trade-off 'efficiency-flexibility-resilience' in disruption management. *International Journal of Production Research*, *52*(7), 2154–2172.

Jacobs, B. C., Lee, C., O'Toole, D., & Vines, K. (2014). Integrated regional vulnerability assessment of government services to climate change. *International Journal of Climate Change Strategies and Management*, *6*(3), 272–295.

Jüttner, U., & Maklan, S. (2011). Supply chain resilience in the global financial crisis: An empirical study. *Supply Chain Management: An International Journal*, *16*(4), 246–259.

Kamalahmadi, M., & Mellat-Parast, M. (2016). Developing a resilient supply chain through supplier flexibility and reliability assessment. *International Journal of Production Research*, *54*(1), 302–321.

Kamalahmadi, M., & Mellat-Parast, M. (2016a). A review of the literature on the principles of enterprise and supply chain resilience: Major findings and directions for future research. *International Journal of Production Economics*, *171*, 116–133.

Ketokivi, M. A., & Schroeder, R. G. (2004). Perceptual measures of performance: Fact or fiction? *Journal of Operations Management*, *22*(3), 247–264.

Kleindorfer, P. R., & Saad, G. H. (2005). Managing disruption risks in supply chains. *Production and Operations Management*, *14*(1), 53–68.

Kline, T. J. (2005). *Psychological testing: A practical approach to design and evaluation.* Sage Publications, USA.

Kolk, A., & Pinkse, J. (2004). Market strategies for climate change. *European Management Journal*, *22*(3), 304–314.

Krishnan, R., Martin, X., & Noorderhaven, N. G. (2006). When does trust matter to alliance performance? *Academy of Management Journal*, *49*(5), 894–917.

Kwon, I. W. G., & Suh, T. (2004). Factors affecting the level of trust and commitment in supply chain relationships. *Journal of Supply Chain Management*, *40*(1), 4–14.

Lindell, M. K., & Whitney, D. J. (2001). Accounting for common method variance in cross-sectional research designs. *Journal of Applied Psychology*, *86*(1), 114–121.

Liu, F., Song, J. S., & Tong, J. D. (2016). Building supply chain resilience through virtual stockpile pooling. *Production and Operations Management, 25*(10), 1745–1762. DOI: 10.1111/poms.12573.

Malhotra, N. K., Kim, S. S., & Patil, A. (2006). Common method variance in IS research: A comparison of alternative approaches and a reanalysis of past research. *Management Science, 52*(12), 1865–1883.

Malone, D. W. (1975). An introduction to the application of interpretive structural modeling. *Proceedings of the IEEE, 63*(3), 397–404.

Mogre, R., Talluri, S., & D'Amico, F. (2016). A Decision Framework to Mitigate Supply Chain Risks: An Application in the Offshore-Wind Industry, *IEEE Transactions on Engineering Management, 63*(3), 316–325.

Morgan, R. M., & Hunt, S. D. (1994). The commitment-trust theory of relationship marketing. *The Journal of Marketing, 58*(3), 20–38.

Munoz, A., & Dunbar, M. (2015). On the quantification of operational supply chain resilience. *International Journal of Production Research, 53*(22), 6736–6751.

Norton, T., Ryan, M., & Wang, F. (2015). *Business Action for Climate-Resilient Supply Chains: A Practical Framework for identifying priorities to Evaluating Impact.* BSR Working Paper. BSR, San Francisco

Nunnally, J. (1978). *Psychometric methods.* McGraw-Hill, USA.

Oliver, C. (1997). Sustainable competitive advantage: Combining institutional and resource-based views. *Strategic Management Journal, 18*(9), 697–713.

Papadopoulos, T., Gunasekaran, A., Dubey, R., Altay, N., Childe, S. J., & Fosso-Wamba, S. (2017). The role of big data in explaining disaster resilience in supply chains for sustainability. *Journal of Cleaner Production, 142*, 1108–1118.

Park, S. H., & Ungson, G. R. (2001). Interfirm rivalry and managerial complexity: A conceptual framework of alliance failure. *Organization Science, 12*(1), 37–53.

Park, S. J., Cachon, G. P., Lai, G., & Seshadri, S. (2015). Supply chain design and carbon penalty: monopoly vs. monopolistic competition. *Production and Operations Management, 24*(9), 1494–1508.

Pettit, T. J., Fiksel, J., & Croxton, K. L. (2010). Ensuring supply chain resilience: Development of a conceptual framework. *Journal of Business Logistics, 31*(1), 1–21.

Podsakoff, P. M., MacKenzie, S. B., Lee, J. Y., & Podsakoff, N. P. (2003). Common method biases in behavioral research: A critical review of the literature and recommended remedies. *Journal of Applied Psychology, 88*(5), 879–903.

Podsakoff, P. M., & Organ, D. W. (1986). Self-reports in organizational research: Problems and prospects. *Journal of Management, 12*(4), 531–544.

Ponomarov, S. Y., & Holcomb, M. C. (2009). Understanding the concept of supply chain resilience. *The International Journal of Logistics Management, 20*(1), 124–143.

Premkumar, G., & King, W. R. (1994). Organizational characteristics and information systems planning: An empirical study. *Information Systems Research, 5*(2), 75–109.

Priem, R. L., & Swink, M. (2012). A demand-side perspective on supply chain management. *Journal of Supply Chain Management, 48*(2), 7–13.

Purvis, L., Spall, S., Naim, M., & Spiegler, V. (2016). Developing a resilient supply chain strategy during 'boom' and 'bust'. *Production Planning & Control, 27*(7–8), 579–590.

Ravichandran, T., & Lertwongsatien, C. (2005). Effect of information systems resources and capabilities on firm performance: A resource-based perspective. *Journal of Management Information Systems, 21*(4), 237–276.

Redman, C. L. (2014). Should sustainability and resilience be combined or remain distinct pursuits? *Ecology and Society, 19*(2), 37–44.

Ryu, H. S., Lee, J. N., & Choi, B. (2015). Alignment between service innovation strategy and business strategy and its effect on firm performance: An empirical investigation. *IEEE Transactions on Engineering Management, 62*(1), 100–113.

Sheffi, Y. (2005). Building a resilient supply chain. *Harvard Business Review, 1*(8), 1–4.

Shibin, K. T., Dubey, R., Gunasekaran, A., Luo, Z., Papadopoulos, T., & Roubaud, D. (2018). Frugal innovation for supply chain sustainability in SMEs: Multi-method research design. *Production Planning & Control, 29*(11), 908–927.

Singh, A. K., & Garg, A. (2015). Impact of information integration on decision-making in a supply chain network. *Production Planning & Control, 26*(12), 994–1010.

Sirmon, D. G., Gove, S., & Hitt, M. A. (2008). Resource management in dyadic competitive rivalry: The effects of resource bundling and deployment. *Academy of Management Journal, 51*(5), 919–935.

Srinivasan, R., & Swink, M. (2018). An investigation of visibility and flexibility as complements to supply chain analytics: An organizational information processing theory perspective. *Production and Operations Management*, 27(10), 1849–1867.

Steiger, R., & Mayer, M. (2008). Snowmaking and climate change: Future options for snow production in Tyrolean ski resorts. *Mountain Research and Development*, 28(3), 292–298.

Sushil (2012). Interpreting the interpretive structural model. *Global Journal of Flexible Systems Management*, 13(2), 87–106.

Tabachnick, B. G., & Fidell, L. S. (2007). *Experimental designs using ANOVA*. Thomson/Brooks/Cole, USA.

Tang, C. S. (2006). Perspectives in supply chain risk management. *International Journal of Production Economics*, 103(2), 451–488.

Tatham, P., & Kovács, G. (2010). The application of "swift trust" to humanitarian logistics. *International Journal of Production Economics*, 126(1), 35–45.

Tokar, T. (2010). Behavioral research in logistics and supply chain management. *The International Journal of Logistics Management*, 21(1), 89–103.

Wagner, S. M., & Bode, C. (2008). An empirical examination of supply chain performance along several dimensions of risk. *Journal of Business Logistics*, 29(1), 307–325.

Warfield, J. N. (1974). Toward interpretation of complex structural models. *IEEE Transactions on Systems, Man and Cybernetics*, 5, 405–417.

Welty, B., & Becerra-Fernandez, I. (2001). Managing trust and commitment in collaborative supply chain relationships. *Communications of the ACM*, 44(6), 67–73.

Wieland, A., & Marcus Wallenburg, C. (2013). The influence of relational competencies on supply chain resilience: a relational view. *International Journal of Physical Distribution & Logistics Management*, 43(4), 300–320.

Williams, B. D., Roh, J., Tokar, T., & Swink, M. (2013). Leveraging supply chain visibility for responsiveness: The moderating role of internal integration. *Journal of Operations Management*, 31(7), 543–554.

Wu, F., Yeniyurt, S., Kim, D., & Cavusgil, S. T. (2006). The impact of information technology on supply chain capabilities and firm performance: A resource-based view. *Industrial Marketing Management*, 35(4), 493–504.

Wu, L. Y. (2010). Applicability of the resource-based and dynamic-capability views under environmental volatility. *Journal of Business Research*, 63(1), 27–31.

Wu, T., Huang, S., Blackhurst, J., Zhang, X., & Wang, S. (2013). Supply chain risk management: An agent-based simulation to study the impact of retail stockouts. *IEEE Transactions on Engineering Management*, 60(4), 676–686.

Xu, L., & Beamon, B. M. (2006). Supply chain coordination and cooperation mechanisms: An attribute-based approach. *Journal of Supply Chain Management*, 42(1), 4–12.

Zhou, H., & Benton Jr, W. C. (2007). Supply chain practice and information sharing. *Journal of Operations management*, 25(6), 1348–1365.

Zhu, K., & Kraemer, K. L. (2002). E-commerce metrics for net-enhanced organizations: Assessing the value of e-commerce to firm performance in the manufacturing sector. *Information Systems Research*, 13(3), 275–295.

CASE STUDY
Zespri global supply chain integration

Abraham Zhang and Paul Childerhouse

New Zealand kiwifruit industry

The horticultural sector is increasingly becoming a very important export earner for New Zealand. The global supply chains are complex and there is a need to manage these with precision due to the limited shelf life and fragile nature of the products. Zespri is the name and image of the New Zealand kiwifruit industry. The industry currently has 2385 growers and 3240 registered orchards, earning more than NZD$2.4 billion from exports to over 50 countries. Zespri manages and monitors its supply chain to ensure that it consistently provides the "world's finest kiwifruit" to consumers.

Lack of integration

Before Zespri, the New Zealand kiwifruit industry was steadily pacing itself downhill due to all the distributors and exporters trying to survive by selling their fruit at the lowest prices due to the lack of differentiation. Kiwifruit was caught in a supply-driven commodity trap: kiwifruit was available all year round from a variety of sources, but the eating experience was inconsistent. Kiwifruit had a very low penetration as a preferred commonly eaten fruit because the quality of the fruit was compromised. There was poor integration and synchronization between the separate units: growers, pack houses, distributors and exporters.

Zespri formation

In the late 1990s, Zespri was established as the single desk marketer for New Zealand kiwifruit under the Kiwifruit Export Regulations. That critical mass and single supply chain gave Zespri the ability to create something unique in terms of a system that could deliver a differentiated model. Since then, there has been a dramatic improvement to the integration and flow throughout the whole supply chain. Zespri designed a way to funnel money and information through all the phases back to the growers.

The Zespri brand is fundamental to the company's success. The brand is uncompromisingly about quality, because to get a premium price for products, exporters must have consistent quality. The supply chain is the system that protects the Zespri brand from a quality point of view.

DOI: 10.4324/9781315225661-8

The system is essentially layers of standards and each segment of the supply chain is responsible for its part in meeting those standards. Zespri assists with the application of these standards up and down the supply chain, and audits business practices at each level to ensure that its standards are maintained. Also, to help get the quality message through, Zespri offers incentive payments around quality.

Global supply chain integration

Zespri and the kiwifruit industry are now making larger profits than ever, and it is partly because of their internal and external integration. This is enabled by their ability to reach back to the growers and throughout the supply chain to inform all the actors what the consumers want, as well as the professional marketing team working with the distributors to manage and meet the high expectations of today's customers and consumers. This makes Zespri a success, as the abundance of information flow throughout the supply chain has resulted in customers from all over the world increasingly buying kiwifruit because they know to expect exceptional quality.

According to Zespri, "the ZESPRI System" is a supply chain delivery system that acts as the glue that binds the market delivery and production ends of the business together with a shared goal, a shared way of doing business and a shared commitment to mutual success. The Zespri global supply chain is unique in that its branding and quality requirements permeate right through the chain, although Zespri owns very little of it.

Traceability

Every kiwifruit is traceable in the Zespri global supply chain. Zespri growers document their cultivation process in detail (what sort of compost was used, whether pesticides or extra watering were needed, etc.). Every box of Zespri kiwifruit has a unique code. Based on this code, Zespri knows the entire history of the fruit: where it was grown, when it was harvested, where it was packed and when it was shipped.

Clearly, managing such a global supply chain requires impressive information and communications technology (ICT) systems. Since its inception, Zespri has done a lot of custom developments in its ICT systems, predominantly around the supply chain. In the past few years, Zespri further invested over $10 million to enhance supply chain planning. Very recently, a chief digital officer was appointed as part of Zespri's continuous journey to drive business performance through innovative and effective ICT usage.

The use of the internet of things (IoT) is one of the examples showing how Zespri has enhanced its quality and supply chain management through the latest technologies. Now Zespri puts temperature and humidity sensors in kiwifruit pallets to track the storage conditions of kiwifruit in its global supply chain, from pack houses through cold storage to multiple transportation stages to regional warehouses in the markets. Such end-to-end supply chain visibility enables Zespri to monitor the ripening process of its kiwifruit. It allows Zespri to proactively manage the quality of its produce along the supply chain, ensuring a superior consumer experience.

Conclusion

Being part of an integrated supply chain is an aspirational goal for many firms. Achieving this takes many years of continuous improvement and is based on mutual trust and the sharing of benefits by all actors. It has taken Zespri 20 years to design, implement and now optimize its supply chain by staying focused on uncompromising quality and a collective agenda to maximize the value creation and capture of New Zealand's kiwifruit growers. The journey is still ongoing with current investments into IoT to further enhance visibility throughout the chain and development of even more enjoyable varieties to delight consumers.

PART III

Role of emerging technologies and data analytics in global value chains

In Chapter 6, Rema Padman, Ramesh Krishnan and Renu Agarwal introduce integration of information and communications technology (ICT) systems and processes, which draws upon the illustrative example from healthcare delivery to highlight some opportunities with analytics in patient safety initiatives and implications for healthcare supply chains. The emerging megatrends in healthcare and continuing digital transformation of the healthcare sector worldwide has opened new opportunities to improve healthcare delivery and this chapter introduces these new perspectives.

In Chapter 7, Ramesh Krishnan, Phi Yen Phan, Arshinder Kaur and Sanjoy Kumar Paul discuss blockchain and allied technologies for food supply chain risk mitigation. Globalisation of value chain activities, such as sourcing, design, production, distribution and marketing, have improved the benefits and opportunities for stakeholders. However, this has also increased the associated risks due to the complexity and involvement of too many entities. This, especially, matters in food and agricultural value chains, which are facing a number of challenges, including a lack of transparency, variation in quality, high price fluctuation and different government regulations. Underpinning this megatrend and its associated risks, managing global food value chain (GFVC) risks using advanced technologies is becoming important for transformation. Considered as one of the most disruptive technologies of recent times, the impact of blockchain in integration with internet of things and big data analytics ought to be crucial to managing risks in the GFVC. This study is among the few to identify the potential risks associated with GFVC and explores the significant roles of blockchain and its allied technologies in mitigating the identified GFVC risks.

In Chapter 8, Renu Agarwal, Christopher Bajada, Mile Katic and Manjot Singh Bhatia discuss the rise of new management practices and business models as a consequence of technological, process and systems change, and organisational transformations. In this chapter, the authors review the recent trends in management practices for global value chains. They investigate the megatrends in emerging technologies in global value chains and examine the implications these have on the management practices within organisations.

In Chapter 9, Anwara Happy, Kazi Waziur Rahman, Md Maruf Hossan Chowdhury, Mesbahuddin Chowdhury and Moira Scerri illustrate a multi-criteria decision model for mitigating block chain adoption challenges in supply chain, which is proving to be a game changer in supply chain management, with expectations that it may change the competitive landscape

DOI: 10.4324/9781315225661-9

with the global business arena. The authors use study findings to develop a conceptual model, after which the fuzzy analytic hierarchy process is used to prioritize challenges using expert opinion. Theoretical and managerial significance are employed.

A case study concludes Part III. Written by Ray Y. Zhong and Abraham Zhang, it outlines IoT-enabled agri-food supply chain management (ASCM) consisting of three components: smart farming, smart logistics, and smart supply chain visibility and traceability.

6

INTEGRATION OF ICT SYSTEMS AND PROCESSES

Supply chain, process management and patient safety with data analytics to enhance healthcare delivery

Rema Padman, Ramesh Krishnan and Renu Agarwal

Introduction

The advent of supply chain technologies, systems and processes combined with the availability of vast amounts of digital data from internet of things (IoT) devices and sensors in healthcare delivery and advanced data analytic tools have the potential to arm health administrators with actionable insights for planning and strategic decision-making, for both operational improvements and better care delivery (Winters-Miner, 2014). In addition, healthcare providers are facing pressure from governments, consumers and payers to provide better service at lower cost, improving quality of service, ensuring patient safety and reducing medical errors (Mandal and Jha, 2018). However, the involvement of numerous entities, tasks, uncertainties and shared responsibilities makes managing healthcare operations highly complex (Kitsiou et al., 2007). Further, with economic growth across the world, millions of people are demanding affordable healthcare services and healthcare products (Dixit et al., 2019). In the past two decades, the trade of medical devices and pharmaceuticals in the global market has increased by more than four times (Ebel et al., 2013). On the other hand, quality, safety and compliance issues are also increasing within global healthcare value chains.

In this context, a global value chain is defined as the "pattern of organization of production involving international trade and investment flows whereby the different stages of the production process are located across different countries" (OECD, 2018). Ensuring patient safety by reducing medical and medication errors rise to paramount importance within global healthcare value chains, especially during the global COVID-19 pandemic when the number of patients who need treatment goes beyond the maximum capacity of the systems of care (WHO, 2020). Adopting better supply chain practices within the health system could increase overall efficiency of healthcare operations in terms of service level, patient safety, medical errors and inventory management (Dixit et al., 2019; Mathur et al., 2018; Meijboom et al., 2011).

Supply chain management practices have attracted many applications in the healthcare industry (Mathur et al., 2018; Meijboom et al., 2011). The healthcare supply chain involves the

 DOI: 10.4324/9781315225661-10

seamless flow of products and services from multiple suppliers and distributing the product to hospitals to ensure timely availability of resources for healthcare service delivery (Shih et al., 2009). Though the processes involved in the healthcare supply chain are similar to that of other supply chains, the specific characteristics of the healthcare supply chain such as perishability, system dynamics and diversity differentiate the health supply chain from other sectors (Waller, 1999).

Furthermore, it has been highlighted that integration of technology in the healthcare supply chain would also improve communication between clinicians and enable access to healthcare information, thus reducing medical errors and improving patient safety (Ranky, 2006; Tsai and Hung, 2009). This is extremely important in the global context, noting that healthcare delivery organizations are increasingly being challenged to improve patient safety efforts, such as the correct and timely patient identification for medication administration (Newell, 2011). Healthcare information technology includes electronic health records, computerized physician order entry, clinical decision support, patient data management systems, barcode medication administration, automated medication dispensing and electronic incident reporting (Alotaibi and Federico, 2017). This results in a large volume and variety of digital data generation for every individual patient, which includes the past medical history of a patient, current problems and their recovery patterns. In addition, data related to healthcare supply chains comprise inventory, availability and stock levels of all the drugs, medical equipment usage and operations, performance reports of health systems and processes, advancements in medical research, and all financial transactions. The analysis of such large data sets with advanced analytical techniques such as predictive analytics using machine learning and artificial intelligence has the potential to provide valuable insights for strategic decision-making (Malik et al., 2018). An increase in the accuracy of diagnoses, early intervention to disease management and better inventory planning, including timely availability of drugs, are some of the benefits that can be realized (Winters-Miner, 2014). This data can also be used to measure the compliance levels of technologies implemented as well as the effectiveness of technologies, processes and policies that enhance patient safety (Early et al., 2011). However, there are misconceptions and challenges in understanding the compliance levels of technologies implemented for patient safety that require a better understanding. This chapter draws on an illustrative example of a real case study from the United States healthcare delivery setting to highlight some opportunities with analytics in patient safety initiatives (Padman et al., 2013) and implications for the global supply chain in healthcare.

Background to the case study

The National Academy of Medicine (formerly the Institute of Medicine) in the United States published a landmark study in 1999 that reported that at least 44,000 people, and perhaps as many as 98,000 people, die in US hospitals each year as a result of medical errors that could have been prevented (Kohn et al., 1999). For example, patient misidentification is a common, potentially fatal error that is largely preventable. Studies indicate that better tools and procedures to confirm patient identity can help prevent 225,000 deaths per year due to iatrogenic causes (Starfield, 2000). As a result, healthcare accreditation organizations have identified correct patient identification as the primary goal for patient safety in healthcare and recommends the use of automated systems (The Joint Commission, 2019). This increased focus on patient safety has resulted in a number of reliable and useful Positive Patient Identification (PPID) technologies that are being widely deployed. However, improving compliance in the use of PPID technologies faces multiple challenges associated with human factors, process workarounds, supply chain sequences and technology failures (Koppel et al., 2008; Rack et al., 2012).

The case study

PPID technologies, processes and policies enhance patient safety by supporting care providers in reducing medical errors during interventions such as medication management and blood transfusions, and specimen collections, such as for laboratory tests (Early et al., 2011). All these interventions pose significant challenges to the global healthcare supply chain, which is exacerbated by noncompliance with usage requirements and policies. In the case of medication management, PPID aims to provide the right dose of the right medication to the right patient at the right time via the right route, ensuring that the "5 rights" are complied with at all times.

A major pediatric facility in the United States implemented PPID in 2008, reaching a compliance rate of about 85 percent. A new quality and innovation initiative sought to understand the challenges and corresponding solutions to increase it to above 90 percent. In this study, PPID compliance is defined explicitly as "the average, across all units, of the percentage of medications administered using PPID technologies in the inpatient setting." Using medication administration and PPID compliance data from the pediatric facility, interviews and observations, this study identified areas for improvement in PPID compliance, lessons learned and approaches that are generalizable to other clinical settings and healthcare organizations more broadly for improved patient safety initiatives, with implications for smart supply chain management to implement such initiatives.

Methods adopted

The research team applied a three-pronged approach that classified observed issues as driven by people, process or technology challenges (Padman et al., 2013). Through direct observations of medication administration activities by nurses utilizing the PPID technology on the floor and in training sessions; interviews with clinical, administrative and technical staff familiar with the process; technology and human factors; and analysis of recent medication administration and compliance data, several key issues were brought to light. In particular, nursing administrators, pharmacists, database and networking technology staff members were actively involved in every stage of the study, sharing knowledge and insights, testing technologies using time-motion approaches, and providing wireless maps and battery specification documents. Relevant literature presenting recent studies on PPID technologies were also reviewed to obtain a comprehensive understanding of the current status.

People and process

Many studies have reported that understanding the PPID process and its interactions with the human participants and technology components facilitate identification of failure points and subsequent workarounds, recognition and solution of technology and supply chain bottlenecks, and the potential design and implementation of simulation interventions to evaluate new recommendations (McNulty et al., 2009; Mims et al., 2009; Snyder et al., 2010). As shown in Figure 6.1, the PPID process at the pediatric facility had two key sub-processes: pharmacy activity and nurse activity. The pharmacy prepares the medications and nurses administer the medications.

Pharmacy

The pharmacy continuously checks the order entry database for medication orders from physicians, organizes medications into drawers for delivery to nurse carts and makes necessary preparations for specific medications (Alotaibi and Federico, 2017). If the medication does not have a

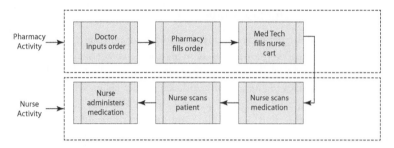

Figure 6.1 Medication management process.

manufacturer barcode, a pharmacy barcode is tested and placed on the medication, and a supply chain error is noted. The medical technician (MT) brings the drawers from the pharmacy to a designated area for nurse carts. Under the supervision of the clinical leader, the MT restocks the nurse carts. If there is an issue with a medication, the nurse contacts the pharmacy and a new delivery is made within 30 minutes, provided there are no supply chain inventory failures (see Figure 6.2).

The process at the pharmacy was well documented. The research team discovered that all barcodes are not tested before they are sent to the floor. If a medication is used in the same form it is received by the pharmacy, then the manufacturer barcode is used. If some preparation is necessary, the pharmacy creates a barcode and scans it to verify that it can be read before attaching it to a medication. This brought to light a potential opportunity for noncompliance.

Nurses

The nurse collects the cart at the beginning of the shift and signs on to the medical administration record (MAR) outside a patient room using the computer on the cart and checks the medications in the drawers against the medications scheduled to be administered. If all medications are accurate and accounted for, the nurse carries the necessary medication to the patient. In addition to the medications, the nurse also removes the PPID device from its charging station on the cart and brings it into the patient room. Assuming that the device has been properly charged, the nurse logs into the PPID device, scans the barcode on the patient's wristband, then proceeds to scan each medication individually. The supply chain of PPID devices and barcode-enabled wristbands to healthcare facilities is another challenge to be included in the patient safety initiative.

The device has many alerts for various circumstances to protect the patient from human/device/application errors. The nurse then uses the device to indicate any changes or specific information about the medication and signs off on all the medications. If any error in scanning occurs, the nurse is required to contact the computer help desk or physically go through the 5 rights and use the MAR on the cart outside the room to confirm the administration of medication. If the device times out, the nurse can log back in and complete the procedure. If the device runs out of power, the nurse should follow the same procedure as if there was a scanning error. The process is depicted in Figure 6.3.

In this process, several opportunities were identified for noncompliance after a nurse receives the medication. When the nurse attempts to log into the device, the waiting time or the lack of a charge could motivate a nurse to use the MAR on the cart instead. Once the nurse logged in, if the barcode on the patient's wristband does not scan, the nurse is required to print a new

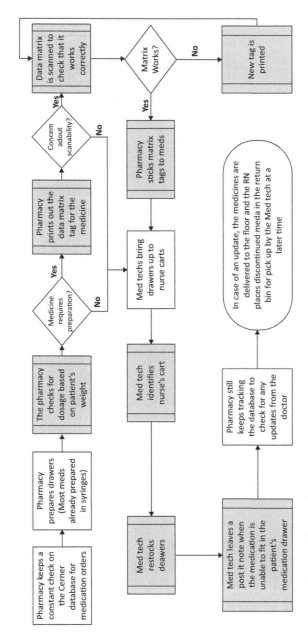

Figure 6.2 Process flow at the pharmacy.

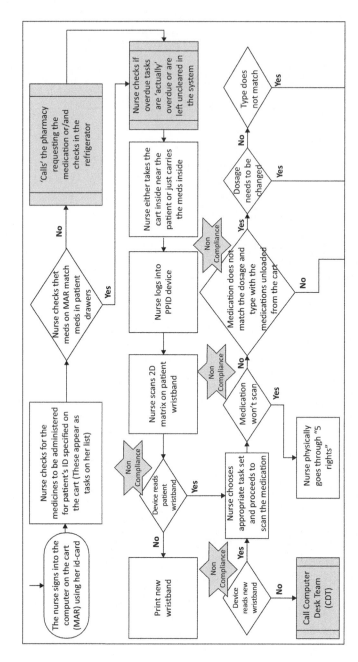

Figure 6.3 Process flow for nurses on floors.

wristband, which is another barrier. If the second wristband does not scan, the nurse is asked to contact the computer help desk. This escalating workload leads to occasional noncompliance and may also affect the inventory of wristbands. Once the patient is scanned, the medication barcode must be scanned. If the barcode on the medication does not scan, there are several steps built into the process so that the nurse can get help. However, once again, it is simpler for the nurse to use the MAR instead.

These practical barriers created resistance to technology for a small fraction of nurses who were against the use of the PPID devices, for reasons ranging from problems with technology and its supply chain challenges, misalignment with workflow, discomfort with the devices and a perception of reluctance to use by older nurses. Nurses are the most important entity in the barcoded medication administration (BCMA) process and they are the last line of defense for patient safety. If the nurses are unwilling or unable to use the devices in a timely and effective manner, it can lead to a serious degradation of system effectiveness as a whole (Hurley et al., 2007). Thus, a summary of people- and process-related reasons for noncompliance were identified as follows:

- Nurses complained that devices were slow.
- The log-in process took too long.
- It is hard to maneuver on the small screen even with the stylus.
- The process to sign off on medications using the MAR application on the computer is much simpler than using the device.
- Administering critical medications that must be given at specific times in specific forms was not easy with the devices.

Technology

Apart from the people and process issues that resulted in noncompliance as described earlier, there were technology issues that were potential areas of concern for PPID compliance. Based on the technologies used in PPID deployment, we examined issues particularly related to the (1) battery, (2) database and (3) wireless network.

Battery-related issues

The handheld device used for PPID had a battery with a discharge time of five to seven hours based on its usage, and a charging time of about three hours. Thus, the battery charge depletes quickly and needs constant charging. This is a cause for concern because low-battery conditions lead to extremely slow response times or no response when communicating with the database, resulting in the nurse administering the medicine without PPID scanning and charting using MAR. Another issue is that the indications of low battery charge are not very evident. There are just two colors of LED used to indicate the battery condition. This does not provide enough warning to the nurse to notice a low battery and immediately put it on charge and get a replacement. Sometimes when a low-battery condition is not noticed soon enough, it will result in dead batteries at the point of use, which not only affects compliance due to lack of a device but also affects the battery life resulting in bad battery performance for future use (Martin et al., 2003). Hence, supply chain management of batteries is an important consideration in the use of PPID devices.

Furthermore, the docking station on the cart to keep the battery charging when the nurse is on rounds to administer medications posed another challenge. Its position, placed inconveniently behind the monitor, and the requirement for the device to be placed in only one particular direction with the application of some force to ensure proper placement on the dock, led the nurse to sometimes not place the handheld device on the docking station for charging, resulting in quicker depletion of charge. Thus, some potential failure points caused by battery-related issues were identified as follows:

- Low battery charge, so the device cannot scan the medication barcode, leading to the nurse signing off on the MAR.
- Low battery charge, causing a lower data transmission rate over the network.

Database-related issues

The handheld device used for PPID constantly interacts with the database to display various kinds of information on the device for the nurse. When the patient barcode is scanned, the database is accessed for patient information, and upon a match, the medication that needs to be administered in the next two-hour window is displayed on the device. Hence, the interaction with the database is a crucial link for the device to function properly, so database issues need to be identified and addressed to improve compliance.

The response time of the database, i.e., the time gap between scanning the barcode on the PPID device and getting data displayed on screen depends on the following factors:

- Time taken for the device to send barcode information to the database. This depends on battery conditions and network availability.
- Time taken for the database to identify the right data (this is the most time-consuming step).
- Time taken for the PPID device to receive data from the database. This depends on how long a patient has been in the hospital and how many medications are to be administered in each time window.

The duration of stay of a patient affects the PPID device response time for accessing patient information. The test patient in pharmacy had the slowest access times since the pharmacy had been using the same test patient for a few years to test the barcodes they print out for scanning. Based on this information, new issues regarding the architecture and implementation of the database need further investigation. These include separation of new and archival data such that the search and look-up can be faster, and caching of data in a local database to reduce network latency and speed up access. Barring these two unresolved issues, this study confirmed that all other database-related issues were identified and resolved at the database level.

Network-related issues

The final link between the handheld device and the health database (addressed earlier) is the network that was examined using the hospital's network layout maps and the interaction of the device with the network. Initially, the PPID device firmware made constant hops between two or more access points; however, this was corrected with updated firmware on the device. Additionally, an upgrade resulted in consistent and high availability of the network throughout the hospital. Hence, all network-related issues were identified and addressed and did not need any further attention.

Data analysis and results

The objective of the data analysis was to detect patterns of interest regarding failure to scan patients and/or medications by unit, personnel, route of administration and other relevant factors, and in the process, obtain deeper insights regarding possible failure modes and effects during the scanning process. Medication administration data was obtained from the data warehouse for the months of September and October 2012. This detailed data included 83,816 records in September and 90,315 records in October and were generated for each instance of medication administration for all patients across all floors in the hospital. This data set contained the following relevant variables: Nurse Unit, Personnel ID, Medication Name, Route of Administration, Source Application Flag (PPID vs. MAR), Date and Time, Positive Medication Identification Indicator (medication scanned or not), Positive Patient Identification Indicator (patient scanned or not), and Scanned? (both scanned or not).

Based on this data, the team identified four different states that were possible during the scanning process, representing the two major steps in the PPID scanning process: scanning the patient and scanning the medicine for that patient. The four states are shown in Table 6.1.

The data was analyzed to identify six high-volume units with a high percentage of potential noncompliance, summarized in Table 6.2. Unit A with the highest volume and unit B with the highest noncompliance were of particular interest for further analysis.

The next level of analysis examined the top five medications that contributed to noncompliance in each unit. Based on the states mentioned in Table 6.1, we observed that the number of noncompliance issues caused by the "Med not Scanned" was comparatively lower than those caused by the "Both not Scanned" and the "Patient not Scanned" states. This contradicted all previous assumptions that the patient was always scanned! Table 6.3 and Table 6.4 show a summary of this analysis across the six units mentioned in Table 6.2 for both months of data.

To get a better understanding of the particular medications that had low compliance, the six units mentioned in Table 6.2 for each type of medicine were analyzed. Furthermore, based on

Table 6.1 PPID scanning states

State of interest	Patient ID	Medication ID	Scanned
Both not scanned	0	0	0
Patient not scanned	0	1	0
Med not scanned	1	0	0
Both scanned	1	1	1

Table 6.2 Units with high volume of medication administration and high noncompliance rate

Unit	September % noncompliance (total administered)	October % noncompliance (total administered)
A	18% (16016)	17% (20173)
B	24% (6417)	21% (6806)
C	20% (8171)	16% (8611)
D	13% (8156)	13% (9989)
E	15% (3931)	13% (3947)
F	13% (547)	16% (476)

Table 6.3 Distribution of noncompliance across various states across six units for September

Unit	Total not scanned	PID 0, MID 1	PID 0, MID 0	PID 1, MID 0
A	2927	0	2313	614
B	1520	7	1191	322
C	1603	128	825	650
D	1101	24	401	676
E	575	0	416	159
F	71	0	60	11

Table 6.4 Distribution of noncompliance across various states across six units for October

Unit	Total not scanned	PID 0, MID 1	PID 0, MID 0	PID 1, MID 0
A	3362	0	2658	704
B	1437	8	1181	248
C	1375	131	583	661
D	1297	81	366	850
E	525	1	378	146
F	77	0	66	11

Table 6.5 Top 5 meds not scanned in Unit A for September

Medication	Percent scanned	Total	MID 0, PID 1	New compliance
Sodium chloride 0.9%	77%	1198	9	99.2%
Acetaminophen	76%	693	33	95.2%
Fentanyl	50%	599	59	90.2%
Lorazepam	72%	455	22	95.2%
Dextrose 5% with 0.9% NaCl	62%	215	1	99.5%

Table 6.6 Top 5 meds not scanned in Unit A for October

Medication	Percent scanned	Total	MID 0, PID 1	New compliance
Dextrose 5% in water	79%	1357	13	99%
Sodium chloride 0.9%	69%	1046	33	96.8%
Fentanyl	77%	759	33	95.7%
Acetaminophen	63%	280	4	98.6%
Albumin human	67%	258	13	95%

our original definition of compliance of those situations when medication was not scanned, we also calculated a new compliance rate based only on the "Med not Scanned" state. The results are shown in Table 6.5 and Table 6.6. Similar results are seen in other units where the rates increase substantially from current levels under the new definition of compliance.

Based on the information in the tables, it is very clear that looking at just the "Med not Scanned" state does not address the compliance challenge. All states needed to be analyzed without prior assumptions about user behavior, as confirmed by the results on the "Both not Scanned" and the "Patient not Scanned" states.

Discussion

Issues in compliance calculation

The reported baseline compliance rate was 84–85 percent, calculated for all cases under the assumption that the patient barcode was scanned and noncompliance arose from medications not being scanned. However, the data analysis found that the majority of the cases for noncompliance issues in many units were due to just the opposite case, i.e., the patient ID was itself not scanned. Hence, a new baseline compliance rate has to be defined, which distinguishes between the various states of scanning. In particular, the compliance rate increased considerably from 80–85 percent to 95–99 percent when considering only medications not being scanned.

Battery policy

For efficient operation of the battery-powered PPID device, battery life has to be checked and the batteries replaced on a periodic basis, and a process to do the same has to be in place. Thus, a battery policy has to be instituted with several specified components to ensure that all batteries are utilized up to their optimal shelf-life so that the impact on compliance or performance drop is minimal. These could include:

- A centralized monitoring system to check how often batteries are replaced, batching the replacement, and providing timely reminders, with respect to battery shelf-life, for replacement.
- An efficient charging mechanism for batteries to last long, better placement of the charging dock on the cart for ease of accessibility, an indicator (beep) if the PPID device itself is placed in the wrong position on the dock, and multicolor LED indicators on the PPID device to signal the battery condition.
- Profiling of battery health condition to ensure quality.
- Tracking the performance of the batteries (essentially aid in performance monitoring).

Time series analysis of data

The current calculation of PPID compliance based on the average of all data across all units does not always provide sufficient information for an insightful analysis because a series or clusters of low values can skew the results. Hence a time series analysis that allows investigation of clusters, autocorrelations and annotations of variance from the expected values can be utilized to directly focus on specific user/technology behaviors and problematic areas as they arise and establish quality control mechanisms instead of scanning through the entire set of information, as was the case with the present analysis.

Benchmarking and governance policy

While interacting with the various teams at the hospital for this study – Network, Database, Hardware, Process and Data Warehouse – it was observed that some of the problem areas had already been identified and fixed by the in-house teams. For example, the Wi-Fi network was optimized, and access point issues were resolved in collaboration with the PPID device manufacturer. Similarly, the database was also upgraded, and several PPID process measurement studies were conducted internally. Hence, a central benchmarking mechanism that can be used to collate results from all departments and record the most recent updates and optimization is necessary to establish a stable governance policy for maintenance and a standardized baseline for compliance rate calculation. This has the potential to improve operations and efficiency.

Finally, a survey across all floors is needed that gives individual nurses an opportunity to highlight issues they face with the PPID. Mapping the results to insights from the technology and process analysis can further enhance compliance improvement, patient safety and supply chain management efforts.

Global supply chain in healthcare for patient safety

Patient safety has begun to be a focus of healthcare supply chains only recently, particularly in the areas of medical devices and pharmaceuticals. Transforming global supply chains to support frontline clinicians is critically needed to improve safety-related outcomes, specifically through regulations affecting sensors, wearables, medical and IoT devices, and radio frequency identification (RFID) technologies, minimizing their need to perform non-value-added search-and-replace and logistic activities and dealing with the associated process and workflow challenges. Pharmacies are also facing big changes in the way drugs are handled in the pharmaceutical supply chain. Systems and technologies to track and trace pharmaceutical products, providing key information about drugs that are bought and sold, and closely monitoring drug shortages that affect patient care and outcomes are rapidly emerging global supply chain issues to investigate further.

Conclusions

Healthcare value/supply chains combined with healthcare information technology have the potential to improve healthcare systems worldwide by reducing costs, enhancing the overall efficiency of administration and, in particular, better patient safety. Combining advanced analytics with a large amount of data generated from the information technology tools and implementation of associated processes would provide useful insights for healthcare decision makers in assessing the compliance of the ever-emerging innovative information and communications technology (ICT) devices and solutions as they are implemented and the supply chain bottlenecks that may need to be resolved.

At a major pediatric facility, barcoded medication administration had been in use since 2008 to assist in PPID. Since its inception, the hospital had sought to increase the use of this application through technology improvements and continuing education efforts. This case study explored the PPID compliance problem from multiple perspectives using qualitative and quantitative approaches that highlighted people, process and technology challenges, and the complex interactions between them. Drawing on and synthesizing data from interviews, observations, technology assessments and actual usage data, the results provide detailed insights and recommendations for healthcare delivery organizations to improve patient safety efforts involving correct and timely patient identification for medication administration, and the supply chain challenges and opportunities resulting from the granular data collection and analysis.

Patient safety initiatives are currently viewed through the lens of in-hospital technologies, workflows and human–computer issues. Extending these to include supply chain challenges, such as availability and maintenance of devices, batteries, nurse carts, medications and all other components necessary to ensure that the medication administration process is completed safely and successfully as described in the case study, is another global supply chain imperative that is yet to be addressed.

Acknowledgments

The first author is grateful to colleagues J. Levin (deceased), D. Sieworek and A. Smailagic, and graduate students A. Katti, S.M. Ketter and K.S. Nanduri for collaborating on the case study presented in this chapter.

References

Alotaibi, Y.K., & Federico, F., 2017. The impact of health information technology on patient safety. *Saudi Med. J.* 38, 1173–1180. https://doi.org/10.15537/smj.2017.12.20631

Dixit, A., Routroy, S., & Dubey, S.K., 2019. A systematic literature review of healthcare supply chain and implications of future research. *Int. J. Pharm. Healthc. Mark.* 13, 405–435. https://doi.org/10.1108/IJPHM-05-2018-0028

Early, C., Riha, C., Martin, J., Lowdon, K.W., & Harvey, E.M., 2011. Scanning for safety: An integrated approach to improved bar-code medication administration. *CIN – Comput. Informatics Nurs.* 29, 157–164. https://doi.org/10.1097/NCN.0b013e3181fc416d

Ebel, T., George, K., Shah, K., & Ungerman, D., 2013. *Building New Strengths in the Healthcare Supply Chain Pharmaceuticals and Medical Products Operations*, McKinsey & Company.

Hurley, A.C., Bane, A., Fotakis, S., Duffy, M.E., Sevigny, A., Poon, E.G., & Gandhi, T.K., 2007. Nurses' satisfaction with medication administration point-of-care technology. *J. Nurs. Adm.* 37, 343–349. https://doi.org/10.1097/01.NNA.0000285114.60689.02

Kitsiou, S., Matopoulos, A., Manthou, V., & Vlachopoulou, M., 2007. Evaluation of integration technology approaches in the healthcare supply chain. *Int. J. Value Chain Manag.* 1, 325–343. https://doi.org/10.1504/IJVCM.2007.015091

Kohn, L.T., Corrigan, J.M., & Donaldson, M.S., 1999. To err is human: building a safer health system. *National Academic Press (US).* https://doi.org/10.17226/9728

Koppel, R., Wetterneck, T., Telles, J.L., & Karsh, B.T., 2008. Workarounds to barcode medication administration systems: Their occurrences, causes, and threats to patient safety. *J. Am. Med. Informatics Assoc.* 15, 408–423. https://doi.org/10.1197/jamia.M2616

Malik, M.M., Abdallah, S., & Ala'raj, M., 2018. Data mining and predictive analytics applications for the delivery of healthcare services: A systematic literature review. *Ann. Oper. Res.* 270, 287–312. https://doi.org/10.1007/s10479-016-2393-z

Mandal, S., & Jha, R.R., 2018. Exploring the importance of collaborative assets to hospital-supplier integration in healthcare supply chains. *Int. J. Prod. Res.* 56, 2666–2683. https://doi.org/10.1080/00207543.2017.1381349

Martin, T.L., Siewiorek, D.P., Smailagic, A., Bosworth, M., Ettus, M., & Warren, J., 2003. A case study of a system-level approach to power-aware computing. *ACM Trans. Embed. Comput. Syst.* 2, 255–276. https://doi.org/10.1145/860176.860178

Mathur, B., Gupta, S., Meena, M.L., & Dangayach, G.S., 2018. Healthcare supply chain management: Literature review and some issues. *J. Adv. Manag. Res.* 15, 265–287. https://doi.org/10.1108/JAMR-09-2017-0090

McNulty, J., Donnelly, E., & Iorio, K., 2009. Methodologies for sustaining barcode medication administration compliance. A multi-disciplinary approach. *J. Healthc. Inf. Manag.* 23, 30–33.

Meijboom, B., Schmidt-Bakx, S., & Westert, G., 2011. Supply chain management practices for improving patient-oriented care. *Supply Chain Manag. An Int. J.* 16, 166–175. https://doi.org/10.1108/13598541111127155

Mims, E., Tucker, C., Carlson, R., Schneider, R., & Bagby, J., 2009. Quality-monitoring program for barcode-assisted medication administration. *Am. J. Heal. Pharm.* 66, 1125–1131. https://doi.org/10.2146/ajhp080172

Newell, S., 2011. Special section on healthcare information systems. *J. Strateg. Inf. Syst.* https://doi.org/10.1016/j.jsis.2011.05.002

OECD, 2018. *Oslo Manual 2018: Guidelines for collecting, reporting and using data on innovation*. OECD publishing. https://doi.org/10.1787/9789264304604-en

Padman, R., Smailagic, A., Sieworek, D., Katti, A., Nanduri, K.S., Morrison-Ketter, S., & Levin, J.E., 2013. *Positive Patient Identification Compliance: A Mixed Methods Patient Safety Analysis.* Technical Report, Heinz College, Carnegie Mellon University.

Rack, L.L., Dudjak, L.A., & Wolf, G.A., 2012. Study of nurse workarounds in a hospital using bar code medication administration system. *J. Nurs. Care Qual.* 27, 232–239. https://doi.org/10.1097/NCQ.0b013e318240a854

Ranky, P.G., 2006. An introduction to radio frequency identification (RFID) methods and solutions. *Assem. Autom.* 26, 28–33. https://doi.org/10.1108/01445150610645639

Shih, S.C., Rivers, P.A., & Sonya Hsu, H.Y., 2009. Strategic information technology alliances for effective health-care supply chain management. *Heal. Serv. Manag. Res.* 22, 140–150. https://doi.org/10.1258/hsmr.2009.009003

Snyder, M.L., Carter, A., Jenkins, K., & Fantz, C.R., 2010. Patient misidentifications caused by errors in standard bar code technology. *Clin. Chem.* 56, 1554–1560. https://doi.org/10.1373/clinchem.2010.150094

Starfield, B., 2000. Is US health really the best in the world? *JAMA.* 284, 483-5. doi: 10.1001/jama.284.4.483. PMID: 10904513

The Joint Commission, 2019. Laboratory National Patient Safety Goals. https://www.jointcommission.org/standards/national-patient-safety-goals/

Tsai, W.H., & Hung, S.J., 2009. A fuzzy goal programming approach for green supply chain optimisation under activity-based costing and performance evaluation with a value-chain structure. *Int. J. Prod. Res.* 47, 4991–5017. https://doi.org/10.1080/00207540801932498

Waller, D.L., 1999. *Operations Management: A Supply Chain Approach.* International Thomson Business Press, London.

WHO, 2020. WHO checklist to ensure hospitals in European region are ready for COVID-19 patients [WWW Document]. URL https://www.euro.who.int/en/countries/kyrgyzstan/news/news/2020/4/who-checklist-to-ensure-hospitals-in-european-region-are-ready-for-covid-19-patients (Accessed June 29, 2020).

Winters-Miner, L.A., 2014. Seven ways predictive analytics can improve healthcare. Elsevier 1–10.

7

BLOCKCHAIN AND ALLIED TECHNOLOGIES FOR FOOD SUPPLY CHAIN RISK MITIGATION IN GLOBAL VALUE CHAINS

*Ramesh Krishnan, Phi Yen Phan, Arshinder
Kaur and Sanjoy Kumar Paul*

7.1 Introduction

Over the past decades, international trade, investment and, especially, production have been increasingly organised to make the supply chains or value chains "global". The term *global supply chain* focuses on managing activities related to the production or material provision of products/services in a production network, whereas *global value chain* emphasises value addition made over the production chain (Marcolin et al., 2016). In this study, these two terms are used interchangeably, and global value chain is preferred over global supply chain, as it includes the aspects of global supply chain. A global value chain (GVC) is defined as a range of activities (e.g. production, delivery and marketing) that firms undertake to bring a product/service from conception to the end consumer (Gereffi and Fernandez-Stark, 2016) across national borders. Within GVCs, different stages of a firm's production process are located and managed across multiple countries (OECD, 2019).

Food value chain management is the management of activities associated with value addition to food products by farmers and manufacturers and the delivery of them through distributors, transporters, wholesalers and retailers to the end customer (Aramyan et al., 2006). The food value chain (FVC) exhibits unique characteristics, such as a long lead-time for agricultural production, the perishable nature of fresh products, geographic variations, seasonality in production and consumption, and variability in product quality and yield, making it highly complex to manage (Amorim et al., 2013). Globalisation of FVC networks has created an opportunity for selling products in the larger international market. However, the very nature of the global food value chain (GFVC) involves stakeholders from different countries, high trade barriers and strict government regulations for import and export of food products in international markets, which have increased the complexity of the GFVC (Siddh et al., 2017), resulting in a greater number of risks in addition to the opportunities created by international markets (Diabat et al., 2012). Furthermore, in the GFVC network, food products are grown, processed and packaged in different geographical sites and transported to multiple countries over the globe, thus increasing the distance and duration of travel for food before it reaches the end

DOI: 10.4324/9781315225661-11

customer, thereby affecting the visibility, quality and safety of the GFVC. In addition, the occurrence of food-related diseases, such as mad cow disease, foot and mouth disease, and bovine spongiform encephalopathy, has resulted in increased consumer concerns towards food traceability, safety and quality (Aung and Chang, 2014; Marucheck et al., 2011; Pennings et al., 2002). These facts highlight the importance of risk management in the GFVC.

The risks associated with the FVC can be broadly classified into supply risk, demand risk, storage and transport risk, financial risk, health risk, social risk, political/institutional risk, and environmental risk. The presence of these risks reduces the resources available to support agricultural production (Singla and Sagar, 2012), agricultural productivity (Rathore et al., 2017), quality of agricultural products (Rathore et al., 2017) and food availability (Saritas and Kuzminov, 2017); increases emissions to the environment (Saritas and Kuzminov, 2017); and causes adverse health impacts to surrounding populations (Yeung and Morris, 2007). Hess et al. (2002) highlighted that not promptly addressing the agricultural risks could result in serious consequences; for example, the decrease in yield and profit from crops could result in farmers exhausting all their savings and eventually selling their land. The more farmers selling land to manage their financial losses and loans, the lower the value of land becomes. This could result in abject poverty, which can, in turn, lead to farmer suicides (Hess et al., 2002). Thus, risks in every stage of the GFVC must be identified and addressed effectively.

Technological innovations have become the forefront of risk management in GVCs. Significantly, Industry 4.0, which is being increasingly observed and adopted, aims towards automatisation, transparency, integrity (Ferrantino and Koten, 2019) and, consequently, risk minimisation of GFVCs. Blockchain is one of the emerging technologies being used to address GVC risks. Blockchain is a distributed ledger technology allowing multiple stakeholders in various locations to access and maintain copies of the same information (Chen, 2018). The technology can transform the value chains, through recording and safeguarding all transactions along every node in the chain, from the production of a product to its distribution and point of sale, such that every stakeholder in the supply chain can track the source, production progress and location of products, and share information within the system (Patel et al., 2017). Blockchain technology benefits risk management in value chains by creating a safer, and more transparent and efficient value chain (Litke et al., 2019; Queiroz and Fosso Wamba, 2019; Takahashi, 2017). For further significant impacts on GFVCs, blockchain could be integrated with other innovative technologies, such as the internet of things (IoT) (Kim et al., 2018) and big data analytics, including machine learning and predictive learning (Tijan et al., 2019).

Much literature has focused on supply chain/value chain risk management, such as risk identification and mitigation strategies (e.g. Prakash et al., 2017; Rathore et al., 2017; Saritas and Kuzminov, 2017). On the other hand, a few studies have strived to link blockchain and its impacts to various aspects of the supply chain, such as meeting supply chain management objectives, in terms of quality, cost, speed, flexibility, and sustainability (Kshetri, 2018); establishing supply chain provenance (Montecchi et al., 2019); enabling authenticity, trust, security and efficiency (Wang et al., 2019); streamlining logistics activities (Tijan et al., 2019); and enhancing supply chain resilience (Min, 2019). However, there has been a lack of studies addressing the role of advanced technologies, in particular blockchain, in GFVC risk management. Therefore, this study aimed to fill this gap and become the first to investigate how blockchain and its allied technologies, such as IoT and big data analytics (including machine learning and predictive analytics), will address the risks presented in the GFVC.

This chapter first explores the risks in the GFVC, then provides a brief review of blockchain before analysing its main characteristics and impacts on value chains. Finally, the chapter discusses how blockchain and its allied technologies contribute to risk management in the GFVC.

7.2 Literature review

7.2.1 Risks in the GFVC

Risk is defined as the "variation in the distribution of possible outcomes, their likelihoods, and their subjective values" (March and Shapira, 1987, p. 1404). The extent of deviation from the planned and expected measure is considered as the severity of risk. The larger the deviation, the larger its impact on business. The presence of risk in one entity affects both the downstream and upstream entities of the GFVC, as they are dependent on each other. *Risk management* in the value chain context has been defined as

> the identification, assessment, treatment, and monitoring of supply chain risks, with the aid of the internal implementation of tools, techniques and strategies and of external coordination and collaboration with supply chain members so as to reduce vulnerability and ensure continuity coupled with profitability, leading to competitive advantage.
>
> *(Fan and Stevenson, 2018, p. 7)*

The literature on risk management in the global food supply chain has evolved over the years, due to its impact on society and natural resources (Gold et al., 2017; Mol and Oosterveer, 2015; Saritas and Kuzminov, 2017). The process of risk management starts with (i) identification of risks across all stages of the value chain; (ii) analysis of risks to understand the scope of addressing these risks and their links to different factors; (iii) prioritisation of risks to rank the identified risks according to the severity of their impacts; (iv) treatment of risks with a holistic approach to addressing the prioritised risks; and, finally, (v) monitoring and undertaking a periodic review of risks to assess future consequences and take remedial actions (Keramydas et al., 2010). As a first step towards addressing GFVC risks, the existing literature is reviewed.

7.2.1.1 Supply risks

Supply risks arise as a result of the inability of an entity to supply the product due to capacity constraints (Lockamy and McCormack, 2010), inability of the supplier to meet the quality requirements stated by the buyers of local and export markets and government regulations, failure in supply of the stated quantity on time (Norrman and Jansson, 2004; Tummala and Schoenherr, 2011), lack of information transparency between the entities (Chopra and Sodhi, 2004; Wagner and Bode, 2014), supplier bankruptcy, production resulting in lower than expected yield, or combinations of these risk factors. The supply risk is not only associated with farmers but also applies to all entities in the GFVC. Delay or failure of supply from one entity impacts all the upstream and downstream entities, which not only results in fluctuation of supply to the market and price of the food product but also impacts the quality of the food product supplied to the market due to the perishable nature of food products (Prakash et al., 2017; Rathore et al., 2017). Additionally, with lack of transparency between entities, the retailers' demands are not known to farmers; in fact, farmers have no visibility of their produce after they sell the produce to the agent or wholesale market, resulting in an over-/undersupply of food products to the market. Further, this over-/underproduction and supply of food products results in huge product waste and fluctuation in the price of agricultural products (Singla and Sagar, 2012).

7.2.1.2 Demand risks

Demand risks are the result of fluctuations in the actual demand of the product. When the demand for a product is overforecasted or underforecasted than the actual demand, it is called demand risk. It severely affects the price and sale of the product (Rathore et al., 2017). Demand risk occurs due to sudden increases or decreases in demand that arise from the introduction of a new product to the market, changing customer preferences in the global market, migration of customers to different geographic locations and market competition (Diabat et al., 2012; Manuj and Mentzer, 2008; Wu et al., 2006). Demand risk is also associated with supply risk. Furthermore, errors in point-of-sale data (Wagner and Bode, 2011), lack of information about new market segments and negligence of important parameters in forecasting models cause demand risk (Chopra and Sodhi, 2004; Wu et al., 2006).

7.2.1.3 Storage and transport risks

The perishable nature of food products requires special arrangements, such as cold storage transport facilities, in order to reduce deterioration rates, maintain product freshness and quality, and, hence, reduce food wastage and revenue loss (Prakash et al., 2017). In addition, due to the globalisation of businesses with the presence of value chain entities across the globe, the storage and transportation of food products have become highly complex and create several risks. The risks associated with storage and transportation include food wastage (due to poor handling during packaging), loading and unloading of food products at multiple locations, unavailability of on-time transport vehicles in supplier locations, pilferage and holding excessive inventory (Rathore et al., 2017). In addition, inadequate capacity and facilities in warehouses and the lack of proper road facilities for interstate transport impact the value chain (Sahay and Mohan, 2003). Furthermore, vehicles used to transport food items long distances emit enormous amounts of greenhouse gases into the environment, contributing to environmental pollution and climate change (Soysal et al., 2014).

7.2.1.4 Environmental risks

Since the last decade, the number of climate-induced disasters has been increasing significantly. Climate change and natural disasters severely affect agricultural productivity and food security across the globe. Climate change is the alteration of the overall temperature and the normal weather pattern of a location or the whole planet for a prolonged period of time. Climate change is a result of the release of greenhouse gases into the environment from the burning of fossil fuels. Climate change poses an enormity of challenges to India's food security (Wheeler and Braun, 2013).

The agricultural sector absorbs 22 percent of economic losses due to the impact from climate change (FAO, 2015); for example, FAO (2015) estimated that the drought in sub-Saharan Africa between 2003 and 2013 resulted in crop and livestock production losses amounting to US$23.5 billion. Similarly, the 2008–2011 drought in Kenya resulted in a total loss of US$10.7 billion, particularly to the agriculture sector. Further, climate change has resulted in the reduction of average and seasonal rainfall, decreased groundwater levels, degradation of soil fertility, spread of pests/diseases and decreased agricultural productivity (Saritas and Kuzminov, 2017; Wang, 2013). All these impacts affect the earning potential of farmers and their ability to supply quality food products (Kumar, 2016). Further, with respect to other entities, natural disasters cause shutdowns of processing plants, closures of warehouses, cancellations of shipments and delayed deliveries (FAO, 2015).

7.2.1.5 Social risks

Social risk focuses on the impacts of human action on GFVC performance and outcome. Social risk includes labour strikes, lack of skill and efficiency of labour, increasing labour costs for agriculture work, lack of awareness among farmers, and theft or damage to facilities and livestock (Diabat et al., 2012; Leat and Revoredo-Giha, 2013; Prakash et al., 2017). The knowledge contribution and effort of employees are the main drivers for the success of a business enterprise. It is important, therefore, to identify the potential risk to the value chain from employees' actions (Clarkson, 1995; McWilliams and Siegel, 2000).

7.2.1.6 Health risks

Health risks focus on the impact of GFVC activities on human health. Due to several food quality and other social issues, consumers have started demanding transparency of information regarding the origin of food products and the inputs used throughout the food life cycles (Aung and Chang, 2014). It is, thus, important to identify the risk to human health associated with food products. The presence of microbiological hazards, such as salmonella and campylobacter bacteria, in food products results in food spoilage and, in some cases, food poisoning (Meikle, 1999; Phillips, 1995). Similarly, the use of fertilisers and pesticides during cultivation and chemicals and preservatives in the food industry that is beyond acceptable limits for food products causes ill effects on human health (Yeung and Morris, 2007). Food quality standards vary for each country and, hence, food products undergo numerous quality inspections when they are shipped to other countries (Yeung and Morris, 2007). These quality inspections can lead to ill effects on food products; for example, irradiation of food products results in the degradation of nutrients in food and, in the case of chicken, it has been found that the flavour and nutrient contents become altered after the irradiation process (IFST, 2015). In addition, if the irradiation process is not done thoroughly, microorganisms, such as bacteria, are left untreated, resulting in a drastic reduction of the shelf life of affected food products (FSAC, 1993).

7.2.1.7 Political/institutional risks

Political/institutional risks focus on risks associated with changing government policies and regulations, in terms of tax, imports/exports and food quality standards (Saritas and Kuzminov, 2017). The government's budget allocation and investment in research and development for the agricultural sector defines the GFVC's performance in a country (Diabat et al., 2012; Leat and Revoredo-Giha, 2013). Due to globalisation, food products are imported from countries where food and labour are available at a cheaper price. This affects the livelihood of local farmers, due to lower prices being assigned to their products (Saritas and Kuzminov, 2017). In addition, in developed countries, the quality requirements of retailers for exported products as well as for locally produced products are much higher than those for developing countries, resulting in large amounts of food wastage at the farmers' end (Devin and Richards, 2018).

7.2.1.8 Financial risks

With increasing international trade and dealings with multiple markets and currencies, the GFVC is facing several financial risks. Price fluctuation is one of the major risks for agricultural products (Singla and Sagar, 2012). With a lack of awareness and ineffective crop planning, farmers often grow the same products their neighbours grow, resulting in an oversupply of a particular product to the market and a sudden fall in the price of the product. Furthermore, with a lack of refrigerated storage facilities, farmers are not able to store food products in order to wait for prices to increase (Sudarevic et al., 2017). Similarly, fluctuating and overvalued currency exchange rates in domestic markets and the varying government tax policies, tariffs and sale costs on export markets limit the export of agricultural products (Berman et al., 2012). In addition, delays in the inflow of money from the sale of exported products pose financial constraints on exporters, which, in turn, affect the smooth flow of business (Chittenden and Bragg, 1997). Due to insufficient financial support and government loans, marginal farmers and small-scale exporters are borrowing money from third parties at higher interest rates. However, with small landholdings and high costs of agricultural inputs, it becomes difficult to repay the borrowings and, hence, the debt increases (Hernández, 2017). Furthermore, with a lack of financial support, small landholders are not able to adopt advanced technologies or hybrid agriculture inputs to improve their yield and revenue (Saritas and Kuzminov, 2017).

These risk factors are summarised in Table 7.1.

Thus, globalisation of the FVC has created the opportunity, even for small farmers in developing countries, to connect with the international market to sell their products. Irrespective of the growing period, food products are made available throughout the year by importing from other countries. While such opportunities have been created by extending local value chains to the global network, so many risks have been introduced, as a consequence, to the GFVC, as summarised in Table 7.1. In order to address some of the risks identified, the next section provides a review, from the literature, of blockchain and its allied technologies.

7.2.2 *Blockchain and allied technologies*

Blockchain is a distributed ledger (database) that records, secures and distributes transactions of physical goods, data, and financial services in a network, and all participants have access to the data (Chen, 2018). Blockchain works in a way that a copy (or partial copy) of the database is distributed to each stakeholder and the stakeholder may make alterations to the database according to accepted rules. The alterations made by different stakeholders are then gathered and stored in the database at a regular interval creating a bundled packet called a "block" (Mattila and Seppälä, 2015). Each block in a blockchain system stores a set of transactions recorded in the database over a given period. These blocks are mathematically chained (connected within a chain) through a hashing function, turned into an immutable record, then shared across the network (Laurence, 2017; Queiroz and Fosso Wamba, 2019; Seebacher and Schüritz, 2017).

7.2.2.1 The role of blockchain in transforming value chains

Recent literature has reported various benefits of blockchain to value chains. In particular, blockchain increases value chain *transparency* through shared visibility of information and transaction flows across the value chain (Min, 2019). In a blockchain system, all stakeholders can access and validate a transaction history, thus enabling transparency across the value chain. Transparency is also gained via increased assurances of product provenance, in terms of how products are produced, stored and delivered to consumers (Kim and Laskowski, 2018). Blockchain is also an effective tool for recording, tracking and tracing every single physical (e.g. products, containers) and digital asset (e.g. orders, barcodes, warranties, invoices) flowing through the value chain (Litke et al., 2019). This enables better cost-savings and faster and more accurate transactions across the chain, consequently contributing to improved *efficiency* of the chain. In addition, the technology provides a robust system for tracing the origin, certifying authenticity, tracking custody and verifying the integrity of products, which helps to ensure *security* and *integrity* across the value chain (Montecchi et al., 2019). Additionally, the impact of blockchain is that it contributes to building better communication and trust-based relationships among related stakeholders in the value chain (Barnard, 2017).

Given these benefits, blockchain is imperative for GFVCs which articulates a strong requirement for product provenance and traceability; for example, tracing the source and production

Table 7.1 List of risk factors for the global food supply chain

Risk category	Risk factor	Reference
Supply risk	Supplier's inability to supply	Prakash et al., 2017; Rathore
	Low quality of supply	et al., 2017
	Failure in reliability of the supplier	Prakash et al., 2017
	Communication failure	
	Supplier bankruptcy	Diabat et al., 2012
	Uncertainty of the yield levels	Singla and Sagar, 2012
Demand risk	Demand volatility	Rathore et al., 2017
	Forecasting error	
	Changing customer preferences	Diabat et al., 2012
	Migration of customers	Prakash et al., 2017
	Point-of-sale data error	
	Distortions in information sharing	
	Entering into new market segment	
Storage and transport risk	Inadequate storage capacity and facilities	Rathore et al., 2017; Saritas and Kuzminov, 2017
	Improper handling during loading and unloading	
	Poor packaging and preservation	
	In-transit loss	
	Unavailability of on-time vehicles	
	Storage of surplus inventory	Diabat et al., 2012
	Underutilised capacity	
Environmental risk	Spread of pests/diseases due to climate change	Leat and Revoredo-Giha, 2013; Singla and Sagar, 2012
	Increasing water pollution and water scarcity	Kumar, 2016; Saritas and Kuzminov, 2017; Wang, 2013
	Degradation of land and biodiversity	
	Land acquisition for landfilling and urbanisation	
	Overfertilisation of crops	
	Transportation emission	
	Natural disaster	Diabat et al., 2012; Singla and Sagar, 2012
Social risk	Malfunctioning in public distribution systems	Leat and Revoredo-Giha, 2013; Rathore et al., 2017
	Theft or risk from outside	
	Lack of skilled labourers	Diabat et al., 2012; Prakash et al., 2017; Rathore et al., 2017
	Labour strike	
	Labour efficiency	Singla and Sagar, 2012
	Lack of awareness among farmers	
	Increasing labour cost	Wang, 2013
Health risk	Development of microbiological hazards	Yeung and Morris, 2007
	Development of chemical hazards	
	Development of technological hazards	
	Growing population and changing food consumption patterns	Saritas and Kuzminov, 2017
	Malnutrition and limited accessibility to food	
	Spread of diseases, such as bird flu	Diabat et al., 2012
	Heavy metal contamination of food products	Cheraghi et al., 2013

(Continued)

Table 7.1 (Continued)

Risk category	Risk factor	Reference
Political/ institutional risk	Degradation of agriculture due to subsidised imports from other countries	Saritas and Kuzminov, 2017
	Lack of investment in research and development	
	Increasing political instability	Diabat et al., 2012; Leat and
	Strict and changing government regulations	Revoredo-Giha, 2013
Financial risk	Fluctuation in currency exchange rates	Sudarevic et al., 2017
	High tariffs and charges for exporting food products	
	Complexity in the inflow of money from sales on export markets	
	Fluctuation in the prices of output or inputs	Leat and Revoredo-Giha, 2013
	Price volatility	Singla and Sagar, 2012

processes of food and food ingredients are significant concerns for all stakeholders from different countries participating in GFVCs. Effective communication and information sharing, which can be facilitated through the implementation of blockchain, are central to the achievement of GVCs (Marcolin et al., 2016).

7.2.2.2 The integration of blockchain and its allied technologies in the value chain

To make full use of blockchain, the technology has to be integrated with other advanced technologies, such as the IoT and big data analytics, which are considered as the basis of the Industry 4.0 revolution (Tijan et al., 2019). Figure 7.1 shows the integration of blockchain with other technologies.

IoT refers to the integration between things (smart objects, i.e. machines and devices) with the internet to provide various services to users (Lee and Lee, 2015). Typical applications of IoT technology include radio frequency identification (RFID), sensing technologies and Global Positioning System (GPS) in logistics management. Blockchain potentially enhances IoT technology, such as managing and connecting IoT devices efficiently and reliably, and enhancing real-time tracking of products from their sources to final delivery (Tijan et al., 2019). On integration with IoT, blockchains create shareable, actionable and permanent records of products' footprints across the supply chain (Wang et al., 2019). Tian (2016) confirmed that integration of blockchain technology and RFID was advantageous, in terms of traceability through the collection and sharing of authentic and trusted data from every stage in the value chain, and guarantees food safety. IoT sensors can enable smart containers or trucks to recognise and report any transgressions to limits, such as temperature and light intensity, as well as other logistic details, which contribute to visibility across the value chain because all data are transmitted and updated onto the blockchain shared database as products move through facilities (Kim and Laskowski, 2018).

A *smart contract* can be considered as a core function of blockchain and is automatically generated by a blockchain system. It works similar to the traditional contract but is automated for self-establishing and self-verifying contractual agreements and obligations and the contract life cycle (ICERTIS, 2018). A smart contract can facilitate exchanges of money, shares, property, etc., in a transparent manner, while eliminating the role of the middleman (Blockgeeks, 2017).

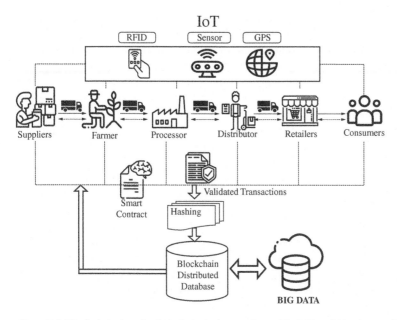

Figure 7.1 Blockchain-based value chain in integration with IoT and big data analytics. (Adapted from Rubio et al., 2018. Icons used in the figure were downloaded from www.flaticon.com.)

A smart contract, thereby, enhances the level of automation and streamlined processes within a supply chain, which is especially useful for complex supply chains with multiple outsourcing arrangements (Barnard, 2017); for example, once products are delivered and confirmed at the final point, an electronic notification triggers the smart contract in blockchain to execute payment for the products (Kim and Laskowski, 2018).

Big data analytics is based on knowledge extracted from the analyses of large volumes of data, using machine learning, predictive analytics and other analytical techniques, which facilitate better decision-making (Ivanov et al., 2019). Big data analytics can help improve supply chain risk management, such as disaster resistance (Papadopoulos et al., 2017). Big data analytics is also the basis for blockchain development (Tijan et al., 2019). In connection with big data analytics, the breadth of the blockchain system could be increased for added value by identifying patterns present in the large amounts of collected data, potentially offering a continuous monitoring and improvement tool for the entire supply chain (Corallo et al., 2018). Rubio et al. (2018) developed a new archetype for a supply chain based on the integration of blockchain with big data. The integration facilitates an integral collaboration between valuable data from the two technologies, which helps attain knowledge of the balance between demand and supply, thereby increasing the supply chain's efficiency and its response capacity to the market.

7.3 Blockchain and its allied technologies to address GFVC risks

As discussed in Section 7.2.1 and presented in Table 7.1, the FVC faces several risks across its stages. Also, as described in Section 7.2.2, the function and application of blockchain and its allied technologies could be applied to address the current risks in the GFVC. This relationship is further elaborated in this section.

Integration of blockchain and allied technologies could benefit the risk management of GFVCs, through improving transparency and visibility, information sharing, demand and supply balancing, and quick response to changes across the value chain (Litke et al., 2019; Queiroz and Fosso Wamba, 2019; Takahashi, 2017). In particular, the traceability mechanisms of blockchain can help manage risks of contamination or counterfeiting across the value chain (Chen, 2018; Toyoda et al., 2017); for example, for contaminated food and food products, blockchain allows identification of the contamination source and can enable a quick and targeted response, such as the strategic removal of tainted products, rather than the recall of the whole product chain (Yiannas, 2017). The case of Chipotle Mexican Grill outlets is an example of blockchain's importance in the GFVC. In 2015, the company suffered a food contamination crisis that resulted in the illness of 55 customers. This led to a loss in reputation and a significant drop in the share price. The problem was due to the lack of accountability and transparency throughout Chipotle's complex supply chain, by which the company could not monitor its multiple suppliers in real time.

There is also a clear implication of blockchain in related value constructs, such as reliable information sharing, cooperation and trust-based relationships between supply chain partners (Queiroz and Fosso Wamba, 2019), which helps safeguard international relationships. As a result, cooperation across the GFVC can prevent risks associated with value chain relationships, such as supply risks. Blockchain also facilitates the measurement of performance and outcomes of value chain activities; for example, it enables accurate measures of product quality in terms of storage conditions and transportation (Kshetri, 2018), thereby reducing related possible risks occurring across the value chain.

In addition, blockchain can mitigate risks associated with manipulations/interventions by intermediaries, such as hacking, loss of data, contractual disputes, instability of financial institutions, costly compliance with government regulations and vulnerability of political turmoil (Bettín-Díaz et al., 2018; Min, 2019). Blockchain-based solutions may help reduce the impact of value chain disruptions and/or increase flexibility for dealing with disruptions through, for example, considering buffering with additional safety stock and enhancing quick response capability to unexpected events, such as disasters or product recall (Min, 2019). In addition, the integrity and security of blockchain data also protects against cybercrime and fraud, which usually result in financial crimes, market manipulations and data breaches (Wang et al., 2019).

The interrelations between blockchain and its allied technologies and GFVC risks are further elaborated in Table 7.2.

Thus, the incorporation of blockchain and its allied technologies in the GFVC addresses most of the risks faced by entities of the GFVC, improving efficiency and ensuring smooth flow of operations.

Based on the preceding discussions, a framework (Figure 7.2) has been proposed that shows how GFVC risks can be addressed with the help of blockchain and its allied technologies.

7.4 Conclusions

Globalisation of the FVC has increased the number of entities involved in the food production process and, hence, increased complexity. Further, due to changing climatic conditions, customer preferences and government regulations, the GFVC faces several risks. In an effort towards addressing these risks, we have reviewed the existing academic literature on GFVC risks and identified the risks that presently exist across the stages of the GFVC. The identified risks are classified across multiple categories: demand risks, supply risks, storage and transport risks,

Table 7.2 Blockchain and allied technologies potential mitigation of GFVC risks

Risk category	Risk addressed	Blockchain's roles (in integration with other allied technologies)
Supply risk	• Supplier's inability to supply • Low quality of supply • Failure in reliability of the supplier • Communication failure • Uncertainty of the yield levels	• Increasing the transparency and visibility of product flow across the value chain ensures the traceability of product provenance from its origin, as well as inducing suppliers to be more responsible for their reliability and product quality. • Using *smart contracts* that self-execute and self-verify agreements and obligations, thus improving compliance between partners, eliminating contractual fraud and increasing the firm's confidence in their supply reliability. • Enabling reliable information sharing and cooperation between value chain partners and creating close partnerships and effective communication channels. • Providing visibility of production processes, thereby enabling quick modification in response to uncertainties, as well as improving the decision-making process. • Incorporating *sensing technologies* and predictive analytics to detect and predict uncertainties, such as climate changes, to avoid production-related risks.
Demand risk	• Demand volatility • Forecasting errors • Changing customer preferences • Point-of-sale data error • Entering new market segment • Distortions in information sharing	• Allowing customers to be aware of product origin and production, increasing their confidence in product safety and quality that promote their purchasing, ultimately leading to an increase in demand. • Integrating *big data* with machine learning enables timely and more accurate information about customer demands and preferences, resulting in more accurate decision-making processes and quick responses to demand uncertainties, as well as minimisation of forecasting errors. • Facilitating streamlined, auditable and immutable data exchange among value chain members. The security and integrity of blockchain data protects against unauthorised access, cybercrime and fraud, securing IT systems.

(Continued)

Table 7.2 (Continued)

Risk category	Risk addressed	Blockchain's roles (in integration with other allied technologies)
Storage and transportation risks	• Inadequate storage capacity and facilities • Improper handling during loading and unloading • Poor packaging and preservation • In-transit loss • Unavailability of on-time vehicles • Storage of surplus inventory • Underutilised capacity	• Integrating with *IoT devices*, such as RFID, and GPS and sensors, to create efficient and real-time traceability systems that allow tracking of shipment status and product custody (e.g. storage condition) during transportation. • Allowing the cascading of orders, invoices, receipts, shipment notifications and other related documents, as well as inventory data, throughout the value chain, thereby, streamlining payments, replenishment, and inventory control. • Enhancing reliable and effective information sharing and cooperation, which results in improved connectivity among different value chain nodes, from processing, warehousing, and distribution. This helps minimise loss/waste, errors, or delay in order fulfilment. • Allowing the automation of data analysis with the help of predictive analytics and artificial intelligence (e.g. demand forecasting, process optimisation) helps in demand forecasting and, hence, in avoiding excessive inventory and underutilisation of production capacity.
Environmental risk	• Spread of pests/diseases due to climate change • Increasing water pollution and scarcity • Overfertilisation of crops • Transportation emission • Natural disasters (earthquakes, volcanic eruptions, cyclones)	• Predictive analytics with real-time weather data (big data) helps in predicting natural disasters and shortens the recovery time. • Enabling more efficient production and logistics process (e.g. smart transportation, elimination of paper records) and product provenance, leading to the minimisation of environmental impacts due to, e.g., emissions from transportation and overfertilisation in agriculture. • Precision farming based on IoT devices helps in controlling the amount of inputs, such as fertiliser and water consumed for the cultivation of agricultural crops.
Social risk	• Malfunctioning in public distribution system • Theft or risk from outside • Lack of skilled labourers • Lack of awareness among farmers • Increasing labour cost	• Tracing every physical asset flowing through the value chain nodes, with the help of *IoT devices*, which helps in minimising theft and damage. • Creating open networks in the blockchain that involve every member in the value chain, including producers (farmers), and creating information and knowledge sharing across the chain, thereby, increasing farmers' awareness.

Table 7.2 (Continued)

Risk category	Risk addressed	Blockchain's roles (in integration with other allied technologies)
Health risk	• Hazards • Growing population and changing food consumption patterns • Spread of diseases, such as bird flu • Heavy metal contamination of food products	• Providing various mechanisms (IoT devices) to monitor and trace the product quality and safety reduces hazards or damages from agriculture. • Dynamic decision-making to decide the delivery location, based on deterioration rate of food product, with the help of IoT devices and artificial intelligence, reduces food waste and food-related diseases.
Political/ institu- tional risk	• Political instability • Government regulations • Changes in environment-related policies	• Involving multiple stakeholders, including government authorities, in the blockchain, with timely information sharing, improves compliance with government regulations and flexibility for dealing with unstable policies. • Due to product provenance and information shared along the value chain, all members are encouraged, or even enforced, to follow environmental-related acts and regulations.
Financial risk	• Changes in the prices of outputs or inputs • Price volatility • High tariffs and charges for exporting food products • Fluctuation in currency exchange rates	• Facilitating (globally) fast information and knowledge sharing (e.g. market price, quality standard) across the value chain, enabling the chain members to have awareness and enact quick responses to the changes in the global market. • With the aid of *big data* analysis, price volatility can be predicted beforehand and planned accordingly. • Increasing cross-border operations efficiency through the disintermediation in cross-border trade settlement.

Note: Consolidated from multiple sources.

environmental risks, social risks, health risks, political/institutional risks and financial risks. We have also discussed the use of blockchain and its allied technologies, such as IoT and big data analytics, in addressing the identified risks. Also, with the emerging GFVC, there is a chance for numerous other risks to arise, which have not been reviewed and addressed in this study. The use of big data and predictive analytics will, however, help to identify the uncertainty present in the market and contribute to wiser decision-making.

Despite the higher cost incurred in implementing technological solutions, the benefits from such integration are significant. Hence, considering the benefits, governments and private organisations must take initiatives to adopt blockchain-based technologies in the GFVC. This will not only improve the efficiency of operations but will also meet the food demand of growing populations. Also, further research should be focused on developing low-cost technological

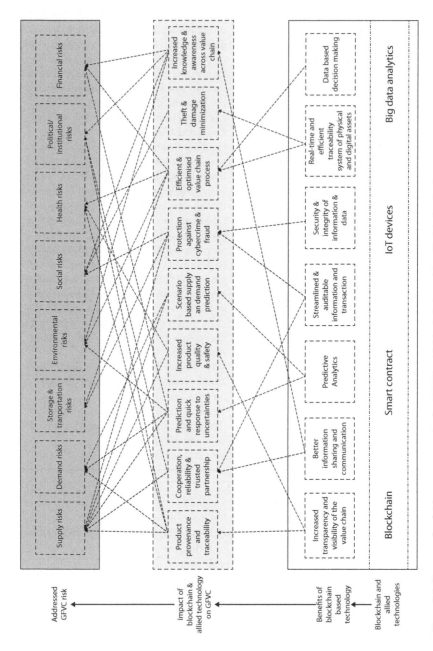

Figure 7.2 Framework of risk management in the GFVC with blockchain and its allied technologies.

solutions, such that small- and medium-scale farmers in developing countries will be able to adopt these technologies and improve their incomes.

References

Amorim, P., Meyr, H., Almeder, C., & Almada-Lobo, B., 2013. Managing perishability in production-distribution planning: A discussion and review. *Flex. Serv. Manuf. J.* 25, 389–413. https://doi.org/10.1007/s10696-011-9122-3

Aramyan, L., Ondersteijn, C. J., Van Kooten, O., & Lansink, A. O. 2006. Performance indicators in agri-food production chains. *Frontis*, 47–64.

Aung, M.M., & Chang, Y.S., 2014. Traceability in a food supply chain: Safety and quality perspectives. *Food Control* 39, 172–184. https://doi.org/10.1016/J.FOODCONT.2013.11.007

Barnard, B., 2017. Maersk, IBM digitalize global container supply chain. *JOC.com* [WWW Document]. JOC. URL https://www.joc.com/maritime-news/container-lines/maersk-line/maersk-ibm-digitalize-global-container-supply-chain_20170306.html (Accessed April 26, 2019).

Berman, N., Martin, P., & Mayer, T., 2012. How do different exporters react to exchange rate changes? *Q. J. Econ.* 127, 437–492. https://doi.org/10.1093/qje/qjr057

Bettín-Díaz, R., Rojas, A.E., & Mejía-Moncayo, C., 2018. *Methodological Approach to the Definition of a Blockchain System for the Food Industry Supply Chain Traceability*. Springer, Cham, pp. 19–33. https://doi.org/10.1007/978-3-319-95165-2_2

Blockgeeks, 2017. What are smart contracts? A beginner's guide to smart contracts [WWW Document]. *Blockgeeks*. URL https://blockgeeks.com/guides/smart-contracts/ (Accessed April 26, 2019).

Chen, Y., 2018. Blockchain tokens and the potential democratization of entrepreneurship and innovation. *Bus. Horiz.* 61, 567–575. https://doi.org/10.1016/J.BUSHOR.2018.03.006

Cheraghi, M., Lorestani, B., Merrikhpour, H., & Rouniasi, N., 2013. Heavy metal risk assessment for potatoes grown in overused phosphate-fertilized soils. *Environ. Monit. Assess.* 185, 1825–1831. https://doi.org/10.1007/s10661-012-2670-5

Chittenden, F., & Bragg, R., 1997. Trade credit, cash-flow and SMEs in the UK, Germany and France. *Int. Small Bus. J. Res. Entrep.* 16, 22–35. https://doi.org/10.1177/0266242697161002

Chopra, S., & Sodhi, M.S., 2004. Managing risk to avoid supply-chain breakdown. *MIT Sloan Manag. Rev.* 46, 53–61.

Clarkson, M.E., 1995. A stakeholder framework for analyzing and evaluating corporate social performance. *Acad. Manag. Rev.* 20, 92–117. https://doi.org/10.5465/amr.1995.9503271994

Corallo, A., Latino, M.E., & Menegoli, M., 2018. From industry 4.0 to agriculture 4.0: A framework to manage product data in agri-food supply chain for voluntary traceability. *Int. J. Nutr. Food Eng.* 12, 146–150. https://doi.org/10.1109/ieem.2014.7058728

Devin, B., & Richards, C., 2018. Food waste, power, and corporate social responsibility in the australian food supply chain. *J. Bus. Ethics* 150, 199–210. https://doi.org/10.1007/s10551-016-3181-z

Diabat, A., Govindan, K., & Panicker, V.V., 2012. Supply chain risk management and its mitigation in a food industry. *Int. J. Prod. Res.* 50, 3039–3050. https://doi.org/10.1080/00207543.2011.588619

Fan, Y., & Stevenson, M., 2018. A review of supply chain risk management: Definition, theory, and research agenda. *Int. J. Phys. Distrib. Logist. Manag.* 48, 205–230. https://doi.org/10.1108/IJPDLM-01-2017-0043

FAO, 2015. *Impact of Natural Hazards and Disasters on Agriculture and Food Security and Nutrition*, FAO report. United Nations.

Ferrantino, M.J., & Koten, E.E., 2019. *Understanding Supply Chain 4.0 and its Potential Impact on Global Value Chains*. Switzerland.

FSAC, 1993. Food safety questions and answers [WWW Document]. *Food Saf. Advis. Cent.* URL https://extension.psu.edu/food-safety-questions-and-answers (Accessed April 19, 2019).

Gereffi, G., & Fernandez-Stark, K., 2016. *Global Value Chain Analysis: A Primer*. Durham, NC.

Gold, S., Kunz, N., & Reiner, G., 2017. Sustainable global agrifood supply chains: Exploring the barriers. *J. Ind. Ecol.* 21, 249–260. https://doi.org/10.1111/jiec.12440

Hernández, E., 2017. Innovative Risk Management Strategies in Rural and Agriculture Finance - The Asian Experience. Food and Agriculture Organization of the United Nations (FAO), Rome. http://www.fao.org/3/a-i6940e.pdf

Hess, U., Richter, K., & Stoppa, A., 2002. Weather risk management for agriculture and agri-business in developing countries. Climate risk and the weather market, financial risk management with weather hedges.

ICERTIS, 2018. How blockchain and smart contracts will change contract management in 2018 [WWW Document]. *ICERTIS*. URL https://www.icertis.com/blog/blockchain-smart-contracts-will-change-contract-management-2018/ (Accessed April 26, 2019).

IFST, 2015. The use of irradiation for food quality and safety - information statement [WWW Document]. *IFST*. URL https://www.ifst.org/resources/information-statements/food-irradiation (Accessed April 19, 2019).

Ivanov, D., Dolgui, A., & Sokolov, B., 2019. The impact of digital technology and Industry 4.0 on the ripple effect and supply chain risk analytics. *Int. J. Prod. Res.* 57, 829–846. https://doi.org/10.1080/00207543.2018.1488086

Keramydas, C., Papapanagiotou, K., Vlachos, D., & Iakovou, E. 2015. Risk Management for Agri-food Supply Chains. *Supply chain management for sustainable food networks*, 255-292. https://doi.org/10.1002/9781118937495.ch10

Kim, H.M., & Laskowski, M., 2018. Toward an ontology-driven blockchain design for supply-chain provenance. *Intell. Syst. Accounting, Financ. Manag.* 25, 18–27. https://doi.org/10.1002/isaf.1424

Kim, M., Hilton, B., Burks, Z., & Reyes, J., 2018. Integrating blockchain, smart contract-tokens, and iot to design a food traceability solution. *2018 IEEE 9th Annual Information Technology, Electronics and Mobile Communication Conference (IEMCON). IEEE*, 335–340. https://doi.org/10.1109/IEMCON.2018.8615007

Kshetri, N., 2018. 1 Blockchain's roles in meeting key supply chain management objectives. *Int. J. Inf. Manage.* 39, 80–89. https://doi.org/10.1016/J.IJINFOMGT.2017.12.005

Kumar, M., 2016. Impact of climate change on crop yield and role of model for achieving food security. *Environ. Monit. Assess.* 188, 1-14. https://doi.org/10.1007/s10661-016-5472-3

Laurence, T., 2017. Blockchain for Dummies. John Wiley & Sons.

Leat, P., & Revoredo-Giha, C., 2013. Risk and resilience in agri-food supply chains: The case of the ASDA PorkLink supply chain in Scotland. *Supply Chain Manag.* 18, 219–231. https://doi.org/10.1108/135985 41311318845

Lee, I., & Lee, K., 2015. The Internet of Things (IoT): Applications, investments, and challenges for enterprises. *Bus. Horiz.* 58, 431–440. https://doi.org/10.1016/J.BUSHOR.2015.03.008

Litke, A., Anagnostopoulos, D., Varvarigou, T., Litke, A., Anagnostopoulos, D., & Varvarigou, T., 2019. Blockchains for supply chain management: Architectural elements and challenges towards a global scale deployment. *Logistics* 3, 5. https://doi.org/10.3390/logistics3010005

Lockamy, A., & McCormack, K., 2010. Analysing risks in supply networks to facilitate outsourcing decisions. *Int. J. Prod. Res.* 48, 593–611. https://doi.org/10.1080/00207540903175152

Manuj, I., & Mentzer, J.T., 2008. Global supply chain risk management. *J. Bus. Logist.* 29, 133–155. https://doi.org/10.1002/j.2158-1592.2008.tb00072.x

March, J.G., & Shapira, Z., 1987. Managerial perspectives on risk and risk taking, Management Science, 33, 1404–1418.

Marcolin, L., Miroudot, S., & Squicciarini, M., 2016. *GVCs, Jobs and Routine Content Of Occupations*. https://doi.org/10.1787/5jm0mq7kr6s8-en

Marucheck, A., Greis, N., Mena, C., & Cai, L., 2011. Product safety and security in the global supply chain : Issues, challenges and research opportunities, *J. Oper. Manag.* 29, 707–720. https://doi.org/10.1016/j.jom.2011.06.007

Mattila, J., & Seppälä, T., 2015. Blockchains as a Path to a Network of Systems: An Emerging New Trend of the Digital Platforms in Industry and Society. No. 45. ETLA Report, 2015

McWilliams, A., & Siegel, D., 2000. Corporate social responsibility and financial performance: Correlation or misspecification? *Strateg. Manag. J.* 21, 603–609. https://doi.org/10.1002/(SICI)1097-0266(200005)21:5<603::AID-SMJ101>3.0.CO;2-3

Meikle, J., 1999. Up to one in five chickens or turkeys contaminated. Food. *The Guardian*. Guard.

Min, H., 2019. Blockchain technology for enhancing supply chain resilience. *Bus. Horiz.* 62, 35–45. https://doi.org/10.1016/J.BUSHOR.2018.08.012

Mol, A.P.J., & Oosterveer, P., 2015. Certification of markets, markets of certificates: Tracing sustainability in global agro-food value chains. *Sustain.* 7, 12258–12278. https://doi.org/10.3390/su70912258

Montecchi, M., Plangger, K., & Etter, M., 2019. It's real, trust me! Establishing supply chain provenance using blockchain. *Bus. Horiz.* 62, 283–293. https://doi.org/10.1016/J.BUSHOR.2019.01.008

Norrman, A., & Jansson, U., 2004. Ericsson's proactive supply chain risk management approach after a serious sub-supplier accident. *Int. J. Phys. Distrib. Logist. Manag.* 34, 434–456. https://doi.org/10.1108/09600030410545463

OECD, 2019. Global value chains. *OECD.* https://www.oecd.org/sti/ind/global-value-chains.htm

Papadopoulos, T., Gunasekaran, A., Dubey, R., Altay, N., Childe, S.J., & Fosso-Wamba, S., 2017. The role of big data in explaining disaster resilience in supply chains for sustainability. *J. Clean. Prod.* 142, 1108–1118. https://doi.org/10.1016/J.JCLEPRO.2016.03.059

Patel, D., Bothra, J., & Patel, V., 2017. Blockchain exhumed. In 2017 ISEA Asia Security and Privacy (ISEASP). IEEE, pp. 1–12. https://doi.org/10.1109/ISEASP.2017.7976993

Pennings, J.M.E., Wansink, B., & Meulenberg, M.T.G., 2002. A note on modeling consumer reactions to a crisis: The case of the mad cow disease. *Int. J. Res. Mark.* 19, 91–100. https://doi.org/10.1016/S0167-8116(02)00050-2

Phillips, C.A., 1995. Incidence of Campylobacter and possible modes of transmission. *Nutr. Food Sci.* 95, 12–17. https://doi.org/10.1108/00346659510076503

Prakash, S., Soni, G., Rathore, A.P.S., & Singh, S., 2017. Risk analysis and mitigation for perishable food supply chain: a case of dairy industry. *Benchmarking* 24, 2–23. https://doi.org/10.1108/BIJ-07-2015-0070

Queiroz, M.M., & Fosso Wamba, S., 2019. Blockchain adoption challenges in supply chain: An empirical investigation of the main drivers in India and the USA. *Int. J. Inf. Manage.* 46, 70–82. https://doi.org/10.1016/J.IJINFOMGT.2018.11.021

Rathore, R., Thakkar, J.J., & Jha, J.K., 2017. A quantitative risk assessment methodology & evaluation of food supply chain. *Int. J. Logist. Manag.* 28, 1272–1293. https://doi.org/10.1108/IJLM-08-2016-0198

Rubio, M.A., Tarazona, G.M., & Contreras, L., 2018. Big data and blockchain basis for operating a new archetype of supply chain. *International Conference on Data Mining and Big Data. Springer, Cham.* 659–669. https://doi.org/10.1007/978-3-319-93803-5_62

Sahay, B.S., & Mohan, R., 2003. Supply chain management practices in Indian industry. *Int. J. Phys. Distrib. Logist. Manag.* 33, 582–606. https://doi.org/10.1108/09600030310499277

Saritas, O., & Kuzminov, I., 2017. Global challenges and trends in agriculture: impacts on Russia and possible strategies for adaptation. *Foresight* 19, 218–250. https://doi.org/10.1108/FS-09-2016-0045

Seebacher, S., & Schüritz, R., 2017. *Blockchain Technology as an Enabler of Service Systems: A Structured Literature Review.* Springer, Cham, pp. 12–23. https://doi.org/10.1007/978-3-319-56925-3_2

Siddh, M.M., Soni, G., Jain, R., Sharma, M.K., & Yadav, V., 2017. Agri-fresh food supply chain quality (AFSCQ): a literature review. *Ind. Manag. Data Syst.* 117, 2015–2044. https://doi.org/10.1108/IMDS-10-2016-0427

Singla, S., & Sagar, M., 2012. Integrated risk management in agriculture: An inductive research. *J. Risk Financ.* 13, 199–214. https://doi.org/10.1108/15265941211229235

Soysal, M., Bloemhof-Ruwaard, J.M., & Van Der Vorst, J.G.A.J., 2014. Modelling food logistics networks with emission considerations: The case of an international beef supply chain. *Int. J. Prod. Econ.* 152, 57–70. https://doi.org/10.1016/j.ijpe.2013.12.012

Sudarevic, T., Radojevic, P., Marjanovic, D., & Dragas, R., 2017. Marketing and financial barriers in agri-food exporting. *Br. Food J.* 119, 613–624. https://doi.org/10.1108/BFJ-05-2016-0183

Takahashi, R., 2017. How can creative industries benefit from blockchain? McKinsey [WWW Document]. McKinsey Co. URL https://www.mckinsey.com/industries/media-and-entertainment/our-insights/how-can-creative-industries-benefit-from-blockchain (Accessed April 26, 2019).

Tian, F., 2016. An agri-food supply chain traceability system for China based on RFID & blockchain technology. In 13th Int. Conf. Serv. Syst. Serv. Manag. ICSSSM. https://doi.org/10.1109/ICSSSM.2016.7538424

Tijan, E., Aksentijević, S., Ivanić, K., & Jardas, M., 2019. Blockchain Technology Implementation in Logistics. *Sustainability* 11, 1–13.

Toyoda, K., Mathiopoulos, P.T., Sasase, I., & Ohtsuki, T., 2017. A novel blockchain-based product ownership management system (poms) for anti-counterfeits in the post supply chain. *IEEE Access* 5, 17465–17477. https://doi.org/10.1109/ACCESS.2017.2720760

Tummala, R., & Schoenherr, T., 2011. Assessing and managing risks using the Supply Chain Risk Management Process (SCRMP). *Supply Chain Manag. An Int. J.* 16, 474–483. https://doi.org/10.1108/13598541111171165

Wagner, S.M., & Bode, C., 2011. An Empirical Examination of Supply Chain Performance Along Several Dimensions of Risk. *J. Bus. Logist.* 29, 307–325. https://doi.org/10.1002/j.2158-1592.2008.tb00081.x

Wagner, S.M., & Bode, C., 2014. Supplier relationship-specific investments and the role of safeguards for supplier innovation sharing. *J. Oper. Manag.* 32, 65–78. https://doi.org/10.1016/j.jom.2013.11.001

Wang, H.H., 2013. Agricultural risks and risk management in the current context of Chinese economy. *Agric. Financ. Rev.* 73, 245–254. https://doi.org/10.1108/AFR-01-2013-0003

Wang, Y., Singgih, M., Wang, J., & Rit, M., 2019. Making sense of blockchain technology: How will it transform supply chains? *Int. J. Prod. Econ.* 211, 221–236. https://doi.org/10.1016/J.IJPE.2019.02.002

Wheeler, T., & Braun, J. von, 2013. Climate change impacts on global food security. *Science* 341, 508–513. https://doi.org/10.1126/SCIENCE.1239402

Wu, T., Blackhurst, J., & Chidambaram, V., 2006. A model for inbound supply risk analysis. *Comput. Ind.* 57, 350–365. https://doi.org/10.1016/J.COMPIND.2005.11.001

Yeung, R.M.W., & Morris, J., 2007. Food safety risk: Consumer perception and purchase behaviour. *Br. Food J.* 103, 170–187. https://doi.org/10.1108/00070700110386728

Yiannas, F., 2017. A new era of food transparency with Wal-Mart center in China. [WWW Document]. *Food Saf. News.* URL https://www.foodsafetynews.com/2017/03/a-new-era-of-food-transparency-with-wal-mart-center-in-china/ (Accessed April 26, 2019).

8

TECHNOLOGICAL TRENDS AND FUTURE MANAGEMENT PRACTICES IN GLOBAL VALUE CHAINS

Renu Agarwal, Christopher Bajada, Mile Katic and Manjot Singh Bhatia[1]

8.1 Introduction

In today's environment, an organisation's position in the market is influenced by its decisions on where its specific business activities are conducted. These days, organisations are increasingly exposed to varying opportunities stemming from advancements in information and communication technologies that enable more effective globalised operations. Whether a business's activity is primarily undertaken domestically or overseas, the business is likely to be part of a global value chain (GVC) that involves a dispersed number of suppliers and production processes for goods and services taking place across multiple countries (Kano et al., 2020). Further, the structure of global value chains is affected by specific country policies, such as flexible labour markets, firm contractual arrangements, and better access to finance and export procedures, amongst many others (Criscuolo and Timmis, 2018). Additionally, goods, services, capital, people, technology and knowledge are easily transferrable across borders, including knowledge spillovers in emerging markets (Zhang et al., 2010). The question remains whether managing and undertaking activities such as global sourcing, global production and assembly or global distribution for development (Taglioni and Winkler, 2016) offer significant outcomes for both incumbents as well as new entrants, despite it not always being an easy path.

Supply chain management has long concerned itself with reducing the variation in delivery mechanisms and outputs, such that the occurrence of events that may impact the smooth running of supply chain operations can be prevented or effectively mitigated. Given the increasing reliance on outsourcing to retain competitiveness with other organisations by way of technology, competencies or networks, organisations can no longer ignore the implications of effective interfirm GVCs (Kano et al., 2020). Indeed, even smaller organisations operating in localised value chains can suffer catastrophic consequences from ineffective value chain operations.

DOI: 10.4324/9781315225661-12

Additionally, with COVID-19 we have seen how easily disrupted GVCs can become and hence the need for resilient value chains (Van Hoek, 2020; Linton and Vakil, 2020). Overseeing the value chain is therefore critical in ensuring minimal disruptions to both consumers and businesses (Gattorna and Ellis, 2020).

The COVID-19 crisis has caused major value chain disruptions, and these can be traced back to basic supply chain risks faced by GVCs (Van Hoek, 2020). To date, organisations can leverage effective use of tools to mitigate supply chain risks, including supply chain design, information systems and network integration mechanisms, each of which contribute to value-enhancing processes for the delivery of products or services (Kano et al., 2020). However, despite these resources, other issues may arise that are compounded by the very nature of GVCs, that is, an increased complexity associated with the vast distances travelled, foreign legislation and international market volatility (UNIDO, 2015; Gereffi, 2018). The challenges are fundamentally different, and whilst the concepts of supply chain integration, collaboration and alignment indeed apply, their application and definitions are also varied when it comes to managing GVCs. Additionally, there has not only been a rise in the material transfers of goods and services (both final and intermediate) but also the transfers of intangibles and immaterial assets between countries, and managing both aspects hinges on possessing management capabilities (De Backer et al., 2017). They require increased focus on exploratory mechanisms associated with finding innovative ways to adapt to changes within GVCs while at the same time retaining the capability to deliver on stringent customer demands associated with lower costs, improved delivery time and customised solutions (UNIDO, 2015). These outcomes hinge on organisations having the right capabilities reflected in best management practices.

In this chapter, we review the recent trends with management practices for GVCs. We investigate the megatrends in emerging technologies in GVCs and examine the implications these technologies have on the management practices necessary within organisations when operating globally. In Section 8.2 we look at the emerging trends and technologies in GVCs, and in Section 8.3 we discuss the appropriate management practices for better managing supply chain activities and propose a theoretical framework. In Section 8.4 we examine the implications for managers and organisations developing capabilities through these management practices. Finally, Section 8.5 provides concluding remarks.

8.2 Emerging trends and technologies in GVCs

Recently, many technologies have come into existence that could have a disruptive and substantial economic impact for organisations within a short time horizon. A few of the potential economically disruptive technologies are the internet of things, cloud technology, advanced robotics, 3D printing and blockchain technologies (Strange and Zucchella, 2017). According to the KPMG/Forbes Emerging Tech Risk survey (2017), the emerging technologies that organisations are most investing in include mobile applications and devices, the internet of things, cloud computing and artificial intelligence (Davenport et al., 2012). However, it is expected that over the next few years, blockchain, digital reality and cognitive automation will gain tremendous traction (Laplume et al., 2016). These technologies are already being adopted in several industries. Some of the technologies have been commercialised for years (e.g. cloud, mobile and social media), while others are relatively immature (e.g. internet of things, 3D printing, cognitive automation and blockchain), and have had an impact on GVC structures, especially on the basis for offering value (Nambisan et al., 2019). Furthermore, the pace at which these new technologies are introduced is accelerating and their adoption will ultimately reshape GVCs, both in the physical sense and in the data world, underpinned by digital sovereignty as the key relevant factor. We describe and discuss the impact of some of the latest technologies in the following.

8.2.1 Additive manufacturing

3D printing, also known as additive manufacturing, has been mostly used in very select applications in manufacturing. However, an increase in the range of materials, improvement in the performance of machinery used, and the decline in prices of materials and printers has resulted in rapid adoption of 3D printing by manufacturers and consumers. In 3D printing, an idea can go directly from a 3D design file to a finished part or product, potentially skipping many traditional manufacturing steps and processes. Furthermore, 3D printing helps in on-demand production, which translates to a number of implications in a supply chain. Implementation of 3D printing can result in a reduction of waste material during the manufacturing process as well as allowing for complex or sophisticated products to be manufactured where traditional manufacturing systems may fail. This will also impact the area of spare parts, which is one of the major costs for companies involved in manufacturing. Scientists have even "bioprinted" organs, using an inkjet printing technique to layer human stem cells along with supporting bioprinted scaffolding (Strange and Zucchella, 2017).

Though demonstrating considerable benefits for organisations operating in GVCs, including an increase in supply chain flexibility and ultimately company performance (Delic and Eyers, 2020; also see "Case study 1"), effective implementation often requires fundamentally changing business processes, such as the manner in which organisations manage and conduct collaborative efforts (Martens et al., 2020; Luomaranta and Martinsuo, 2019). We discuss some of these capabilities in the next section.

Case study 1

Under Armour, a company based in the US, manufactures apparel and footwear. It manufactures most of its products in low-cost countries such as Indonesia and China. Under Armour recently opened a new manufacturing and innovation facility. The facility has technological capabilities such as 3D printing and 3D design. (also known as additive manufacturing technologies). The firm has used such technologies for the manufacturing of Speedform running shoes. The effect of implementing such technologies is that the headcount needed for manufacturing has decreased from 150 to 30. The use of additive manufacturing/3D printing allows close integration in the manufacturing process through the use of innovation, use of new materials and shorter lead times. However, to successfully integrate these technologies, firms need to collaborate with others in redesigning and optimising the supply chain. Also, collaboration will help firms tackle the barriers to additive manufacturing such as cost and production speed. Looking at the benefits, Under Armour is now planning to implement additive manufacturing.

8.2.2 Blockchain technology

Blockchain technology is in the early stages of development. Over the next few years, blockchain technology is expected to disrupt manufacturing by redesigning inefficient manufacturing processes in supply chains and transforming business models. Today, most organisations spend a lot of time and expense in the management of GVCs, which include identification and selection of suppliers, negotiation and enforcement of agreements, tracking of products, and ensuring timely payments. Most of these processes are manual and require e-mails and phone calls. Blockchain has the potential to streamline these processes and operations as it allows information to be shared securely among disparate firms, without any intermediary (Deloitte, 2017). Through process integration, blockchain technology allows all parties in the supply chain to track the products during production and during distribution. Blockchain also supports smart contracts that automatically negotiate and execute agreements, which eliminate the manual processes by slowing the overall processing and increasing overall costs. Blockchain can also help in the improvement of planning by helping to gain real-time visibility of supply chains through process integration. Beyond increased efficiency, blockchain could also fuel the transition toward the democratisation of manufacturing – small production runs of customised products – made possible by 3D printing. Smart contracts on a blockchain network could automatically connect designers, manufacturers and buyers, and then execute the agreement. All participants can gain real-time visibility into the production process and delivery (see "Case study 2"). Risk practitioners across industries recognise blockchain's potential to help organisations manage risks posed by current systems.

However, organisations should understand that while blockchain may drive efficiency in business processes and mitigate certain existing risks, it poses new risks broadly classified under three categories: common risks, value transfer risks and smart contract risks. Blockchain's potential is disruptive. Three-quarters of respondents to a survey said they believe blockchain will be either very important or important to the future of their industry. With the technology's ability to streamline operations, 84 per cent of respondents expect annual cost savings of more than 2.5 per cent by applying blockchain in their organisation (UNIDO, 2013).

Case study 2

Cassava is a crop used for producing beer and is produced in Zambia. The firm BanQu has collaborated with another firm, Anheuser-Busch InBev. BanQu undertook a pilot study by implementing blockchain technology, which involved linking farmers producing Cassava to blockchain. It has helped small farmers to compete on a much larger scale, as blockchain helps to track the lifespan of crops. A similar project has also been implemented by the Chinese firm OriginTrail. The firm produces wine bottles and earlier found that these bottles are mixed with several additives that are harmful. It partnered with TagItSmart in a pilot study and tracked nearly 15,000 bottles of wine. The goal of the project was to use the capabilities of blockchain technology to end illegal wine. To know more details about the wine bottle, consumers scan the QR code on each bottle to extract all the details about the wine bottle. Implementing blockchain can help in the alignment of the supply chain, and this alignment aids to better integrate sourcing, services, etc. The alignment of supply chain members also helps them to achieve competitive advantage. Also, by integrating the processes, all supply chain members can see on another's internal processes, share records, etc., which makes the supply chain aligned to a common objective.

8.2.3 Cloud technology

The use of cloud technology creates a lot of value for businesses as well as customers as it makes the digital world efficient, simple, productive and fast. Firms can manage their IT systems in a flexible manner with the implementation of the cloud. The majority of computational work can be completed remotely and delivered online using the cloud-based resources. This reduces the storage requirements and processing power on devices. Thus, cloud technology can disrupt existing business models further paving the way for new methods which are more flexible, light and mobile. It is expected that by 2025, many firms will be using services offered by cloud technologies, and most IT applications and services will be cloud-enabled. Cloud technology can drive firms towards a better relationship with customers through customer relationship management and collaborative relationships. Through virtual integration, cloud technology provides a flexible and productive way for firms to manage IT systems, and mobile and asset-light business models (Manyika et al., 2013). Cloud technology also acts as a driver for many high-impact technologies such as, but not limited to, the internet of things and mobile internet (Strange and Zucchella, 2017).

Case study 3

One of the key differentiating factors of an airline is the level of service its provides to its customers. This depends to a large extent on the use and deployment of digitisation within its customer service processes. For example, American Airlines wanted to offer its customers digital services and remove any constraints on the current technological platform. American Airlines worked with IBM to migrate key customer applications to the IBM cloud and simultaneously transform these to cloud-based microservices. This has enabled American Airlines to innovate faster with regard to change in customer requirements, and hence deliver more customised and efficient services. This deployment of cloud services has resulted in improved productivity, reliability and decrease in customer response time, ultimately resulting in improved customer satisfaction. It has also helped American Airlines to realise significant savings in upgrading costs of the old technological platform.

8.2.4 Machine learning

With the advent of machine learning, computers can now undertake a lot of the work which would otherwise have been achieved through human effort. For instance, computers can act on "unstructured commands", answer questions put forth in simple language and even go as far as making some elementary judgements. Computers can further understand speech, intentions and actions of humans, and make interpretations. Machine learning also enables the creation of a relationship between worker and machine (Manyika et al., 2013). Therefore, managers can simply interact with computers and ask for any required information, which has the scope for getting more timely and accurate information and ultimately can result in fast and quality decision-making. Computers can also draw conclusions from patterns they recognise within large data sets. Further, computers need not rely on algorithms, which are provided to them. Rather, based on the data, they can adjust the algorithms that enable them to understand those relations which a manager might have overlooked. Moreover, these machines can "learn" more and get smarter as they go along; the more they process big data, the more refined their algorithms become.

Case study 4

The firm Object Computing has used machine learning techniques to help its clients diagnose crop diseases. Farmers have been spending a lot of money on managing crop diseases; however, it is important that they apply the right treatment. Without using the appropriate tools, farmers tend to apply solutions that are ineffective, harmful and have adverse environmental impact. The firm collaborated with a biochemical firm, which was further responsible for delivering recommendations to farmers around the world. The firm implemented the disease classification capabilities by using deep learning capabilities available in the Google machine learning engine. Farmers can take photographs of the crops with diseases, and then get an accurate diagnostic solution. Customer service improved significantly as Object Computing was able to provide precise recommendations to each farmer. In this way, farmers save both money and time through informed decision-making.

8.3 Supply chain management practices and global value chains

Supply chain management traditionally sought to unite the organisational functions of procurement, operations and distribution in an effort to explicitly take into consideration the roles of individuals and organisations both within and external to a particular organisation (Ellram and Cooper, 1990; Jones and Riley, 1985). This involves viewing the supply chain as a network of individuals and businesses that exchange products, services, finances and/or information towards some strategic objective (Mentzer et al., 2001). Indeed, this involved the integration of major business processes through interfunctional coordination and inter- and intrafirm cooperation towards improved customer service and cost savings (Mentzer et al., 2001). Thus, a commonly cited definition of supply chain management is (Mentzer et al., 2001)

> the systemic, strategic coordination of the traditional business functions and the tactics across these business functions within a particular company and across businesses within the supply chain, for the purposes of improving the long-term performance of the individual companies and the supply chain as a whole.

More recently, however, supply chain management has begun to view the entire supply chain from a systems perspective, taking in contributions from a variety of disciplines (including economics and strategic management) in order to better facilitate the challenges facing today's organisations (Ellram and Cooper, 2014; Halldórsson et al., 2015). Such challenges involve synchronising strategic and operational capabilities of the network towards creating value for the customer (Ellram and Cooper, 2014; Min and Mentzer, 2004) whilst keeping abreast of emerging technological trends that bring forth to the limelight productivity enhancements and information transparency.

Global value chains, defined as a "pattern of organisation of production involving international trade and investment flows whereby the different stages of the production process are located across different countries" (OECD/Eurostat, 2018, p. 246), are characterised by increased complexity stemming from the distributed nature of value-adding operations on a global stage. Apart from the pull of low-cost labour, participating in global value chains also offers eligible organisations the opportunity of acquiring new knowledge, capabilities and technologies that they otherwise may not have in the domestic market. In such circumstances, allowing organisations to expand their strategic repertoire towards lucrative capabilities in complementary (or new) industrial contexts further paves the way for value towards increased competitive advantage. However, there is also an opportunity to create (or extend) market share by undertaking global distribution activities through pushing existing competencies and products into new markets abroad.

We have come to recognise that despite the lucrative benefits of participating in global value chains, there are also significant challenges and barriers that can stunt globalisation efforts (Kano et al., 2020). Apart from the more visible challenges resulting from considerable distances in the global supply network, other challenges include country-level trade tariffs arrangements and other duties, international customs protocols, cultural peculiarities, and currency exchange rates. At the same time, megatrends stemming from both technology and customer-driven factors in relation to product performance and customisation, to name a few, also prove to be a daunting exercise for organisations to contend with. Thus, not only do organisations need to service the disparate needs of various customer groups in a cost effective and timely manner, there is an underlying need to do this at a global level whilst simultaneously creating and appropriating value in the process to retain viable operational and economic performance. In addition, organisations are not alone in this pursuit of global dominance either, that is, there are also competing GVCs. Thus, it is not enough to merely navigate through these challenges; organisations operating in GVCs must also be able to do this better than others.

To this end, in light of the material transfers of goods and services (both final and intermediate), the transfers of intangibles and immaterial assets between countries, as well as emerging technologies, we next discuss three fundamental capabilities organisations can leverage in order to effectively participate in GVCs, namely (1) global supply chain integration, (2) global supply chain alignment and (3) global supply chain collaboration (Subramani and Agarwal, 2013).

8.3.1 Global supply chain integration

Adams et al. (2014), citing Chen et al. (2009), describe supply chain integration as a set of activities that involve "restructuring firm processes to better distribute, align, and utilize both internal and external resources" (p. 302). In general, this involves integrating knowledge and information flows between both customer and supplier networks as well as those internal to the firm itself (Schoenherr and Swink, 2012). Greater integration between GVC participants is said to improve problem-solving capabilities, sensing new opportunities for growth and operational productivity (Flynn et al., 2010; Schoenherr and Swink, 2012). Process integration can help firms in the standardisation of tasks (Deloitte, 2017) as well as tracking of products during production and delivery (Cognizant, 2017). Similarly, virtual integration allows firms to do the work remotely, thereby reducing the storage and processing requirements. However, increased supply chain integration capabilities can also induce rigidities as interdependencies between GVC participants strengthen (Sorenson, 2003), thus undermining the opportunities supply chain integration fosters in the first place. For GVCs, this means carefully balancing the degree of integration amongst customers and suppliers (Das et al., 2006) whilst maintaining strong internal integration capabilities (Schoenherr and Swink, 2012) that can help facilitate the dynamic reconfiguration of resources and processes required to leverage external knowledge and information. Such reconfiguration efforts rely on inter-/intrafirm connectivity and the simplification of business processes (Chen et al., 2009).

8.3.2 Global supply chain alignment

Strategic alignment has long been considered a major driver for both operational (Swink et al., 2005) and supply chain (Ralston et al., 2015) competitive excellence. Alignment, in the case of supply chains, typically refers to achieving a strategic fit with regard to "objectives, structures and processes within and between different functions and members in a supply chain" (Wong et al., 2012). For the case of both domestic and global supply chains, this poses a significant challenge given the almost inevitable variation in strategic imperatives amongst supply chain participants (e.g. commoditised parts supply vs. specialised engineered-to-order products). For this reason, there is a general consensus amongst authors that the characteristics of each so-called logic that guides capability investments in partner organisations should be extracted so that appropriate alignment mechanisms can be adopted to suit. In this case, other, more generic mechanisms can include performance management by virtue of performance indicators and incentive systems (Selviaridis and Spring, 2018); development of informal relationships (Shub and Stonebraker, 2009); and business process management (McAdam and McCormack, 2001), for example, value-based management (UNIDO, 2013) and collaborative relationships (Deloitte, 2017; c.f. Skipworth et al., 2015). To participate in the global exchange of knowledge, goods and services are no longer merely an operational concern. Organisations are increasingly seeking new competencies abroad and, counter to what strategy literature once condemned, are now beginning to outsource key strategic capabilities. As von Delft et al. (2019) mention, this then requires close integration with an organisation's business model – moving value chain members from arms-length transaction-style relationships to those that require careful alignment with the core logic that underpins the very existence of organisations.

8.3.3 Global supply chain collaboration

Collaboration is defined here as "the ability to work across organizational boundaries to build and manage unique value-added processes to better meet customer needs" (Fawcett et al., 2008). According to Fawcett et al. (2008), this involves "the sharing of resources –information, people, and technology – among supply chain members to create synergies for competitive advantage" (p. 93). It is thus conceptually distinct from supply chain integration and alignment as a higher-order capability that enables firm-level longevity through the effective reconfiguration of a firms' resource pool. Organisations need to maintain collaborative relationships among themselves to achieve the desired objectives. In such situations, information sharing plays a very crucial role as it can result in increased coordination, product tracking, etc. (Strange and Zucchella, 2017). However, the desired results do depend on information quality. As a capability, then, supply chain collaboration ensures the right alignment and integration practices are undertaken at the right time towards leveraging the knowledge, technology and processes of the GVC network of which the organisation forms a part. Indeed, such a capability, though hailed for its potentially lucrative benefits in bolstering innovation (Jimenez-Jimenez et al., 2019), productivity (Soosay et al., 2008) and sustainable competitive advantage (Cao and Zhang, 2011) – particularly when both customers and suppliers are involved (Vereecke and Muylle, 2006), and when internationalisation is key (Chavan and Agarwal, 2016) – involves much more than leveraging external competencies and resources.

From a configurational perspective, supply chain alignment and supply chain integration capabilities present themselves as key antecedents of supply chain collaborative capability (Cao et al., 2010). However, both "lower level" capabilities depend on the willingness of participants to share sensitive information and the focal firm's ability in effectively disseminating this information towards appropriating value for both its own customers and the fellow members of the GVC. Indeed, cultural, financial, political and legal peculiarities between the many cultures involved in a GVC further complicate the issue. As illustrated in Figure 8.1 and in the context of GVCs, these three primary components of supply chain collaborative capabilities (Cao et al., 2010) (nested in strategic alignment and integration capabilities) appear additive in their adoption by organisations. For instance, collaborative communication can facilitate the cultural alignment amongst GVC participants towards greater information-sharing capabilities – both of which provide for the necessary context in order for effective knowledge creation and diffusion amongst organisations. In

Figure 8.1 The role of emerging technologies and management practices in shaping GVCs.

addition, emerging information technologies have become a key enabler of supply chain collaboration (Agarwal et al., 2014), allowing for greater connectivity amongst GVC participants and thus improved capabilities in disseminating and analysing information (Fawcett et al., 2011) (some of which were discussed earlier). However, as Jimenez-Jimenez et al. (2019) demonstrate, the impact of IT on supply chain performance is governed by the capabilities in the focal organisation regarding information sharing, collaborative communication and joint knowledge creation – demonstrating the role of management practices in facilitating effective technology adoption in GVCs.

The same can also be said for the operational management practices an organisation is adopting. As the outcomes of some large-scale studies on so-called structured management practices would suggest, the effective implementation of routine operational practices, including from a wider organisational context, for instance, the adoption of key performance indicators and human resource management practices, is a key determinant of performance (Bloom et al., 2012; Agarwal et al., 2013; Agarwal et al., 2014). Equally, they impact the performance of value chains themselves (Beske-Janssen et al., 2015; Taticchi et al., 2013). A key learning from such studies includes the complementary nature of management practice adoption (Bloom and Van Reenen, 2007), thus the more an organisation adopts, the better its performance will be and the significant role it plays in achieving competitive parity in an increasingly dynamic and turbulent market environment over the long term (Bloom et al., 2018). Though these practices are proven to be an important ingredient in organisational performance, the adoption of practices leaves much to be desired. We discuss the implication of this next.

8.4 Implications for managers and management practices

There are several implications for managers and businesses with regard to emerging technologies. Since many of the technologies discussed here are new and emerging, it is hard to find people with relevant skills and capabilities who can work well with all these technologies across GVCs whilst ensuring maximised benefits are attained (Grundke et al., 2017). Furthermore, as production is internationally fragmented (De Backer and Miroudot, 2013), best management practices for GVCs lack prominence and require consolidation, and the use cases of these emerging technologies are nearly non-existent (Kano et al., 2020). The firms that want to make use of these emerging technologies to drive innovation practices would need to provide an environment where people are encouraged to experiment; failing is a source of learning and experimental boundaries are tested (De Backer et al., 2017).

In the case of additive manufacturing, there are many advantages when it comes to society and business. Firstly, products made using the additive manufacturing result in less waste, do not need to be transported and are consistent with a more sustainable environmental agenda (Manyika et al., 2013). From an organisational perspective, product designers can make use of 3D printing and quickly reach a large number of customers (Shipp et al., 2012). The use of 3D printing may further see a shift in the share of sales of products such as toys, accessories used in local production or dedicated 3D printing centres. There are certain regulatory challenges that should be considered from a policy perspective as well, including the approval of new materials for use, assigning legal liability related to issues and safeguarding intellectual property protections.

With blockchain technology, managers need to take a strategic view about the problems that it can address. To gain insights on the potential applications of this technology, gain relevant experience and for mutual benefit, managers need to collaborate and partner with external organisations (Sati, 2018). Further, organisations also need to decide the platform to be adopted for the implementation of blockchain technology (public or private platform). In this regard, managers will be required to choose the platform which is best suited for each use case, further taking into account the requirement of speed, security, privacy and functionality. Managers should further recognise that benefits of this technology are visible in the long run and require a cultural change in organisations (Kshetri, 2018).

Finally, the internet of things is going to challenge the ways businesses work due to the level of innovation and technical skills that are required (Nambisan et al., 2019). The benefits that can be obtained using the internet of things will not be easy to obtain for managers due to the high initial costs of hardware required for appropriate implementation (communication tags, RFID devices, etc.). Partnerships will be required among companies with capabilities in sensors and manufacturers of the machines and products. Business leaders will also need to identify employee functions that could be performed more efficiently or more effectively on a mobile platform. They will need to consider how performance could be enhanced by enabling increased mobility, augmenting worker knowledge and capabilities, or facilitating collaboration and social interaction.

Whilst clearly demonstrating novel opportunities for organisations, the adoption of these technologies is not always a matter of technical implementation. As mentioned, the majority of these technologies require effective collaboration and integration practices amongst GVC members, and internally within the firm, in order to be leveraged by organisations. Such practices rely on lower-level operational activities that (1) aid in the collaborative efforts of GVC members (Beske-Janssen et al., 2015; Taticchi et al., 2013) and (2) facilitate firm-level innovation capabilities necessary to promote effective change (Agarwal et al., 2014). Such activities often include risk management and performance management to promote effective collaborative efforts, human resource management to equip people with the necessary skills and environment to perform, and data-driven decision-making for effective capability investments. Though, as is demonstrated in "Case study 5", the adoption of these management practices remain insufficient. Thus, prior to implementing any of these emerging technologies, organisations would benefit from a stable foundation of structured management practices that lay the groundwork for effective capability investments, not least global performance.

Case study 5

Figure 8.2 illustrates the Australian experience of supply chain–related management practices. Each of these practices in the figure are scored on a 0 to 1 scale, where 1 represents the maximum score on a specific dimension of management practice. Firms score highest on risk management practices and lowest on data decision-making management practices. Overall the scores on each dimension are quite low, suggesting that although Australian firms have a significant dependence on their supply chains, the management practices reflect the relatively little emphasis that firms place on quality supply chain activities. More emphasis is placed on risk mitigation than on people, quality and

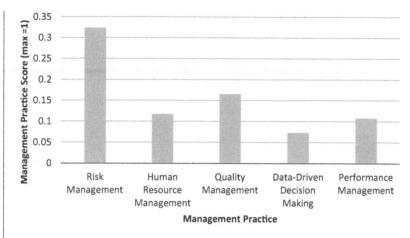

Figure 8.2 Management practices of supply chain activities.

performance management. The use of data in decision-making scored the lowest suggesting that informed decisions based on the use of data is not a common practice amongst Australian firms.

8.5 Conclusion

The global value chain revolution requires fresh thinking in light of emerging megatrends. Twentieth-century paradigms are insufficient when applied to twenty-first century challenges. The megatrends in global value chains is pivoted upon emerging technology trends and on the efficacy and effectiveness of best management practices deployed to manage a global economy which produces and exchanges goods in a way that has never been more dynamic or more interconnected. With increased risks due to disruption of global supply chains as evident from the unprecedented challenges of COVID-19, fragmentation of production internationally, lack of integration of end-to-end processes, shortage of skills, and emerging technologies providing better technological collaborative platforms for operations of global value chains, better management capabilities, practices and processes are paramount. In an attempt to reshape future global value chains, firms, which are global or are looking for internationalisation, must deploy emerging technologies, coupled with best management practices of collaboration, integration and alignment, as well as personnel practices (Zhang et al., 2010), to drive innovative outcomes.

Note

1 All authors contributed equally.

References

Adams, F. G., Richey JR, R. G., Autry, C. W., Morgan, T. R. & Gabler, C. B. 2014. Supply chain collaboration, integration, and relational technology: How complex operant resources increase performance outcomes. *Journal of Business Logistics*, 35, 299–317.

Agarwal, R., Brown, P. J., Green, R., Randhawa, K. & Tan, H. 2014. Management practices of Australian manufacturing firms: Why are some firms more innovative? *International Journal of Production Research*, 52, 6496–6517.

Agarwal, R., Green, R., Tan, H., Randhawa, K. & Brown, P. 2013. Determinants of quality management practices: An empirical study of New Zealand manufacturing firms. *International Journal of Production Economics*, 142, 1, 130–145.

Beske-Janssen, P., Johnson, M. P. & Schaltegger, S. 2015. 20 years of performance measurement in sustainable supply chain management–what has been achieved? *Supply Chain Management: An International Journal*, 20, 664–680.

Bloom, N., Genakos, C., Sadun, R. & Van Reenen, J. 2012. Management practices across firms and countries. *The Academy of Management Perspectives*, 26, 12–33.

Bloom, N., Mahajan, A., Mckenzie, D. & Roberts, J. 2018. Do management interventions last? Evidence from India. *American Economic Journal: Applied Economics*, 2, 2, 198–219. See https://www.aeaweb.org/articles?id=10.1257/app.20180369

Bloom, N. & Van Reenen, J. 2007. Measuring and Explaining Management Practices Across Firms and Countries. *The Quarterly Journal of Economics,* 122, 4, 1351–1408. https://doi.org/10.1162/qjec.2007.122.4.1351

Cao, M., Vonderembse, M. A., Zhang, Q. & Ragu-Nathan, T. 2010. Supply chain collaboration: Conceptualisation and instrument development. *International Journal of Production Research*, 48, 6613–6635.

Cao, M. & Zhang, Q. 2011. Supply chain collaboration: Impact on collaborative advantage and firm performance. *Journal of Operations Management*, 29, 163–180.

Chavan, M. & Agarwal, R. 2016. The efficacy of linkages for relational capability building and internationalization - Indian and Australian mining firms. *International Journal of Business and Economics*, 15, 1, 51–78.

Chen, H., Daugherty, P. J. & Roath, A. S. 2009. Defining and operationalizing supply chain process integration. *Journal of Business Logistics*, 30, 63–84.

Cognizant. 2017. *Blockchain in Manufacturing: Enhancing Trust, Cutting Costs and Lubricating Processes Across the Value Chain*. Digital System and Technology Report, November 2017.

Criscuolo, C. & Timmis, J. 2018. *GVC Centrality and Productivity: Are Hubs Key to Firm Performance?* OECD Productivity Working Papers, 2018–14, OECD Publishing, Paris.

Das, A., Narasimhan, R. & Talluri, S. 2006. Supplier integration—finding an optimal configuration. *Journal of Operations Management*, 24, 563–582.

Davenport, T. H., Barth, P. & Bean, R. 2012. How big data is different. *MIT Sloan Management Review*, 54, 1, 43–46.

De Backer, K., Destefano, T. & Moussiegt, L. 2017. The links between global value chains and global innovation networks – An exploration. OECD Science, Technology and Innovation Policy Papers April 2017 No. 37.

De Backer, K. & Miroudot, K. 2013. *Mapping Global Value Chains*. OECD Trade Policy Papers, No. 159, OECD Publishing, Paris. doi:10.1787/5k3v1trgnbr4-en

Delic, M. & Eyers, D. R. 2020. The effect of additive manufacturing adoption on supply chain flexibility and performance: An empirical analysis from the automotive industry. *International Journal of Production Economics*, 228, 107689.

Deloitte. 2017. *Beyond the Noise: The Megatrends of Tomorrow's World*. Deloitte Consulting Group, July 2017.

Ellram, L. M. & Cooper, M. C. 1990. Supply chain management, partnership, and the shipper-third party relationship. *The International Journal of Logistics Management*, 1, 1–10.

Ellram, L. M. & Cooper, M. C. 2014. Supply chain management: It's all about the journey, not the destination. *Journal of Supply Chain Management*, 50, 8–20.

Fawcett, S. E., Magnan, G. M. & Mccarter, M. W. 2008. A three-stage implementation model for supply chain collaboration. *Journal of Business Logistics*, 29, 93–112.

Fawcett, S. E., Wallin, C., Allred, C., Fawcett, A. M. & Magnan, G. M. 2011. Information technology as an enabler of supply chain collaboration: a dynamic-capabilities perspective. *Journal of Supply Chain Management*, 47, 38–59.

Flynn, B. B., Huo, B. & Zhao, X. 2010. The impact of supply chain integration on performance: A contingency and configuration approach. *Journal of Operations Management*, 28, 58–71.

Gattorna, J. & Ellis, D. 2020. *Transforming Supply Chains - Realign Your Business to Better Serve Customers in a Disruptive World*. Pearson EducationHarlow, UK.

Gereffi, G. 2018. *Global Value Chains and Development – Redefining the contours of 21st Century Capitalism*. University Printing House, Cambridge, UK.

Grundke, R., Jamet, S., Kalamova, M., Keslair, F. & Squiccariani, M. 2017. Skills and value chains: A characterisation. OECD Science, Technology and Industry Working Papers 2017/05. Available at: https ://www.oecd-ilibrary.org/docserver/cdb5de9b-en.pdf?expires=1595472522&id=id&accname=guest &checksum=5291DDAC6CFB4E9F522B0DDC8AAEE7D3

Halldórsson, Á., Hsuan, J. & Kotzab, H. 2015. Complementary theories to supply chain management revisited–from borrowing theories to theorizing. *Supply Chain Management: An International Journal*, 20, 574–586.

Jimenez-Jimenez, D., Martínez-Costa, M. & Sanchez Rodriguez, C. 2019. The mediating role of supply chain collaboration on the relationship between information technology and innovation. *Journal of Knowledge Management*, 23, 548–567.

Jones, T. C. & Riley, D. W. 1985. Using inventory for competitive advantage through supply chain management. *International Journal of Physical Distribution & Materials Management*, 15, 16–26.

Kano, L., Tsang, E. W. K. & Yeung, H. W. 2020. Global value chains: A review of the multidisciplinary literature. *Journal of International Business Studies*, 51, 577–622.

Kshetri, N. 2018. 1 Blockchain's roles in meeting key supply chain management objectives. *International Journal of Information Management*, 39, 80–89.

Laplume, A. O., Peterson, B. & Pearce, J. M. 2016. Global value chains from a 3D printing perspective. *Journal of International Business Studies*, 47, 5, 595–609.

Linton, T. & Vakil, B. 2020. Coronavirus is proving we need more resilient supply chains. *Harvard Business Review*. Available at: https://hbr.org/2020/03/coronavirus-isproving-that-we-need-more-resilient-s upply-chains#comment-section

Luomaranta, T. & Martinsuo, M. 2019. Supply chain innovations for additive manufacturing. *International Journal of Physical Distribution & Logistics Management*, 50, 1, 54–79. https://doi.org/10.1108/IJPDLM -10-2018-0337

Manyika, J., Chui, M., Bughin, J., Dobbs, R., Bisson, P., & Marrs, A. (2013). *Disruptive Technologies: Advances that Will Transform Life, Business, and the Global Economy* (Vol. 180). McKinsey Global Institute, San Francisco, CA.

Martens, R., Fan, S. K. & Dwyer, R. J. 2020. Successful approaches for implementing additive manufacturing. *World Journal of Entrepreneurship, Management and Sustainable Development*, 16, 2, 131–148. https://do i.org/10.1108/WJEMSD-12-2019-0100

Mcadam, R. & Mccormack, D. 2001. Integrating business processes for global alignment and supply chain management. *Business Process Management Journal*, 7, 113–130.

Mentzer, J. T., Dewitt, W., Keebler, J. S., Min, S., Nix, N. W., Smith, C. D. & Zacharia, Z. G. 2001. Defining supply chain management. *Journal of Business Logistics*, 22, 1–25.

Min, S. & Mentzer, J. T. 2004. Developing and measuring supply chain management concepts. *Journal of Business Logistics*, 25, 63–99.

Nambisan, S., Zahra, A. & Luo, Y. 2019. Global platforms and ecosystems: Implications for international business theories. *Journal of International Business Studies*, 50, 9, 1464–1486.

OECD/EUROSTAT. 2018. *Oslo Manual 2018: Guidelines for Collecting, Reporting and Using Data on Innovation* (4th ed.) The Measurement of Scientific, Technological and Innovation Activities, OECD Publishing, Paris/Eurostat, Luxembourg, https://doi.org/10.1787/9789264304604-en

Ralston, P. M., Blackhurst, J., Cantor, D. E. & Crum, M. R. 2015. A structure–conduct–performance perspective of how strategic supply chain integration affects firm performance. *Journal of Supply Chain Management*, 51, 47–64.

Sati, M. 2018. Deloitte Insights Tech Trends 2018. Available at: https://www2.deloitte.com/content/dam/ insights/us/articles/Tech-Trends-2018/4109_TechTrends-2018_FINAL.pdf

Schoenherr, T. & Swink, M. 2012. Revisiting the arcs of integration: Cross-validations and extensions. *Journal of Operations Management*, 30, 99–115.

Selviaridis, K. & Spring, M. 2018. Supply chain alignment as process: Contracting, learning and pay-for-performance. *International Journal of Operations & Production Management*, 38, 732–755.

Shipp, S. S., Gupta, N., Lal, B., Scott, J. A., Weber, C. L., Finnin, M. S. & Thomas, S. 2012. *Emerging global trends in advanced manufacturing*. Institute for Defence Analysis, Alexandria, VA.

Shub, A. N. & Stonebraker, P. W. 2009. The human impact on supply chains: Evaluating the importance of "soft" areas on integration and performance. *Supply Chain Management: An International Journal*, 14, 31–40.

Skipworth, H., Godsell, J., Wong, C.Y., Saghiri, S. & Julien, D. 2015. Supply chain alignment for improved business performance: An empirical study. *Supply Chain Management: An International Journal*, 20, 511–533.

Soosay, C. A., Hyland, P. W. & Ferrer, M. 2008. Supply chain collaboration: Capabilities for continuous innovation. *Supply Chain Management: An International Journal*, 13, 160–169.

Sorenson, O. 2003. Interdependence and adaptability: Organizational learning and the long–term effect of integration. *Management Science*, 49, 446–463.

Strange, R. & Zucchella, A. 2017. Industry 4.0, global value chains and international business. *Multinational Business Review*, 25, 3, 174–184. doi:10.1108/ MBR–05–2017–0028

Subramani, P. & Agarwal, R. 2013. Opportunities and pitfalls associated with coordination structures in supply chain management: An exploratory case study. *International Journal of Supply Chain Management*, 2, 4, December 2013, 17–31.

Swink, M., Narasimhan, R. & Kim, S.W. 2005. Manufacturing practices and strategy integration: effects on cost efficiency, flexibility, and market-based performance. *Decision Sciences*, 36, 427–457.

Taglioni, D. & Winkler, D. 2016. *Making Global Value Chains Work for Development*. Trade and Development series. World Bank, Washington, DC. doi:10.1596/978-1-4648-0157-0. License: Creative Commons Attribution CC BY 3.0 IGO.

Taticchi, P., Tonelli, F. & Pasqualino, R. 2013. Performance measurement of sustainable supply chains: A literature review and a research agenda. *International Journal of Productivity and Performance Management*, 62, 782–804.

UNIDO. 2013. *Emerging Trends in Global Manufacturing Industries*. United Nations Industrial Development Organization., Vienna. See https://www.unido.org/sites/default/files/2013-07/Emerging_Trends_U NIDO_2013_0.PDF, accessed 12 Oct 2020

UNIDO. 2015. *Global Value Chains and Development*. United Nations Industrial Development Organization. Available at: https://www.unido.org/sites/default/files/2016-03/GVC_REPORT_FINAL_0.PDF

Van Hoek, R. 2020 Research opportunities for a more resilient post-COVID-19 supply chain – closing the gap between research findings and industry practice. *International Journal of Operations and Production Management*, 40, 4, 341–355.

Vereecke, A. & Muylle, S. 2006. Performance improvement through supply chain collaboration in Europe. *International Journal of Operations & Production Management*, 26, 1176–1198.

Von Delft, S., Kortmann, S., Gelhard, C. & Pisani, N. 2019. Leveraging global sources of knowledge for business model innovation. *Long Range Planning*, 52, 101848.

Wong, C., Skipworth, H., Godsell, J. & Achimugu, N. 2012. Towards a theory of supply chain alignment enablers: A systematic literature review. *Supply Chain Management: An International Journal*, 17, 419–437.

Zhang, Y., Li, H., Li, Y. & Zhou, L. 2010. FDI spillovers in an emerging market: The role of foreign firms' country origin diversity and domestic firms' absorptive capacity. *Strategic Management Journal*, 31, 9, 969–989.

9

BLOCKCHAIN ADOPTION CHALLENGES IN SUPPLY CHAIN

Anwara Happy, Kazi Waziur Rahman, Md. Maruf Hossan Chowdhury, Mesbahuddin Chowdhury and Moira Scerri

Introduction

Today's supply chains are inherently complex in nature and consist of geographically disjointed entities competing to serve diverse consumers worldwide (Lambert and Enz, 2017; Saberi et al., 2019b). Globalisation, diverse regulatory policies, and varied cultural and human behaviour in supply chain networks make it a daunting task to evaluate information and manage risk across these complex networks (Ivanov et al., 2019; Saberi et al., 2019b). Inefficient transactions, fraud, pilferage, and poorly performing supply chains lead to a lack of trust amongst business partners, necessitating the need for collaboration, better information sharing, and verifiability systems to be in place to tackle these issues (Saberi et al., 2019b). In this regard, blockchain is considered as a potential solution to address these issues. Blockchain is expected to speed up the processes of information sharing and make it a more reliable system (Kamble et al., 2019).

Recent studies (from 2015 onward) embark on demonstrating the usefulness of adopting blockchain technology in supply chains (Wang et al., 2019b; Queiroz et al., 2019; Wang et al., 2019a). Some of the potential benefits highlighted in the operations and supply chain management (OSCM) literature are (i) to improve transparency, authenticity, trust and security (Wang et al., 2019b; Queiroz et al., 2019); (ii) to improve efficiency and reduce cost/waste (Wang et al., 2019b); (iii) to extend visibility and product traceability (Wang et al., 2019a); (iv) supply chain digitalisation and disintermediation (Wang et al., 2019a); and (v) the ability to automate the process through the introduction of smart contracts (Wang et al., 2019a).

While the literature portrays the positive aspects of transforming supply chains through the adoption of blockchain applications, significant challenges exist with its implementation. First, and one of the most important challenges, is the current infancy level of blockchain technology (Wang et al., 2019b). Due to its infancy, there is a lack of understanding of the technicalities of how and where the technology is best deployed and a skills shortage, both of which contribute to the scepticism and low level of confidence for individual users to adopt blockchain technology (Wang et al., 2019b; Wang et al., 2019a). At present, only large global firms such as Unilever, Walmart and Sainsbury are investing in and trialling the use of blockchain technology to improve the transparency (and sustainability) of their supply chain with expected financial rewards to follow (Cole et al., 2019). The second key challenge is the complexities of integrating all supply chain partners using blockchain technology (Wang et

    DOI: 10.4324/9781315225661-13

al., 2019b). Particularly, in a global supply chain context, complexity arises when needing to comply with diverse laws, regulations and institutions (Wang et al., 2019a). In addition to that, one of the real hurdles that are evident in the implementation stage is that all partners must be convinced of the benefits of sharing data and be prepared to invest time, human and financial resources to a project which they do not consider to be high. Many partners may not be willing to share their data with all. Third, integrating all supply chain partners into the system based on blockchain technology needs financial support and infrastructural investments (Chang et al., 2019).

A brief review of recent literature suggests that studies just embark on identifying potential challenges of adopting blockchain technology for a supply chain. No empirical research has yet been conducted to identify and prioritise those challenges to develop effective strategies. Considering this gap in the literature, the aim of this study is at identifying and prioritising the challenges of blockchain adoption in the global supply chain.

In line with the research objective, our study uses an extensive literature review to identify blockchain adoption challenges and use these challenges to develop a conceptual model. Then we use the fuzzy analytic hierarchy process (AHP) technique to prioritise the challenges using expert opinion. Theoretical and managerial significance are discussed.

Blockchain-based supply chain

This section outlines the potential aspect of blockchain technology and its application to supply chains. It also outlines a blockchain structure and possible areas for managing information in a blockchain-based supply chain. Evidence shows that the blockchain-based supply chain has emerged significantly in the last five years, showing many benefits in various supply chain activities (Saberi et al., 2019b; Roeck et al., 2020).

Blockchain is an evolving technology rooted in cryptography (unique codes to keep information safe in computer networks); it was conceived and popularised by Nakamoto (2008). In a seminal paper, Nakamoto showed how this technology could be applied to develop a cryptocurrency (bitcoin). Conceptually, blockchain is a chain of decentralised computer–terminal–participants ("nodes") that are linked together through a key access system (Nowiński and Kozma, 2017). The linking of nodes enables direct contracting between buyer and seller (peer-to-peer) for making a transaction without the need for traditional intermediaries and creates an unalterable transactional ledger (Letourneau and Whelan, 2017). A ledger is a book or computer file that records transactions. Blockchain is also known as distributed ledger technology (DLT) (Ramachandran and Rehermann, 2017).

The breakthrough of DLT is the advancement of the paper ledger to the trusted electronic ledger. The electronic ledger enables direct communication across supply chain actors without the involvement of a centralised body or intermediaries. Consequently, blockchain-based supply chain actors can save time and money that would otherwise be absorbed by intermediaries (Saberi et al., 2019b; Verhoeven et al., 2018). From this perspective, the following four dominant actors play a significant role in the blockchain-based supply chain (Saberi et al., 2019b):

1. *Registrars,* who provide unique identities to actors in the network.
2. *Standard organisations*, which define standard schemes, technological requirements and blockchain policy.
3. *Certifier*, who provides certifications to actors for supply chain network participation.
4. *Actors*, including suppliers, manufacturers, retailers and customers.

There are use cases that present investments in blockchain technology projects throughout a range of economies, industries and supply chains. For example, small island economies (Allessie et al. 2019) are leading the charge when it comes to the whole economy/industry implementations. For example, Aruba is developing an Etheruem-based platform for travel bookings, promoting direct bookings and disintermediating large foreign-owned intermediaries who keep a large percentage of the transaction in fees (Kwok and Koh, 2019). The Caribbean islands have issued and promoted the use of a regional government-endorsed cryptocurrency (Callahan, 2018), while the Vanuatu government announced the digital national plan which will see the issuance and roll out of Volcano Coin (VCoin) as a way to promote tourism and develop the digital economy (Access Wire 2018). Government officials are articulating the vision for VCoin to become a universal payment digital currency for immigration, tourism, aviation, gaming and real estate industries within Vanuatu and the South Pacific region.

Blockchain technology also has significance for the telecommunications industry in four specific areas. First, blockchain technology is viewed as the "new generation of access technology selection mechanism required for the enablement of 5G networks" (p. 15). Second, the communication and authentication of machines and devices will see blockchain technology guide production processes in the era of the internet of things (IoT). The third use of blockchain technology stands to improve fraud detection and reduce the incidence of roaming fraud, where a subscriber accesses communication resources from a third-party telco and where they are not able to charge the subscriber, yet are still committed to paying the third-party telco for the provision of services. Lastly, telcos are using blockchain technology through an eSIM solution with identity and authentication based on cryptographic identity.

The financial services sector, which is known to spend millions of dollars automating front-end systems measuring advantageous time savings in nanoseconds, has the opportunity to realise an estimated saving of $20 billion annually by focusing on the automation of back-end systems. Settlement processing, regularity reporting and cross-border payments are the main areas identified for cost savings. However, the replacement of paper certificates, letters of credit, recording of property transactions, and validation and transfer of luxury goods have also been areas cited for blockchain technology. Fanning and Centers (2016) also predict the disruptive elements of blockchain technology will have an impact on foreign exchange transactions and auditing functions, both of which should prepare for the disruptive effects to take hold in the near future.

Blockchain technology is also viewed as a solution in the healthcare sector. Blockchain technology connects independently managed healthcare stakeholders who are open to collaboration without ceding control to a central organisation or intermediaries. According to Kuo et al. (2017), they view the preservation and continuous availability of records such as electronic health records, improvements to privacy and security with real-time processing of information in insurance claims in particular, and the immutable audit trail of critical information surrounding client-centred data and consent as the key drivers for acceptance of the technology in the industry.

In the logistics sector, Di Gregorio et al. (2017) report a number of cases within shipping, where there has been a move by carriers and terminal operators to streamline the process of mandatory reporting of verified gross mass (VGM) data before loading using blockchain technology (Hellenic Shipping News 2017). In addition the work done by IBM-Maersk to move to paperless processing is being replicated by the Ports of Rotterdam and Antwerp, realising the reduction of fraud, costs and time delays. As well as this, the Malaysian Institute of Supply Chain Innovation in collaboration with universities is addressing fragmentation, low information sharing and frequent details by using blockchain solutions to improve the less-than-container load (LTCL).

Supply chain management is the enabler for coordinating and integrating key business processes that add value to customers and other stakeholders (Lambert and Cooper, 2000). The main focus of these integrations among the value creation activities (source to produce, market, purchase, and consume goods and services) in the supply chain is to achieve a desired level of performance that can lead to gaining a competitive advantage (Cooper et al., 1997; Gunasekaran and Kobu, 2007). From this perspective, blockchain technology can facilitate the integration of value creation activity and thereby hold the key to enabling the realisation of long-term and sustained competitive advantage (Tian, 2016; Yiannas, 2018).

Blockchain technology enables transparency between supply chain actors by making visible transactions to anyone participating in the supply chain network and providing security, durability and process integrity (Hasan and Salah, 2018; Saberi et al., 2019b). Many organisations, such as Bosch, IBM, Microsoft, Samsung, Toyota and Visa, are embracing blockchain technologies in their supply chain (Letourneau and Whelan, 2017). For example, the Commonwealth Bank of Australia, Wells Fargo and Brighann Cotton successfully applied blockchain technology in the first trade transaction between two independent banks (Ramachandran and Rehermann, 2017). To make this operation successful, they applied a combination of the IoT and smart contracts on a blockchain platform (Ramachandran and Rehermann, 2017).

The IoT, also called the internet of everything or the industrial internet, is a new technology paradigm (Qian, 2018). The IoT is recognised as one of the significant areas of future technology increasingly receiving attention from a wide variety of industries (Makhdoom et al., 2019). The use of IoT is contributing to the economy around the world and improving the quality of consumers' life. The expected contribution of IoT is predicted at about US$7.1 trillion in the global economy by 2020 (Lund et al., 2014). The following are the five IoT technologies widely used for the development of IoT-based products and services (Qian, 2018): radio frequency identification (RFID), wireless sensor network (WSN), middleware, cloud computing and IoT application software.

Similarly, the concept of smart contracts is increasingly receiving attention in global supply chains. Smart contracts is a software application that stores rules (if this happens, then that occurs) for negotiating the terms of contracts between trading partners. Smart contracts can automatically verify and execute the contract based on the agreed terms recorded on the blockchain platform (Ryan, 2017). To this end, smart contracts enable automating complex multistep processes as per the contract's terms in a transparent, secure and traceable manner. The transparent transaction processes enable all parties to save time and money simultaneously, improving supply chain performance (Gatteschi et al., 2018). Blockchain provides reliability, traceability and authenticity of the information flows across the supply chains (Letourneau and Whelan, 2017). It provides consumers with the capability of verifying the provenance relating to products or processes in the supply chain (Saberi et al., 2019b). For example, Letourneau and Whelan (2017) indicate a conceptual link between the traditional supply chain and blockchain transaction. According to Saberi et al. (2019b), a general graphic presentation of a traditional supply chain transformation to a blockchain-based supply chain is shown in Figure 9.1.

However, despite these use cases, blockchain is in its infancy in the supply chain practices, and the widespread adoption of blockchain is only the first step of a very long journey (Letourneau and Whelan, 2017; Queiroz and Wamba, 2019). It is expected that the next generation blockchain could address many problems, some of which include the passage of a typical contract of sale, security and loan arrangement, or lease of applications across a supply chain (Gatteschi et al., 2018; Ryan, 2017; Letourneau and Whelan, 2017). The following section examines the challenging factors that affect blockchain adoption in the supply chain.

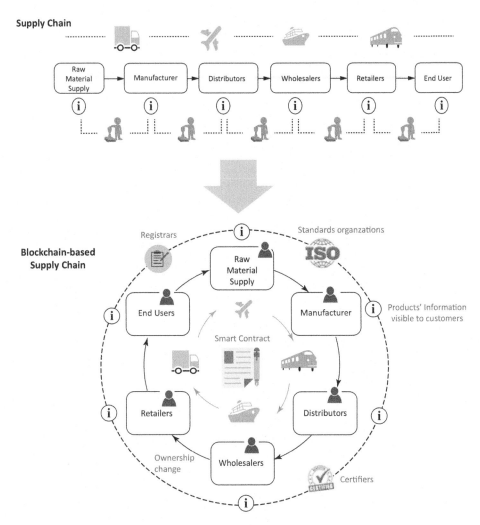

Figure 9.1 A blockchain-based supply chain.

Blockchain adoption challenges

This section provides an extensive literature review on blockchain adoption challenges in supply chains and provides a list of challenges. Within the last five years the literature has explored the possibilities of adopting blockchain into the supply chain (Tian, 2016; Wu, 2017; Lyu, 2018). The published research addressed numerous advantages related to blockchain adoption across the supply chain (Saberi et al., 2019b; Francisco and Swanson, 2018). Many researchers have identified that a substantial change will occur across supply chains around the globe due to the disruptive and transformative properties of blockchain technologies (Collomb and Sok, 2016; Tapscott and Tapscott, 2017; Letourneau and Whelan, 2017). These transformation effects will disrupt how supply chain processes are currently managed (Nowiński and Kozma, 2017) and will profoundly affect the nature of value creation activities in the supply chain (Tapscott and Tapscott, 2017).

Table 9.1 Blockchain misconceptions and factual realities

General misconception	Vs	Factual reality
By definition, blockchain is distributive ledger technology.		Blockchain technology is formed with the idea of distributive ledger technology and (DLT) do not often follow (BC) technology.
Blockchain only uses bitcoin.		Bitcoin is a cryptocurrency and an application of blockchain technology.
Smart contract legally binds two parties.		Without a separate contractual agreement paper smart contracts are not legally enforceable.
Blockchain is the best database for business solutions.		Traditional database creation is faster and one single point of control, ideal for enterprises that rely on performance.
In the blockchain, transactional data are absolutely secured.		Depends on architecture, as in the public blockchain privacy is the biggest concern.

One of the key barriers to adopting blockchain technology is the hype and misconceptions arising from the volatility of bitcoin. Lu et al. (2019) point out four key misconceptions and sought to clarify things by presenting corresponding factual realities. These are shown in Table 9.1.

A recent Deloitte survey on blockchain attitudes amongst the C-suite show executives believe blockchain is overhyped, and are concerned about how blockchain may disrupt their industry and the potential loss of competitive advantage that arises from not using blockchain technology. In contrast, to the positive use cases and the attitudes surrounding blockchain, there is relatively limited literature that indicates the challenges to blockchain adoption in the supply chain (Saberi et al., 2019b; Queiroz and Wamba, 2019). To investigate blockchain technology and its relationship to sustainable supply chain management, Saberi et al. (2019b) discussed four significant barriers relating to blockchain adoption in the supply chain. The barriers were classified as intra-organisational barriers, inter-organisational barriers, system-related barriers and external barriers. These barriers lead to blockchain adoption challenges that need to be overcome before implementation in complex supply chains is likely to increase (Saberi et al., 2019b).

The complexity of supply chains is the result of the involvement of multiple numbers of partners (one too many or many too many) and a series of related activities (coordinating, planning, and controlling of product and services) occurring through the network (Büyüközkan and Göçer, 2018; Chowdhury and Quaddus, 2016). Due to such complexity, the lack of visibility in shipping or transporting goods or services from one part of the world to another is challenging. Blockchain adoption could minimise such visibility by enabling open access to members of the supply chain, thereby improving transparency, traceability, accountability, knowledge sharing and integration with upstream and downstream partners (Martinez et al., 2019; Rahmanzadeh et al., 2020). In this regard, however, building the technological infrastructure to be made available to the entire supply chain or industry is challenging (Queiroz and Wamba, 2019; Saberi et al., 2019b; Chowdhury, 2016). Furthermore, the high cost of compliance and upgrading of legacy systems is challenging many supply chains and industries (Nikolakis, 2018).

Blockchain technology can support vital information sharing in the supply chain such as data collection, data storage and management, and it can also aid environmental supply chain sustainability (Saberi et al., 2019b). The application of blockchain in the supply chain can improve recycling, reduce carbon emissions and ensure fraud prevention in the supply chain. Blockchain technology has the potential to contribute to social supply chain sustainability. For example, the blockchain-based Social Plastic project contributes to improving the supply chain (Saberi et al., 2019b). Figure 9.2 demonstrates blockchain-based logistics activities in the supply chain.

However, many challenges must be overcome in order to adopt blockchain technologies in supply chains. Such challenges include technology implementation challenges, business process challenges, lack of government policies, lack of top management support, high costs, lack of ethical and safe practice, lack of skilled people, and lack of knowledge (Saberi et al., 2019b). Based on the literature review, the following challenges have been identified:

- Implementation challenges: To implement blockchain technology in the supply chain, it is essential to build blockchain-compatible infrastructure across the supply chain. As blockchain in its infant stage, there is a lack of appropriate business models, and relatively limited trained people and expertise are available. For instance, such an infrastructure building is quite a costly operation.
- Operational challenges: To gain day-to-day operational success by adopting blockchain in the supply chain, a better understanding of supply chain integration is vital through the entire supply chain. Supply chain integration relates to both internal and external integration. Supply chain integration is a broader concept. All partners in the supply chain needed to understand the scalability of integration to execute their major business processes across the supply chain.
- Business process challenges: The application of blockchain could create value in the business process through the entire supply chain. However, selecting the appropriate design in the business process is relatively challenging in the supply chain.
- Legal challenges: Lack of industry involvement and safe practice make it harder to adopt blockchain in the supply chain. More important, jurisdictional problems as the ledger can span multiple locations, and it is possible to fall under different regulations.
- Sustainability challenges: Blockchain adoption in the supply chain requires a large scale of IT infrastructure building, which initiates electricity consumption challenges. In some stages, it is challenging to adopt blockchain in the supply chain due to individual, privacy, and ethical issues.

Based on the review of literature, blockchain adoption challenges in the supply chain are presented in Table 9.2.

Methodology

The aim of this study is to identify the crucial challenges which hinder the process of mass blockchain adoption in the supply chain. In line with the research objective, we conducted an extensive literature review to identify blockchain adoption challenges in the supply chain. Then we sought opinions from three experts to validate the findings from literature and categorise the challenges. The challenges have been categorised into five major categories, which comprise a total of 23 sub-categories (see Figure 9.3), depending on their relevancy.

Once the challenges were categorised, based on expert opinion, we prioritised the blockchain adoption challenges in the context of the global supply chain using the fuzzy AHP technique. The fuzzy AHP method is explained in the next section.

Fuzzy AHP application and data computation

AHP was first introduced by Saaty (1988) as a decision-making tool in the field of economics and management. AHP has been widely used by many researchers and professionals around the world to identify the best alternative, especially when decision-makers must consider several

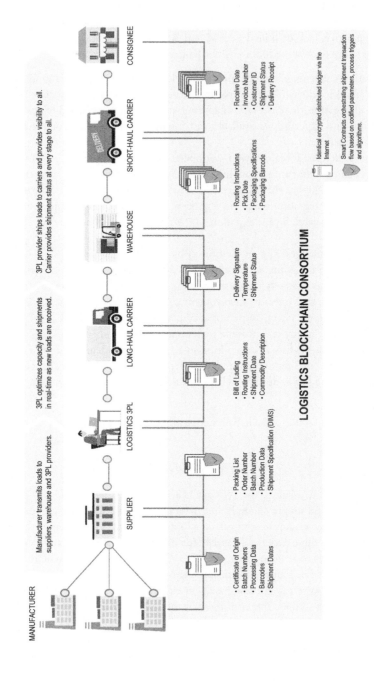

Figure 9.2 Blockchain–based logistics and supply chain operations.

Table 9.2 Blockchain adoption challenges in the supply chain

Challenge	Description	Reference
Technology	Adopting new technology in an attempt to market oneself as an early adopter without a proper strategy creates many issues.	Saberi et al. (2019), Dobrovnik et al. (2018), Queiroz and Wamba (2019)
Operational issues	Due to multiple entities and many business processes in the supply chain, deploying a consensus mechanism is challenging. As such, *trust, shortage of professionals, anonymity concern, lack of device authenticity, lack of scalability and immutability* are major operational challenges for implementing blockchain in the supply chain.	Mackey et al. (2019), Feng et al. (2018), Wang et al. (2019a), Casino et al. (2019)
Infrastructure	Requires large-scale investment in technological infrastructure.	Queiroz and Wamba (2019), Saberi et al. (2019), Baker and Steiner (2015)
Cost	The high cost is a significant issue due to building technological infrastructure across the supply chain.	Saberi et al. (2019), Kamble (2019), Nikolakis (2018)
Legal implications issues	Lack of business models and best practices for implementing new technologies are major challenges. These include *jurisdiction, contract enforceability, legal practitioners' knowledge, identify theft and liability of customer risk issues.*	Chang et al. (2019), Queiroz et al. (2019), Jacob and Buer (2016)
Implementations	Lack of business model and best practice for implementing the new technology.	Dobrovnik et al. (2018), Saberi et al. (2019), Verhoeven et al. (2018)
Training	Lack of trained people to implement the technology.	Saberi et al. (2019), Francisco and Swanson (2018)
Knowledge and expertise	Lack of knowledge and expertise to encounter troubleshoot issues after implementation of the technology.	Saberi et al. (2019), Verhoeven et al. (2018)
Governance issues	Data integrity and data provenance are key challenges in the blockchain adoption supply chain. These include *compliance policy and guidance, bill of lading, governance procedure establishment, a variation on digital flow and physical flow of goods.*	Casino et al. (2019), Saberi et al. (2019), Mackey et al. (2019), Figorilli et al. (2018), Chang et al. (2019)
Integration	Challenges of integrating sustainable supply chain practice through blockchain technology	Haddud et al. (2017), Saberi et al. (2019)
System deployment	System development is another challenge for blockchain adoption in the supply chain. The challenges include *blockchain structure design, integration with partner, data security and sharing and management disinterest.*	Chang et al. (2019), van Engelenburg et al. (2019), Figorilli et al. (2018)

(Continued)

Table 9.2 (Continued)

Challenge	Description	Reference
Collaboration, communication, and coordination	Lack of collaboration, communication and coordination among the supply chain partners.	Saberi et al. (2019), Verhoeven et al. (2018)
Security	System-related security is one of the big challenges.	Saberi et al. (2019)
Top management support	Lack of top management support and commitment.	Saberi et al. (2019)
Sustainability issues	Challenges of integrating sustainable supply chain practices through blockchain technology. The challenges include *ecologically unfriendly, power consumption, double spending risk and employee ethics.*	Nikolakis et al. (2018), Fu et al. (2018), Pankowska (2019), Saberi et al. (2019), Carter and Rogers (2008)
Awareness of customer	Lack of customer awareness relating to blockchain technology adoption in the supply chain.	Saberi et al. (2019)
Government policy	Lack of government policy.	Saberi et al. (2019)
Ethical and safe practice	Lack of industry involvement in ethical and safe practice.	Saberi et al. (2019)

criteria. Decision-makers make a decision by providing quantitative value from a pre-existing numerical scale (1, 2, 3, …, 9) to rank options based on whichever best meets the decision-making criteria (Chang, 1996).

Fuzzy AHP is more applicable in situations when a decision cannot be made precisely as there is more complexity associated with surrounding environments. Experts can make precise decisions when the situation is more known to the expert, but the majority of the times, human judgement is imprecise. Bellman and Zadeh (1970) first introduced fuzzy set theory to more accurately explain qualitative, vague, inconsistent and fuzzy information. This study led Chang (1996) to propose fuzzy extent analysis methodology and all the computational work was conducted through online software. The fuzzy AHP is explained in the following with some results as an example. The pairwise comparison matrix can be expressed as in Figure 9.4. The fuzzy triangular scale and the linguistic terms used for the comparison matrix are presented in Table 9.3.

Elements of a complete pairwise comparison matrix used in the fuzzy AHP method are triangular fuzzy numbers where the first component (l) is the least number, the second component (m) is the mean of numbers and the third component (u) is the maximum number (Ayhan, 2013).

To ensure the reliability of AHP results, the consistency ratio (CR) of pairwise comparison metrics is salient. The CR for each matrix is derived from dividing the consistency index (CI) of each matrix by the random index (RI):

$$CR_g = \frac{CI_g}{RI_g}$$

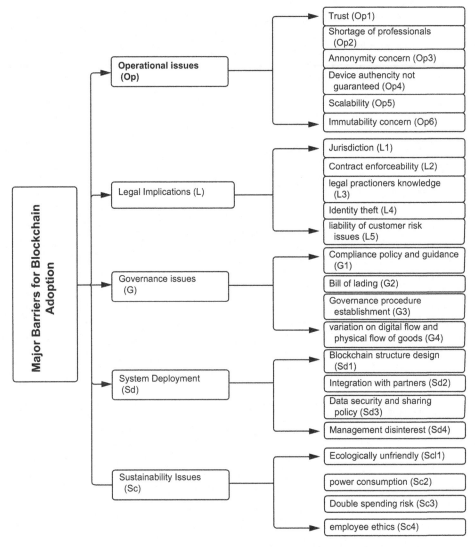

Figure 9.3 Hierarchical structure of blockchain adoption challenges in the supply chain.

$$\tilde{A} = \begin{bmatrix} 1 & \tilde{\alpha}_{12} & \cdots & \tilde{\alpha}_{1n} \\ \tilde{\alpha}_{21} & 1 & \cdots & \tilde{\alpha}_{2n} \\ \vdots & \vdots & \ddots & \vdots \\ \tilde{\alpha}_{n1} & \tilde{\alpha}_{n2} & \cdots & 1 \end{bmatrix}$$

Figure 9.4 A pairwise comparison matrix.

Table 9.3 Fuzzy triangular scale and linguistic terms

Code	Linguistic variables	L	M	U
1	Equally important	1	1	1
2	Intermediate value between 1 and 3	1	2	3
3	Slightly important	2	3	4
4	Intermediate value between 3 and 5	3	4	5
5	Important	4	5	6
6	Intermediate value between 5 and 7	5	6	7
7	Strongly important	6	7	8
8	Intermediate value between 7 and 9	7	8	9
9	Extremely important	9	9	9

In Table 9.4, the random indices for fuzzy pairwise comparison matrices were developed, according to Gogus et al. (1997), by initiating 400 random matrices. Only 10% of consistency variations are allowed. The software automatically detects any inconsistency and allows the decision to be modified manually (Radionovs et al., 2016).

The pairwise comparison matrix has been constructed for the main criteria and sub-criteria concerning the main objective. For example (the following example was generated after taking the mean value of triangular fuzzy numbers given to a criterion in respective to others):

$$\text{Operational} = \begin{bmatrix} 1.000, & 1.000, & 1.000 \\ 0.143, & 0.167, & 0.200 \\ 0.200, & 0.289, & 0.500 \\ 0.167, & 0.775, & 4.000 \\ 0.143, & 0.183, & 0.250 \end{bmatrix}$$

$$\text{Shortage of skill professionals} = \begin{bmatrix} 1.000, & 1.000, & 1.000 \\ 5.000, & 5.988, & 6.993 \\ 3.003, & 4.464, & 5.988 \\ 0.200, & 0.867, & 4.000 \\ 5.000, & 5.988, & 6.993 \\ 2.000, & 3.003, & 4.000 \end{bmatrix}$$

Results and discussion

The results of the software interface are provided next (Table 9.5, Figures 9.5 and 9.6).

From Table 9.6, it is evident that the criterion Op2, Op5, Sd1, G4 and G3 are the top five important factors, and comparing their weights to other differences is quite significant. One major issue requires clarification 0 weight of some criteria. It means, as per experts in comparison to the prioritised 15 criteria, those criteria are not necessary or relevant enough to our main issues. One of the main reasons for adopting Chang's extended analysis is when computing the comparison result, it deploys the intersection operation which allows the fuzzy intersection

Table 9.4 Random index

N	1	2	3	4	5	6	7	8	9	10	11	12	13	14	15
RI^g	0	0	0.1796	0.2627	0.3597	0.3818	0.4090	0.4164	0.4348	0.4455	0.4536	0.4776	0.4691	0.4804	0.4880

Table 9.5 Priorities of main criteria with respect to goal

Rank	Name	Weight
1	Operational issue	0.354
4	Legal implications	0.056
2	Governance issue	0.337
3	System deployment	0.252
5	Sustainability issue	0

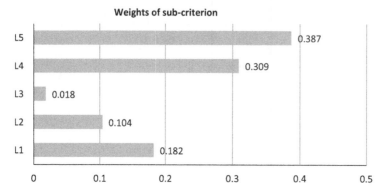

Figure 9.5 Priorities with respect to legal implications.

result to be zero. The representation of the corresponding criteria may raise confusion about their zero weight as to how it is possible that criteria of a decision-making process have no importance. The explanation comes with fuzzy logic in a comparison matrix: if one criterion carries the least weight among others, it also means the criteria have no importance and can be represented with zero importance (Özdağoğlu and Özdağoğlu, 2007). The research objective is based on a topic that ultimately represents an uncertain environment and decision-making with absolute certainty not possible for the decision-makers, which motivated the authors to follow Chang's extended fuzzy AHP method.

Based on the final weight calculation total, 15 challenges have been ranked and found to be more responsible for halting the process of blockchain adoption in the supply chain.

Considering the sub-criteria of our study, we identified Op2 (shortage of professionals) is ranked 1 with an importance weight equal to 15.1158%. We also found that Op5 (scalability issue) is ranked 2, which carries an importance weight equal to 13.275%. Similarly, we identified Sd1 (blockchain structure/design) as ranked 3 with a 9.2988% importance weight. Our findings are consistent with the literature, as authors such as Makhdoom et al. (2019) and Saberi et al. (2019a) asserted that as blockchain adoption in the supply chain is in the infancy stage, the professional shortage and scalability are important challenges to adopt blockchain in the supply chain. The prioritised of 15 challenges with respect to their weight-based rank are presented in Table 9.6.

Blockchain in the global supply chain is in the infancy stage, and most firms are yet to go beyond analyses leading to the adoption phase (Queiroz and Wamba, 2019). Blockchain adoption has gained a relative pace in the global supply chain, focusing on enormous potential over recent years. However, existing literature on the blockchain provides relatively limited priorities

Summary Weight

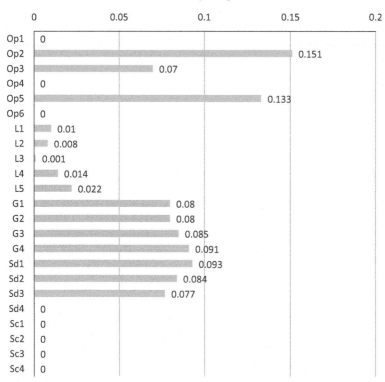

Figure 9.6 Summary of priorities with respect to the objective.

Table 9.6 Prioritised blockchain adoption challenges in the supply chain

Code	Challenges	Weight	Rank
Op2	Shortage of professionals	0.151158	1
Op5	Scalability	0.13275	2
Sd1	Blockchain structure/design	0.092988	3
G4	Variation between digital transaction and physical flow	0.091664	4
G3	Governance procedure	0.085261	5
Sd2	Integration with partners	0.082152	6
G2	Bill of lading	0.080543	7
G1	Compliance policy and guidance	0.079532	8
Sd3	Data security and sharing policy	0.07686	9
Op3	Anonymity concern/data quality not guaranteed	0.070092	10
L5	Liability of customer risk issue	0.021672	11
L4	Identity and information theft	0.017304	12
L1	Jurisdiction	0.010192	13
L2	Contract enforceability	.005824	14
L3	Legal practitioners' insufficient knowledge	.001008	15

on blockchain adoption challenges in the supply chain (Janssen et al., 2020; Saberi et al., 2019b; Biswas and Gupta, 2019; Queiroz and Wamba, 2019). In terms of blockchain adoption challenges in the supply chain, our findings bring important insights by prioritising 5 significant challenges and 15 sub-challenges accordingly to take the adoption decision in the global supply chain. In addition, to overcome such challenges, blockchain technology can bring the most important change and strategies in supply chain design, activities and product flow. In particular, the findings of this study add a useful contribution to the existing body of knowledge in this field.

Conclusion

The emerging technology blockchain is still in its infancy stage. Expert predicts it will serve an essential role in the value creation activities of the global supply chain. However, numerous challenges inhibit blockchain adoption in the global supply chain. This study examines the blockchain adoption challenges in the supply chain. Our study found 23 challenges regarding blockchain adoption, which are classified under five groups: implementation challenges, operational challenges, business process challenges, legal challenges and sustainability challenges. In an effort to prioritise the identified challenges, we find that the shortage of professionals, scalability and system architecture are the top three challenges of blockchain adoption in the supply chain. Supply chain managers needed to take proactive and rapid moves to mitigate the most significant blockchain adoption challenges to improve supply chain operations and transparency, visibility, and sustainability in the global supply chain. This study is expected to add to the existing knowledge and academic literature by extending the insight of blockchain adoption challenges in the supply chain. The proposed model in this chapter may serve as a framework for managers to prioritise blockchain adoption challenges in the supply chain management. The prioritisation of challenges will assist managers in designing effective and efficient strategies to mitigate the most important challenges. Despite the numerous merits of this study, some limitations need to be addressed in future research. This study is based on a literature review and a small number of experts' opinions. Further, empirical study may be conducted by incorporating data from different and many respondents encompassing different supply chain members. Future research may also be conducted to develop a decision model that can determine the most effective and efficient strategies to mitigate blockchain adoption challenges in the global supply chain.

References

Allessie, D., Janssen, M., Ubacht, J., Cunningham, S., van der Harst, G., Bolívar, R. & Scholl, H. J. 2019. The consequences of blockchain architectures for the governance of public services: A case study of the movement of excise goods under duty exemptions. *Information Polity: The International Journal of Government & Democracy in the Information Age*, 24, 487–499.

Ayhan, M. B. 2013. A fuzzy AHP approach for supplier selection problem: A case study in a gear motor company. *International Journal of Managing Value and Supply Chains*, 4(3), pp. 11–23.

Baker, J. & Steiner, J. 2015. Blockchain: The solution for transparency in product supply chains. *Provenance*, London, UK.

Bellman, R. E. & Zadeh, L. A. 1970. Decision-making in a fuzzy environment. *Management Science*, 17, B-141–B-164.

Biswas, B. & Gupta, R. 2019. Analysis of barriers to implement blockchain in industry and service sectors. *Computers & Industrial Engineering*, 136, 225–241.

Büyüközkan, G. & Göçer, F. 2018. Digital supply chain: Literature review and a proposed framework for future research. *Computers in Industry*, 97, 157–177.

Callahan, D. 2018. *Taming the beloved beast: how medical technology costs are destroying our health care system*. Princeton University Press, New Jersey, USA.

Carter, C. R. & Rogers, D. S. 2008. A framework of sustainable supply chain management: Moving toward new theory. *International Journal of Physical Distribution & Logistics Management*, 38, 360–387.

Casino, F., Dasaklis, T. K. & Patsakis, C. 2019. A systematic literature review of blockchain-based applications: Current status, classification and open issues. *Telematics and Informatics*, 36, 55–81.

Chang, D.-Y. 1996. Applications of the extent analysis method on fuzzy AHP. *European Journal of Operational Research*, 95, 649–655.

Chang, S. E., Chen, Y.-C. & Lu, M.-F. 2019. Supply chain re-engineering using blockchain technology: A case of smart contract based tracking process. *Technological Forecasting and Social Change*, 144, 1–11.

Chowdhury, M. M. H. & Quaddus, M. 2016. Supply chain readiness, response and recovery for resilience. *Supply Chain Management: An International Journal*, 21, 709–731.

Cole, R., Stevenson, M. & Aitken, J. 2019. Blockchain technology: Implications for operations and supply chain management. *Supply Chain Management*, 24, 469–483.

Collomb, A. & Sok, K. 2016. Blockchain/distributed ledger technology (DLT): What impact on the financial sector? *Communications & Strategies*, 93–111, 212, 214.

Cooper, M. C., Lambert, D. M. & Pagh, J. D. 1997. Supply chain management: More than a new name for logistics. *The International Journal of Logistics Management*, 8, 1–14.

Di Gregorio, R. & Nustad, S. S. 2017. Blockchain adoption in the shipping industry. Master's thesis, Copenhagen Business School.

Dobrovnik, M., Herold, D. M., Fürst, E. & Kummer, S. 2018. Blockchain for and in Logistics: What to adopt and where to start. *Logistics*, 2, 18.

Fanning, K. & Centers, D. P. 2016. Blockchain and its coming impact on financial services. *Journal of Corporate Accounting Finance*, 27, 53–57.

Feng, L., Zhang, H., Chen, Y. & Lou, L. 2018. Scalable dynamic multi-agent practical byzantine fault-tolerant consensus in permissioned blockchain. *Applied Sciences (Switzerland)*, 8, 1919.

Figorilli, S., Antonucci, F., Costa, C., Pallottino, F., Raso, L., Castiglione, M., Pinci, E., Del Vecchio, D., Colle, G., Proto, A. R., Sperandio, G. & Menesatti, P. 2018. A blockchain implementation prototype for the electronic open source traceability of wood along the whole supply chain. *Sensors (Switzerland)*, 18, 3133.

Francisco, K. & Swanson, D. 2018. The supply chain has no clothes: Technology adoption of blockchain for supply chain transparency. *Logistics*, 2, 2.

Fu, B., Shu, Z. & Liu, X. 2018. Blockchain enhanced emission trading framework in fashion apparel manufacturing industry. *Sustainability (Switzerland)*, 10, 1105.

Gatteschi, V., Lamberti, F., Demartini, C., Pranteda, C. & Santamaría, V. 2018. Blockchain and smart contracts for insurance: Is the technology mature enough? *Future Internet*, 10, 20.

Gogus, O. & Boucher, T. O. 1997. A consistency test for rational weights in multi-criterion decision analysis with fuzzy pairwise comparisons. *Fuzzy Sets and Systems*, 86, 129–138.

Gunasekaran, A. & Kobu, B. 2007. Performance measures and metrics in logistics and supply chain management: A review of recent literature (1995–2004) for research and applications. *International Journal of Production Research*, 45, 2819–2840.

Haddud, A., DeSouza, A., Khare, A. & Lee, H. 2017. Examining potential benefits and challenges associated with the Internet of Things integration in supply chains. *Journal of Manufacturing Technology Management*, 28, 1055–1085.

Hasan, H. R. & Salah, K. 2018. Blockchain-based proof of delivery of physical assets with single and multiple transporters. *IEEE Access*, 6, 46781–46793.

Ivanov, D., Dolgui, A. & Sokolov, B. 2019. The impact of digital technology and Industry 4.0 on the ripple effect and supply chain risk analytics. *International Journal of Production Research*, 57, 829–846.

Jacob, J. & Buer, T. 2016. Population-based negotiation of contract clauses and transportation request assignments. *IFAC-PapersOnLine*, 49, 1862–1867.

Janssen, M., Weerakkody, V., Ismagilova, E., Sivarajah, U. & Irani, Z. 2020. A framework for analysing blockchain technology adoption: Integrating institutional, market and technical factors. *International Journal of Information Management*, 50, 302–309.

Kamble, S., Gunasekaran, A. & Arha, H. 2019. Understanding the Blockchain technology adoption in supply chains-Indian context. *International Journal of Production Research*, 57, 2009–2033.

Kuo, T.-T., Kim, H.-E. & Ohno-Machado, L. 2017. Blockchain distributed ledger technologies for biomedical and health care applications. *Journal of the American Medical Informatics Association*, 24, 1211–1220.

Kwok, A. O. J. & Koh, S. G. M. 2019. Is blockchain technology a watershed for tourism development? *Current Issues in Tourism*, 22, 2447–2452.

Lambert, D. M. & Cooper, M. C. 2000. Issues in supply chain management. *Industrial marketing management*, 29, 65–83.

Lambert, D. M. & Enz, M. G. 2017. Issues in supply chain management: Progress and potential. *Industrial Marketing Management*, 62, 1–16.

Letourneau, K. B. & Whelan, S. T. 2017. Blockchain: Staying ahead of tomorrow. *The Journal of Equipment Lease Financing (Online)*, 35, 1–6.

Lu, H., Huang, K., Azimi, M. & Guo, L. J. I. A. 2019. Blockchain technology in the oil and gas industry: A review of applications, opportunities, challenges, and risks. 7, 41426–41444.

Lund, D., MacGillivray, C., Turner, V. & Morales, M. 2014. Worldwide and regional internet of things (IoT) 2014–2020 forecast: A virtuous circle of proven value and demand. International Data Corporation (IDC), Tech. Rep, 1.

Lyu, G. C., L. & Huo, B. 2018. Logistics resources, capabilities and operational performance: A contingency and configuration approach. *Industrial Management and Data Systems*.

Mackey, T. K., Kuo, T. T., Gummadi, B., Clauson, K. A., Church, G., Grishin, D., Obbad, K., Barkovich, R. & Palombini, M. 2019. 'Fit-for-purpose?' – Challenges and opportunities for applications of blockchain technology in the future of healthcare. *BMC Medicine*, 17, 68.

Makhdoom, I., Abolhasan, M., Abbas, H. & Ni, W. 2019. Blockchain's adoption in IoT: The challenges, and a way forward. *Journal of Network and Computer Applications*, 125, 251–279.

Martinez, V., Zhao, M., Blujdea, C., Han, X., Neely, A. & Albores, P. 2019. Blockchain-driven customer order management. *International Journal of Operations & Production Management*, 39, 993–1022.

Nakamoto, S. 2008. Bitcoin: A peer-to-peer electronic cash system, *Self-Published Paper*, 1–9.

Nikolakis, W., John, L. & Krishnan, H. 2018. How blockchain can shape sustainable global value chains: An Evidence, Verifiability, and Enforceability (EVE) Framework. *Sustainability (Switzerland)*, 10(11), 3926.

Nowiński, W. & Kozma, M. 2017. How can Blockchain technology disrupt the existing business models? *Entrepreneurial Business and Economics Review*, 5, 173–188.

Özdağoğlu, A. & Özdağoğlu, G. 2007. Comparison of AHP and fuzzy AHP for the multi-criteria decision making processes with linguistic evaluations. *İstanbul Ticaret Üniversitesi Fen Bilimleri Dergisi Yıl*, 1, 65–85.

Pankowska, M. 2019. Information technology outsourcing chain: Literature review and implications for development of distributed coordination. *Sustainability (Switzerland)*, 11(5), 1460.

Qian, Y., Jiang, Y., Chen, J., Zhang, Y., Song, J., Zhou, M. & Pustišek, M. 2018. Towards decentralized IoT security enhancement: A blockchain approach. *Computers and Electrical Engineering*, 72, 266–273.

Queiroz, M. M., Telles, R. & Bonilla, S. H. 2019. Blockchain and supply chain management integration: A systematic review of the literature. *Supply Chain Management: An International Journal*, 25(2), 241–254.

Queiroz, M. M. & Wamba, S. F. 2019. Blockchain adoption challenges in supply chain: An empirical investigation of the main drivers in India and the USA. *International Journal of Information Management*, 46, 70–82.

Radionovs, A. & Užga-Rebrovs, O. 2016. Fuzzy analytical hierarchy process for ecological risk assessment. *Information Technology and Management Science*, 19, 16–22.

Rahmanzadeh, S., Pishvaee, M. S. & Rasouli, M. R. 2020. Integrated innovative product design and supply chain tactical planning within a blockchain platform. *International Journal of Production Research*, 58, 2242–2262.

Ramachandran, V. & Rehermann, T. 2017. Can blockchain technology address de-risking in emerging markets? (No. 30364). The World Bank.

Roeck, D., Sternberg, H. & Hofmann, E. 2020. Distributed ledger technology in supply chains: A transaction cost perspective. *International Journal of Production Research*, 58, 2124–2141.

Ryan, P. 2017. Smart contract relations in e-Commerce: Legal implications of exchanges conducted on the Blockchain. *Technology Innovation Management Review*, 7, 14–21.

Saaty, T. L. 1988. What is the analytic hierarchy process? Mathematical models for decision support. Springer.

Saberi, S., Kouhizadeh, M. & Sarkis, J. 2019a. Blockchains and the supply chain: Findings from a broad study of practitioners. *IEEE Engineering Management Review*, 47, 95–103.

Saberi, S., Kouhizadeh, M., Sarkis, J. & Shen, L. 2019b. Blockchain technology and its relationships to sustainable supply chain management. *International Journal of Production Research*, 57, 2117–2135.

Tapscott, D. & Tapscott, A. 2017. How blockchain will change organizations. *MIT Sloan Management Review*, 58, 10.

Tian, F. 2016. An agri-food supply chain traceability system for China based on RFID & blockchain technology. 2016 13th international conference on service systems and service management (ICSSSM). IEEE, 1–6.

van Engelenburg, S., Janssen, M. & Klievink, B. 2019. Design of a software architecture supporting business-to-government information sharing to improve public safety and security. *Journal of Intelligent Information Systems*, 52(3), 595–618.

Verhoeven, P., Sinn, F. & Herden, T. T. 2018. Examples from Blockchain implementations in logistics and supply chain management: Exploring the mindful use of a New Technology. *Logistics*, 2, 20.

Wang, Y., Han, J. H. & Beynon-Davies, P. 2019a. Understanding blockchain technology for future supply chains: A systematic literature review and research agenda. *Supply Chain Management: An International Journal*, 24, 62–84.

Wang, Y., Singgih, M., Wang, J. & Rit, M. 2019b. Making sense of blockchain technology: How will it transform supply chains? *International Journal of Production Economics*, 211, 221–236.

Wu, H., Li, Z., King, B., Miled, Z. B., Wassick, J. & Tazelaar, J. 2017. A distributed ledger for supply chain physical distribution visibility. *Information (Switzerland)*, 8(4), 137.

Yiannas, F. 2018. A new era of food transparency powered by blockchain. *Innovations: Technology, Governance, Globalization*, 12, 46–56.

CASE STUDY

Internet of things (IoT)–enabled agri-food supply chain management: A New Zealand case

Ray Y. Zhong and Abraham Zhang

New Zealand agri-food businesses

The agricultural sector is a pillar of the New Zealand economy. It involves over 7500 types of animal products and 3800 types of dairy products that feed over 40 million people. Traditionally, a variety of agri-food businesses attempt to optimize their own operations with little collaboration with upstream and downstream business entities. Much waste and loss occur in the interfaces between different business entities. Over the past three decades, the focus on single echelons such as food production shifted to holistic supply chains, with their greater efficiency and effectiveness. More and more agri-food businesses have started to realize the importance of integrating and coordinating activities across the whole supply chain. These activities typically include farm/orchard production, harvesting, pack house sorting and packaging, cold storage, transportation, customs clearance for imports/exports, market distribution, and sales to final customers. The term *agri-food supply chain management* (*ASCM*) invokes the efficient and effective management of all these supply chain activities to keep up the safety and quality of various agri-food products and satisfy customer requirements.

Challenges for New Zealand agri-food businesses

New Zealand's agri-food businesses face the common challenges inherent in the agri-food products. ASCM is more challenging than its counterpart in typical manufactured products, as agri-food products raise additional concerns, such as food safety and perishability. In addition, though agricultural harvesting is seasonal, consumption is throughout the year. A biological production process is susceptible to pests, diseases, and extreme weather conditions. In a global agri-food supply chain, the complexities are compounded. The quality and safety of agricultural products heavily relies on efficient and effective ASCM.

DOI: 10.4324/9781315225661-14

156

Internet of things (IoT)–enabled solutions

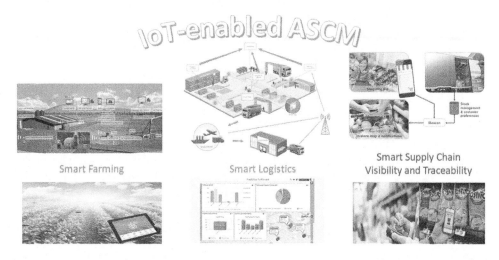

Smart Farming · Smart Logistics · Smart Supply Chain Visibility and Traceability

For overcoming these challenges, we envision internet of things (IoT)–enabled ASCM consisting of three components: smart farming, smart logistics, and smart supply chain visibility and traceability. A good example of smart farming is the National Animal Identification and Tracing (NAIT) scheme implemented by the New Zealand government in the early 2010s. Under the scheme, all cattle and deer in New Zealand are required by law to be traced using radio frequency identification (RFID) ear tags for disease control. Smart farming will allow farmers to monitor and control more and more farm activities on the smartphones. For instance, smart irrigation can be made possible by deploying sensors to monitor soil moisture. The data from the sensors is transmitted to a cloud and accessed by a mobile application that facilitates the management of remote-controlled irrigation equipment. The mobile app makes irrigation decisions by simultaneously evaluating soil moisture and weather forecasts that are provided by an external app.

Smart logistics uses innovative IoT-based applications to increase the agility, sustainability, and efficiency of various logistics operations. Many agri-food products perish or are otherwise wasted in the transportation and storage stages. IoT technology can monitor the storage conditions and maturity level of agri-food products. Combined with the use of big data analytics, it can predict the remaining shelf life of agri-food products for the purposes of proactive inventory management and promotion and sales decisions.

Smart supply chain visibility and traceability will not only benefit business operations, but also enable consumers to make more informed purchase decisions. Using a smartphone to scan a 2D barcode on a product label, a consumer can instantly acquire information on the source, harvest date, storage warehouse, logistics history, date on which it was put on the shelf, etc. It will help New Zealand-based agribusinesses to differentiate their products to command a premium price because of the country's reputation as a high-quality producer. In case of a concern about product safety, a product recall can be managed more effectively and efficiently using IoT to quickly identify and trace affected products.

Recommendations

A few large New Zealand and regional agribusiness firms have pioneered or are testing IoT-enabled solutions. To reap the potential benefits of IoT and minimize the associated implementation risks, we suggest potential users carefully consider the following areas of strategic importance before they commit to an IoT implementation.

- System interoperability: A supply chain needs to integrate the different IT systems used by multiple stakeholders. A risk posed by supply chain and IT integration is becoming locked into a technology or IT platform. To minimize risk, one may consider IT system architecture that is built on open sources and poses less risk of interoperability issues.
- Big data analytics: IoT-based solutions generate a huge amount of data from a network of widely deployed smart objects. Big data analytics and visualization are necessary for uncovering patterns in data for better decision-making.
- "Cloud first" IT strategy: Cloud-based technologies have the advantage of virtually integrating spatially dispersed supply chain activities using minimum resources, substantially reducing the amount of capital required for implementing IoT solutions and reducing the associated investment risks.

Conclusion and managerial implications

Despite a promising future, one should not blindly jump into an IoT implementation in ASCM without understanding its costs, benefits, risks, and challenges. Like other IT technologies, it is an enabler – it could transform one's supply chain operations, but it is not an Aladdin's lamp. If a business is heading in the right direction and its processes are streamlined, IoT applications can make it even more successful. However, if it has not sorted out the fundamental issues in operations strategy, human resource management, organizational culture, and business processes, it should not expect IoT technologies to rescue its future.

PART IV

Megatrends in global value chains

In Chapter 10, Brian Wixted and Martin J. Bliemel illustrate that global value chains are not always global. Despite, a burgeoning genre of analysis focused on global value chains (GVCs), there is still yet to emerge a clear picture of their geographic structure or indeed how their pattern differs between "industries." The lack of clarity extends to questioning whether GVCs are truly global or only regionalised. This study uses inter-country input–output data to develop a "global value architecture" analysis across 22 industries. It reframes each industry as a trade complex, which considers the supply of foreign value added from inter-country and inter-industry sources. This meso-level analysis sits between the micro level (e.g. firm or product) and macro level (aggregated national trade) and enables industry-specific insights in a global context. Analysis of the 22 trade complexes reveals three distinct archetypes of what we call global value architectures (GVAs). The GVA archetypes are the sparsely interconnected "exo-nets," the globally highly interconnected "global factory" and a "fusion" archetype that is interconnected within regions with few inter-regional ties. The GVA has implications for how global value chains and trade relations can be managed by individual firms or on behalf of sectors by their government representatives, as elaborated in the accompanying case study.

In Chapter 11, Martin Bliemel, Brian Wixted and Göran Roos link the interconnectedness and innovativeness of global value chains. There is a strong conceptual link between the structure of GVCs and innovativeness. However, evidence of the link has largely been limited to the study of GVCs in industries that are purported to be innovative, and the studies have largely been at the level of an individual firm or product. This sampling bias and level of analysis creates a lack of an objective measure of innovativeness, which would enable generalisation to other firms in a given industry and with which to perform inter-industry comparison. This chapter extends the typology of global value architectures by Wixted and Bliemel to use the same trade data to quantify the structures of 22 industry complexes via a measure of significant sourcing pathways per economy (SPE). The SPE results are used to rank the industries according to their level of interconnectedness and then reveal how this measure of trade complex structure correlates to well-established innovation measures based on research and development intensity, alliancing and modularity. These correlations suggest that measures of trade in GVCs are complementary to these innovativeness measures. It is proposed that these innovativeness measures can be replaced by the measure of SPE, as it is a more objective, replicable and thus reliable

DOI: 10.4324/9781315225661-15

measure of innovativeness which also explicitly accounts for the dispersion of innovation across regions, thereby representing the aggregate structure of all GVCs of a given industry.

Next in Chapter 12, Daria Taglioni, Deborah Winkler and Jakob Engel illustrate that how countries engage with GVCs determines how much they benefit from them. For an effective and sustainable strategy of GVC participation, governments must identify key binding constraints and design the necessary policy and regulatory interventions, including investing in infrastructure and capacity building. Countries that understand the opportunities that GVCs offer and adopt the appropriate policies to mitigate the risks associated with them have the opportunity – through GVCs – to boost employment and productivity in agriculture, manufacturing and services. The new policy framework that allows developing countries to maximise the gains from GVC integration is one in which a "whole supply chain approach" must be adopted. This reflects the fact that in a world economy where GVCs play a dominant role, imports matter as much as, if not more than, exports, and in which the flows of goods, services, people, ideas and capital are interdependent and must be assessed jointly. However, within the context of increased automation in many of the entry stages of GVC production in most industries, as well as rising protectionism in advanced countries, developing countries' efforts to engage and upgrade in GVCs face a more challenging global trading landscape than in the past.

Chapter 13, presented by Menaka Arudchelvan and Ganeshan Wignaraja, undertakes a comparative, micro-level analysis of joining global supply chain trade in selected developing Asian economies to improve our understanding of fragmentation of manufacturing across borders. It uses a large-scale firm-level data set collected by the World Bank to investigate micro-level behaviour in supply chains in developing Asian economies and to explore policy implications. The findings suggests that firm size (reflecting economies of scale to overcome entry costs) matters for joining supply chain trade with large firms playing the dominant role in Asian economies. Meanwhile, small- and medium-sized enterprises (SMEs) make a small contribution to supply chain trade relative to the sectors' employment contribution. However, firm size is not the whole story. Efficiency – particularly investment in building technological capabilities and skills – and access to commercial bank credit also influence joining supply chain trade. The chapter suggests that governments can facilitate SMEs joining supply chain trade through a market-oriented strategy, modern physical infrastructure, streamlined regulations and efficient business support services.

Global value chains and least developed countries are discussed in Chapter 14 by Jodie-Anne Keane. Whilst the mainstream literature posits a range of new trade opportunities created by the fragmentation of global production and increase in intermediate goods trade, there is a notable absence of critical reflection on contemporaneous upgrading processes of GVCs and the role of international support measures. The absence of critical reflection is surprising in view of the automaticity of upgrading processes posited through GVC participation. The available empirical evidence, explored in this chapter drawn from comparative GVC case studies of the participation by selected least developed countries (LDCs), is more suggestive of upgrading avenues closed rather than opened. Within this context, the upgrading process for LDCs trading within contemporary GVCs requires bridging divergent governance structures, demanding heighted governance capabilities. This pressure demands a commensurate response from the international support architecture, not all aspects of which are adequately reflected in the recent universal adoption of the Sustainable Development Goals.

Koen De Backer and Sébastien Miroudot wrote Chapter 15 titled "Mapping of GVCs, services and intangible assets." The chapter first reviews the recent developments in input–output analysis and discusses the new indicators available for researchers together with their strength and weaknesses. Using the World Input-Output Database (WIOD) – 43 countries and 56 industries from the year 2000 to 2014 – the chapter then uses some of these indicators to provide a broad mapping of GVCs, focusing on dispersion of income along the value chain and what is the role of different countries and industries. De Backer and Miroudot then discuss three determinants of income in GVCs: the role of services and how in particular wholesale and retail as well as interactions with customers shape some value chains; the role of intellectual assets and how income is also captured or maintained in other segments of the value chain on the basis of intangible capital; and the role of business ecosystems and how cooperative value chains as opposed to captive value chains offer an alternative model to create and retain value in GVCs. In a final section, the chapter draws some implications from the new findings.

Next, Quan Zhao, Wenwen Shen, Wei Zhang and Jimena Sotelo in Chapter 16 discuss GVCs from a trade and investment perspective. Global trade and investment have been key factors in shaping GVCs. The current stagnation of trade is a concern at the global level. The estimated trade growth at 1.7 percent and global GDP growth at 2.2 percent in 2016 are the lowest since the financial crisis of 2009. The contribution of trade to output growth seems to be at a stake after having experienced a trade growth that doubled that of global GDP during 1985–2007, which was still barely standing during the last four years. However, globalisation is taking new forms and with that trade and GVCs. Structural transformations such as the shortening of GVCs, digitalisation of trade and servicification might be playing a role in trade slowdown.

Chapter 17 from Mark Matthews assesses a broad range of literature in order to take stock of current understanding of the relationships between industrial strategy, innovation and GVCs. The aim is to focus attention on these important relationships and to suggest a way forward in improving our understanding of how GVCs are shaped by, and also shape, national industrial strategies and innovation performance. As such, a set of issues are addressed in combination in a way that is relatively unusual. In highlighting these important connections, the intention is that the future treatment of industrial strategy, innovation and GVCs will less fragmented and, as a result, more accurately reflect political, economic and technologies realities. Given the breadth of the literature covered in this practitioner-oriented "stocktake," which must cover work on industrial strategy, innovation and GVCs, the flow of the argument has not been disruptive with exhaustive references to the literature. An extensive list of the sources drawn upon is provided in the "References." The aim is to distil the main messages and lessons from the broad body of literature in order to focus on how best to move forward in the future when translating this academic understanding into practical initiatives.

Two case studies are presented to complete Part IV. The first case study, written by Brian Wixted and Martin Bliemel, is a meso-level GVC analysis of Korean shipbuilding. Korean trade policymakers are concerned with increased talk about trade wars and the impact of trade tariffs on one of the country's major industries, shipbuilding. To understand which countries to target for specific trade policies, the first challenge is to understand who their significant trade partners are for this industry (in this case the suppliers of input to shipbuilding, not the buyers of finished vessels).

The second case study, with Martin Bliemel, Brian Wixted and Göran Roos, explores GVCs' vulnerability to disruption. Despite the benefits of modularisation and highly interconnected GVCs, recent natural disasters have provided evidence that global supply chains can be quite vulnerable to interruptions.

10

GLOBAL VALUE CHAINS ARE NOT ALWAYS GLOBAL

The 'global factory' and 'exo-net' value architectures

Brian Wixted and Martin Bliemel

Introduction

Globalisation is fast moving, constantly changing and in flux. Thanks to economic policy transformations in a growing list of countries, advances in telecommunication, transportation (including containerisation) and international trade agreements, it is becoming easier for firms to efficiently source and integrate components from specialist suppliers almost anywhere in the world. The effects of globalisation are often expressed as a net increase in the global trade of goods and especially in intermediate goods (Cattaneo et al. 2010), and more complex structural patterns of trade (e.g., IBM 2011; Dolphin & Nash 2012). This phenomenon is especially relevant to growing debates on innovation localisation (see e.g. Bathelt et al. 2004 on clusters), international supply chains (also referred to as global production networks, global value chains, etc.; e.g. Sturgeon 2002; Coe et al. 2008; Dedrick et al. 2010) and their change. The recent fundamental changes to global production and innovation are only in part related to the rising strength of the so-called BRIICS economies (Brazil, Russia, Indonesia, India, China and South Africa; see OECD 2009). Likewise, the new strength in Asia and the challenges in the US and Eurozone economies only partially explain the destabilisation of the long-accepted wisdom that national production and international trade patterns are essentially stable and slow to change (see e.g. Wolff 2000).

There are, however, inherent challenges to studying such a broad phenomenon as globalisation and international trade, notably, the choice of an appropriate theoretical lens and level of analysis at which to operationalise a theory. For instance, Ernst (2002, p. 503) argues that globalisation "poses some important puzzles that need to be addressed in a revised agglomeration theory." In contrast, rather than prescribe a specific theory, Gereffi (2005, p. 160) warns that globalisation scholars have to be "academic interlopers [because] no single academic field can encompass it."

In context of an increasingly globalised world, this chapter is driven by an observed need for a conceptual clarification of what industries are and what their global trade linkages reveal about them. More specifically, this chapter explores the research question of which structural patterns of trade or 'value architectures' can be derived from observations at the level of inter-industry

 DOI: 10.4324/9781315225661-16

and inter-country production sourcing pathways. Our interest is in the global organisation of trade, focusing on the products of industries, not on the technologies (such as production technologies or the advances in product technologies) embedded in them (cf. Pavitt 1998).[1]

In order to elucidate these value architectures, this research draws on value chain studies, which are often illustrated with examples at the firm level (aka *micro* level) and analysed using data at the economy level (aka *macro* level), or are focused on individual industries or economies without considering how inter-connected global trade has become. As a result, these studies do not simultaneously capture inter-industry and inter-country relationships as also noted in a review by Ernst (2002), creating a gap between the micro and macro levels of analysis. In order to address this micro–macro gap, this study analyses industries at the meso level by using data about inter-industry *and* inter-country trade linkages. More specifically, this study uses input–output tables (I-O tables) from the Organisation for Economic Co-operation and Development (OECD) as the basis for a model of global trade to identify and quantify global value architectures across 22 trade complexes. Trade complexes are defined here as the trade network structure of a particular industry incorporating all source inputs but disaggregated by each source country. To clarify, trade complexes include a focal industry, as well as supplier industries to that industry, and are therefore more encompassing than agglomerations of organisations within only one industry. The trade complex definition and level of analysis is therefore distinct from industries (i.e. homogeneous sets of firms that compete on the basis of similar or substitutable products).

Our analysis suggests that aggregating foreign inputs by country offers a promising method for qualitatively differentiating value architectures, where value architectures are the archetypes of trade complexes. More specifically we visualise the architectures by drawing out only the significant sourcing pathways. In a subsequent study (see Chapter 11), we use these pathways to derive a quantitative measure with which we highlight important network patterns *across industries* and their correlation with popular *measures of innovation*. While the data we have analysed is relatively old (2000) it is more detailed than subsequent data sets. We therefore consider it to be a benchmark study, one providing the baseline from which other studies can assess changes across time.

When comparing the trade complexes of the 22 industries, this study reveals striking differences across industries. Some are truly globalised, while others remain highly regionalised, despite the globalisation rhetoric across the media and literature. By overlaying the 22 trade complexes onto geographic maps, we distinguish three archetypes of global value architectures – global factories, fusion and exo-nets – with which we can categorise each of the 22 manufacturing industries according to such architectural forms.

Literature review

There is much literature relevant to research related to the structure of global trade, value chains and innovation. For instance, recent reviews in the modularity literature emphasise inter-firm or within-industry levels (Colfer & Baldwin 2010; Campagnolo & Camuffo 2010), but have not yet stretched the level of analysis further towards the macro level (i.e., a meso level). For example, some empirical studies analyse entire value chains of a single product (Apple's iPod; Dedrick et al. 2010), a single industry (Turkina et al. 2016) or single economic region, or a more focused combination thereof. We cannot do all studies justice, and must risk being 'interlopers' (Gereffi 2005). Even within subfields related to research on global value chains (GVCs), the key concepts and evidence are "scattered across a number of fields in management, economics, and engineering" (Colfer & Baldwin 2010, p. 1), each of which offers their own interpretation.

Perhaps one of the most important and challenging aspects to maintaining conceptual clarity is setting clear boundaries around the phenomenon of interest and defining the relevant level of analysis. While, the GVC concept is most intuitively described by the interfaces between firms, products and modules, its measurement usually occurs at the macro scale of activity (e.g. net trade per economy). This disconnect across micro- and macro-levels is exemplified by an OECD report (2013), which includes macro-economic studies that draw on illustrative examples at the micro-level phenomenon to support arguments about how trade occurs at a global level (net imports or exports per economy). This can be somewhat confusing because the micro-level GVC terminology permeates macro-level arguments and implies measurement across multiple steps in the value chain, despite measures only reflecting a single step in the value chain (e.g., Cattaneo et al. 2010; Timmer et al. 2012; OECD 2013). Thus, the literature is organised here around the level of analysis.

Micro-level research on GVCs

The micro level of analysis is closest to the origins of near-decomposability (Simon 1962) and studies how a firm or its products are modularised and organised. Research at this level explains how products are assemblies of separable components with interfaces that are codified and standardised such that the components and sub-assemblies can be sourced from an open market. In reality, assembling components also often requires complex coordination of interface design and other tasks. Therefore, research at this level includes emphasis on the interrelation of components and their functions (Sako 2005), of product designs (see Novak & Eppinger 2001), and of tasks (see Minondo & Requena-Silvente 2013) and activities (Hobday 1998; Davies 2003, 2004). Taken together, micro-level work can bounded by the interest in firms, their interrelations (Wang & von Tunzelman 2000) and functions (Sturgeon 2008).

While early micro-level research focused on operations within a firm boundary, more recent studies highlight that components are often sourced from outside the firm. The value added by most modern firms is increasingly proportionate to internal research and development (R&D) and to in-house sales and marketing, and decreasingly proportionate to in-house manufacturing. Plotting the proportion of value added of these activities in this sequence results in the 'smile curve' (Baldwin & Evenett 2015) that graphically highlights increased sourcing of low value-added components, offset by a commensurate increase in high value-added R&D and sales.

This externalisation of production is reflected in research about the 'modularisation of production' and 'modularisation in inter-firm systems' (Takeishi & Fujimoto 2003). These inter-firm systems (Brusoni, Jacobides & Prencipe 2001) can then be investigated through a lens of the hierarchical and transactional nature between firms (Baldwin 2007; Luo et al. 2012), which link together to form value chains. These value chains include upstream and downstream relations, and have been labelled global commodity chains (GCCs) (e.g. Gereffi & Korzeniewicz 1994), GVCs (e.g. Gereffi et al. 2005; Dedrick et al. 2010), modular production networks (e.g. Sturgeon 2002 and 2003) or global production networks (GPNs) (e.g. Ernst 2002; Henderson et al. 2002). We recognise that each of these terms has a specific meaning but each contributes to the overall field of analysing the network patterns of international trade.

This extension from a firm to its GVC stretches the level of analysis beyond the traditional micro level to include suppliers, often across economic regions (Fields 2006). For example, Dedrick et al. (2010) break down an Apple iPod to list Broadcom, Samsung, TDK, Toshiba–Matsushita Display and Toshiba amongst others as suppliers of the major components. Similarly, Ali-Yrkkö et al. (2011) break down a Nokia mobile phone into its processors, display, integrated circuits, camera, memory, battery, other components, and software. They suggest that, on the basis of the suppliers' locations, Finland captures 34% of final value, with the rest of the EU capturing an additional 9.3%, America capturing 9.1% and Asia 8.3% of the final value. Luo et al. (2012) provide a more regional focus by examining Japanese automotive and electronics manufacturing using inter-firm level data. Their dependency structure matrices provide a rich picture of the interconnectedness within either industry and of the various levels of suppliers within Japan. However, such a regional focus then means that there is less attention on the global context of these industries.

Overall, we find that much of the micro-level literature about value chains is written as case studies of firm–product combinations, value chain–product combinations or industry–product combinations. Indeed, a considerable portion of the GVC literature is focused on the operation of the system (Sturgeon 2002; Gereffi et al. 2005; Sturgeon et al. 2008; Ponte & Sturgeon 2014) without operationalising interactions. While these case studies provide a lot of depth, they are not intended to be generalisable across industries and thus do not express the degree to which components are sourced across a broad range of suppliers and regions in quantitative terms that enable direct comparison of industry or region. To address the lack of comparability across industries and regions, Sturgeon (2008) calls for research devoted to industry independent functions and governance activities, albeit at the firm level. Without an established overarching framework of inter-industry and inter-regional patterns of sourcing, researchers, managers and policymakers alike risk overconfidently importing findings from conceptually 'near' industries, such as from Silicon Valley to Bangalore (Saxenian 2001). In comparison, the present study attempts to systematically classify quantifiable differences in sourcing patterns across industries (e.g. the archetypical form of their value architecture). For more quantitative analysis of global trade structures and their correlates, see Chapter 11 in this book.

Macro-level research on GVCs

By measuring net trade per economy, these macro-level studies also do not differentiate industries, and thus are not a good fit with studying the interconnectedness of regions across industries and of industries across regions.

Macro-level studies typically focus on country specialisation in relation to other explanatory factors (see for example the recent recommended measures; Ahmad et al. 2017). For example, Hidalgo and Hausmann (2009, p. 931) examine how a given economy's trade structure correlates to income level and growth. As noted by Minondo and Requena-Silvente (2013), such studies may contain inter-industry trade data, but the aggregation at the macro level is done in a way that excludes consideration or explanation of how trade structures vary across industries.

Other macro-level studies related to GVC cover 'fragmentation' (e.g. Jones & Kierzkowski 1990, 2001; Arndt 1998). These studies show that trade in parts and components has been increasing, and argue that this is due to reductions in transportation and communications costs. Despite the general appeal of the concept, the empirical research has focused predominantly on electronics and motor vehicle industries (e.g. Feenstra 1998; Hummels et al. 2001; Chen et al. 2005; Athukorala & Yamashita 2006; Luo et al. 2012).

Finally, of note there is 'complex networks' analysis of trade, which uses network analysis concepts (scale-free distributions, centrality, density, etc.) to measure trade patterns (see e.g. Smith & White 1992; Kastelle 2008; De Benedictis & Tajoli 2010, 2011). Collectively, these studies highlight the heterogeneous distribution of structural measures of trade patterns across a broad range of industries. While the measures of network structure (Amador & Cabral 2017; Criscuolo & Timmis 2018) or intermediate trade (Soo 2018) are useful to identify and parameterise industries, they lack a qualitative appreciation of geography. For instance, an industry's structural core can be determined by the inter-country connections that maintain a density threshold of 0.9 (e.g. De Benedictis & Tajoli 2010). Such a purely network structural measure does not qualify each relationship's relative level of trade, resulting in countries being included in the core that arguably only add marginal value to the industry.

Bridging the micro–macro gap: The missing muddled middle of GVC research

To say there is a muddle over the middle of GVC studies is not intended as a criticism against researchers studying GVCs. Researchers have been working from both ends of the spectrum – the micro and the macro, both implying the existence of a middle 'territory' of GVCs. This mixing of perspectives presents the opportunity to focus our effort on synthesising the middle – GVCs at the global 'industry' structure level. The muddle over the middle level between micro and macro levels of analysis can be highlighted in a number of ways.

Most clearly, Amador and Cabral (2016) provide an extensive review of the literature regarding the measurement of global value chains and clearly reveal that prior research has focused on trade in parts, changes in the foreign content of production and trade in value-added. Their review also shows that there is no clear attention to the structure of trade at an industry level (as done here). The literature since has not filled this gap. As an example, the edited volume by De Marchi et al. (2017) links GVC analysis through case studies, *cluster* identification and *multinational* firms. Such work is a deepening of the mixing micro and meso views suggested by Ernst (2002, p. 505), who comments: "We thus need to shift the focus of our analysis away from the *industry and the individual firm* to the level of a network flagship and its evolving GPN." While this more macro shift in focus includes multiple geographies, it remains centred on a focal 'network flagship' firm and the group of organisations to which it is connected, and is thus only a minor extension from the micro level.

At the macro level, research has also begun to recognise the need to bridge the micro–macro gap. As stated by the OECD (2013, p. 24):

> Until recently, [measurement of GVCs] mainly involved case studies of specific products [...] Evidence on GVCs at the aggregate level has been limited, and until recently there was little internationally comparable data on the importance of GVCs across economies. However, the OECD has addressed the measurement of GVCs during the past years, and new data and indicators on GVCs have been developed for a large number of OECD and non-OECD economies.

Interestingly, while the OECD recognises the importance of creating comparable data across GVCs (and by implication industries), its emphasis remains at the economy level.

A handful of value chain studies have aggregated micro-level data to the meso level. One such approach is provided by analysing the structure of specialised production within an industry of similar firms. For example, Fujimoto (2007; building on Fujimoto and Oshika 2008) analyses Japanese manufacturing firms and their interrelations to conclude that industries in Japan have a comparative advantage in integrated products, not just the production of specialised components. However, Fujimoto's study is limited regarding systematic comparison across regions. It only provides detail about the Japanese economy, and its measures are constructed around a 5-point Likert scale in a survey, which thus includes some degree of subjectivity of the participating managers.

For GVC studies at the meso level, the conundrum is being as inclusive of other industries and regions as micro-level studies, without aggregating away the qualitative texture and quantitative differences, as seen in macro-level studies. When aggregated beyond a micro level, inclusion of sources from other industries risks overwhelming the analysis and the ability to simultaneously distinguish the industry and region of origin. With these risks in mind, there is therefore an untapped opportunity to increase the scope from *what* products firms make to include *how* they make those products, *where* the production occurs and *with whom* (as also advocated by Ernst 2002 and Luo et al. 2012).

Empirical challenges in bridging the micro–macro gap

Firm-level studies suggest that transactions take many different forms and include complex practices such as relational contracts, concurrent sourcing (or tapered integration), and two-way vertically permeable boundaries. Sector-level studies, in turn, focus on networks of related firms and describe stable and recurring patterns in the flows of goods and knowledge within a sector. Formal network methods have been used to study flows of knowledge *but, because of data limitations, transactions and flows of goods have not received as much attention.*

(Luo et al. 2012, p. 6, emphasis added)

The preceding quote aptly summarises the value chain literature regarding industry structure and notes the empirical gap in the literature that we aim to fill. It also notes the need to expand the scope from firms to sectors and industries, thus implying subsequent expansion to globally distributed industries and economies. This latter challenge was also highlighted by Ernst (2002), who argues that in order to bridge the micro–macro gap, we are required to consider linkages and trade within an industry, across industries *and* across economic boundaries. There are several challenges in achieving this. First, we need relatively clear boundaries of each industry in order to study the flows between them. Second, we also need to separate out where geographically these industries and suppliers are located. As indicated in our introduction, the terms 'industries' and 'sectors' can be somewhat fuzzy due to the multilevel nature of those terms and in the literature. 'Industries' is usually limited to homogeneous sets of firms with similar products (e.g. Brusoni, Jacobides & Prencipe 2009).

To avoid the industry vs. sector debate, we introduce the term *trade complex*, which includes supplier industries to a given industry (e.g. according to International Standard Industrial Classification of All Economic Activities [ISIC] categories) and is observable via the international sourcing pathways within and across industries, including reciprocal flows. Thus, *trade complex* boundaries include the immediate sources to an industry and geographically differentiate each source economy. Trade complexes are also distinct from industry architectures. The latter concept is challenging because it "embraces the *entire* structure of the supporting value chain, and the *full range* of institutions involved" (Brusoni, Jacobides & Prencipe 2009, p. 210, emphasis added). Inclusion of the entire system's structure and institutions is empirically impractical because value chains feed into themselves across industries, resulting in encompassing the circular flow of the entire global economy (Leontieff 1991).

Trade complexes are conceptually similar to systems of production (Baldwin 2008), and incorporate the components and the structure derived from the interactions between the components, where the nodes are industries within economies and the interactions are the significant *inter-* and *intra-industry* sourcing pathways between economies' industries. This analysis is done simultaneously for all economies and their industries for which there is data. In comparison to systems of production, the trade complex is more precise about the boundaries of the system being analysed: geographically inclusive of all countries (for which data is available) and inclusive of suppliers across all industries, albeit limited to only one step of the value chain.

In targeting this meso level, it is important to trade off multiple potential foci, for example design and specialisation (e.g., Fujimoto 2007; Baldwin 2007), hierarchies of transactions (e.g., Luo et al. 2012) or knowledge-based vs transactional interactions (e.g., Rosenkopf & Schilling 2007). We trade off capturing granularity of individual firm trade and multiple tiers in the value chain in favour of differentiating sourcing patterns across each industry's trade complex. The breadth of economic activities and economies included in our analysis allows for generalisation while also facilitating industry or economy specific analysis. This scope is similar to Rosenkopf and Schilling's (2007) analysis of the strategic alliance structure across multiple industries, but using trade data and with the additional benefit of considering geography.

Methodology

Methodological framing

Before delving into the technical aspects of our methodology and analysis, we first operationalise the meso level employed to capture the inter-industry and inter-country linkages. Because there are multiple possible analytical perspectives on global trade at the meso level, it is important to note their variations.

A key element of meso-level analysis of GVCs, following Los, Timmer and De Vries (2015), is that it reveals something about industry boundaries and country boundaries. A building block towards multi-industry multi-region GVC analysis is to start the analysis with a single country and industry, follow all the (significant) input linkages (country and industry) and then iteratively keep following the inputs to those activities (country and industry). The result is a complex matrix that is representative of the value network for the focal economy and industry, with the risk of ending up in loops via the circular flow of the entire global economy (Leontieff 1991). Such an approach is elaborated on in the case study on Korean shipbuilding (later in Part IV).

At the opposite end of the scale to these building blocks is analysis of economic blocs for particular industries. This highly aggregated variant can be visually displayed in different forms such as in Los et al. (2015) and OECD publications (e.g. OECD 2010 and Miroudot et al. 2009), wherein they investigate global regional (triad) trade (Asia, Europe and the Americas). Thus, this type of analysis aggregates all the trade within and across the three major regions, but it is simpler with real dollar figures than I-O coefficients. At this level of analysis, the scale of the flows is what matters. A taxonomy of industry structure is not possible at this level because the transaction structure of each industry would be the same: there will always be six international flows plus the three Rest Of World (ROW) flows.

This study introduces and operationalises a *middle* approach between these two, framed around trade complexes – focusing on significant imported input pathways across *all* countries within a global industry to develop a taxonomy of global industries. These multi-region multi-industry visualisations will follow from the following analysis.

Methodology

Our analysis of international sourcing pathways involves three steps by which we reduce raw trade data into trade complexes.

1. First, we construct a large multi-industry inter-country input–output (ICIO) model, including all the major OECD countries plus the large non-OECD countries of China

and Brazil (see also Yamano & Ahmad 2006; Wixted, Yamano & Webb 2006; Guo, Webb & Yamano 2009 for a series of working papers published by OECD about its I-O data). The ICIO model is thus a specific form of an interregional model (see Polenske 1995 and Polenske & Hewings 2004 for definitions of different I-O model types).

2. Second, using data from the ICIO model, we identify the significant inter-country sourcing links for each economy and industry, which together form a trade complex. Although the I-O model contains input and output data (inputs becoming outputs), final market segments (consumers, exports, etc.) and value added (e.g. labour) we focus on a standard demand pull modelling of intermediate goods sourcing because it is more indicative of input use in an industry; any given industry's output patterns may include diverse markets.

3. Third, we visualise and categorise the structure of these significant international sourcing pathways for each trade complex.

Step 1: Inter-country input–output model construction

Input–output data has been collected for decades (see Augusztinovics 1995), but attempts at harmonising the data between OECD countries is relatively recent dating back to the early 1990s (see Wixted et al. 2006). As explained by the OECD, "The most unique feature of the OECD input–output tables is that they break down inter-industrial transaction flows of goods and services into those that are domestically-produced and those that are imported, and into intermediate and capital goods" (Yamano & Ahmad 2006, p. 5). In other words, the ICIO models are unique in their emphasis on transactions of intermediate goods within a framework that includes horizontal transactions (e.g. multilateral partners), and can accommodate vertical trade (e.g. production and value chains). This vertical or inter-industry trade is necessary to include when analysing value-add and modularity as it relates to global trade. For instance, vehicles are not made up only of the outputs of the motor vehicle industry, but also components made of steel, aluminium, plastics, fabrics, electronics, glass and outputs of various other industries, which themselves are distributed around the globe. Focusing on international transactions allows identification of higher value transactions. Our use of ICIO tables also allows us to capture important *inter*-industry activity, similar to Wixted and Cooper (2007), who showed that significant trade activity existed *between* the two trade complexes related to information and communications technology (ICT). Our use of large ICIO models advances trade research done to date, in that no other studies have compared intra- and inter-industry trade across so many economies and 'industries' at an *industry's meso level*.

Our analysis follows on from the development of a series of ICIO[2] models (Wixted & Cooper 2007; Wixted 2009) that are based on the harmonised OECD I-O database (see Wixted et al. 2006 and Yamano & Ahmad 2006 for details). The harmonised OECD data removes many but not all the inconsistencies with using I-O tables between countries. This series of models includes a single-transactions matrix that summarises all intra- and inter-industry trade data between national industries and across borders, and thus integrates inter-industry and international trade. We follow the process for creating these kinds of matrices from the OECD data provided elsewhere (Cooper 2000; Wixted et al. 2006; Wixted & Cooper 2007; Wixted 2009) and only briefly summarise the Wixted ICIO model here.

The OECD provides two important input–output tables for each economy: a domestic (industry-by-industry) trade table and an imports (industry-by-industry) table. Both include intermediate goods transactions. The domestic table also includes 'value added' components such as labour and taxes (etc.) and forward linkages (consumption and exports). To transform these two tables into an ICIO matrix for each economy, each industry's total imports in the imports table must be redistributed according to the inter-regional pattern of trade for that economy. This inter-regional pattern of trade was compiled using the Bilateral Trade Database (BTD) by the OECD, for which all the industry classifications matched with the industries in the I-O tables. The BTD identifies the aggregate trade into a given industry from each economy in the OECD database. Therefore the inter-country regional pattern of trade will be different for each economy and each industry. By combining the two I-O tables (domestic and imports) and the BTD data, we create an industry-by-industry matrix for *each* pair of trade partners, resulting in the single large Wixted ICIO matrix. In this matrix, the domestic tables make up the diagonal of the ICIO matrix and each of the inter-economy trade tables fill in each side of the diagonal.

The Wixted model consists of 48 industries integrated across 24 economies listed. Of the 48 industries in the full model, we focus on 22 manufacturing-based trade complexes.[3] The other industries are non-manufacturing related, such as real estate, utilities, education and health, and remain important to consider when calculating the relative proportion of inputs of any one industry or economy. The overall data set thus consists of an economy-by-economy table (22 × 24 economies) in which each of these economy blocks in the matrix contains an industry-by-industry sub-matrix (48 × 48 cells). The main diagonal of the matrix contains the domestic I-O tables (i.e. intra- and inter-industry trade flows within each domestic economy), and the remaining cells contain data on trade between industries across economies. The overall size of the transaction matrix is [(48 × 48) × 24] × 22, approximately 1.2 m cells.

This massive matrix is not entirely representative for all trade between these economies, as certain trade flow assumptions were required for some services. Although "goods [still] represent the bulk of trade flows while services make up the bulk of GDP," services represent an increasing proportion of trade and GDP (Cattaneo et al. 2010, p. 32). Unfortunately, data on services trade was insufficient to analyse trade patterns of service industries. In order to overcome this data availability challenge, we follow Wixted (2009) to approximate the contribution of services trade to each manufacturing industry. For analysis of services trade, particularly for more recent years, the World Input-Output Database (WIOD) is more complete (see Timmer 2012). Neither data set is perfect, and includes limitations with respect to the number of countries or distinct industries in the data set. Our preference is for the OECD data which includes fewer countries but many more industries.

The most recent update of the OECD I-O database contains national tables for around 50 economies for the mid-2000s.[4] Our data is for 2000 or the nearest available year.[5] For international trade data availability reasons our study is limited to analysis of 22 economies plus an extra 2 source economies [Mexico and a "Rest of World" (ROW) region]. According to World Bank data,[6] concerning the average GDP per economy from 2003 to 2006, 13 of these economies are in the top 20 and 19 are in the top 40 GDP for this time range. Thus we believe these economies are representative of the industrialised global economy. The 24 economies in our model are summarised in Table 10.1 and visualised in darker grey in Figure 10.1. We prefer to arrange the economies in the figures in a roughly global geographic but Asia–Americas centred pattern due to the substantial pan-Pacific trade.

As briefly outlined earlier and described in greater detail elsewhere (e.g., Yamano & Ahmad 2006; Wixted et al. 2006; Wixted & Cooper 2007; Wixted 2009), we convert the raw data of dollars spent on inputs, labour, taxes etc. in each economy into a set of coefficients for each industry. These coefficients represent the proportion that is imported and domestically produced for each dollar of output for each industry and every economy. Once analysed through input-output methodologies, a new set of 'results' tables is produced which captures some of the circular flows in the economy: each dollar of extra production in a particular industry requires supplies from other industries which requires a marginal increase in production in those other industries, which in turn requires a marginal increase in production in those other industries, etc. Calculation of the results follows the net multiplier technique developed by Cooper (2000)

Table 10.1 Economies in our I-O model

Australia	Greece	Spain
Austria	Hungary	United Kingdom
Canada	Italy	United States
Czech Republic	Japan	Brazil
Denmark	Korea	China
Finland	Netherlands	Chinese Taipei (Taiwan)
France	Norway	Mexico★
Germany	Poland	ROW★★

★Complete I-O-tables were unavailable at the time of model construction, but Mexico was included as a supplier country due to its significance within the North American system.
★★Included in the modelling as a residual supplier region but not shown in the figures for clarity.

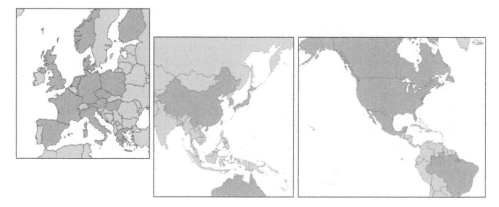

Figure 10.1 Map of economies in our I-O model.

and requires every industry to be analysed recursively until all the relative contributions and coefficients for each industry are resolved.

Because larger economies generally import a smaller share of production than smaller economies, a further normalisation is required. Rather than calculate country shares of imports on the basis of all output, we normalised using the value of imports for each economy. To illustrate the result of this normalisation, consider a small economy with limited local activity in a particular industry. The net multiplier calculations may show that for this industry, this economy requires 80 cents of its output dollar to be spent on imports (from any industry), thus capturing internally only 20 cents of each output dollar. This is an extreme example but not unrealistic. Alternatively, an industry in a large economy with an extensive network of suppliers to that industry may only require 10 cents of its output dollar to be imported, capturing the remaining 90 cents of each output dollar. Thus, without a normalisation step to correct for this, imports to smaller economies would be over-emphasised and imports to larger economies under-represented.

Step 2: Isolating significant sourcing pathways from the model

In the 'trade networks' literature it is common to analyse the complete network (e.g. De Benedictis & Tajoli 2010) and to include every trade transaction, however small. By including every minute transaction, visualisations would become too cluttered (see e.g. Turkina et al. 2016), since sourcing pathways of some scale tend to exist between every pair of developed economies (see also Serrano et al. 2007 and De Benedictis & Tajoli 2010). We seek to make the meso-level aggregation more meaningful by selecting only the significant[7] sourcing pathways in the model. This parsimonious selection is essential to explore differences in the value chain structures and to explore the extent to which such data can be used to quantify trade intensity for each trade complex.

In order to analyse the relationships between economies within a trade complex, we first isolate significant sourcing pathways for each industry's trade complex. As a reference value, if trade was shared evenly across 20 economies, each would capture 5%. This '20' is representative of the post-war period up until the late 1980s early 1990s, for which it can be argued that roughly there were about 20 major industrialised economies. Also, the OECD commenced with 20 economies (some of which were small) in 1960, with Italy, Japan and Australia joining soon thereafter. Thus, at face value, 5% serves as a minimum reference value below which trade is likely to be less significant.

We build on this relatively intuitive reference value to establish a more statistical minimum threshold above which to consider sourcing pathways to be part of the trade complex. To do so, we first investigate whether the distribution of all the economy-to-economy sourcing pathways in each industry follows a scale-free distribution, as also observed in the macro-economic literature on trade (e.g. Hidalgo & Hausman 2009; Panagariya & Bagaria 2013), as well as at the micro level (e.g. Uzzi 1996). For each industry's trade complex, we plot the proportion of sourcing pathways that exceed a range of thresholds against that range of thresholds, resulting in a classic L-shaped or 'long-tail' distribution graph. To test for a power-law or scale-free distribution, we then re-scale these curves into a log–log format, and test their fit against a straight line. Across all industries, the R^2 value of this line ranges between 0.773 and 0.910, with an average of 0.833, and significant well below 1%,[8] confirming our expectation that global sourcing patterns follow a scale-free distribution.

A logical threshold above which we capture the core sourcing pathways and filter out the 'long tail' of lower value sourcing pathways can be specified at the 'elbow' in the L-shaped curve. This elbow is defined by the point at which the slope of the distribution curve is closest to (negative) unity (−1). This is the point on the curve at which the long tail starts. Up to this threshold, adding another x% of links to the network adds more than x% of the trade volume. Vice versa, beyond this threshold, adding another x% of links to the network adds less than x% of the trade volume. For reference, Panagariya and Bagaria (2013) comment that "frequently, the top five partners [out of an average of 203 partners, e.g. ~2.5%] account for half of the exports and imports, while the bottom half account for less than 1 per cent of the trade in either direction" (2013: 1179). Similarly, Bernard et al. (2009) find that over 90% of imports and exports with the US are accounted for by just the top 5% of firms engaged in international trade.

Starting with our intuitive minimum reference value of 5%, we include tests for 10% and 15% thresholds in our search for the elbow in the L-curve. We find that in 21 out of 22 industry trade complexes, the 10% threshold comes closest to the elbow. Only in the petroleum industry is the 5% threshold closest to the elbow.[9] For 10 out of the 22 complexes the 15% threshold was closer to the elbow than the 5% threshold, but was never closer than the 10% threshold.[10] Thus, we employ a 10% threshold across all complexes, because a higher threshold could miss significant sourcing pathways, and a lower threshold could include too many insignificant sourcing pathways in isolating the core structure of the trade complex. Using only the sourcing pathways over 10%, we retain a parsimonious set of relationships from which we can derive the trade structure of each trade complex, thereby also enabling the development of archetypes (i.e. three forms of global value architecture); our step 3. See also Figure 3 in the Korean shipbuilding case study later in Part IV.

Step 3: Visualisation of trade complexes and identification of global value archetypes

To examine the overall organisation of a trade complex, we visualise and illustrate the patterns of significant sourcing pathways.[11] Our goal here is to explore the patterns of trade links through the lens of geography, which helps us infer properties of the trade complex. We refine the categorisation criteria provided by Wixted (2009) and categorise the figures into three *value architecture* groups: exo-nets, fusion and global factories. For each of our three classes of trade we discuss one example.

Exo-nets are architectures in which there are two separate 'worlds': Europe and the Asia–Americas. Each world has one dominant trade partner, usually Germany and the US. These architectures may have up to two 'bridges,' where bridges are defined as significant trade flows between the two worlds. An exemplar of the exo-net global value architecture is the iron and steel industry's trade complex, as shown in Figure 10.2a. This industry clearly has few pathways between countries within each of the two worlds, and has no pathways across worlds.

In contrast, global factories have globally distributed and interconnected production and international flows of intermediate goods, and resemble an 'elaborate international factory' (Cohen 2002, p. 22). Whereas some others define global factories at the level of the firm and its relations (e.g. Buckley 2009), the notion of global factory adopted here is at the trade complex level. Global factories have three interconnected 'worlds' (i.e. Europe, Asia and the Americas), with significant trade between them. There is also significant trade within each world, as evidenced by the number of pathways between countries within each world, including bilateral sourcing pathways. The global factory label indicates trade complexes in which the final product is a result of goods and services being sourced from around the world. These complexes have eight or more bridges, including at least one bilateral sourcing pathway, as for instance the 'office, accounting and computing machinery' industry's global factory global value architecture, shown in Figure 10.2b.

Between exo-nets and global factories are the 'fusion' global value architectures. Fusion architectures typically include the same separation of two worlds (Europe and Asia–Americas) as the exo-nets, but have two or more bridges between them, neither of which are bilateral. Like global factories, they often have one or two bilateral pathways, but these remain within the

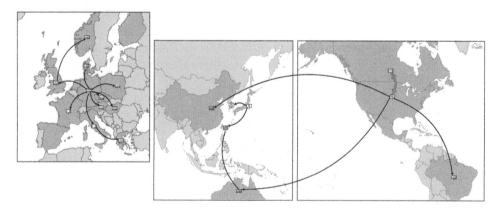

Figure 10.2a The exo-net global value architecture for the iron and steel industry's trade complex.

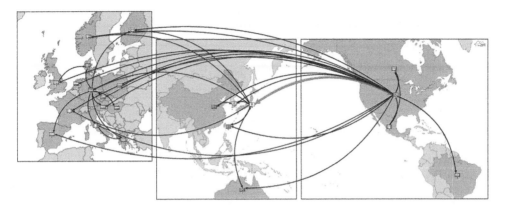

Figure 10.2b The global factory global value architecture for the office, accounting and computing machinery industry's trade complex.

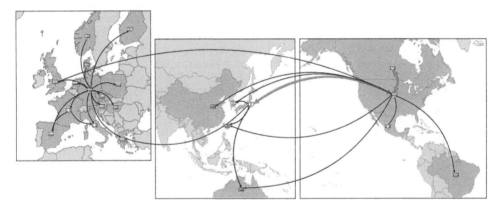

Figure 10.2c The fusion global value architecture for the motor vehicles, trailers and semi-trailers industry's trade complex.

Asia–Americas world (usually Canada–US or Japan–US). For example, the motor vehicles, trailers and semi-trailers industry's trade complex has two worlds that are interconnected by only two bridges (shown in Figure 10.2c). Each of the worlds also includes several internal interconnections, thus shifting away from the hub-and-spoke structure seen in many exo-nets.

With these criteria for each global value architecture in mind, we can classify each of the 22 OECD standard statistical industry categories in the data set,[12] as summarised in Table 10.2.

Discussion

Whether using OECD data from 1995, 2000 or the WIOD data from 2012, the preceding analysis and the visualisation of each industry's trade complex[13] reveals that each industry's complex can have very different forms and architectures, despite much of the rhetoric of globalisation across all sectors. The persistence of the distribution of exo-nets, fusion or global factories across all industries across three decades of data confirm that a more measured tone is required when researching GVCs in any particular industry.

For example, two of the most commonly studied global industries and GVCs (automobiles and ICT) have entirely different architectures. Based on the volume of extant literature on these

Table 10.2 Global value architectures for 22 industry trade complexes

Industry trade complex	Count of worlds and bridges	Global value architecture
Iron and steel	2 worlds, 0 bridges	Exo-net
Other non-metallic mineral products	2 worlds, 0 bridges	Exo-net
Textiles, textile products, leather and footwear	2 worlds, 0 bridges	Exo-net
Fabricated metal products, except machinery and equip	2 worlds, 0 bridges	Exo-net
Food products, beverages and tobacco	2 worlds, 1 bridge	Exo-net
Pulp, paper, paper products, printing and publishing	2 worlds, 1 bridge	Exo-net
Chemicals excluding pharmaceuticals (industrial & other)	2 worlds, 1 bridge	Exo-net
Manufacturing nec; including furniture	2 worlds, 1 bridge	Exo-net
Rubber and plastics products	2 worlds, 1 bridge	Exo-net
Machinery and equip nec (aka industrial machinery)	2 worlds, 2 bridges	Exo-net
Wood and products of wood and cork	2 worlds, 2 bridges	Exo-net
Coke, refined petroleum products and nuclear fuel	2 worlds, 2 bridges	Exo-net
Non-ferrous metals	2 worlds, 3 bridges*	Exo-net
Railroad equipment & transport equip nec	2 worlds, 2 bridges**	Fusion
Motor vehicles, trailers and semi-trailers	2 worlds, 2 bridges**	Fusion
Electrical machinery and apparatus, nec	2 worlds, 3 bridges	Fusion
Pharmaceuticals	2 worlds, 3 bridges	Fusion
Building & repairing of ships and boats	2 worlds, 5 bridges	Fusion
Medical, precision and optical instruments	2 worlds, 8 bridges	Fusion
Aircraft and spacecraft	2 worlds, 8 bridges, incl. a bilateral France–US bridge	Global factory
Radio, television and communication equipment	3 worlds, 9 bridges	Global factory
Office, accounting and computing machinery	3 worlds, 15 bridges	Global factory

Note: nec, not elsewhere classified.
* The global value architecture for the non-ferrous metals trade complex was classified as exo-net because the bridges links are all between different pairs of EU and Asia–Americas countries (Germany to Brazil, United States to Great Britain, Canada to Norway), and its network structure is sparse – for each economy where there is data – there is only slightly more than 1 significant trade pathway.
** We classify the global value architectures for these trade complexes as fusion, because despite having only two bridges between EU and Asia–Americas, they have many intra-regional pathways, both trans-Pacific and within Europe, that makes them closer to global factories (as observable in Figure 10.2c).

industries, one might be inclined to believe they are similarly interconnected and might completely overlook their differences when conducting GVC research at the micro or macro levels. The preceding analysis also reveals interesting differences between industries that have similar products: for example, non-ferrous metals have more bridges than either iron and steel or fabricated metal products. Vice versa, we also find architectural similarities across industries with different products interesting: for example, shipbuilding and precision instruments both have fusion value architectures but completely dissimilar physical scales of products and production.

As illustrated in the accompanying case study, having a clearer understanding of the context in which a given firm or industry manages its GVC can help resolve interdependencies with adjacent industries and GVCs. Visualising and managing these interdependencies become viable at the meso level. The interdependencies are occasionally lumped together as the 'circular flow' concept (Leontieff 1991), which does not provide actionable insights regarding how to manage inter-regional and inter-industry trade across multiple regions and industries. With the recent anxieties about trade wars and tariffs, such insights may enable higher-quality negotiations by governments and firms, should free trade agreements break down. Because of the qualitative differences across archetypes, restrictions to free trade may have a greater impact on eco-nets than global factories, because alternative sourcing pathways are not readily available.

The preceding analysis and categorisation of global value architectures also enables researchers to recognise the specific context of their research, thus permitting moderation of their results by industry. For instance, conclusions drawn from GVC research in the ICT industry may be less generalisable to pharmaceuticals, despite both being research intensive. Similarly, our findings caution against generalising from aircraft GVCs to shipbuilding or motor vehicle GVCs, despite all three being about transportation.

Conclusions

In summary, our review of the literature relevant to global value chains and production complexity reveals that there is considerable work at the micro level (firms) and macro level (economy-wide). However, without knowledge of the middle there is a notable leap of faith when extrapolating from a single firm's GVC to generalising about global economic trade, as exemplified by the OECD report (2013) mentioned earlier. Likewise, there is a gap when extrapolating from a single regional industry to global economic trade (e.g. Fujimoto 2007; Luo et al. 2012). Thus far, there has been little research that bridges this micro–macro divide. In response to this meso-level gap, we introduce a relatively novel meso level of analysis – the trade complex – which we use to analyse a large multi-industry ICIO model. We then explore what differences the inter-industry global trade data can qualitatively reveal about value architectures across each industry. For each of the 22 manufacturing industries in our model, we have categorised the architecture of the trade complex (as an exo-net, fusion or global factory). Despite frequent comments about industries being global, the vast majority of industries have a sparse exo-net structure that is vulnerable to supply chain interruptions and changes to trade agreement. Only three of the 22 industries can be classified as a global factory.

In Chapter 11 in this book we pursue a number of questions which we found to be particularly interesting arising from these results. Particularly, how do these results correlate to measures of innovation and the numerous industry taxonomies produced within the innovation studies field.

We recognise that ICIO analysis emphasises trade and production modularisation and does not (per se) capture knowledge linkages (e.g. strategic alliances and licensing agreements). Thus, we believe multiple further research opportunities exist that build directly on the conceptual and methodological approaches provided here. These opportunities include studying the non-manufacturing industries, domestic industries or taking a finer-grained analysis of inter-industry linkages (e.g. a meso-level analysis that is closer to the micro level, as with Figure 5 of the Korean shipbuilding case study). Whereas our primary analysis aggregated sourcing by economy, such aggregation could also be done by industry.

The two big pieces of work that are obvious follow ups to this chapter would be, first, using the WIOD data to track the evolution of trade complexes across time. Second, as newer data sources become available, we also find the notion of studying the emergence of the *global office* and global services trade of imminent interest.

Acknowledgements

This chapter has a long history and we need to thank many people who have contributed directly and indirectly to its development. Versions have been presented in seminars at the Department of Innovation, Industry, Science and Research (Australian Government); the Centre for Industry and Innovation Studies; University of New South Wales (UNSW) Business School in Sydney; and the South Australian Department of State Development. A number of individuals (including Gerald Hage and Fredrik Tell) have also commented on different versions, to whom we are immensely grateful. We specifically acknowledge the thoughtful and deeply useful comments of Paul Nightingale on a previous version of this work.

Notes

1 In comparison to Geels (2002) multi-level perspective, this study focuses only on a single type of tangible interaction and not on the layering of intangible interactions or rules in socio-technical regimes.
2 This analysis work predates the publication of the World Input-Output Database, but as explained later that ICIO data trades off more countries for fewer manufacturing industries.
3 Exactly the same approach could be taken to analysing service sector activities, but it would require a completely separate paper to explain the results.
4 http://stats.oecd.org/index.aspx.
5 For four industries, the 2000 model had relatively few economies (in brackets): aerospace (8), non-ferrous metals (9), pharmaceuticals (9) and other transportation equipment (8). For these four industries, we used the 1995 model, which increased the economies per model to 13, 12, 13 and 17, respectively. The OECD input–output tables and country notes for the 1995 and 2000 data are available at www.oecd.org/sti/inputoutput.
6 http://data.worldbank.org/indicator/NY.GDP.MKTP.CD.
7 We use the term *significant* in a quasi-statistical sense because there are arguably fewer economies than required to create a meaningful statistical threshold. However, we use statistics to justify our choice of threshold.
8 For the 16 industries in the WIOD data, the R-squared values ranged from 0.770 to 0.982, with an average of 0.834, and significant well below 1%.
9 In the WIOD data, 14/16 industry complexes in the elbow were closest to a threshold of 10%, with only coke and refined petroleum and nuclear fuel as well as mining and quarrying being closer to 5%.
10 For the WIOD data, the 5% threshold was closer to the elbow than the 15% threshold in all 16 industry complexes.
11 Flows from the Rest of the World (ROW) are not represented on the figures since, across all complexes, trade with the ROW is above the threshold of 10% of imports for most economies, and their inclusion in the figures would diminish their clarity and add little to the analysis. When modelling input–output flows, the direction of the trade relationships in the matrices is the direction of the monetary flows (i.e. from buyer to seller). Corresponding imports flow in the opposite direction (i.e. from producer to consumer). While it would be technically correct for the direction of the arrows to represent the monetary flows, our experience tells us that the visualisations are more intuitive for readers if the direction of the arrows represents the trade of goods. Significant bilateral trade is indicated by double-ended arrows, for which we doubled their thickness to make them easier to identify.
12 Using the WIOD data, there were a few more bridges between worlds and slightly more bilateral sourcing pathways. However, our classification remained largely unchanged versus the OECD comparables.
13 Available from the authors upon request.

References

Ahmad, N., Bohn, T., Mulder, N., Vaillant, M. & Zaclicever, D. 2017, '*Indicators on global value chains*', OECD Statistics Working Papers, No. 2017/08, OECD Publishing, Paris.
Ali-Yrkkö, J., Rouvinen, P., Seppälä, T. & Ylä-Anttila, P. 2011, 'Who captures value in global supply chains? Case Nokia N95 Smartphone', *Journal of Industry, Competition and Trade*, vol. 11, no. 3, pp. 263–278.

Amador, J. & Cabral, S. 2016, 'Global value chains: A survey of drivers and measures', *Journal of Economic Surveys*, vol. 30, no. 2, pp. 278–301.

Amador, J. & Cabral, S. 2017, 'Networks of value-added trade', *The World Economy*, vol. 40, no. 7, pp. 1291–1313.

Arndt, S.W. 1998, 'Super-Specialization and the gains from trade', *Contemporary Economic Policy*, vol. 16, no. 4, pp. 480–485.

Athukorala, P.-c. & Yamashita, N. 2006, 'Production fragmentation and trade integration: East Asia in a global context', *The North American Journal of Economics and Finance*, vol. 17, no. 3, pp. 233–256.

Augusztinovics, M. 1995, 'What input-output is about', *Structural Change and Economic Dynamics*, vol. 6, no. 3, pp. 271–277.

Baldwin, C.Y. 2007, 'Where do transactions come from? Modularity, transactions, and the boundaries of firms', *Industrial and Corporate Change*, vol. 17, no. 1, pp. 155–195.

Baldwin, R.E. & Evenett, S.J. 2015, 'Value creation and trade in 21st century manufacturing', *Journal of Regional Science*, vol. 55, no. 1, pp. 31–50.

Bathelt, H., Malmberg, A. & Maskell, P. 2004, 'Clusters and knowledge: Local buzz, global pipelines and the process of knowledge creation', *Progress in Human Geography*, vol. 28, no. 1, pp. 31–56.

Bernard, A.B., Jensen, J.B. & Schott, P.K. 2009, 'Importers, exporters and multinationals: A portrait of firms in the U.S. that trade goods,' Chapter 14, pp. 513–552, in T. Dunne, J.B. Jensen and M.J. Roberts (Eds.) *Producer Dynamics: New Evidence from Micro Data.* University of Chicago Press, Chicago, IL.

Brusoni, S., Jacobides, M.G. & Prencipe, A. 2009, 'Strategic dynamics in industry architectures and the challenges of knowledge integration', *European Management Review*, vol. 6, no. 4, pp. 209–216.

Brusoni, S., Prencipe, A. & Pavitt, K. 2001, 'Knowledge specialization, organizational coupling, and the boundaries of the firm: why do firms know more than they make?', *Administrative Science Quarterly*, vol. 46, no. 4, pp. 597–621.

Buckley, P.J. 2009, 'The impact of the global factory on economic development', *Journal of World Business*, vol. 44, no. 2, pp. 131–143.

Campagnolo, D. & Camuffo, A. 2010, 'The concept of modularity in management studies: A literature review', *International Journal of Management Reviews*, vol. 12, no. 3, pp. 259–283.

Cattaneo, O., Gereffi, G. & Staritz, C. 2010, *Global value chains in a postcrisis world: A development perspective*, The World Bank.

Chen, H., Kondratowicz, M. & Yi, K.-M. 2005, 'Vertical specialization and three facts about US international trade', *The North American Journal of Economics and Finance*, vol. 16, no. 1, pp. 35–59.

Coe, N.M., Dicken, P. & Hess, M. 2008, 'Global production networks: Realizing the potential', *Journal of Economic Geography*, vol. 8, no. 3, pp. 271–295.

Cohen, S.S. 2002, 'Mapping Asian integration: Transnational transactions in the Pacific Rim', *American Asian Review*, vol. 20, no. 3, p. 1.

Colfer, L. & Baldwin, C. 2010, *The Mirroring Hypothesis: Theory, Evidence and Exceptions Lyra Colfer The Mirroring Hypothesis: Theory, Evidence and Exceptions*, Harvard Business School Working Paper.

Cooper, R.J. 2000, 'An extension of the block spatial path approach to analysis of the influence of intra and interregional trade on multiplier effects in general multiregional input-output models', Chapter 15, pp. 303–327, in, A. Reggiani (Ed.) *Spatial Economic Science, New Frontiers in Theory and Methodology.* Springer, Berlin.

Criscuolo, C. & Timmis, J. 2018, *GVCs and Centrality: Mapping Key Hubs, Spokes and the Periphery*, OECD Publishing, Paris.

Davies, A. 2003, 'Integrated solutions: The changing business of systems integration', Chapter 16, pp. 333–368, in A. Prencipe, A. Davies and M. Hobday (Eds.) *The Business of Systems Integration*, Oxford University Press, Oxford, UK.

Davies, A. 2004, 'Moving base into high-value integrated solutions: A value stream approach', *Industrial and Corporate Change*, vol. 13, no. 5, pp. 727–756.

De Benedictis, L. & Tajoli, L. 2011, 'The world trade network', *The World Economy*, vol. 34, no. 8, pp. 1417–1454.

De Marchi, V., Di Maria, E. & Gereffi, G. 2017, *Local Clusters in Global Value Chains: Linking Actors and Territories Through Manufacturing and Innovation*, Routledge, Abingdon.

Dedrick, J., Kraemer, K.L. & Linden, G. 2010, 'Who profits from innovation in global value chains?: A study of the iPod and notebook PCs', *Industrial and Corporate Change*, vol. 19, no. 1, pp. 81–116.

Dolphin, T. & Nash, D. 2012, *Complex New World: Translating New Economic Thinking into Public Policy*, Institute for Public Policy Research, London, UK.

Ernst, D. 2002, 'Global production networks and the changing geography of innovation systems. Implications for developing countries', *Economics of Innovation and New Technology*, vol. 11, no. 6, pp. 497–523.

Feenstra, R.C. 1998, 'Integration of trade and disintegration of production in the global economy', *Journal of Economic Perspectives*, vol. 12, no. 4, pp. 31–50.

Fields, G. 2006, 'Innovation, time, and territory: Space and the business organization of Dell Computer', *Economic Geography*, vol. 82, no. 2, pp. 119–46.

Fujimoto, T. 2007, 'Architecture-based comparative advantage—a design information view of manufacturing', *Evolutionary and Institutional Economics Review*, vol. 4, no. 1, pp. 55–112.

Fujimoto, T. & Oshika, T. 2008, 'Empirical analysis of the hypothesis of architecture-based competitive advantage and international trade theory', 중소기업연구, vol. 30, no. 4, pp. 1–16.

Geels, F.W. 2002, 'Technological transitions as evolutionary reconfiguration processes: A multi-level perspective and a case-study', *Research Policy*, vol. 31, no. 8–9, pp. 1257–1274.

Gereffi, G. 2005, 'The global economy: Organization, governance, and development', *The handbook of economic sociology*, vol. 2, pp. 160–182.

Gereffi, G., Humphrey, J. & Sturgeon, T. 2005, 'The governance of global value chains', *Review of International Political Economy*, vol. 12, no. 1, pp. 78–104.

Gereffi, G. & Korzeniewicz, M. 1994, *Commodity Chains and Global Capitalism*, Praeger Publishers, Westport, CT.

Guo, D., Webb, C. & Yamano, N. 2009, '*Towards harmonised bilateral trade data for inter-country input-output analyses: statistical issues*', OECD Science, Technology and Industry Working Papers, No. 2009/04.

Henderson, J., Dicken, P., Hess, M., Coe, N. & Yeung, H.W.-C. 2002, 'Global production networks and the analysis of economic development', *Review of International Political Economy*, vol. 9, no. 3, pp. 436–464.

Hidalgo, C.A. & Hausmann, R. 2009, 'The building blocks of economic complexity', *Proceedings of the National Academy of Sciences*, vol. 106, no. 26, pp. 10570–10575.

Hobday, M. 1998, 'Product complexity, innovation and industrial organisation', *Research Policy*, vol. 26, no. 6, pp. 689–710.

Hummels, D., Ishii, J. & Yi, K.-M. 2001, 'The nature and growth of vertical specialization in world trade', *Journal of International Economics*, vol. 54, no. 1, pp. 75–96.

IBM. 2011, *Capitalizing on Complexity – Insights from the Global Chief Executive Officer Study*, IBM Global Business Services, Somers, New York.

Jones, R. & Kierzkowski, H. 1990, 'The role of services in production and international trade: A theoretical framework,' in R. Jones and A. Krueger (eds.) *The Political Economy of International Trade: Festschrift in Honor of Robert Baldwin*, Basil Blackwell, Oxford.

Jones, R. & Kierzkowski, H. 2001, 'A framework for fragmentation', Chapter 2, pp. 17–34, in S. Arndt and H. Kierzkowski (eds.) *Fragmentation: New Production Patterns in the World Economy*, Oxford University Press, New York.

Kastelle, T. 2008, '*Analysing the Evolution of International Trade: A Complex Networks Approach*,' Unpublished PhD Thesis, School of Business, The University of Queensland.

Leontief, W. 1991, 'The economy as a circular flow', *Structural Change and Economic Dynamics*, vol. 2, no. 1, pp. 181–212.

Los, B., Timmer, M.P. & de Vries, G.J. 2015, 'How global are global value chains? A new approach to measure international fragmentation', *Journal of Regional Science*, vol. 55, no. 1, pp. 66–92.

Luo, J., Baldwin, C.Y., Whitney, D.E. & Magee, C.L. 2012, 'The architecture of transaction networks: A comparative analysis of hierarchy in two sectors', *Industrial and Corporate Change*, vol. 21, no. 6, pp. 1307–1335.

Minondo, A. & Requena-Silvente, F. 2013, 'Does complexity explain the structure of trade?', *Canadian Journal of Economics/Revue canadienne d'économique*, vol. 46, no. 3, pp. 928–955.

Miroudot, S., Lanz, R. & Ragoussis, A. 2009, '*Trade in intermediate goods and services*', OECD Trade Policy Working Paper No. 93.

Novak, S. & Eppinger, S.D. 2001, 'Sourcing by design: Product complexity and the supply chain', *Management Science*, vol. 47, no. 1, pp. 189–204.

OECD. 2009, *Globalisation and Emerging Economies: Brazil, Russia, India, Indonesia, China and South Africa*, OECD Publishing, Paris.

OECD. 2010, *Perspectives on Global Development 2010: Shifting Wealth*. OECD Publishing, Paris.

OECD. 2013, *Interconnected Economies: Benefiting from Global Value Chains*, OECD Publishing, Paris.

Panagariya, A. & Bagaria, N. 2013, 'Some surprising facts about the concentration of trade across commodities and trading partners', *The World Economy*, vol. 36, no. 9, pp. 1165–1186.

Pavitt, K. 1998, 'Technologies, products and organization in the innovating firm: What Adam Smith tells us and Joseph Schumpeter doesn't', *Industrial and Corporate Change*, vol. 7, no. 3, pp. 433–452.

Polenske, K.R. 1995, 'Leontief's spatial economic analyses', *Structural Change and Economic Dynamics*, vol. 6, no. 3, pp. 309–318.

Polenske, K.R. & Hewings, G.J. 2004, 'Trade and spatial economic interdependence', *Papers in Regional Science*, vol. 83, no. 1, pp. 269–289.

Ponte, S. & Sturgeon, T. 2014, 'Explaining governance in global value chains: A modular theory-building effort', *Review of International Political Economy*, vol. 21, no. 1, pp. 195–223.

Rosenkopf, L. & Schilling, M.A. 2007, 'Comparing alliance network structure across industries: Observations and explanations', *Strategic Entrepreneurship Journal*, vol. 1, no. 3–4, pp. 191–209.

Sako, M. 2005, 'Modularity and Outsourcing' Chapter 12 in Prencipe, A., Davies, A., & Hobday, M. (Eds.) *The Business of Systems Integration*. Oxford University Press, Oxford.

Saxenian, A. 2001, *Bangalore: the Silicon Valley of Asia?*. Centre for Research on Economic development and Policy Reform, Working paper 91, Berkeley, CA.

Serrano, M.Á., Boguñá, M. & Vespignani, A. 2007, 'Patterns of dominant flows in the world trade web', *Journal of Economic Interaction and Coordination*, vol. 2, no. 2, pp. 111–124.

Simon, H. 1962, 'The architecture of complexity', *Proceedings of the American Philosophical Society*, vol. 106, pp. 467–482.

Smith, D.A. & White, D.R. 1992, 'Structure and dynamics of the global economy: Network analysis of international trade 1965–1980', *Social Forces*, vol. 70, no. 4, pp. 857–893.

Soo, K.T. 2018, 'Country size and trade in intermediate and final goods', *The World Economy*, vol. 41, no. 2, pp. 634–652.

Sturgeon, T., Van Biesebroeck, J. & Gereffi, G. 2008, 'Value chains, networks and clusters: Reframing the global automotive industry, *Journal of economic geography*, vol. 8, no. 3, pp. 297–321.

Sturgeon, T.J. 2002, 'Modular production networks: A new American model of industrial organization', *Industrial and Corporate Change*, vol. 11, no. 3, pp. 451–496.

Sturgeon, T.J. 2003, 'What really goes on in Silicon Valley? Spatial clustering and dispersal in modular production networks', *Journal of Economic Geography*, vol. 3, no. 2, pp. 199–225.

Sturgeon, T.J. 2008, 'Mapping integrative trade: Conceptualising and measuring global value chains', *International Journal of Technological Learning, Innovation and Development*, vol. 1, no. 3, pp. 237–257.

Tajoli, L. & De Benedictis, L. 2010, 'Comparing sectoral international trade networks', *Aussenwirtschaft*, vol. 65, no. II, pp. 53–73.

Takeishi, A. & Fujimoto, T. 2003, 'Modularization in the car industry', Chapter 13, in A. Prencipe, A. Davies, & M. Hobday (eds.) *The Business of Systems Integration*, Oxford University Press, Oxford.

Timmer, M., Erumban, A., Los, B., Stehrer, R. & De Vries, G. 2012, 'New measures of European competitiveness: A global value chain perspective', *World Input-Output Database*, Working Paper, vol. 9, p. 2012.

Timmer, M., Erumban, A.A., Gouma, R., Los, B., Temurshoev, U., de Vries, G.J., Arto, I.a., Genty, V.A.A., Neuwahl, F. & Francois, J. 2012, *The World Input-Output Database (WIOD): Contents, Sources and Methods*, Institue for International and Development Economics.

Turkina, E., Van Assche, A. & Kali, R. 2016, 'Structure and evolution of global cluster networks: Evidence from the aerospace industry', *Journal of Economic Geography*, vol. 16, no. 6, pp. 1211–1234.

Uzzi, B. 1996, 'The sources and consequences of embeddedness for the economic performance of organizations: The network effect', *American Sociological Review*, vol. 61, pp. 674–698.

Wang, Q. & von Tunzelmann, N. 2000, 'Complexity and the functions of the firm: Breadth and depth', *Research Policy*, vol. 29, no. 7–8, pp. 805–818.

Wixted, B. 2009, *Innovation System Frontiers: Cluster Networks and Global Value*, Springer, Heidelberg.

Wixted, B. & Cooper, R.J. 2007, 'The evolution of OECD ICT inter-cluster networks 1970–2000: an input-output study of changes in the interdependencies between nine OECD economies', in K.D.a.G.H. R. Cooper (ed.), *Globalization and Regional Economic Modeling*, Springer, Heidelberg, pp. 153–182.

Wixted, B., Yamano, N. & Webb, C. 2006, '*Input-output analysis in an increasingly globalised world: Applications of OECD's Harmonised International Tables*', OECD STI Working Paper, No. 2006/7, OECD Publishing, Paris.

Wolff, E. 2000, 'How persistent is industry specialization over time in industrialized countries?', *International Journal of Technology Management*, vol. 19, no. 1-2, pp. 194–205.

Yamano, N. & Ahmad, N. 2006, '*The OECD input-output database: 2006 edition*', OECD STI Working Paper, No. 2006/8, OECD Publishing, Paris.

11

LINKING THE INTERCONNECTEDNESS AND INNOVATIVENESS OF GLOBAL VALUE CHAINS

Martin Bliemel, Brian Wixted and Göran Roos

Introduction

In a globally connected business environment, the mantra for many is to innovate or die. Barring the existence of favourable and monopolistic trade agreements, tariffs or embargos, if your company does not source and produce the most innovative products or services, or does not use the most innovative efficient and effective production processes, then it will only be a matter of time until your business fails. Advances in telecommunication, transportation (including containerisation) and international trade agreements can work for or against anyone. The aggressiveness by which firms focus on producing and distributing innovative products applies across almost all industries. For manufacturing-based firms, and increasingly for service-based firms, this push to innovate and distribute globally has resulted in two primary strategies: specialisation and systems integration (Hobday, Davies & Prencipe 2005).

These two interrelated strategies create an inherent link between innovation and trade as indicted by DeBresson over 20 years ago. But what do they look like when played out at the level of an industry? What can we deduce about innovativeness from analysing the trade data of multiple industries at a global scale? Is it possible to create an objective measure to benchmark the relative level of innovativeness for any given industry? Can this measure be used to benchmark innovativeness across industries?

In this chapter we explore how a structural measure of industry complexes relates to measures of innovation. As in the previous chapter, trade complexes are defined as the trade network structure of a particular industry incorporating all source inputs but disaggregated by each source country. Trade complexes thus include more than a given industry, but include inter- and intra-industry trade as well. In essence, they reveal the global distribution of production. We then correlate our measure against the best established indicators of innovativeness.

Our analysis consistently reveals a relationship between the global distribution of production and multiple indicators of innovativeness across 22 manufacturing industries, our proposed measure of trade intensity to other industry classifications and indices. The measure derived here reveals rankings across industries that are strikingly similar to rankings based on the research and development (R&D) intensity from the Organisation for Economic

DOI: 10.4324/9781315225661-17

Co-operation and Development (OECD), modularity (Rosenkopf & Schilling 2007) and Pavitt's (1984) taxonomy. Such rankings are useful when exploring under-researched industries, and when making comparisons about each industry's relative trade intensity and innovativeness. Based on our findings, we discuss what our measures of the global distribution of production tell us about the relative innovativeness of industries and suggest implications for innovation studies.

Literature review

Global value chains (GVCs) have been studied from a plethora of perspectives, and their empirical analysis continues apace. The different methodologies reflect the different interests of researchers. For instance, the World Bank (2017) is interested in economic development and impact. Nielsen (2018) represents an interest in firm-level data on business involvement in international trade. To address the aforementioned questions about investigating a relationship between structural patterns of trade in GVCs and degrees of innovativeness of that GVC or industry, we are more closely aligned with network-based studies. Recent network studies include Cingolani et al. (2018), which represents a stream of work analysing complete global trade networks at the 'industry' level. Similarly, Criscuolo and Timmis (2018) examine centrality and peripheries in networks. Both of these are nearest to our own interests (see Chapter 10). Despite this rise in quantitative network analysis of GVCs, there remains little empirical work that links GVCs to innovation indices beyond case studies (see De Marchi et al. 2017) or early exploratory analysis (see Wixted 2009).

As articulated more elaborately in Chapter 10, the lack of empirical studies that objectively compare the network structure of GVCs across industries is likely to be an artefact of the lack of research at the meso level. The meso level includes inter-industry and inter-country trade that simultaneously reflects how individual firm's GVCs are structured (i.e. micro-level analysis), while also reflecting the globally aggregated structure of trade (i.e. macro-level analysis). Such aggregations of trade across national borders are clearly useful for national trade policy. However, the trade-off of macro-level analysis is that it can obscure the ability to identify the sourcing pathways of specific components from supplier industries or firms, which is important to consider for managers and academics interested in the broader phenomenon of trade and innovation.

Other areas related to studying the relationship between the global distribution of production and innovation include innovation systems (e.g. Lundvall 1992; Cooke 2001) and technological innovation systems (e.g. Markard & Truffer 2008; Bergek et al. 2008). Many of these are geographical-bounded studies of the interplay of organisations that foster innovation. In that sense, such studies do not reveal the inter-regional structure of the system or GVC that produces the innovation. Nor do they explore the degree of innovativeness of whatever is being produced. By definition, innovation systems are assumed to produce something with a requisite level of innovativeness, or else they would be a broader category of production systems with less emphasis on innovation.

An important concept in innovation systems research is its emphasis on the separability of components and activities within a system or region (e.g. von Hippel 1990 or Carlsson 2006). We draw on this concept, noting that it has rarely been extended to the level of inter-regional trade (aka the meso level). Only a handful of studies approach a meso level to include comparison of multiple global industries without geographic distinction (e.g. Rosenkopf & Schilling 2007). The separability or modularity of components and sub-components that are sourced via GVCs is a core attribute of many modern globally distributed value chains.

Systems of trade and innovation

In this study, we employ a meso level at which we can being to disentangle global trade into *what* products are traded, *where* the production occurs and *with whom* trade occurs (as also advocated by Ernst 2002 and Luo et al. 2012), regardless of the degree of innovativeness. The who and where aspects are incorporated in some innovation studies at the meso level (e.g. industry or cluster, as in Bathelt, Malmberg & Maskell's 2004 suggested framework).

To explore the relationship between the geographic distribution of production (where and who) for each industry (what) and the degree of innovativeness (of the what) we look to logic provided by DeBresson (e.g. 1996). DeBresson conducted hundreds of interviews and collected thousands of surveys at the firm level on innovation and indicates a correlation between domestic trade. His analysis included multiple industries *and* their trade, albeit *within* a given region (e.g. DeBresson 1996; DeBresson & Xioping 1996). While his work is at a different level of analysis than GVCs, we are inspired by DeBresson's (1996) tome, which uses innovation input–output tables of a number of countries, including the Italian economy, covers thousands of Italian manufacturers across 29 industries, and reveals a high correlation (0.836) between domestic trade patterns and innovation. DeBresson (1996, p. 115) offers an output-oriented explanation for the correlation – ceteris paribus, more innovative products will be in greater demand than less innovative ones: "[The] innovative output of one supplier industry will likely be used in greater proportion by a [downstream] industry that consumes more of that supplier's [innovative] output."

While this correlation is certainly interesting, DeBresson's work focussed only on individual economic regions with limited ranking across industries. For example, he provides a ranking of the top 10 industries according to innovative output and number of domestic suppliers, but specific to Italy (e.g. Table 7.3 in DeBresson 1996, p. 112). As such, he does not provide a complete scale or ranking across industries at a global scale.

DeBresson's work with Xioping includes some comparison across countries, such as his scatter plot of multiple industries for three economies (Italy, China and France) which contrasts the number of domestic economic linkages against innovation frequency or innovative product sales (depending on the data availability; see Figure 6 in DeBresson & Xioping 1996, p. 196). Their analysis again reveals a correlation between domestic trade and innovativeness, for which they offer an additional explanation to the aforementioned one, which is a precursor to the systems integration strategy we know today (DeBresson & Xioping 1996, p. 197):

> The most plausible explanation for the above relationship between economic linkages and innovative activity is a simple one, the more varied the enterprise's information network is, the more likely it is to combine production factors in a new way for new uses. Innovation, as Schumpeter stressed, requires first and foremost new combinations. [...] If the entrepreneur is in contact with a variety of potential input suppliers, he has more opportunities to innovate. Conversely, if he has a variety of potential market outlets for his products, he has greater possibilities for innovative variation.

This input-oriented explanation is at the firm level and offers a complementary logic to DeBresson's (1996) output-oriented explanation: Having more linkages enables more innovative combinations of inputs. This holds under the assumption of a matching increase in absorptive capacity since the absorptive capacity of a firm determines its ability to make use of the new information it receives. If the information inflows increase beyond the firm's absorptive capacity, then the firm will still not do any better.

While these correlations between trade and innovativeness are intriguing, the limited number of countries and variation across the countries leaves the reader with puzzle pieces rather than a complete picture. For example, in DeBresson and Xioping (1996) research 'economic linkages' were between organisations and not at a global level. And, their measure of innovativeness incorporates the subjectivity of the managers responding to their interviews and surveys. Researchers are left to wonder, Are these patterns generalisable to more countries and more industries. How robust are these pattern using less subjective data? Beyond a likelihood of producing something innovative, how is the degree of innovativeness related to these patterns of sourcing?

Measures of trade and innovation intensity

Scattered through the literature are various attempts at operationalising industry attributes in terms of the skill, task or modularity intensiveness of industry products. For example, Minondo and Requena-Silvente (2013) employ a measure of skill intensity based on the number of occupations related to International Standard Industrial Classification of All Economic Activities (ISIC) four-digit industry codes as a proxy for product complexity.

While these measures are good at capturing what occurs within an industry, they don't necessarily capture the interconnections across industries and regions, and thus only cast some light onto the question of how industries are interconnected and concentrated at a global level. Vice versa, analysis of trade data (like ours) directly captures the latter, but only indirectly captures the bigger picture of innovation complexity. The merits (and scope for future research) of *inter*-industry and *inter*-country trade data analysis are also aptly summarised by Panagariya and Bagaria (2013, p. 1179):

> A complementary explanation for the concentration in trade is in terms of international specialisation in the production of components that has been made possible by the fragmentation of previously vertically integrated production processes. A country may specialise in the exports of a few final products that it assembles using the components that it imports. This will produce some concentration in both exports and imports.

To explore how the distribution of global production may be related to the degree of innovativeness across industries, we draw on three indices and categorisations of innovation intensity and complexity: (i) the OECD's (1997) R&D intensity, (ii) measures based on alliancing and modularisation (Rosenkopf & Schilling 2007), and (iii) Pavitt's classic sectoral taxonomy (1984). The OECD measure and Pavitt's taxonomy are well established in the literature as indicators of innovativeness. The measures by Rosenkopf and Schilling remain contested, as explained in greater detail later but provide another emerging benchmark of innovativeness across multiple industries.

Methodology and analysis

In this section, we explain how we build on an earlier typology of global value architectures (GVAs) (see Chapter 10) to quantify the intensity of the interconnections of each industry, as an indicator of innovation complexity. By innovation complexity, we mean the degree to which the production of goods by an industry is dependent on a large number of highly interdependent inputs. We then also benchmark our measure against other industry level measures related to innovation.

The method follows three general steps:

1. We start with the same data, method and inter-country input–output (ICIO) model as Wixted (2009) and Wixted and Bliemel (Chapter 10, this volume) by which significant sourcing pathways were isolated for each of 22 industry complexes.
2. The trade structure of each industry complex is operationalised as a trade link intensity measure, which is a count of the significant pathways per industry, normalised by the number of economies that have significant trade pathways in that industry complex.
3. The league table of trade intensity across all industries is then compared to the afore-mentioned benchmarks of innovativeness measures (e.g. OECD, Pavitt, and Rosenkopf & Schilling).

Step 1: Isolation of significant sourcing pathways

This step is comprised of the two steps in Chapter 10, including the construction of the Wixted model from the OECD input–output data, from which we isolate only the significant sourcing pathways per economy across all 22 manufacturing industries in the 1995 and 2000 OECD input-output tables. Our measure is based on 'significant' trade links that account for at least 10 per cent of the imported value (foreign value-added) of an industry *in a particular country* – cumulatively forming the trade complex. The isolated relationships reveal the structure of the trade complex (see Chapter 10 for graphics) and emphasise the core portion of the value-add structure of trade. They should not be interpreted as representing *net volumes* or *scale* of trade. Our measure provides a new perspective on the patterns of global sourcing and should not be confused with long-running existing debates on *net* trade.

Step 2: Normalisation of trade intensity per economy

The second step is to count the total number of significant sourcing pathways and normalise it by the number of economies available in the model, repeated for each of the 22 industries. This normalisation results in a measure of significant sourcing pathways per economy (or SPE for short) that reflects the level of complexity and interconnectedness of each industry complex. The averaging to a per-economy basis accommodates industries for which the raw data by OECD did not include the full matrix of countries. For instance, for non-ferrous metals, pharmaceuticals, aerospace and transportation equipment, fewer than 10 economies were available in OECD's 2000 data set, so the data set for 1995 was used for these industries, with 12, 13, 13 and 17 economies, respectively. This approach can also accommodate ICIO models of different dimensions, such as ones based on the World Input-Output Database (WIOD),[1] which has a different number of countries and industries.

Each economy's transaction intensity or SPE value is also directly analogous to the average in-degree centrality measure used in social network analysis. To explore robustness of this measure across time and data sets, we compare the SPE measures based on OECD data against SPE measures using WIOD data (Timmer et al. 2012). While the WIOD data offers more recent data and more countries, it manages this partly by amalgamating important industry categories, thereby obfuscating critical differences across some industries. For example, the two electronics industries and 'precision and optical equipment' in the OECD data are treated as one 'electrical and optical equipment' industry in the WIOD data. Similarly, WIOD does not separate pharmaceuticals from the broader chemicals classification. Furthermore, the WIOD categorisation for 'Basic and Fabricated Metals' incorporates two OECD industries, as does WIOD's 'Machinery nec' industry. Mapping the vehicular industries across the two databases is particularly problematic because OECD's distinction between 'motor vehicles,' 'aerospace,' railroad equipment and transport nec and 'shipbuilding' are treated as a single unified category in WIOD.

Such trade-offs maximise geographic coverage yet miss important industry differences. Nonetheless, we have repeated our analysis using WIOD data for 2008 as an additional robustness check and have not found any major differences in the results. Table 11.1 summarises the SPE levels for all the manufacturing industries in the Wixted model (ranked by SPE) and the WIOD model, both using the 10 per cent threshold for 'significance' of pathways.

Overall, the WIOD data show the same general sequence of industries in terms of SPE. In addition to the differences between models (i.e. industry classifications and regions), the

Table 11.1 Significant sourcing pathways per economy (SPE) by industry complex and model

Wixted model/OECD industry name	*SPE*	*WIOD model/industry name*	*SPE*
Iron and steel	0.82	Basic Metals and Fabricated Metal	1.38
Coke, refined petroleum products and nuclear fuel	0.82	Coke, Refined Petroleum and Nuclear Fuel	0.97
Other non-metallic mineral products	0.95	Other Non-Metallic Mineral	1.25
Food products, beverages and tobacco	0.95	Food, Beverages and Tobacco	1.33
Wood and products of wood and cork	1.00	Wood and Products of Wood and Cork	1.28
Pulp, paper, paper products, printing and publishing	1.00	Pulp, Paper, Paper, Printing and Publishing	1.53
Chemicals excluding pharmaceuticals (Industrial & other)	1.00	Chemicals and Chemical Products (including Pharmaceuticals)	1.53
Textiles, textile products, leather and footwear	1.00	Average for (1) Textiles and Textile Products, and (2) Leather, Leather and Footwear	1.64
Fabricated metal products, except machinery and equip	1.05	Basic Metals and Fabricated Metal	1.38
Non-ferrous metals	1.08	Basic Metals and Fabricated Metal	1.38
Manufacturing nec; including Furniture	1.09	Manufacturing, Nec; Recycling	1.63
Rubber and plastics products	1.23	Rubber and Plastics	1.70
Building & repairing of ships and boats	1.36	(not distinguishable from other vehicular industries)	—
Motor vehicles, trailers and semi-trailers	1.36	(not distinguishable from other vehicular industries)	—
Medical, precision and optical instruments	1.41	Electrical and Optical Equipment	1.78
Machinery and equip nec (aka industrial machinery)	1.41	Machinery, Nec	1.48
Electrical machinery and apparatus nec	1.45	Machinery, Nec	1.48
Railroad equipment & transport equip nec	1.53	Transport Equipment	1.60
Radio, television and communication equipment	1.57	Electrical and Optical Equipment	1.78
Pharmaceuticals	1.69	(integrated into Chemicals and Chemical Products)	n/a
Office, accounting and computing machinery	1.77	Electrical and Optical Equipment	1.78
Aircraft and spacecraft	1.85	(not distinguishable from other vehicular industries)	—

Note: nec, not elsewhere classified.

overall increase in SPEs in the WIOD data reflects the increased levels of globalisation in 2008 versus the OECD data from 2000 (see also Figure 3 in Los, Timmer & de Vries 2015 for a trend analysis).

Step 3: Comparison of SPE and innovativeness

The third step is to examine the relationship between trade intensity and indices of innovation. The purpose of this step is to explore whether an index based on trade link intensity is representative of the relative 'innovativeness' of industries. Innovativeness is typically perceived as something that is primarily based on knowledge or its manifestation as a technology or product. As such, knowledge and technology are related to the products and to their production, but remain distinct concepts. We acknowledge that linking innovativeness and trade might appear to confuse the knowledge and technologies embedded in products with the production of those products. However, the global organisation of production remains conceptually distinct from the level of technology and knowledge innovativeness in the products being produced. These are separate but related key features of global value chains and studying their relationship is the motivation for this study.

As revealed in the earlier analysis and GVA typology by Wixted and Bliemel (Chapter 10, this volume), there are significant differences across industries in terms of how interconnected various regions are, and how interconnected the three 'worlds' are (Europe, Asia and the Americas). Some of these trade relations are governed by (i) natural resource constraints or endowments of each country and (ii) industry- or firm-specific trade agreements. When qualitatively comparing the exo-nets against the global factories, a theme of low-tech versus high-tech products emerges. This is in part due to the cost-to-value curve of shipping raw materials vs. high-tech goods; commodity ores and metals often compete on cost to the purchaser and are sourced due to geographic proximity and delivery speed (for metals), while computer components compete on value for the purchaser and are often sourced from around the globe. More important, the degree to which an industry's trade complex is interconnected is a factor of the technological composition of the industry's products. High-tech products are usually not just a single high-tech component; they are complex assemblies of *multiple* high-tech components (Dedrick, Kraemer & Linden 2010; Ali-Yrkkö et al. 2011).

All of the preceding arguments, include DeBresson's explanations, suggest a correlation between trade and innovativeness. There are, however, also arguments and evidence to the contrary. For instance, recent work by Piccardi and Tajoli (2018) on the complexity of products and the centralisation of their export networks finds that more complex products actually have more centralised networks. The key difference between the research in this chapter and theirs is whether the trade is imports or exports. As noted in their conclusions,

> even if global value chains increase connectivity by generating many [sourcing] trade links between countries exchanging parts and inputs, the complex goods resulting from this organization are eventually exported by the final assembler, giving rise to a centralized structure of [export] trade.
>
> *(Piccardi and Tajoli 2018, p. 10)*

To quantitatively explore whether SPE can be used as an index of innovativeness across industries, we benchmark three indices and categorisations of innovation intensity and complexity: (i) the OECD's R&D intensity, (ii) measures based on alliancing and modularisation (Rosenkopf & Schilling 2007), and (iii) Pavitt's classic sectoral taxonomy (1984).

SPE versus R&D intensity

Our first benchmarking of the SPE measure is against R&D intensity. As part of its bi-annual Science, Technology and Industry Scoreboard, the OECD (the same source as our data) provides an R&D intensity measure of manufacturing industries.[2] This measure has long been held to be a useful index of innovativeness when assuming that firms invest their own resources into their own innovations. While the number of industries is insufficient to derive a statistically significant correlation, the SPE measure does appear to increase with R&D intensity,[3] as shown in Figure 11.1.

It has long been observed that there is a relationship between innovativeness and *volume* of *exports*, wherein innovating economies export to emerging economies until it becomes more cost effective for the innovation to be produced elsewhere (Krugman 1979). Here we are concerned with a slightly different hypothesis – that the innovativeness of an industry is related to the *structure* of the *imports* required to produce the innovation. The null hypothesis is that there is no mathematical relationship linking (sourcing) trade and innovativeness. Based on Figure 11.1, this is easily rejected, with an indication that there is at least a linear fit ($R^2 = 73.38$).

Furthermore, we observe that an exponential relationship slightly improves the fit ($R^2 = 75.67$). The exponential relationship suggests that there may be limits to how globally interconnected an industry can be. R&D intensity may increase well above 10 per cent, but one can only have so many significant sourcing relationships before running out of countries. Also visible in Figure 11.1 is that a number of trade complexes have a similar number of SPEs but have differing levels of R&D. Aerospace is a prime example with similarly high levels of SPE to other industries, but disproportionately high levels of R&D intensity.

The curve in Figure 11.1 echoes DeBresson's (1996) comments that more innovative outputs from one industry are more likely to be inputs to multiple other industries. There are of course exceptions to this pattern, such as shipbuilding, which has disproportionately more trade-significant sourcing pathways for such a low R&D intensity industry. OECD data shows that patent-

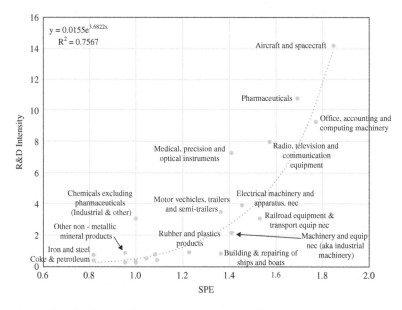

Figure 11.1 Significant trade pathways per economy (SPE) versus R&D intensity.

ing is increasing at a slower pace in the maritime industry than in the economy more generally (Corbett et al., 2016) although the difference between different subsectors is substantial with defence shipbuilding showing an R&D expense of some 10 per cent of turnover (Bekkers et al. 2009). Variation from the curve simply acknowledges that trade linkages may be driven by factors other than innovation (e.g. trade agreements, tariffs, strategic relationships, cost-to-value of shipping commodities).

SPE versus modularisation and alliancing

Amador and Cabral (2016, p. 280) present the argument that "technology is a key driver of GVCs [and] makes it possible that parts and components produced in factories in different parts of the world perfectly combine in sophisticated final products." Despite this argument, their survey of measures of global value chains does not return to the topic of parts being shipped and traded globally. Blyde (2014) and Amador and di Mauro (2015) also avoid discussions of modular-/modularity-based GVCs. We can only speculate that their omission of modularity-based measures is because such measurement is problematic. Aside, it may be interesting to note that changing production technologies can impact sourcing pathways. An example is GE's Advanced Turboprop (ATP), where the engine design team reduced 855 separate parts down to just 12 and as a result more than a third of the engine is 3D printed with the associated reduction of the supply chain.[4] See also the case study associated with this chapter for a closer look at the modularisation in aerospace, associated vulnerabilities to GVC disruption and the impact of disintermediating sources by 3D printing.

Modularity has its roots in 'near-decomposability' (Simon 1962), and is the concept that larger systems can be broken down into multiple interrelated components or modules that can be 'mixed and matched' (Baldwin & Clark 1997). The implication is that modularisation enables faster iteration of variations of the whole, and can lead to greater performance and accelerated product innovation, because firms can "rapidly respond to altered business conditions by recombining diverse divisional resources and product-market domains" (Galunic & Eisenhardt 2001, p. 1244). In other words, modularisation is linked to innovation via Schumpeterian innovation through recombination of modules, consistent with the proposition put forward by DeBresson and Xioping (1996). Adoption of modularisation as a strategy to increase the diversity of modules, and their combinations can occur in many ways, ranging from open markets providing the modules, to modules being collaboratively produced with suppliers (e.g. Song, Ming & Wang 2013), through to modules being developed in-house and then outsourced to strategic suppliers while maintaining full control over IP (e.g. Chanaron 2001).

Modularisation may be operationalised in three ways: in terms of product (i) components, (ii) organisational units or (iii) the production-related activities these units perform. An example of how products and their production are simultaneously modularised within a larger system can be found in GE's multimodal production plant in Pune, India. This manufacturing plant can deploy the same 1500 employees and footprint to pivot cleanly from production of jet engines and locomotive technology to wind turbines and water treatment equipment as demand changes (Toner et al. 2015). Another rule of thumb for how much to modularise and how to bundle components into modules or submodules is that the number of modules is approximately the square root of the number of components in the systems (Lean Management Institute 2012 cited in Qiao, Efatmaneshnik, Ryan & Shoval 2017).

While differences exist in some settings, these three forms of modularisation are generally correlated (Sanchez & Mahoney 1996; Brusoni & Prencipe 2001; MacCormack, Baldwin & Rusnak 2012). Despite these nuances between different forms of modularity, the core premise remains the same: modularisation creates transactions across firm boundaries (Baldwin 2008; Luo et al. 2012), thus further cementing a relationship between innovation and trade.

Despite several advances in modularity research, the "biggest challenge in empirical research on modularity is quantifying modularity" (Cebon, Hauptman & Shekhar 2008, p. 382). Instead of benchmarking against a modularity measure per se, we compare our index against measures provided by Rosenkopf and Schilling (2007), including their Innovation Activity Separability (IAS) variable and their small-world quotient of strategic alliances within an industry, both of which are proxies for modularity. For the IAS variable, their intention was that it "captures the degree to which the industry is considered to be characterised by innovation activities that can be separated across multiple firms (as, for example, when the industry is characterised by interfirm product modularity" (p. 193). However, their IAS measure includes three limitations. Firstly, it is not a conventional scale (i.e. Likert style), but based on votes in a survey in which "respondents were asked to nominate the 10 industries with the highest level" (p. 193). While their voting process may reveal the rank of each industry by modularity, it may not accurately reflect their relative level of modularity. Secondly, the IAS measure is based on subjective nominations requested from of a 'set of 13 scholars,' for which it remains questionable how many scholars responded to their request and how much each scholar was an expert across all industries. Thirdly, the voting criteria contained a blend of (i) IAS and (ii) product modularity, despite their article's emphasis on IAS. Despite these limitations, we believe their measures provide reasonable safeguards against biases and subjectivity, and cover a broad range of industries to provide another useful robustness check against which to benchmark or calibrate our SPE-based index.

The small-world quotient is the degree to which the network is clustered and has longer path lengths in comparison to a random network graph of the same size (Watts & Strogatz, 1998). Rosenkopf and Schilling (2007) create a small world quotient based on strategic alliance data and thus less subjective than their IAS measure. It represents the degree to which the aggregate strategic alliance pattern of all firms in a given industry represents one interconnected 'world' or whether the industry is fragmented into many smaller and lessor interconnected clusters. This measure is conceptually analogous to our notion of a global factory, but does not include weightings of each relationship or geographic specificity. Plots of SPE versus the IAS measure (Figure 11.2) and small-world quotient (Figure 11.3) indicate the degree to which

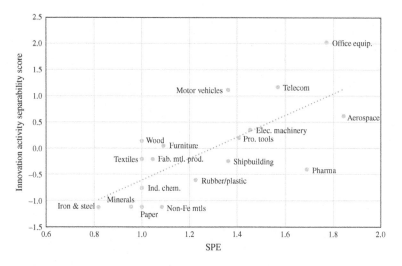

Figure 11.2 Significant trade pathways per economy (SPE) versus Innovation Activity Separability (IAS).

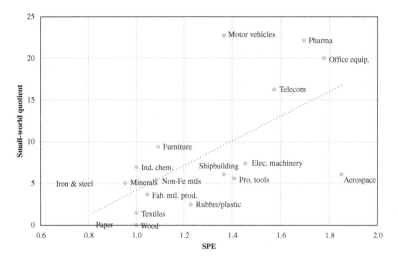

Figure 11.3 Significant trade pathways per economy (SPE) versus small-world quotient.

SPE is correlated with their measures. In absence of a more sophisticated theory linking trade and innovativeness, we default to a linear relationship, with the null hypothesis being 'no relationship.' Overall, both graphs lend further evidence towards a relationship between the global distribution of production and innovativeness.

Lastly, we compare SPE to Pavitt's (1984) taxonomy, noting his dual of 'scale' category (bulk materials and assembly). In comparison to the other benchmarks, Pavitt's initial work is based on one country for innovations between 1945 and 1979. So, it unsurprising that it is only a *good* fit and not a perfect fit. However, *that it is a fit at all is important.*

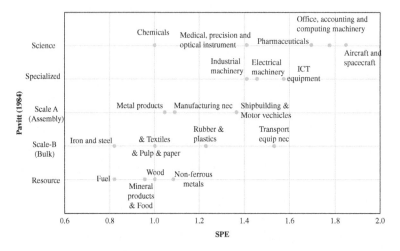

Figure 11.4 Significant trade pathways per economy (SPE) grouped by Pavitt (1984).

Discussion

By focussing on only the significant sourcing pathways, we make a methodological contribution: quantifying the structure of industry complexes and GVCs by calculating the significant sourcing pathways per economy (SPE). This methodological contribution forms the foundation for direct quantitative comparison of industries' structures (e.g. how much percentage-wise more globally networked is industry X vs industry Y) and for subsequent analysis of innovativeness across industries. As a robustness check, we repeat our analysis using WIOD data. While their model includes more regions, it is less granular about industries. Nonetheless, we find the SPE index is generally consistent across data sets.

Perhaps the most significant contribution is the benchmarking of the SPE measure against the various innovation indices and categories, supporting our proposition that it can be a reliable and objective proxy for innovativeness across industries. The three comparisons of (inter- and intra-industry) sourcing pathway intensity lend consistent support that industries which have a higher proportion of international value-add to supplies from a larger number of source countries also tend to be industries with greater levels of innovativeness. This consistent pattern is despite there being significant differences between these three benchmark measures. Some measures are more directly related to innovation (R&D intensity), and others are incidental to innovation and knowledge (alliancing). Some measures are based on objective data (R&D intensity, alliancing), while others are based on expert's knowledge (IAS, Pavitt). Predominantly, these measures and classifications are based on what happens *within* an industry. The only one that is somewhat inclusive of inter-industry relations is the small-world quotient of strategic alliances. Our comparisons of SPE against these benchmarks reinforce that there can be no perfect index that captures the multidimensionality of product complexity. Further, research is required to compare these metrics to the Product Complexity Index developed by ElMaraghy and Urbanic (2003) and Urbanic and ElMaraghy (2006) at the plant level and the Product Complexity Index (PCI) developed by Hidalgo and Hausmann (2009) at the level of global trade. However, the support for a link between trade pathways and innovation is consistent across all three benchmarks. We thus argue that the SPE measure appears to be a reliable and objective proxy measure for innovation complexity in a global era. Furthermore, we believe it can be used across time to analyse changes at the industry and global levels.

Empirical implications

Because of the similarities between SPE and the three measures of innovativeness, we believe that the rank order of industries according to SPE in Table 11.1 provides a guide to measure the innovativeness of each industry in a way that is more objective than the three benchmarks used. To guide and simplify our discussion of the empirical implications of this relationship, we frame the discussion using each of the three archetypes of global value architecture – global factory, fusion and exo-net (see also Chapter 10 for a more elaborate explanation of the typology). Using this categorisation, we explore how the different indices' arguments are aligned within each category.

We acknowledge that some industries do not neatly follow this categorisation because they deviate from the curves shown in the above figures. For example, for the R&D intensity benchmark shown in Figure 11.1, chemicals (industrial and other) along with medical and optical instruments stand out as being off the curve. Meanwhile, for both the Innovation Activity Separability and small-world quotient benchmarking shown in Figures 11.2 and 11.3, aerospace and pharmaceuticals do not follow the general pattern. Finally, for the benchmarking against Pavitt's taxonomy, shown in Figure 11.4, one of the more obvious variants is chemicals. Pavitt classified it as science-based; later the OECD suggests it is scale-based, more precisely bulk-scale-based. Over time, as new production methods are introduced, products that were previously scale-based may become less dependent on scale, as with the introduction of flow chemistry. This means that the categorisation may change over time. It could be argued that the classification challenges relating to chemicals can be explained by considering whether the innovation is related to the production process, as with scale-based petrochemicals, or whether the innovation is related to the chemical itself, as with science-based pharmaceutical molecules.

Pharmaceuticals are also a peculiar industry, with their own tariff-free structure (i.e. the Uruguay Round) and extreme emphasis on R&D and high value per unit, with relatively few raw ingredients and intermediate goods, where imports and exports are predominantly finished goods. As noted by Kiriyama (2011, p. 24):

> More than 70% of the exports to [high-income countries] are finished goods [and finished goods] exports to [low- and middle-income countries] occupy more than half of such exports. A major exception is China, over 70% of whose exports are intermediate goods.

At any rate, these deviations from the generalised pattern provide interesting areas for a future research agenda.

Despite these variations, our analysis and plots suggest that the classifications are consistently mapped onto the three global value architectures as follows in Table 11.2. The first column is the GVA type and the second column reflects the quantitative measure and range according to OECD and Rosenkopf and Schilling (2007). Pavitt's categorisation is added as a third column because is it not a quantifiable measure and reveals how his five industry classes map onto the three GVA types.

Global factories (aerospace, radio, television and communication equipment, office, accounting and computing machinery) are characterised by high SPE levels and high R&D intensity. The investment in R&D-related knowledge and coordination in this industry is evident at the level of product architectures (Boeing 787 or smartphones/tablets) and at the level of individual components (e.g. screens or chips). These each require a considerable amount of investment in both knowledge creation and innovation development. Higher orders of specialisation open up opportunities for knowledge sharing within alliances as well as international trade of the specialised components. As products become more knowledge intensive and complex there are greater opportunities for a division of labour, including innovation activities, and systems integration (Hobday et al. 2005). Such higher levels of complexity and interconnections are also observed

Table 11.2 Innovation characteristics of global value architectures (GVAs)

GVA	Innovation measure	Pavitt's categorisation
Global factory	High R&D intensity High/medium IAS Spider web/hybrid alliance network structure	Science based (except chemicals in Pavitt's original)
Fusion	Medium R&D intensity Medium and high IAS Hybrid alliance network structure	Specialised supplier Scale A – assembly
Exo-nets	Low R&D intensity Low IAS Disconnected alliance network structure	Scale B – bulk materials Supplier dominated/resource intensive

in Minondo and Requena-Silvente's (2013) analysis of occupational complexity, wherein aerospace, electronics, precision instruments and pharmaceuticals are at the top of their list. The last two of these are high in our fusion category.

In regards to Pavitt's taxonomy, there is an important distinction to make regarding knowledge sources versus more tangible sources. In Pavitt's taxonomy, science-based firms relied on internal knowledge sources and knowledge gained through collaboration with universities. While this remains true for individual firms, the organisation of the trade complexes reveals that bringing innovative products to market requires global factories that source tangible inputs from well beyond the firm's boundaries. Our result may be interpreted as another manifestation of the trend for R&D-intensive firms to focus their resources on R&D and marketing while outsourcing and offshoring labour-intensive activities (i.e. manufacturing). This trend is visualised in the 'smile curve' (Baldwin & Evenett 2015; Office of the Chief Economist 2018). Labour intensity in manufacturing is continuously declining (Tregenna 2008) and in the period 1985–2014 there has been a shift of manufacturing from labour-intensive to skill-intensive activities in developed countries (Wood 2017).

Fusion architectures (railroad equipment & transport equip nec; motor vehicles, trailers and semi-trailers; electrical machinery and apparatus nec; pharmaceuticals; building & repairing of ships and boats; medical, precision and optical instruments) are characterised by mid-range SPE levels which reflect their structure comprising two moderately interconnected worlds. In comparison to global factories, this reflects regionalisation of the production, as perhaps influenced by trade policies specific to that industry or the relatively high cost of shipping modules around the world. For example, the cost of shipping $1 million of microchips is much lower than the cost of shipping $1 million of railroad equipment.

This group of industries is a 'mixed bag' of science-based, specialised suppliers and the scale-based auto industry. However, these industries have relatively similar (medium) levels of R&D intensity. This group includes specialised high-value contract jobs of custom shipbuilding and repairs, and lower-value contract jobs of mass-produced railroad equipment. While traditional studies of the medical, precision and optical instruments 'industry' emphasise the geography of the innovators, it may be a fusion trade complex due to the *inter-industry* links with electronics industries. The mix of industries in this category suggests that each has its own particular dynamics – that integrate it more into the global economy than the exo-nets but less than the global factories – across all the dimensions of R&D, alliance building and innovation generally.

Notably, the motor vehicles industry is in this category and is not a global factory. This suggests that the complexity of the motor vehicle industry may actually be lower than it is perceived to be (c.f. high IAS scores). Some of the differences between perceptions versus the reality of modularisation and complexity in the automotive industry come down to whether only the tier 1 suppliers' modules are considered, or also the tier 2 and 3 submodules and components, as the latter have been shown to have higher PCI scores than the finished vehicles (extracted from the Observatory of Economic Complexity, https://atlas.media.mit.edu/en/rankings/product/hs07/?year_range=2011-2016). This discrepancy makes it a peculiar case study, thus reinforcing the high level of attention it has received in academic literature, particularly the global value chains literature. Despite the modest levels of trade links, the strategic alliances in this industry are densely interconnected and the tiers of suppliers and the application of modularity in this industry have been extensively analysed (cf. Cabigiosu, Zirpoli & Camuffo 2013).

Similarly, the pharmaceuticals industry has received considerable attention over a very long time by innovation scholars. Our SPE indicator ranks pharmaceuticals higher than perhaps might be expected for the production of this kind of product. Nevertheless, it has fewer trade links than would be suggested by other measures of innovation (R&D intensity, alliance measures; Minondo and Requena-Silvente 2013). The process to get a drug approved across jurisdictions can be long and complicated, involving prolonged research; licencing and distribution royalty payments; multi-site clinical trials and data exchange; and complex partnership agreements related to patenting costs, marketing and production costs. While trade in the intermediate components to a particular drug are relatively low (foreign value add), our trade link indicator is not excessively out of step with the other innovation metrics and suggests that the trade routes for pharmaceuticals are more complicated than expected.

Exo-nets are characterised by low levels of R&D intensity, low IAS, disconnected alliance networks and activities that Pavitt/OECD associate with bulk production, and 'supplier dominated' and resource-based industries. In these industries the innovation is done by the tier 1 suppliers and then migrates into the resource extraction industry. This is mostly a push innovation rather than pull innovation. These industries are at the little-studied end of the innovation spectrum. That is not to say they are uninteresting (cf. Hirsch-Kreinsen 2008 and Hirsch-Kreinsen & Jacobson 2008). Their study remains focused on the creation of innovation and the sources of knowledge, but usually does not extend to global production systems. There is fertile territory to explore the policy connections between global innovation and trade complexes, especially the potential for specific structures around productivity competitiveness. It is possible that the low SPE levels are more related to the sequential flow of goods in these industries than to a lack of developing and emerging economies in the Wixted ICIO model (replication using WIOD's data also had lower SPE levels than other industries).

Methodological implications

The empirical contributions have methodological and practical implications. Methodologically, trade statistics that appear as rows in a table or lines on a map can be easily misunderstood. While they appear to represent an *average* industry or firm in a given country, that mindset is mistaken; *aggregates* are not representative of *averages*. As seen in our selection of significant sourcing pathways per economy and with many other economic phenomena, power laws apply (Andriani & McKelvey 2007). Bernard, Jensen and Schott (2009) suggests 90 per cent of imports and exports with the US are accounted for by just the top 5 per cent of US firms, i.e. aggregates are more representative of industry 'outliers' than industry averages. A similar argument can be made for the geography of production. Parilla and Berube's (2013) analysis shows that production within North America is not evenly distributed. Instead, out of all the cities in North America (Canada, Mexico and US) there are just 19 automotive, 16 electronics and 14 aerospace city-based clusters which produce more than $100 million in value. While we cannot interpolate our data to reveal city-to-city or firm-to-firm connections, the scale-free nature of trade gives us the confidence to assume that the significant links presented here can be understood as being representative of connections between these top-trading firms in their respective cities.

Our research has two major implications for industry-level research. First, the methodology and SPE index developed here may enable further analysis of similar data in order to explore the evolution of different 'complexes.' For instance, other years of OECD data may be used to explore how these global trade complexes evolved over time, similar to Los et al. (2015), but with more qualitative texture. Such longitudinal analysis may cast some light into the impact of changes in trade agreements, trends towards outsourcing to lower wage economies or disruptions to supply chains (including but not limited to natural disasters and revolutionary changes in production processes and production technologies embedded in capital equipment, such as the aforementioned 3D printing example above and featured in the case study about GVC disruptions, later in Part IV). This longitudinal methodological implication is not exclusive to global trade. For example, using data such as that developed by the Brookings Institution's (see Parilla & Berube 2013) one may be able to explore the evolution of complexes that are internal to countries. Such analysis would also enable comparisons between national and international patterns of trade and innovation.

Secondly, and perhaps most importantly, our empirical contributions can aid in contextualising more detailed analysis of industry structures and dynamics, or studies that focus more on specific regions. Such future research may include virtually any inter-industry comparison (case study or quantitative), where the industry is considered to be a moderating factor. We hope that future inter-industry research can move beyond binary dummy variables and include relative measures or rankings such as the SPE-based index provided in Table 11.1. For context to our argument, a longstanding default index for studies of innovation, technology management and industry evolution is R&D intensity. R&D intensity is conventionally something that is driven by the internal resources of a firm or region, moderated by the industry. However, with the explosion of inter-firm and inter-regional connections, and opening of the innovation process into a system of innovation, such an internally oriented metric may be reaching the end of its utility. Similar limitations have been observed about recent decades of cluster studies, that are "excessively inward looking and [result in] an ensuing unfortunate downplay of crucial external linkages" (Maskell 2014, p. 833). Thus, based on our comparison with other innovation taxonomies and metrics, we believe our index can add more inter-industry and inter-country nuance to research on innovation intensity.

We would thus welcome further research in two distinct directions. More research explicitly combining a focus on GVCs and innovation geography along the lines of Rutherford and Holmes (2008) and Sturgeon, Van Biesebroeck and Gereffi (2008) would be valuable. Second, cross-sectoral analysis of the innovation systems that lie behind the trade complexes/GVC structures would be very valuable. In particular, the exo-nets may lend themselves to being studied for how their structure and productivity is influenced by very specialised policy. In comparison, the complex nature of products and firms in global factories may be beyond the control of any given policy. There may also be valuable insights to be had from combining our type of GVC analysis with economic complexity analysis (for discussion around related insights from economic complexity analysis, see e.g. Reynolds et al. 2018 and Roos et al. 2018).

Implications for practice and policy

As hinted in the aforementioned implications, each industry may have policies specific to it, in addition to general policies. A major challenge of policymakers is to coordinate and synchronise policies so they can have their intended consequences (Weber & Rochracher 2012). For instance, there are multiple ways to circumvent trade tariffs, including reclassification of goods to another industry (aka tariff engineering)[5] or by routing shipments through another country (aka transshipment) (Feenstra & Hanson 2004). Other strategies include relocating the manufacturing into the foreign market to operate within it instead of importing into it. For instance, China encourages manufacturers to set up shop within China by imposing high trade tariffs, while simultaneously requiring them to collaborate with a domestic manufacturer, thus posing a risk of diffusion of intellectual property. Likewise, venture capital markets and R&D tax policies can influence where companies fund and conduct their R&D, separately from their manufacturing operations. Ultimately, there are many trade-related levers for policymakers to pull and coordinate to try to accrue more short- or long-term benefits in the form of import tariffs, R&D tax incentives, corporate income tax, job creation and personal income tax.

The challenge in coordinating multiple policies to stimulate a country's innovativeness also fits the generalisation of Ashby's (1956, 1958) law of requisite variety, which is a general principle that applies to any system, whether economic, social, mechanical or biological. It has practical relevance for systems that need to survive and grow in uncertain, turbulent environments and it is central to the design of governance systems. It has been claimed that Ashby's law is as fundamental to the disciplines of management and economics as Newton's laws are to physics (Senge et al. 1994). Ashby's law was derived from mathematical analysis, but expressed in words it is very simple: control can only be obtained if the internal regulatory mechanism of a system is as diverse as the environment with which it interacts. The key word is 'requisite'; if the control system is too complex, the system will not operate efficiently. Vice versa if it lacks sufficient internal differentiation, it might not be able to cope with variable supply and demand of the variety of resources in the environment (e.g. variance and diversity in product markets, labour markets, capital markets), and the system might fail entirely. An expression of this law linked to innovation policy would be that the diversity and coordination of government policies must match the dynamics of change in the countries' operating environments. This requires simultaneous consideration of policies across multiple levels of government, across a broad range of international trade partners and industries.

Limitations

This study includes several methodological limitations. While our evidence suggests that there is a connection between GVC structure and innovation via modularity theory, more theoretical and empirical research is needed to conclusively connect them. We are very aware that modularity has proven to be a difficult concept to operationalise in research and practice (see the excellent survey of the literature by Campagnolo & Camuffo 2010 and Cabigiosu et al. 2013). We would hope to see a greater effort in the future to define and develop industry-level modularity measures that could be used to benchmark aggregate data such as those developed in this study. We concede, however, that perhaps modularity is too difficult a concept and we might need to revisit attempts at measuring complexity (see e.g. Wang & von Tunzelmann 2000).

Conclusions

In summary, we introduced a measure of trade intensity, significant sourcing pathways per economy (SPE), with which to quantitatively compare and index 22 manufacturing industries. We believe such an index or league table of industries can enable quantifiable and direct comparison of the interconnectedness of industries. For instance, this table allows us to not only say *that* one industry is more interconnected than another but also be able to describe *relatively* how much more interconnected it is.[6] As robustness checks, we benchmark our SPE index against (i) OECD's R&D intensity, (ii) Rosenkopf and Schilling's modularisation metrics (2007), and (iii) Pavitt's innovation taxonomy, and find that they reinforce the SPE measure. This supports DeBresson's hypothesised correlation between trade and innovativeness, and provides further evidence that as trade pathway complexity increases, so too does the underlying knowledge intensity. Such a link opens up many interesting avenues for future research and is aligned with the insights from economic complexity analysis.

While the SPE index adds support to the trade–innovativeness link, we recognise that the link is not perfect. Nor do we expect it to be. The variation of results across the SPE measure and the three benchmarks adds to the richness of methods and theoretical lenses with which researchers can analyse GVCs. In our discussion section, for each of the three global value architecture archetypes, we explore industries for which the metrics diverge, and suggest new areas of research.

Acknowledgements

This chapter has a long history and we need to thank many people who have contributed directly and indirectly to its development. Versions have been presented in seminars at the Department of Innovation, Industry, Science and Research (Australian Government); the Centre for Industry and Innovation Studies; University of New South Wales (UNSW) Business School in Sydney; and the South Australian Department of State Development. A number of individuals (including Gerald Hage and Fredrik Tell) have also commented on different versions, to whom we are immensely grateful. We specifically acknowledge the thoughtful and deeply useful comments of Paul Nightingale on a previous version of this work.

Notes

1 The World Input-Output Database was developed by an international consortium funded by the European Commission and released in May 2012 at http://www.wiod.org/. In comparison to the 1.2 m cells in our model, the WIOD database contains [(35 × 35) × 41] × 41, approximately 2.1 m cells.
2 http://dx.doi.org/10.1787/sti_scoreboard-2013-en. We use the 2000 data to correspond to our ICIO model.
3 This might look to some readers as an echo of Vernon's (1979, 1992) theory of technology and trade, even though his work was based on volumes of exports and imports not the patterns of value-add linkages.
4 https://www.ge.com/reports/mad-props-3d-printed-airplane-engine-will-run-year/.
5 https://www.strtrade.com/news-publications-232-301-tariff-strategies-avoid-reduce-071118.html.
6 The average SPE using the OECD data was 1.26, whereas the average using WIOD data was 1.52. The latter data includes nearly twice as many economies, yet showed values in the same range as the former.

References

Ali-Yrkkö, J., Rouvinen, P., Seppälä, T. & Ylä-Anttila, P. 2011, 'Who captures value in global supply chains? Case Nokia N95 Smartphone', *Journal of Industry, Competition and Trade*, vol. 11, no. 3, pp. 263–278.

Amador, J. & Cabral, S. 2016, 'Global value chains: A survey of drivers and measures', *Journal of Economic Surveys*, vol. 30, no. 2, pp. 278–301.

Amador, J., & Di Mauro, F. 2015, *The Age of Global Value Chains: Maps and Policy Issues*, Centre for Economic Policy Research (CEPR), London, UK

Andriani, P. & McKelvey, B. 2007, 'Beyond Gaussian averages: Redirecting international business and management research toward extreme events and power laws', *Journal of International Business Studies*, vol. 38, no. 7, pp. 1212–1230.

Ashby, W.R. 1956, *An Introduction to Cybernetics*, Chapman & Hall, London.

Ashby, W.R. 1958, 'Requisite Variety and its implications for the control of complex systems', *Cybernetica*, vol. 1, no. 2, pp. 83–99.

Baldwin, C.Y. 2008, 'Where do transactions come from? Modularity, transactions, and the boundaries of firms', *Industrial and Corporate Change*, vol. 17, no. 1, pp. 155–195.

Baldwin, C.Y. & Clark, K.B. 1997, 'Managing in an age of modularity', *Harvard Business Review*, vol. 75, pp. 84–93.

Baldwin, R.E. & Evenett, S.J. 2015, 'Value creation and trade in 21st century manufacturing', *Journal of Regional Science*, vol. 55, no. 1, pp. 31–50.

Bathelt, H., Malmberg, A. & Maskell, P. 2004, 'Clusters and knowledge: Local buzz, global pipelines and the process of knowledge creation', *Progress in Human Geography*, vol. 28, no. 1, pp. 31–56.

Bekkers, F., Butter, M., Anders Eriksson, E., Frinking, E., Hartley, K., Hoffmans, D., Leis, M., Lundmark, M., Masson, H., Rensma, A., van der Valk, T. & Willemsen, G. 2009, *Development of a European Defence Technological and Industrial Base Main report TNO report: Final*, European Commission, DG Enterprise and Industry, Delft, Netherlands.

Bergek, A., Jacobsson, S., Carlsson, B., Lindmark, S. & Rickne, A. 2008, 'Analyzing the functional dynamics of technological innovation systems: A scheme of analysis', *Research Policy*, vol. 37, no. 3, pp. 407–429.

Bernard, A.B., Jensen, J.B. & Schott, P.K. 2009, 'Importers, exporters and multinationals: A portrait of firms in the U.S. that trade goods', in T. Dunne, J. B. Jensen, and M. J. Roberts (eds.), *Producer Dynamics: New Evidence from Micro Data*, Chicago University Press, Chicago.

Blyde, J.S. (ed.) 2014, *Synchronized Factories: Latin America and the Caribbean in the Era of Global Value Chains*, Springer Nature, Heidelberg, Germany.

Brusoni, S. & Prencipe, A. 2001, 'Unpacking the black box of modularity: Technologies, products and organizations', *Industrial and Corporate Change*, vol. 10, no. 1, pp. 179–205.

Cabigiosu, A., Zirpoli, F. & Camuffo, A. 2013, 'Modularity, interfaces definition and the integration of external sources of innovation in the automotive industry', *Research Policy*, vol. 42, no. 3, pp. 662–675.

Campagnolo, D. & Camuffo, A. 2010, 'The concept of modularity in management studies: A literature review', *International Journal of Management Reviews*, vol. 12, no. 3, pp. 259–283.

Carlsson, B. 2006, 'Internationalization of innovation systems: A survey of the literature', *Research Policy*, vol. 35, no. 1, pp. 56–67.

Cebon, P., Hauptman, O. & Shekhar, C. 2008, 'Product modularity and the product life cycle: new dynamics in the interactions of product and process technologies', *International Journal of Technology Management*, vol. 42, no. 4, pp. 365–386.

Chanaron, J.J. 2001, 'Implementing technological and organisational innovations and management of core competencies: Lessons from the automotive industry', *International Journal of Automotive Technology and Management*, vol. 1, no. 1, pp. 128–144.

Cingolani, I., Iapadre, L. & Tajoli, L. 2018, 'International production networks and the world trade structure', *International Economics*, vol. 153, pp. 11–33.

Cooke, P. 2001, 'Regional innovation systems, clusters, and the knowledge economy', *Industrial and Corporate Change*, vol. 10, no. 4, pp. 945–974.

Corbett, J.J., Johnstone, N., Strodel, K. & Daniel, L. 2016, *Environmental Policy and Technological Innovation in Shipbuilding*, OECD Publishing, Paris.

Criscuolo, C. & Timmis, J. 2018, *GVCs and Centrality: Mapping Key Hubs, Spokes and the Periphery*, OECD Publishing, Paris.

DeBresson, C. (ed.) 1996, *Economic Interdependence and Innovative Activity an Input-Output Analysis*, Edward Elgar, Cheltenham, UK.

DeBresson, C. & Hu, X. 1996, *The Localisation of Clusters of Innovative Activity in Italy, France and China*, Chapter 8 in Innovation, Patents and Technological Strategies, OECD Publishers, Paris.

De Marchi, V., Di Maria, E. & Gereffi, G. 2017, *Local Clusters in Global Value Chains: Linking Actors and Territories Through Manufacturing and Innovation*, Routledge, Abingdon.

Dedrick, J., Kraemer, K.L. & Linden, G. 2010, 'Who profits from innovation in global value chains?: A study of the iPod and notebook PCs', *Industrial and Corporate Change*, vol. 19, no. 1, pp. 81–116.

ElMaraghy, W.H. & Urbanic, R.J. 2003, 'Modelling of manufacturing systems complexity', *CIRP Annals*, vol. 52, no. 1, pp. 363–366.

Ernst, D. 2002, 'Global production networks and the changing geography of innovation systems. Implications for developing countries', *Economics of Innovation and New Technology*, vol. 11, no. 6, pp. 497–523.

Feenstra, R.C. & Hanson, G.H. 2004, 'Intermediaries in entrepot trade: Hong Kong re-exports of Chinese goods', *Journal of Economics & Management Strategy*, vol. 13, no. 1, pp. 3–35.

Galunic, D.C. & Eisenhardt, K.M. 2001, 'Architectural innovation and modular corporate forms', *Academy of Management Journal*, vol. 44, no. 6, pp. 1229–1249.

Hidalgo, C.A. & Hausmann, R. 2009, 'The building blocks of economic complexity', *Proceedings of the National Academy of Sciences*, vol. 106, no. 26, pp. 10570–10575.

Hirsch-Kreinsen, H. 2008, '"Low-tech" innovations', *Industry and Innovation*, vol. 15, no. 1, pp. 19–43.

Hirsch-Kreinsen, H. & Jacobson, D. 2008, *Innovation in Low-tech Firms and Industries*, Edward Elgar Publishing, Cheltenham, UK.

Hobday, M., Davies, A. & Prencipe, A. 2005, 'Systems integration: A core capability of the modern corporation', *Industrial and Corporate Change*, vol. 14, no. 6, pp. 1109–1143.

Kiriyama, N. 2011, *Trade and Innovation: Pharmaceuticals*, OECD Trade Policy Papers, No. 113, OECD Publishing, Paris.

Krugman, P. 1979, 'A model of innovation, technology transfer, and the world distribution of income', *Journal of political economy*, vol. 87, no. 2, pp. 253–266.

Los, B., Timmer, M.P. & de Vries, G.J. 2015, 'How global are global value chains? A new approach to measure international fragmentation', *Journal of Regional Science*, vol. 55, no. 1, pp. 66–92.

Lundvall, B.-Å. (ed.) 1992, *National Systems of Innovation: Towards a Theory of Innovation and Interactive Learning*, Pinter, London, UK.

Luo, J., Baldwin, C.Y., Whitney, D.E. & Magee, C.L. 2012, 'The architecture of transaction networks: A comparative analysis of hierarchy in two sectors', *Industrial and Corporate Change*, vol. 21, no. 6, pp. 1307–1335.

MacCormack, A., Baldwin, C. & Rusnak, J. 2012, 'Exploring the duality between product and organizational architectures: A test of the "mirroring" hypothesis', *Research Policy*, vol. 41, no. 8, pp. 1309–1324.

Markard, J. & Truffer, B. 2008, 'Technological innovation systems and the multi-level perspective: Towards an integrated framework', *Research Policy*, vol. 37, no. 4, pp. 596–615.

Maskell, P. 2014, 'Accessing remote knowledge—the roles of trade fairs, pipelines, crowdsourcing and listening posts', *Journal of Economic Geography*, vol. 14, no. 5, pp. 883–902.

Minondo, A. & Requena-Silvente, F. 2013, 'Does complexity explain the structure of trade?', *Canadian Journal of Economics/Revue canadienne d'économique*, vol. 46, no. 3, pp. 928–955.

Nielsen, P.B. 2018, 'The puzzle of measuring global value chains–The business statistics perspective', *International Economics*, vol. 153, pp. 69–79.

OECD. 1997, *Technology and Industrial Performance*, OECD Publishing, Paris.

Office of the Chief Economist. 2018, *Industry Insights − Globalising Australia: Chapter 3, Manufacturing and the Smile Curve*, Canberra, ACT.

Panagariya, A. & Bagaria, N. 2013, 'Some surprising facts about the concentration of trade across commodities and trading partners', *The World Economy*, vol. 36, no. 9, pp. 1165–1186.

Parilla, J. & Berube, A. 2013, *Metro North America: Cities and the Metros as Hubs of Advanced Industries and Integrated Goods Trade*, Brookings Institution, Washington, DC.

Pavitt, K. 1984, 'Sectoral patterns of technical change: Towards a taxonomy and a theory', *Research Policy*, vol. 13, no. 6, pp. 343–373.

Piccardi, C. & Tajoli, L. 2018, 'Complexity, centralization, and fragility in economic networks', *PloS One*, vol. 13, no. 11, e0208265.

Qiao, L., Efatmaneshnik, M., Ryan, M. & Shoval, S. 2017, 'Product modular analysis with design structure matrix using a hybrid approach based on MDS and clustering', *Journal of Engineering Design*, vol. 28, no. 6, pp. 433–456.

Reynolds, C., Agrawal, M., Lee, I., Zhan, C., Li, J., Taylor, P., ... & Roos, G. 2018, 'A sub-national economic complexity analysis of Australia's states and territories', *Regional Studies*, vol. 52, no. 5, pp. 715–726.

Roos, G., Shroff, Z., Gamble, H., Taylor, P., Mares, T., Esvelt-Allen, R. & Baird, A. 2018, *Smart Specialisation − Insights for a Future Industry Policy*, Economic Development Board of South Australia. Adelaide, South Australia, Australia: Government of South Australia.

Rosenkopf, L. & Schilling, M.A. 2007, 'Comparing alliance network structure across industries: Observations and explanations', *Strategic Entrepreneurship Journal*, vol. 1, no. 3–4, pp. 191–209.

Rutherford, T. & Holmes, J. 2008, "The flea on the tail of the dog': Power in global production networks and the restructuring of Canadian automotive clusters', *Journal of Economic Geography*, vol. 8, no. 4, pp. 519–544.

Sanchez, R. & Mahoney, J.T. 1996, 'Modularity, flexibility, and knowledge management in product and organization design', *Strategic Management Journal*, vol. 17, no. S2, pp. 63–76.

Senge, P.M., Kleiner, A., Roberts, C. & Ross, R.B. 1994, *The Fifth Discipline Fieldbook*, Nicholas Brearley, London.

Simon, H. 1962, 'The architecture of complexity', *Proceedings of the American Philosophical Society*, vol. 106, pp. 467–482.

Song, W., Ming, X. & Wang, P. 2013, 'Collaborative product innovation network: Status review, framework, and technology solutions', *Concurrent Engineering*, vol. 21, no. 1, pp. 55–64.

Sturgeon, T., Van Biesebroeck, J. & Gereffi, G. 2008, 'Value chains, networks and clusters: Reframing the global automotive industry', *Journal of economic geography*, vol. 8, no. 3, pp. 297–321.

Timmer, M., Erumban, A.A., Gouma, R., Los, B., Temurshoev, U., de Vries, G.J., Arto, I.a., Genty, V.A.A., Neuwahl, F. & Francois, J. 2012, *The World Input-Output Database (WIOD): Contents, Sources and Methods*, Institute for International and Development Economics.

Toner, M., Ojha, N., de Paepe, P. & Simoes de Melo, M. 2015, *A Strategy for Thriving in Uncertainty: How Leaders Prepare and Adapt to Succeed in an Impossible to Predict World*, Bain and Company. Published online https://www.bain.com/insights/a-strategy-for-thriving-in-uncertainty/ Last retrieved 24 June 2021.

Tregenna, F. 2008, 'The contributions of manufacturing and services to employment creation and growth in South Africa', *South African Journal of Economics*, vol. 76, pp. S175–S204.

Urbanic, R.J. & ElMaraghy, W.H. 2006, 'Modeling of manufacturing process complexity', in H. ElMaraghy and W. H. ElMaraghy (eds.), *Advances in Design* (pp. 425–436). Springer, London.

von Hippel, E. 1990, 'Task partitioning: An innovation process variable', *Research Policy*, vol. 19, no. 5, pp. 407–418.

Wang, Q. & von Tunzelmann, N. 2000, 'Complexity and the functions of the firm: Breadth and depth', *Research Policy*, vol. 29, no. 7–8, pp. 805–818.

Watts, D.J. & Strogatz, S.H. 1998, 'Collective dynamics of 'small-world' networks', *Nature*, vol. 393, no. 6684, pp. 440–442.

Weber, K.M. & Rohracher, H. 2012, 'Legitimizing research, technology and innovation policies for transformative change: Combining insights from innovation systems and multi-level perspective in a comprehensive 'failures' framework', *Research Policy*, vol. 41, no. 6, pp. 1037–1047.

Wixted, B. 2009, *Innovation System Frontiers: Cluster Networks and Global Value*, Springer, Heidelberg.

Wixted, B. & Bliemel, M. 2019, '*Global value chains are not always global – The 'global factory' and 'exo-net' value architectures'*, This volume.

Wood, A. 2017, '*Variation in structural change around the world, 1985–2015: Patterns, causes and implications*', WIDER Working Paper 2017/34, ISBN 978-92-9256-258-8, Available at SSRN: https://ssrn.com/abstract=2920560

World Bank. 2017, *Measuring and Analyzing the Impact of GVCs on Economic Development*, The World Bank, Washington, DC.

12

MAXIMIZING THE DEVELOPMENTAL BENEFITS OF GVC INTEGRATION WHILE ADDRESSING EMERGING CHALLENGES

Jakob Engel, Daria Taglioni and Deborah Winkler

12.1 Introduction

Global value chain (GVC) participation can provide countries with the opportunity to industrialize more rapidly. Firms in developing countries that are able to connect with GVCs often produce more and higher-quality jobs, provide better opportunities for domestic suppliers to trade, benefit from increased exports, and, finally, experience higher productivity gains (Baldwin and Lopez-Gonzalez 2015, Taglioni and Winkler 2016, Criscuolo and Timmis 2017). Flows of knowledge and technology from high-income countries to low- and middle-income countries is central to GVCs' role in supporting these countries' industrialization and development prospects (Inomata and Taglioni 2019).

From the perspective of a developing country's policymaker, effectively integrating a GVC-led development strategy into economic policymaking and therefore how to maximize the benefits from technology transfer, knowledge spillovers, and increased value addition is a central concern (Elms and Low 2013, Gereffi 2018, World Bank 2019). Policymakers need to put in place appropriate policies to ensure that participation in GVCs benefits domestic society through more and better-paying jobs, better living conditions, and social cohesion. Finally, with increasing automation of GVC production in most industries and products, and rising protectionist forces in advanced countries, developing countries' efforts to engage and upgrade in GVCs face increasing challenges (Rodrik 2018, Hollweg 2019).

This chapter addresses how countries can more effectively benefit from GVCs, especially in the context of increased automation and growing skepticism about the gains from globalization. Section 12.2 discusses the importance of GVC participation for developmental outcomes. Section 12.3 focuses in particular on "upgrading" as the mechanism through which GVC-related gains can be realized and discusses differing upgrading trajectories depending on income levels. Section 12.4 presents an analysis of the factors likely to influence countries' upgrading trajectories. Sections 12.5 and 12.6 address some of the risks presented by increased automation

DOI: 10.4324/9781315225661-18

and the growth of protectionism and economic nationalism as well as some of the policy solutions, and section 12.7 concludes the chapter.

12.2 Why GVCs matter for development

Companies used to make things primarily in one country, but nowadays a single finished product often results from manufacturing and assembly in multiple countries, with each step in the process adding value to the final product (Baldwin 2013). As a result, GVCs lower the threshold and costs for individual countries to develop. Low- and middle-income countries can now industrialize by joining GVCs without the need to build their own value chain from scratch, as Japan and the Republic of Korea had to do in the 20th century (Engel and Taglioni 2017).[1] The reductions in costs that have arisen enables low- and middle-income countries to focus on specific tasks in the value chain, rather than producing the entire product, while still reaching the scale necessary to produce profitably thanks to their access to global markets intermediated by GVCs (Grossman and Rossi-Hansberg 2008, Lanz et al. 2011).

Through GVCs, countries trade more than products; they trade know-how and make things together. These flows of knowledge and technology from high-income countries to low- and middle-income countries are integral to the relevance of GVCs for development. Low- and middle-income countries can benefit from foreign-originated patents; trademarks; marketing expertise; organizational models; and operational, managerial, and business practices. Large multinational corporations (MNCs) establish highly sophisticated processes and flows where parts and components produced in geographically distant facilities can be seamlessly integrated and customized for different world markets (Gereffi et al. 2005, Saliola and Zanfei 2009).

To facilitate the integration of low- and middle-income countries into GVCs, MNCs often take an active role in improving local innovation systems and worker competencies. The Samsung Group –which employs 369,000 people in 510 offices worldwide – worries about shortages of technical and engineering skills in Africa and how those shortages affect its efforts to embed its African workforce in Samsung's global production networks (ACET 2014). Other corporations are also investing in building the skill base in low- and middle-income countries (Dunbar 2013).[2]

Countries that adopt the appropriate policies to benefit from GVC participation and mitigate the risks associated with them have the opportunity to boost employment and productivity in agriculture, manufacturing, and services. The policy framework that allows developing countries to maximize the gains from GVC integration is one in which imports matter as much as, if not more than, exports, and in which the flows of goods, services, people, ideas, and capital are interdependent and must be assessed jointly (Baldwin and Lopez-Gonzalez 2015, Taglioni and Winkler 2016).

This in turn does not need to lead to job losses. While job creation and labor productivity growth are sometimes viewed as competing goals, as higher labor productivity enables firms to produce a larger amount of value added without necessarily increasing the number of workers at the same rate (static productivity effects), GVC integration in many cases leads to more net jobs but at a lower job intensity (Cali and Hollweg 2015). This has strong potential for productivity gains via several transmission channels (dynamic productivity effects), which go in hand with increased labor demand caused by more vertical specialization and higher output in GVCs.

12.3 What are the characteristics of recent upgrading trajectories?

"Upgrading" occurs when a firm increases its rents through new or more sophisticated products, improved production processes, or the integration of new value-added functions. This is the primary means through which GVC participation supports developmental outcomes. Drawing on earlier work by Humphrey (2004), Taglioni and Winkler (2016) differentiate three types of economic upgrading based on productivity, comparative advantage, skills, and capabilities: product upgrading, which entails moving into more sophisticated products within an existing value chain; functional upgrading, involving increasing the value-added share by moving toward more sophisticated tasks; and intersectoral upgrading, which involves moving into new supply chains with higher value-added shares.

The ability of firms to upgrade is determined by improving skills of workers (skills upgrading), improving the absorptive capacity and technology of firms (capital upgrading), and increasing productivity in existing tasks (process upgrading). Lead firms have an important role here by setting detailed specifications and requirements that exceed local norms and create opportunities for improving capabilities, technology, and assets. However, this is not always the case: often the complexity of GVCs and the power dynamics within their governance structures can lead to processes of downgrading or stagnation (Rossi 2013, Blazek 2016).

While heterogeneity exists in how countries participate and upgrade in GVCs, some regularities in development trajectories can be identified. In Table 12.1 we sketch some of these regularities observed from fieldwork and case-study literature. Reflecting their comparative advantage, low-income countries tend to engage in GVCs in industries of limited complexity, such as agriculture and manufacturing. These are also industries in which buyer–seller relations tend to be at arm's length more frequently than in other settings. Firm size is not a constraint, so that also small firms can easily engage.

Firms in middle-income countries that integrate into GVCs, focus primarily on advanced manufacturing and/or professional, modern services, including pre- and post-production high value-added services. In these GVCs, buyer–seller relations tend to be more relational, captive or hierarchical, as substantial knowledge transfer takes place. The size of participating firms tends to be medium to large, particularly in manufacturing (Cusolito, Safadi, and Taglioni 2016), and competition between firms is based on non-price features, such as quality, degree of customization, or responsiveness and timeliness in delivery to clients.

Finally, once countries reach high-income status, the engagement of firms in GVCs is predominantly focused on tasks of coordination, and high value-added services, such as research and developments (R&D) and branding. Firms are primarily buyers of inputs and components and sellers to end markets, and/or engaged in modular relationships. These firms' comparative advantage is based on offering highly specialized products at the technology frontier.

Table 12.1 Trajectories in GVC engagement

	Low income	*Middle income*	*High income*
Industry complexity	Agriculture and light manufacturing	Advanced manufacturing and services	Coordination of manufacturing and services, R&D, branding
Buyer–seller relations	Market relations	Relational/captive/ hierarchical	Primarily buyer, modular
Firm size	Small	Large	Lead firms, conglomerates
Mode of competition	Price-to-quality competitiveness	Increasingly diversified, non-price competitiveness	Highly specialized, technology frontier

Source: Engel and Taglioni (2017).

12.4 What factors are likely to influence countries' engagement in GVCs?

There is a broad literature on the factors that are likely to influence countries' abilities to upgrade within GVCs, though this is primarily based on case studies, with few econometric analyses conducted until recently. However, there is growing evidence that open economies tend to grow faster and have higher income levels than closed economies (Wacziarg and Welch 2008, Gill and Kharas 2015).

Taglioni and Winkler (2016) argue that there are five main transmission channels through which GVC participation could lead to higher output, productivity and value added: backward and forward linkages; the creation of pro-competitive market restructuring effects; technology spillovers; minimum scale achievements that amplify pro-competitive effects; and through labor market effects including demand for skilled workers and their training, as well as turnover when trained workers move to local firms.

Kummritz et al. (2017) identify three main channels that link value chain integration to productivity. These are the role of (i) foreign direct investment (FDI), (ii) exporting, and (iii) importing inputs. In the case of FDI, the impact of spillovers on productivity is not conclusive (Görg and Greenaway 2004, Paus and Gallagher 2008). In the case of the link between exporting and economic upgrading, Bernard and Jensen (1999) demonstrated that exporters outperform non-exporters in the same sector and country in terms of productivity, skills, and wages. This has led to a question of whether this is driven by self-selection or learning-by-exporting (LBE) effects. In the case of the former, the assumption is that only more productive firms can absorb additional trade costs. The LBE literature argues that exporting improves the productivity of firms over time. These findings have been most robust for developing countries and nascent industries. Recent literature has questioned the robustness of these early LBE studies (see Clerides et al. 1998, but LBE effects have been found by Lileevea and Treffler (2007) for Canada and Fernandes and Isgut (2015) for Colombia.

Finally, for the third channel, the role of importing inputs on productivity, there is a breadth of literature, albeit primarily focused on developed countries. There are three main feedback loops through which importing is linked to competitiveness: its impacts on productivity, on innovation, and on skills. In the case of productivity, several studies have shown that easier access to imports tends to improve firm productivity. Grossman and Rossi-Hansberg (2008) show that offshoring can entail productivity gains similar to technological progress for offshoring nations through lower input costs. Amiti and Konings (2007) show that a 10 percent fall in input tariffs leads to a 12 percent improvement in productivity for importing firms in Indonesia. Bas (2012) demonstrates that for a sample of Argentinian firms, input tariffs facilitate entry into export markets. In the case of innovation, MacGarvie (2006), drawing on French trade and citation data, and Bøler et al. (2015), using a sample of Norwegian firms, find importers to be more innovative and profitable. Finally, there is an emerging literature showing that skills are relevant for importing and complementary to it. Koren and Csillag (2011) show that importing more sophisticated machinery, which requires higher skills to operate, in turn increases returns to skills.

To actually test the effects of GVC participation on its ability to enable countries' economic upgrading, Kummritz et al. (2017) use foreign value added in exports and domestic value added re-exported by third countries as measures of backward and forward GVC integration, respectively, and domestic value added generated by a specific sector as the measure of economic upgrading. Using a standard fixed effects model, they test the impact of a series of national characteristics that may be associated with economic upgrading via GVC participation to capture a country's infrastructure, connectivity, investment and trade policy, business climate and institutions, financial and labor markets, skills and education, and innovation and product standards, as well as labor, social, and environmental standards.

Using the Organisation for Economic Co-operation and Development (OECD) Inter-Country Input–Output (ICIO) database for 61 countries and 34 industries in 1995, 2000, 2005, and 2008–2011, Kummritz et al. (2017) found that overall GVC integration increases a country's domestic value added. Splitting the sample into income groups, they found that this does not substantially change results, though GVC integration as a buyer (i.e. via foreign value added embodied in exports) is more significant for low-income and lower middle income countries, while for upper middle income and high-income countries selling into GVCs has a greater impact. On the buyer side, airfreight infrastructure and road network quality are of particular importance, while connectivity, education and skills, and the level of standards compliance are most important for countries selling into GVCs. This leads the authors to conclude that the policy areas hypothesized to be significant for economic upgrading within GVCs do in fact largely have the expected impact.

Boffa et al. (2016) build on these findings to focus specifically on the relationship between GVC integration and the "middle income trap," and – more broadly – the role of GVC integration in supporting countries graduating to a higher income level. As can be seen in Figure 12.1, the magnitude of the correlation between GVC integration and GDP per capita depends on income status and the type of integration. Moving from these findings of correlation, the authors use a logit (probit) model for income group transitions and found that GVC integration increases GDP per capita but that gains diminish as income increases. Similarly, growth in output per capita is highest for lower income groups. Certain channels between GVC integration depend on industry similarity with linkages assumed to be easier when trade is intra-industry. Boffa et al. (2016) also found that manufacturing leads to higher GDP gains

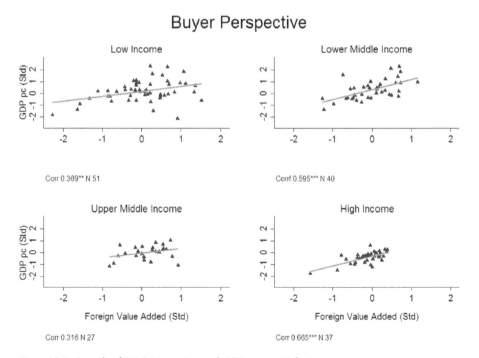

Figure 12.1 Growth of GVC integration and GDP per capita by income category.

for buyers, but for services both types of integration – forward and backward – lead to similar GDP increases.

However, the aforementioned studies – while providing an important foundation for a better understanding of what variables are significant for upgrading – suffer from two main limitations. First, due to the lack of value-added trade data prior to 1990, they only allow assessments of the last 25 years. Second, the studies provide a helpful overview of what kind of institutions and policies are associated with upgrading and income transitions, but they do not specify the global conditions under which specific types of institutions and policies lead to greater gains from GVC participation. While some of these opportunities may have been available 20 years ago, they may no longer be available for new entrants today, or even feasible, given that most late industrializers nowadays tend to be small both geographically and economically, as well as distant from end markets and the current hubs of global economic activity.

12.5 GVC participation in the context of technical progress and globalization skepticism

As the aforementioned study by Boffa et al. (2016) has pointed out, there is a positive and significant relationship between GDP per capita and integration into GVCs, though this correlation diminishes at higher income levels. This points to questions around the gains of GVC trade for workers in countries at the middle- to high-income threshold. Over the past few years there has been a proliferation of reports by the Oxford Martin School (Berger and Frey, 2016), Brookings (West 2015), McKinsey (Chui et al. 2015), and KPMG (2016), was well as numerous papers (see Autor 2015, Beaudry et al. 2016, Eden and Gaggi 2015, Morikawa 2016, Pikos and Thomsen 2016) investigating the impact of technological change on production, trade, and labor markets. The authors focus particularly on the rapid technological advances in automation, big data analytics, and digitization, as well as manufacturing responses to climate change and other environmental- and resource-related risks, including transitions toward additive manufacturing through 3D printing technologies and the growth of the circular economy paradigm that is likely to require manufacturers to design products for several cycles of disassembly and reutilization.

As Antràs (2015) notes, GVCs are characterized by four features: customized production; sequential production decisions going from the buyer to the suppliers; high contracting costs; and global matching of goods, services, production teams, and ideas. All four of these point to the significant power that multinational corporations coordinating GVCs have in the selection of where geographically to locate individual production tasks. Technological improvements are likely in each of these cases to both increase the sophistication of buyer demands and the level of supplier capabilities required to meet them. A full exploration of these issues is beyond the scope of this chapter, but given their implications for the relationship between GVC participation and declining economic growth and structural stasis experienced by many middle-income countries, it is worth addressing these developments in the context of the preceding discussion.

First, the workforce skills required to participate in manufacturing of even relatively unsophisticated products is likely to increase substantially, requiring not only higher levels of education but also the "cross-domain" skills and tacit knowledge necessary for using new equipment, think computationally and analytically, and high levels of technical and engineering knowledge. For many middle-income countries this will require a fundamental upgrading of education systems, research institutions, and innovation systems. As such, the already diminishing advantage that labor-abundant, low-wage countries currently possess for low-skill manufacturing is likely to diminish further.

Second, and related to the previous point, the incentives to "reshore" production to developed economies given both the need for highly skilled workers and – more important – the ability to automate many tasks could become even greater in coming years, a trend likely to be reinforced by the rapidly growing political backlash against globalization and rising economic nationalism in many Western countries (Artuc et al. 2019). Seventy percent of clients surveyed in a recent study believe automation and the developments in 3D printing will encourage companies to move their manufacturing closer to home, with North America seen as having the most to gain from this trend, while China has the most to lose (Oxford Martin School 2016). In this context, the rapidly growing importance of the trade in data and information, even within production and manufacturing, is likely to further increase the modularity of work processes and is likely to bypass all but the most sophisticated middle-income countries.

Collectively, these issues may reinforce trends toward "premature deindustrialization" (Rodrik 2016) with countries running out of industrialization opportunities sooner and at lower levels of income compared to earlier industrializers – a trend that has hit Latin American middle-income countries particularly hard, both economically and in terms of risk toward political stability and democratization. Thus, while it was only recently that firms and governments in developed and developing economies were coming to terms with the fact that the "GVC revolution" required a fundamental rethinking of trade and more broadly industrial development, these new disruptive technological changes will again require new policies and strategies to adapt.

This in turn points to challenges for ensuring that the gains from GVC trade for industrializing countries in fact benefit workers and households, and points to the increasingly complex aspects of the political economy of globalization, particularly for industrializing countries.

12.6 Policy frameworks

While policies need to adapt to a rapidly changing world, it remains valid that, for an effective and sustainable strategy of GVC participation, some areas of policy remain relevant. Identifying binding constraints and designing the necessary policy and regulatory interventions will help achieve distinct objectives and address country-specific challenges to

i.   Participate in GVCs, including attracting foreign direct investment and facilitating domestic firm entry into GVCs.
ii. Expand and strengthen existing GVC participation, including promoting economic upgrading and densification, and strengthening domestic firms' absorptive capacity.
iii. Ensure sustainability and transform GVC participation into inclusive growth by fostering economy-wide productivity spillovers, social upgrading, and welfare improvements.

By integrating their domestic firms (suppliers and final producers) into GVCs, developing countries can help their economies industrialize. Taglioni and Winkler (2016) suggested how to assess various aspects of GVC participation (including the rate, strength, and consistency across sectors and industries) and, thus, how to identify key policy needs. They suggest "strategic questions" and approaches to addressing such policy needs and offer "policy options." These are summarized in Figures 12.2 to 12.4.

First, countries must find ways to enter global production networks (Figure 12.2). Those avenues include ways to attract foreign investors, as well as strategies to enhance the participation of domestic firms in GVCs. Suggestions for entering GVCs encompass measures to ensure that the country can offer world-class connectivity to the global economy and create a friendly business climate for foreign tangible and intangible assets.

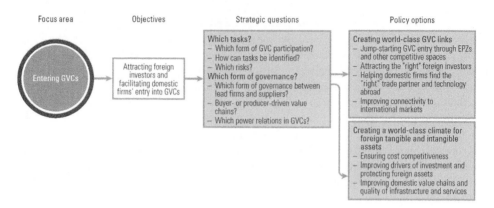

Figure 12.2 A policy framework for entering GVCs.

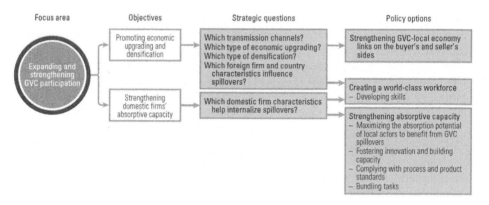

Figure 12.3 Policies for strengthening participation in GVCs.

Figure 12.4 Policies for turning GVC participation in sustainable development.

However, GVC participation is a necessary but not sufficient condition for development. Although GVCs open doors, they are not a panacea. Most of the hard work still has to be done domestically, with pro-investment, pro-skills, pro-jobs, and pro-growth reforms. Creating demand for high-productivity workers must be matched with a supply of capable workers who have the relevant skills. In other words, when thinking about the first step in facilitating GVC entry, policymakers must have a clear road map of how entry will lead to strengthened and broader participation and economic and social upgrading. Policymakers must keep a keen eye on the workforce's competencies and how they match up with foreign investment.

Expanding and strengthening participation in GVCs (Figure 12.3) requires countries to leverage their position and enhance domestic production, achieving higher value addition through economic upgrading and densification. The concept of economic upgrading is largely about gaining competitiveness in higher value-added processes, products, tasks, and sectors. Densification involves engaging more local actors (firms and workers) in the GVC network. Raising domestic labor productivity and skills contributes to the overall goal to increase a country's value added that results from GVC participation.

Finally, countries also need to tackle the challenge of turning GVC participation into sustainable development (Figure 12.4). Three areas of sustainable development are important: macroeconomic sustainability, social sustainability, and environmental sustainability. Not only are they important development objectives per se, but they also ensure the sustainability of a GVC-centric approach to development. Labor market–enhancing outcomes for workers at home and more equitable distribution of opportunities and outcomes create social support for a reform agenda aimed at strengthening a country's GVC participation. Climate-smart policy prescriptions can mitigate the challenges for firms from climatic disruptions, as those firms seek to ensure the long-term predictability, reliability, and time-sensitive delivery of goods necessary to participate in global value chains. Because climatic disruption can impair firms' ability to access inputs and deliver final products, countries' preparedness is an increasingly critical factor in firms' location decisions.

Within this context, policymakers should consider the following issues as priority:

- *Investing in digital technologies* – Newcomers should not favor manufacturing over services and innovation functions, and early developers and newcomers alike should balance policies that support connectivity infrastructure building and the deployment of leading information and communications technologies (ICTs), with those that support the development of a domestic ICT sector.
- *GVCs and the enabling environment* – To be competitive in the new ICT-dominated environment, countries and companies will need to be part of global production and knowledge networks, upgrade infrastructure and connectivity systems, and ensure regulatory certainty.
- *Human capital* – Countries will need to develop the needed talent through technical skills acquisition and, crucially, also develop soft skills (managerial skills, strong foreign-language skills, etc.)
- *Reducing barriers to knowledge* – They will also need to reduce barriers to foreign skilled personnel and services. One dimension of this can be mutual recognition arrangements for professional services that help facilitate the movement of global talent into the home country. Reducing barriers to knowledge also includes establishing robust intellectual property rights to attract technology-intensive foreign investors.
- *Focus on workers* – It is important for policymakers to ensure that the link between productivity and distribution, and between economic and social impacts works. This requires ensuring social cohesion with policies that focus on workers and not just jobs. For example, retraining, education, supporting mobility, and income could be associated with well-targeted and nondistortive vertical interventions. Policies for openness should be bundled with social, governance, and infrastructural support at the regional level. This also applies to industrialized countries, and includes supporting workers that have suffered wage cuts or job loss due to technical progress and globalization.
- *Deep integration agreements with knowledge clusters* – New technologies, new processes, and new products require a fair amount of decodification and recodification according to innovative criteria. As such they tend to arise from existing knowledge clusters where the pool

of skills and support functions is at the same time deep and broad. The activity of decodification and codification of new processes also implies that such clusters are natural standard-setting bodies. Hence the role of knowledge clusters can be self-reinforcing.

- *Contract enforcement and governance* – Cutting-edge digitally powered goods and services are likely to be outsourced based on sophisticated contractual arrangements. This means that areas such as contract enforcement and the rule of law are again important foundational areas.
- *Infrastructure investment* – This can help prevent the wedge between the networked countries, individuals, and firms, and the non-networked created by the digital revolution. Physical, digital, and institutional infrastructure connects global hubs with peripheral countries, cities with both smaller centers and rural areas, and opens opportunities, ensuring that the development potential of the digital technologies reaches a large fraction of the world population. Without infrastructure investment, the matching of technologies, services, and talents at the global level unleashed by the interplay between digital innovation and globalization would lead to negative distributional impacts, including shifts in global income toward the networked (countries, individuals, firms) and a task remuneration structure that further tilts away from production functions to services, innovation, and core R&D functions.

12.7 Conclusion

This chapter has surveyed the relationship between GVC participation and economic development. Specifically, it examined the channels and circumstances through which GVC engagement may assist countries in advancing their economic development objectives. Within this context, it is useful to restate a few of the key assumptions underpinning this chapter. First, the types of policies and the quality of institutions required for successful GVC participation play an important role in determining economic development. However, graduating to high-income status remains difficult: the types of capabilities, policies, investment decisions, and institutional processes required are highly complex and interact in unpredictable and dynamic ways. Moreover, they are often unique to the respective country, sector, and product context. Furthermore, emergent technological changes are likely to further complicate the ability of countries to integrate into and upgrade within GVCs.

This in turn informs a series of more specific policy recommendations of how to move toward a less zero-sum view of the emergent paradigm of industrial development in an age likely to be dominated by disruption and increasing automation. For one, policymakers and companies in the digital era – in developed and developing countries alike – will need to focus on the key features of the 21st-century economy. This includes the interplay between technological (digital) innovation and globalization (increased connectivity and GVCs), and strengthening an environment conducive to diversification, innovation, and productivity in the era of digital innovation.

Acknowledgments

The authors would like to thank the Commonwealth Secretariat for permission to use the article that was commissioned as part of the online publication *Future Fragmentation Processes: Effectively Engaging with the Ascendency of Global Value Chains*. The views expressed in this chapter are those of the authors and should not be attributed to the World Bank, its executive directors, or the countries they represent.

Notes

1 See Baldwin (2012) as well as the key works in the literature on Asian "developmental states" (Amsden 1992, Wade 2004, Johnson 1995).
2 For example, Lucent Technologies supports education and a range of learning programs, including promoting educational reform, science and math, and developing teachers and young leaders, in 16 countries throughout Africa, Asia, Europe, and Latin America; Nike and the United Kingdom's Department for International Development run a program to support access to economic assets for adolescent girls; Microsoft provides support to incorporate information technology (IT) into the daily lives of young people in the Philippines, Poland, the Russian Federation, and South Africa; CISCO provides funds, expertise, and equipment to create national networks of IT training centers in India, Mexico, Palestine, and South Africa, in addition to the work of the Cisco Networking Academy, which has 10,000 academies in 165 countries; finally, Nokia enhances life skills and leadership skills of young people in several countries, including Brazil, China, and Mexico.

References

ACET. 2014. *African Transformation Report: Growth with Depth*. Accra, Ghana: ACET.

Amiti, M. and Konings, J. 2007. Trade liberalization, intermediate inputs, and productivity: Evidence from Indonesia. *American Economic Review*, *97*(5), pp. 1611–1638.

Amsden, A.H. 1992. *Asia's Next Giant: South Korea and Late Industrialization*. Oxford, United Kingdom: Oxford University Press on Demand.

Antras, P. 2015. *Global Production: Firms, Contracts, and Trade Structure*. Princeton, NJ: Princeton University Press.

Artuc, E., Christiaensen, L. and Winkler, H.J. 2019. *Does Automation in Rich Countries Hurt Developing Ones?: Evidence from the US and Mexico*. The World Bank.

Autor, D. 2015. Why are there still so many jobs? The history and future of workplace automation. *Journal of economic perspectives*, *29*(3), pp. 3–30.

Baldwin, R. 2013. Trade and industrialization after globalization's second unbundling: How building and joining a supply chain are different and why it matters. In *Globalization in an Age of Crisis: Multilateral Economic Cooperation in the Twenty-First Century* (pp. 165–212). University of Chicago Press.

Baldwin, R. and Lopez-Gonzalez, J. 2015. Supply-chain trade: A portrait of global patterns and several testable hypotheses. *The World Economy*, *38*(11), pp. 1682–1721.

Baldwin, R.E. 2012. *Global Supply Chains: Why They Emerged, Why They Matter, and Where They are Going*. CEPR Discussion Paper No. DP9103.

Bas, M. 2012. Input-trade liberalization and firm export decisions: Evidence from Argentina. *Journal of Development Economics*, *97*(2), pp. 481–493.

Beaudry, P., Green, D.A. and Sand, B.M. 2016. The great reversal in the demand for skill and cognitive tasks. *Journal of Labor Economics*, *34*(S1), pp. S199–S247.

Berger, T. and Frey, B. 2016. *Digitalisation, Jobs and Convergence in Europe: Strategies for Closing the Skills Gap* (Vol. 50). Oxford: Oxford Martin School.

Bernard, A.B. and Jensen, J.B. 1999. Exceptional exporter performance: Cause, effect, or both? *Journal of International Economics*, *47*(1), pp. 1–25.

Blažek, J. 2016. Towards a typology of repositioning strategies of GVC/GPN suppliers: the case of functional upgrading and downgrading. *Journal of Economic Geography*, *16*(4), pp. 849–869.

Boffa, M., Kumritz, V., Santoni, G., Taglioni, D. and Winkler, D. 2016 "Overcoming the Middle-Income Trap: The Role of GVC Integration for Climbing-Up the Income Ladder." Mimeo.

Bøler, E.A., Moxnes, A. and Ulltveit-Moe, K.H. 2015. R&D, international sourcing, and the joint impact on firm performance. *American Economic Review*, *105*(12), pp. 3704–39.

Calì, M. and Hollweg, C. 2015. *The Labor Content of Exports in South Africa and Botswana*. World Bank Policy Research Working Paper No. 23828. The World Bank.

Chui, M., Manyika, J. and Miremadi, M. 2015. Four fundamentals of workplace automation. *McKinsey Quarterly*, *29*(3), 1–9.

Clerides, S.K., Lach, S. and Tybout, J.R. 1998. Is learning by exporting important? Micro-dynamic evidence from Colombia, Mexico, and Morocco. *The Quarterly Journal of Economics*, *113*(3), pp. 903–947.

Criscuolo, C. and Timmis, J. 2017. The relationship between global value chains and productivity. *International Productivity Monitor*, *32*, pp. 61–83.

Cusololito, A.P., Safadi, R. and D. Taglioni 2016. *Inclusive Global Value Chains: Policy Options for Small and Medium Enterprises and Low-Income Countries*. Washington, DC: World Bank.

Dunbar, M. 2013. *Engaging The Private Sector in Skills Development*. HEART (Health & Education Advice and Resource Team) Oxford: Oxford Policy Management.

Eden, M and Gaggl, P. 2015. *On The Welfare Implications of Automation*. World Bank Policy Research working No. 7487.

Elms, D.K. and Low, P. 2013. *Global Value Chains in a Changing World*. Geneva: World Trade Organisation.

Engel, J. and Taglioni, D. 2017. *The Middle-Income Trap and Upgrading Along Global Value Chains*. Global Value Chain Report, pp. 119–139.

Fernandes, A.M. and Isgut, A.E. 2015. Learning-by-exporting effects: Are they for real? *Emerging Markets Finance and Trade, 51*(1), pp. 65–89.

Gereffi, G. 2018. *Global Value Chains and Development: Redefining the Contours of 21st Century Capitalism*. Cambridge, United Kingdom: Cambridge University Press.

Gereffi, G., Humphrey, J. and Sturgeon, T. 2005. The governance of global value chains. *Review of International Political Economy, 12*(1), pp. 78–104.

Gill, I. and Kharas, H. 2015. *Middle Income Traps: A Conceptual and Empirical Survey*. World Bank Policy Research Working Paper No. 6594.

Görg, H. and Greenaway, D. 2004. Much ado about nothing? Do domestic firms really benefit from foreign direct investment? *The World Bank Research Observer, 19*(2), pp. 171–197.

Grossman, G.M. and Rossi-Hansberg, E. 2008. Trading tasks: A simple theory of offshoring. *American Economic Review, 98*(5), pp. 1978–1997.

Hollweg, C.H. 2019. Global Value Chains and Employment In Developing Economies. Global Value Chain Development Report 2019, pp. 63–82.

Humphrey, J. 2004. "*Upgrading in Global Value Chains*." World Commission on the Social Dimensions of Globalization Working Paper No. 28. Geneva: ILO.

Inomata, S. and Taglioni, D. 2019. Technological progress, diffusion, and opportunities for developing countries: Lessons from China. *Global Value Chain Development Report*, 83–101.

Johnson, C. A. 1995. *Japan, Who Governs?: The Rise of the Developmental State*. New York: WW Norton & Company.

Koren, M. and Csillag, M. 2011. *Machines and Machinists: Capital-Skill Complementarity from an International Trade Perspective*. CEPR Discussion Paper No. DP8317.

KPMG. 2016. *Future State 2030: The Global Megatrends Shaping Governments*. London: KPMG.

Kummritz, V., Taglioni, D. and Winkler, D. 2017. "*Economic Upgrading through Global Value Chain Participation: Which Policies Increase the Value Added Gains?*" World Bank Policy Research Working Paper No. 8007. Washington, DC: World Bank.

Lanz, R. and Miroudot, S. 2011. Intra-firm trade: Patterns, determinants and policy implications. OECD Trade Policy Papers, No. 114. Paris: OECD Publishing.

Lileeva, A. and Treffler, D. 2007. "*Improved Access to Foreign Markets Raises Plant-Level Productivity… For Some Plants.*" NBER Working Paper No. 13297. Washington, DC: NBER.

MacGarvie, M. 2006. Do firms learn from international trade? *Review of Economics and Statistics, 88*(1), pp. 46–60.

Morikawa, M. 2016. "*The Effects of AI and Robotics on Business and Employment: Evidence from a Survey on Japanese Firms.*" RIETI Discussion Paper, 16-E–066.

Paus, E.A. and Gallagher, K.P. 2008. Missing links: Foreign investment and industrial development in Costa Rica and Mexico. *Studies in Comparative International Development, 43*(1), pp. 53–80.

Pikos, A.K and Thomsen, S.L. 2016. "*Rising Work Complexity But Decreasing Returns*". IZA Discussion Paper No. 9878.

Rodrik, D. 2016. Premature deindustrialization. *Journal of Economic Growth, 21*(1), pp. 1–33.

Rodrik, D. 2018. *New Technologies, Global Value Chains, and Developing Economies* (No. w25164). National Bureau of Economic Research.

Rossi, A. 2013. Does economic upgrading lead to social upgrading in global production networks? Evidence from Morocco. *World Development, 46*, pp. 223–233.

Saliola, F. and Zanfei, A. 2009. Multinational firms, global value chains and the organization of knowledge transfer. *Research Policy, 38*(2), pp. 369–381.

Taglioni, D. and Winkler, D. 2016. *Making Global Value Chains Work for Development*. Washington, DC: World Bank.

Wacziarg, R. and Welch, K.H. 2008. Trade liberalization and growth: New evidence. *The World Bank Economic Review*, *22*(2), pp. 187–231.

Wade, R. 2004. *Governing the Market: Economic Theory and the Role of Government in East Asian Industrialization.* Princeton, NJ: Princeton University Press.

West, D.M. 2015. *What Happens If Robots Take the Jobs? The Impact of Emerging Technologies on Employment and Public Policy.* Centre for Technology Innovation at Brookings. Washington, DC: Brookings.

World Bank. 2019. *World Development Report 2020: Trading for Development in the Age of Global Value Chains.* Washington, DC: World Bank.

13

REGIONALISM AND SMES

A firm-level perspective on GVCs and FTAs

Menaka Arudchelvan and Ganeshan Wignaraja

13.1 Introduction

East Asian countries are increasingly linked with each other as well as the world economy. Outward-oriented development strategies have enabled East Asian countries to become more prosperous but also become more economically integrated with each other in a process known as regionalism. A key indicator of economic interdependence, the share of a region's trade conducted within it, rose in East Asia from one-third to over half between the 1980s and early 2000s (ADB, 2009). Emerging East Asian regionalism has been underpinned by two important arrangements: (1) the spread of market-led global value chains (GVCs)[1] since the 1980s and (2) a network of bilateral and regional free trade agreements (FTAs) since the 2000s. GVC activity has driven the region's rise as a global manufacturing hub based on trade in parts and components. Meanwhile, increasingly comprehensive FTAs have been concluded by East Asian countries to support GVC activity through preferential trade liberalization and trade rules against a back-drop of rising protectionism and stalled multilateral trade negotiations. While there is a growing regionalism literature exploring the dynamics of GVCs and FTAs in East Asia (e.g. ADB 2009, Kuroiwa and Heng 2008, Kuroiwa 2009, Kawai and Wignaraja 2013, Ing, Richardson, and Urata 2019, Petri and Plummer 2020), an understudied area is the behavior of firms including small and medium enterprises (SMEs) under these arrangements. There is scant research on important research questions in East Asia such as what are the characteristics of SMEs that are able to participate in GVCs, what are the characteristics of SMEs that successfully use FTA preferences, and what impedes SMEs from using FTA preferences.[2] In part, the lack of studies on these issues may reflect the paucity of firm-level data on East Asian countries.

This chapter attempts to address these research questions through a micro-level analysis in a bid to contribute to the literature on regional economic integration. Drawing on insights from related studies of international economics and the microeconomics of technical change, it examines the characteristics of SMEs that have successfully internationalized through participation in GVCs and FTAs using enterprise survey data on 234 Malaysian exporters and importers collected in 2012. Malaysia is an interesting case study as it is an upper-middle income regional economy with a long and notable presence in both GVC and FTA activities. To the best of our knowledge, this is probably the only study that has attempted to examine the regionalization of SMEs in an East Asian country both in terms of participation in GVCs and in FTAs. Section

DOI: 10.4324/9781315225661-19

13.2 reviews relevant theoretical and empirical work related to firm-level participation in GVCs and the use of FTA preferences. Section 13.3 discusses the data used in the empirical analysis and some summary statistics. Section 13.4 looks at the findings on SME characteristics related to GVC participation. Section 13.5 discusses the findings on SME characteristics associated with FTA use and looks at the barriers faced by SMEs to using FTAs. Finally, Section 13.6 concludes the chapter.

13.2 Literature review

13.2.1 Global value chain participation

Several related strands of literature in international economics and the microeconomics of technical change have provided insights on GVCs and the role of firms, particularly SMEs. The fragmentation of production approach – as found in seminal works by Jones and Kierzkowski (1990) and Arndt and Kierzkowski (2001) – refines these insights. It shows how increasing returns and the advantages of specialization of factors within firms encourage the location of different stages of production across geographical space connected by service links. Products traded between firms in different countries are components rather than final goods. Two alternative approaches have been used to quantify the magnitude of fragmentation trade. One uses national trade data obtained from the United Nations trade data reporting system to identify trade in parts and components (e.g., Ng and Yeats 2003, and Athukorala 2011). It suggests that East Asia's trade is increasingly made up of parts and components trade, suggesting that global production networks are growing in importance. Another approach – relying on input–output tables to trace value added in production networks – suggests that value added seems a more accurate means of capturing production network activity than trade data (e.g., Koopman, Powers, Wang, and Wei 2010, and WTO and IDE-JETRO 2011). Neither approach, however, sheds light on factors affecting firms joining supply chains. Case studies show that large multinational corporations (MNCs), which use the region as an international production base, drive the process of production fragmentation (Kuroiwa and Heng 2008; Kuroiwa 2009).

Another related strand of literature is the "new new" trade theory of Melitz (2003) and Helpman et al. (2004), which emphasizes firm heterogeneity in international trade (i.e., firms are considered different in terms of efficiency and fixed and variable costs when involved in trade). Accordingly, only a few highly efficient firms are able to export and invest overseas as only they are able to make sufficient profits to cover the large trade costs required for overseas operations.

Finally, the technological capability and national innovation systems approach reveals a different channel through which firm behavior affects export performance. Focusing on innovation and learning processes in developing countries, proponents emphasize the acquisition of technological capabilities as a major source of export advantage at the firm level (Bell and Pavitt 1993, Lall 1992, Iammarino et al. 2008). The underlying evolutionary theory of technical change emphasizes that difficult firm-specific processes and complex interactions with institutions are needed to absorb imported technologies efficiently (Nelson and Winter 1982).

Implicit in most of the aforementioned theories is the notion that SMEs are at a disadvantage in participating in supply chains compared with larger firms. Compared to larger firms, SMEs face many challenges in the global environment. Ting's (2004) analysis of Malaysian SMEs identified five key challenges: lack of access to finance, human resources constraints, limited or no ability to adopt technology, lack of information on potential markets and customers, and global competition. He also argued that there is a high risk SMEs will be wiped out if they do not increase their competitiveness in the new, rapidly changing world of globalization. Given these challenges, the probability of SMEs joining supply chains (as direct exporters, indirect exporters, or overseas investors) is lower than that of large firms.

There is very little empirical literature on the characteristics of SMEs that participate in production networks, but a study by Harvie, Narjoko, and Oum (2010) is one of the few that consider this issue. They utilize the results from an Economic Research Institute for ASEAN and East Asia survey on SME participation in production networks, conducted over a three-month period at the end 2009 in most economies of the Association of Southeast Asian Nations (ASEAN). The results suggest that size, productivity, foreign ownership, and to some extent innovation efforts and managerial attitude are the key characteristics of SMEs in production networks. Rasiah, Rosli, and Sanjivee (2010) also consider the characteristics of SMEs in value chains, with particular focus on Malaysia. They find that SME size and labor productivity are positively and significantly associated with firms that participate in global value chains.

Wignaraja (2015) is the third study that addresses the characteristics of SMEs in global supply chain trade. The study utilizes the World Bank's Enterprise Survey data of 5900 manufacturing enterprises data from five ASEAN economies. The results find that in the late 2000s, large firms were the leading players in supply chain trade in ASEAN economies, while SMEs were relatively minor, but since the late 2000s there has been an increase in the participation of SMEs. More developed ASEAN economies such as Malaysia and Thailand, which are more established in production networks, have higher SME export shares than other ASEAN economies. The study also finds that firm heterogeneity matters in relation to firm-level participation in supply chains. The econometric analysis finds that size, foreign ownership, educated workers, experienced chief executive officers (CEOs), building of technological capabilities, and access to commercial bank credit all positively affect the probability of SME participation in supply chains. By contrast, age has a negative relationship.

Finally, a recent study using firm-level data from World Bank Enterprise Surveys (Lanz et al. 2018) found that digital connectivity, captured by whether a firm has a website or not, facilitates the participation of manufacturing SMEs from developing countries in GVCs. SMEs with a website were found to import a higher share of their inputs used for production and export a higher share of their sales as compared to SMEs without a website. Additionally, beyond digital connectivity at the firm level, the study also found evidence to suggest that countries with a higher share of population with fixed broadband subscriptions have higher share SMEs participating in GVCs. Therefore, investing in information and communications technology (ICT) infrastructure, creating a regulatory and policy environment conducive to e-commerce, and providing SMEs and workers with the digital skills and knowledge to use ICTs efficiently are broad policy options to be considered to increase SME participation in GVCs.

13.2.2 *Free trade agreement preference utilization*

One of the major challenges to researching the impact of FTAs is the lack of published information on trade flows (or individual business transactions) enjoying tariff preferences. Transaction records on exports and imports for preferential tariff purposes are filed with the authorities of origin, such as national customs authorities or trade ministries, but not published. Thailand is one exception to this norm, publishing annual information on FTA preference use, albeit in the Thai language. Using Thai data, Chirathivat (2008) has shown that the overall actual utilization rate for Thailand's FTA partners has been rising and nearly doubled (from 16% to 27%) during 2005–2008. The 2008 utilization rates of Thailand's partners vary by market, with 72%

for the Thailand–Australia FTA and 28% for the ASEAN Free Trade Area (AFTA). Using data from Thai secondary sources, Kawai and Wignaraja (2013) have shown that the overall actual utilization rate for Thailand's FTA partners rose further to around 61% in 2011, while the FTA utilization rate for the Thailand–Australia FTA increased to 91% and AFTA to 52%. Tambunan and Chandra (2014) narrow in on SMEs in ASEAN. In their scan of economic literature and government-supported programs they found that SMEs are by far the least active economic actors in the region to make use of the flourishing trade agreements.

In the absence of published data on preference utilization, micro-level information obtained from interviews with firms as well as large-scale enterprise surveys can be useful. In an early study, Kumar (1992) interviewed 15 trading companies and manufacturers in Kuala Lumpur, Singapore, and Jakarta to identify possible impediments to a successful implementation of AFTA in the future. Kumar reported that the main bottlenecks were likely to be non-tariff barriers (standards, testing procedures, and customs procedures), a lack of information about the Common Effective Preferential Tariff (CEPT) scheme of ASEAN, domestic investment regulations, and subsidy schemes.

The Asian Development Bank (ADB) and the Asian Development Bank Institute (ADBI) have also conducted comprehensive enterprise surveys in recent years on the business impact of FTAs in several Asian countries (Kawai and Wignaraja 2011). The economies of Japan, the People's Republic of China (PRC), the Republic of Korea, and three Southeast Asian countries (Singapore, Thailand, and the Philippines) were included in the first round of surveys of 841 firms, with 28% indicating they used FTA preferences. Interestingly, the average FTA use among the three Southeast Asian economies was reported to be somewhat lower than for manufacturing giants like Japan and the PRC. Furthermore, only 20% of the sampled firms said that multiple rules of origin (ROOs) significantly added to business costs. Weighing up the firm-level evidence, the study concluded that concerns about the Asian FTA "noodle bowl" effect on business might have been overstated at the time of the surveys.[3] Nonetheless, the study noted the risk of an Asian noodle bowl problem in the future with the growing number of FTAs in the region.

Some studies have explored the factors affecting FTA use at the firm level using econometric analysis. Using a sample of Japanese firms, Takahashi and Urata (2008) examined the influence of several enterprise characteristics (e.g., firm size, trading relations with FTA partners, the ratio of overseas sales to total sales, overseas business bases, and manufacturing membership) on FTA use. Firm size and trading relations with FTA partners were found to be positive and significant parameters. The authors concluded that large firms were more likely to use FTAs, reflecting the costs of such practices, and that trading experience in FTA markets also influenced the likelihood of FTA use.

In their study of Japanese multinational corporations (MNCs), Hiratsuka et al. (2009) tested the relationship between firm size and FTA use, and various enterprise characteristics (e.g., the share of local inputs among total inputs, the share of imports with zero tariffs, and sector and country dummy variables). One key finding was that large firm size (proxied by employment) positively correlated with FTA use. Another was that firms actively engaged in international fragmentation are likely to use FTAs for exports.

These econometric studies provide useful insights into the determinants of FTA use at the firm level. However, they also focus on firms from Japan – a developed industrial economy with relatively well-functioning markets and institutions – from which it is difficult to extrapolate to newly industrializing economies. Furthermore, there may be methodological gaps in these studies. For instance, in Takahashi and Urata (2008) the exclusive use of dummy variables as regressors resulted in a model with weak explanatory power. On the other hand, Hiratsuka et al. (2009) employed a sophisticated panel data analysis of a large sample of Japanese MNCs, but only a few explanatory variables were explored, which could contribute to omitted-variable bias in the results.

Factors affecting firm-level FTA use in Indonesia, Malaysia, and the Philippines were considered by Wignaraja (2014). Econometric analysis using firm-level data produced some interesting results. Key results included firm-heterogeneity matters in FTA use. Acquiring knowledge about FTAs through in-house efforts and actively forging links with FTA support institutions, building technological capabilities, and membership of industrial clusters show up as significant factors affecting the likelihood of firm-level regional trade agreement (RTA) use. A lack of information about FTAs and the absence of FTAs with major trading partners are the main reasons for non-use of RTAs.

Additionally, Song et al. (2019) in their analysis of CEO attitudes on the intention of exporting firms to utilize preferential tariffs in FTAs found that a CEO's knowledge and positive attitudes toward FTAs enhance intentions to use. This result further reinforces the need for improving business support and business buy-in for RTAs. Although there is a perception that the formation of FTAs by design will increase exports, evidence suggests that on the contrary, many exporting firms are still not aware of the advantages of FTAs' preferential tariffs. Policymakers, therefore, need to encourage CEOs and top managers to develop business models utilizing FTA schemes.

13.3 Data and exploratory analysis

In 2012, ADB and ADBI developed and conducted a survey of 234 exporters and importers in Malaysia. Manufacturing firms and in particular textiles and garments, food and beverages, wood and wood products, electronics and components, and automotive parts firms were targeted. The survey was conducted across Malaysia, covering firms in the northern, central, and southern regions.

Firms in the sample were asked whether they used tariff preferences in FTAs for exports, imports, or both, and whether they were part of the regional/global supply chain. These questions, along with those covering firm characteristics, form the basis of this analysis on the characteristics of SMEs that have internationalized through GVCs and FTAs.

The survey included both exporters and importers, and the majority of firms (216) were importers compared with 86 exporters (see Appendix Table 13.A.1). Of these firms, 69 were both exporters and importers of goods. The firms were distributed across five key manufacturing sectors and were predominantly small firms – 88.5% of the firms in the sample were small firms with fewer than 100 employees.

GVC participation was found to be positively correlated to size, with over 86% of giant firms engaged in production network trade compared to less than 20% of SMEs. Similarly, the use of FTA preferences is also positively related to size.

Narrowing in on SMEs, we consider the first and second research questions: SME characteristics related to participation in GVCs and FTA use. This is initially considered in the form of a t-test that looks at the difference in means between firms in/not in GVCs and firms using/not using FTA preferences. The results are shown in Table 13.1.

There are five noteworthy findings. First, SMEs in production networks and those utilizing FTAs are much larger than other SMEs. The average size of SMEs in production networks is 30 employees, twice the average size of SMEs not in production networks. The size of SMEs

Table 13.1 t-Test for SME participation in GVCs and FTA use

SME characteristics	GVC participation			FTA use		
	Yes	No	t-test	Yes	No	t-test
Size	30.41	15.01	2.88***	28.71	14.91	2.67***
Age	10.62	10.86	0.15	10.89	10.79	0.07
Proportion of firms in electronics	0.36	0.35	0.09	0.24	0.38	−1.84*
Proportion of firms in auto	0.26	0.20	0.70	0.33	0.18	2.00*
Central location	0.38	0.31	0.87	0.47	0.28	2.20**
Proportion of firms that are foreign owned	0.15	0.02	2.29**	0.09	0.03	1.29
Proportion of firms with a technology license from a foreign-owned company	0.44	0.10	4.07***	0.27	0.13	1.91*
R&D spending as a share of total sales	25.79	6.84	3.70***	15.60	8.97	2.02**
Proportion of firms with ISO certification	0.28	0.07	2.78***	0.20	0.09	1.77*
Export share of total sales	39.36	9.61	4.50***	31.89	10.59	3.66***
Proportion of raw materials imported	33.59	8.81	4.10***	30.78	8.67	3.70***
Labor productivity (turnover in million ringgit per employee)	15,166	7515	0.76	10,956	1760	1.96*
Knowledge of FTAs				0.38	0.19	2.43**

Source: Authors' calculations based on ADB/ADBI survey data.
Note: ***, **, and * indicate significance at the 1%, 5%, and 10% levels, respectively.
FTA = free trade agreement, GVC = global value chain, R&D = research and development.

utilizing FTA preferences (29 employees) is also almost twice as large as SMEs not utilizing preferences (15 employees).

Second, SMEs with foreign ownership are on average more likely to participate in production networks than domestically owned SMEs. However, there is no significant difference in foreign ownership among users and non-users of FTAs.

Third, technological capability, as measured by ISO certification, holding of a technology license from overseas, and R&D spending as a share of total sales, is also a significant point of difference among SMEs in GVCs/users of FTA preferences and other SMEs.

Fourth, SMEs with a greater outward orientation, that is a greater share of exports to sales, greater proportion of imported raw materials, and exports to multiple countries, are more likely to participate in GVCs and utilize FTA preferences than other SMEs.

Finally, given the high tariff barriers, firms in the auto sector are more likely to use FTA preferences. The data also suggest that a greater number of firms in the electronics sector are non-users of FTAs than users. This could be explained by the free trade zones in Malaysia, which have been set up to foster the electronics sector. Firms in these sectors have no incentive to use preferences available in FTAs since they are exempt from the country's normal customs barriers and other constraining legislation.

13.4 Global value chain participation

Having identified some key characteristics that differentiate GVC participants/SMEs utilizing FTA preferences from other SMEs in our sample, it is of interest to investigate the extent to which some of these characteristics are related to GVC participation.

13.4.1 The model

The characteristics related to SME participation in GVCs are examined by a probit regression. The GVC participation model is specified as

$$GVC_{participation} = F(\alpha_o + \alpha_1 SIZE + \alpha_2 AGE + \alpha_3 ELECTRONICS + \alpha_4 LOCATION$$

$$+ \alpha_5 TECHLICENSE + \alpha_6 FOREIGNOWNERSHIP$$

$$+ \alpha_7 R\&D + \alpha_8 ISO + \alpha_9 LABORPRODUCTIVITY)$$

The variables and the expected direction of association are described next.

$GVC_{participation}$ is the dependent variable. It takes on the value of 1 if the firm responds positively to the question "is your firm part of a regional/global supply chain" or is 0 otherwise.

SIZE measures the number of permanent employees. Even among SMEs, i.e., firms with fewer than 100 employees, it is expected that bigger firms are more likely to participate in production network trade (i.e., a positive relationship). Larger SMEs can benefit from economies of scale and therefore set a lower price than their smaller counterparts. Additionally, larger SMEs are likely to have greater access to resources, including finances that are important for SME growth. Therefore, size is positively related to participation in GVCs.

AGE is measured as the number of years the SME has been in operation. We are ambivalent about the direction of causation. Older firms have more accumulated experience in production and tacit knowledge, making them more likely to participate in production networks. However, it is also possible that a firm's maturity may cause it to become set in its ways and less inclined to participate in production networks. Younger firms, on the other hand, might be more active in seeking out new sources of information and knowledge, and therefore better able to realize the opportunities from GVCs.

ELECTRONICS is a dummy variable taking on the value of 1 if the firm is in the electronics sector or 0 otherwise. The sector variable is expected to be positively related to GVC participation since electronics accounts for around 60% of Malaysia total exports and the sector is heavily exposed to GVCs.

LOCATION takes on a value of 1 if the firm is located in central Malaysia or 0 otherwise. SMEs located in central Malaysia are more likely to have greater access to transportation, infrastructure, and information and communication technologies and therefore are better able participate in GVCs. A central location is expected to be positively associated with GVC participation.

A firm's exposure to foreign technology is captured by the *FOREIGN OWNERSHIP* and *TECHNOLOGY LICENSE* variables. *FOREIGN OWNERSHIP* is a dummy variable taking on the value of 1 if the firm has some level of foreign ownership or 0 otherwise. Technology license is also a dummy variable, taking on the value of 1 if the firm uses technology licensed from a foreign-owned company (excluding office software) or is 0 otherwise. Both foreign ownership and holding a foreign technology license would give domestic firms access to knowledge of international production, technology, management know-how, and sophisticated international networks and therefore are expected to be positively related to GVC participation.

Firm-level investment in learning is captured by the two technology variables *R&D* and *ISO*. These variables are expected to be positively related to production network participation. Research and development is measured as the share of R&D spending to sales. *ISO* is a dummy variable taking on the value of 1 if the firm has ISO certification or is 0 otherwise. Firm-level effort in investing in R&D and technology is expected to improve the quality of the product or service and increase the competitiveness of the firm in getting invited to participate in GVCs.

Finally, *LABOR PRODUCTIVITY*, measured as annual sales turnover in a million ringgits per employee is expected to be positively related to GVC participation. Productive firms are better able to compete against other firms in gaining a foothold onto the production chain following on from Bernard and Jensen's (1999) argument that there is a cost involved in participating in the export market/production network. But even after entering a GVC, productive firms are more likely to maintain their foothold by learning and adapting their product as per market needs (Clerides, Lach, and Tybout 1996).

13.4.2 Results

The regression results are summarized in Table 13.2 as a baseline specification (equation i) and alternative specifications (equations ii–iv). In the discussion that follows we will be referring to

Table 13.2 Probit model of factors influencing participation in GVCs

	Malaysia			
	(i)	*(ii)*	*(iii)*	*(iv)*
Size	0.0142	0.0092	0.0085	0.0088
	(0.00)***	(0.00)**	(0.00)*	(0.00)*
Age	−0.0141	−0.0111	−0.0098	−0.0078
	(0.01)	(0.01)	(0.01)	(0.01)
Electronics	0.0743	−0.0083	−0.0796	−0.0618
	(0.22)	(0.24)	(0.25)	(0.25)
Location	0.2687	0.3685	0.3070	0.2242
	(0.22)	(0.22)*	(0.24)	(0.25)
Tech license		0.9629	0.8665	0.8760
		(0.31)***	(0.31)***	(0.31)***
Foreign ownership		0.3996	0.0435	0.0192
		(0.5)4	(0.54)	(0.54)
R&D			0.0156	0.0164
			(0.01)***	(0.01)***
ISO			0.3466	0.3557
			(0.34)	(0.34)
Labor productivity				0.0000
				(0.00)
Constant	−1.1483	−1.3258	−1.4981	−1.5464
	(0.21)***	(0.22)***	(0.22)***	(0.23)***
N	207	207	207	207
Wald Chi²	12.98	29.64	38.48	40.4
Pseudo R²	0.07	0.15	0.22	0.23

Source: Authors' calculations based on ADB/ADBI survey data.
Notes: Dependent binary variable: 1 = firm part of production network.
Standard errors are reported in parentheses. ***, **, and * indicate significance at the 1%, 5%, and 10% levels, respectively.
The Pearson correlation coefficient matrix can be found in the Appendix (see Table 13.A.1).

the full model (equation iv). The pseudo R^2 in equations (i) and (iv) suggests that the regressions explain about 20% of the variation in the data.

The results suggest that firm size is positive and significant, and even among SMEs, it is the larger firms that are more likely to participate in GVCs. For example, the probability of participating in GVCs increases from 16% to 22% when firm size increases from 25 to 50 employees. It increases further from 29% to 37% when firm size increases from 75 to 100 employees. The results suggest economies of scale are important in overcoming the initial fixed costs of entering and maintaining a foothold in a GVC.

The foreign technology license variable is also positively significant. Having a foreign technology license increases GVC participation by 20%. R&D expenditure as a proportion of sales also has a considerable effect on SME participation in GVCs. An increase in the R&D-to-sales ratio from 10% to 30% increases the probability of participation from 15% to 23%. An R&D-to-sales ratio of 50% increases the probability of participation to 35%.

The results suggest that size and technological capability are positively associated with SME participation in GVCs.

13.5 Free trade agreement use

13.5.1 The model

In seeking out the SME characteristics related to FTA utilization we use a probit model. The FTA use model is specified as:

$$FTA_{USE} = F(\alpha_o + \alpha_1 SIZE + \alpha_2 AGE + \alpha_3 AUTO + \alpha_4 LOCATION$$

$$+ \alpha_5 FOREIGNOWNERSHIP + \alpha_6 EXPORTSHARE$$

$$+ \alpha_7 PROPORTIONOFRAWMATERIALSIMPORTED$$

$$+ \alpha_8 KNOWLEDGEOFFTA)$$

The hypotheses and variables in the model are described below.

FTA_{USE} is the dependent variable. It takes on a value of 1 if the firm responds positively to the question "does your firm use tariff preference in FTAs for exports, imports, or both," or is 0 otherwise.

SIZE is measured by the number of permanent employees and is expected to be positively related to FTA use. The larger the SME, the more resources it is likely to have to meet the associated costs of using FTAs.

AGE is measured as the number of years the SME has been in operation. Once again, we are ambivalent about the direction of causation. Older firms may be more experienced in navigating trading rules and utilizing FTAs, but could also be set in their ways and less inclined to utilize preferential tariff rates. Alternatively, younger firms might be more active in taking advantage of the opportunities made available through FTAs.

LOCATION takes on a value of 1 if the firm is located in central Malaysia or 0 otherwise. A firm's geographical location is expected to be positively associated with FTA use. Firms concentrated in major industrial centers are more likely to use FTAs than geographically isolated firms, for two reasons. First, geographical clusters of networked firms are characterized by information spillovers and exchanges (including know-how on tariff preferences, rules of origin, and origin administration). Second, public and private sector FTA support institutions are more likely to provide technical assistance to firms in major industrial centers.

The sectoral dummy *AUTO* takes on the value of 1 if the firm is in the auto industry or is 0 otherwise. Auto imports in Malaysia attract a high tariff and therefore firms engaging in auto trade have a greater incentive to use preferences available in FTAs. This variable is therefore expected to be positively correlated with FTA use.

The variables *FOREIGN OWNERSHIP, EXPORT SHARE OF SALES*, and *PROPORITON OF RAW MATERIALS IMPORTED* capture the extent to which the firm is outward oriented. These variables are expected to be positively related to FTA use. The greater the outward orientation the higher the likelihood the firm is aware of international markets and trade regulations (including import tariffs, FTA preferences, rules of origin, and custom procedures). Additionally, firms with higher exposure to international trade have more to gain for using preferences made available in FTAs.

KNOWLEDGE OF FTA is a dummy variable taking on the value of 1 if a firm has some knowledge of FTAs or 0 otherwise. The variable captures the firm's proactive efforts in better understanding FTAs. FTA texts are complex, lengthy legal documents requiring significant investment in specialist skills (e.g., trade law, customs procedures, and business strategy) to derive the benefits of FTAs. Given this, firms that invest time in acquiring relevant in-house FTA expertise and that actively build linkages with FTA support institutions are more likely to be equipped to take advantage of FTA provisions.

13.5.2 Results

The regression results of factors affecting the use of FTAs are summarized in Table 13.3 with a baseline specification (equation i) and alternative specifications (equations ii–iv). In the discussion that follows we will be referring to the full model (i.e., equation iv). The pseudo R^2 in equation (iv) suggests that the regressions explain about 20% of the variation in the data.

Similar to the GVC model, size is significantly and positively associated with FTA use, suggesting once again that even among a group of SMEs it is the larger firms that are more likely use FTA preferences. The model suggests that the probability of use increases from 17% to 25% as the firm size increases from 25 to 50 employees. It increases further from 34% to 44% as firm size increases from 75 to 100 employees.

FTA use among firms in the auto industry is also significant and positive, with the probability of using FTA preferences increasing by 15% for firms in the auto industry. SMEs located in central Malaysia are also more likely to use FTAs than geographically isolated firms. The probability of using FTA preferences increases by 19% if the SME is located in central Malaysia, highlighting the greater availability of support and technical assistance in major industrial centers and the scope for information spillovers and exchanges between firms.

Exposure to international trade, as captured by the export share of sales, and the proportion of raw materials imported are positive indicators of FTA use. The probability of FTA use increases from 24% to 30% when the export share of total sales increases from 50% to 75%. Similarly, as the proportion of raw materials increases from 50% to 75%, the probability of FTA use increases from 31% to 43%. Finally, a firm's investment in acquiring knowledge to use FTAs also increases the probability of use by 12%.

This is a very interesting result suggesting that an SME's use of FTAs is largely related to its capability in terms of understanding FTA provisions, access to financial and human resources captured by size, exposure to trade captured by the proportion of raw materials imported, and firm location and sector.

Table 13.3 Probit model of factors influencing FTA use

| | Malaysia | | | |
	(i)	*(ii)*	*(iii)*	*(iv)*
Size	0.0125	0.0135	0.0106	0.0103
	(0.00)★★★	(0.00)★★★	(0.00)★★	(0.00)★★
Age	−0.0110	−0.0118	−0.0075	−0.0081
	(0.01)	(0.014)	(0.01)	(0.01)
Auto	0.4716	0.4321	0.6732	0.6119
	(0.23)★★	(0.24)★★	(0.25)★★★	(0.26)★★
Location		0.5142	0.8069	0.7889
		(0.21)★★	(0.23)★★★	(0.24)★★★
Foreign ownership			−0.6325	−0.5235
			(0.56)	(0.57)
Export share of sales			0.0062	0.0082
			(0.00)	(0.00)★
Proportion of raw materials imported			0.0157	0.0135
			(0.00)★★★	(0.00)★★★
Some knowledge				0.4884
				(0.25)★
Constant	−1.0303	−1.2227	−1.7589	−1.8764
	(0.18)★★★	(0.20)★★★	(0.25)★★★	(0.27)
N	207	207	207	207
Wald Chi²	14.72	20.64	47.33	51.16
Pseudo R²	0.07	0.10	0.22	0.24

Source: Authors' calculations based on ADB/ADBI survey data.
Notes: Dependent binary variable: 1 = use of FTA preferences.
Standard errors are reported in parentheses. ★★★, ★★, and ★ indicate significance at the 1%, 5%, and 10% levels, respectively.
The Pearson correlation coefficient matrix can be found in the Appendix (see Table 13.A.1).

13.5.3 *Firm-level barriers to FTA use and desired support*

The perceived barriers by SMEs to using FTAs and the support sought is the final research question. The survey results suggest that the most significant barrier to FTA use among SME firms is lack of information, with 114 SMEs ranking lack of information as one of their top three reasons for not using FTAs (see Figure 13.1). Two other major barriers are that firms do not see the need to use FTAs and are not interested in trading with current FTA partners.

To encourage greater FTA use, the SMEs in the sample would like the government to provide more information on the implications of FTAs for businesses; more training on the FTAs under implementation; and enhanced consultations before, during, and after FTA negotiations (see Figure 13.2). This suggests there is a real role for public policy in addressing limited FTA use.

13.6 Conclusion

In an attempt to shed light on the micro-level aspects of regionalism in East Asia, this chapter evaluated the characteristics of SMEs that have successfully participated in GVCs and FTAs in

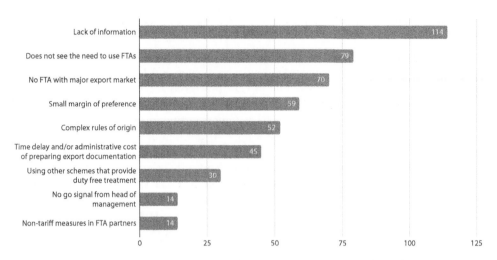

Figure 13.1 Impediments to FTA use. (Source: Authors' calculations based on ADB/ADBI survey data.)

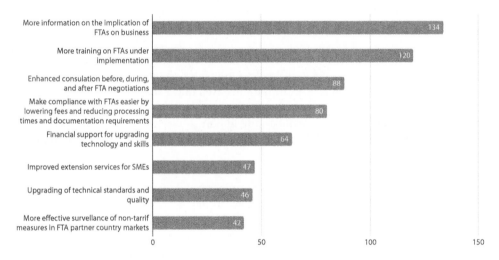

Figure 13.2 Services requested by firms to adjust to FTAs. (Source: Authors' calculations based on ADB/ADBI survey data.)

Malaysia using enterprise survey data. It sought to improve our understanding of regionalization of SMEs and to contribute to the scant literature on regional economic integration.

Three findings come out of the analysis. First, SME size matters in GVC participation. Even among SMEs, firm size was found to be positively and significantly associated with participation in GVCs. This key result highlights that economies of scale and firm resources, which are positively linked with size, are important in overcoming the initial fixed costs of entering the value chain. In addition to size, technological capability of enterprises, as captured by the ownership of a foreign technology license and R&D share of sales, was found to be positively and significantly associated with SME participation in GVC trade. This suggests that the extent to which a firm actively engages in improving its technology, production, and processes positively influences its participation in GVCs. Surprisingly, foreign ownership was not found to be a significant predictor of value chain participation.

Second, size was also found to be positively associated with FTA use, capturing perhaps the costs associated with understanding the complex and lengthy legal documents. In addition to size, a good understanding of FTA provisions and exposure to trade results in greater use of FTAs. Firms that invest time in acquiring relevant in-house FTA expertise and that actively build linkages with FTA support institutions were found to be more likely to use FTAs. The study also found a positive and significant relationship between exposure to trade, as measured by export share of sales and the proportion of raw materials imported, and FTA use. This result is not surprising since the greater the outward orientation, the higher the likelihood the firm is aware of international markets and trade regulations (including import tariffs, FTA preferences, rules of origin, and customs procedures). Additionally, firms with higher exposure to international trade have more to gain from using the preferences made available in FTAs. Firms located in central Malaysia are also more likely to use FTA preferences, highlighting perhaps the greater availability of support and technical assistance in major industrial centers and the scope for information spillovers and exchanges between firms.

Finally, the descriptive analysis on the barriers to FTA use found that lack of information is the predominant reason for not utilizing preferences under an FTA. Other top responses included not seeing the need to use FTAs and not being interested in trade with the current FTA partners.

The preceding results reinforce what researchers have known from micro-level studies of international trade: importing technology from abroad and investment in R&D are positively related to business internationalization. Given this, a conducive business environment with effective business support institutions and programs for internationalization of SMEs is vital. Support services to facilitate the import of technology from abroad as well as assistance for stimulating research and development seem particularly beneficial for SME entry into GVCs.

Additionally, the "lack of information" barrier to FTA use can be addressed by providing more information on the implications of FTAs on businesses, more training on FTAs under implementation, and enhanced consultations before, during, and after FTA negotiations.

A combination of public and private institutional support services is an effective means of delivering such services to SMEs. This would involve close coordination among the following intuitions: the Ministry of Trade and Customs, business and industrial associations, and chambers of commerce. With these policies in place, SMEs in Malaysia and Asia may internationalize more efficiently and access the global market.

This was the first study, to our knowledge, to consider the characteristics of firms that participate in GVCs and utilize FTA preferences. Some limitations in the data and methodology should be noted. First, given the small sample size, the statistical power of the estimation is reduced, leading to the possibility of a type II error, where the significance of a variable under consideration is incorrectly dismissed. Second, the GVC participation model and the FTA preference use model are static as only cross-sectional data were available. As panel data becomes available over time, we will become increasingly able to investigate the changes in policy and enterprise responses. Finally, there are other factors that may influence participation in GVCs and FTA preference use, such as trade policies, domestic regulations, infrastructure, and business support services. Attempting to incorporate these policy factors in future econometric work may provide additional insights. Thus, the results should be interpreted with caution.

Appendix

Table 13.A.1 Characteristics of surveyed firms

	Count	*%*
Type of traders		
Exporters only	17	7.3
Importers only	147	62.8
Export and import	69	29.5
No answer	1	0.4
Size		
Small	207	88.5
Large	20	8.5
Giant	7	3
Sector		
Textiles and garments	49	20.9
Food and beverages	26	11.1
Wood and wood products	23	9.8
Electronic products and components	87	37.2
Automotive and parts	47	20.1
Other	2	0.9
Foreign ownership		
Foreign owned	24	10.3
Domestically owned	210	89.7
Total number of respondents	234	100

Source: Authors' calculations based on ADB/ADBI survey data.

Notes

1　Also known as global supply chain trade and production network trade.
2　The few studies include Harvie, Narjoko, and Oum (2010); Rasiah, Rosli, and Sanjivee (2010); Wignaraja (2014, 2015); and Lanz et al. (2018).
3　The "noodle bowl" refers to the observation that multiple rules of origin in overlapping Asian FTAs may raise transaction costs for businesses, particularly SMEs, for using tariff preferences in FTAs.

References

Arndt, W., and H. Kierzkowski. 2001. *Fragmentation: New Production Patterns in the World Economy*. Oxford, UK: Oxford University Press.

Asian Development Bank (ADB). 2009. *Emerging Asian Regionalism: A Partnership for Shared Prosperity*. Manila: Asian Development Bank.

Athukorala, P. 2011. Production Networks and Trade Patterns in East Asia: Regionalization or Globalization? *Asian Economic Papers* 10(1):65–95.

Bell, M., and K. Pavitt. 1993. Technological Accumulation and Industrial Growth. *Industrial and Corporate Change* 2(2): 157–209.

Bernard, A. B., and J. Bradford Jensen. 1999. *Exporting and Productivity*. NBER Working Papers No. 7135. Cambridge, MA: National Bureau of Economic Research.

Chirathivat, S. 2008. ASEAN's Strategy toward an Increasing Asian Integration. In *East Asian Economies and New Regionalism*, edited by A. Shigeyuki and B. Nidhipraba. Kyoto, Japan: Kyoto University Press.

Clerides, S., S. Lach, and J. Tybout 1996. Is Learning-by-exporting Important? Micro-dynamic Evidence from Colombia, Mexico and Morocco. Finance and Economics Discussion96–30. Board of Governors of the Federal Reserve System (United States).

Harvie, C. 2010. East Asian Production Networks—the Role and Contribution of SMEs. *International Journal of Business and Development Studies* 2(1):27–62.

Harvie, C., D. Narjoko, and S. Oum. 2010. Firm Characteristic Determinants of SME Participation in Production Networks. ERIA Discussion Paper Series 2010–11. Jakarta: Economic Research Institute for ASEAN and East Asia.

Helpman, E., M. J. Melitz, and S. R. Yeaple. 2004. Export versus FDI with Heterogeneous Firms. *American Economic Review* 94(1): 300–316.

Hiratsuka, D., K. Hayakawa, K. Shino, and S. Sukegawa. 2009. Maximising the Benefits from FTAs in ASEAN. In *Deepening East Asian Integration, ERIA Research Report* 2008–1, edited by J. Corbett and S. Umezaki. Jakarta: Economic Research Institute for ASEAN and East Asia.

Iammarino, S., R. Padilla-Perez, and N. von Tunzelmann. 2008. Technological Capabilities and Global–Local Interactions: the Electronics Industry in Two Mexican Regions. *World Development* 36(10): 1980–2003.

Ing, L.Y., M. Richardson and S. Urata, eds. 2019. *East Asian Integration: Goods, Services and Investment.* London: Routledge.

Jones, R. W., and H. Kierzkowski. 1990. The Role of Services in Production and International Trade: A Theoretical Framework. In *The Political Economy of International Trade: Essays in Honour of R.E. Baldwin*, edited by R.W Jones and A. O. Krueger. Oxford, UK: Basil Blackwell.

Kawai, M., and G. Wignaraja, eds. 2011. *Asia's Free Trade Agreements: How Is Business Responding?* Cheltenham: Edward Elgar.

Kawai, M., and G. Wignaraja. 2013. *Patterns of Free Trade Areas in Asia.* Policy Studies No. 65. Honolulu: East-West Center.

Koopman, R., W. M. Powers, Z. Wang, and S.-J. Wei. 2010. *Give Credit where Credit is Due. Tracing Value Added in Global Production Networks.* National Bureau of Economic Research Working Paper No. W16426. Cambridge, MA: NBER.

Kumar, S. 1992. Policy Issues and the Formation of the ASEAN Free Trade Area. In *AFTA: The Way Ahead*, edited by P. Imada and S. Naya. Singapore: Institute of Southeast Asian Studies.

Kuroiwa, I., ed. 2009. *Plugging into Production Networks! Industrialization Strategies in Less Developed Southeast Asian Countries.* Singapore: Institute of Southeast Asian Studies (ISEAS).

Kuroiwa, I., and T. M. Heng, eds. 2008. *Production Networks and Industrial Clusters: Integrating Economies in Southeast Asia.* Singapore: ISEAS.

Lall, S. 1992. Technological Capabilities and Industrialization. *World Development* 20(2): 165–186.

Lanz, R., Lundquist, K., Mansio, G., Maurer, A., and Teh, R. 2018. *E-Commerce and Developing Country-SME Participation in Global Value Chains.* World Trade Organization Staff Working Paper ERSD-2018-13. Geneva: World Trade Organization.

Melitz, M. J. 2003. The Impact of Trade on Intra-industry Reallocations and Aggregate Industry Productivity. *Econometrica* 17(6): 1,695–1,725.

Nelson, R. R., and S. G. Winter. 1982. *An Evolutionary Theory of Economic Change.* Cambridge, MA: Belknap/Harvard University Press.

Ng, F., and A. Yeats. 2003. *Major Trade Trends in East Asia—What are their Implications for Regional Cooperation and Growth?* World Bank Policy Research Working Paper 3084. Washington, DC: World Bank.

Petri, P.A and M.G Plummer. 2020. *East Asian Decouples from the United States: Trade War, COVID-19 and New East Asian Trade Blocs.* Working Paper 20-6. Washington, DC: Peterson Institute for International Economics.

Rasiah, R., M. Rosli, and P. Sanjivee. 2010. The Significance of Production Networks in Productivity, Exports and Technological Upgrading: Small and Medium Enterprises in Electric-Electronic, Textile-Garments, Automotives and Wood Products. In *Integrating Small and Medium Enterprises (SMEs) into the More Integrated East Asia*, edited by T. T. Vo, D. Narjoko, and S. Oum. Jakarta: ERIA.

Song, Joon-Heon, and Moon, Hee-Cheol. 2019. Exploring the Intention of FTA Utilization by Exporting SMEs: Evidence from South Korea. *Journal of International Logistics and Trade*, 17(1): 1–11.

Takahashi, K., and S. Urata. 2008. *On the Use of FTAs by Japanese Firms.* RIETI Discussion Paper Series 08-E-002. Tokyo: Research Institute of Economy, Trade and Industry.

Tambunan, T., and Chandra, A. C. 2014. Utilisation Rate of Free Trade Agreements (FTAs) by Local Micro-, Small- and Medium-Sized Enterprises: A Story of ASEAN. *Journal of International Business and Economics* 2(2): 133–163.

Ting, O. K. 2004. SMEs in Malaysia: Pivot Points for Change. Available at http://www.mca.org.my

Wignaraja, G. 2014. The Determinants of FTA Use in Southeast Asia: A Firm-level Analysis. *Journal of Asian Economics* 35: 32–45.

Wignaraja, G. 2015. Factors Affecting Entry into supply Chain Trade: An Analysis of Firms in Southeast Asia. *Asia and the Pacific Policy Studies*, 2(3, March): 623–42.

WTO and IDE-JETRO. 2011. *Trade Patterns and Global Value Chains in East Asia: From Trade in Goods to Trade in Tasks*. Geneva: World Trade Organization and Tokyo: Institute for Developing Economies-Japan External Trade Organization.

14

GLOBAL VALUE CHAINS AND LEAST DEVELOPED COUNTRIES

Influencing value chain governance and upgrading processes

Jodie-Anne Keane

14.1 Introduction

For late industrialisers, particularly the least developed countries (LDCs), the challenges of facilitating integration with global value chains (GVCs) through tax and other fiscal incentives, whilst directing efforts to facilitate upgrading processes, in view of severe capacity and capability constraints are undoubtedly formidable. LDC is an internationally recognised category of countries identified based on their progress in relation to national income, human development and economic vulnerability by the United Nations Committee for Development in triennial reviews. Currently, there are 46 LDCs which face severe structural impediments to their sustainable development.

Since the category of LDCs was created in 1971, the international trade and development architecture has evolved in order to enable the more effective integration of LDCs into the global trading system. There is recognition that inducement of entry into the modern export sector requires facilitation through the creation of economic rents within the form of tariff preferences (Keane, 2013). However, as the global trading system has evolved, preference erosion has reduced the value of tariff rents for LDCs. This has led to calls for renewed thinking on the appropriate trade-related international support measures for LDCs. For example, it is generally recognised that the rise of the emerging Asian economies – including China – and their integration within the global trading system has led to competition at entry-level positions within GVCs becoming fierce, with available shares of value added becoming less over time (Baldwin, 2012).

There are other challenges, however, in view of the re-framing of the role of the state in terms of either an enabler or a facilitator of business as opposed to the main arbiter of rules and regulations, with globalisation necessitating an internalisation of the state and an associated squeezing of fiscal space for public policy (Jessop, 2006; Moran et al., 2009). In order to keep pace with the process of globalisation, countries remain under pressure to provide climates conducive to investment as well as profit maximisation. Coupled with enhanced competition amongst nation states for the labour-intensive stages of production, the mobility of capital is

DOI: 10.4324/9781315225661-20

seen both directly and indirectly, to exert a strong downward pressure on public policy frameworks, especially within LDCs.

Only a limited number of LDCs have been able to effectively engage with the modern export sector and vertically fragmented trade as manifested within GVCs. This includes within archetypal GVCs such as the textiles and clothing industry – the focus of this chapter. Whilst the available evidence on upgrading through engagement with GVCs is mixed and highly temporally, as well as context specific, there are few detailed comparative analyses of upgrading processes for LDCs within GVCs. Through the comparative analysis undertaken in this chapter, it is shown how a greater focus on trade governance within GVC-driven trade is required to account for the ability of some LDCs to enter and achieve certain upgrading processes, compared to others.

Nowadays, there is an imperative for governments to understand the causal drivers of global production networks in terms of their competitiveness dynamics (optimising cost-capability ratios, market imperatives and financial discipline) and risk environments (Yeung and Coe, 2014). However, careful mediation is required, since the strategies adopted by actors in terms of reconfiguring their global production networks affects development outcomes in particular industries and countries (Yeung and Coe, 2014). The widely referred to structure of value chain governance, developed by Gereffi et al. (2005), posits that certain types of governance structures, which exist between firms, are derived from the technological characteristics of the production process. Therefore, different structures provide for certain upgrading opportunities, in part due to the nature of technology and the potential for lead firms to take a more hands-on role with their suppliers. However, given the disruptive process of technological development, greater consideration is required in relation to how firm-level governance structures are influenced in practice by public policy frameworks, to achieve developmental objectives like technological upgrading.

In order to explore these aspects, this chapter integrates comparative analyses of the integration process of two LDCs (Bangladesh and Cambodia) with GVCs within the textiles and clothing industry, an industry which is considered to be the archetypal stepping stone into the modern export sector and which has tended to exhibit buyer-driven tendencies. Both LDCs entered the textiles and clothing value chain through utilising the trade preferences available to them. However, the integration process in the case of Bangladesh was rather more directive as opposed to the facilitative approach adopted in Cambodia, which means that value chain governance structures were influenced so as to achieve specific objectives, and as a consequence, outcomes in terms of upgrading processes have been divergent.

This chapter is organised as follows. In Section 14.2, the concept of value chain governance is introduced. In Section 14.3, the structure of the textiles and clothing value chain is described and the contrasting experiences of upgrading processes analysed. Finally, this article concludes with reference to the demands for enhanced governance capabilities within LDCs in view of the divergent trade governance structures apparent within GVC-driven trade, not all aspects of which have been fully elaborated upon in this contribution.

14.2 Structures of value chain governance

The current architecture of the global trading system was created at a time when the political economy of the General Agreement on Trade and Tariffs (GATT) centred on a prisoner's dilemma tariff setting game: in order to shift from high tariffs towards low tariffs, all parties had to act in concert and be punished for non-compliance (Baldwin, 2012). Later, agreement was reached under the auspices of The United Nations Conference on Trade and Development

(UNCTAD) on the need for a Generalised System of Preferences (GSP) towards developing countries. The decision reached by the international community consisted of a recognition that a form of infant industry protection could be conveyed towards LDCs through a tariff preference.[1]

Since it was created in 1979, the GSP has become more refined and LDCs better defined. Some players such as the European Union (EU) have gone even further to define needs, through the graduation of major developing economies from its GSP on income grounds (Stevens et al., 2011). The associated structures of the trade architecture created in the postwar period, enabled the entrance of some LDCs into GVCs, as documented in this chapter. However, whilst the global trade architecture established enabled the entry of some LDCs into GVCs, it has not been sufficient to enable upgrading. Many LDCs, particularly in sub-Saharan Africa and in other parts of Asia, have failed to adequately gain a foothold in the modern export sector, which demands greater consideration of the appropriate frameworks to facilitate their participation.

Within the mainstream assimilation of the GVC literature, a major area neglected is the role institutions play in overcoming coordination problems, moreover, how enhanced state capacity is required for enforcement of competition policies (Ravenhill, 2014). This is an obvious need in view of the strong control exerted by the lead firm drivers of GVCs, with an increasing proportion of global trade manifesting as intra-firm transfers (UNCTAD, 2013a). As summarised by Keane (2017), only recently have institutional variables and public policy frameworks been paid greater attention within GVC analysis, as opposed to being relegated to the 'background'. Although global public policy aspects, notably social and environmental ones, have achieved greater prominence since the adoption of the SDGs, the operationalisation of these goals across fragmented regulatory spheres remains unclear.[2]

The dominant framework used to understand value chain governance and upgrading opportunities (Gereffi et al., 2005) refers only to the coordination of activities between firms, whereas in the earlier literature the interplay between local inter-firm networks, business associations and public–private institutions was recognised (Humphrey and Schmitz, 2001). For example, as discussed by Humphrey and Schmitz (2001), whilst the cluster literature focused on firm proximity, the literature on innovation systems was more concerned with the role of the knowledge system with reference to the business school of thought on GVCs (e.g. Porter, 1985). The role of these aspects in enabling, or disabling, the codification of knowledge derived from undertaking specific activities is downplayed within the Gereffi et al. (2005) classification because the focus is on global rather than local linkages. Instead, within the Gereffi et al. (2005) framework, the upgrading process results from interaction with buyers – a form of learning-by-exporting – though the exact mechanisms are not detailed and hence a certain degree of automaticity is assumed.

The comparative GVC analysis presented in the following section shows why this unquestionable approach can be misleading, especially given the process of technological development, which means greater consideration of the interaction between firm-specific governance structures and public policy frameworks. In relation to aspects of external value chain governance – negotiated by governments for the private sector[3] – such as trade policy, only recently has its influence on value chain outcomes and upgrading strategies, specifically within the textiles and clothing sector, been explored (Curran and Nadvi, 2015). This includes measures applied at the border such as tariffs, as well as product specifications on shares of domestic value added, like rules of origin.[4] However, a greater focus is required on how external value chain structures are crafted specifically so as to influence value chain development and development outcomes, moving across different levels of public policy formulation.

14.3 Structure of governance in the textiles and clothing value chain

Generally, the textiles and clothing GVC is considered one of the quintessential 'buyer-driven' value chains. Over time, particular segments of the GVC and stages of production have become increasingly concentrated, which has served to consolidate the position of firms within stages and tiers of production. As quantitative trade restrictions have been removed in developed country markets, the end result has been increased consolidation at the firm and country level. Buyers have modified their strategies towards lead time management, production flexibility, and product quality and delivery – away from [tariff] rent capture.[5] Globally, these shifts have been expressed through a decline in unit prices and increased pressure in the sector, as geographies of global sourcing have become more complex and multi-layered; more recently, trade policy developments have begun to influence the institutional context within which production and work – the role of labour – are organised (Pickles et al., 2015).

Because of the evolution of the industry globally, it is important to take stock and reflect on how LDCs have fared in view of recent transformations of the industry. The conventional understanding is that the garment sector, as a sub-sector of the textiles and clothing value chain, is buyer-driven. This is because production is coordinated by decentralised, globally dispersed production networks coordinated by lead firms who control value-added activities such as design and branding, but outsource all or most of the manufacturing process to a global network of suppliers.[6] Producers are integrated into the value chain based on their respective capabilities. These relate not only to labour costs but increasingly to other aspects of production, including logistics and supply chain management, compliance issues, and avoidance of reputation risks.[7]

More recently, because of the challenges associated with moving towards taking control of some of the downstream functions within the textiles and clothing value chain, the traditional route of upgrading posited (which involves domestic firms incrementally taking over the functions provided by lead firms) – moving from original equipment manufacturing (OEM) to original design manufacturing (ODM) and then original brand manufacturing (OBM), as described in Gereffi (1999) – has been replaced by other opportunities to increase the range of services offered to lead firms, without necessarily resulting in a step-change position within the value chain.

Specifically, within the textiles and clothing sector, a distinction between a country that specialises in Cut, Make, and Trim (CMT) (Tier 1) as compared to another that is a full package supplier that takes control of the assembly of the product, including the sourcing of inputs as well as delivery to customers (Tier 2), is now made. However, the implication of these shifts in potential upgrading trajectories – the closing of some routes and opening of others – has not been adequately explored within the literature to date. On the other hand, movement by CMT producers into certain types of activities so as to become a full package supplier may generate other spillover effects through enhancing logistics capabilities.

The experience obtained with managing logistics could serve to attract similar basic activity functions of other industries. However, major questions remain as to the ability to functionally upgrade – to change the specific function of firms' existing specialisations within the value chain. The two LDC case studies explored in this chapter explore these aspects further. Whilst the two case-study countries entered the textiles and clothing GVC in similar ways, they have experienced very different outcomes in terms of upgrading processes.

14.3.1 Position of Bangladesh and Cambodia

Nowadays, both Cambodia and Bangladesh feature among the world's largest exporters of textiles and clothing, though Bangladesh is by far the powerhouse in absolute terms.[8] Cambodia entered into the clothing, or garment, node of this GVC during the 1990s and is located within the CMT node or first tier. In comparison, Bangladesh is considered to be a package contractor in the supplier tier, or second tier. Since CMT producers normally make garments using the fabric supplied by their end customer (the buyer), or a designated intermediary, the experience of Bangladesh demonstrates how firms were encouraged to move into the production of textiles so as secure a position as a package contractor.

As discussed by UNCTAD (2013) over time, Bangladesh has increased the share of local value added within its clothing exports to around 30 per cent (the same level as Viet Nam) and this is attributed to government policies which encouraged investment in the domestic textiles industry. Developing backward linkages has enabled the sourcing of domestic textiles and fabric inputs, domestically. This has enabled firms to reduce their reliance on intermediaries. In comparison, the available evidence suggests Cambodian firms remain positioned within the CMT node of the value chain and integrated within triangular manufacturing networks, with a reliance on East Asian intermediaries, and now increasingly China, for inputs.

The main buyers in the EU and US markets differ in the size of their orders, which has implications for the kinds of services leveraged from suppliers. Generally, US buyers tend to be more prescriptive. This includes dictating the manufacturers' choice of fabrics (Roberts and Thoburn, 2003). As discussed by Savchenko (2012), orders from US mass market retailers – the main buyers from Cambodia – are large and price is the most important criteria. Hence, this may be characterised as a price-driven value chain, where the opportunities for upgrading are low. In comparison, orders from the EU tend to be smaller, demand more variation and have different standards for quality. Bangladesh predominantly supplies the EU market. Some of the same branded manufacturers source both from Bangladesh and Cambodia and supply both the EU and US (e.g. GAP). However, there are important differences in relation to the sourcing mechanisms, which combined with different country capabilities, has implications for upgrading processes and likely trajectories.

14.3.2 Upgrading processes

The upgrading process currently so widely referred to in the GVC literature posits a trajectory beginning with product and process upgrading and then onto functional and inter-sectoral upgrading (Gereffi, 1999; Lee and Chen, 2000; Kaplinsky and Morris, 2001; Humphrey and Schmitz 2001, 2004). The upgrading trajectory posited is therefore largely based on the more qualitative analysis of the process by which structural and industrial transformation was achieved by first-tier newly industrialised countries (NICs) within a short period of time (by historical standards) and which has been described in detail by in-depth individual country case-study analysis.

However, although the trajectory followed – from original equipment assembling (OEA) to own brand manufacturing (OBM) – was possible at that time, in that region, within particular value chains, accessing specific markets, major questions remain regarding the extent to which it may be replicable across other countries, including the LDCs. The external trade environment has dramatically changed for late entrants compared to at the time of the emergence of the East Asian NICs. Non-reciprocal trade relations between, for example, the EU and African, Caribbean, and Pacific (ACP) countries, have ended. Similarly, quantitative restrictions on specific product lines, such as textiles and clothing, have been removed, as World Trade Organization (WTO) members facilitated the entry of countries like China within the global trading system.

The combined effect of these changes, coupled with the tight control of particular functions by lead firms, means some types of upgrading processes may simply no longer be achievable.

The creation of tiers of suppliers and intermediaries may create added layers of barriers to entry. Because of this realisation there are increased efforts to untangle just exactly what it means to upgrade within GVCs. Attempts have been made to assign quantitative indicators to the qualitative GVC upgrading typology so widely referred to in the literature:[9]

- *Product upgrading*: improving quality.
- *Process upgrading*: performing certain tasks better and increasing efficiency.
- *Functional upgrading*: acquiring skills that enable movement towards another node or higher value-added level or function within the value chain.
- *Inter-sectoral upgrading*: using skills acquired to move into another sector, e.g. from textiles and clothing into footwear production.

In addition, Bernhardt and Milberg (2011) distinguish between economic and social upgrading. Within their framework economic and social upgrading are defined as follows:

- *Economic upgrading*: trade performance, as indicated by export unit values and market shares.
- *Social upgrading*: employment and wage growth.

The analytical approach of Bernhardt and Milberg (2011) seeks to link economic and social upgrading to a particular node of production. This is as opposed to considering the movement of labour (and investors) across and into new functions. Although the results from Bernhardt and Milberg (2011) are insightful, the ability to monitor these processes over time remains challenging: movement from one functional position can only be known through detailed case-study analysis. And, a major omission is the failure to consider skills development within their framework.

The upgrading of producers' capabilities and skills base – part of technological advancement more broadly – is necessary to sustain societal upgrading over time and to promote knowledge spillovers across sectors. Facilitating this complex and potentially disruptive process requires leveraging policy instruments in relation to the management of trade, investment policy and interaction with elements of a national innovation strategy (NIS). The presence, or absence, of more directive approaches adopted in view of specific developmental objectives are clearly apparent within the comparative analysis of upgrading processes for Bangladesh and Cambodia within the textiles and clothing GVC, introduced in the following sections.

14.3.3 Upgrading processes in Bangladesh

The availability of domestic inputs and strong backward linkages enables specialisation in the knitwear segment of the value chain. This, in turn, enables Bangladesh to benefit from duty-free market access, which creates a margin of around 12 per cent on the final retail value of the product (Curran and Nadvi, 2015). Within the EU market, in particular, these sales have grown. The reasons for better performance apparent in the EU market for knitwear compared to the US are explained by Curran and Nadvi (2015) in relation to tariff reductions made available: the US suspended duty-free access after the Rana Plaza building collapse and in view of poor labour rights and working conditions in factories.

Increased exports are an indicator of process upgrading. Analysis of trends combined with that of employment levels and skills development can help to identify how increases in exports were achieved. The analyses of Bernhardt and Milberg (2011) find that the number of workers employed in the sector in Bangladesh increased to 1 million in 1998 from 720,000 in 1993, but success in the industry is generally put down to low wages. However, in 2006 minimum wages were revised for the first time in 12 years by a massive 78.8 per cent (Yunus and Yamagata, 2014). According to the World Bank (2014), the minimum wage for garment workers was updated in December 2013 and the minimum salary for entry-level workers, Grade 7, increased to Tk 5300 (US$68) per month – this is a 76.7 per cent rise compared to the previous level of Tk 3000 (US$38).

Regarding skills development, Mottaleb and Sonobe (2011) and Alam and Natsuda (2013) pay particular attention to the education level of factory managers. They argue that the education level of entrepreneurs matters most for the future development of the sector, not a general increase in the skill level of workers. Their analysis is based on the outcomes from the Desh–Daewoo collaboration, a strategic partnership between South Korean investors (Daewoo) and domestic entrepreneurs (Desh) to bring investment into the textiles and clothing industry as well as provide specific training (in South Korea) for the employees of the domestic company.

The initial Desh–Daewoo agreement included training of managers and workers by Daewoo, in return for payment of a marketing fee by Desh Garments (Yunus and Yamagata, 2014). This involved Desh sending 150 critical personnel to Daewoo's production plant in Pusan in 1979 (and covering these costs except hosting and production-line training) with Daewoo being repaid for its training through a 3 per cent royalty on eventual sales by Daewoo and an additional 5 per cent for marketing, given its knowledge of global marketing chains. Hence, the agreement was based on the provision of marketing and technical assistance in order to be beneficial to all trading partners.

However, contrary to expectations, many of the Desh–Daewoo trainees did not become garment manufacturers but instead became traders, acting as the intermediaries between manufacturers and foreign buyers.[10] Traders who received this formal training abroad were able to provide higher-value services for domestic manufacturers and contributed more to their growth.[11] Through the actions of the traders, domestic firms were able to reduce their reliance on Daewoo as an intermediary.

The acquisition of competitiveness in the sector was based on a number of institutional and political arrangements that ensure compliance and high levels of effort (Khan, 2013). This process of engaging with a buyer-driven GVC so as to benefit from rapid product and process upgrading and access high-value end markets is conceptualised within the GVC governance typology developed by Gereffi et al. (2005). However, the creation of the appropriate incentive structures and institutional force, exerted by the state, required to ensure the flow of tacit and explicit forms of knowledge and information is more clearly demonstrated in the case of Bangladesh and the interpretation provided by Khan (2013).

Daewoo firms had a specific interest in transferring garment 'know-how' to Bangladesh, given that they had a textile business that needed to sell fabrics to a competing garment-producing company.[12] A combination of targeted institutional arrangements, backed by enforcement mechanisms, was utilised: Daewoo had incentives to transfer tacit knowledge, since it would not be paid until Desh began exporting. In this regard, Khan (2013) makes an explicit link between the integration approach with the textiles and clothing GVC with the effective management of learning rents, given the preferential market access conferred to Bangladesh – an LDC – compared to South Korea.

The dominant presence of domestic firms is recognised as a distinctive feature of production in Bangladesh (Yamagata, 2009). It is atypical in comparison to other LDCs engaged with this value chain and results from a more directive approach towards the management of foreign direct investment (FDI) in the sector. Fiscal benefits directed towards the textile and clothing GVC have been managed. Tax incentives decline after the initial year of establishment: from

100 per cent after the first two years of a firm's establishment to 50 per cent for two years more before reaching 25 per cent in the fifth year (Astarloa et al., 2012). Generally, problems with firms opening and closing in order to benefit from fiscal incentives seem less problematic than in the case of Cambodia. There are other challenges, however, related to capital flight.[13] It is generally recognised that Bangladesh is starved of tax revenues, with one of the smallest tax-to-GDP ratios in the world (though comparable to Cambodia) at about 10 per cent (Allchin, 2014; UNCTAD, 2013b). As discussed by UNCTAD (2013), Bangladesh does not have an established set of transfer pricing rules or the ability to implement such rules, which can result in arbitrary decisions.

The most up-to-date summary of functional upgrading processes in the sector for Bangladesh is undertaken by Alam and Natsuda (2013). They find that most firms are engaged in what they term FOB-1 and FOB-2 production. The terms are defined as follows:

- FOB-1 is a step above CMT production, whereby producers take responsibility for the sourcing of intermediate materials and production.
- FOB-2 includes the sourcing of intermediate materials and the undertaking of all levels of production and design.

Out of the 70 firms surveyed, 85 per cent (56 firms) were involved with FOB-1 production, 6 per cent (4 firms) involved with FOB-2 production and 9 per cent (6 firms) with traditional CMT arrangements. They note that only 4 of the 70 firms surveyed offered finished products to retailers. This includes providing all necessary production material, including design and branding. Although they do not distinguish between the end markets for these products, they do note that "most of the garment firms in Bangladesh are owned by domestic entrepreneurs who have limited capital, less experience, and little knowledge to carry out all necessary stages of production" (Alam and Natsuda, 2013: 27). Overall, therefore, they conclude that whilst there is evidence of functional upgrading from CMT to FOB-1 production, the ability of firms to upgrade to FOB-2 is doubtful. They make reference to broad-based productive constraints, including weak infrastructure as the reasons for this.

Regarding the movement of skilled labour within the sector, in the case of Bangladesh, overall there is a greater tendency for foreign enterprises to simply be replaced by indigenous domestic enterprises as service providers, manufacturers and material suppliers (Yamagata, 2006). Skills development remains on the job, with limited institutional links to vocational skills development bodies or incentive structures. In 2013, it was estimated that a shortage of skilled labour equated to around 25 per cent of the total labour force in the sector, and just to maintain average rates the industry needs to attract around a hundred thousand skilled workers.[14]

Given these huge demands for labour, it is surprising that there has been a failure to integrate workforce development within factory management systems. The available evidence suggests process upgrading has been achieved without a commensurate increase in the skills base, as proxied by workers' skill endowments. However, since the four main stages of production in the textiles and clothing sector include distribution and sales, the fact that domestic firms have successfully penetrated the domestic market provides evidence of functional upgrading. This is because there is evidence of a large number of domestic branded retailers on the domestic market. This strategy of shifting towards the domestic market after supplying the export market is referred to as a process of 'strategic recoupling' (Butollo, 2015).

The process of strategic recoupling results from domestic firms building on benefits related to their local embeddedness (supplier networks, institutional support and relationships) in order to gain new market opportunities as brand name companies in the domestic market. This option may be more amenable in the domestic market given ties to local wholesale traders (as described by Navas-Alemán, 2011). It seems this route towards upgrading has been pursued by domestic firms within Bangladesh, which constitutes a form of functional upgrading.

14.3.4 *Upgrading processes in Cambodia*

For some, Cambodia is considered to be an 'economic upgrader' within the textiles and clothing sector based on its performance between 2009 and 2011 (Bernhardt and Milberg, 2011). This is because economic upgrading was achieved with social upgrading, as indicated by both an increase in market share and the unit value of exports. Despite the optimism of Bernhardt and Milberg (2011), evidence to the contrary is presented by Asuyama et al. (2013), who show how the unit value of garment exports from Cambodia increased between 2001 and 2003, but thereafter followed a gradual decline – for the 2002–2008 period as a whole, the unit value declined by 23 per cent.

Given the different views posited regarding Cambodia's export performance, trade and unit data was sought directly from the Ministry of Commerce, Cambodia (Figure 14.1). This data confirms a decline in the unit value of Cambodia's clothing exports to US$35.25/dozen in 2012 from a high of US$46.26/dozen in 2004 [prior to the end of the Multifibre Agreement (MFA) period] and starting point of US$41.49/dozen in 2000.[15] It therefore updates and confirms the findings of Asuyama et al. (2013), but not those of Bernhardt and Milberg (2011). It is therefore difficult to concur that Cambodia has indeed been an economic upgrader.

In order to substantiate these findings further, a comparison of unit values between Cambodia and Bangladesh was undertaken (Table 14.1). These results confirm that the unit value of textiles and clothing exports into the US market from Cambodia are slightly lower compared to Bangladesh, and have declined over time. These findings are suggestive of different positions within the US market being occupied by Bangladesh and Cambodia within the overall textiles and clothing GVC; with a higher position being occupied by Bangladesh, as an FOB-1 supplier, compared to Cambodia, which occupies the CMT node.

Globally, Cambodia increased its world market share in clothing from 0.5 per cent in 2000 to 1.1 per cent in 2013 (WTO, 2014). Within the US market, Cambodia's predominant destination, however, a decline in market share occurred from 2.4 per cent in 2013 to 2.3 per cent in 2013.[16]

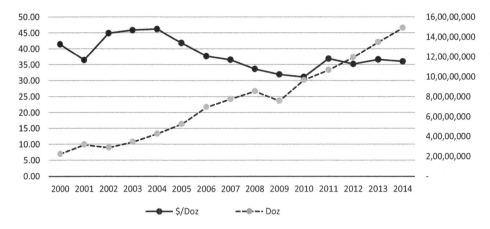

Figure 14.1 Cambodian clothing exports: total and unit value.

Table 14.1 Comparison of unit values: Cambodia and Bangladesh

Year	Cambodia			Bangladesh		
	Volume (million square metre equivalent)	Value (US$ million)	Unit value	Volume (million square metre equivalent)	Value (US$ million)	Unit value
2008	910.423	2385.821	2.621	1664.657	3537.458	2.125
2009	888.360	1887.773	2.125	1622.746	3522.803	2.171
2010	1002.693	2243.455	2.237	1866.908	4063.359	2.177
2011	1097.761	2622.022	2.389	1749.767	4652.865	2.659
2012	115.364	2568.996	2.303	1764.632	4621.587	2.619
2013	1131.519	2587.479	2.287	1944.621	5104.875	2.625
2014	1087.416	2515.928	2.314	1888.160	5004.948	2.651

Source: Otexa Major Shipping Report, each year, general imports per country (http://otexa.trade.gov/m sr_archive/msr_archive.htm); adapted from Keane (2016).
Note: Total of all aggregations.

Overall, Cambodia has not upgraded according to the results of the selected indicator of product upgrading – the combination of unit value and market share analysis.

Bernhardt and Milberg (2011: 38) find an "unambiguous case of social upgrading in Cambodia." This results from a doubling of real wages and a 60-fold increase in employment from the late 1990s to the late 2000s.[17] What is absent from their analysis is the fact that recent wage increases have been driven predominantly by political economy considerations. There were organised strikes during the elections held in 2013. Increasingly, unions have become affiliated with the opposition Cambodia National Rescue Party (CNRP). Wage increases in the sector have been motivated to reduce conflicts within the sector and to politically appease unions, as opposed to being implemented based on a performance review process and incentive structure.[18]

There is some evidence of on-the-job training. Based on analysis of the IDE-JETRO firm-level surveys undertaken in 2003 and 2009, around 75 per cent of the surveyed firms provided formal training to their employees. Interestingly, this incidence of training is considerably higher than that of Bangladesh (12.6 per cent in 2002 and 31.5 per cent in 2008).[19] There is anecdotal evidence that firms have begun to replace foreign managers with national employees. For example, Asuyama and Neou (2014) find around two-thirds of firms recruited Cambodian supervisors. However, they describe how these moves may be motivated more by a desire to reduce wages for managers, rather than a concerted effort to develop local skills.

According to Asuyama et al. (2013) most top managers in firms are foreign nationals and of Chinese nationality: 30 per cent from mainland China, and 15 and 21 per cent from Hong Kong and Taiwan, respectively. They found only 8 per cent of managers had Cambodian nationality. By ethnicity, 77 per cent of top managers answered that they were Chinese, whatever their geographical origin (Asuyama et al., 2013).

Cambodia's pattern of industrial development – led by a labour-intensive industry – is similar to that of neighbouring countries in East Asia, but a major difference is that industrial development has been pursued without a strong industrial policy in place (Yamagata, 2006).[20] Factors to attract FDI into the sector include the permitting of 100 per cent foreign ownership and the ability to import capital goods without duty and other tax incentives. As discussed by UNCTAD

(2013c), Cambodia has one of the most liberal investment regimes in developing Asia. Incentives include a 9 per cent concessionary corporate tax, tax holiday of up to 8 years, tax exemption for reinvestment, import duty exemption and export tax exemption (Asuyama and Neou, 2014). Investors are free to exit from a venture in accordance with the investment law, so long as the Council for the Development of Cambodia (CDC) is informed and all obligations, including those due to the Ministry of Finance, settled.[21] Once the investor has been officially allowed to dissolve the enterprise, the remaining assets can be transferred overseas or reused in Cambodia. Hence, firms can dissolve and reopen so long as the CDC signs off and statutory duties are met.

No requirements are specified such as the formulation of partnerships or joint ventures with domestic firms. The current objective regarding SMEs' development includes the mandate "to upgrade their position and support the integration of SMEs into global value chains" (RGC, 2013: 28). However, although the Government-Private Sector Forum (GPSF) discusses private sector development concerns at the highest level and decisions could be translated into formal law-making processes, its membership comprises mainly large foreign-invested enterprises and not SMEs. The role of business associations as forming a crucial bridge in terms of public–private interactions and as intermediate institutions performing an integral role within national innovation strategies was not recognised at the time of GVC integration.

Since most major managerial decisions to do with local manufacturing are almost exclusively made outside Cambodia, the degree of domestic autonomy within the sector is invariably limited (Ear, 2013). Overall, there is no evidence suggestive of any fundamental change in the functional position of Cambodian firms, and managers, within the overall textiles and clothing GVC. There is also no evidence of Cambodian firms selling onto the domestic market as part of a strategic decision to move into their own brand production. Functional upgrading processes have therefore been limited.

14.3.5 Summary of identifiable upgrading processes

Despite being inserted within the archetypal textiles and clothing GVC in similar ways – being predominantly driven by trade preferences – there are some major differences in the upgrading processes experienced in Bangladesh and Cambodia, as summarised in Table 14.2. These differences are related to the ability to move into higher value-added activities within the textiles and clothing value chain in the case of Bangladesh; this is as opposed to remaining at the same node, as in the case of Cambodia, despite more than two decades of participation.

These differences in turn have been related to the process of knowledge acquisition within the sector, related to the management of the integration process with the textiles and clothing value chain which took a more directive form in the case of Bangladesh compared to Cambodia. There are major differences in the degree of trade openness, management in relation to investment, and linkages with domestic firms and entrepreneurs in Bangladesh compared to Cambodia. The combined effect of which has influenced the divergent upgrading trajectories apparent.

Bringing these aspects into analyses of upgrading within GVCs means considering how specific firm-level interactions may need to be directly influenced in order to unlock particular learning opportunities, given developmental objectives. Because of differences in the types of knowledge that may be transferred (tacit and non-tacit) within firm-specific value chain structures, it becomes clear that GVCs often don't meet innovation systems unless proactive measures are taken and a combination of facilitative and directive approaches are adopted. Particular institutional set-ups may be required to release opportunities, with all of the political economy challenges and considerations related to effective rent management.

Table 14.2 Identifiable upgrading processes

Upgrading processes	Cambodia	Bangladesh
Product upgrading: increase in unit values and market share	Decline in unit values apparent	Overall increase (woven products) and higher unit values compared to Cambodia
Process upgrading: improving the efficiency of production and unit costs	Increased employment	Increased employment
Employees skill level, years of education, vocational training	Weak evidence of skill premium; limited vocational trading	Limited; skills shortages
Employees' years of experience, movement of labourers towards higher skilled positions; remuneration	Limited Increased wages driven by political motivations	Critical role of entrepreneurs/traders in entry
Functional upgrading: Movement into a higher value-added activity, including sales on the domestic market	Not apparent	Movement towards 2nd tier FOB supplier Sales on domestic market

These aspects of external value chain governance, related to the institutional frameworks encompassing trade, taxation, investment and finance, go beyond the role of the global trading system ascribed to within the Sustainable Development Goals (SDGs). Within SDG17 – Means of Implementation – the role of the WTO references a commitment to the achievement of duty-free, quota-free market access by LDCs. This objective was agreed under the Doha Round of negotiations, nearly two decades ago, and before the full entry of China into the WTO. As this chapter has sought to elucidate, enhanced market access alone is unlikely to ease the formidable trade and development challenges of LDCs both entering and upgrading within GVCs.

14.4 Conclusion

Because the new trade opportunities posited within GVCs are often posited without critical reflection on contemporaneous upgrading processes, this chapter has demonstrated why effective value chain governance matters: the stimulation of upgrading processes requires a more pro-active approach by governments than typically assumed within the GVC literature. Whilst the global trade architecture has provided specific market access opportunities for LDCs, which has provided a foothold into the modern export sector, the comparative experiences of the LDCs reviewed in this chapter has shown how passive integration with the textiles and clothing GVC has disabled rather than enabled particular upgrading opportunities.

In relation to trade and investment policy, two opposite sides of a continuum have been described, ranging from facilitative (positive functional) to directive (positive selective).[22] More directive approaches, rather than assuming knowledge spillovers, recognise their more rivalrous nature and the need for more proactive measures to stimulate spillovers, which do not occur automatically. Tacit knowledge spillovers between lead firms and their suppliers require close interaction in order for knowledge acquisition to occur.

Through the comparative analysis undertaken in this chapter, it is shown how a greater focus on how trade is governed within GVC-driven trade is required to account for the ability of some LDCs to enter and achieve certain upgrading processes compared to others. This ability is related to how governments have influenced relationships between firms in order to achieve developmental objectives. Such approaches require careful mediation and consideration of the specific learning opportunities which may be unlocked through more directive approaches and the incentive structures in place for different actors within the GVC to realise these.

The main policy implications which arise from the analyses relate to the need to better understand how power is exercised through value chains, how they are governed and potential leverage points. The need to effectively govern value chains through more directive approaches has been demonstrated in view of the rivalrous nature of knowledge spillovers. However, there are some major challenges in terms of doing so within the current fragmented global trade, investment and finance regime. All governments are struggling in relation to taxation issues, including transfer pricing issues and base profit shifting within a highly fragmented regulatory context.

More fundamentally, however, there is a need to more explicitly define what type of knowledge spillover may occur through engagement with particular types of GVCs, then the specific leverage points and scope to influence these. This requires greater understanding of the types of technologies, organisational form and interactions with human capital formation processes which might best realise desired knowledge spillovers to support LDCs development objectives.

Notes

1 See Keane (2011).
2 See Keane and Baimbill-Johnson (2017).
3 See Keane (2012).
4 For example, rules of origin specifically state the amount of domestic value added which must be embodied within exports in order to benefit from reduced tariffs.
5 See Curran and Nadvi (2015).
6 See Pickles et al. (2015).
7 This view was expressed by several key informants as "where the market is heading."
8 The textiles sector comprises chapters 50 to 60 and 63 of the Harmonised System, whilst the clothing sector comprises chapters 61 and 62 of the same classification.
9 See Kaplinsky and Morris (2001); Humphrey and Schmitz (2004).
10 Motteleb and Sonobe (2011) also note that generally there is very little information available on the role local traders play in industrial development in developing countries, and moreover that the economic literature is silent on this.
11 See Mottaleb and Sonobe (2011) and Alam and Natsuda (2013).
12 See Khan (2013).
13 The challenge of capital flight is discussed in the World Bank's (2012b) growth strategy document *Towards Accelerated, Inclusive and Sustainable Growth: Opportunities and Challenges*. Despite foreign capital inflows including donor support, it is acknowledged that growth rates will be hard to maintain without addressing the incentives to invest (World Bank, 2012b: 24). Bangladesh has a similar level of inequality to Cambodia, our major case study, as measured by the Gini coefficient, which is 0.46 and 0.43, respectively. The bottom 40 percent of households according to the World Bank (2012b: 96) suffered a decline in their income share between 1988 and 2000, whilst the top ten increased their share. The overriding challenge relates to incentives for productive investments.
14 The results are presented in UNCTAD (2013b) with reference to other studies undertaken in the sector.
15 This information obtained from the Ministry of Commerce is based on per dozen/clothing exports. It is therefore a highly aggregate category which is used for customs purposes.
16 Estimated based on a comparison of the top ten importers into the US market of textiles and clothing between 2013 and 2014, and information obtained from Otexa and US Shippers Report.

17 According to their estimates, employment in the sector increased 60-fold, or by 5824.7 percent from the late 1990s to 2000s; wages increased by 84.5 percent over the same period.

18 Because of wage increases in this sector, the government is under increasing pressure to review wage levels more generally, as discussed in the World Bank (2014) in its Cambodia Economic Update, which includes the section "Improving Pay for the Public Sector."

19 See Asuyama and Neou (2014).

20 Cambodia was drawn into the buyer-driven garment GVC based almost entirely on inward investment (Natsuda et al., 2010).

21 It is necessary to obtain a tax certification from the tax department in this regard. See UNCTAD (2013b).

22 With reference to Lall (1997).

Bibliography

Alam, M.D. and Natsuda, K. (2013) '*The Competitive Factors of the Bangladeshi Garment Industry in the Post-MFA Era*', Ritsumeikan Center for Asia Pacific Studies Working Paper 13003, Japan: Ritsumeikan Asia Pacific University.

Allchin, J. (2014) Bangladesh: Infrastructure, Corruption and the Struggle to Diversify, *Financial Times*, 03 June 2014, [accessed 20 January 2015] (http://blogs.ft.com/beyond-brics/2014/06/03/bangladesh-infrastructure-corruption-and-the-struggle-to-diversify/).

Astarloa, B.D., Eaton, J., Krishna, K., Aw-Roberts, B.Y., Rodriguez-Clare, A. and Tybout, J. (2012) '*Born-to-Export: Understanding Export Growth in Bangladesh*', International Growth Centre Working Paper, London: London School of Economics.

Asuyama, Y., Chhun, D., Fukunishi, T., Neou, S. and Yamagata, T. (2013) 'Firm Dynamics in the Cambodia Garment Industry: Firm Turnover, Productivity growth and Wage Profile under Trade Liberalisation', *Journal of the Asian Pacific Economy* 18(1): 51–70.

Asuyama, Y. and Neou, S. (2014) 'Cambodia: Growth with Better Working Conditions', in T. Fukunishi and T. Yamagata (eds.) *The Garment Industry in Low-Income Countries*, Hampshire: Palgrave McMillan.

Baldwin, R. (2012) 'WTO 2.0: Global governance of supply-chain trade', *CEPR Policy Insight No. 64* [accessed 14 June 2014] (http://www.cepr.org/sites/default/files/policy_insights/PolicyInsight64.pdf).

Bernhardt, T. and Milberg, W. (2011) '*Economic and Social Upgrading in Global Value Chains: Analysis of Horticulture, Apparel, Tourism and Mobile Telephones*', Capturing the Gains Working Paper 2011/6, Brooks World Poverty Institute: University of Manchester.

Butollo, F. (2015) 'Growing Against the Odds: Government Agency and Strategic Recoupling As Sources of Competitiveness in the Garment Industry of the Pearl River Delta', *Cambridge Journal of Regions, Economy and Society*, 8(3): 521–536.

Curran, L. and Nadvi, K. (2015) 'Shifting Trade Preferences and Value Chain Impacts in the Bangladesh Textiles and Garment Industry', *Cambridge Journal of Regions, Economy and Society*, 8(3): 459–474.

Ear, S. (2013) 'Cambodia's Gar hgg1qgah1q1hment Industry: A Case Study in Governance', *Journal of Southeast Asian Economies* 30(1): 91–105.

Frederick, S. and Staritz, C. (2012) 'Apparel Industry Developments after the MFA Phase-out' in Lopez-Acevedo, G. and Robertson, R. (Ed) *Sewing Success? Employment and Wage Effects of the end of the Multi-fibre Arrangement (MFA)*, Washington, DC: The World Bank.

Gereffi, G. (1999) 'International Trade and Industrial Upgrading in the Apparel Commodity Chain', *Journal of International Economics*, 48(1): 37–70.

Gereffi, G. and Frederick, S. (2010) *The Global Apparel Value Chain, Trade and the Crisis: Challenges and Opportunities for Developing Countries*, World Bank Policy Research Paper 5281, Washington, DC: World Bank [accessed 5 May 2012] (http://elibrary.worldbank.org/doi/pdf/10.1596/1813-9450-5281).

Gereffi, G., Humphrey, J. and Sturgeon, T. (2005) 'The Governance of Global Value Chains', *Review of International Political Economy* 12: 78–104.

Guimbert, S. (2010) '*Cambodia 1998–2008: An Episode of Rapid Growth*', World Bank Policy Research Working Paper 5271, Washington DC: World Bank.

Humphrey, J. and Schmitz, H. (2001) '*Developing Country Firms in the World Economy: Governance and Upgrading in Global Value Chains*', INEF Report 61, Duisburg: Institut für Entwicklung und Frieden.

Humphrey, J. and Schmitz, H. (2004) 'Chain Governance and Upgrading: Taking Stock', in Schmitz, H. (ed.) *Local Enterprises in the Global Economy*, Cheltenham: Edward Elgar.

Jessop, B. (2006) 'State- and regulation-theoretical perspectives on the European Union and the Failure of the Lisbon agenda', *Competition and Change*, 10: 141–161.

Kamau, P. (2009) *Upgrading and Technical Efficiency in Kenyan Garment Firms: Does Insertion in Global Value Chains Matter?* PhD Thesis, Nairobi: Institute of Development Studies.

Kaplinsky, R. and Morris, M. (2001) 'A Handbook for Value Chain Analysis', paper prepared for the International Development Research Centre [accessed 14 May 2008] (http://asiandrivers.open.ac.uk/documents/Value_chain_Handbook_RKMM_Nov_2001.pdf).

Keane, J. (2012) 'The Governance of Global Value Chains and the Effects of the Global Financial Crisis Transmitted to Producers in Africa and Asia', *Journal of Development Studies* 48(6): 783–797.

Keane, J. (2013) 'Rethinking Trade Preferences for sub-Saharan Africa: How can trade in tasks be the potential lifeline?' *Development Policy Review* 31(4): 443–462.

Keane, J. (2016) The New Trade / New Growth Nexus for Late Industrialisers: Exploring Learning-by-Doing Processes for Garment (Cambodia, Bangladesh) and Cut-Flower (Kenya, Ethiopia) Exporters: Integrating Global Value Chain and Firm-Level Analyses. PhD Thesis. SOAS, University of London [accessed 10 August 2020] (http://eprints.soas.ac.uk/23647).

Keane, J. and Baimbill-Johnson, R. (2017) *Future Fragmentation: Effectively engaging with the ascendency of Global Value Chains*, London: Commonwealth Secretariat.

Khan, M. (2013) 'Technology Policies and Learning with Imperfect Governance', in Stiglitz et al. (eds.) *The Industrial Policy Revolution 1: The Role of Government Beyond Ideology*, London: Palgrave.

Lall, S. (1997) 'Selective Policies for Export Promotion: Lessons from the Asian tigers', *Research for Action 43*, World Institute for Development Economics Research, Helsinki: United Nations University.

Lee, J. and Chen, J. (2000) 'Dynamic Synergy Creation with Multiple Business Activities: Toward a Competence-based Growth Model for Contract Manufacturers', in Sanchez, R. and Heene, A. (eds.) *Research in Competence-based Management*, London: Elsevier.

Moran, M., Rein, M. and Goodin, R. (2009) *The Oxford Handbook of Public Policy*, Oxford: Oxford University Press.

Mottaleb, K.A. and Sonobe, T. (2011) 'An Inquiry into the Rapid Growth of the Garment Industry in Bangladesh', *National Graduate Institute for Policy Studies (GRIPS) Discussion Paper 11-10*, Tokyo: GRIPS.

Navas-Alemán, L. (2011) 'The Impact of Operating in Multiple Value Chains for Upgrading: The Case of the Brazilian Furniture and Footwear Industries', *World Development* 39(8): 1386–1397.

Neilson, J. Pritchard, B. and Wai-chung Yeung, H. (2014) 'Global Value Chains and Global Production Networks in the Changing International Political Economy: An introduction', *Review of International Political Economy*, 21(1): 1–8.

Pickles, J., Plank, L., Staritz, C. and Glasmeier, A. (2015) 'Trade Policy and Regionalisms in Global Clothing Production Networks', *Cambridge Journal of Regions, Economy and Society* 8(3): 381–402.

Pietrobelli, C. and Saliola, F. (2008) 'Power Relationships along the Value Chain: Multinational Firms, Global Buyers and Performance of Local Suppliers', *Cambridge Journal of Economics* 32(6): 947–962.

Ponte, S. and Sturgeon, T. (2014) 'Explaining Governance in Global Value Chains: A Modular Theory-Building Effort', *Review of International Political Economy* 21(1): 195–223.

Porter, M. (1985) *The Competitive Advantage: Creating and Sustaining Superior Performance*, New York: Free Press.

Raikes, P. Jensen, M.F. and Ponte, S. (2000) 'Global Commodity Chain Analysis and the French Filiere Approach: Comparison and Critique', *Economy and Society* 38(3): 390–417.

Ravenhill, J. (2014) Global Value Chains and Development, (21) – Issue 1: Global Value Chains and Global Production Networks in the Changing International Political Economy.

Roberts, S. and Thoburn, J. (2003) 'Adjusting to Trade Liberalisation: The Case of Firms in the South Africa textile sector', *Journal of African Economies* 12(1): 74–103.

Royal Government of Cambodia (2013) *Rectangular Strategy for Growth, Employment, Equity and Efficiency Phase III*, Phnom Penh: Royal Government of Cambodia [accessed 10 June 2014] (http://www.ilo.org/wcmsp5/groups/public/---asia/---ro-bangkok/---sro-bangkok/documents/genericdocument/wcms_237910.pdf)

Savchenko, Y. (2012) The Rise of Small Asian Economies in the Apparel Industry, in Acevedo, L.G. and Robertson, R. (eds) *Sewing Success? Employment and Wages Following the End of the Multi-Fibre Arrangement*, Washington, DC: World Bank.

Schmitz, H. and Knorriga, p. (2001) 'Learning from Global Buyers', *Journal of Development Studies* 37(2): 77–205.

Stevens, C., Bird, K., Keane, J., Kennan, J., te Velde, D.W. and Higgins, K. (2011) '*The Poverty Impact of the Proposed Graduation Threshold in the Generalised System of Preferences (GSP) Trade Scheme*', London: ODI (http://bit.ly/odi-gsp-fullreport).

UNCTAD (2013a) *World Investment Report: Global Value Chains: Investment and Trade for Development*, Geneva: United Nations Conference on Trade and Development [accessed 14 March 2014] (http://unctad.org/en/publicationslibrary/wir2013_en.pdf).

UNCTAD (2013b) *Bangladesh: Sector-Specific Investment Strategy and Action Plan*, Geneva: United Nations Conference on Trade and Development [accessed 10 June 2014] (unctad.org/Sections/diae_dir/docs/diae_G20_Bangladesh_en.pdf).

UNCTAD (2013c) *Cambodia: Sector-Specific Investment Strategy and Action Plan*, Geneva: United Nations Conference on Trade and Development [accessed 10 June 2014] (http://unctad.org/Sections/diae_dir/docs/diae_G20_Cambodia_en.pdf).

WTO (2014) *World Trade Report*, Geneva: World Trade Organisation.

World Bank (2014) 'Coping with Domestic Pressures and Gaining from a Strengthened Global Economy', *Cambodia Economic Update April 2014*, Washington D.C.: World Bank.

Yamagata, T. (2006) '*The Garment Industry in Cambodia: Its Role in Poverty Reduction through Export-orientated Development*', IDE Discussion Paper No. 62. Tokyo: Institute of Development Economics [accessed 10 March 2009] (http://ir.ide.go.jp/dspace/bitstream/2344/131/5/ARRIDE_Discussion_No.062_yamagata.pdf).

Yamagata, T. (2009) 'Industrialisation cum Poverty Reduction', in T. Shiraishi, T. Yamagata and S. Yusuf (eds.) *Poverty Reduction and Beyond: Development Strategies for Low Income Countries*, Houndmills: Palgrave McMillan.

Yeung, H. and Coe, N. (2014) 'Toward a Dynamic Theory of Global Production Networks', *Economic Geography* 91(1): 29–58.

Yunus, M. and Yamagata, T. (2014) 'Bangladesh: Market Force Supersedes Control', in Fukunishi, T. and Yamagata, T. (ed.) *The Garment Industry in Low-Income Countries: An entry point of industrialisation*, Hampshire: Palgrave McMillan.

15

MAPPING OF GVCS, SERVICES AND INTANGIBLE ASSETS

Koen De Backer and Sébastien Miroudot

15.1 Introduction

Global value chains (GVCs) have changed the way we look at world trade and production. While trade has traditionally been regarded upon as the exchange of products fully manufactured in one country and competing with varieties from other economies, international trade is now understood as being mostly about exchanges of intermediate products and capital goods within international production networks. Instead of industries from different countries competing to sell products in the international marketplace, the literature on GVCs has introduced a different perspective on international production by describing how, in the process of bringing final products to consumers, a variety of producers interact, co-operate and compete across different stages of production that take place in different countries.

Empirical research on GVCs was initially limited to case studies describing in detail the activities needed in order to produce a good or a service. Case studies focused on in the first place on specific products, such as Apple's iPod or notebook PCs from Lenovo and Hewlett-Packard in the seminal paper by Dedrick et al. (2008). In addition, GVC analysis has also been conducted for a broader category of products belonging to the same industry. For example, the work of Gary Gereffi started with the study of the apparel value chain (Appelbaum and Gereffi, 1994).

More recently, the analysis of GVCs has largely benefitted from new theoretical and empirical developments in the field of input–output analysis, in particular, to answer questions at the aggregate or sectoral level. Developed by Wassily Leontief in the 1930s, the input–output model describes inter-industry relationships within an economy and how output from one industry becomes an input in another industry. As such, GVC analysis is already of an aggregate nature and because it looks at the process of transforming raw materials and processed intermediates into final products, it is very similar to input–output analysis. In one of the first papers documenting the rise of vertical trade and international supply chains, Hummels et al. (2001) rely on input techniques to assess the foreign content of exports in ten Organisation for Economic Co-operation and Development (OECD) countries. With the development of inter-country input–output (ICIO) tables[1] at the end of the 2000s, a new literature has emerged with new indicators tracing value added across countries and industries.

DOI: 10.4324/9781315225661-21

The chapter first reviews the recent developments in input–output analysis and discusses the new indicators available for researchers together with their strength and weaknesses. Using the World Input-Output Database (WIOD) – 43 countries and 56 industries over the period 2000–2014 – the chapter then uses some of these indicators to provide a broad mapping of GVCs, focusing on the dispersion of income along the value chain and the role of different countries and industries.

The chapter then discusses three determinants of income in GVCs: the role of services and how, in particular, wholesale and retail as well as interactions with customers shape some value chains; the role of intellectual assets and how income is also captured or maintained in other segments of the value-chain on the basis of intangible capital; and the role of business ecosystems and how co-operative value chains as opposed to captive value chains offer an alternative model to create and retain value in GVCs. In a final section, the chapter draws some implications from the new findings.

15.2 Input–output analysis: An aggregate perspective on global value chains

15.2.1 New insights on trade in value-added, GVC participation and linkages

Global input–output tables have been used to calculate new indicators characterising the involvement of countries and industries in GVCs. At the beginning, researchers have focused primarily on the concept of trade in value-added. Indeed, an important implication of the rise of GVCs is that trade statistics measured in gross terms are not able to reflect the contribution of each economy to the generation of value added. When a good crosses borders multiple times at different stages of processing, the total value of the good (including the intermediate inputs) is recorded each time, leading to an important double or multiple counting that inflates trade statistics. Moreover, the contribution of the suppliers of inputs located in other countries is not acknowledged in the exports of a given country, introducing some bias in terms of who really benefits from trade. Building on the work of Hummels et al. (2001), Koopman et al. (2014) have proposed a decomposition of gross exports based on an inter-country input–output table. Foster-McGregor and Stehrer (2013), as well as Los et al. (2015), have provided alternative formulas in what is now a growing literature on trade in value-added.

While understanding the double counting in gross exports is an important empirical issue, trade in value-added also implies that any final good consumed in a given country embodies some foreign value added. Another approach then consists in fully decomposing final demand according to the country and industry of origin of value added, i.e. where the primary factors of production (labour and capital) were used in the first place. Formulas to provide such decomposition are part of the core input–output model developed by Leontief. Johnson and Noguera (2012) assess the value-added content of bilateral trade using this approach. In addition, they introduce the value added to gross exports ratio (VAX), which can be understood as a measure of the double counting in international trade.

It should be noted that only the last approach (i.e. starting from final goods and services) provides estimates of the value added in trade consistent with GDP (i.e. the value added measured in each economy). The concept of gross exports includes both final and intermediate products, and some intermediates are still 'travelling' in what is sometimes 'circular trade' (i.e. inputs exported by an economy coming back embodied in a more processed good or service to the same economy). As a consequence, one can measure the domestic value-added in gross exports but never fully disentangle the double counting from the foreign value-added at the country level (Nagengast and Stehrer, 2016).

Measures of trade in value-added terms start from the final demand estimate of the contribution of each country in the global value chain. The results are conceptually close to GVC analysis where a final product is described as resulting from different production stages performed in different countries. Timmer et al. (2013) introduced the concept of 'GVC income' based on a full decomposition of the final demand for manufacturing goods by country of origin of value added.[2] Such decomposition can, for example, show the contribution of France, Japan or the US in the final demand for cars in Germany. The value added by France, Japan or the US may originate in inputs used by German car manufacturers in their domestic sales or embodied in imported cars. This calculation sums up all the value added originating in these foreign economies.

Also derived from the literature on trade in value-added, the concept of 'participation in GVCs' aims at providing a single metric that takes into account both the contribution of countries supplying inputs at the beginning of the value chain and countries using these inputs at the end of the value chain (i.e. close to final demand). Backward participation in GVCs is defined as the share of foreign value-added in exports, while forward participation in GVCs is measured through the domestic value-added in the exports of third countries. Koopman et al. (2014) suggested adding the two measures to derive an index of participation in GVCs.

Building on input–output analysis, other indicators used in the analysis of GVCs are based on the concepts of 'backward linkages' and 'forward linkages'. The backward linkages refer to the impact of an increase in demand for one industry (in one country) on the demand for inputs in all other industries (and countries), while the forward linkages look at the impact of an increase in the supply of one industry (in one country) on the production in all other industries (and countries). As explained by Fally (2012), the backward linkages can be interpreted as a measure of the length of the value chain or average number of production stages required to produce a good or a service in the industry for which it is calculated. Moreover, Antràs et al. (2012) show that the forward linkages have a different interpretation: they indicate the distance to final demand (i.e. the average number of production stages before consumption takes place) and therefore measure the 'upstreamness' of a given industry (in a given country).[3]

15.2.2 Some caveats, however

While input–output techniques provide a powerful tool for the analysis of GVCs, they have some weaknesses related both to the level of aggregation of input–output tables and to some of the assumptions in the underlying model. The level of aggregation of tables matters because for each industry in each country there is a single function of production. All firms are assumed to produce an output based on the same mix of domestic and foreign inputs. This assumption becomes an issue when there is a high heterogeneity among producers within the same industry. One example of heterogeneity is related to differences among firms involved in exports and firms focusing on the domestic market. The latter tend to use fewer foreign inputs than the former. When exporting firms are in addition mostly processing foreign inputs (e.g. processing trade in China or Mexico), not taking into account this heterogeneity can lead to an important bias in the measurement of the foreign value-added embodied in exports (Koopman et al., 2012). Closely related to this are the differences between foreign affiliates (i.e. affiliates of multinational enterprises) and purely domestic – often small to medium-sized enterprises (SMEs) – companies (see Cadestin et al., 2018).

More fundamentally, the fact that the whole value chain is analysed with a single production function for each industry, with fixed proportions for intermediate inputs and factors of production (the 'Leontief production function'), creates an aggregation bias that tends to overestimate the value created at the last stage of production (Nomaler and Verspagen, 2014). For the same industry, the way an input is produced (upstream in the value chain) may be different from the way a final good is produced (downstream in the value chain). But the input–output framework assumes that the production function is the same (as long as the input and the final product belong to the same industry). The same production structure is repeated all along the value chain in the absence of a specific input–output table for each stage of production.

More generally, international input–output tables require extensive output, value-added and trade data at the country and industry level that are not available for all economies. They are also built based on many assumptions and require many estimates to fill the gaps in official data. Some caution should therefore be taken into account when analysing GVC indicators derived from input–output frameworks. They concern estimates that suffer from an aggregation bias, more or less serious depending on the degree of heterogeneity among firms and products within each industry.

15.3 Mapping global value chains with inter-country input–output tables

In this section, we propose a new mapping of six global value chains based on the concept of 'GVC income' described by Timmer et al. (2013). The analysis derives additional insights by focusing on the regional character of GVCs (and distinguishing between final demand at home and abroad) and by linking this to an OECD dataset on business functions (which makes it possible to identify the specialisation of countries in terms of activities within each industry).

15.3.1 Data and methodology

The analysis is based on the World Input-Output Database (WIOD), updated in November 2016. The database is described in Timmer et al. (2015) and information on the update can be found in Timmer et al. (2016). It consists of a set of world input-output tables covering 43 countries[4] and a model for the rest of the world for the period 2000–2014. Details are available for 56 industries in the International Standard Industrial Classification of All Economic Activities Revision 4 (ISIC Rev. 4). The tables are built according to the 2008 version of the System of National Accounts.

While the database has information on all industries in all countries, we focus on six manufacturing GVCs and use regional groupings to simplify the presentation of results. The six industries analysed are food and beverages (C10 to C12 in ISIC Rev. 4, 'Manufacture of food products, beverages and tobacco products'); textiles and apparel (C13 to C15, 'Manufacture of textiles, wearing apparel and leather products'); pharmaceuticals (C21, 'Manufacture of basic pharmaceutical products and pharmaceutical preparations'); computer and electronics (C16, 'Manufacture of computer, electronic and optical products'); automotive industry (C29, 'Manufacture of motor vehicles, trailers and semi-trailers'); and aeronautics, shipbuilding and railway equipment (C30, 'other transport equipment').

The data are combined with information on business functions coming from labour force surveys. A description of these data can be found in Miroudot and Cadestin (2017). The business function is a new statistical unit of analysis proposed in the GVC literature to better characterise the activities of workers within firms and industries (Sturgeon et al., 2013). It builds on the value chain as described by Michael Porter (1985) and the distinction between the primary or core activity of the firm (its operations) and a number of support functions: research and development (R&D), IT support, logistics, marketing, sales, marketing and administrative support. It sheds light on functional specialisation in GVCs (Timmer et al., 2019).

The GVC income is calculated by decomposing final demand in the industries corresponding to the six GVCs previously listed. We first calculate the 'global Leontief inverse' (L) (i.e. a world matrix of total inputs requirements), measuring all the inputs required both directly and indirectly (the indirect inputs being the inputs used upstream to produce the direct inputs) as a share of output in all industries and countries. This matrix is then multiplied by a vector of value-added ratios to gross output to obtain value-added shares and multiplied by the world final demand in each of the six industries to obtain column vectors that indicate the contribution of each industry and each country to the global value chain. We can also multiply the matrix by the foreign final demand (removing the domestic consumption in each economy) to have a different contribution that focuses only on products consumed abroad. We call this alternative indicator 'GVC income in foreign final demand'. Also, instead of working with the world final demand, we can focus on final demand in three regions – North America, Europe and Asia – to look at regional differences in GVCs. In this case, the vector of final demand only takes into account the countries belonging to these regions.

All data in the WIOD tables are in current US dollars and the results of the decomposition are values in dollars. We present them as shares to look at the evolution over time. Ideally, the analysis should be carried out in constant prices, but input–output information is generally not provided with volumes and prices.[5]

15.3.2 Results: GVC income

Figure 15.1 summarises the main results when looking at the contribution of China, the EU, Japan, Korea and the US to the GVC income in each of the six industries. The EU is split between the 15 economies part of the EU before the start of the period (EU15) and the economies that joined more recently (EU enlargement). Other economies for which there are detailed results in the WIOD data set are part of 'other developed countries' (Australia, Canada, Switzerland and Norway) or 'other emerging economies' (Brazil, India, Indonesia, Mexico, Russia, Turkey and Taiwan).

While the results reflect the specialisation of certain economies in specific industries (e.g. Japan in computer and electronics, or China in textiles and apparel), Figure 15.1 illustrates clearly why it is relevant to talk about 'global value chains'. Production in each of these industries is really global, not only because Figure 15.1 has aggregated the final demand from all countries but also because production takes place with value added from all over the world (Figure 15.3 will allow us to confirm this by removing the domestic final demand).

There are also some common trends in all GVCs. The shift to Asia and the rise of China is common to the six industries. Even in the pharmaceuticals industry, there is a growing share of GVC income for China between 2000 and 2014. But not surprisingly, the highest increase is found in computer and electronics, other transport equipment (aeronautics, shipbuilding and railway equipment), textiles and apparel, and the automotive industry. While not as impressive as for China, other emerging economies and EU enlargement countries also benefit from higher shares of GVC income in almost all industries between 2000 and 2014.

Since the data are presented as shares, it means that developed countries (EU15, Japan, US and other developed countries) account for a lower share of GVC income. However, in absolute terms, these countries have increased their GVC income: they have a smaller share of a much bigger pie. But in relative terms, there was a redistribution of GVC income.

15.3.3 Results: GVC income in regional value chains

Notwithstanding the global character of production, the results in Figure 15.1 hide to some extent the regional nature of GVCs. That is why in Figure 15.2 the final demand is this time

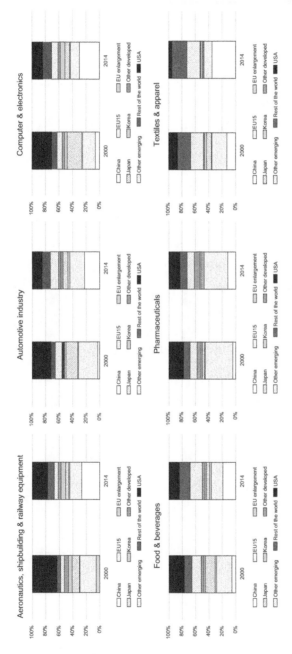

Figure 15.1 GVC income in 2000 and 2014, contribution by country (%). (Source: Calculations by the authors based on WIOD, November 2016 update.)

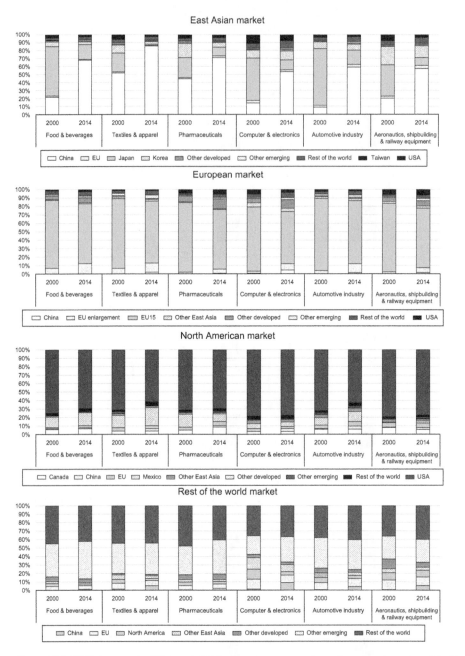

Figure 15.2 GVC income in 2000 and 2014, share by country in each regional market (%). (Source: Calculations by the authors based on WIOD, November 2016 update.)

split according to the region of consumption of products (East Asia, Europe, North America or the rest of the world).

In Figure 15.2, the regional nature of GVCs becomes much clearer. When a final product is sold in East Asia, it has mostly Asian value added; when it is sold in the EU, it has predominantly European value added, and so on. Still, a non-negligible share of value added is extra-regional, confirming the 'global' nature of GVCs. This share has even increased between 2000 and 2014, indicating that GVCs are becoming more global (Los et al., 2015).

Within each market, there are also important changes over time. In East Asia, there is a clear shift between Japan and China, particularly in the automotive industry, computer and electronics, and the food and beverages GVCs. Again, the income derived from GVCs has increased significantly between 2000 and 2014, and Japan has lost a market share that it could not have kept in a much bigger East Asian market now dominated by Chinese consumers. Even Korea has diminishing shares with the rise of China. But Korea has increased its share of GVC income for computer and electronics, which is quite remarkable in the context of growing Chinese final demand.

In the EU, the core countries at the origin of the European construction tend to maintain their share of GVC income. EU enlargement countries have increased their contribution to EU value chains, particularly in the automotive industry and in computer and electronics. But overall they still account for a relatively low overall share of the GVC income in Europe, due to their small size as compared to the larger economies in the EU15 group.

In the North American market, there are mixed results for Mexico. While China in East Asia or EU enlargement countries in the EU have increasing shares of GVC income in all industries, it is not the case for Mexico in North America. The country is catching up in the automotive industry, in textiles and apparel, and food and beverages but has not increased its share of GVC income in the other industries. In these other industries, the US has largely maintained its GVC income. It means that the decreasing shares that were observed in Figure 15.1 for the US in most industries are explained by a loss in GVC income in extra-regional markets.

As the regional character of GVCs in Figure 15.2 is to some extent driven by the size of the final demand in domestic markets, Figure 15.3 calculates the GVC income without the domestic contribution, i.e. the value added by domestic firms in products sold domestically. It means that when a car is sold in the US, only the contribution of countries other than the US is taken into account. The value added by US producers to products sold in the US is omitted (but the value added by Mexican and Canadian producers is kept in the calculation for the North American market).

Figure 15.3 is overall not very different from Figure 15.2. The absolute numbers for GVC income are – not surprisingly – significantly smaller when removing the domestic contribution (for example, total GVC income for the textiles and apparel industry in East Asia is US$240 million without the domestic contribution, as opposed to US$436 million when it is included). But the allocation of GVC income across countries remains largely the same. For example, China still accounts for more than 80 per cent of GVC income in the textiles and apparel industry when only taking into account the sales in other East Asian economies and no longer the sales in China. It means that the results are not driven by domestic outcomes and that when focusing on the value added that has been traded we really see international production networks.

There are, however, differences between Figure 15.3 and Figure 15.2. For example, while China maintains its GVC income share in the textiles and apparel industry, the story is different for the automotive industry. Due to product characteristics but also policies supporting domestic producers, the car manufacturing industry is less 'globalised' than other GVCs (Van Biesebroeck and Sturgeon, 2010). China accounts for a much smaller share of GVC income in Figure 15.3 as compared to Figure 15.2 (60 per cent against 20 per cent). One could argue that the car manufacturing industry is nascent in China and not yet well established in other countries in the region, but the same is observed for the US in the North American market. The US share of GVC income is above 60 per cent when including US value added in US final demand and

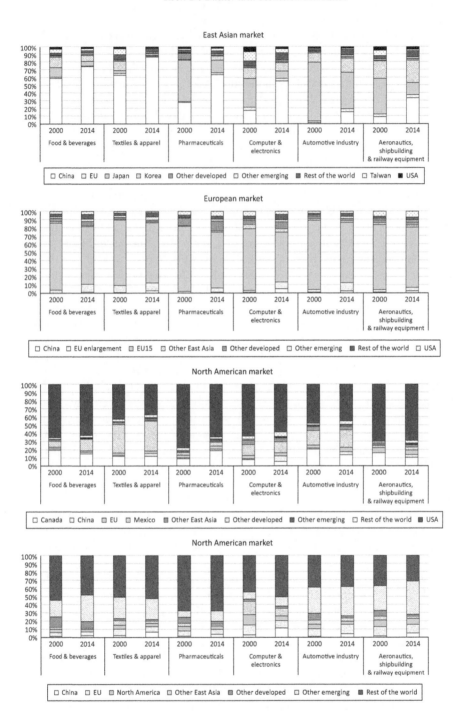

Figure 15.3 GVC income without the domestic VA in domestic final demand, in 2000 and 2014, share by country in each regional market (%). (Source: Calculations by the authors based on WIOD, November 2016 update.)

below 50 per cent when only taking into account US value added in Canadian and Mexican final demand.

The lower shares of income for the US imply higher shares for Mexico and Canada in the automotive GVC. It is also the case in textiles and apparel where the important role of Mexico is shown in Figure 15.3. Generally speaking, the calculation of the GVC income without the domestic value-added in domestic final demand provides more insights on the international specialisation of countries and global part of GVCs.

For the EU, high shares of GVC income are still observed for the EU15 group, but because data are at the level of EU Member States and 'domestic' does not remove the intra-EU trade, the exercise of removing the domestic VA in domestic final demand does not change the results too much. But it also highlights the high degree of economic integration within the EU.

15.3.4 Results: GVC income and functional specialisation

Finally in Figure 15.4, a further decomposition is introduced based on business functions. The GVC literature assumes that countries specialise in different activities in the value chain and often refers to the business functions described by Porter (1985). The GVC income previously described identifies the contribution of the US or China to the textiles and apparel industry, but this contribution could be of a very different nature, such as branding and marketing in the US and assembly in China. Based on labour force surveys and the composition of occupations by country and industry, the OECD has created a data set that allows decomposing the value-added in each country and industry according to the business activity it contributes to. These data are used in Figure 15.4 to check whether there is a specialisation in activities or business functions in GVCs, i.e. functional specialisation.

The answer is that there is such specialisation, but again it is important to distinguish the place of consumption. For example, in the EU, assembly and core manufacturing activities still play a significant role for textiles and apparel products sold in the European market. But in other markets, the EU value added is more in R&D and IT support functions, as well as management and administrative support functions. The same is observed for the US, but interestingly US companies exporting to or selling in Asia are as much involved in operations as those focusing on the North American market. It is only in the European market that US value added is more in the support services functions and less in core manufacturing.

Still looking at the textiles and apparel GVC, 'other developed economies' (a group with Australia, Canada, Norway and Switzerland) are even more focused on R&D in products sold in North America and not at all on operations. These data clearly point to the specialisation in specific business functions when it comes to extra-regional exports of value added.

The GVC literature has often emphasised that there is a 'smile curve'[6] with developing countries specialising in the assembly of products or core manufacturing activities in the middle of the value chain and developed countries focusing on higher value-added activities at both ends (R&D, design, logistics, marketing, sales). Figure 15.4 reveals such patterns but also highlights three important aspects that may not be well captured in the smile curve. First, the specialisation of countries in business functions is not complete. We can see that China derives on average more GVC income from operations than from R&D and IT support. But differences in shares are relatively small. In all GVCs and in all countries, companies need a similar mix of business functions to carry out their activities. Firms specialising in core manufacturing also require logistics, IT, administrative support and if some of these business functions are outsourced, they are often outsourced in the domestic economy. Therefore, we can only see slight differences in

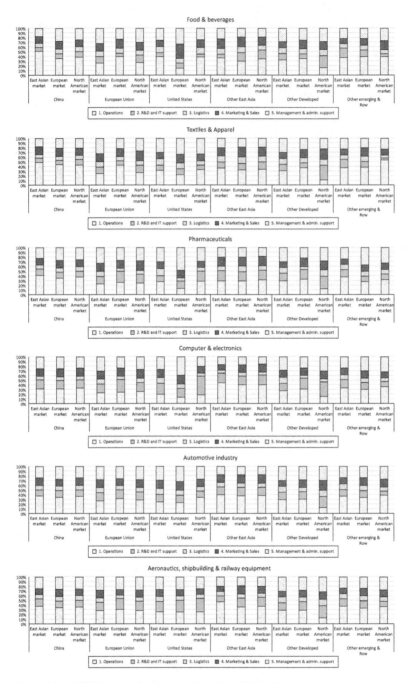

Figure 15.4 GVC income by business function, 2014, share by country in each regional market (%).
(Source: Calculations by the authors based on WIOD, November 2016 update.)

the mix of business functions highlighting some specialisation in one activity rather than the other.

Second, as illustrated with EU operations in the textiles and apparel value chain for products sold in the EU, there is also a regional dimension in this specialisation in business functions. It is generally outside their 'native' market that countries appear more specialised in specific types of activities.

Last, Figure 15.4 confirms the role of the 'non-core' manufacturing activities in deriving income from manufacturing GVCs. The share of GVC income going to operations is on average around 30 per cent with differences across industries. It is higher for the traditional industries, such as textiles and apparel or food and beverages, and lower for high-tech sectors, such as computer and electronics. But even in the textiles and apparel GVC, the share of GVC income going to services support functions is higher than 60 per cent. It points out the important role of services and intangible assets in determining the distribution of income in the value chain.

15.4 The determinants of income in GVCs

As illustrated in the previous sections, the benefits that countries and companies draw from GVCs are indeed unevenly distributed across the value chain. The results have confirmed that pre-production (R&D, design, etc.) and post-production (marketing, logistics, etc.) are creating more value added than pure production activities. This section aims to shed light to what extent do particular services and intellectual assets determine the location of production activities across countries and industries. As such, the discussion links the literature on GVCs with the growing literature on servitisation of national economies.

15.4.1 Services as value-creating activities

From Adam Smith (1776) to the latest growth theories, the division of labour has been at the heart of explanations of productivity growth. GVCs are just the next level in the international division of labour. They have contributed to the upward shift in productivity observed from the mid-1990s to the mid-2000s. Trade, and not just the information and communications technology (ICT) revolution, has increased growth (Feenstra et al., 2013).

In this process, the first role that was identified for services in the value chain is the role they play in linking manufacturing activities across countries.[7] In order to manage production processes that are geographically split, companies need services such as transport, communication, logistics and finance (Jones and Kierzkowski, 2001). Without these service links, there would be no global value chain.

But services are not just the glue in global value chains (Low, 2013). There are important services inputs that go beyond linking activities across countries. For example, any value chain starts with some R&D, design and engineering activities that are service inputs when outsourced. At the other end of the value chain are also found other services such as marketing and distribution that are per se important production stages and not just links in the value chain. Therefore, the service links can be seen as part of a broader category of services inputs that are not only support functions to enable the value chain but also important inputs in key stages of production.

Some of these service inputs are horizontal in the sense that they are needed by any type of company in any value chain, while others are specific to certain value chains in the manufacturing sector. For example, Gereffi and Fernandez-Stark (2010) discuss in detail GVCs in business services by explicitly distinguishing between horizontal activities (e.g. business consulting, market intelligence, legal services, accounting, training, marketing and sales) and vertical activities (e.g. investment research in the finance sector, risk management for insurance services, industrial engineering for specific manufacturing sectors, clinical tests in the health and pharmaceutical industry).

It is now acknowledged that services are increasingly tradable and that potential welfare gains from trade liberalisation in services are as high as in the manufacturing sector (Gervais and Jensen, 2013). Trade theory has evolved to add to the classic framework explaining trade in goods new theories explaining trade in tasks (Grossman and Rossi-Hansberg, 2008; Baldwin and Robert-Nicoud, 2014). Trade in tasks accounts for the fact that not only final goods are traded but also intermediate goods and services through offshoring.

An important result from this literature is that trade in tasks leads to productivity through an effect analogous to factor-augmenting technological change, thus highlighting that services are also adding value through trade. Growth theories have also emphasised that trade in intermediate goods and services improves the allocation of capital and labour across sectors and countries (Jones, 2011).

Moreover, firms producing goods are increasingly selling them together with services (De Backer et al., 2015; Cadestin and Miroudot, 2017). These services are generally needed for the customer to make use of the product. For example, machines are exported with installation, engineering, maintenance and repair services. There is an export contract that covers both goods and services as part of an integrated system or solution. The bundle is generally proposed as a cost-saving solution for the customer. This phenomenon, known as 'servitisation' (Vandermerwe and Rada, 1988), allows firms to add more value and to create a long-term relationship with customers that will generate income not only when the good is sold but all along its life until it is replaced. Consumers also benefit by not having to deal with multiple companies and avoiding the hassle of getting all the needed services separately over time.

But the story would not be complete without also emphasising that the servitisation of manufacturing goes together with digitalisation and the innovation of new business models where companies push customer service to new levels. The consumer himself can become associated with the production process through a community or through tailored solutions. As such, the servitisation is not just the result of more people working in services or a higher share of value added originating in the service sector. It is a shift towards more productive and more customer-centric production models where value can be seen as co-created with consumers. This result is highlighted in the recent literature suggesting looking at services as part of a 'service science' (Dermirkan et al., 2011; Cinquini et al., 2013).[8]

This servitisation is therefore not limited to manufacturing sectors. The way services industries operate has also changed in the recent period. In the financial, transport, telecoms, distribution and other business services sectors, companies have broadened the range of services they provide and created new types of relationships with customers. For example, banks offer a variety of services through 'packages' that combine insurance services, payment services, legal services, access to advice or investment tools, etc. Telecom operators provide 'triple play' or 'quad play' services that combine fixed telephony, mobile services, access to internet, television and additional digital content – in some cases through third parties – while also renting the required hardware. Services companies themselves provide more services and solutions closer to consumers' needs.

15.4.2 *The role of intangible assets*

Intangible assets or knowledge capital (OECD, 2013b) are a second determinant of GVC income. The higher levels of value creation in certain upstream and downstream activities are typically dependent on highly tacit, non-codified knowledge in areas such as original design, and the creation and management of cutting-edge technology and complex systems, as well as management or organisational know-how. Success in GVCs is increasingly based on innovation and the ability to supply sophisticated and hard-to-imitate products and services. Innovation, in turn, is dependent on intangible assets such as brands, basic R&D, design and the complex integration of software with business models and organisational structures.

OECD (2013a) research has shown that the positive link between intangible assets and success in GVCs with countries heavily investing in knowledge-based capital were likely to create and capture more value from their exports. In addition, the empirical analysis also showed that more and better intangible assets promoted the export competitiveness of countries and industries internationally.

Investments in knowledge capital drive productivity growth and determine the extent to which the final product of a value chain can be differentiated in consumer markets. In addition, intangible assets allow companies to shape the architecture of GVCs and to capture a larger share of the value. Superior capabilities allow firms to innovate and compete in their own markets segment but also to change the competitive conditions of the whole value chain. For example, much of the success of recent Apple products is due to specific design features which allow Apple to govern the whole value chain.

Intangible assets are much broader than investments in R&D, which in the past were typically considered as the basis for innovation and competitiveness. In general, different types of intangible assets play a role in GVCs: (a) computerised information – software and databases; (b) innovative property – R&D and non-R&D innovative expenditures including copyrights, designs and trademarks; and (c) economic competencies – brand equity, firm-specific skills (technological and managerial), networks and organisational structures. The value that a firm creates within a GVC critically depends on the difficulty for rivals to supply similar or substitutable products. When a product is easy to replicate, e.g. when it is not tacit, or when it is not protected by intellectual property rights (IPRs), rival firms can easily develop substitutes for the inputs that a firm provides to a GVC.

Economic competencies, which include firm-specific skills such as superior management, brand equity and organisational structure, are, in general, more tacit forms of knowledge and may therefore be more difficult to replicate than innovative property or computerised information. In practice, it is often the complex combination of multiple intangible assets that acts as the source of firms' competitive advantage. For example, some firms integrate simulations of product design and workplace organisation based on large computerised data sets – often referred to as 'big data' – to achieve faster product introduction and greater efficiency. Nevertheless, even a cutting-edge technology may not be a sustainable source of value in a GVC if it can easily be replicated by rivals.

15.4.3 Co-operation between firms and business ecosystems

In addition to interactions with customers and the benefits of investing in knowledge and capabilities, the recent literature also emphasises that income can be created with competitors or with other firms in a co-operative environment. Individual firms no longer compete as stand-alone entities but increasingly through a complex portfolio of partnerships. The (academic) research on co-operation between firms is vast and growing, discussing the different forms, motives, activities (R&D, innovation, production), strategies, etc. of inter-firm relationships. Instead of discussing the most important conclusions of this research,[9] this chapter aims to provide some insights on how firms are co-operating in their (global) value chains.

The 'relational value chain' is one of the five types of value chain governance described in the seminal paper by Gereffi et al. (2005). This type of value chain is based on trust and mutual dependence as well as also knowledge sharing (generally complex information that creates some kind of community). This relational value chain is also close to a more recent strand of the literature focusing on 'business ecosystems'. As explained by Moore (1993), companies are not members of a single industry; they evolve in some kind of 'ecosystem' at the intersection of many industries. In this context, they build a competitive advantage through a cooperative network.

As noted by Nokia's CEO in 2011, analysing the reasons why his company could not face the competition of Apple, Android and new entrants in the mobile phone industry: "Our competitors aren't taking our market share with devices; they are taking our market share with an entire ecosystem". Nokia was a very efficient and innovative firm, but it suddenly realised that it could not produce something similar to the iPhone or Android phones because it did not have all the partners and the technological environment brought by Apple and Google to the industry.

Platforms are very powerful types of ecosystems, and while very popular today in the digital economy they are in fact not so new. The creation of Visa in 1976 was also a cooperative effort in the banking industry to develop consumer credit cards. The central point is that value is created both through co-operation and competition. This aspect cannot be well captured in empirical data but can also explain how firms capture a high share of the GVC income and are able to maintain this advantage over time.

15.5 Conclusion and policy implications

World trade, investment and production are increasingly structured around GVCs. While the international fragmentation of production across countries is not new, the increasing scale and scope of GVCs is very different from the past. The growth of GVCs has increased the interconnectedness of economies and led to a growing specialisation in specific activities and stages in value chains, rather than in entire industries. In addition, trade in GVCs involves extensive flows of intermediate goods and services.

There is a need to better understand how global value chains work, how they affect economic performance and what policies can help countries in drawing the benefits from engagement in global value chains. In addition to product/industry case studies, the rapid growing input–output analysis on GVCs allows for more aggregate insights. This chapter has focused on the concept of GVC income – i.e. how much value added and income countries create within GVCs globally and within more regional value chains. The results show how the creation of value changes along the value chain and how this value dispersion is dependent on different business functions within industries and countries.

In addition, the chapter has discussed how services, intangible assets, new business models and ecosystems are increasingly affecting the growth of GVCs. Companies increasingly include these determinants in their (GVC) strategies to cooperate with GVC partners, stay abreast of competitors and capture value from their activities in GVCs.

While GVCs are the result of companies' strategies, government policies are significantly affected by the emergence and growth of GVCs. The effects are not only visible for trade policy, where the emergence of GVCs calls for a reassessment of a range of trade policies, but also for investment policies, innovation policies, and a range of framework and structural policies that affect how and to what extent countries, including emerging and developing economies, can draw benefits from their engagement in global value chains.

The OECD, together with other international organisations, has in recent years published ample works enlarging the evidence base of GVCs and discussing the policy implications of GVCs across a broad range of domains. They will continue to do so, as this work is far from finished.

Notes

1 Inter-country (or multi-regional) input-`output tables (ICIOs or MRIOs) link national accounts across countries in order to identify inter-industry relationships not only within a given country but also with industries located in other economies. When including all countries in the world, the tables provide a summary of all domestic and international transactions in the world economy. Examples of global ICIO include the World Input-Output Database (WIOD) project, the OECD–WTO Trade in Value Added (TiVA) initiative and EORA, a global MRIO developed by the University of Sydney.

2 They focus on manufacturing industries because the GVC framework describes production processes that are more relevant for this sector. To analyse services industries, alternative models are needed (Miroudot and Cadestin, 2017).

3 De Backer and Miroudot (2013) provide estimates of the participation in GVCs, length of value chain and distance to final demand for a large number of countries and industries, using the OECD–WTO TiVA database.

4 In addition to the 28 EU economies, the WIOD data set covers Australia, Brazil, Canada, China, India, Indonesia, Japan, Korea, Mexico, Norway, Russia, Switzerland, Taiwan, Turkey and the US. There is in addition a 'rest of the world' with data aggregated for all other economies in the world.

5 The previous edition of the WIOD database included tables in previous year prices. But these data have not been updated for the 2016 release. They also have methodological issues, as in the absence of detailed price information for all inputs used in all industries, the construction of I-O tables in constant prices is quite challenging.

6 The concept of the smile curve was first introduced in the 1990s by Stan Shih, the founder and CEO of Acer, in the context of the computer and electronics industry. See Baldwin and Evenett (2012).

7 The growing importance of services as intermediate inputs – and more broadly, the whole discussion about manufacturing and services – suffers to some extent from measurement and classification error. Outsourcing of services activities is more common today than it was in the past, not only entire service functions but also individual services tasks. For example, in-house service activities that have been outsourced by vertically integrated manufacturing companies (cleaning, transport, etc.) are now better reflected in the available statistics on services, while before they were hidden in manufacturing data.

8 The term 'service science' was first introduced by IBM and was then relabelled 'Service Science, Management and Engineering' (SSME). It is now promoted within an industry consortium called the 'Service Research and Innovation Institute' (SRII) to which all major IT companies belong.

9 Overview articles/books of this heterogeneous and vast research have been provided in the management and strategy literature, e.g. Li (2015).

References

Antràs, P., D. Chor, T. Fally and R. Hillberry (2012), "Measuring the upstreamness of production and trade flows", *American Economic Review*, 102/3, pp. 412–416, http://dx.doi.org/10.1257/aer.102.3.412.

Appelbaum, R.P. and G. Gereffi (1994), "Power and profits in the apparel commodity chain", in E. Bonacich et al. (eds.), *Global Production: The Apparel Industry in the Pacific Rim*, Temple University Press, Philadelphia, PA, pp. 42–64.

Baldwin, R. and S. Evenett (2012), "Value creation and trade in 21st century manufacturing: What policies for UK manufacturing?", in D. Greenaway (ed.), *The UK in a Global World: How Can the UK Focus on Steps in Global Value Chains that Really Add Value?*, CEPR, London, pp. 71–128.

Baldwin, R. and F. Robert-Nicoud (2014), "Trade-in-goods and trade-in-tasks: An integrating framework", *Journal of International Economics*, 92/1, pp. 51–62, http://dx.doi.org/10.1016/j.jinteco.2013.10.002.

Cadestin, De Backer, Desnoyers-James, Miroudot, Rigo and Ye. (2018). "*Multinational Enterprises and Global Value Chains, New Insights on the Trade-Investment Nexus*", OECD, Science, Technology and Industry Working Paper, No. 2018/05, https://doi.org/10.1787/194ddb63-en.

Cinquini, L., A. Di Minin and A. Varaldo (eds.) (2013), *New Business Models and Value Creation: A Service Science Perspective*, Springer-Verlag, Mailand, http://dx.doi.org/10.1007/978-88-470-2838-8.

De Backer, K., I. Desnoyers-James and L. Moussiegt (2015), "*Manufacturing or Services – That is (not) the Question: The Role of Manufacturing and Services in OECD Economies*", OECD Science, Technology and Innovation Policy Paper, No. 19, OECD Publishing, Paris, http://dx.doi.org/10.1787/5js6 4ks09dmn-en.

De Backer, K. and S. Miroudot (2013), "*Mapping Global Value Chains*", OECD Trade Policy Papers, No. 159, OECD Publishing, Paris, http://dx.doi.org/10.1787/5k3v1trgnbr4-en.

Dedrick, J., K. Kraemer and G. Linden (2008), "Who profits from innovation in global value chains? A study of the iPod and notebook PCs", Paper prepared for the Sloan Industry Studies Annual Conference, Boston, MA.

Demirkan, H., J. Spohrer and V. Krishna (eds.) (2011), *The Science of Service Systems*, Springer, New York, http://dx.doi.org/10.1007/978-1-4419-8270-4.

Fally, T. (2012). "*Production Staging: Measurement and Facts*", University of Colorado-Boulder, August.

Feenstra, R., B. Mandel, M. Reinsdorf and M. Slaughter (2013), "Effects of terms of trade gains and tariff changes on the measurement of US productivity growth", *American Economic Journal: Economic Policy*, 5/1, pp. 59–93, http://dx.doi.org/10.1257/pol.5.1.59.

Foster-McGregor, N. and R. Stehrer (2013), "Value added content of trade: A comprehensive approach", *Economics Letters*, 120/2, pp. 354–357.

Gereffi, G. and K. Fernandez-Stark (2010), "The offshore services value chain: Developing countries and the crisis", in O. Cattaneo, G. Gereffi and C. Staritz (eds.), *Global Value Chains in a Postcrisis World: A Development Perspective*, The World Bank, Washington, DC.

Gereffi, G., J. Humphrey and T. Sturgeon (2005), "The governance of global value chains", *Review of International Political Economy*, 12/1, pp. 78–104.

Gervais, A. and B. Jensen (2013), "*The Tradability of Services: Geographic Concentration and Trade Costs*", NBER Working Papers, No. 19759, National Bureau of Economic Research.

Grossman, G. and E. Rossi-Hansberg (2008), "Trading tasks: A simple theory of offshoring", *American Economic Review*, 98/5, pp. 1978–1997, http://dx.doi.org/10.1257/aer.98.5.1978.

Hummels, D., J. Ishii and K.-M. Yi (2001), "The nature and growth of vertical specialization in world trade", *Journal of International Economics*, 54/1, pp. 75–96, https://doi.org/10.1016/S0022 -1996(00)00093-3.

Johnson, R. and G. Noguera (2012), "Accounting for intermediates: Production sharing and trade in value added", *Journal of International Economics*, 86/2, pp. 224–236, http://dx.doi.org/10.1016/j.jinteco.2011 .10.003.

Jones, C.I. (2011), "Intermediate goods and weak links in the theory of economic development", *American Economic Journal: Macroeconomics*, 3/2, pp. 1–28, http://dx.doi.org/10.1257/mac.3.2.1.

Jones, R. and H. Kierzkowski (2001), "A framework for fragmentation", in S. Arndt and H. Kierzkowski (eds.), *Fragmentation: New Production Patterns in the World Economy*, Oxford University Press, New York, NY, pp. 17–34.

Koopman, R., Z. Wang and S.-J. Wei (2012), "Estimating domestic content in exports when processing trade is pervasive", *Journal of Development Economics*, 99/1, pp. 178–189, http://dx.doi.org/10.1016/j.jd eveco.2011.12.004.

Koopman, R., Z. Wang and S.-J. Wei (2014), "Tracing value-added and double counting in gross exports", *American Economic Review*, 104/2, pp. 459–494, http://dx.doi.org/10.1257/aer.104.2.459.

Li, D. (2015), *International Strategic Alliances*, Oxford University Press, Oxford, UK.

Los, B., M. Timmer and G. de Vries (2015), "How global are global value chains? A new approach to measure international fragmentation", *Journal of Regional Science*, 55/1, pp. 66–92, http://dx.doi.org/10.1111 /jors.12121.

Low, P. (2013), "*The Role of Services in Global Value Chains*", Real Sector Working Paper, Fung Global Institute.

Miroudot, S. and C. Cadestin (2017), "*Services in Global Value Chains: From Inputs to Value-Creating Activities*", OECD Trade Policy Papers, No. 197, OECD Publishing, Paris, http://dx.doi.org/10 .1787/465f0d8b-en.

Moore, J.F. (1993), "Predators and prey: A new ecology of competition", *Harvard Business Review*, 71/3, pp. 75–86.

Nagengast, A.J. and R. Stehrer (2016), "Accounting for the differences between gross and value added trade balances", *The World Economy*, 39/9, pp. 1276–1306, http://dx.doi.org/10.1111/twec.12401.

Nomaler, O. and B. Verspagen (2014), "*Analysing Global Value Chains Using Input-Output Economics: Proceed with Care*", UNU-MERIT Working Paper Series, 2014–070, United Nations University.

OECD (2013a), "*Interconnected Economies – Benefiting from Global Value Chains*", OECD Publishing, Paris, http://dx.doi.org/10.1787/9789264189560-en.

OECD (2013b), "*Supporting Investment in Knowledge Capital, Growth and Innovation*", OECD Publishing, Paris, http://dx.doi.org/10.1787/9789264193307-en.

Porter, M. (1985), *Competitive Advantage: Creating and Sustaining Superior Performance*, The Free Press, New York.

Smith, A. (1776), *An Inquiry into the Nature and Causes of the Wealth of Nations*, Strahan and Cadell, London

Sturgeon, T., P.B. Nielsen, G. Linden, G. Gereffi and C. Brown (2013), "Direct measurement of global value chains: collecting product- and firm-level statistics on value added and business function outsourcing and offshoring", in A. Mattoo, Z. Wang and S.-J. Wei (eds.), *Trade in Value Added: Developing New Measures of Cross-Border Trade*, CEPR and World Bank, Washington, DC, pp. 291–321.

Timmer, M.P., E. Dietzenbacher, B. Los, R. Stehrer and G.J. de Vries (2015), "An illustrated user guide to the world input–output database: The case of global automotive production", *Review of International Economics*, 23, pp. 575–605, http://dx.doi.org/10.1111/roie.12178.

Timmer, M.P., B. Los, R. Stehrer and G.J. de Vries (2013), "Fragmentation, incomes and jobs: an analysis of European competitiveness", *Economic Policy*, 28/76, pp. 613–661, http://dx.doi.org/10.1111/1468-0327.12018.

Timmer, M.P., B. Los, R. Stehrer and G.J. de Vries (2016), "An Anatomy of the Global Trade Slowdown based on the WIOD 2016 Release", GGDC research memorandum number 162, December.

Timmer, M.P., S. Miroudot and G.J. de Vries (2019), "Functional Specialisation in Trade", *Journal of Economic Geography*, 19/1, pp. 1–30.

Van Biesebroeck, J. and T.J. Sturgeon (2010), "Effects of the 2008–09 crisis on the automotive industry in developing countries: A global value chain perspective", in O. Cattaneo, G. Gereffi and C. Staritz (eds.), *Global Value Chains in a Postcrisis World*, The World Bank, Washington, pp. 209–244, http://dx.doi.org/10.1596/978-0-8213-8499-2.

Vandermerwe, S. and J. Rada (1988), "Servitization of business: Adding value by adding services", *European Management Journal*, 6/4, pp. 314–324.

16

GLOBAL VALUE CHAIN AT A CROSSROADS

A trade and investment perspective[1]

Quan Zhao, Wenwen Sheng, Wei Zhang and Jimena Sotelo

16.1 Introduction

Trade and investment have been key drivers for the emergence and evolution of global value chains (GVCs). Technological advances coupled with the removal of policy barriers led to reduced costs for cross-border trade and increased foreign direct investment (FDI), making it possible to organize production and distribution across different parts of the world along the value chains.

The increased GVC activities have been an underpinning trend in the global economy for the past decades. However, recent figures suggest that it may have arrived at a crossroads. Global trade and investment growth, often seen as key indicators for GVC activities, are witnessing a significant slowdown in the decade following the financial crisis.

Trade figures show that world merchandise trade grew by 3.0% in 2018, just above the 2.9% increase in world GDP over the same period. This is in sharp contrast to the two decades before the financial crisis: during 1985–2007, global trade has been growing at twice the rate of global GDP. FDI activity has also continued a downward trend since 2013. The average annual growth of global FDI inflow was around 8% in 2000–2007, but plunged to just 1% in post-crisis years from 2008–2018.

Multiple factors are contributing to this tectonic shift in global economic landscape, including the increasing trade tension among the world's largest trade nations, disruptive new technologies and business models that reshaped supply chains, as well as evolutions in intra-regional and inter-regional GVC activities.

These new developments will have a significant impact on the future of GVCs. Through a trade and investment lens, this chapter reviews the underpinning trends that have shaped GVCs formulation and growth, examines whether the slowdown in GVC activities are due to cyclical or structural factors, and attempts to explore issues that will determine the future evolution of GVCs.

DOI: 10.4324/9781315225661-22

Section 16.2 of this chapter focuses on the linkages between global trade, investment and GVC activities. It reviews the fundamental role of trade and investment in enabling fragmented production and distribution across the globe, formulating and shaping GVC in the decades up to the turning point.

Section 16.3 focuses on the recent stagnation in trade and investment and their implications for GVCs. It examines the structural factors that are behind the slowdown in trade and invest growth, including the impact of technologies, shortening of the value chains, servicification of manufacturing and rising labor cost in emerging economies, as well as shifts in the trade policies.

Section 16.4 explores issues that will determine the future evolution of GVCs, taking into account the current trade tension and rapid evolution in technologies that will have an impact on future GVCs and associated megatrends. It will also discuss ways to make GVCs more inclusive and sustainable, enabling more developing countries to participate and benefit from GVCs.

Technological advances and GVC-related policies are two story lines embedded in each section, as both are key determinants shaping the global value chains. The interplay between these two factors have created conditions for the birth of GVCs and will shed light on its future megatrends.

16.2 Trade and investment as engines for GVC formulation and growth

Trade and investment are essential for GVCs. In fact, GVC participation is defined and measured as the share of a country's exports that is part of a multistage trade process, by adding to the foreign value added used in a country's own exports and the value added supplied to other countries' exports (UNCTAD, 2013).

Over the past decades, global trade and GVC activities have grown in tandem. It is difficult to separate the drivers behind increases in international trade from those behind the fragmentation of production (Antras et al., 2012; De Backer and Miroudot, 2014). The same is true for the expansion of FDI, which is the reflection of increased GVC activities by multinational corporations. International trade and investment have enabled GVC activities, which in turn spurred more cross-border flow of goods, services and capital.

It is widely accepted that the key drivers for the international fragmentation of production could be attributed to reduced costs for transport and deployment of new information communications technology (ICT) and associated technological solutions, and removal of policy barriers to trade and investment. These factors have changed the nature of economic globalization by deepening GVC specializations geographically (by including more countries, in particular emerging economies), sectorally (by not only transforming manufacturing but also increasingly services industries) and functionally (by including not only production and distribution but also reach and development and innovation).

16.2.1 Decline of trade costs enables fragmentation of production

Economists have well explained how declining trade costs due to technological progress facilitate the formulation of GVCs, such as the unbundling theory proposed by Baldwin (2006). Broadly defined trade costs include all costs incurred in getting a good to a final user other than the marginal cost of producing the good itself. Trade costs therefore may consist of transportation costs, information costs, contract enforcement costs, costs associated with the use of different currencies, legal and regulatory costs, and local distribution costs (Anderson and Wincoop, 2004).

Trade costs matter to trade flows and is of particular importance in the context of GVCs, as the segmentation of production across the world involves import and export of intermediate products, and sophisticated GVC operations may require parts and components to cross borders multiples times. Accumulation of associated trade costs may amount to a significant determinant for the success of GVC operations.

The determining effect of trade costs on GVCs is reflected in the heterogeneity of different sectors in GVC participation, as trade costs vary significantly across the sectors (Hoekman, 2014). Trade costs vary by a factor larger than four between the highest (food products) and the lowest (mining). Overall, trade costs increase the import price by a margin of 20% to the international price of competing imports (averaged across all sectors in 2011), 17% for non-tariff costs and 3% for tariff costs, including a 2.5% preference margin (Escaith, 2017).

Advancements in transportation and ICT have led to a dramatic fall in trade costs and "flattening of the world." Containerization made it easier for products to be shipped and transported rapidly at low cost. Research by the World Trade Organization (WTO) (2018) shows that international trade costs declined by 15% between 1996 and 2014, and the trend was similar for trade among developed ("North–North") and between developed and developing ("North–South") countries (Figure 16.1).

Reduced trade costs have allowed multinational companies to break apart production processes and relocated segments of production abroad, which has contributed to the rapid expansion and deepening of GVCs.

16.2.2 Reduction of policy barriers to trade and investment

Reduction of policy barriers has been an important driver of trade, in general, and of GVC growth, in particular. Rounds of trade negotiations under the General Agreement on Tariffs and Trade (GATT) have brought down tariffs across both developed and developing countries. The pace of globalization has significantly accelerated since the end of the Cold War. Significant tariff reductions in developing countries have brought them closer into the GVC production: from 1990 to 2014, the average tariff in emerging economies has reduced from more than 35% to around 10% (Figure 16.2). This has enabled developing countries to import intermediary inputs at a lower cost, and attracted multinationals to offshore production to take advantage of lower labor and land costs.

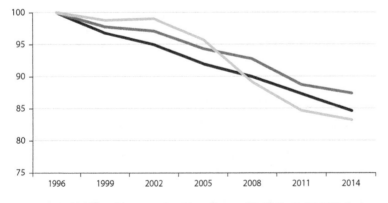

Figure 16.1 Overall trade costs, 1996–2014. (Source: World Bank-ESCAP database on International trade costs.)

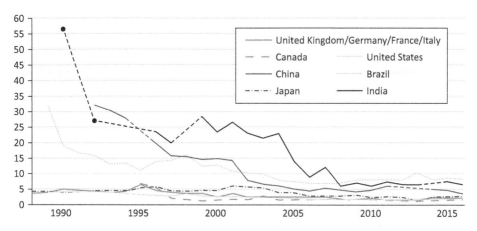

Figure 16.2 Tariff reduction in developed and developing economies. Note: Shows word's ten largest economics, 2016. Rates are weighted by trade value. Dotted lines indicate years when data are not available. (Source: World Bank DataBank.)

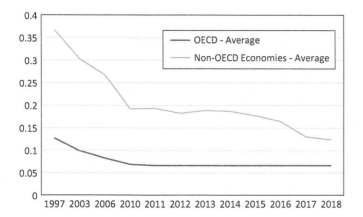

Figure 16.3 OECD FDI Regulatory Restrictiveness Index. (Source: OECD Statistics.)

Regional integration has also been a key factor for GVC growth. Value chain trade is highly regionalized, supported by a combination of deep regional trade agreements (RTAs), bilateral investment treaties (BITs) and unilateral reforms. The reduction of tariffs, especially for manufactured goods, and the gradual lowering of nontariff barriers not only facilitated trade in goods and services but also have a positive impact on boosting cross-border investment (Grossman and Rossi-Hansberg, 2008).

Liberalization of cross-border investment is another key contributor for GVCs. Since the 1980s, developing countries have gradually opened their industries to foreign investment and removed investment restrictions (Figure 16.3). Rapid reduction in FDI restrictiveness in developing countries in the first decade of the millennium has allowed investors, in particular multinationals from developed countries, to increasingly organize and disperse their production processes on a global scale.

Apart from liberalization measures, cross-border investment is also facilitated by the increasing number of BITs, which contributed to safeguarding the interests of the investors. As of the end of 2017, there were more than 3200 BITs signed, with participation of almost every country in the world (UNCTAD, 2017). BITs provide legal commitments to secure fair and equitable treatment for foreign investors, decreasing investment risk and facilitating cross-border investment.

Trade and investment liberalization alone cannot ensure participation in GVC. Institutional quality is another fundamentally important factor, as efficiency of institutions can influence the enforceability of contracts and protection of property rights, thus reducing uncertainties and increasing profitability (Alfaro et al., 2004; Hsiao and Shen, 2003). Institutional quality in the host countries play a crucial role in determining the local sourcing strategies of foreign investors. Countries with better institutions, such as stronger property rights and rule of law, are able to better participate in GVCs. This also applies to regions within a country, for example, cities in China that score better on property rights and government efficiency are more likely to have firms involved in GVCs. The wave of increased GVC activities has also pushed for reforms and improvements in institutional quality of the developing countries, which paves the way for their long-term sustainable development.

16.2.3 Trade and investment nexus for advanced GVCs

Trade and investment are historically viewed as separate tracks and can be substitutive to each other. However, as GVCs evolved into more sophisticated production networks across different countries, a stronger trade–investment nexus is needed to ensure functioning of GVCs.

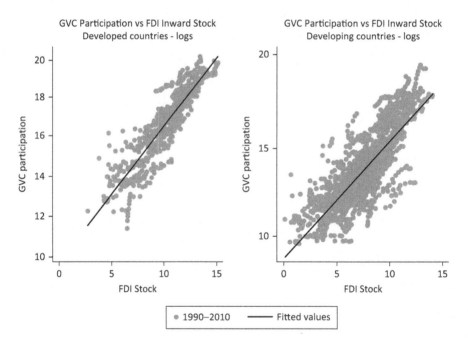

Figure 16.4 Correlation between levels of inward FDI stock and GVC participation. (Source: OECD (2013).) Note: Data for 187 countries over 20 years. The regression of the annual GVC participation growth on the annual FDI inward (stock) growth yields a positive and significant correlation (at the 5 per cent level) both for developed and developing countries (R2 = 0.77 and 0.44, respectively). The correlation remains significant considering the two time periods 1990 - 2000 and 2001 - 2010 separately. Regressions use lagged (one year) inward FDI (stock) growth rates and include year fixed effects to account for unobserved heterogeneity.

This trade and investment nexus requires greater depth of openness and coordination among countries. Services, intellectual property rights (IPRs), investments and standards are becoming increasingly important to ensure unimpeded flow of goods, services, capital and IP (Baldwin 2013).

These linkages between value chains, trade and operation of multinational companies (responsible for the lion's share of global FDI) in generating value-added trade is confirmed by a series of quantitative analysis. As shown in Figure 16.4, the correlation between bilateral FDI stock in host countries and their GVC participation rates is strongly positive, and the country-level relationship is strong for both developed and developing countries.

16.3 GVC at a crossroads: Global trade and investment slowdown and its implication on GVCs

The global financial crisis of 2008–2009 marked a turning point in global trade and foreign direct investment. In the decade after the crisis, growth in global trade and investment have stagnated. Along with the subdued trade and investments, global GVC participation rate (as a share of GDP) has dropped significantly, and as of 2017 has not returned to pre-crisis levels: 0.1289 in 2017 compared to 0.1343 in 2007.

This downward trend leads to the critical question: Have GVCs arrived at a crossroads? As trade and investment are the key parameters for GVC activities, the following sections will answer this question through examining the underlying factors behind sluggishness in trade and investment growth in the recent decade: Are they caused by the cyclical elements such as weakening demand, or is there a deeper structural shift that may imply a fundamental change in GVC evolution?

16.3.1 Post-crisis slowdown in global trade and investment growth

Although world trade bounced back after the financial crisis, the growth of global trade was only 3% in 2018, against an average of 6%–7% in the pre-crisis years. Trade was on average growing twice as fast as global GDP growth from the 1990s until the financial crisis, and in the decade after the financial crisis, trade growth was barely catching up with GDP growth (Figure 16.5).

A similar slowdown is observed in global FDI flows. FDI activity has continued a downward trend since 2013. The average annual growth of global FDI inflow has been around 8% in 2000–2007, but it plunged to just 1% in post-crisis years from 2008–2018 (Figure 16.6). In 2018, global FDI flow continued its slide, declining for the third consecutive year by 13% to $1.3 trillion.

To a certain extent, the declining FDI flows in 2018–2019 can be attributed to the large repatriations of accumulated foreign earnings by US firms following the tax reforms in 2017. However, according to the United Nations Conference on Trade and Development (UNCTAD) World Investment Report 2019, discounting the fluctuations caused by the tax reform and the increase in cross-border mergers and acquisitions (M&A), the underlying FDI trend – which discounts for the volatility caused by one-off transactions and swings in intra-firm financial flows – was still negative. Average annual growth in the underlying trend, which was above 10% until a decade ago, has since stagnated at less than 1%.

At the same time, the fall in global FDI contrasted with the trend in other cross-border capital flows. Total capital flows increased from 5.6% to 6.9% of GDP, as bank lending and portfolio investment (mostly debt) compensated for the FDI slump. As FDI flows are usually

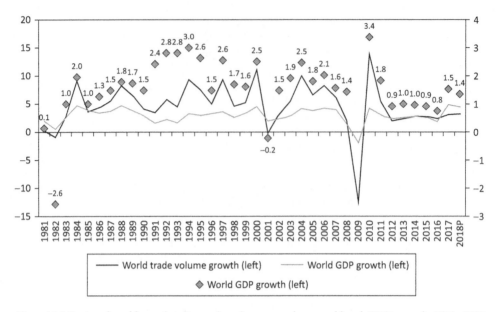

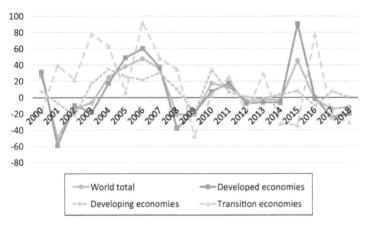

Figure 16.5 Ratio of world merchandise trade volume growth to world real GDP growth, 1981–2018. (Source: WTO and UNCTAD for trade, consensus estimates for GDP.)

Figure 16.6 Annual growth of FDI inflow, by region and economy, 2000-2018 (%). (Source: UNCTAD World Investment Report 2019.)

seen as having greater positive growth impact for host countries, e.g., less volatile than com-mercial bank loans and portfolio flows, and convey greater knowledge spillover, the drop in FDI has important implications for industrial development and financial stability in develop-ing countries.

Growth in GVC activities has slowed with the stagnation in trade and FDI. From 1990 until 2010, the share of foreign value added (FVA) in total exports – a proxy for estimating GVC activities – rose continuously, contributing to the growth in global trade in the last decade. The rise was gradual, around 7 percentage points in 20 years, but steady without interruptions.

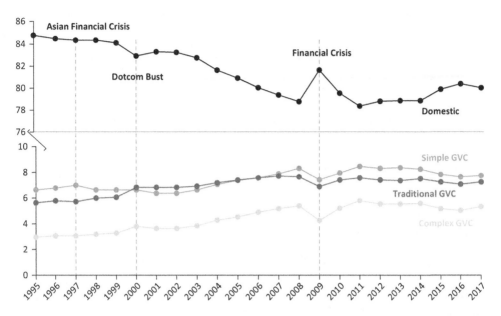

Figure 16.7 Trends in production activities as a share of global GDP, by type of value-added creation activity, 1995–2017. (Source: WTO Global Value Chain Development Report 2019.)

However, FVA in global trade peaked in 2010–2012 after two decades of continuous increases (Figure 16.7). For the first time in 30 years, the growth of GVC activities has come to a halt, with UNCTAD's GVC data showing FVA down 1 percentage point to 30% of trade in 2017. This reverse in the trend of GVCs is consistent with the slowdown in FDI activities, with the close correlation confirming the impact of the key role played by multinational enterprises on GVC production.

16.3.2 *What is behind the trade and investment slowdown?*

Various papers have studied the slowdown in trade and investment, attempting to determine whether it is a cyclical or structural issue. The impact of cyclical factors on GVCs may be temporary, but the effects of structural shifts could be persistent and have overwhelming effects on the evolution of GVCs in the long run.

While it is difficult to draw a clear line between cyclical and structural factors impacting GVC, it is widely acknowledged that cyclical factors relate to the periods of expansion or recession in business cycles, such as growth in demand and supply. Structural factors, on the other hand, relate to more long-term trends such as changes in technologies and factors of production that impact GVC structure, changes in policy trends, changes in the trade composition (services versus goods), or a shift between demand components (consumption versus investment).

Research points to various factors behind the post-crisis slowdown in global trade and investment growth. Beneath the cyclical factors, some structural elements have emerged, which may explain the persistent trends and shed light on the future direction of GVC evolution.

First, cyclical change remains a major explanation for the trade and investment slowdown, notably the weak demand in the advanced economies and more recently in emerging and developing economies. Ten years after the global financial crisis, global growth remains subdued.

The world economy is projected to grow at 3.2% in 2019, more than 1.7 percentage points lower than it was during the upswing prior to the global financial crisis.

Investment and demand for consumer durables have been subdued across advanced and emerging market economies as firms and households continue to hold back on long-range spending. For advanced economies, amid high policy uncertainty and weakening prospects for global demand, industrial production decelerated, particularly for capital goods. As high-income countries account for over 60% of global imports, their lingering weak demand inevitably affects the recovery in global trade.

Emerging economies are also struggling to absorb the impact of the weaker-than-expected outlook for domestic demand. In China, the weakening external demand have added pressure to an economy already in the midst of regulatory strengthening to rein in high dependence on debt.

Second, the slowdown in trade and investment could also reflect a deeper, structural change undergoing in major emerging markets and developing economies. These changes include increased import substitution, rising wages and other production costs in developing countries, as well as a shift in their economic growth models.

Some studies argue that, to a certain extent, the trade stagnation could be explained by the trend of import substitution for intermediate products with local supply in developing Asia. According to the estimation by the Asian Development Bank (2017), the ratio of China's intermediate goods imports to manufactured exports, which represents a crude proxy for GVC trade, fell from 63% to about 38% between 2000 and 2015. For the Republic of Korea, this ratio also fell from 49.5% to 39.6% (Figure 16.8). This suggests that GVC participation has helped to develop local supply capacity, and increasingly intermediary inputs are sourced locally rather than imported from abroad.

On the supply side, with higher minimum wage regulations and strengthened environmental policies, production costs have been rising gradually in emerging markets, which makes their comparative advantage in production costs less pronounced and thus less attractive destinations for multinational companies to outsource production.

Take labor costs for example. The average hourly wage in emerging economies was esti-mated to be around 2% of the Unites States' average in 2000, but has risen to 9% in 2015

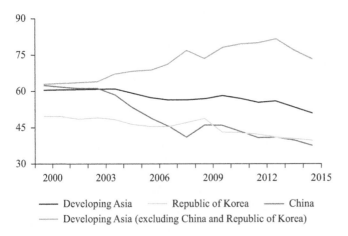

Figure 16.8 Share of imported intermediate goods to manufacturing exports (%). (Source: ADB (2017) estimation based on data from the United Nations.)

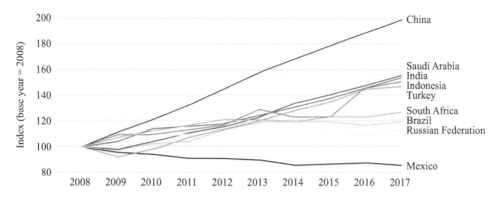

Figure 16.9 Average real wage index for emerging G20 countries, 2008–2017. (Source: ILO estimates.)

(World Economic Forum, 2012). Figure 16.9 shows the rising labor costs in China, where average real wages almost doubled between 2008 and 2017. In fact, all emerging G20 countries except Mexico experienced significant positive growth in average real wages over this period.

A projection from PwC (2013) estimates that wage costs in emerging economies will keep increasing and converging to those in developed economies up to 2030. This trend, coupled with increasing automation, is a significant structural factor that will shape GVCs in the coming years.

On the demand side, China's transformation from an export-and-investment-led growth model to consumption-led growth also has an impact on GVCs. Fueled by expanding middle-class consumption, corporate deleveraging, growing imports and a services trade deficit, China's imports has been growing at a faster pace than its exports. Its current account surplus has slipped from 10.3% of its GDP in the third quarter of 2017, to just 0.4% in the third quarter of 2018.

As one of the global factories and a regional economic powerhouse, transformation of China's trade has repercussions around the world in the near term, especially for its trade partners as well as on commodity prices. However, in the longer term, this transition and rebalancing toward less trade surplus will provide a more stable environment for GVC development.

At the global level, trade between major economies has also been leaning toward greater balance, with declining goods trade surpluses with the US and the European Union, and declining deficits with Japan and Korea (IMF, 2019). The trend toward more balanced trade is likely to continue in the near future with far-reaching implications for the rest of the world.

Third, new technologies reduce labor intensity in modern manufacturing, making it less appealing for multinationals to outsource. GVCs essentially started as a form of labor arbitrage, relocating manufacturing to locations with low labor costs. However, as manufacturing becomes more technology and capital intensive, the share of labor in overall production cost is constantly on the decline. Higher technology content also requires more skilled labor. In many developing countries, while unskilled labor is abundant, skilled workers are in short supply and do not necessarily represent a comparative advantage.

Automation is a growing part of manufacturing. It is widely acknowledged that a major part of tasks that are suitable for offshoring are also suitable for automation, such as in the production of motor vehicles and other transportation equipment (Autor et al., 2016). As the technologies advance, there is more evidence that autonomous robots have reduced offshoring, and efficiency-seeking FDI may flow back from low- and middle-income countries to high-income countries.

The application of automation has prompted some lead firms to reshore labor-intensive manufacturing activities. For example, Foxconn, the world's largest contract electronics manufacturer known for making iPhones, is expected to open a new $10 billion factory in Wisconsin, using advanced robots to make LCD panels.

Similar evidence is also coming from Europe. Based on firm-level data for 3313 manufacturing companies across seven European countries, Kinkel et al. (2015) found that firms using industrial robots in their manufacturing processes are less likely to offshore production activities outside Europe. Hallward-Driemeier and Nayyar (2018) find a nonlinear relationship between the intensity of robot use in high-income countries and FDI from high-income countries to low-/medium-income countries between 2003 and 2015. It is worth noticing that as automation further advances, this on-shoring trend might spread from manufacturing to other sectors, including food production and even certain service industries such as customer centers and previously outsourced back-office operations, which increasingly can be handled by artificial intelligence.

Last but not the least, services trade has been increasing at a higher growth rate than goods trade, but their role in GVCs has been vastly underestimated. Understanding the role of services in GVCs remains a challenge, as existing services trade data does not fully capture cross-border digital trade, which is perhaps the most dynamic area in global trade. Nor does it provide a full picture on services supplied through commercial presence (Mode 3 of services trade). Value creation by foreign affiliates is the most important form of services trade and account for over half of global services trade. This trade, however, is treated as part of domestic economic activity, as cross-border transactions are not reflected through this statistic.

Despite the efforts of some countries to collect these data on a global scale, services share in world total trade in goods and services (23% in 2018) is much lower than the services share in global GDP (65% in 2017). The significant discrepancy between domestic and international transactions indicates the gap in understanding the role of trade in services in GVCs.

Apart from the missing information on services trade, tools to measure GVC activities also require a substantive update. The indicators commonly used to analyze countries' participation in international production networks are either based on international trade data or international input–output tables, which have their weaknesses and might deflate the importance of GVCs. Customs data provides little information on production processes or origin of intermediary inputs used in the production. Input–output tables, on the other hand, are constrained by the high degree of sectoral aggregation and the proportionality assumption (the allocation of trade flows by country of origin and destination). This offers low resolution measurement of production fragmentation and creates an aggregate downward bias, which results in lower estimation of the shares of foreign content.

16.3.3 Increasing protectionism may have long-term impact on GVCs

After more than a half-century of efforts to lower barriers for international trade and investment, trade tensions are coming back to dominate the headlines. Protectionist measures undertaken by the world's leading trade nations have put global trade at risk and significantly increased uncertainty for international trade and the world economy.

In 2018, the US enacted several waves of tariff increases on a wide range of products, sectors and countries. As of October 2019, import tariffs increased from 2.6% to 16.6% on 12,043 products covering $303 billion (12.7%) of annual US imports. These measures represent the most comprehensive protectionist trade policies implemented by the US in the postwar era due to the sizes of the countries involved, the magnitude of the tariff increases and the breadth of tariffs across sectors.

In response, several countries imposed retaliatory tariffs on US exports. These countermeasures increased tariffs from 6.6% to 23% on 2931 export products covering $96 billion (6.2%) of 2017 annual US exports (Fajgelbaum et al., 2019).

There is evidence that trade distortions are at a historically high level. The WTO's Monitoring Report on G20 Trade Measures shows that the trade coverage of new import-restrictive measures introduced by G20 economies between October 2018 and May 2019 has increased by more than three-and-half times since May 2012 when the report started including trade coverage figures (Figure 16.10).

On the investment front, 2018–2019 has also witnessed a turning point in the policy environment. Since 2017, restrictions on foreign ownership, based on national security considerations or strategic considerations, have been on the rise. New investment measures adopted in the past two years indicate a more critical stance toward foreign investment (Figure 16.11).

In 2018, for instance, out of 112 measures affecting foreign investment adopted by 55 economies, more than one-third introduced new restrictions – the highest number for two decades. They are mainly in the areas of limiting foreign ownership of critical infrastructure, core technologies and other sensitive business assets. On top of that, at least 22 large M&A deals were withdrawn or blocked for regulatory or political reasons – twice as many as in 2017.

In an era of interconnected markets and supply chains, the cost of protectionism can be higher than generally understood, and trade tensions are likely to have significant contagion effects around the world. Today, two-thirds of world trade is in intermediate inputs rather than finished goods and services (McKinsey, 2019). Tariffs are cumulative when intermediate inputs are traded across borders multiple times, and even small tariff increases can add up and have a sizeable impact on GVC operations.

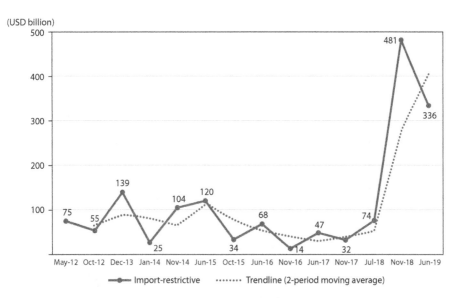

Figure 16.10 Trade coverage of new import-restrictive measures in each reporting period (not cumulative). (Source: WTO Secretariat.) Note: These figures are estimates and represent the trade coverage of the measures (i.e. annual imports of the products concerned from economies affected by the measures) introduced during each reporting period and not the cumulative impact of the trade measures.

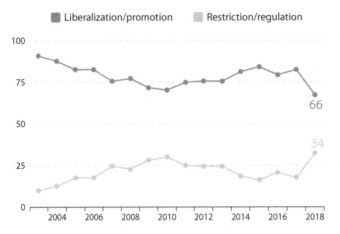

Figure 16.11 Changes (%) in national investment policies, 2003–2018. (Source: UNCTAD World Investment Report 2019.)

Traditionally, trade tensions are limited to certain products and sectors: tariff lines are carefully picked to avoid backfiring on consumers and domestic firms that rely on imported inputs. In a total trade war, however, it is difficult to escape backfire damages – firms might end up paying tariffs on their imported inputs and then face tariffs again in the exporting county on the full value of their exports, including on those same inputs. Tariffs can add up to a significant level by the time the finished good reaches customers, dampening demand and affecting production and investment at all stages of a value chain.

This effect is especially strong when the foreign content of manufactured goods is high, as is the case, for example, for electronic products. What is more, in the context of GVCs, currency interventions (competitive depreciation), which aim at gaining the price advantage for exporters, may lose relevance as a solution to tariff hikes, since any export advantage gained from a cheaper currency is at least partially eroded by the cost of more expensive imported inputs.

16.4 Emerging megatrends and future evolution of GVCs

As discussed in the previous sections, technological advances and GVC-related policy changes were the key factors shaping GVCs in the past and they will remain determining factors for the emerging megatrends and future of GVC evolution.

16.4.1 COVID-19's disruptive impact on global supply chains

The year 2020 started with a global health crisis that spread throughout the world, bringing severe disruptions to economic activities. Global merchandise trade volume is estimated to drop by 14% between the first and second quarters (WTO), and global FDI flows are expected to decrease by up to 40% in 2020 (UNCTAD).

The drastic falls in trade and investment show that the pandemic has had a traumatic impact on GVCs, and some of the effects may linger for years. Disruption in supply and contraction in demand have rendered an extremely challenging and unpredictable business environment for the coming years. Companies responded by halting investments and taking measures to decrease their dependency on extended supply chains. Governments introduced policies that aimed at reshoring production, especially production of critical medical supplies.

It is estimated that the three major supply chain trade hubs (China, EU and US) account for 63% of world supply chain imports and 64% of supply chain exports. The decreased demand for inputs by these large economies will lead to lower exports of raw materials, parts and components by their partners, thus transmitting the effects of shutdown globally through the supply chains. Overall, COVID-19 will reduce global exports of manufacturing inputs by at least $228 billion. (ITC, 2020).

Trade data in the early stage of the pandemic show that supply chain disruption mainly affects machinery, plastics and rubber, chemicals and electronic equipment industries. Services sectors, such as travel, tourism and retail services, have also seen tremendous impact, with the number of international tourists estimated to fall between 60% and 80% in 2020 (UNWTO). Other services key to GVCs, including transportation and logistics, may also see long-lasting impacts due to strengthened health requirements such as quarantines, inspections and social distancing. These measures are likely to remain for months and years until a global solution has been found to curb the pandemic.

16.4.2 Technology will have a mixed effect on future GVCs

Technology advances will have a mixed effect on value chains. On the one hand, technology will provide GVCs with better tools for more efficient value chain management. For example, the internet of things (IoT) cuts the cost of tracking components across borders and allows for more efficient organization of value chains, and blockchain provides solutions for trust-related issues and has the potential to increase transparency across value chains – particularly relevant to avoid supply shocks due to stockpiling in times of crisis. 5G allows for high-speed, low-latency massive communication that can bring new applications such as autonomous vehicles, virtual reality and remote medical care.

On the other hand, technology also contributes to the restructuring of value chains, and in many instances, shortening of value chains. Automation reduces some of the incentives for GVCs to relocate to lower-wage countries; digital technologies, advanced robotics, 3D printing (additive manufacturing), big data and other ICTs will transform manufacturing processes, as well as related services and business models, with wide-ranging implications for international production and GVCs. The case of 3D printing is remarkable, especially in the context of the COVID-19 pandemic. This emerging technology was key to bridging the gap between offer and supply, allowing for the production of protective medical equipment closer to consumption markets.

Technology advances lead to more services being used, increasing the share of services in both inputs and outputs in manufacturing processes. This so-called servicification will also have transformative effects on value chains: more services will be used and traded. As some of them could be supplied remotely, especially digitally traded services, new services value chains will emerge. The broad composition of trade in services has changed dramatically over the years as Internet penetration has increased: while "other commercial services" represented a third of global services exports in 1990, today this category accounts for more than half of services exports in the world. The value of ICT-enabled services grew by a factor of 1.6 between 2008 and 2018, reaching $2.964 billion in 2018.

These services value chains could be established business models such as outsourcing centers handling travel and payroll operations, or they could be more sophisticated networks of cooperation between software engineers, graphic designers, and financial and logistics experts to develop a platform using block chain technology to manage goods and information flows. The new business models enabled by digital technologies are often more responsive to customer needs, providing tailor-made solutions and focusing on generating new demand. They also blur the line between production and consumption, as customers often share their data and expectations and become part of the production process.

International trade itself is also being transformed by new technologies and business models, notably cross-border e-commerce. Global e-commerce sales reached an estimated $29 trillion in 2017, and the share of consumers buying from abroad rose from 15% in 2015 to 21% in 2017 (UNCTAD, 2019).

Cross-border business-to-consumer (B2C) e-commerce, in which products are shipped in parcels from suppliers overseas directly to the consumers, are reshaping global trade and with it the distributed value chains. On the one hand, disintermediation eliminates a number of players in the traditional distribution value chain, such as importers, wholesalers and retailers; on the other hand, e-commerce is also creating new value chains with new players such as online retailers, e-payment providers and express delivery services. Digital platforms will play an increasing role in shaping the global economy, and increasingly they will act as infrastructure that enable the flow of goods, services, data and capital in the digital era, especially as they expand from the matchmaking or marketplace business to also include their own logistics and payment providers. This poses significant regulatory challenges, as reflected in the increased debate on data, privacy, cybersecurity, competition, taxation and transparency, as well as values and ethics.

16.4.3 GVCs in the new trade policy era

Significant deterioration of the global trade environment has been the key feature of the global economy in recent years. Trade is back in the headlines with increasing trade tensions and rising protectionist measures. These will not only raise the costs of trade but also affect companies' production and investment decisions, and thus have a disruptive impact on GVCs.

The trade war between US and China, the world's first and second largest trade nations, has significant ramifications around the world. If the US and China fail to reach an agreement, global trade is likely to return to high tariff zones. From February 2018 when the US applied the first round of Section 201 tariffs on solar panels and washing machines to December 2019, the average US tariff on Chinese imports increased from 3.1% to 24.3%. Chinese tariffs on US imports increased from 8% to 25.9%.

Increasing tariffs impose additional costs for traders, and in order to absorb these costs, companies may consider minimizing the impact of tariffs through restructuring value chains. This will have a mixed impact on the FDI flows between the US and China. On the one hand, it might dampen the efficiency-seeking FDI – investments that are typically associated with offshore production. Efficiency-seeking FDI has been the bulk of global FDI flows between developed and developing economies since the 1990s, which took advantage of differences in production costs such as lower labor and land costs, loose environmental standards and cheaper natural resources (Hummels et al., 2001).

On the other hand, trade tensions might boost market-seeking FDI. Multinational companies can serve foreign markets via exports, local establishment or a combination of the two. Serving a market with exports bears trade costs, but saves the cost of operating an establishment in a foreign country. Serving a market with FDI bears the cost of overseas operations, but saves on trade costs. Therefore, the higher the trade costs, the more attractive it will be for a firm to serve a foreign market through production on site and the lower will be the gains from economies of scale at home.

A prolonged trade war will compel multinational firms reconsider their production and distribution decisions to overcome the increased trade costs. However, restructuring the established supply chain implies a considerable cost in itself. Breaking up the existing GVC linkages means investing to build new production facilities and developing new partnerships. This is perhaps the reason why in the September 2019 survey by the US-China Business Council, despite over 80% of respondents claiming that their business with China has been impacted by trade tension, 97% are making profits in China and 87% have no plans to leave the Chinese market.

As has been widely argued by trade economists, protectionism is not the solution for trade disputes. The root cause of increasing populism and dissatisfaction with globalization is the widening income gap both in developed and developing countries. Benefits from trade are not evenly distributed among the countries and within countries among different income groups. Evidence shows that GVC benefits on labor markets are uneven: in both developed and developing countries, GVCs tend to benefit skilled labor and negatively impact unskilled labor. This is why rather than raising tariffs, governments should invest in providing remedies to the population impacted by GVC, such as social security and skill development programs.

Growing protectionism may also have repercussions around the world, including in developing countries. Rising protectionism may stir up similar sentiments in developing countries, which may lead to a slowing of domestic reforms that are essential for increased participation in GVC. This could lead to slowing the implementation of trade facilitation, increased protectionism in investment and services sectors, and increased restrictions on data.

Strengthening the multilateral trade system is a way to address the rising protectionism. Despite a lack of progress in multilateral talks since the beginning of the Doha Development Agenda of 2001, WTO members did manage to agree on the Information Technology Agreement (ITA) and its expansion in 2015, which captures 97% of world trade in ITA products, and eliminates 89% of tariff lines by 2019. The Trade Facilitation Agreement (TFA) is expected to reduce trade costs by an average of 14.3% and boost global trade by up to $1 trillion per year, providing renewed impetus to GVC activities.

Further efforts could be directed toward reforming the WTO system, updating its rulebook to address the new challenges in global trade and revitalizing its negotiation functions. In this regard, WTO members are actively pursuing results in the negotiations on fishery subsidies and services trade domestic regulation, as well as plurilateral initiatives such as e-commerce; micro, small, and medium enterprises (MSMEs); and investment facilitation for development.

Digital trade has been the focus of trade talks in recent years. Since 2017, G20 has held Digital Economy Ministers meetings annually, engaging members in discussions on issues such as taxation, competition and cybersecurity. The ongoing plurilateral negotiation at the WTO on e-commerce could also bring multilateral solutions to address the new challenges in rising digital trade, such as customs duties on electronic transmission, e-signatures, consumer protection, cross-border information flows, data localization and disclosure of source codes.

Last but not the least, better measurement and study of GVC activities could contribute to better-informed policies. Traditional statistical approaches toward gross trade figures are inadequate and often lead to "double counting" of the value of intermediate goods. The value of final products is usually attributed to the last country of origin instead of allocating to different countries where those intermediates are from, which leads to bias in assessing, for example, bilateral trade imbalances. Joint efforts of the WTO members to advance measuring trade in value added (TiVA) terms can present a more objective and comprehensive picture of global trade. In addition to trade in goods, TiVA will also facilitate the understanding of the contribution of services in domestic production and their value-added contribution to trade.

16.4.4 Increasing role of regional value chains

In the past decade, with rapid economic growth and regional integration, intra-regional GVC activities in Asia grew faster than in North America, especially in complex GVC participation. GVC linkages between developing Asia and developed countries in North America and Europe have also increased. However, the importance of North America and Europe as both destinations of Asia's GVC exports and sources of Asia's GVC imports has declined.

While inter-regional linkages between developing and developed economies might see a further decline, intra-regional value chains among the developing world will likely further strengthen, especially in the context of the rising trade tensions. Moreover, the shock in global value chains thanks to the pandemic has made some companies turn to "nearshoring" as a way to have more control over the production of both goods and services. As developing countries cumulate experiences, capital and know-how, their capacity to organize production inter-regionally rather than intra-regionally also increases. This, however, is to be taken with a grain of salt, as current GVC research focuses on the flow of goods and much of the services and knowledge inputs, which are key factors for GVC, are not well captured.

Indeed, efforts to further advance regional value chains are being undertaken by governments across the world, notably reflected in the increased pace of regional trade agreements. The conclusion of the Regional Comprehensive Economic Partnership (RCEP) agreement, the African Continental Free Trade Area (AfCFTA) and the strengthened Pacific Alliance are all examples of efforts to further develop regional value chains through reducing trade barriers.

The RCEP has great potential to enhance regional value chains in Asia. The RCEP-participating countries account for almost half of the world's population, over 30% of global GDP and over a quarter of world exports. The agreement is expected to come into force in early 2022 when the signatories complete the ratification processes.

In general, comprehensive RTAs can boost GVC trade and have particular impact on GVC-intensive sectors. The depth of trade agreements is reflected in both their coverage, i.e., covering not only goods trade, but also services, intellectual property, movement of capital, persons and more recently information, and also their quality, going beyond the applied regime to further reduce trade barriers. Studies show that there's a positive correlation between the depth of regional trade agreements and increased trade in intermediate goods. Deep RTAs will stimulate the development of regional value chains by providing more common disciplines that facilitate the operation of economic activities spanning multiple borders.

16.4.5 Toward more inclusive and sustainable value chains

GVCs offer opportunities for developing countries to participate in the global supply chain instead of building the whole chain from the scratch themselves (Baldwin, 2011). However, with the exception of "factory Asia," the greater part of the developing world remains outside of GVC activities. The majority of developing countries only have limited roles in today's GVCs, mostly as suppliers of raw materials and markets for lower-end products.

More inclusive and sustainable GVCs would mean greater participation of developing countries in GVC activities and their greater share in creating and retaining value added. It would also mean more environmentally friendly approaches to production and consumption, such as through a circular economy, and new business models in which ownership of products are replaced with access to use, licenses and memberships.

Taking the share of developing countries in global trade and investment as proxy for their participation in GVCs, it is encouraging to see that both shares have been rising over the past decade. Developing economies accounted for 44% of global trade and 54% of global FDI in 2018, higher than a decade ago.

Despite the growing share of developing economies in global trade and investment, growth has been imbalanced, with developing Asia spearing ahead in rapid increases in GVC activities, while others, least developed countries (LDCs) in particular, have seen marginal change. The share of LDCs in global exports remains less than 1%. To make GVCs more inclusive, low-income countries need to be better integrated into GVC networks.

Africa so far has not been a significant player in GVCs, except as a source of raw materials. However, in the coming decade, Africa might see an increased role in GVCs as its manufacturing capacity increases. The accelerated pace of regional integration in Africa is already contributing to increased regional trade: the Southern African Development Community (SADC) and the Common Market for Eastern and Southern Africa (COMESA) saw their intra-regional shares in global trade through RTAs increase by around 10 percentage points in the past ten years. The advancement of the African Continental Free Trade Agreement (AfCFTA) will forge a large market covering a population of 1.2 billion people and GDP of USD 2.6 trillion, attractive to global businesses and investment. With the increasing productivity, trade and FDI, Africa is poised to play a larger role in the future of GVCs.

More inclusive and sustainable GVCs also means that developing countries need to generate and retain more value added in GVCs, in other words, to move up the value chains. Experiences from Asia suggest that this could be a viable path to development: countries start with simpler and less technology-intensive value chains such as apparel, and as they build capital and expertise, production and export of apparel is gradually overtaken by higher value-added products such as electronics and machineries. Vietnam's exports of electrical machinery, for example, increased almost 30-fold between 2008 and 2018, and the country saw the fastest growth in merchandise exports among developing countries in the past decade, with average annual growth of 14.6%.

In this process of moving up from lower to higher value-added exports, being part of GVCs is crucial. WTO studies show that the higher the technology (knowledge) intensity of a sector, the more significant the increase of complex GVC activities. In the technology-intense value chains, the share of foreign value added is often higher than simple value chains. Thus, GVC linkages are especially important for high-tech sectors, such as electronics, and it is in these areas that highly complex value chains have developed ranging across many countries.

Many challenges remain for developing countries to take advantage of and benefit from GVC participation. These challenges may include inadequate infrastructure, underdeveloped supply capacity, lack of skills and know-how, as well as lack of a conducive policy environment, notably higher trade costs and less attractive FDI policies. Reducing supply chain barriers to trade could improve GDP by almost 5% and trade by 15%, thus contributing to GDP growth six times more than removing all tariffs (World Economic Forum, 2013). The striking difference has to do with the elimination of resource waste versus the mere reallocation of resources if tariffs are eliminated. More importantly, efficiency gains from reducing supply chain barriers are more evenly distributed across nations.

Thus, further reducing trade costs is key for increased participation of developing countries in value chain production. Despite the fact that trade costs have seen significant reductions across both developed and developing countries in the past decades, high trade costs in low-income countries remain a factor hampering their participation in GVCs. The World Bank (2017) found that trade costs in high-income countries for the manufacturing sector were 82%, compared with 98% in the upper middle-income group, 125% in the lower middle-income group and 227% in the low-income group (Figure 16.12).

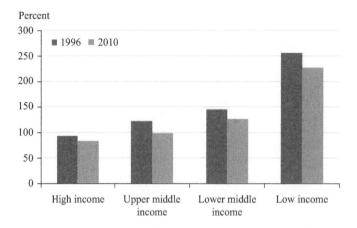

Percent

Figure 16.12 Trade costs in manufacturing, 1996 and 2010, by income group. (Source: UNESCAP-World Bank trade costs database.)

Research shows how as trade costs fall, developing countries tend to join and move up the value chain (Zi, 2018). Further, lowering tariffs, but probably most important, removing non-tariff measures (NTMs) and opening services sectors will help low-income countries better integrate into regional and global value chains.

Trade costs in services sectors, in particular services relevant to manufacturing, are key to boosting value chain activities. Converted to tariff equivalents for comparison purposes, trade costs in services are in general higher than tariffs on goods (Egger et al., 2018). Empirical studies have also shown that reduced transportation and communication costs can help developing countries join and move up existing value chains.

Foreign investment plays an important role in value chain participation, as foreign invested companies are the active players in not only import and export, but also knowledge and technology transfer. Developing countries need to continue improving the efficiency of their institutional framework, including increasing transparency, streamlining procedures, liberalizing more sectors to foreign investment, providing better investor services and strengthening property right protection. These will help hedge against reduction in global FDI flows, reducing uncertainties and increasing attractiveness for foreign investment.

Box 16.1 Future trends in GVC evolution

Technology advancement and GVC-related policies will remain two key factors shaping GVCs in the coming decade.

Some technologies contribute to GVC growth: the IoT cuts the cost of tracking/interaction and allows for more efficient organization of value chains, blockchain provides trusted solutions, 5G provides high speed, and low-latency massive communication enables new GVC applications.

Others may result in shortening of value chains: automation and robotics reduce labor demand thus the need to relocate production, digital technologies replace physical interactions with bits, additive manufacturing enables distributed manufacturing, and new business models shift demand from product ownership to its access.

Services will play an increasing role in GVCs. Increasing the share of services in both inputs and outputs (servicification) will result in more services being used and traded. Cross-border B2C e-commerce will continue to expand and transform value chains in the supply of consumer products.

Digital platforms increasingly act as infrastructure that enable the flow of goods, services, data and capital. This poses significant regulatory challenges, and policy debate will increasingly focus on new issues such as data, privacy, cybersecurity, competition, taxation and transparency, as well as values and ethics.

The world is entering an era of rising protectionism and geopolitical tension, which results in greater policy uncertainty that has negative effects on GVC growth. Prolonged trade wars increase trade costs and may result in restructuring in certain value chains, with significant costs to producers and consumers. Efficiency-seeking FDI (investments in offshore production) might see a greater decline.

Regional value chains will see accelerated growth, especially in Asia and Africa. Intra-regional value chains among developing countries are likely to further strengthen while inter-regional linkages between developing and developed economies might see a decline.

Sustainability and inclusiveness will become important themes in GVCs, advocating for more environmentally friendly approaches to production and consumption, a circular economy and new business models.

Developing countries will continue to reform and connect to value chains, as they tackle the challenges in infrastructure, supply capacity, knowledge and skills, and further reduce trade costs and attract FDI.

16.5 Conclusion

Trade and investment have formulated and shaped GVCs. Reduced transportation and communication costs, coupled with tariff reductions, services and investment liberalization, in particular in developing countries, have enabled distributed and coordinated production. Multinationals seeking to benefit from lower production costs have offshored to developing countries, bringing them into GVCs.

GVC activities have reached a peak in the years before the financial crisis. The decade after the crisis is characterized by a slowdown in global trade, investment and GVC activities. Apart from cyclical economic downturn, a number of structural changes have emerged that may have long-term implications for GVC evolution, including growing wages and other production costs in emerging economies, new technologies reducing labor intensity in modern manufacturing, China's transition from an export-and-investment-led growth model to a consumption-led growth, trade rebalancing, and a reduction in trade surplus of the leading exporters, as well as a slowdown in trade and investment liberalization and rising protectionism as the result of increased inequality.

Technology and policies will remain the long-term key factors shaping GVCs in the coming decade. However, the COVID-19 global pandemic has had a short-term disruptive impact on GVC activities, sharply reducing both global supply and demand for goods and services, and draining FDI flows. Until a global solution is found for the pandemic, its presence will significantly accelerate the structural transformation towards shorter supply chains.

Trade tensions will continue to have a significant impact on GVC activities. A prolonged trade war between the US and China will bring global trade back to high tariff zones. This may compel companies to minimizing the impact through restructuring value chains. However, in an era of interconnected markets and supply chains, the cost of restructuring can be higher than generally understood. Rather than raising tariffs, governments should invest in education and providing remedies. A strengthened multilateral system may help bring trade back to normal, through updating its rulebook to address the new challenges and ensuring trade norms.

Regional value chains might see faster growth, with the possibility of declining interregional linkages between developing and developed economies and increasing intraregional value chains among the developing world. GVCs should become more inclusive and sustainable, through greater participation of developing countries and their greater share in creating and retaining value added. Africa might see an increased role in GVCs with strengthened manufacturing capacity and increased regional integration. Further reducing trade costs by cutting tariffs, opening services and investment, improving institutional capacity, and investing in education and skills are key for increased participation of developing countries in future GVCs.

Note

1 The views expressed in this article are those of the authors alone and not the institutions they work at.

Bibliography

Ahmad, N., Bohn, T., Mulder, N, Vaillant, M., and Zaclicever, D. (2017). *Indicators on Global Value Chains: A Guide for Empirical Work*. OECD Statistics Working Papers, No. 2017/08, OECD Publishing, Paris.

Alfaro, Laura, Chanda Areendam, Sebnem Kalemli-Ozcan, and Selin Sayek (2004). FDI and economic growth: The role of local financial markets. *Journal of International Economics*, 64, 89–112.

Amador, J. and Cabral, S. (2014). *Global Value Chains: Surveying Drivers and Measures*. Technical report, ECB Working Paper.

Anderson J. and E. van Wincoop (2004). Trade costs. *Journal of Economic Literature*, 42, 691–751

Antras, P., Chor, D., Fally, T., and Hillberry, R. (2012). Measuring the upstreamness of production and trade flows. *American Economic Review*, 102(3), 412–416.

Asian Development Bank. (2017). *Changing Patterns of Trade and Global Value Chains in Postcrisis Asia*. ADB Briefs NO.76.

Autor, D., D. Dorn, and G. Hanson. (2016). The China shock: Learning from labor- market adjustment to large changes in trade. *Annual Review of Economics*, 8, 205–240.

Baldwin, R. (2006). *Globalisation: The Great Unbundling(s)*. Study for Economic Council of Finland, 20 September. Graduate Institute of International Studies, Geneva.

Baldwin, R. (2011). *Trade and Industrialisation after Globalisation's 2nd Unbundling: How Building and Joining a Supply Chain are Different and Why It Matters*, NBER Working Paper Series No. 17716, Cambridge, MA.

Baldwin, R. (2013). Trade and industrialization after globalization's second unbundling: How building and joining a supply chain are different and why it matters. In Robert C. Feenstra and Alan M. Taylor (eds.), *Globalization in an Age of Crisis: Multilateral Economic Cooperation in the Twenty-First Century*, pp. 165–212. Chicago, IL: University of Chicago Press.

Baldwin, R. (2016). *The Great Convergence: Information Technology and the New Globalisation*. Harvard University Press, Cambridge, MA.

BDI. (2020). Export Controls and Export Bans over the Course of the Covid-19 Pandemic, 29 April 2020, Available at https://www.wto.org/english/tratop_e/covid19_e/bdi_covid19_e.pdf

Buckley, P. J. and Casson, M. C. (2009). The internalisation theory of the multinational enterprise: A review of the progress of a research agenda after 30 years. *Journal of International Business Studies*, 40(9), 1563–1580.

Borensztein, E., De Gregorio, J., and Lee, J.-W. (1998). How does foreign direct investment affect economic growth? *Journal of International Economics*, 45, 115–135.

Caves, R. E. (1971). International corporations: The industrial economics of foreign investment. *Economica*, 38(149), 1–27.

Colen, L., Persyn, D., and Guariso, A. (2016). Bilateral investment treaties and FDI: Does the sector matter? *World Development*, 83, 193–206.

De Backer, K., and Miroudot, S. (2014). *Mapping Global Value Chains*, ECB Working Paper No. 1677, Frankfurt am Main.

Dunning, J. H. (1998). Location and the multinational enterprise: A neglected factor? *Journal of International Business Studies*, 29(1), 45–66.

Egger, P. H., Larch, M., Nigai, S., and Yotov, V. Y. (2018). *Trade Costs in the Global Economy: Measurement, Aggregation and Decomposition*, Staff Working Paper, Geneva: World Trade Organization (WTO).

Escaith, Hubert (2017). *Accumulated Trade Costs and Their Impact on Domestic and International Value Chains*. WTO Global Value Chain Development Report 2017.

Fajgelbaum, P. D., Goldberg, P. K., Kennedy, P. J., and Khandelwal, A. K. (2019). *The Return to Protectionism*, National Bureau of Economic Research W25638, March 2019.

Gangnes, B., A. C. Ma, and A. Van Assche (2011). "Global Value Chains and the Transmission of Business Cycle Shocks", mimeo.

Gereffi, G. and T. Sturgeon (2013). Global value chain-oriented industrial policy: The role of emerging economies. In D. K. Elms and P. Low (eds.), *Global Value Chains in a Changing World*. Geneva: WTO Secreteriat.

Grossman, G. and E. Rossi-Hansberg (2008). Trading tasks: A simple theory of offshoring. *American Economic Review*, 98(5), 1978–1997.

Hallward-Driemeier, Mary and Gaurav Nayyar. (2018). *Trouble in the Making? The Future of Manufacturing-Led Development*. Washington, DC: World Bank.

Hanson, G. H., Mataloni Jr, R. J., and Slaughter, M. J. (2005). Vertical production networks in multinational firms. *The Review of Economics and Statistics*, 87(4), 664–678.

Hoekman, Bernard. (2014). *Supply Chains, Mega-Regionals, and the WTO*. Washington, DC: Center for Economic Policy Research.

Hsiao, C. and Shen, Y. (2003). Foreign direct investment and economic growth: The importance of institutions and urbanization. *Economic Development and Cultural Change*, 51, 883–896.

Hummels, D., Ishii, J., and Yei, K. (2001). The nature and growth of vertical specialization in world trade. *Journal of International Economics*, 54, 75–96.

Hymer, S. (1976). *The International Operations of National Firms, a Study of Foreign Direct Investment*. Cambridge: MIT Press.

International Monetary Fund (IMF). (2019). *The People's Republic of China: 2019 Article IV Consultation-Press Release*, Staff Report; and Statement by the Executive Director for the People's Republic of China. IMF Staff Country Reports, 2019.

International Monetary Fund (IMF), The World Bank, and The World Trade Organization (WTO). (2017). *Making Trade an Engine of Growth for All: The Case for Trade and for Policies to Facilitate Adjustment.*

International Trade Centre. (2020). SME Competitiveness Outlook 2020: COVID-19: The Great Lockdown and its Impact on Small Business. ITC, Geneva.

Kinkel, Steffen, A. Jager, and Christoph Zanker. (2015). The effects of robot use in European manufacturing companies on production off-shoring outside the EU. June. 22nd International Annual EurOMA Conference, At Neuchâtel, Switzerland.

Lewis, Colin. (2014). Robots are starting to make offshoring less Attractive. *Harvard Business Review*. May 12.

Markusen, J. R. (1995). The boundaries of multinational enterprises and the theory of international trade. *The Journal of Economic Perspectives*, 9(2), 169–189.

McKinsey Global Institute (2019). Globalization in Transition: The Future of Trade and Value Chains, January 2019.

Nordås, H. K., E. Pinali, and M. G. Grosso. 2006. "Logistics and Time as a Trade Barrier."

OECD. (2019). *Trade in the Digital Era*, OECD Going Digital Policy Note, OECD, Paris.

PwC (2013). Global Wage Projections. http://www.pwc.fr/fr/publications/ressources-humaines/global-wage-projections-to-2030.html

UNCTAD (United Nations Conference on Trade and Development). (2013). *World Investment Report 2013.* Geneva: UNCTAD.

UNCTAD (United Nations Conference on Trade and Development). (2017). *World Investment Report 2013.* Geneva: UNCTAD.

UNCTAD (United Nations Conference on Trade and Development). (2019). *World Investment Report 2013.* Geneva: UNCTAD.

UNCTAD, O. W. (2013). *Implications of Global Value Chains for Trade, Investment, Development and Jobs.* Joint report of the OECD, WTO, UNCTAD for G20 Leaders' Summit.

Wohlers Associates. (2019). *Wohlers Report 2019*, cited in World Economic Forum (2020). *3D Printing: A Guide for Decision-Makers.* Geneva.

World Bank. (2015). How are trade costs evolving and why? In *Aid for Trade at a Glance 2015: Reducing Trade Costs for Inclusive, Sustainable Growth.* OECD, WTO.

World Bank. (2017). *Measuring and Analyzing the Impact of GVCs on Economic Development.* Washington, DC: The World Bank.

World Economic Forum. (2012). *New Models for Addressing Supply Chain and Transport Risk.* Geneva: World Economic Forum.

World Economic Forum. (2013). *Enabling Trade Valuing Growth Opportunities.* Geneva: World Economic Forum.

World Trade Organization. (2008). *World Trade Report 2008: Trade in a Globalizing World.* Geneva: WTO.

World Trade Organization. (2018). *WTO World Trade Report 2018: The Future of World Trade: How Digital Technologies are Transforming Global Commerce.* Geneva: World Trade Organization.

World Trade Organization. (2019). *Global Value Chain Development Report 2019: Technological Innovation, Supply Chain Trade, and Workers in a Globalized World (English).* Washington, D.C.: World Bank Group.

World Trade Organization. (2019). *World Trade Statistical Review 2019.* Geneva: World Trade Organization.

Yi, K. M. (2009). The collapse of global trade: The role of vertical specialisation. In R. Baldwin and Evenett (eds.), *The Collapse of Global Trade, Murky Protectionism and the Crisis: Recommendations of the G20.* London: CEPR.

Zi, Y. (2018). Trade costs, global value chains and economic development. *Journal of Economic Geography*, 5, 249–291.

17

INNOVATION, INDUSTRIAL STRATEGY AND GLOBAL VALUE CHAINS

Mark Matthews

Introduction

This chapter considers the relationships between innovation, industrial strategy and global value chains (GVCs). It advocates transitioning to a more integrated approach to government innovation policy and industrial strategy that brings in the GVC dimension 'centre-field' whilst also recognising the importance of geo-strategic and national security concerns in this 'internationalised' stance.

This argument pivots on recognising what the rapidly developing evidence-base on the structure and performance of GVCs and the public policy insights that emerge from this work can do to improve the efficacy of government innovation policy and industrial strategy. As things currently stand, these aspects of public policy are struggling for relevance. Traditional innovation policy has been too narrowly couched around core national science and technology concerns to capture the broader range of, often international and non-innovation, factors that influence the likelihood of policy success. However, the response of transitioning to a broader 'industrial strategy' framing (as was attempted in the UK up to early 2021 before being abandoned as a formal title after a change in Prime Minister) is of constrained relevance and effectiveness because it overlooks the fundamental importance of GVCs in providing opportunities for boosting industrial activity. In short, both innovation policy and industrial strategy have been 'too national' in their approach. The focus on 'national innovation systems' and on industrial strategy decoupled from GVCs has created a parochial definition of the problem that, in turn, directs attention away from important opportunities (and threats) associated with the real-world GVC context in which industry operates. If policymakers continue to assume away the GVC dimension, then they risk perpetuating the self-imposed restrains to policy effectiveness that have dogged public policy to date.

As is so often the case, success in 'internationalising' innovation policy and industrial strategy rests on presenting enough evidence to convince policymakers that mindsets now need to change. Thanks to the path-breaking empirical work of the Organisation for Economic Co-operation and Development (OECD) aimed at mapping GVCs, this evidence base is now emerging. This creates the conditions for a paradigm shift in innovation policy and industrial strategy. In this new paradigm, innovation policy and industrial strategy are internationalised via

 DOI: 10.4324/9781315225661-23

a consideration of how GVCs stimulate innovation and act as conduits for cross-border transfers of intellectual property and know-how.

This chapter makes the case for this new internationalised policy stance towards innovation and industrial strategy, and draws attention to the type of evidence that will assist this transition in policy thinking. Whilst much new empirical work on the innovation dimension to GVCs now needs to be done, at least the data now starting to appear creates the conditions for progress. Indeed, current political developments (notably in the US–China tensions over trade, technology and national security) mean that the transition to a more integrated approach should not be delayed further. As the previous globalisation trajectories that drive GVC evolution shift to more nationalistic stances that consider *both* commercial and national security aspects within the same framing, the established 'decoupled' approach of treating innovation, industrial strategy, national security and GVC participation separately is no longer tenable.

The time is therefore ripe for improving the accuracy of our understanding of how GVCs function by drawing together how innovation and industrial strategy are shaped by GVC participation and, in turn, shape the structure and performance of GVCs.

Insights from the literature

There are currently a limited number of published academic and policy studies concerned with the relationships between innovation and GVCs (or global supply chains as they are sometimes referred to). Significantly, the bulk of the studies of GVCs have had a focus on developing rather than advanced industrial economies.[1] This developing country emphasis is also reflected in the emerging work on the innovation–GVC relationship, which tends to explore the implications for developing rather than developed economies. In other words, how to enter GVCs, or upgrade GVC contributions, rather than how to maximise the benefits from well-established GVC participation or, indeed, pursue strategies to configure GVCs around national interests and at the global technological frontier.

The most useful empirical work (by far) on the innovation–GVC relationship is currently being produced by the OECD, which has been driving both the focus on GVCs and the major advances in international data required to explore this area (discussed later). In this formative stage in the development of the literature on the innovation–GVC nexus, these relationships are currently addressed indirectly when specific aspects of the broader interplay of trade and GVCs or trade and innovation are considered – we still need a joined-up approach. It is plausible that we will start to see an increase in the academic literature on the GVC–innovation nexus due to the recent availability of better data on GVCs and, as a result, growing recognition of the ways in which innovation and GVCs are interrelated. Hopefully, this chapter will contribute to this emerging area of study and policy practice.

When considering the relationship between innovation and GVCs, the first point to stress is that global research and development (R&D) expenditure is highly skewed and dominated by the US and China (which overtook Japan several years ago), as demonstrated in Figure 17.1. This is an important context for considering the links between innovation and GVCs simply because these major economies are also key nodes in GVCs. Most maps of specific GVCs, whilst characteristically complex with various loops, have key nodes in the major R&D spending economies. The same large economies feature in most GVCs, but usually with relatively low foreign value-added content of their exports.

These asymmetries in R&D are highly significant for GVC participation. This is because, when embodied in the imports of smaller economies, there is effectively a leverage of the broader global R&D system via the knowledge spillovers generated by GVCs. The ability to

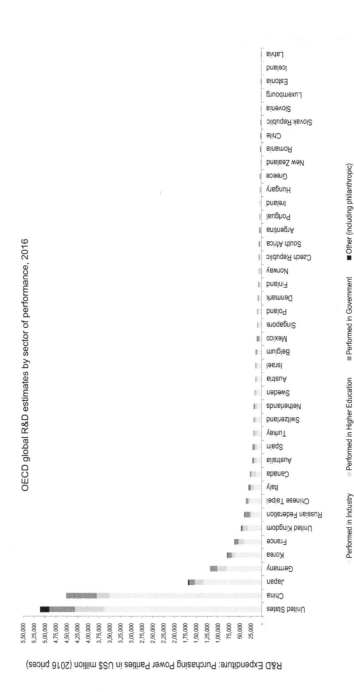

Figure 17.1 The highly skewed distribution of global R&D. (Source: Data from OECD Main Science and Technology Indicators.)

exploit these knowledge spillovers is an important aspect of the return on investment in internationally engaged business and innovation.

The literature identifies two basic types of GVCs: buyer-driven and producer-driven. The former is based on a strong purchasing power and market presence (usually from large corporations). This allows a set of value-added inputs to be brought together; a large retail corporation exemplifies this situation. A buyer-driven GVC tends not to involve high-technology–driven value added, so is less relevant to innovation policy. In contrast, a producer-driven GVC has a much closer relationship with innovative activities. The system of value-added contributions tends to be driven by efforts to increase the rents received by returns from proprietary knowledge, practical know-how and intellectual property rights. Consequently, producer-driven GVCs are the most logical GVC configurations from which to explore the relationships between innovation and GVC participation.

The following framework for analysing how innovation relates to GVCs emerged from early work carried out from a developing economies' perspective and stems from the contributions of Kaplinsky and Morris (2000) and has more recently been emphasised in the OECD's comprehensive discussion of GVCs (OECD 2013a).

This GVC upgrading framework focuses on the strategies via which companies (and entire countries) can upgrade their value-added contributions to GVCs. Four strategies are identified, as summarised in OECD (2013a):

- *Process upgrading* is achieved when firms can undertake tasks with significantly greater efficiency and lower defect rates, and process more complex orders than their rivals. This tends to rely on firm-specific management skills and flexible organisational structures.
- *Product upgrading* is achieved when firms can supply higher value-added products than their rivals owing to their superior technological sophistication and quality and also introduce novel products faster than rivals. This tends to rely on introducing advanced production technology, effective quality management and good designs.
- *Functional upgrading* is achieved when firms can provide competitive products or services in new segments or activities of a GVC that are associated with higher value added. For firms previously specialised in production, this means becoming competitive in upstream or downstream activities such as design or marketing. This requires sophisticated technologies and design capabilities together with strong marketing, brand visibility and extensions in retail and collaboration networks.
- *Chain upgrading* is achieved when firms are able to participate in new GVCs that produce higher value-added products or services, often leveraging the knowledge and skill acquired in the current chain.

Lenovo's acquisition of IBM's PC branch is an example of functional upgrading because this allowed sophisticated R&D capabilities to be acquired and built upon, extending Lenovo's value-added profile (OECD 2013a).

These four strategies are viewed as sequential in the sense that upgrading GVC participation is most easily achieved by prioritising each in turn (OECD 2013a). Evidence considered in this OECD analysis of GVC upgrading supports this perspective. Notably, like many other countries, China's domestic value-added export content in electrical and optical machinery declined over the years 1995 to 2005, reflecting the low margins associated with a focus on assembling products designed elsewhere. However, since 2005 this value-added export content has started to increase as Chinese firms in this industry started to build up their own product design capability, i.e. started moving up through the GVC upgrading process. This upgrading trajectory has resulted in China accounting for 25% of global value added in electronics exports by 2011 (OECD 2013a).

This finding highlights the ways in which a specific country's GVC upgrading strategy (if successful) can impact negatively on other countries' shares of global value-added in specific markets.

The concept of 'end-market upgrading' has also been suggested as a variation to chain upgrading in lifting GVC value-added contributions (Fernandez-Stark et al. 2013). This involves efforts to move into new higher value end markets by diversifying around an established market presence. For example, textile suppliers diversifying away from making general clothing to supply more specialised, higher value-added garments for medical, defence and other uses.

In general terms, the literature on GVC upgrading suggests that whilst there are elements of learning-by-doing in GVC participation (Gereffi 1999), upgrading value-added participation requires strong strategic intent and capabilities. It becomes increasingly more difficult to move from the process, through to product and then on to functional and chain upgrading in GVCs. Whilst the Chinese electronics industry has achieved GVC upgrading, industries in other technologically strong economies have not. South Korea, Germany and the US did not manage to increase their value-added content of electronics exports over the period that China was able to achieve this (OECD 2013a). Evidence from developing economies in Asia highlights the feasibility of upgrading value added in GVCs by moving from process upgrading through to product upgrading and then on to more ambitious GVC engagement. This upgrading trajectory requires increases in innovation capability alongside a range of other GVC-related business competencies – and this, in turn, requires very strong strategic intent and capability.

As the prominence of work on GVCs has increased following, in particular, the release of the OECD Trade in Value Added (TiVA) data in 2013,[2] policy-oriented studies of innovation policy have started to make an explicit link between innovation and GVCs. The 2015 OECD report 'The Innovation Imperative' highlighted the following issues:

- The openness to international flows of capital, goods, people and knowledge associated with the increasing importance of GVCs is also essential to innovation.
- Globalisation increases the size of accessible markets for investors and facilitates specialisation and competition, in turn facilitating the diffusion of innovations globally – thereby enhancing the long-term productivity yield from innovation.
- Tariff and non-tariff barriers to trade that affect imports are also, in effect, a tax on exports due to GVC inter-dependencies. This impact is compounded when GVCs repeatedly cross national borders. This, in turn, can impact on innovation performance because national innovation capability rests in part on the technologies and knowledge-based services imported and also on the intellectual property (IP) and know-how embodied in many imports.

Consequently, the OECD lists GVC participation as one of the framework conditions for effective innovation, especially with regard to strengthening the factors of production (OECD 2015). As a joint World Trade Organization (WTO/OMC) and United Nations Conference on Trade and Development (UNCTAD) paper prepared for a 2013 G20 Leaders' Summit stressed, GVCs are an international channel for ideas, knowledge and innovations embodied in intermediate goods, services and production methods (OECD 2013b). This position paper also stressed the ways in which modern complex GVCs are made possible by technological advances in transport and communications – these provide the necessary framework conditions by reducing logistical and coordination transaction costs.

As a result of this work, there is now growing recognition that national innovation performance rests, in part, on the technology and know-how embodied in imports, i.e. export performance is built on value-added enabled by imports. Awareness of the importance of this issue is long standing. For example, Coe and Helpman (1995) estimated the contribution to total factor productivity from the foreign R&D stock embodied in imports. More recent analyses have calculated that this embodied R&D can make a stronger contribution to productivity growth than domestic R&D for smaller economies (Achrya and Keller 2009). These transnational flows are treated as knowledge spillovers in the economics and business strategy literature – where trade in technology-intensive goods exists, so too can these spillovers.

Consequently, one of the key insights that a GVC analysis gives to industrial strategy and national innovation support (as reflected in the earlier discussion of upgrading strategies) is that these strategies must be 'global value chain aware'. This means understanding which industries rely on the spillovers associated with imports for their export competitiveness. Whilst discussions of chain dependency may not always highlight the innovation and technology dimension, whether explicit or implicit, chain dependency is of central importance to innovation performance.

Another insight from the literature is that the likelihood of a country lifting its value-added contribution to GVCs is greatest when innovation is defined broadly to encompass non-technological dimensions and is part of a wider strategy to improve GVC participation. The evidence to support this contention is that R&D and technological capability alone are insufficient to upgrade GVC participation.

One reason for this is the 'smiling curve' perspective developed as a strategic positioning framework in the computer industry, initially by the founder of Acer (Shih 1996). It emphasises the way in which the greatest value-added in a GVC is achieved upstream in R&D and design and downstream in marketing and services related to the product (notably aftermarket services). The actual production of the product and associated physical supply chain logistics are the lowest value-added segments in the GVC.

This sort of value-added profile is also relevant to industries such as aerospace, where similar thinking led to the strategy of shifting from designing, building and selling aero engines to selling the thrust provided by the engines and retaining ownership of the capital asset (i.e. selling the capital services rather than the product itself). Whilst technological capabilities were involved in this strategic transition (high engine reliability, modular designs that allowed fast repairs, sophisticated failure risk prediction software, etc.), the guiding principle is that a different value chain configuration would increase value added.

From an industrial strategy and innovation policy perspective, this profile of value added in a GVC suggests that the likelihood of success in upgrading performance is increased by integrating the higher value-added upstream R&D and design capabilities with downstream marketing and aftermarket services. This requires a systemic business strategy that is able to function effectively in different national contexts, usually requiring cross-cultural and other internationally focused skills. Simply spending more on R&D and on technological aspects of innovation will be insufficient to achieve an effective upgrade in value-added GVC participation.

In contrast to the insights emerging from the GVC literature, the plethora of studies of 'national innovation systems' have encouraged a rather parochial inward-looking perspective that has discouraged a focus on how GVCs are a reflection of what is in effect an 'international innovation system'.[3] Arguably, this situation has arisen because innovation has been partially decoupled from broader business realities, and this decoupling has encouraged a scrutiny of the functional arrangements for science and innovation within countries at the expense of attention paid to how innovation targets GVC participation and how the effectiveness of innovation is shaped by GVC participation.

The academic literature on GVCs has not helped in this respect because it has had a dominating concern with developing country economies with relatively little attention paid to the ways in which the major global economies use their science and innovation capability to act as 'architects' of GVCs. The greater the attention paid to how GVCs shape progress at the global innovation frontier, the greater the potential to counterbalance the 'national' dimension to innovation (systems) with a realistic grasp of the international dimension. Indeed, it is not too much of a stretch to argue that the system of GVCs, when coupled with networks of academic collaboration (and arguably also scientific and industrial espionage), *is* in many respects *the* international innovation system.

Put succinctly, a country's innovation capability is strongly influenced by the nature and extent of its participation in GVCs. This is because the GVCs you operate in are conduits for the transfer of IP, know-how and technology, and also long-term competitive strategy insights. Furthermore, innovative activity *itself* often relates to either winning or retaining positions in GVCs or, indeed, to efforts to reconfigure and/or introduce new GVCs.

Crucially, however, the ways in which a country (or individual firms) both *benefit from* GVC participation and also strategically *target* GVC participation involve a close 'braiding together' of scientific, technological and a wide range of general business capabilities in ways that are not captured by more narrowly 'innovation'-focused strategies and policy stances per se. Consequently, these important interdependencies between innovation and GVCs *mediated by this range of business capabilities* can be used by policymakers to reinvigorate approaches to public support for innovation framed as part of industrial strategy.

Given this opportunity, one puzzle is why government approaches to industrial strategy, such as the UK's recent stance,[4] do target this 'braiding' together of scientific, technological and a wide range of general business capabilities but almost totally ignore the GVC participation dimension (Stojanovic and Rutter 2017). Whether or not GVCs are considered has major consequences for whether industrial strategy actually works in practice. Seeking to perpetuate a myth that exports all go to final demand (which they don't) and that exports don't rely in many cases on what a nation imports (which they do) is clearly a risky endeavour likely to create opportunities for various 'nasty surprises' in policy delivery. The 'theory' framing industrial strategy does not stand tests against relevant evidence.

Broadening the scope of the assessment to cover geostrategic and national security concerns

There has been a reluctance, aside from amongst political scientists, international relations and national security researchers, to acknowledge and explore the nexus between innovation capability and national security.[5] This reluctance has directed attention away from the national security dimensions of GVC structure and performance as reflected in economic work on free trade, and also to an extent on science and innovation – where national security aspects can be viewed as a distraction from concerns with letting the markets that drive trade work effectively.

This national security dimension covers both explicit and more implicit and ambiguous dimensions. The explicit dimensions, which are now being brought to the forefront in US–China relationships, are directly concerned with limiting technology transfers where there are national security and, particularly now, cybersecurity concerns. This involves direct scrutiny of how supply chains can act as 'unwanted' technology transfer conduits.

The more implicit and ambiguous dimensions emerge when considering the relevance of the well-established literature on strategic trade theory and the innovation–GVCs relationship. Strategic trade theory focuses on the ways in which technologically sophisticated nations are able to build economically powerful industries via science and innovation capability using forms of funding and subsidies that avoid the restrictions addressed in trade agreements (see Tyson 1992). 'Launch aid' for new civil aircraft is an excellent example of strategic trade theory in action. For large complex systems like an aircraft, there is a well-known process via which design, development and final assembly costs decrease with cumulative experience. This is a complex process via which 'feedback' innovation takes place – actually assembling and testing the systems drives a multitude of design changes 'upstream' as the overall system design and its manufacturing processes (and extended supply chains) are optimised.

The result is that it can take up to 200 aircraft production 'lessons' to debug and speed up production to the point that the product is commercially viable. This means that the systems integrators (like Airbus and Boeing) pay considerable attention to their anticipated and actually achieved learning curve gradients. The steeper the learning curve, the lower the investment risk exposure. The learning curve is used in sales negotiations with customers (the larger the order, the larger the price discount in part to reflect the learning curve gains). A failure to achieve expected learning curve productivity gains can be catastrophic – and has led to large company financial failures.

Learning curves, and the associated product and process innovations they are associated with, are a classic justification for government launch aid – and hard-fought political battles over 'unfair' subsidies to trade. Indeed, Airbus would not have existed, and become a major competitor to Boeing, without European launch aid. The European Commission has long-standing objections to the ways in which the US has leveraged NASA and Department of Defense R&D and demonstrator programs to support civil industry. As a 2010 European Commission trade negotiation briefing note argued:

> So-called "military" and "space" subsidies provide considerable benefits for Boeing's civil aircraft business. Department of Defence and NASA subsidies for military and space assignments have helped Boeing develop technologies (e.g. composites) which the company in turn transfers without any cost to its civil aircraft production to improve and manufacture the necessary technology. Boeing also makes use of DOD centres and testing facilities to work on the design and wings of its civil planes. Those subsidies have for instance enabled Boeing to develop the technologies used in its B-787 and other civil aircraft models. This reduces, and effectively subsidises, Boeing's production costs and puts Airbus at a competitive disadvantage.[6]

This learning curve–based and defence innovation spin-off dimension is also relevant to Industry 4.0 (as advanced automation and pervasive data sharing in manufacturing supply chains are labelled). This is because advanced simulation modelling can have a dramatic impact on learning curve performance, especially when new technologies are being introduced. The greater the ability of advanced simulation models to optimise product designs and processes before actual physical fabrication and assembly, the further the progress along a virtual learning curve of productivity improvement (see Matthews 2006). This means that the so-called First of a Kind (FOAK) system produced, which could be something as large as a new power station design, may be equivalent to the experience gained from five or six system design-and-build debugging cycles. This ability to substitute cheaper virtual design debugging for real design debugging can give a decisive cost advantage.

The result is that Industry 4.0 has the potential to reduce the investment risks faced when new complex technological systems are produced. This, in turn, impacts upon the GVCs that feed these new product systems. However, it is the systems integrators (like Airbus and Boeing) who control the advanced simulation technologies that make this possible – this capability is not necessarily evenly distributed across GVCs. This is partly because the sophistication of these advanced simulation technologies stems from advanced defence applications, access to which is strictly controlled internationally. More generally, the dual-use characteristics of much cutting-edge science and innovation means that the 'science powers' are especially well-positioned to use their very substantial defence innovation budgets to support domestic industries and the associated GVCs (hence influencing the countries their managed GVC's *avoid* for national security reasons).

Consequently, there is a clear link between the insights from strategic trade theory, which stem from an understanding of how competitive advantage in innovation is achieved and contemporary challenges faced in the relationship between innovation and GVCs. These are discussed in more detail later in the next section titled 'State-owned enterprises and GVC upgrade strategies'.

One strategically important issue highlighted in the literature pertinent to innovation strategies and GVCs is that of the deliberate targeting of 'choke point' technologies, (McKinsey & Co 2010). This strategic approach is associated with technologically sophisticated Japanese corporations that identify opportunities to take positions in GVCs that allow them to dominate the market with key technology-intensive components widely used in GVCs. For example, the highly specialised substrates and bonding chemicals used in microprocessor fabrication. The economic value of this strategic approach stems from understanding where to look for such opportunities and then positioning within GVCs in a manner intended to limit the ability of new competitors to enter these choke point markets.

State-owned enterprises and GVC upgrade strategies

Some nations are actively shaping their GVCs rather than passively reacting to them, and are using state-owned enterprises (SOEs) to achieve this (OECD 2013b). China's 'Belt and Road' strategy is particularly interesting in this context because it can be interpreted as a forthright state emulation of the ways in which large multinational enterprises act as GVC architects but also benefit from the distinctive Chinese economic development strategy (Macaes 2016). As Macaes (2016) observes:

> China wants its industrial policy to be sufficiently coordinated with those countries that occupy other segments and chains. In return, China can offer cheap financing and its experience of an economic model that has proved very successful in boosting industrialization and urbanization on an unprecedently fast time scale.

In effect, the Chinese approach is to leverage its demonstrated capability in strategy, organisation and investment finance, together with appropriate inter-governmental agreements, to reconfigure entire sections of GVCs *in ways that suit China*. As such, this can be thought of as a form of an explicitly transnational industrial policy founded upon GVC-focused opportunities (Macaes 2016). Whilst the long sweep of history tells us that this type of transnational industrial strategy is not new (the UK's rise to industrial pre-eminence was linked to earlier GVC architectures facilitated by empire-building), the re-emergence of this highly strategic approach in a highly globalised economy is noteworthy.

The aforementioned issues therefore have implications for the delivery of national innovation and industrial strategies that extend beyond approaches based on market mechanisms and into the territory of strategic trade theory via the use of subsidies for R&D and innovation to shape GVC participation. This issue is addressed from the perspective of trade agreements in a report by the International Centre for Trade and Sustainable Investment (ICTSD) and World Economic Forum (WEF) (2016), highlighting how trade negotiations can impact on a nation's innovation capabilities and future potential. The report stresses that the current trade agreement architecture was designed before the internet revolution and that innovation-related considerations were not at the front of the mind when the WTO was formed in 1994. Consequently, there is no single overarching WTO agreement that covers innovation, and different aspects of innovation are touched upon in a range of WTO agreements.

The conclusion from the ICTSD–WEF (2016) work is that specific aspects of innovation-related policies and measures are impacted upon by different aspects of trade agreements, principally:

- Domestic R&D support and incentives/subsidies
- Protection and enforcement of intellectual property rights
- Commercialisation of publicly funded research
- Transfer of technology and know-how
- Government procurement
- Technical standards
- Competition policy
- Policy/regulatory frameworks and general infrastructure

The complexity of these interdependencies between trade agreements and innovation performance can lead to unintended consequences (both positive and negative). These interdependencies also create an environment in which governments can use multi-pronged strategies for supporting innovation (including strategic GVC positioning initiatives by SOEs) that generate competitive advantage in GVCs in ways that circumnavigate and/or use both bilateral and multilateral trade agreements.

Consequently, one advantage of adopting a GVC-focused approach is that it forces attention on the combined effects of trade *and* innovation considerations. The availability of better data on GVCs in general and an improved understanding of how innovation shapes and is shaped by GVCs will help to improve understanding of the various ways in which the specifics of trade agreements and SOE-orchestrated GVC shaping strategies can impact upon innovation performance via the interdependencies inherent in GVCs.

Communicating what GVCs are to non-specialists is hard

Perhaps *the* major challenge faced when considering the industrial strategy, innovation and GVC nexus is that there is currently no 'actionable' analytical picture of the GVC system. 'Actionable' in this context means results from analysing data that are sufficiently accurate and relevant to allow practical decisions to be made. There are now very useful data sets that allow GVCs to be mapped and analysed using input–output methods applied at the global level, notably (but not limited to) the OECD *Trade in Value Added* (TiVA) data set and the *World Input–Output Database* (WIOD). However, the availability of the new data sets does not mean that an actionable analytical picture now exists (the system is just too complex to make this an easy task).

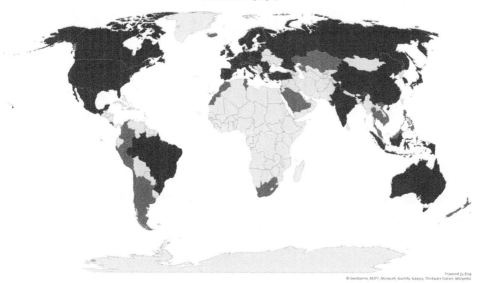

Country-by-country GVC mapping coverage in 2020:
OECD and WIOD data coverage in black, OECD only coverage in dark grey, no detailed country-by-country GVC data coverage from these sources in light grey

Figure 17.2 Where we can currently trace global value chains. (Source: Data from OECD Trade in Value Added Database and the World Input Output Database.)

Aside from the great complexity of the GVC system, one additional limitation is simply that much of the global economy is still an 'unmeasured space' in GVC terms. Figure 17.2 illustrates this point by comparing the coverage of two widely used datasets that can be used to analyse GVCs, the OECD TiVA data set and the WIOD. As is clear, almost all of Africa and a significant proportion of Asia are not covered by data that allows a country-by-country picture of GVCs to be built. These 'unmapped' economies (for which trade data are available but not the reliable input–output data to be combined with trade data to map GVCs) are lumped together as a residual consideration in the major GVC data sets used to balance out the inter-country flows between the 'measured' economies.

For the measured economies for which GVC participation can be tracked, we can generate summary profiles of a particular industry in a particular country (see Figure 17.3). These four UK sector examples (manufacture of other transport equipment; manufacture of computer, electronic and optical products; construction; and manufacture of rubber and plastic products) highlight the great diversity in these summary profiles regarding the balance of 'downstream' value chain destinations (domestic and international) distinguishing between intermediate and final consumption in each case.[7] We can profile the balance of imports and exports from and into GVCs for all industries in a country and we can estimate the full value-added 'flow-through' links between all countries and all other countries created by GVCs; see Figure 17.4 for a depiction of the manufacture of other transport equipment (which includes aerospace) in this GVC context. But what we cannot currently do is provide a more 'forensic' evidence base that allows us to trace these highly complex economic flows in a 'step-by-step' basis. The GVC system is so complicated that representing this sheer complexity in a meaningful way is extremely difficult.

As an illustration of this sheer complexity, the average UK industry connects directly with 153 other GVC streams. A sample of the 'second-order' connections via which each industry's down-

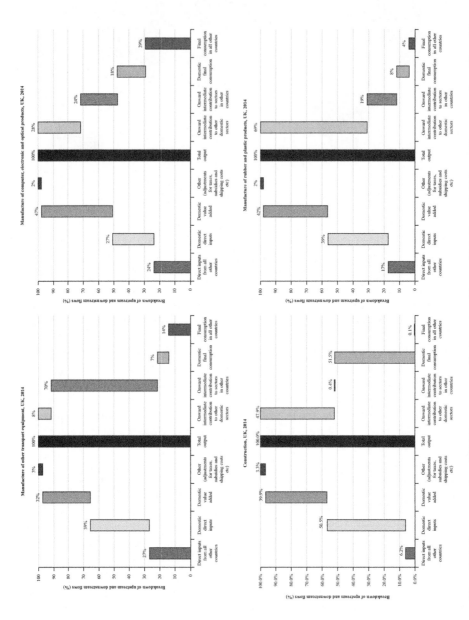

Figure 17.3 Some examples of GVC summary profiles by sector. (Source: Data from World Input Output Database. Use of the World Input Output Database is acknowledged at the developer's request by citing Timmer et al., 2015.)

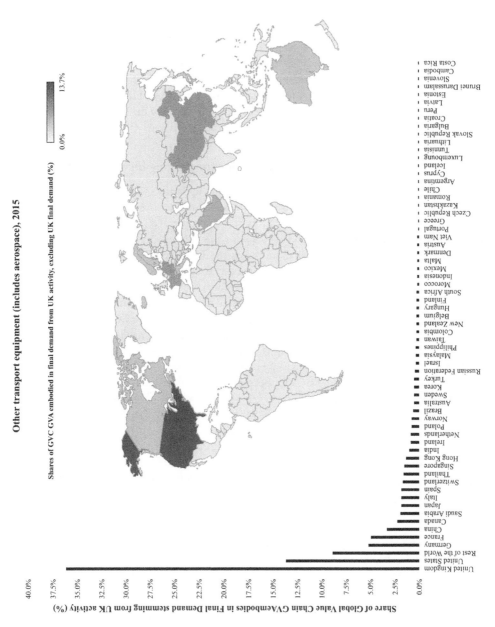

Figure 17.4 An example of a sector-based GVC system map. (Source: Data from the OECD Trade in Value Added Database.)

stream flows merge with others in the system of GVCs leads to a jump to an average of over 40,000 value streams (265 second-order GVC connections for every first-order connection).[8] In short, we can look at one end of the system of GVC 'pipes' or the other end, but not currently the 'middle', the intermediate 'work-in-progress' flow structure of GVCs as they loop through a myriad of different national economies. Whilst pictures of these very complicated flows can be generated, it is hard to make much sense of them from a decision-making perspective.

These shortcomings in our current ability to analyse GVCs in a manner of use to non-specialists have a knock-on impact on the ability to disseminate an appreciation of the industrial strategy/innovation and GVC relationship. This is simply because there is a lack of clarity of what the system of GVCs *actually looks like*. Consequently, success in developing more 'fit for purpose' data visualisation and interactive GVC mapping tools stands to make a profound con-tribution to industrial strategy in general, and to our understanding of the relationships between innovation and GVCs in particular. Better maps of GVCs will allow the implications for innova-tion and industrial strategy to be grasped more fully than at present.

Observations and suggestions for moving forward

The main message to emerge from the literature bearing upon the industrial strategy, innovation strategy and GVC relationship is that upgrading value-added performance in GVCs is first and foremost a matter of competitive strategy in its broadest sense. R&D and innovation strategies alone are a necessary but not a sufficient basis for upgrading GVC participation. Integrated approaches to knowledge-based capital, treated as the key intangible asset, are central to this competitive strategy. R&D and innovation contribute to this broader intangible asset but do not dominate its functional ability. However, this knowledge-based capital also needs to be deployed as part of an overarching competitive strategy focused clearly on upgrading GVC participation.

Such a strategy will work most effectively if GVCs are treated *themselves* as the entities being targeted – something that is only feasible if the appropriate data and analytical methods are avail-able. If one cannot grasp what something is then it is hard to marshal the necessary resources to develop appropriate strategic responses. Hence the importance of the empirical work that the OECD is now leading. Unless GVCs become more 'visible' and understandable to senior policymakers, this strategic shift will be very hard to achieve. Once this visibility is present, and the national economic (and security) ramifications easily grasped, then such a shift in strategy will be both intuitive and relatively easy to accomplish.

Finally, as is implicit in the arguments and evidence reviewed in this chapter, but made explicit in a stocktaking seminar held as part of G20 preparations under the Australian presi-dency, "GVCs create opportunities for fast growth, but they also raise the penalties for the wrong policies" (OECD 2014b). Given the intertwining of innovation strategies and GVC participation, this cautionary note also applies to industrial strategy and innovation policy. If innovation policy pays little or no attention to the opportunities and threats created by GVCs, then the wrong innovation policies may result. For example, (as stressed earlier) an excessive emphasis on what happens within national borders to the exclusion of global connectivity can lead to opportunities to exploit transnational knowledge spillovers being overlooked.

Playing out the implications for innovation and industrial strategy

The interconnections between innovation and GVCs mean that any national policy framework for innovation should ideally factor in this international connectivity. For example, any analysis of fluctu-ations in levels of business enterprise R&D (BERD) that ignores the GVC dimension in preference for purely domestic considerations will be of limited efficacy in informing government policy and national innovation strategy. This is because the business considerations that influence business R&D budgets can relate more strongly to the GVC dimension than to purely domestic economic considerations, and not necessarily in ways that are explained by macroeconomic factors. If a company is trying to position itself to win work as part of a GVC feeding into a major multinational enterprise, then it will characteristically seek to lift its innovation capability to secure that position in the value chain. This may involve an increase in R&D spending. In addition, all participants in a specific GVC stand to benefit from knowledge spillovers generated within that system of relationships – this can amount, in itself, to a useful return on investment on efforts to join a GVC.

It is also worth bearing in mind that the R&D and innovation 'embodied' in imports play a key role in national competitiveness. In those GVCs that are innovation based or strongly innovation influenced, the innovations achieved in any particular country are contributions to this broader global system, and, in turn, countries will benefit from the R&D embodied in these imports. The ways in which national innovation capability leverages upstream knowledge-based capabilities (including innovation but not limited to innovation) means that any focus on exports but not on securing the necessary imports that allow industrial activity to take place creates an imbalance that can distort decision-making. Governments can play an important role here by exploiting opportunities to facilitate access to dual-use technologies and other imported strategic assets that, in turn, enable exports (and associated domestic value added) that would not otherwise be possible.

A GVC focus encourages innovation strategy to consider not just how exports will be achieved and the associated domestic value added increased (or protected), but how imports embodying technology and know-how will be leveraged to achieve this enhanced export performance. In other words, recognition of the importance of GVCs encourages a more systemic approach to the global economy that considers the indirect/embodied drivers of competitiveness – not just the drivers that exist within a national boundary. One implication for policy-makers is that more attention should be paid to this international leverage dimension, including measures that capture this leverage (e.g. calculate the value of other countries' R&D embodied in the imports that contribute to export performance). Such measures are now feasible using a combination of OECD TiVA and R&D data.

The caveat to this impact of GVCs on innovation strategy is that the literature also stresses that improvements in innovation performance alone, in isolation from a broader set of knowledge-based competencies, is less powerful in improving GVC participation than a broader knowledge-based approach. GVCs may provide opportunities to leverage the global innovation effort (to the extent that this is embodied in trade flows), but exploiting those opportunities requires more complex strategies to be successful.

Also, innovation impacts on GVCs via disruptive technological advances (that can make some GVCs obsolete) and via choke point strategies that secure a competitive advantage at key nodes in GVCs. That said, the existing literature on the innovation–GVC nexus does not directly address the disruptive technology issue. There is little attention paid at present to how advanced automation and simulation technologies (Industry 4.0) will impact on GVCs. This latter aspect is better dealt with in the literature on such developments, and work remains to be done on the specific implications for GVCs.

The key role of knowledge spillovers in the innovation–GVC relationship

Knowledge spillovers are an important influence on innovation effectiveness. They explain both why geographical clusters of firms and innovative activity exist (co-location allows these spillovers to be exploited) and why some clusters perform better than others. A start-up firm in a cluster with strong knowledge spillovers is more likely to succeed commercially than one located in a weaker cluster. Better face-to-face advice is available to help start-ups avoid the myriad of risks faced. This advice is based on previous local experience, i.e. geographically specific and therefore particularly valuable. This dimension explains why the 'serial entrepreneurs' found in high-performing innovation clusters play such an important role helping to spot new business opportunities and in driving down the investment risks faced when innovating.[9]

Knowledge spillovers are also an important aspect of GVCs because inter-firm transactions also create opportunities for knowledge transfers to take place. Indeed, as this chapter has stressed, large technologically sophisticated multinational corporations deliberately cultivate knowledge spillovers because they strengthen the competitiveness of their GVCs.

This alignment between the role of knowledge spillovers in both geographically specific innovation clusters and geographically dispersed GVCs suggests that a focus on knowledge spillovers could provide a unified framework for understanding the relationships between GVCs and international academic research collaboration networks. Such a framework would help to explain how GVCs and international academic research collaboration networks interface in the innovation domain – that is to say, wherever GVCs involve innovation-related knowledge spillovers that interconnect with academic collaborations.

The main challenge is that, rather like friction in engineering, these knowledge spillovers cannot be easily measured directly – we can only measure the effects (positive and negative) that they have on innovation performance. In other words, recognition of the importance of GVCs encourages a more systemic approach to the global economy that considers the indirect/embodied drivers of competitiveness – not just the drivers that exist within a national boundary.

More generally, adding an explicit GVC dimension to a national innovation strategy would also have the advantage of encouraging a more integrated approach to innovation and trade policy. The GVC focus makes it clear that innovation policy and trade policy are more closely coupled than traditional stances might suggest. Consequently, adopting a more holistic approach would help to reduce the risk of unintended consequences for innovation performance stemming from the details of trade agreements. The suggested policy 'ecosystem' framework together with a focus on international knowledge spillovers is a possible solution to this challenge to develop a more holistic approach.

Conclusions

Public policy in general can be thought of as a process of investing in trying to obtain more preferable odds of things happening in an uncertain world. More specifically, better odds of things happening that we want to happen and worse odds of things happening that we don't want to happen. From this perspective, the nexus between innovation and GVCs, and how this nexus plays into industrial strategy, is a matter of lifting the odds of increased GVC participation (with consequent benefits in terms of trade, investment, employment and productivity growth) whilst decreasing the odds of damaging consequences from GVC participation. These damaging consequences lie in such things as loss of IP and know-how through forced technology transfer, industrial espionage and exacerbated debt.

The future accuracy and usefulness of our understanding of GVCs will hinge upon the extent to which we can achieve an effective conceptual and empirical integration of innovation, industrial strategy, national security, and GVC structure and performance. In the future, GVC

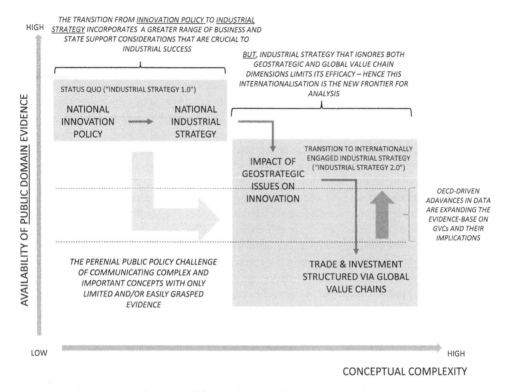

AVAILABILITY OF PUBLIC DOMAIN EVIDENCE

HIGH

THE TRANSITION FROM <u>INNOVATION POLICY</u> TO <u>INDUSTRIAL STRATEGY</u> INCORPORATES A GREATER RANGE OF BUSINESS AND STATE SUPPORT CONSIDERATIONS THAT ARE CRUCIAL TO INDUSTRIAL SUCCESS

BUT, INDUSTRIAL STRATEGY THAT IGNORES BOTH GEOSTRATEGIC AND GLOBAL VALUE CHAIN DIMENSIONS LIMITS ITS EFFICACY – HENCE THIS INTERNATIONALISATION IS THE NEW FRONTIER FOR ANALYSIS

STATUS QUO ("INDUSTRIAL STRATEGY 1.0")

NATIONAL INNOVATION POLICY → NATIONAL INDUSTRIAL STRATEGY

IMPACT OF GEOSTRATEGIC ISSUES ON INNOVATION

TRANSITION TO INTERNATIONALLY ENGAGED INDUSTRIAL STRATEGY ("INDUSTRIAL STRATEGY 2.0")

OECD-DRIVEN ADAVANCES IN DATA ARE EXPANDING THE EVIDENCE-BASE ON GVCs AND THEIR IMPLICATIONS

THE PERENIAL PUBLIC POLICY CHALLENGE OF COMMUNICATING COMPLEX AND IMPORTANT CONCEPTS WITH ONLY LIMITED AND/OR EASILY GRASPED EVIDENCE

TRADE & INVESTMENT STRUCTURED VIA GLOBAL VALUE CHAINS

LOW — HIGH

CONCEPTUAL COMPLEXITY

Figure 17.5 Diagrammatic depiction of the key features of the recommended policy stance.

configurations (the countries and industries that GVCs loop through) will be shaped more explicitly by concerns over 'dual-use' (military–civil) technologies, providing an impetus for the academic community to do a better job of the 'scholarship of integration' in this important area of inquiry. Progressing the empirical mapping and analyses of GVCs in ways that inform our understanding of these interrelationships between innovation/industrial strategy and national security is a logical starting point for this integrative initiative. Figure 17.5 summarises the key features of this proposed transition to a more internationalised and geostrategically aware policy stance regarding GVCs. It highlights the importance of improving the evidence base on the innovation, industrial strategy and GVC nexus in order to address the challenge of communicating these conceptually complex issues to policymakers. Without this effective communication there is a risk that the public policy that stands to gain so much from greater awareness of the GVC dimension to innovation and industrial strategy will get stuck in a policy 'groundhog day' of repeated but relatively futile interventions – *futile* because the problems are misdiagnosed.

A 'risk-aware' industrial strategy that does not shy away from these downsides to GVC participation when addressing the upsides is, therefore, the best way to proceed in public policy. 'Panglossian' policy stances that pretend that GVC participation does not have a downside in these terms will just increase the odds of nasty surprises and are therefore best avoided.

One message for the advocates of the 'government can't pick winners' argument against industrial strategy as a whole is that the strong 'dual use' interconnects between civil and military innovation mean that the directions taken by innovation are influenced by military and national security objectives. The long-term, high uncertainty and therefore high investment risk projects via which national security aims are pursued are non-market resource allocations that shape the directions taken in innovation. Today, both 'spin-in' (civil into national security) and 'spin-out' (national security into civil) are prominent features of this 'braiding' together of civil and military innovation trajectories. The 20-plus years strategic planning time horizons (sometimes as long as 40 years) found in some aspect of weapons systems innovation planning mean that civil innovation is inevitably shaped by the military dimension.

Given this aspect, pure market resource allocations do not drive innovation and, as this examination of the industrial strategy, innovation and GVC nexus has highlighted, GVCs are being shaped by national security concerns. This means that an industrial strategy does make sense from a public policy perspective (because the international economy is not a market-driven 'level playing field) – winners are being picked by the major science and innovation powers and this will continue to be the case. One lesson from the UK Industrial Strategy, which is noteworthy of its ignoring of the GVC dimension to the trade–innovation relationship, is that these exclusions are made at the cost of a less effective policy stance when theory is translated into actual policy practice. As this chapter argues, bringing the GVC–innovation nexus centrally into the industrial strategy enriches both the industrial strategy and the execution of innovation support. This 'rounded' stance encompassing the market-driven factors in GVCs and also national security and strategic trade dimensions that shape and are shaped by innovation will be more effective in using public funding to improve the odds of more desirable futures eventuating and decreasing the odds of less desirable futures eventuating.

Moving forward

Moving forward, the following steps would be useful.

Firstly, provide 'graspable' analyses that help policymakers' mindsets to factor in the GVC dimension to a range of decision-making. 'Step-through' GVC traces that provide a more granular picture of how GVCs are structured would help in this regard. At present we only have access to 'into the pipes' and 'out of the pipes' evidence, with a massive gap in understanding of the structure of the system of pipes itself.

This structural analysis of GVCs could usefully highlight the different types of national positioning in GVCs. For example, *confluence economies* where a large number of GVCs converge in final demand/consumption; *source economies* where resource extraction initiates GVCs; *router/ pivot economies* where several GVCs loop through and combine and then spread out again; and *portal* economies where imports enter GVCs rather than go straight to final demand. Singapore is a good example of a GVC router-/pivot-oriented industrial strategy using innovation capability in combination with locational and regulatory and tax advantages.

Secondly, augment this 'step through' GVC picture by adding data on innovation activities in order to better understand how innovation enables the range of 'GVC aware' industrial strategy approaches noted earlier.

Thirdly, start to draw out the important ways in which it is actually cities and their surrounding functional economic regions that are driving GVC participation, including when enabled by innovation, rather than national economies per se. Around 80 per cent of global value added is generated by cities (Dobbs et al. 2011) and GVCs loop through these cities. Whilst national economies provide the tax, tariff and non-tariff trade and national security innovation capability that shapes GVCs, precisely where (geographically) in these economies GVCs loop through tends to be influenced by cities and their regions. In other words, many of the key nodes in the system of GVCs are city regions, not countries per se.

This 'place-based' focus on innovation capability has grown in importance over the last two decades or so, more recently given expression in the 'Smart Specialisation' concept promoted in particular in the EU policy framework. However, place-based thinking has tended to become *parochial thinking* – emphasising a tight 'within boundaries' geographical focus on science and innovation capabilities at the expense of the national and most importantly global connectivity that tends to determine actual performance in both science and in innovation.

Consequently, the collation of place-based bottom-up data is most useful when it meshes what is happening within a given geographical area and the collaborative scientific activities and GVC-related innovation activities that connect that geography with many others. This perspective highlights the importance of doing more to map GVCs from the bottom up using sub-national data sources able to capture GVC connectivity at the local level. Only then will it be possible to develop a balanced approach that integrates the local functional geographies with the international GVC connectivity that, in combination, are so central to innovation.

The most useful way forward in empirical understanding of the relationships between industrial strategy, innovation and global value chains is to build an evidence base bottom up from cites and their regions – drawing out how they are connected as a complex network. The economic performance of national economies is the result of a 'co-evolution' of the system of GVCs that connects cities and their regions and the system of trade agreements and strategic/national security arrangements around which states organise their relationships with each other.

Acknowledgements

This chapter draws in part on a literature review paper commissioned to inform the development of Innovation and Science Australia's strategic advice to the Australian government through its 2030 Strategy for Australia's Innovation System. It also draws on subsequent work commissioned by the UK's Smart Specialisation Hub and a range of other projects for government carried out by the author as Special Advisor to Steer Economic Development. The author thanks the following people for their comments and advice during the preparation and finalisation of papers upon which this chapter draws: Ross Burton, David Crook, John H Howard, Don Scott-Kemmis, Simon Pringle, Stuart Thompson. Thanks also to Caitriona Lacy and Daniel Matthews for assisting with the collation of the literature reviewed in the papers upon which this chapter draws, and to three anonymous referees for useful comments on the initial draft of this chapter. Most importantly, thanks to John H Howard and Roy Green for liaising over the inclusion of this chapter in the book.

Notes

1 As there are numerous publications on the developing economy aspects of GVCs this literature is detailed in the references to sources at the end of this chapter, but is not cited in detail as the focus of the chapter is on broader and different concerns.
2 The new data collates much (but not all) of available national input-output data to create an international input-output database that is then used to trace complex patterns of value-adding via GVCs.
3 See Nelson (1993) for a seminal contribution, also Lundvall (1992) and Lundvall et al (2002)
4 Whilst the UK abandoned the Industrial Strategy label in early 2021 in preference for a 'Build Back Better' policy stance, with a stronger emphasis on closing regional economic imbalances on the post-COVID era, the underlying principles remain in place.
5 Dick Samuel's book *Rich Nation, Strong Army* (Samuels, 1996) is an excellent example of research that goes to the heart of this nexus between national industrial prowess and national security – a focus now clearly evident in China's industrial strategy stance.
6 Quote taken from European Commission (2010).
7 These 'waterfall' depictions of sector value chain characteristics emulate a graphical depiction used in Stojanovic and Rutter (2017).

8 Authors calculations using the World Input Output Database.
9 There is an extensive literature on the importance of knowledge spill-overs on innovation effectiveness. Audretsch and Feldman (2004) provide an especially useful overview of this literature from a management strategy perspective.

Bibliography

Acharya, R. C. and Keller, W. (2009). Technology Transfer through Imports. *Canadian Journal of Economics*, 42(4): pp. 1411–1418.

Andrews, D. (2013). Raising the Returns to Innovation: Structural Policies for a Knowledge-based Economy, *OECD Economics Department Policy Notes. No. 17*, Paris.

Arndt, S. and Kierzkowski, H. (2001). *Fragmentation: New Production Patterns in the World Economy*. Oxford, UK: Oxford University Press.

Arvis, J.-F., Mustra, M. A., Ojala, L., Shepherd, B. and Saslavsky, D. (2012). *Connecting to Compete 2012: Trade Logistics in the Global Economy*. Washington, DC: World Bank Group.

Audretsch, D. B. and Feldman, M. P. (2004). Knowledge Spillovers and the Geography of Innovation. In J.V. Henderson and F. F. Thisse (eds.), *Handbook of Urban and Regional Economics: Cities and geography*, Volume 4. Amsterdam: Elsevier.

Bair, J. (2005). Global Capitalism and Commodity Chains: Looking Back, Going Forward. *Competition and Change*, 9(2): pp. 153–180.

Bair, J. and Gereffi, G. (2001). Local Clusters in Global Chains: The Causes and Consequences of Export Dynamism in Torreon's Blue Jeans Industry. *World Development*, 29(11): pp. 1885–1903

Baldwin, R. (2012). *Global Manufacturing Value Chains and Trade Rules. The Shifting Geography of Global Value Chains: Implications for Developing Countries and Trade Policy*. Geneva: World Economic Forum.

Baldwin, R. and Lopez-Gonzalez, J. (2013). *Supply-Chain Trade: A Portrait of Global Patterns and Several Testable Hypotheses*. NBER Working Papers. No. 18957.

Baldwin, R. E. (2012). *Global Supply Chains: Why They Emerged, Why They Matter, and Where They Are Going*. Centre for Economic Policy Research. Discussion Papers. No. 9103.

Bamber, P. et al. (2014). *Connecting Local Producers in Developing Countries to Regional and Global Value Chains: Update*. OECD Trade Policy Papers. No. 160. Paris: OECD Publishing.

Belderbos, R. et al. (2016). *Where to Locate Innovative Activities in Global Value Chains: Does Co-location Matter?* OECD Science, Technology and Industry Policy Papers. No. 30, Paris: OECD Publishing.

Beltramello, A., De Backer, K. and Moussiegt, L. (2012). *The Export Performance of Countries within Global Value Chains (GVCs)*. OECD Science, Technology and Industry Working Papers. No. 02, Paris: OECD Publishing.

Benavente, D. (2014). *Measurement of Trade and Innovation: Issues and Challenges*. E15Initiative. Geneva: International Centre for Trade and Sustainable Development (ICTSD) and World Economic Forum.

Bhatia, K. (2012). Case-study 1: General Electric Corporation – Advanced Manufacturing in Perspective. In *The Shifting Geography of Global Value Chains: Implications for Developing Countries and Trade Policy*. Global Agenda Council on the Global Trade System, Geneva: World Economic Forum.

Braga, Carlos Primo Primo. (March 2016). *Innovation, Trade and IPRs: Implications for Trade Negotiations*. Working Paper, East-West Center Workshop on Mega-Regionalism – New Challenges for Trade and Innovation.

Cattaneo, O., Gereffi, G. and Staritz, C. (2010). *Global Value Chains in a Post-crisis World: A Development Perspective*. Washington, DC: The World Bank.

Coe, D. T. and Helpman, E. (1995). International R&D spillovers. *European Economic Review*, 39(5): pp 859–887.

Curtis, J. M. (2016). *Trade and Innovation: Policy Options for a New Innovation Landscape. E15 Expert Group on Trade and Innovation* – Policy Options Paper. E15 Initiative. Geneva: International Centre for Trade and Sustainable Development (ICTSD) and World Economic Forum.

De Backer, K. and Miroudot S. (2013). *Mapping Global Value Chains*. OECD Trade Policy Papers. No. 159, Paris: OECD Publishing.

De Backer, K. and Yamano N. (2012). *International Comparative Evidence on Global Value Chain*. OECD Science, Technology and Industry Working Papers. 2012/03, Paris: OECD Publishing.

Dicken, P. (2003). *Global Shift: Reshaping the Global Economic Map in the 21st Century*, 4th edition, London: Sage.

Dicken, P. (2007). *Global Shift: Mapping the Contours of the World Economy*. London: Sage Publishing.

Dicken, P., Kelly, P., Olds, K. and Yung, H. W.-C. (2001). Chains and Networks, Territories and Scales: Towards a Relational Framework for Analysing the Global Economy. *Global Networks*, 1(2): pp. 89–112.

Dobbs, R et al. (2011). *Urban World: Mapping the Economic Power of Cities.* McKinsey & Co.

Elms, D. K. and Low, P. (eds.) (2013). *Global Value Chains in a Changing World*, WTO Publications for Fung Global Institute, Nanyang Technological University and the World Trade Organization, Geneva.

European Commission (2010). *Support to Boeing and Airbus: Separating the Myths from the Facts.* Briefing sheet.

Farfan, O. (2005). *Understanding and Escaping Commodity-Dependency: A Global Value Chain Perspective.* Washington, DC: The World Bank Group.

Feenstra, R. (1998). Integration of Trade and Disintegration of Production in the Global Economy. *Journal of Economic Perspectives*, 12(4): pp. 31–50.

Fernandez-Stark, K., Bamber, P. and Gereffi, G. (2013). *Costa Rica in the Offshore Services Global Value Chain: Opportunities for Upgrading*, Duke University Center on Globalization, Governance and Competitiveness, Durham, NC.

Fine, B. and Deraniyagala. (2001). New Trade Theory versus Old Trade Policy: A Continuing Enigma. *Cambridge Journal of Economics*, 25: pp. 809–825.

Flavey, R. Foster, N. and Greenaway, D. (2002). North-South Trade, Knowledge Spillovers and Growth. *International Economic Review*, 43(2): pp. 393–407.

Gereffi, G. (1994). The Organization of Buyer-Driven Global Commodity Chains: How U.S. Retailers Shape Overseas Production Networks. In G. Gereffi and M. Korzeniewicz (Eds.), *Commodity Chains and Global Capitalism*. Westport: Greenwood Press, pp. 95–122.

Gereffi, G. (1999). International Trade and Industrial Upgrading in the Apparel Commodity Chain. *Journal of International Economics*, 48, pp. 37–70.

Gereffi, G. and Christian, M. (2009). *Trade, transnational corporations and food consumption: a global value chain.* Durham, NC: Duke University.

Gereffi, G., and Fernandez-Stark, K. (2010). The Offshore Services Value Chain: Developing Countries and the Crisis, in Cattaneo, Gereffi, and Staritz (2010).

Gereffi, G. and Fernandez-Stark, K. (2011). *Global Value Chain Analysis: A Prime.* 1st ed. Durham, NC: Duke University.

Gereffi, G., Fernandez-Stark, K. and Psilos, P. (2011). *Skills for Upgrading: Workforce Development and Global Value Chains in Developing Countries*, Duke Center on Globalization, Governance and Competitiveness and the Research Triangle Institute, Durham, NC.

Gereffi, G., Humphrey, J. and Sturgeon, T. (2005). The Governance of Global Value Chains. *Review of International Political Economy*, 12(1): pp. 78–104.

Gereffi, G. and Kaplinsky, R. (Eds.). (2001). The Value of Value Chains: Spreading the Gains from Globalisation. *IDS Bulletin*, 32(3): 1.

Gereffi, G. and Korzeniewicz, M. (Eds.) (1994). *Commodity Chains and Global Capitalism*. Westport, CT: Greenwood Press.

Gereffi, G. and Memodovic, O. (2003). *The Global Apparel Value Chain: What Prospects for Upgrading by Developing Countries?* United Nations Industrial Development Organization (UNIDO).

Gereffi, G. and Sturgeon T. (2013). Global Value Chain-Oriented Industrial Policy: The Role of Emerging Economies. In D. K. Elms and P. Low (Eds.), *Global value chains in a changing world*. Geneva: World Trade Organization.

Gibbon, P. (2001). Upgrading Primary Production: A Global Commodity Chain Approach. *World Development*, 29(2): pp. 345–363.

Gibbon, P. (2003). Value-Chain Governance, Public Regulation and Entry Barriers in the Global Fresh Fruit and Vegetable Chain into the EU. *Development Policy Review*, **21**(5–6): pp. 615–625. September.

Gibbon, P. (2004). *The Commodity question: new thinking on old problems*, UNDP Occasional Paper.

Gibbon, P. and Ponte, S. (2005). *Trading Down: Africa, Value Chains, and the Global Economy*. Philadelphia, PA: Temple University Press.

Glachant, M. (2013). *Greening Global Value Chains: Innovation and the International Diffusion of Technologies and Knowledge*, OECD Green Growth Papers, 2013–05, Paris: OECD Publishing.

Gnywali, D. and Park, B.-J. (2011). Co-Opetition between Giants: Collaboration with Competitors for Technological Innovation. *Research Policy*, 40(5): pp. 650–663.

Grossman, G. and Helpman, E. (1989). Product Development and International Trade. *Journal of Political Economy*, 97, pp. 1261–1283.

Henderson, J., Dicken, P., Hess, M., Coe, N. and Yeung H. W.-C. (2002). Global Production Networks and the Analysis of Economic Development. *Review of International Political Economy*, 9(3): pp. 436–464.

HM Government. (2018). *Building our Industrial Strategy: Building a Britain Fit for the Future.* White Paper.

Hummels, D., Rapoport, D. and Yi, K.-M. (1998). Vertical Specialisation and the Changing Nature of World Trade. *Federal Reserve Bank of New York Economic Policy Review*, pp. 79–99.

Humphrey, J. (2003). Globalisation and Supply Chain Networks: The Auto Industry in Brazil and India. *Global Networks*, 3(2): 121–141.

Humphrey, J. and Memodovic, O. (2003). *The Global Automotive Industry Value Chain: What Prospects for Upgrading by Developing Countries?* Sectoral Studies Series. Vienna: United Nations Industrial Development Organization.

Humphrey, J. and Schmitz, H. (2000). *Governance and Upgrading: Linking Industrial Cluster and Global Value Chain Research.* IDS Working Paper. 120, Brighton: Institute of Development Studies, University of Sussex.

Humphrey, J. and Schmitz, H. (2001). Governance in Global Value Chains. *IDS Bulletin*, 32: 19–29.

Humphrey, J. and Schmitz, H. (2002). How Does Insertion in Global Value Chains Affect Upgrading in Industrial Clusters? *Regional Studies*, 36(9): 1017–1027.

ICTSD and WEF (2016) *Trade and Innovation: Policy Options for a New Innovation Landscape.* Joint International Centre for Trade and Sustainable Investment (ICTSD) and World Economic Forum (WEF) report.

INSEAD, WIPO, and Cornell University. (2013). *The Global Innovation Index 2013: The Local Dynamics of Innovation.* Geneva, Ithaca, and Fontainebleau.

Jacobides, M., Knudsen T. and Augier M. (2006). Benefiting from Innovation: Value Creation, Value Appropriation and the Role of Industry Architectures. *Research Policy*, 35: pp. 1200–1221.

Kaplinsky, R. (1998). *Globalisation, Industrialisation and Sustainable Growth: The Pursuit of the nth Rent.* IDS Discussion Paper No. 365. Brighton: Institute of Development Studies, University of Sussex.

Kaplinsky, R. (2006). How Can Agricultural Commodity Producers Appropriate A Greater Share of Value Chain Incomes? In A. Sarris and D. Hallam (Eds.), *Agricultural Commodity Markets and Trade: New Approaches to Analyzing Market Structure and Instability.* Cheltenham: Edward Elgar and FAO.

Kaplinsky, R. and Morris, M. (2000). *A Handbook for Value Chain Research*, prepared for the IDRC, Sussex: Institute of Development Studies.

Keane, J. A. (2012). The Governance of Global Value Chains and the Effects of the Global Financial Crisis Transmitted to Producers in Africa and Asia. *Journal of Development Studies*, 48(6), pp. 783–797.

Kimura, S. (2007). *The Challenges of Late Industrialization: The Global Economy and the Japanese Commercial Aircraft Industry.* London: Palgrave Macmillan.

Kiriyama, N. (2012). *Trade and Innovation: Synthesis Report.* OECD Trade Policy Papers 135.

Kogut, B. (1985). Designing Global Strategies: Comparative and Competitive Value Added Chains. *Sloan Management Review*, 26(4): pp. 15–28.

Koopman, R., Powers, W., Wang, Z. and Wei. S. (2010). Give Credit Where Credit is Due: Tracing Value-added in Global Production Chains. NBER Working Paper. No. 16426, Cambridge, MA.

Kowalski, P. et al. (2015). *Participation of Developing Countries in Global Value Chains: Implications for Trade and Trade-Related Policies.* OECD Trade Policy Papers. No. 179, Paris: OECD Publishing. http://dx.doi.org /10.1787/5js33lfw0xxn-en

Levy, F. and Murnane, R. (2004). *The New Division of Labor: How Computers Are Creating the Next Job Market.* Princeton, NJ: Princeton University Press.

Lopez-Gonzalez, J., Kowalski, P. and Achard, P. (2015). *Trade, Global Value Chains and Income Inequality*, OECD Trade Policy Papers, No. 182, OECD Publishing.

Low, P. (2013). The Role of Services in Global Value Chains in Elms and Low (2013).

Lundvall, B.-Å. (1992). *National Systems of Innovation: Towards a Theory of Innovation Learning.* London: Pinter Publishers.

Lundvall, B.-Å, Johnson, B, Andersen, E. S. and Dalum, B. (2002). National Systems of Production, Innovation and Competence-Building. *Research Policy* 31(2): pp. 213–231.

Macaes, B. (2016). *China's Belt and Road: Destination Europe.* Carnegie Europe. November.

Maskus, K. E. and Saggi, K. (2013). *Global Innovation Networks and their Implications for the Multilateral Trading System.* E15Initiative. Geneva: International Centre for Trade and Sustainable Development (ICTSD) and World Economic Forum.

Matthews, M. L. (2006). *Managing Uncertainty and Risk in Science, Innovation and Preparedness: Why Public Policy Should Pay More Attention to Financial and Geopolitical Considerations.* Discussion Paper commissioned by the Federation of Australian Scientific and Technological Societies (FASTS). August. Canberra.

Matthews, M. L. (2018). Rural Innovation Outcomes and Global Value Chains. *Research Report 1: Performance Review of the Rural Innovation System.* Canberra: Howard Partners Pty Ltd.

McKinsey & Co. (2010). Global Grid. *McKinsey Quarterly.* June.

Miroudot, S., Rouzet, D. and Spinelli, F. (2013). *Trade Policy Implications of Global Value Chains: Case Studies.* OECD Trade Policy Papers. No. 161, Paris: OECD Publishing.

Nelson, R. R. (1993). *National Innovation Systems: A Comparative Analysis.* Oxford: Oxford University Press.

OECD (2012). *Intangible Assets, Resource Allocations and Growth: A Framework for Analysis.* OECD Economics Department Working Papers, No. 989, Paris: OECD.

OECD (2013a). *Interconnected Economies: Benefiting from Global Value Chains.* Paris: OECD Publishing.

OECD (2013b) *Implications for Global Value Chains for Trade, Investment, Development and Jobs.* Joint paper for the G20 Leaders Summit. Paris.

OECD. (2014a). *Developing Countries Participation in Global Value Chains and its Implications for Trade and Trade-Related Policies.* OECD internal document to be issued as an OECD Trade Policy Paper in 2015.

OECD. (2014b). OECD Stocktaking Seminar on Global Value Chains. In *G20 Australian Presidency.* 5 May 2014. Paris: OECD Headquarters.

OECD. (2015). *The Innovation Imperative: Contributing to Productivity, Growth and Well-Being.* Paris: OECD Publishing.

OECD. (2017). The Links between Global Value Chains and Global Innovation Networks: An Exploration. OECD Science, Technology and Industry Policy Papers. No. 37, Paris: OECD Publishing.

OECD, UNCTAD, and WTO. (2013). *Implications of Global Value Chains for Trade, Investment, Development and Jobs.* Prepared for the G-20 Leaders Summit Saint Petersburg (Russian Federation).

Palpacuer, F. (2000). Competence-Based Strategies and Global Production Networks: Discussion of Current Changes and Their Implications for Employment. *Competition and Change,* 4(4): pp. 353–400.

Ponte, S. and Gibbon, P. (2005). Quality standards, conventions and the governance of global value chains. *Economy and Society,* 34(1): 1–31.

Samuels, R. J. (1996). Rich Nation, Strong Army: National Security and the Technological Transformation of Japan. Cornell Studies in Political Economy. Ithaca, NY: Cornell University Press.

Shepherd, B. (2013). *Global Value Chains and Developing Country Employment, A Literature Review.* OECD Trade Policy Papers. No. 156, OECD Publishing,

Shepherd, B. and Stone, S. (2013). *Global Production Networks and Employment: A Developing Country Perspective.* OECD Trade Policy Papers. No. 154, OECD Publishing, Paris.

Shih, S. (1996) *Me-Too is Not My Style.* ACER Foundation, 136. Chinese Taipei.

Sinclair-Desgagné, B. (2013). *Greening Global Value Chains: Implementation Challenges.* OECD Green Growth Papers. No. 04, Paris: OECD Publishing.

Spence, M. (2009). *Negotiating Trade, Innovation and Intellectual Property: Lessons from the CARIFORUM EPA Experience From a Negotiator's Perspective.* UNCTADICTSD. Project on IPRs and Sustainable Development Policy Brief No.4.

Stojanovic, A. and Rutter, J. (2017). *Frictionless Trade: What Brexit Means for Cross-Border Trade in Goods.* London: Institute for Government.

Sturgeon, T. (2009). From Commodity Chains to Value Chains: Interdisciplinary Theory Building in an Age of Globalization. In J. Bair (Ed.), *Frontiers of Commodity Chain Research.* Stanford, CA: Stanford University Press, pp. 110–135.

Sturgeon, T., Van Biesebroeck, J. and Gereffi, G. (2008). Value Chains, Networks, and Clusters: Reframing the Global Automotive Industry. *Journal of Economic Geography,* 8(3): 297–321.

Timmer, M., Erumban, A., Los, B., Stehrer, R. and de Vries, G. (2014). Slicing Up Global Value Chains. *Journal of Economic Perspectives,* 28(2): pp. 99–118.

Timmer, M. P., Dietzenbacher, E., Los, B., Stehrer, R. and de Vries, G. J. (2015). An Illustrated User Guide to the World Input–Output Database: the Case of Global Automotive Production. *Review of International Economics,* 23: 575–605.

Tyson, L. D' Andrea (1992). *Who's Bashing Whom?: Trade Conflict in High-Technology Industries.* Washington, DC: Institute for International Economics.

Veugelers, R. (2013). Innovative Firms in Global Value Chains. In *Innovation for Growth – i4g.* Policy Brief No.21, October 13. European Commission.

Zanfei, A. (2000). Transnational Firms and the Changing Organization of Innovative Activities. *Cambridge Journal of Economics,* 24: pp. 515–542.

CASE STUDY

Meso-level GVC analysis of Korean shipbuilding

Brian Wixted and Martin Bliemel

Introduction

Management of global value chains (GVCs) is a coordinated effort by the companies participating in the GVCs as well as by governments who impose trade policy instruments such as tariffs, quotas, antidumping or other barriers. In some cases, when a tariff or other barrier is imposed on a given industry in a given country by another country, that country then attempts to mitigate losses by retaliating by imposing barriers in another industry against the other country or by passing on the barrier to overseas suppliers of the given industry in other countries. This case illustrates how the Korean government may explore how to react to a trade barrier on its shipbuilding industry.

Challenge

Korean trade policymakers are concerned with increased talk about trade wars and the impact of trade barriers on one of the country's major industries, shipbuilding.

Solutions

When a country is subjected to a trade barrier in an industry in which it has high exports, one solution is to impose a reciprocal trade barrier against the offending country. This is usually done across industries, selecting an industry in which the net imports are high. Another, less confrontational, measure is to pass on the barriers and associated costs to suppliers of the same industry. To understand which other countries and industries may be affected by passing on such barriers, they need to understand who their significant trade partners are for this industry (in this case the suppliers of input to shipbuilding, not the buyers of finished vessels).

Implementation steps

When reviewing the trade data for inputs to all domestic industries (left column of Figure C1.1), Korean policymakers may identify the top domestic source industries (middle column of Figure C1.1). This reveals that the industry is quite reliant on domestic iron and steel, and machinery

DOI: 10.4324/9781315225661-24   312

and equipment industries, which are relatively self-supporting within the country. In other words, Korean shipbuilding appears to be relatively economically sovereign. However, exploring the international source industries (right column of Figure C1.1) indicates that these source industries are reliant on importing materials from mining (energy and non-energy related) and on Iron and Steel, thus revealing a more complex picture of critical trade partners. This brings to light the question of finding an appropriate balance of economic sovereignty versus playing a key role in a globally connected industry.

In comparison, investigating the GVC structure at the macro level reveals relatively little actionable information. As shown in the economic-bloc analysis in Figure C1.2, the global shipbuilding industry is massive and that all major economic blocs are interconnected. What the figure does imply is that fumbling a trade partnership could mean being left out as the rest of the industry circumvents the Korean contribution to the industry.

To illustrate this point, Figure C1.3 shows the proportion (x-axis) of all global trade pathways related to shipbuilding, below a given level of percent of sourcing (y-axis) across all countries in the model. The distribution has an 84.6 R^2 with a log-log model. Setting a threshold of 10 percent (y-axis) above which a trade pathway is 'significant' would retain a focus on approximately 7 percent of all 'significant' country–country sourcing pathways.

When overlaying only these 'significant' pathways onto a map, the policymakers observe Korea's 'place' in the industry, globally, shown in Figure C1.4. This visualisation reinforces that major sources to Korean shipbuilding come from Japan and the US. Meanwhile, Korean shipbuilding also appears to be a significant supplier only to the Greek shipbuilding industry, relative to the size of the Greek economy. This confirms the combined message of Figures C1.1 and C1.2 that Korean shipbuilding is a 'small fish in a big ocean' that is more reliant on others than others are of it (as a buyer of imports). Thus, if trade wars did start, passing on trade barriers to the Korean shipbuilding industry may not carry much weight on an international stage.

To get more actionable insights, Korean policymakers need to probe deeper to identify which other industries are directly affected if barriers are passed on or reciprocated. This means omitting the global context and investigating only the Korean shipbuilding sourcing pathways that are significant (i.e. that have over 10 percent of the Korean industry's trade). This time only the relationships to *and* from Korean shipbuilding are considered, from which to select those over 10 percent. This reveals the following structure, shown in Figure C1.5, where the arrow thickness represents the relative intensity of trade.

Conclusion and implications

The analysis culminating in Figure C1.5 confirms that iron and steel imports from China and Japan are significant. To recoup losses on shipbuilding export due to a trade barrier, policymakers may consider passing on barriers or tariffs to China and Japan's steel imports or seek lower cost sources from other nearby countries should steel trade relationships with China and Japan buckle. Other significant imports are observed, including machinery and equipment from Japan and the US. These other imports may also be targets for Korea to impose barriers.

However, *the multiplexity of trade relations across industries and countries paints a complex picture of trade. If policymakers cannot agree on free trade, they must consider trade barrier policies that can be contagious across industries and countries.* For example, if Korea imposed barriers on their Japanese or US suppliers of machinery and equipment industries, how might suppliers of navigation systems (included in the 'Medical, precision and optical instruments' industry) in those countries react? If they refused to supply to Korean shipbuilders out of collegiality to those affected by a Korean

Korean Domestic Industries	Korean Shipbuilding Value Chain - domestic	Korean Shipbuilding Value Chain - imports
Agriculture, hunting, forestry and fishing	Agriculture, hunting, forestry and fishing	Agriculture, hunting, forestry and fishing
Mining and quarrying (energy)	Mining and quarrying (energy)	Mining and quarrying (energy)
Mining and quarrying (non-energy)	Mining and quarrying (non-energy)	Mining and quarrying (non-energy) (Rest of World, Australia)
Food products, beverages and tobacco	Food products, beverages and tobacco	Food products, beverages and tobacco
Textiles, textile products, leather and footwear	Textiles, textile products, leather and footwear	Textiles, textile products, leather and footwear
Wood and products of wood and cork	Wood and products of wood and cork	Wood and products of wood and cork
Pulp, paper, paper products, printing and publishing	Pulp, paper, paper products, printing and publishing	Pulp, paper, paper products, printing and publishing
Coke, refined petroleum products and nuclear fuel	Coke, refined petroleum products and nuclear fuel	Coke, refined petroleum products and nuclear fuel
Chemicals excluding pharmaceuticals	Chemicals excluding pharmaceuticals	Chemicals excluding pharmaceuticals
Pharmaceuticals	Pharmaceuticals	Pharmaceuticals
Rubber & plastics products	Rubber & plastics products	Rubber & plastics products
Other non-metallic mineral products	Other non-metallic mineral products	Other non-metallic mineral products
Iron & steel	Iron & steel	Iron & steel (Japan, China, Rest of World)
Non-ferrous metals	Non-ferrous metals	Non-ferrous metals
Fabricated metal products, except machinery & equipment	Fabricated metal products, except machinery & equipment	Fabricated metal products, except machinery & equipment
Machinery & equipment, nec	Machinery & equipment, nec	Machinery & equipment, nec
Office, accounting & computing machinery	Office, accounting & computing machinery	Office, accounting & computing machinery
Electrical machinery & apparatus, nec	Electrical machinery & apparatus, nec	Electrical machinery & apparatus, nec
Radio, television & communication equipment	Radio, television & communication equipment	Radio, television & communication equipment
Medical, precision & optical instruments	Medical, precision & optical instruments	Medical, precision & optical instruments
Motor vehicles, trailers & semi-trailers	Motor vehicles, trailers & semi-trailers	Motor vehicles, trailers & semi-trailers
Building & repairing of ships & boats	Building & repairing of ships & boats	Building & repairing of ships & boats
Aircraft & spacecraft	Aircraft & spacecraft	Aircraft & spacecraft
Railroad equipment & transport equip nec.	Railroad equipment & transport equip nec.	Railroad equipment & transport equip nec.
Manufacturing nec; recycling (include Furniture)	Manufacturing nec; recycling (include Furniture)	Manufacturing nec; recycling (include Furniture)
Production, collection and distribution of electricity	Production, collection and distribution of electricity	Production, collection and distribution of electricity
Manufacture of gas; distribution of gaseous fuels through mains	Manufacture of gas; distribution of gaseous fuels through mains	Manufacture of gas; distribution of gaseous fuels through mains
Steam and hot water supply	Steam and hot water supply	Steam and hot water supply
Collection, purification and distribution of water	Collection, purification and distribution of water	Collection, purification and distribution of water
Construction	Construction	Construction
…	…	…

Figure C1.1 Korean shipbuilding across two steps in its GVC.

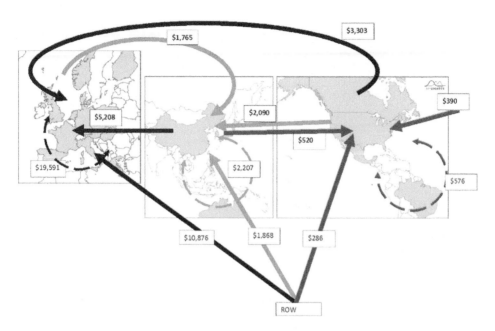

Figure C1.2 Shipbuilding as a global industry across three economic blocs (USD millions, as at 2000).

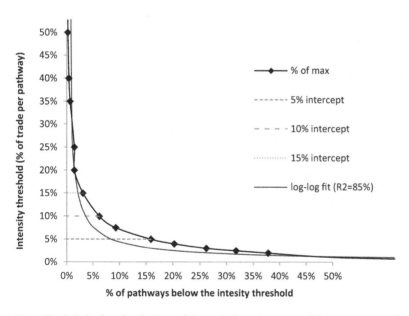

Figure C1.3 Scale-free distribution of the trade intensity across all inter-country pathways in the global shipbuilding industry complex.

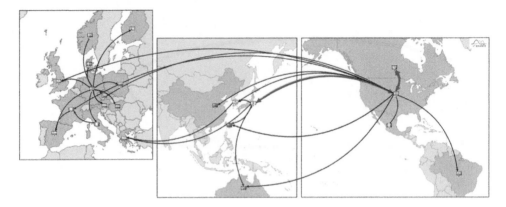

Figure C1.4 Trade complex for the shipbuilding industry, globally.

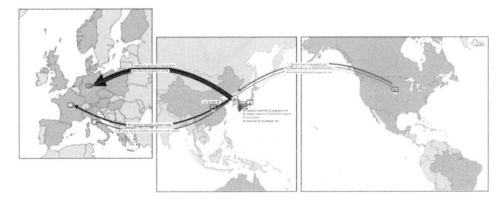

Figure C1.5 Significant imports and importers of Korean shipbuilding.

trade barrier, who else could the Korean shipbuilders turn to? Here at least, Korean shipbuilders may have alternative suppliers of medical, precision and optical instruments in Germany. These alternatives in this industry give Korean policymakers a few more risk mitigation strategies if they were to pass on a trade barrier to the Japanese and US suppliers of the steel, and machinery and equipment industries.

As a Korean policymaker, how would you react to an imposed barrier to exporting Korean ships? Would you pass on the barrier to your suppliers, if so, which from which country? If those countries then reciprocate, what alternatives do you have to continuing an escalation of reciprocal barriers? What would you recommend to Korean shipbuilders? How do you think you could renegotiate the trade barrier on their behalf? Or, would you recommend each exporter and importer fend for themselves?

As managers of Korean shipbuilders, which changes to your pricing or supply chain structure will you have to consider if a barrier is imposed against your exports? Can subsequent trade barriers by Korea on your suppliers make your ships and your business competitive again? Should you lobby the Korean government to impose barriers within your industry, potentially adding strain to your relationships with your suppliers? Or do you encourage Korean policymakers to pick a different industry in which to impose barriers, risking the trade wars spilling across industries?

As a point of reference by which to consider the domino effects of imposing trade barriers, the bilateral trade between the US and Canada is worth investigating. Imposing a trade tariff on Canadian steel has direct implications for the profitability of farmers in the US.[1] The follow-on pains by US farmers escalated further when Canada threatened retaliatory tariffs on US agricultural products to counter the tariffs on Canadian steel, causing US politicians to argue for trade quotas instead of tariffs.[2] These effects instantly also spilled over to trade with Mexico and other upstream and downstream industries.

Notes

1 https://www.cbc.ca/news/world/trump-steel-tariffs-canada-u-s-allies-1.4686734, accessed 9 July 2019.
2 https://www.cbc.ca/news/business/u-s-steel-quotas-tariffs-1.5037411, accessed 9 July 2019.

CASE STUDY

GVC vulnerability to disruption

Martin Bliemel, Brian Wixted and Göran Roos

Introduction

Despite the benefits of modularisation and highly interconnected global value chains (GVCs), recent natural disasters have provided evidence that global supply chains can be quite vulnerable to interruptions. Risks in supply chains leading to interruption are not limited to natural disasters and can include fires and financial ruin (see Natarajarathinam et al., 2009). Simchi-Levi et al. (2014) have recently suggested it is the low-end commodity producers that expose higher-value system integrators to the greatest risks. For example, the Thai floods in 2011 disrupted electronics and auto supply chains across the globe – particularly affecting hard drive supplies (Tibken, 2011). Likewise, the Japanese earthquake in 2011 disrupted auto production from Japan to North America to Sweden (Glinton, 2011), as discussed in a National Public Radio interview between Glinton (interviewer) and Handler (auto industry expert).

GLINTON: So what's happens when one piece of that chain is gone?

Ms. HANDLER: You end up with nothing. In order to build a car, you have to have every piece. There is not one piece that you can say well, I'll add that later.

GLINTON: Not one piece. But there are factories all over the world making car parts.

Ms. HANDLER: If you have a part that is not being made due to a factory being down or something being down, you can't just go to the factory next door and say hey can you make this widget.

We start with examining the inputs to each industry and assess their vulnerability to disruptions in the supply of seven types of input:

(i)   Technologies: all transport, machinery and electronics industry classifications
(ii) Chemicals: chemicals, coke and petroleum, rubber and plastics etc.
(iii) Commodities: agriculture, mining and wood
(iv) Metals: iron, steel and non-ferrous
(v)   Semi-processed: food, beverages and tobacco etc.
(vi) Services: all service sectors
(vii) Self: intra-industry sourcing, separately accounted for from the above

DOI: 10.4324/9781315225661-25

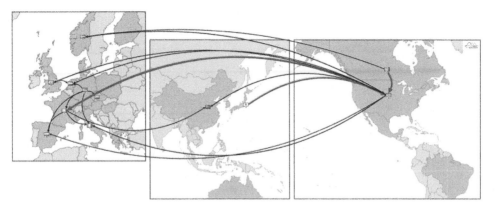

Figure C1.6 The global factory value architecture for the aerospace trade complex.

For each industry, we can then plot the relative proportion of these types of imports, as visualised in Figure C1.6, with the industries listed in order of their significant sourcing pathways per economy (SPE), type input as per columns, and the percentage of inputs as per the magnitude of the bar and noted percentage. Multiple factors are immediately evident from Figure C1.6. Industries are highly dependent on suppliers within the same industry, as represented by the 'self' column, with an average proportion of 40.9% of their value add coming from within the same industry. Vice versa, inter-industry sourcing is also substantial: on average, ~60% of value add is sourced across other industry complexes.

Highly interconnected industries (e.g. SPE >1.3) are highly reliant on inter-industry imports of 'technologies,' averaging 33.8% of their value-add being sourced from technology industries. In comparison, for less interconnected industries (e.g. SPE <1.3), sourced 'technologies' only represent 6% of value add. These recursive intra- and inter-industry flows indicate that vulnerabilities may be of particular importance in industries that resemble global factories. Aerospace tops the SPE list and has surprisingly similar inter-industry sourcing patterns to shipbuilding, in that roughly 60% of the value add from imported modules are intra-industry (e.g. fuselage sections, etc.), and the next most significant import type is technology at 28.2%.

Aerospace

Other than ICT related industries, aerospace is the only other trade complex that is a global factory, as visualised in Figure C1.7. The trade complex has proportionately more significant sourcing pathways per economy than other industries and has three significant bilateral pathways.

This structure evolved due to two trends in the aerospace industry, occurring around the mid- to late 1990s. On the one hand, the number of commercial aerospace production hubs contracted.[1] On the other hand, the remaining firms progressively outsourced. For example, between 1990 and 2000 the share of imports in the US net output (i.e., the foreign value-added) for the aerospace trade complex rose from 9% to 17% (see Wixted, 2009). The Boeing 777 entered into service in the mid-1990s and so provides a useful benchmark for a discussion of the supply chain for that time period, and is analysed by Pritchard and MacPherson (2005). In their analysis, they find that 30% of the build cost for the 777 was imports (Pritchard and MacPherson 2005, p. 3). The imports from Japan include substantial aircraft components

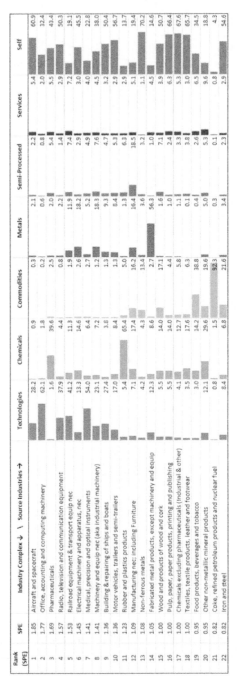

Rank (SPE)	SPE	Industry Complex ↓ \ Source Industries →	Technologies	Chemicals	Commodities	Metals	Semi-Processed	Services	Self
1	1.85	Aircraft and spacecraft	28.2	0.9	0.3	2.1	2.2	5.4	60.9
2	1.77	Office, accounting and computing machinery	62.1	1.8	0.2	0.6	0.8	2.0	32.4
3	1.69	Pharmaceuticals	1.6	39.6	2.5	2.0	5.4	5.5	43.4
4	1.57	Radio, television and communication equipment	37.9	4.4	0.8	2.2	1.4	2.9	50.3
5	1.53	Railroad equipment & transport equip nec	41.2	11.3	1.9	11.9	7.4	7.2	19.1
6	1.45	Electrical machinery and apparatus, nec	13.3	14.6	2.6	18.2	2.9	3.0	45.5
7	1.41	Medical, precision and optical instruments	54.0	6.4	2.7	5.2	4.9	4.0	22.8
8	1.41	Machinery and equip nec (aka industrial machinery)	23.1	7.2	1.2	18.3	7.6	4.5	38.0
9	1.36	Building & repairing of ships and boats	27.4	3.8	1.3	9.3	4.7	3.2	50.4
10	1.36	Motor vehicles, trailers and semi-trailers	17.0	8.4	1.3	8.4	5.3	2.9	56.7
11	1.23	Rubber and plastics products	5.4	65.4	5.0	1.3	6.3	2.9	13.7
12	1.09	Manufacturing nec; including Furniture	7.1	17.4	16.2	16.4	18.5	5.1	19.4
13	1.08	Non-ferrous metals	4.2	4.3	13.4	3.6	3.2	1.1	70.2
14	1.05	Fabricated metal products, except machinery and equip	12.3	8.6	2.7	56.3	1.0	4.5	14.6
15	1.00	Wood and products of wood and cork	5.5	14.0	17.1	1.6	7.1	3.9	50.7
16	1.00	Pulp, paper, paper products, printing and publishing	5.5	14.0	4.4	1.0	2.4	6.3	66.4
17	1.00	Chemicals excluding pharmaceuticals (industrial & other)	4.1	12.7	5.8	1.1	3.3	5.3	67.6
18	1.00	Textiles, textile products, leather and footwear	3.5	17.6	6.3	0.1	3.8	3.0	65.7
19	0.95	Food products, beverages and tobacco	3.0	14.2	38.8	0.4	2.6	6.5	34.5
20	0.95	Other non-metallic mineral products	12.1	29.6	19.6	5.0	5.3	9.6	18.8
21	0.82	Coke, refined petroleum products and nuclear fuel	0.8	1.5	92.3	0.3	0.1	0.8	4.3
22	0.82	Iron and steel	8.4	6.8	21.6	3.4	2.3	2.9	54.6

Figure C1.7 Relative proportion of imported value add by industry.

(Pritchard and MacPherson, 2005, p. 6–7), including fuselage sections, wing sections and fairings, internal bulkheads, beams and ribs, and various external doors.

Furthermore, aerospace is witnessing what could be called super-modularity[2] in commercial aerospace. Wixted (2009) discussed the Airbus A380 super-jumbo, where wings and other parts are moved across Europe and the globe. Boeing's 787 program (first commercial flight on 26 October 2011) outsourced even more of the airframe. Various publications reveal that of the main body of the aircraft, Boeing is now only building the tail, while large sections of the airframe come from Italy and the wings from Japan (Peterson, 2011; Lamba and Elahi, 2012). Japan alone is producing approximately 35% of the value going into 787s (Pritchard and MacPherson, 2004). Aircraft engines also "account for up to a third of the value of a new jet" (The Economist, 2014); are usually sourced from GE (US), Pratt & Whitney (Canada), or Rolls Royce (Great Britain); and are themselves globally modularised products.[3] It is thus possible that the aerospace industry with its super-modularity is even more complex than the iconic iPhone production system and the electronics industry.

Challenge

The preceding analysis reveals that firms must not only consider where geographically they are sourcing their inputs from but also which industries they are sourcing from. Suppliers can cease to be available due to business failure, logistical issues or exclusive trade agreements with competitors. Picture yourself as the competitor to the newly formed GE-Safran Aircraft Engines joint venture, CFM. How would you react? Do you aim to form a similar joint venture and larger modules, in an attempt to gain more credibility and scale in the industry with the aim to secure larger deals with the final aircraft assembler and to attract better suppliers? Or, do you disaggregate your operations with the aim of supplying sub-modules to these suppliers of the final aircraft assemblers? Whichever way you decide, what risks do you face if your supply chain agreements are short term or do not have an exclusivity clause? How can you manage secondary dependencies on your supplier's suppliers?

Solution and implementation steps

Following the preceding analysis, managers of supply chains can become more cognisant of potential risks of experiencing a shock to the supply chain, and how it might cascade through the entire global value chains or architectures of sourcing. Some of these supply chain risks can be managed by diversifying the supply chain to multiple competing suppliers. Alternatively, some supply chain risks can be disintermediated by creating your own organisation at the next step in the supply chain (either becoming a super- or sub-module developer). Lastly, another strategy is to use new innovations in manufacturing methods to completely skip part of the supply chain, and source commodities and raw materials to 3D print into modules as GE did, simultaneous to investing in the manufacturers of the 3D printers (Kellner, 2017).

Notes

1 It is much harder to access data on military aircraft and so the literature typically focuses on commercial aviation.
2 Super-modules are sub-assemblies of modules. The aircraft are now assembled much like a computer from a globally distributed supply system with some of these components physically massive.
3 See pp. 14–15 of https://www.safran-aircraft-engines.com/sites/snecma/files/brochure_sae_-lessent iel_va_0.pdf

References

Glinton, S. 2011, 'Japan Disaster Breaks Auto Supply Chain. National Public Radio', *National Public Radio*. https://www.npr.org/2011/03/22/134755634/Japan-Disaster-Breaks-Auto-Supply-Chain

Kellner, T. 2017, 'An Epiphany of Disruption: GE Additive Chief Explains How 3D Printing Will Upend Manufacturing', *GE Reports*. https://www.ge.com/reports/epiphany-disruption-ge-additive-chief-explains-3d-printing-will-upend-manufacturing

Lamba, N. & Elahi, E. 2012, 'When supply chain strategy does not match supply chain capabilities: Lessons that can be learnt from the supply chain of Boeing 787', *Cases on Supply Chain and Distribution Management: Issues and Principles*, IGI Global, pp. 159–177.

Natarajarathinam, M., Capar, I. & Narayanan, A. 2009, 'Managing supply chains in times of crisis: A review of literature and insights', *International Journal of Physical Distribution & Logistics Management*, vol. 39, no. 7, pp. 535–573.

Peterson, K. 2011, 'A wing and a prayer: Outsourcing at Boeing', Reuters. http://graphics.thomsonreuters.com/11/01/Boeing.pdf

Pritchard, D. & MacPherson, A. 2004, '*Outsourcing US commercial aircraft technology and innovation: implications for the industry's long term design and build capability*', Canada–United States Trade Center Occasional Paper No. 29. Department of Geography, Buffalo, NY.

Pritchard, D. & MacPherson, A. 2005, 'Boeing's diffusion of commercial aircraft design and manufacturing technology to Japan: Surrendering the US aircraft industry for foreign financial support', Canada–United States Trade Center Occasional Paper No. 30. Department of Geography, Buffalo, NY, p. 3.

Simchi-Levi, D., Schmidt, W. & Wei, Y. 2014, 'From superstorms to factory fires: Managing unpredictable supply chain disruptions', *Harvard Business Review*, vol. 92, no. 1–2, pp. 96–101.

The Economist 2014, 'Gearing up for a fight', *The Economist*. https://www.economist.com/business/2014/01/25/gearing-up-for-a-fight

Tibken, S. 2011, 'Thai floods Jolt PC supply chain', *Wall Street Journal*. https://www.wsj.com/articles/SB10001424052970203658804576636951367373290

Wixted, B. 2009, *Innovation System Frontiers: Cluster Networks and Global Value*, Springer, Heidelberg, Germany.

PART V

Implications

Finally, Part V draws the chapters and perspectives together to consider implications for global value chains. In Chapter 18, Steven A. Melnyk, Norma Harrison and Derek Friday explore how the developments discussed in this book apply to supply chain management practitioners and researchers. To do so, the following questions are the focus: What changes are taking place in the supply chain due to the factors discussed in this book? How will these changes affect the theory and practice of supply chain management?

DOI: 10.4324/9781315225661-26

18

SUPPLY CHAIN MANAGEMENT AT AN INFLECTION POINT

A final perspective

Steven A. Melnyk, Norma Harrison and Derek Friday

Overview

In differential calculus, an inflection point on a continuous plane curve is where the curve changes from being concave to convex or vice versa. When applied to business, a point of inflection denotes a period of significant change. It is a period in which past practice, perspectives and frameworks are no longer as attractive or relevant. In reviewing the various chapters of this book, it should be obvious to the reader that supply chain management is at an inflection point.

In this summary chapter, we will explore how the developments discussed in this book apply to supply chain management practitioners and researchers. To do so, we will focus on themes discussed either directly or indirectly in the preceding chapters of this book. Central to this discussion are the following two questions:

- What changes are taking place in the supply chain due to the factors discussed in this book?
- How will these changes affect the theory and practice of supply chain management?

To address these two questions, this chapter is organized as follows. In the first section, we will examine the changes now taking place in supply chain management. The key message in this section is that there is a fundamental transformation in suppliers from being cost-driven and tactical to being value-driven and strategic. This section will also identify the four critical traits of this new supply chain. The second section will examine the impact of the new supply chain for practitioners. The message is simple – a new type of supply chain demands a new class of supply chain manager. The third and final section will conclude this chapter by returning to the theme of supply chain management at the point of inflection.

The "new" supply chain

Since the term was first introduced in the *Financial Times* in 1982,[1] the supply chain and how it is perceived within the firm has greatly changed. Initially, managers outside of the supply chain saw it as *tactical*, consisting of terms such as planning horizons, capacity, advanced delivery notices and Lean.

DOI: 10.4324/9781315225661-27

At the heart of a supply chain was a combination of boxes, trucks, factories and shipping orders. CEOs and senior managers only became aware of their supply chains when there was a disruption, especially one that made the news. They learned the hard way that supply chain disruptions can hurt their firm operationally and strategically. Thanks in large part to academic research, they also learned that a supply chain disruption was often followed by a 40 percent drop in their stock price that took nearly two years to recover. This led to an interesting phenomenon – the attractiveness of the "invisible" supply chain: Since the only time senior management ever heard about a supply chain is when something went wrong, the "best" supply chain must be one that they never heard about.

As can be seen in the chapters presented in this book, it is evident that this view is changing and changing radically. Managers and corporate leaders are starting to recognize supply chains are becoming customer-focused, value-driven and strategic (Stank, Autry, Daugherty, & Closs, 2015). This change can be attributed to the following factors:

- *Increasing rate of technological advances that are rooted in the supply chain.* The media is awash with articles about the internet of things (IoT), 3D printing, big data analytics and autonomous vehicles (self-driving trucks and cars) (Hofmann & Rüsch, 2017; Schniederjans, Curado, & Khalajhedayati, 2019). These new technologies are changing how firms design, build and deliver products, and how they interact with their customers. Tire manufacturer Pirelli has introduced sensors into truck tires that collect information about the durability and performance of their products. This is allowing Pirelli to offer its customers new capabilities for better vehicle protection and control and should lead to better tire designs in the future. Similarly, Amazon is experimenting with 3D printing on trucks so that goods can be built as they are being delivered to its customers, while online clothier M-Tailor draws on the improved photographic power of cell phones to help its customers design, make and deliver shirts specifically configured to their unique physical characteristics.
- *Acceptance of complexity as a business driver.* In the past, complexity[2] was viewed as something that added cost, inconvenience and had to be avoided. However, research in the hospitality industry indicates hotels gain a competitive advantage by raising the complexity of their products to protect markets from competitors. With aid from technology advancements, hotels are able to increase the complexity of supplier markets while lessening complexity for end users/customers (Crichton & Edgar, 1995). Now, firms recognize that the demand for complexity is being driven by their customers. If a customer is willing to pay for something done in a unique way, the firm can make the customer aware of the hidden costs and dangers, but ultimately, it needs to deliver. In part, the ability of the supply chain to deal with this increased demand for complexity is being enhanced by the aforementioned new technologies.
- *New competitive pressures.* How a firm serves and interacts with its customers is being influenced by the experiences and expectations of "The New Customer" and interactions with other providers such as especially Amazon. This has given rise to the *Amazon effect* – the impact exerted on both customers and firms by Amazon's relentless emphasis on quickly connecting its customers to new and innovative solutions (Melnyk & Stanton, 2017). Once Amazon rolls out a new service, its customers come to expect the same level of service from their other providers. For example, at the Supply Chain Outlook Summit held in Chicago in November 2015, a supplier of industrial equipment explained that when one of its customers was told that there would be no customer service on weekends, the customer threatened to pull out of negotiations. Suppliers noted that if Amazon provides 24-hour customer support on the weekend, customers will expect a similar service from other

providers, including equipment suppliers. Dealing with the Amazon effect often requires changes to the supply chain.

- *New methods of dealing with customers.* Increasingly, the customers of business-to-business (B2B) and business-to-consumer (B2C) businesses expect to be able to place orders and find information seamlessly through various means, whether through brick-and-mortar retail locations, online or through smart phone apps. This "buy from anywhere, anytime and on any device" mentality has led to the emergence of the omni-channel (Melacini, Perotti, Rasini, & Tappia, 2018; Murfield, Boone, Rutner, & Thomas, 2017). To a large extent, the success or failure of delivering the omni-channel experience depends on the supply chain system and its leadership.

- *Recognition that cost is no longer enough.* Traditionally, the primary focus of the supply chain has been on one competitive driver – costs. Lowest cost was often held as the primary indicator of supply chain performance. That view is now changing. As noted in the MIT Sloan Management Review (Melnyk, David, Spekman, & Sandor, 2010), supply chains can achieve more than just cost reductions; they can offer improved security, innovation, responsiveness, sustainability, resilience and quality. To understand the competitive value of these other outcomes, consider the impact of Zara on retail apparel. The fast fashion producer became a global powerhouse by emphasizing responsiveness at a time when its competitors were focused on cost, and, therefore, outsourcing to low-cost countries such as China.

- *Customer demands for greater supply chain visibility.* Customers, especially in North America and Europe, demand assurances that their products are being produced safely and without adverse impact (Ahmed, Khalid, Islam, & Abro, 2019; LeBaron & Gore, 2019). Companies such as Disney now recognize that they are accountable for actions taken anywhere in their supply chain, whether those involve first-tier or fourth-tier suppliers. That is one reason why Disney announced in 2013 that it was pulling production out of Bangladesh, Pakistan, Ecuador, Venezuela and Belarus due to concerns over safety standards for supply chain workers in these countries.

When these and other changes are taken as a whole, what we see is a transformation of the supply chain from that of a necessary evil, and a source of risk, to a strategic asset that enhances a firm's competitiveness in the marketplace by offering one or more of the following three advantages:

- Deliver goods and services faster, better and cheaper (the lowest form of competitive advantage).
- Enable the firm to address customer needs that are currently being met poorly.
- Enable the firm to address customer needs currently not being met at all (highest form of advantage).

One result of this change in customer base is the increased importance of supply chain visibility. Visibility, something previously demanded by the corporate buyer as a way of dealing with supply chain risk, is now demanded by the consumer. When prior chapters talk about visibility, transparency, the IoT and blockchain, they are dealing with this emerging theme of supply chain visibility and transparency, which is rapidly growing in importance.

Traits of the new supply chain

In reviewing the prior chapters contained in this book, it becomes evident that there is a new supply chain – strategic and value-driven. This new supply chain is characterized by four critical, distinguishing traits. These are illustrated in Figure 18.1.

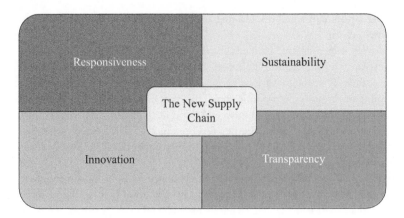

Figure 18.1 Critical traits of the "new" supply chain.

The first trait, responsiveness, emphasizes the shift in focus from cost as dominant driver to responsiveness. Responsiveness emphasizes speed – the ability to respond quickly to changing customer and technological requirements (Yang, Xie, Yu, & Liu, 2019). This trait is best epitomized by businesses such as Amazon. This company has been continuously reducing the time needed to deliver products for its Prime members – from two days to now one day and in some cases less than two hours. The second trait is sustainability. As noted previously in this chapter, today's consumers are increasingly aware of the importance of sustainability. They want goods and services that are produced and delivered in ways consistent with the triple bottom line of people/planet/ profit. To achieve these objectives, we need supply chains that are transparent – supply chains where the provenance or chain of custody can be easily established and made visible to any inter- ested party. Developing such attributes has been greatly simplified by the emergence of block- chain, Big Data, improved analytics and technological advances such as the IOT. Finally, there is innovation. Innovation here means more than simply product innovation. It encompasses such areas as process innovation, business model innovation and supply chain innovation (Hahn, 2019).

Before leaving this discussion, it is important that we recognize the role of operational excel- lence. It is our position that the new supply chain does not eliminate the need for operational excellence. Rather, it builds upon it and expects it. The prior four traits only become important when the firm and its supply chain can deliver on the implied promises. Delivering on those promises requires operational excellence.

The changing face of supply chain practice

The new supply chain requires not only a new way of viewing it but also a new "type" of man- ager – a supply chain leader. To understand this shift, it is important to compare the traits of the traditional supply chain manager with those of the new supply chain leader.

The "traditional" supply chain manager

Traditional supply chain managers emphasize the importance of technical and functional skills in project management, risk management, stakeholder management and decision-making (Shou & Wang, 2017). This current generation of supply chain managers can be effectively character- ized by the following traits:

- *Strong functional orientation.* These are managers who feel most comfortable working with other similar people. Interactions with other functions are handled through hand-offs, best described as decisions that are "thrown over the wall" to other groups with little or no input from them.
- *Strong focus on cost.* Cost reduction is the universal benchmark. But just as no good deed goes unpunished, this can have unintended consequences, as was learned by one major farm equipment manufacturer after it implemented a world-class Lean/Just-in-Time system with the stated goal of driving down costs. Unfortunately, a laser focus on cost reduction adversely affected the manufacturer's ability to be responsive during a time when demand was greatly changing (thus hurting the company's competitive position in the short term). Putting great emphasis on cost performance metrics (unit manufacturing costs, labor productivity, machine utilization and output) is a thing of the 1960s (Armistead, 1992).
- *Strives for supply chain excellence.* The goal to develop a best-in-class supply chain on specific measurements, such as cost, may not necessarily result in better overall corporate performance, especially if the goals of the supply chain are not aligned with the strategy of the business.
- *Strong focus on execution.* This supply chain is focused on implementing decisions made elsewhere in the firm (e.g., by top management, marketing, finance or engineering), often without having any real input or impact on those decisions.
- *Speaks a language that is very functionally oriented.* Current supply chain managers speak their own language, one that is rooted in terms like capacity, throughput, bottlenecks, inventory and ppm. This language hinders the ability of current supply chain managers to effectively interface with the other functions of the firm and with top managers who measure performance in different ways.
- *Strives to simplify and avoid complexity.* In the traditional supply chain, complexity is seen as something that adds cost and lead time, and must be resisted whenever possible.
- *Deliberate decision-making.* The traditional supply chain manager believes that it takes time to make decisions.
- *Optimal solutions are the best.* There is something "attractive" about an optimal solution. As will be shown later on, optimal is often situation specific. Change is often not conducive to optimization.
- *Stability.* Stability is highly valued.
- *Toolsmiths.* Many current supply chain leaders are well grounded in solutions that they can quickly apply to any situation or problem. They are masters of ERP, MRP, DDMRP, Six Sigma, Total Quality Management (TQM), Theory of Constraints (TOC), and Lean/Just-in-time (Armistead, 1992; Foster & Ogden, 2008).

What we have here is a broad brushed view of the "typical" supply chain manager. But while these traits might help get things done, they are not the traits needed by leaders of the new strategic supply chain. Research has indicated a need for additional skills not directly tied to technical training and functional expertise, and have extended the number of skill categories to include global awareness, corporate strategy, cultural empathy, cross-cultural team building, global negotiation skills, ethical understanding of conducting business in foreign countries and self-confidence (Harvey, Kiessling, & Akdeniz, 2014).

Traits of an emerging supply chain leader – Strategic in focus; outside/in in orientation

Several predictions are made on emerging supply chain megatrends influential in driving change (Stank et al., 2015). The emerging supply chain leader, traits strongly hinted at by the 2015

Deloitte Study of Supply Chain Talent (Marchese & Dollar, 2015), has a very different set of skills and orientations. Arguably, leadership is a vital profession skill set for middle- and senior-level supply chain managers (Shou & Wang, 2017). Following are the traits of an emerging supply chain leader:

- *Excels at managing at the interfaces.* The new supply chain leader recognizes that they must work with other functions within the firm. Specifically, they must be prepared to engage with groups such as engineering, marketing, finance, accounting and top management. This engagement is bidirectional. On the one hand, they need to understand the requirements of these other groups since their needs must be translated into capabilities that the supply chain must provide. On the other hand, the new supply chain leader must be prepared to educate these other groups on the capabilities of the supply chain – what the supply chain can and cannot do. They must also be able to communicate how actions taken by these other groups affect the performance of the supply chain. For example, they must be able to show how promotions can adversely affect the ability of the supply chain to ensure that there is adequate stock on the shelf once the promotion becomes active. If a change in supply chain capabilities is required, then it is the responsibility of the new supply chain leader to communicate to the other areas how long it will take and what it will cost. In other words, the new supply chain leader must excel at educating, informing and coordinating.
- *Focus on asking the "right" question, rather than on the "right" solution.* This is where critical thinking shines. As Charles F. Kettering, the brilliant designer and engineer at General Motors, once said, "a problem well stated is a problem half solved." Here, the supply chain leader is more interested in ensuring that there is a clear and concise understanding of the desired outcome, rather than focusing on a specific solution. This means ensuring that everyone understands what the goal is, and then soliciting the input of the various members of the supply chain to identify how best to achieve this goal. The solution becomes secondary to the desired outcome because it is driven by this outcome.
- *Strives for business excellence, rather than supply chain excellence.* Here, the goal is to help the firm better compete at the business model rather than the supply chain level. The business model, which can be viewed as a highly operational restatement of the strategy (see Figure 18.2), identifies three critical components that must be consistently maintained in alignment for the firm to compete:
  - *The key customer.* The customer is the ultimate judge of what is produced. Here, the new supply chain leader must identify who it is that the firm is specifically targeting – whose needs will it try to profitably satisfy.
  - *The value proposition.* This is what the firm offers to attract and retain key customers.
  - *Capabilities.* These are the resources, skills, processes and assets that the firm draws on to deliver the value proposition that is expected by its key customers. It is here that the supply chain resides, along with corporate processes, measurement, capacity and corporate culture. The new supply chain leader understands that it is their task to ensure that what the key customers expect, what the firm has promised and what the supply chain can deliver are continuously in alignment over time.
- *Outside/in as compared to inside/out.* A strategic supply chain leader views the capabilities of the supply chain through a different lens. The traditional lens is from the inside/out, where the leader understands what the supply chain can and cannot do, and tries to convince key customers that this is what they really want (Baden-Fuller, 1995). The new, strategic lens is

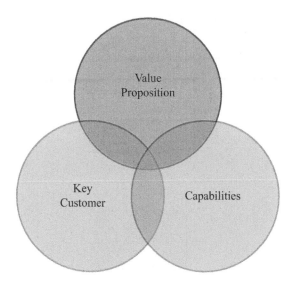

Figure 18.2 The business model.

from the outside/in: It looks at what the key customers want and what type of outcomes they wish to achieve. These new leaders understand that it is these key customers who drive the firm, its strategy and ultimately the supply chain. This identification with key customers takes its most immediate form in terms of how communication is implemented – through measures and metrics.

- *Effective at communicating with others in terms of performance measurement, measures and metrics.* To effectively communicate within the firm, the new supply chain leader must recognize the importance of measures and metrics as communication. Measures and metrics, as noted by Magretta and Stone (2002), restate the business strategy and the business model into what each group or person must do to achieve this strategy. Increasingly, we are recognizing that effective communication within the firm occurs at this level, not in terms of measures such as capacity, throughput, utilization and production process model (ppm). Furthermore, in many cases, the new supply chain leader takes this emphasis on performance to a new level by adopting the customers' own measures as their own. When this occurs, communication is immediately enhanced between the supply chain and the customer since both are using the same set of measures. More important, supply chain impact can be seen immediately since these actions can be translated into how they affect the performance of the customer. Since both parties are using the same measures, the opportunity for conflict is minimized.
- *Recognizes the need for complexity, but still strives to identify and eliminate complications.* Since the new supply chain leader closely knows and identifies with the key customer, there is an acceptance of the need for complexity. Complexity is a trait that comes from the key customer and is something that the supply chain must be able to accommodate. The leader does try to communicate the downside risks of complexity through a *cost of complexity approach* (see Figure 18.3). As shown in this figure, responding to a customer's demand for changes, complexity is often not a zero-cost option – it can and does create real costs, costs that have to be paid for, either by the customer or the firm. By exposing the customers to the costs of complexity, we are essentially educating the customer about the impact of complexity. However, the leader can differentiate between complexity, which comes from

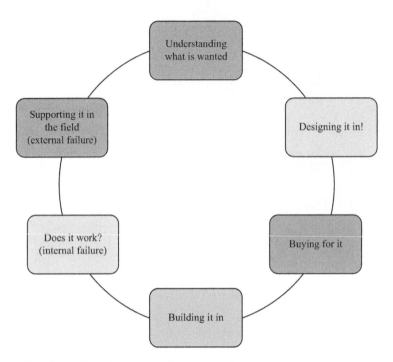

Figure 18.3 Cost of complexity – a total cost approach.

the customer, and a complication, which occurs because of the actions of people within the supply chain.[3]

- *Recognizes and accepts the presence of uncertainty and change.* As Knight first noted in 1921, uncertainty and risk are very different concepts. Risk involves events about which you have prior insight and experience; uncertainty does not. Uncertainty is a major trait of the new supply chain. Supply chain uncertainty is viewed as a continuum ranging from complete certainty to radical uncertainty, where movement along the continuum determines the natural state of nature (probability and risk) influencing supply chain decision-making (Vilko, Ritala, & Edelmann, 2014). After all, you never have enough time, the information is never complete or sufficiently accurate, and something is always changing before you make your decision.
- *Fast decision-making is the key.* This trait is the natural complement of the prior trait. In this environment, you do not have the time to wait until changes shake out. Rather, you must make decisions quickly and be willing to live with the fact that you will be wrong on occasion. This is becoming the natural state of affairs. While selecting optimal alternatives is important, there is a need for competencies in generating new ideas, knowledge and information about targeted customers to quickly adjust/make decisions (Zhan & Tan, 2020). As one manager put it, "you make decisions quickly, you fail fast, you learn quickly, you move on and you repeat."
- *Strives for robust rather than optimal systems.* Optimality is nice. However, in many cases, optimality results in fragile systems. That is, if things have not changed from the conditions that were used to derive the optimal solution, all is well. However, as soon as something changes in the environment, the optimal system sputters. Instead, the goal should be a robust system, one that may not generate optimal performance but is able to respond to changes without

extracting a severe penalty in performance. Robust systems are the natural complement to the preceding trait.

- *The focus is on the future.* In this new environment of change and uncertainty, the past is viewed as a lesson to be learned, and not as the basis for punishment. As one manager interviewed by a member of the research team put it, "The past is something you cannot do anything about. Learn from it; get over it; focus rather on the future." That is the attitude assumed by the new supply chain leader. This focus and concern about the past is also reflected in planning. The new supply chain leader recognizes the importance of that basic supply chain dictum – today's supply chain is the result of investments made in the past; tomorrow's supply chain will be the result of investments made today!

The challenge

The evidence, as summarized in Table 18.1 is clear. While there will always be a demand for tacticians and fire fighters, the new strategic supply chain needs a different type of leader, perhaps a chief supply chain officer (CSCO), who is well prepared by skills, temperament and preparation to sit at the same table as the CEO, CIO, the CFO and the other similar leaders.

Table 18.1 Comparing supply chain leaders

Traits	Traditional supply chain manager	Strategic supply chain leader
Orientation	Functional; strongly internal	Cross-boundary; coordination
Performance stance	Cost/cost minimization	Outcome-driven/revenue maximization
Definition of excellence	Supply chain excellence	Business excellence
Stance	Focus on execution	Asking the right question Making sure the desired outcome is understood and made inevitable
Dealing with the customer	Inside/out	Outside/in
Communication	Very functionally oriented Capacity, throughput, bottlenecks, inventory, production process model (ppm)	Performance measures and metrics Use the customer's metrics as ours
Complexity	Strives to eliminate or simplify complexity	Accepts complexity as a fact of life that must be mastered Strives to eliminate unnecessary complications
Uncertainty	Desires stability; manage change	Accepts uncertainty and change
Decision-making style	Deliberate	Fast decision-making
Desired types of solutions	Optimal	Robust
Overall stance	Toolsmiths – masters of tools	Problem masters – define the problem that the rest of the supply chain will focus on

The challenge that emerges from this comparison of the traditional and new supply chain manager is basically how to develop this new class of leader. Most institutions, whether they are universities, colleges or professional societies, have excelled at developing effective traditional supply chain managers. They have excelled at developing toolsmiths; the new supply chain demands strategic problem masters. For example, in many instances, teaching students Python has occurred at the expense of exposing them to the skills of critical thinking. The challenge is how to bridge this gap in talent development. This challenge has become more pressing given the current talent shortage – a shortage caused by retirement and by the shift in supply chain skills and focus.

The changing face of supply chain research

The new supply chain is not only changing the face of supply chain practice; it is also changing the face of supply chain research. By reviewing the chapter contained in this book, the informed reader can identify five major directions for future research: (1) sensing, (2) scaling, (3) security, (4) social and (5) strategy. In this section, we will review these developments and explore their implications for research.

Sensing – Predictive analytics

Sensing refers to the ability of the organization to sense or identify important potential developments before they occur. Sensing is a dynamic capability that reflects a supply chain's ability to actively learn about customers, competitors and the environment, to allow for an understanding of market conditions and development of forecasting capabilities (Aslam, Blome, Roscoe, & Azhar, 2018). Sensing becomes particularly important when the rate of organizational/environmental change increases. Sensing indicates both threats and opportunities. Sensing gives the organization and its supply chain time to anticipate and prepare for the change. Sensing is to the organization what looking out into the distance is for the driver. When it comes to driving, it is generally recognized that the faster the speed of the vehicle, the further off into the distance you, as the driver, have to look.

Currently, several potentially important areas for future research can be identified:

- *Sensing and predictive analytics.* Of the various areas of sensing, this one is the most developed (Li & Wang, 2017). Here we are interested in exploring the intersection of analytics, big data, and technology in order to be able to quickly identify developments hidden in the data.
- *Using the supply chain as a source of sensing.* The supply chain (both upstream and downstream) is in contact with industry (competitors, government, technology providers – to name a few). Consequently, it is possible that they can help management identify new threats, developments and opportunities. Research in this area would focus on what firms are currently doing, preconditions to using suppliers and customers as sources of sensing information (is trust enough?), and the conditions under which supply chain sensing is most and least appropriate.
- *Better understanding of the process of effective sensing.* Sensing involves more than simply developing and applying predictive analytical procedures. It can be envisioned as a process that starts with the generating of data (being it through predictive analytics or data secured from the supply chain). Potential steps in this process can include vetting (assessing the data for accuracy and degree to which it is trustworthy), aggregation (pooling the data to identify potential trends), assessment (evaluating the results to determine what items must be acted

on now versus being delayed to some future point), transmission and filtering (understanding how the organization as a whole evaluates and acts on the data), and, finally, action. This is a process that has largely gone unstudied. We do not know what factors either facilitate or inhibit the passage of information through the prior described process (especially in those cases where the data points to a conclusion that is at odds with the internally held beliefs of the organization). For example, Corera (2011) noted that the British secret service (MI6) had firm evidence indicating that the United States was targeted for a large-scale terrorist attack. This information was passed on to their American counterparts in the summer of 2001, but then it was dismissed as being unlikely to occur.

Scaling

Sensing can be envisioned as being the trigger to action. However, in responding, the organization must deal with the challenge of scaling. Scaling refers to the process of changing the two dimensions of capacity – volume and capabilities (what the processes can and cannot do) both within the firm and within the upstream supply chain. To compete in the supply chain described by Figure 18.1, the firm must be able to scale its capacity both quickly and at low cost. This challenge has yet to be explored in greater detail by operations and supply chain management researchers. For example, researchers now recognize that cybersecurity is no longer a technical/computer information technology issue; it is a management/system issue (Melnyk, Peters, Spruill & Sullivan, 2018). Furthermore, it is no longer a corporate/internal issue but a supply chain issue.

Security

Like scaling, security is a complex construct. It refers to the ability of the organization and its supply chain to preserve integrity and quality. However, in today's environment, the attributes of integrity and quality refer to two different assets – product/services and data/digital assets. When viewed from this perspective, research into supply chain transparency/visibility and the application of blockchain (as discussed in this book) can be regarded as examples of security-focused research. Yet, more is needed, especially in the area of data or cybersecurity. It is an issue that requires the involvement of the various participants of the supply chain. Yet, as noted by Melnyk et al. (2018), this may not be possible, especially in the case of small to medium-sized enterprises. Overall, more research is needed in this area.

Social

It is tempting, in this new digital age of big data, predictive analytics, improved operations research procedures and advances in technology, to argue that managers should be willing to let the systems manage day-to-day decisions (*self-thinking supply chains*) (Calatayud, Mangan, & Christopher, 2019). Yet, in these situations, it is important to recognize the words of George Santayana (1905), philosopher, essayists, and writer, who observed that "those who cannot remember the past are condemned to repeat it." From history, we know that the real advantages offered by management are only realized when management has time to learn about the new technology and its capabilities and limitations. We also know from history that management always lags behind technology. Finally, we now recognize that management is not always economically driven but is rather the result of complex, dynamic social processes (Abrahamson, 1991; Abrahamson & Rosenkopf, 1990, 1991, 1993; Mintzberg, 1973; Reed, 1984).

That is, for the critical decisions, the results of the procedures such as predictive analytics are simply one input into the decision-making process. This is a process that is influenced by numerous other factors such as the decision-maker's attitudes towards risk (Abdel-Basset, Gunasekaran, Mohamed, & Chilamkurti, 2019), the performance measurement system (Melnyk, Stewart, & Swink, 2004), bounded rationality (Simons, 1955), escalation of commitment (Bazerman & Moore, 2017), satisficing behavior (Baumol & Quandt, 1964) and probability weighting (Tversky & Kahneman 1992), to name a few. Consequently, if we are to improve the effectiveness of decision-making in this "new" age, it is imperative that more research be devoted to how decision-making and the resulting decisions are affected by social and personal issues and factors (and how they affect the process). We have already seen the impact of the social issues when we discussed how the American intelligence community rejected the evidence provided by British intelligence.

Strategy

This final dimension recognizes the shift in research focus from supply chain as tactical to supply chain as strategic – a recognition that the supply chain and how it performs influences the customer (and consumer). The supply chain influences what the firm can (and cannot) offer and how it is delivered. In its delivery, the supply chain has a significant impact on the moments of truth delivered by the firm (Carlzon, 1987). This means a shift in research focus from the tactical to the strategic. The danger here lies in the ability of big data, predictive analytics and technology to encourage research that focuses on the tactical side. More research is needed on the strategic rather than the tactical side. As previously noted in the Deloitte Study (Marchese et al., 2015), this is not only demanded by the shift in supply chains described in this chapter; it is also being demanded by recruiters and firms.

Conclusion: Supply chain at the inflection point

Yes, supply chain management is at an inflection point – at a critical point of change. It is at a point where whatever has been done in the past in terms of research and practice may no longer be as relevant. However, the point we wish to make in this last chapter is that these changes have not only affected the relevancy of past research; they have created new, exciting opportunities for future research. This chapter has attempted to lay out the nature of the changes and the implication of these changes for both the theory and practice of supply chain management.

As we conclude, it is important to recognize the new opportunities that we are now faced with – opportunities to do research that is attractive and impactful to both academic researchers and practitioners. At this time, we should view the opportunities in the same way that Howard Carter first viewed the treasures of King Tutankhamun on November 1922 when he made the first breach into the tomb. What asked what he saw, he replied:

What can you see?

I replied, "Yes, wonderful things."

Notes

1 Keith Oliver, the top British logistician and consultant, first used the terms "supply chain" and "supply chain management" in a public interview conducted by Arnold Kransdorff of the *Financial Times* on June 4, 1982.

2 Complexity, in this context, is different from complication. Complexity derives from the customer – it is whatever the customer wants in terms of the product. It differs from complication, which is something that we, as supply chain managers, do to ourselves. For example, the firm acquires a new company. This means that we are faced by the challenge of what to do with the new part numbers and bills inherited from the acquisition. A common response is to simply take the old part numbers and to add a modifier to it. The danger – we are now exposed to the potential problem of having a part having two or more different part numbers. This is complication.

3 See footnote 2.

References

Abdel-Basset, M., Gunasekaran, M., Mohamed, M., & Chilamkurti, N. (2019). A framework for risk assessment, management and evaluation: Economic tool for quantifying risks in supply chain. *Future Generation Computer Systems*, 90, 489–502.

Abrahamson, E. (1991). Managerial fads and fashions: The diffusion and rejection of innovations. *The Academy of Management Review*, 16, 586–612.

Abrahamson, E., & Rosenkopf, L. (1990). When do bandwagon diffusions roll? How far do they go? And when do they roll backwards: A computer simulation. *Academy of Management Best Paper Proceedings*, 1, 155–159. Briarcliff Manor, NY 105010–8020, USA.

Abrahamson, E., & Rosenkopf, L. (1991). Trickle-down and trickle-up diffusion processes. Simulating the impact of reputation on two-stage diffusion models. *Proceedings of the Annual Meeting of the Academy of Management*, Miami Beach.

Abrahamson, E., & Rosenkopf, L. (1993). Institutional and competitive bandwagons: Using mathematical modeling as a tool to explore innovation diffusion. *Academy of Management Review*, 18(3), 487–517.

Ahmed, U., Khalid, N., Islam, D. M. Z., & Abro, Z. (2019). Abuse, emotions, and workload in the distribution business: Implications for employees' engagement. *International Journal of Advanced and Applied Sciences*, 6(8), 90–99.

Armistead, C. (1992). The changing role of supply chain operations managers. *Logistics Information Management*, 5(2), 10–16.

Aslam, H., Blome, C., Roscoe, S., & Azhar, T. (2018). Dynamic supply chain capabilities: How market sensing, supply chain agility and adaptability affect supply chain ambidexterity. *International Journal of Operations and Production Management*, 38(12), 226–2285.

Baden-Fuller, C. (1995). Strategic innovation, corporate entrepreneurship and matching outside-in to inside-out approaches to strategy research 1. *British Journal of Management*, 6(1), S3–S16.

Baumol, W. J., & Quandt, R. E. (1964). Rules of thumb and optimally imperfect decisions. *American Economic Review*, 54(2), 23–46.

Bazerman, H. M. & Moore, A. D. (2017). *Judgement in managerial decision making* (Eighth Edition). United Kingdom: Wiley Custom.

Calatayud, A., Mangan, J., & Christopher, M. (2019). The self-thinking supply chain. *Supply Chain Management: An International Journal*, 24(1), 22–38.

Carlzon, J. (1987). *Moments of truth*. Cambridge, MA: Ballinger.

Corera, G. (2011). *The art of betrayal: Life and death in the British Secret Service*. Hachette, UK.

Crichton, E., & Edgar, D. (1995). Managing complexity for competitive advantage. *International Journal of Contemporary Hospitality Management*, 7(2/3), 12–18.

Foster, S. T., & Ogden, J. (2008). On differences in how operations and supply chain managers approach quality management. *International Journal of Production Research*, 46(24), 6945–6961.

Hahn, G. J. (2019). Industry 4.0: A supply chain innovation perspective. *International Journal of Production Research*, 1–17.

Harvey, M., Kiessling, T., & Akdeniz, L. (2014). The evolving role of supply chain managers in global channels of distribution and logistics systems. *International Journal of Physical Distribution & Logistics Management*, 44(8/9), 671–688.

Hofmann, E., & Rüsch, M. (2017). Industry 4.0 and the current status as well as future prospects on logistics. *Computers in Industry*, 89, 23–34.

Knight, F. H. (1921). *Risk, uncertainty, and profit*. Boston, MA: Hart, Schaffner & Marx; Houghton Mifflin Company.

LeBaron, G., & Gore, E. (2019). Gender and forced labour: Understanding the links in global cocoa supply chains. *The Journal of Development Studies*, 1–23.

Li, D., & Wang, X. (2017). Dynamic supply chain decisions based on networked sensor data: an application in the chilled food retail chain. *International Journal of Production Research*, 55(17), 5127–5141.

Magretta, J., & Stone, N. D. (2002) *What management is: How it works and why it's everyone's business*. New York: Free Press.

Marchese, K., Dollar, B. (2015). Deloitte supply chain talent of the future: Findings from the Third Annual Supply Chain Survey. https://www2.deloitte.com/us/en/pages/operations/articles/supply-chain-talent-of-the-future-survey.html. Accessed January 15, 2020.

Melacini, M., Perotti, S., Rasini, M., & Tappia, E. (2018). E-fulfilment and distribution in omni-channel retailing: A systematic literature review, *International Journal of Physical Distribution & Logistics Management*, 48(4), 391–414.

Melnyk, S. A., David, E. W., Spekman, R. E., & Sandor, J. (2010). Outcome-driven supply chains, *MIT Sloan Management Review*, 51(2, Winter), 33.

Melnyk, S. A., Peters, C., Spruill, J., Sullivan, K. W. (2018). Implementing cybersecurity in DoD supply chains. NDIA White Paper (Manufacturing Division). July. Accessed http://www.ndia.org/-/media/sites/ndia/divisions/manufacturing/documents/cybersecurity-in-dod-supply-chains.ashx?la=en

Melnyk, S. A., & Stanton, D. J. (2017). The customer-centric supply chain. *Supply Chain Management Review*, 20(12), 28–39.

Melnyk, S. A., Stewart, D. M., & Swink, M. L. (2004). Metrics and performance measurement in operations management: Dealing with the metrics maze. *Journal of Operations Management*, 22(3), 209–281.

Mintzberg, H. (1973). *The Nature of Managerial Work*. New York: Harper and Row.

Murfield, M., Boone, C. A., Rutner, P., & Thomas, R. (2017). Investigating logistics service quality in omni-channel retailing. *International Journal of Physical Distribution & Logistics Management*, 47(4), 263–296.

Reed, M. I. (1984). Management as a social practice. *Journal of Management Studies*, 21(3), 273–285.

Santayana, G. (1905) *The life of reason: Reason in common sense*. Scribner's, p. 284.

Schniederjans, D. G., Curado, C., & Khalajhedayati, M. (in press). Supply chain digitisation trends: An integration of knowledge management. *International Journal of Production Economics*.

Shou, Y., & Wang, W. (2017). Multidimensional competences of supply chain managers: An empirical study. *Enterprise Information Systems*, 11(1), 58–74.

Stank, T., Autry, C., Daugherty, P., & Closs, D. (2015). Reimagining the 10 megatrends that will revolutionize supply chain logistics. *Transportation Journal*, 54(1), 7–32.

Tversky, A., Kahneman, D. (1992). Advances in prospect theory: Cumulative representation of uncertainty. *Journal of Risk and Uncertainty*, 5(4), 297–323.

Vilko, J., Ritala, P., & Edelmann, J. (2014). On uncertainty in supply chain risk management. *The International Journal of Logistics Management*, 25(1), 3–19.

Yang, J., Xie, H., Yu, G., & Liu, M. (2019). Turning responsible purchasing and supply into supply chain responsiveness. *Industrial Management & Data Systems*, 119(9), 1988–2005.

Zhan, Y., & Tan, K. H. (2020). An analytic infrastructure for harvesting big data to enhance supply chain performance. *European Journal of Operational Research*, 281(3), 559–574.

INDEX

Page numbers in **bold** denote tables, those in *italic* denote figures.

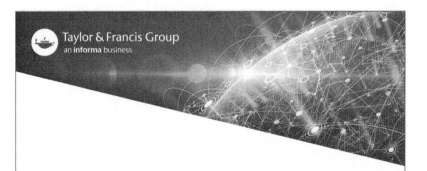